IUCN	International Union for the Conservation of Nature and Natural Resources		POTWs	Publicity Owned Treatment Works
IWC	International Whaling Commission		PPPA	Poison Prevention Packaging Act
			PRP	Potentially Responsible Parties
LAER	Lowest Achievable Emission Rate		PSD	Prevention of Significant Deterioration
LDAs	Localizer-Type Directional Aids		PSES	Pretreatment Standard for Existing Sources
			PUD	Planned Unit Development
MACT	Maximum Available Control Technology		PWS	Public Water System
MCL	Maximum Contaminant Level			
MCLG	Maximum Contaminant Level Goals		RACT	Reasonably Available Control Technology
MMPA	Marine Mammal Protection Act		RCO	Responsible Corporate Officer
MPRSA	Marine Protection, Research, and Sanctuaries Act		RCRA	Resource Conservation and Recovery Act
			RICO	Racketeer Influenced and Corrupt Organizations Act
NAAQSs	National Ambient Air Quality Standards		ROD	Record of Decision
NAFTA	North American Free Trade Agreement			
NCP	National Contingency Plan		SARA	Superfund Amendments and Reauthorization Act
NEPA	National Environmental Policy Act		SCRAP	Students Challenging Regulatory Agency Procedures
NESHAPs	National Emissions Standards for Hazardous Air Pollutants		SDWA	Safe Drinking Water Act
NETF	National Environmental Trust Fund		SEC	Securities and Exchange Commission
NFMA	National Forest Management Act		SEIS	Supplemental Environmental Impact Statement
NGOS	Nongovernmental Organizations		SIPs	State Implementation Plans
NGPSA	Natural Gas Pipeline Safety Act		SNUR	Significant New Use Rule
NMFS	National Marine Fisheries Service		SPCC	Spill Prevention, Control and Countermeasure
NOC	Notice of Commencement		SSAs	Sole-Source Aquifers
NPDES	National Pollutant Discharge Elimination System			
NPL	National Priorities List		TCDD	2, 3, 7, 8-tetrachlorodibenzo-p-dioxide
NRC	Nuclear Regulatory Commission		TCE	Trichloroethylene
NRDC	Natural Resources Defense Council		TCP	2, 4, 5-trichlorophenol
NSF	National Science Foundation		TSCA	Toxic Substances Control Act
NSPSs	New Source Performance Standards		TSD	Treatment, Storage and Disposal
NWRS	National Wildlife Refuge System		TSS	Total Suspended Solids
			TVA	Tennessee Valley Authority
OAU	Organization of African Unity			
OCS	Outer Continental Shelf		UCC	Uniform Commercial Code
OCSLA	Outer Continental Shelf Lands Act		UIO	Underground Injection Control
OECD	Organization for Economic Cooperation and Development		UN	United Nations
OEP	Office of Environmental Policy		UNCED	United Nations Conference on the Environment and Development
OMB	Office of Management and Budget		UNEP	United Nations Environmental Program
OPA	Oil Pollution Act		USEPA	United States Environmental Protection Agency
OSHA	Occupational Safety and Health Administration		USFS	United States Forest Service
OSM	Office of Surface Mining		USTs	Underground Storage Tanks
OTR	Office of Trade Representative			
			VMT	Vehicle Miles Traveled
PANE	People Against Nuclear Energy		VOCs	Volatile Organic Compounds
PCBs	polychlorinated biphenyls			
PM	Particulate Matter		WHO	World Health Organization
PMN	Premanufacture Notice		WTO	World Trade Organization
			WWF	Worldwide Fund for Nature

LAW AND
THE ENVIRONMENT

FRONA M. POWELL

Indiana University

WEST
WEST EDUCATIONAL PUBLISHING COMPANY
An International Thomson Publishing Company

Publisher/Team Director: Jack W. Calhoun
Senior Acquisitions Editor: Rob Dewey
Developmental Editor: Susanna C. Smart
Production Editor: Sharon L. Smith
Sr. Marketing Manager: Scott D. Person
Production House: BookMasters, Inc.

Library of Congress Cataloging-in-Publication Data

Powell, Frona M.,
    Law and the environment / Frona M. Powell.
        p.   cm.
    Includes index.
    ISBN 0-538-87874-6
    1. Environmental law—United States.   I. Title.
    KF3775.P69   1997
    344.73′046—dc21   97-13286
                                                       CIP

2 3 4 5 6 7 8   DI   4 3 2
Printed in the United States of America

International Thomson Publishing

CONTENTS

Preface   xi

1   ENVIRONMENTAL ETHICS, LAW, AND POLICY   1

Introduction   1

A Brief History of Environmental Law   1

Defining "Environmental Law"   2

Environmental Values and Goals   3
Who Should Speak for the Environment?   8 / *Economics and Regulation*   12

Valuing the Natural Environment   13

Market-Based Incentives v. Command and Control Regulation   15

Problems Associated With Risk Assessment   16

Who Should Regulate?   18

Law and the Future: Where Should We Go From Here?   21

Comments and Conclusion   24

2   THE AMERICAN LEGAL SYSTEM: SOURCES OF LAW AND RULES OF PROCEDURE   27

Introduction   27

Civil Cases in General   27

General Sources of Law   28
Constitutional Law   28 / *Treaties*   31 / *State and Federal Statutes*   31
Executive Orders   32 / *Administrative Law*   32 / *Common Law*   32

Court Structure   38
State Court Systems   33 / *Federal Court System*   38

Steps in a Civil Law Suit (Civil Procedure)   39
The Adversary System   39 / *Commencing the Action—The Complaint and Summons*   40 / *The Defendant's Answer*   40 / *Motion for Summary Judgment*   41 / *Appeals*   42

Conclusion   43

3 INTRODUCTION TO THE LAW OF PROPERTY   47

Introduction   47

The Nature of Property   48
Acquisition of Property   49 / Legal Categories of Property   51 / Acquisition of Real Property   53 / Scope of Interests in Real Property   56 / Kinds of Ownership   62 / Easements and Covenants   65

Summary   70

4 COMMON LAW REMEDIES FOR ENVIRONMENTAL HARMS   75

Introduction   75

Tort Law   76

Trespass   76

Nuisance   80
Public nuisance   83

Negligence   84

Cause in Fact   87

Proximate Cause   90

Injury   90

Multiple-Party Toxic Torts Cases   91

Defenses to Negligence   92

Strict Liability   93

Summary   96

5 ENVIRONMENTAL LIABILITY IN THE SALE OR LEASE OF PROPERTY, PRODUCT LIABILITY, AND INSURER LIABILITY FOR ENVIRONMENTAL HARM   103

Introduction   103

Contract Law   104
CERCLA Liability   104 / General Principles   104 / Environmental Audits   106

Contract Warranties and Disclaimers   107
Indemnification Agreements   110 / Disclaimers of Liability and the "As Is" Clause   110 / Implied Warranties of Habitability   113 / Residential and

Commercial Leases   113 / Expanding Landlord and Tenant Liability   116
Avoiding Environmental Liability   117

Product Liability Law   119
Defenses in Product Liability Actions   122

Insurer Liability for Environmental Damages   123
Standard CGL Policy Language   124 / Techniques of Contract
Interpretation   124 / CGL Policy Language   125

Summary and Conclusion   128

6

LAND USE REGULATION AND REGULATORY TAKINGS   133

Introduction   133

Zoning   133
Authority to Zone Under Police Power   134 / Establishing
Planning Authority   136 / Regulating Land Use under the Zoning
Code   137 / Exceptions from Zoning Regulations   137 / Subdivision
Regulations   139

State Controls of Land Development   140

Wetlands Regulations   140
No Net Loss Policy   141 / State Wetlands Protection   142 / Flood Plain
Regulation   142

Standards of Review   142

Constitutional Issues in Land Use Regulation   144
Zoning and Discrimination   144

Land Use Regulations and the "Takings" Issue   145
Fifth Amendment Requirements   145 / "Regulatory" Takings   146
Takings Analysis: When Does a Taking Occur?   150

Summary and Conclusion   128

7

FEDERALISM AND THE ENVIRONMENT   157

Introduction   157

The Commerce Clause   157
The Commerce Clause as a Source of Federal Regulatory Power   158
The "Dormant Commerce Clause" and State Regulation of Out-of-State
Waste   163 / The Balancing Test   167 / The State as a "Market
Participant"   168

Federal Pre-Emption of State Laws Affecting the Environment   169

Express (Manifest) Intention to Pre-Empt State Law   169 / Pre-Emption of State Law by Congressional Intent   172 / State Law Incompatible with Congressional Intent   173 / State Laws Interfering with Policy Objectives of Federal Law   174 / Summary of the Pre-Emption Doctrine   174

Federal Public Land Laws   175

Federal Land Management Legislation   178 / The National Environmental Policy Act and Endangered Species Act   179 / The Surface Mining Control and Reclamation Act of 1977   179 / The Coastal Zone Management Act   180 / Federal Wildlife Protection Acts   180 / Wilderness Protection Laws   181 / Summary of Federal Land Management Laws   181

8   PRINCIPLES OF ADMINISTRATIVE LAW   185

Introduction   185

The "Delegation Doctrine": Scope of Agency Authority   186

The Administrative Procedure Act   187

General Framework of the APA   187 / Rule Making v. Adjudication   187 / Rule Making Under the APA   188 / Deference to Agency Opinion   188 / Application of the Delegation Doctrine   191 / Procedures for Rule Making Under the APA   194

Other Statutes Affecting Rule Making   195

Judicial Review of Agency Decision Making   195

Is Agency Action Subject to Review?   196 / The Issue of "Standing"   197 / "Timing" Issues in Judicial Review   201 / The Scope of Judicial Review   201

Summary and Review   209

9   THE NATIONAL ENVIRONMENTAL POLICY ACT AND THE ENDANGERED SPECIES ACT: ENVIRONMENTAL LAWS REGULATING GOVERNMENT ACTIONS   213

Introduction   213

The National Environmental Policy Act (NEPA)   214

Section 101   214 / The Council on Environmental Quality   215 / "Action-Forcing Provisions" of NEPA   215 / Threshold Requirements for the EIS   218 / Scope and Timing of the EIS   221 / Contents of the EIS   225 / Evaluation of NEPA   228

The Endangered Species Act   229

History and Purposes   229 / Key Provisions: The Listing Procedures of Section 4   233 / Section 7: Application to Federal Agencies   234 / Section 9:

*The "Takings" Prohibition   234 / Evaluation of the Endangered Species
Act   237*

Summary   241

10

CONTROLLING AIR POLLUTION   245

Introduction   245

The Clean Air Act of 1970   246
*Overview of the Clean Air Act   246 / Sources of Air Pollution   247
National Ambient Air Quality Standards (NAAQSs)   247 / State
Implementation Plans   250 / Nonattainment Areas   253 / New Source
Performance Standards   254 / The Permit Program   255 / The PSD
Program   255 / Hazardous Air Toxics   258 / Acid Rain Provisions   261
Stratospheric Ozone Protection   261 / Mobile Source Fuels and Fuel
Additives   262 / Motor Vehicle Provisions   263 / Indoor Air
Pollution   263 / Radon Gas and Indoor Air Quality Research Act   264
Noise Pollution and Abatement Act   264*

Policy Implications of the Clean Air Act   264

Standard Setting Under the Clean Air Act   266

11

THE CLEAN WATER ACT   273

Introduction   273

History of Federal Water Pollution Control   273

Overview of the Clean Water Act   274
*Pollution Discharge Prohibition   275 / NPDES Exclusions   279 / Citizen
Suit Provision   281 / Permit Program Conditions   282 / Monitoring and
Reporting Requirements   282 / Technology-Based Limitations   282*

Control of Conventional Pollutants   283
*Best Available Technology (BAT)   284 / Water Quality Standards   284
Toxicants and Nonconventional Pollutants   285 / New Source Performance
Standards (NSPS)   285 / Variances   285 / Pretreatment and Indirect
Dischargers   288 / Effluent Limitations for Publicly Owned
Treatment Works   288*

Protecting Wetlands   289
*Section 404 Permit Program   289 / Other Government Mechanisms
for Wetlands Protection   293*

Nonpoint Source Pollution   293
Stormwater discharge   293

Oil and Hazardous Substances Spills   294

Ocean Dumping   294
Enforcement of the Clean Water Act   295

The Safe Drinking Water Act   295
1996 Amendments   296

Summary and Discussion   296

12   REGULATING TOXIC SUBSTANCES AND PESTICIDES   303

Introduction   303

The Federal Insecticide, Fungicide, and Rodenticide Act (FIFRA)   304
*FIFRA: An Overview   305 / Cost-Benefit Analysis under FIFRA   305
Pesticide Registration   305 / Trade Secrets and Use of Data   306
Pesticide Tolerance in Food: The Federal Food, Drug, and Cosmetic
Act (FFDCA)   306 / The Food Quality Protection Act of 1996 and
Repeal of the Delaney Clause   307 / 1996 Amendments to FIFRA   307
Special Registrations   308 / Classification and Certification under
Section 3   308 / Minor Use Registrations   308 / Removal of Pesticides
from the Market   309 / Effect of Cancellation of Registration   311 / State Authority
to Regulate Pesticides   312 / Enforcement and Penalties   312
FIFRA and Other Laws   312*

The Toxic Substances Control Act   313
*Screening New Chemicals   314 / Approval of the PMN   315 / Testing
Requirements   316 / Information Gathering and Reporting   320 / Regulation
of Existing Chemicals   321 / The Asbestos Hazard Emergency Response Act
(AHERA)   325 / Regulating PCBs   325 / Radon and Lead-Based
Paint   325 / Biotechnology   326 / Importers and Exporters   326*

Other Federal Laws Regulating Chemicals   326

Comparison of FIFRA and TSCA   327

The Problem of Risk Assessment in Controlling Toxic Substances   327
A Critical Analysis of TSCA and FIFRA   328

13   REGULATING SOLID AND HAZARDOUS WASTE   333

Introduction   333

An Overview of RCRA   334
*Structure of the Act   334 / Section 3001: What is Hazardous Waste?   335
Hazardous Waste under EPA Definition   338 / Generator of Waste
Requirements   339 / Small Quantity Generators   340 / The Hazardous
Waste Manifest   340 / Transporter Requirements   341 / The Hazardous*

*Materials Transportation Act   341 / Standards for Treatment, Storage, and
Disposal (TSD) Facilities   342 / Land Disposal Restrictions   343 / Permit
Requirements for TSD Facilities   343 / Medical Waste   343 / State
Hazardous Waste Programs   343 / Enforcement Mechanisms and Citizen Suit
Provisions   344 / Restraining Imminent or Substantial Endangerment to
Health or the Environment   345 / Underground Storage Tanks   347*

**The Comprehensive Environmental Response, Compensation, and
Liability Act (CERCLA)   348**
*Introduction   348 / Basic Structure of the Act   349 / The National Priorities
List and the National Contingency Plan   349 / Defining Hazardous Substances
under CERCLA   349 / Definition of Terms: "Release" and "Facility"   349
CERCLA Response Actions   350 / Liability of Potentially Responsible Parties
under CERCLA   350 / Defenses to CERCLA Liability   354 / Recoverable
Response Costs   355 / Community Right to Know   355 / Lender Liability
under CERCLA 356*

Comments and Summary   359

14

**ENFORCING ENVIRONMENTAL LAWS: ISSUES IN CRIMINAL
AND CORPORATE LIABILITY   365**

Introduction   365
*Compliance Issues   366 / Voluntary Compliance as Regulatory
Policy   366*

Civil v. Criminal Liability   366

Establishing Criminal Intent   367
Proving "Knowledge" under RCRA's Criminal Enforcement Provision   368

Issues in Corporate Liability   371
*The Rule Limiting Corporate Liability   371 / Corporate Criminal
Liability   372 / Personal Liability of Corporate Directors and
Managers   375 / Corporate Shareholder Liability and Successor
Liability   376 / Some Defenses to Environmental Enforcement Actions   378
Sentencing Problems and Other Enforcement Issues   380 / Environmental
Audits and the Corporate Defendant   381 / Prosecution under RICO for
Environmental Crimes   381 / Securities Violations   382 / Bankruptcy Law
and the Environment   383*

Illustrating Issues: The Case of the *Exxon Valdez*   383
*The Prosecution of Captain Hazelwood   384 / The Corporate
Defendants   385 / The* Exxon Valdez *Debate: What Did We Learn?   385
The CERES Principles   386*

15

INTERNATIONAL LAW AND THE ENVIRONMENT   389

Introduction   389

International Environmental Concerns   389

Sources of International Environmental Law   390

International Treaties and Conventions   392
*The Stockholm Conference   392 / The Montreal Protocol   393
Basel Convention   393 / The 1992 Earth Summit   394*

Trade and the Environment   395
*Environmental Implications of International Trade Agreements   396 / Trade
Agreements in General   396 / The General Agreement on Tariffs and Trade
(GATT)   397 / Environmental Implications of NAFTA   402*

Extraterritorial Application of U.S. Domestic Laws   405
*Legal Actions by Foreign Citizens in U.S. Courts   408 / Impact of U.S. Laws
Abroad   409 / The Global Environment and Problems of Enforcement   410*

Emerging Protection for the Environment—ISO 14000   410
Direct Regulation of Products   411

Summary and Conclusion   414

APPENDICES   **419**
   A: Court Systems   419
   B: Sample Hazardous Waste Form and the Superfund Process   423
   C: Environmental Principles and Laws   427

INDEX   437

PREFACE

Several years ago, my colleagues in the Business Law Department at the Indiana University School of Business encouraged me to develop an introductory environmental law course for undergraduate students. Because I had previously concentrated my research in real estate law, an area of law which increasingly demands an understanding of environmental law and policy issues, I was glad to undertake the project. This book grew out of my experiences in developing and teaching that course.

As a teacher developing a new course, I began with the recognition that this would be the first law course for many of my students. The students would come from a variety of backgrounds with different experiences and perspectives. Their reasons for taking the class would differ and their future career plans would be varied. For these reasons, I decided to develop a course where students could explore a number of legal topics and issues while focusing on policy issues affecting the environment.

I define *environmental law* broadly for purposes of the course and this book. I believe that common law, constitutional law, legal procedure, administrative law, and contract law principles, in addition to state and federal regulatory policy, all play a role in the development and implementation of environmental law and policy. The study of these topics will give students an opportunity to see the breadth of the legal system and its impact on environmental policy making. For this reason, this book not only provides an overview of administrative law and federal environmental statutes and regulatory policy, it also includes chapters introducing the legal process, examining the basic concepts of property and contract law affecting the environment, and discussing the constitutional issues affecting the environment.

The first chapter sets the stage by raising some basic policy issues that underlie environmental policy making. Because some students are unfamiliar with the legal process in general, Chapter 2 provides an introduction to law and the legal system. Chapter 3 examines principles of American property law, and Chapter 4 examines common law theories, such as trespass, nuisance, negligence, and strict liability, which are a basis for recovering damages for environmental harm in civil cases. Chapter 5 looks at some contract law issues which may be important in resolving environmental disputes, including the issue of insurer liability for environmental harm. Chapter 6 considers land use regulation and the constitutional "takings" issues. Chapter 7 addresses other important constitutional issues in environmental regulation.

The second half of the book focuses on administrative law (Chapter 8) and major federal environmental laws passed in the last three decades. These include the National Environmental Policy Act and Endangered Species Act (Chapter 9), the Clean Air and Clean Water acts (Chapters 10 and 11), TSCA and FIFRA (Chapter 12), and CERCLA and RCRA (Chapter 13). The book ends with two topics I've found to be of particular interest to undergraduate students—criminal law and the environment (Chapter 14) and international environmental law (Chapter 15).

This book will be of special interest to new teachers of environmental law. While environmental law may first appear to be a subject of overwhelming complexity, I have found that the legal issues often distill into a few simple and yet profoundly important policy questions. Some of these questions are raised in Chapter 1: What are our environmental goals and values? Why should we protect the environment? If we should protect the environment, how do we know what to protect? Who should decide—the courts, the legislature, or the administrative agency? If we decide to regulate to protect the environment, how should we best implement that decision? How do we determine and resolve the costs and benefits of environmental protection? How do we determine risk? Many of these questions are raised in the cases and discussions throughout the book.

There are many people I would like to thank. First, a thank you to two people at West Publishing, Al Bruckner, who persuaded me to undertake this project and guided and encouraged me in the early days, and Susan Smart, who has always been available with advice and support.

The following reviewers gave of their time and expertise, and I appreciate their helpful comments and suggestions.

Mary C. Keifer
Ohio University

Dennis L. Soden
University of Texas–El Paso

E. Paul Richitt
University of Nevada–Las Vegas

Donald F. McCabe
Southern Illinois University–Edwardsville

Sharon S. Tisher
University of Maine

Marlene C. McGuirl
George Washington University

Toni Ristau
University of New Mexico

James M. Robertson
University of Oklahoma

Mary Ellen Perri
SUNY–Farmingdale

Thank you to Mike Phillips for his suggestions in Chapter 1, and to Geoff Grodner for his help in chronicling the Bloomington-Westinghouse PCB dispute, included in the instructor's manual that accompanies this book. Special thanks to John Powell for his input into Chapters 10 and 11, Terry Pennington for Chapter 13, and Eric Richards for his input and assistance in Chapter 15. I also want to express my gratitude to my colleagues at the Indiana University School of Business and at the Wharton School of the University of Pennsylvania, the Environmental Section of the Academy of Legal Studies in Business, and particularly Professor Mary Keifer at Ohio University, for their support and encouragement during my tenure as a business law faculty member and teacher of environmental law.

Finally, I would like to thank my family, especially Ron, Grace, Aaron, Alison, my parents and mother- and father-in-law, and my friends Lorelei, Linda, Rosemary, and Sandy who have encouraged me throughout this project. Without your support, this book would not have been possible.

F.M.P.

1

ENVIRONMENTAL ETHICS, LAW, AND POLICY

INTRODUCTION

Far from being static, law evolves and changes to reflect society's current goals and values. No area of law more vividly illustrates this fact than environmental law. This chapter provides a brief historical background and introduces some broad policy issues, ethical perspectives, and economic concerns that underlie environmental rule making and outlines judicial decisions that interpret and apply those rules.

A BRIEF HISTORY OF ENVIRONMENTAL LAW

In the last part of this century, federal and state governments adopted major legislation to address specific environmental problems in response to immediate and dramatic events. In the 1960s, for example, the American public became increasingly concerned about the problems associated with environmental pollution. Lake Erie was dying; an oil spill that coated the beaches near Santa Barbara, California, killed large numbers of land and ocean animals; and the public learned of the deadly effects of DDT. These and other events combined to create a climate of ecological concern that led in 1969 to the adoption of the **National Environmental Policy Act** (NEPA), which addressed the need for a national environmental policy, and in 1970 to the creation of the **Environmental Protection Agency** (EPA).

The 1970s have been called the "environmental decade." In 1970, Congress enacted the **Clean Air Amendments,** now known as the **Clean Air Act** (CAA). In 1972, Congress substantially amended the Federal Water Pollution Control Act to create the **Clean Water Act** (CWA), with the goal that all waters in the United States would be safe for swimming by 1983. In 1972, Congress also strengthened the regulation of pesticides under the **Federal Insecticide, Fungicide, and Rodenticide Act** (FIFRA). Congress passed the **Safe Drinking Water Act** (SDWA) in 1974 and enacted the **Resource Conservation and Recovery Act** (RCRA) and **Toxic Substances Control Act** (TSCA). In 1980, the **Comprehensive Environmental Response, Compensation, and Liability Act** of 1980 (CERCLA, or "**Superfund**") was adopted following the discovery of substantial toxic chemical contamination at Love Canal, New York.

Most of these major environmental anti-pollution laws have subsequently been amended. In 1990, CERCLA was amended to add the **Oil Pollution Act of 1990** (OPA) following the massive oil spill of the tanker *Exxon Valdez* in Prince William Sound, Alaska. This and other amendments addressed problems in the original act as well as new problems.

Passage of major environmental laws in the 1970s and 1980s reflected a new public commitment to environmental protection. Laws like the **Endangered Species Act** (ESA), Marine Mammal Protection Act, and Wild and Scenic Rivers Act were adopted or strengthened in order to protect public lands, wildlife, and wilderness areas. Laws protecting coastal zones and protecting the oceans from pollution were also passed.

Today, environmental concerns seem to be shifting toward global issues. Problems like global warming and acid rain have captured the public's attention and have been addressed to some extent through laws and treaties. In the future, issues of sustainable development and cross-boundary environmental concerns will likely come to the forefront of debates.

Environmental laws were sometimes adopted following heated debate over how best to address particular environmental problems, how to balance the costs and benefits of environmental protection, and how to prioritize environmental concerns. That debate continues. For this reason, to understand environmental law, it is essential to be aware of some of the factors influencing its development.

The law reflects *choices* made by legislative bodies, courts, the executive branch, and administrative agencies. These policy choices were in turn influenced by many factors, including political concerns, ethical perspectives, economic considerations, and perceptions of risk. This chapter explores some of these concerns and includes some different points of view on the issues.

Presented in this chapter are only some of the questions which policy makers, environmentalists, business and industry leaders, and ultimately the average citizen must consider if progress is to be made toward meeting present and future environmental challenges. As you consider the issues presented, bear in mind that there are no easy answers and many different responses to environmental policy concerns.

DEFINING "ENVIRONMENTAL LAW"

As a preliminary matter, it is important to define the scope of environmental law as that term is used in this book. To some, the study of environmental law is the study of major environmental laws passed in the last third of this century. Acts like the CAA, Clean Water Act, and CERCLA, which are designed to address the problems of national air, water, and land pollution, are clearly important sources of environmental law. As the term is used in this text, however, environmental law is not limited to pollution control, species protection, and natural resources conservation laws. It also covers the fundamental legal rules governing private ownership and use of land and natural resources, and the allocation of liability for environmental harm. To the extent constitutional issues affect the natural environment, those issues are also treated as issues of environmental law.

In keeping with this broad definition of "environmental law," this text examines legal rights and duties which arise under traditional common law, state law, and federal statutory law. These include traditional property rights (Chapter 3), common law remedies for harm to property (Chapter 4), contract law issues affecting parties' environmental rights and duties (Chapter 5), and constitutional issues which question the balance between state and federal environmental regulation and the responsibilities of individual landowners in utilizing natural resources (Chapters 6 and 7).

ENVIRONMENTAL VALUES AND GOALS

Assuming that the law should implement society's ideas about how humans relate to their environment, how do humans define that relationship? Why should humans value the natural environment? The answers to these questions are important because they help determine environmental goals. These questions evoke different responses, depending on an individual's ethical and ecological perspectives.

One obvious answer is that we should protect the natural environment because it is in our own *self-interest* to do so. Human beings, as a part of the natural world, depend on the planet for survival because we must eat and breathe. A safe and healthy environment is valuable to human happiness. To foul the earth and pollute the air and water is like sitting on the limb of a tree and sawing it off at the trunk.

In her famous book *Silent Spring,* Rachel Carson makes this point when she argues that humans are recklessly polluting the earth with pesticides without understanding the ultimate effect of the chemicals. Carson is angered that poisonous chemicals are available to be used indiscriminately by persons who are unaware of their potential for harm. She asserts that humans are entitled a safe environment.

Excerpt from *Silent Spring* by Rachel Carson

The history of life on earth has been a history of interaction between living things and their surroundings. To a large extent, the physical form and the habits of the earth's vegetation and its animal life have been molded by the environment. Considering the whole span of earthly time, the opposite effect, in which life actually modifies its surroundings, has been relatively slight. Only within the moment of time represented by the present century has one species—man—acquired significant power to alter the nature of his world.

During the past quarter century this power has not only increased to one of

Excerpted from "The Obligation to Endure," Silent Spring by Rachel Carson. Copyright © 1962 by Rachel L. Carson. Copyright © renewed 1990 by Roger Christie. Reprinted by permission of Houghton Mifflin Company. All rights reserved.

disturbing magnitude but it has changed in character. The most alarming of all man's assaults upon the environment is the contamination of air, earth, rivers, and sea with dangerous and even lethal materials. This pollution is for the most part irrecoverable; the chain of evil it initiates not only in the world that must support life but in living tissues is for the most part irreversible. In this now universal contamination of the environment, chemicals are the sinister and little-recognized partners of radiation in changing the very nature of the world—the very nature of its life. Strontium 90, released through nuclear explosions into the air, comes to earth in rain or drifts down as fallout, lodges in soil, enters into the grass or corn or wheat grown there, and in time takes up its abode in the bones of a human being, there to remain until his death. Similarly, chemicals sprayed on croplands or

Excerpt from Silent Spring *by Rachel Carson (continued)*

forests or gardens lie long in soil, entering into living organisms, passing from one to another in a chain of poisoning and death. Or they pass mysteriously by underground streams until they emerge and, through the alchemy of air and sunlight, combine into new forms that kill vegetation, sicken cattle, and work unknown harm on those who drink from once pure wells. As Albert Schweitzer has said, "Man can hardly even recognize the devils of his own creation."

It took hundreds of million of years to produce the life that now inhabits the earth—eons of time in which that developing and evolving and diversifying life reached a state of adjustment and balance with its surroundings. The environment, rigorously shaping and directing the life it supported, contained elements that were hostile as well as supporting. Certain rocks gave out dangerous radiation; even within the light of the sun, from which all life draws its energy, there were short-wave radiations with power to injure. Given time—time not in years but in millennia—life adjusts, and a balance has been reached. For time is the essential ingredient; but in the modern world there is no time.

The rapidity of change and the speed with which new situations are created follow the impetuous and heedless pace of man rather than the deliberate pace of nature. Radiation is no longer merely the background radiation of rocks, the bombardment of cosmic rays, the ultraviolet of the sun that have existed before there was any life on earth; radiation is now the unnatural creation of man's tampering with the atom. The chemicals to which life is asked to make its adjustment are no longer merely the calcium and silica and copper and all the rest of

the minerals washed out of the rocks and carried in rivers to the sea; they are the synthetic creations of man's inventive mind, brewed in his laboratories, and having no counterparts in nature.

To adjust to these chemicals would require time on the scale that is nature's; it would require not merely the years of a man's life but the life of generations. And even this, were it by some miracle possible, would be futile, for the new chemicals come from our laboratories in an endless stream; almost five hundred annually find their way into actual use in the United States alone. The figure is staggering and its implications are not easily grasped—500 new chemicals to which the bodies of men and animals are required somehow to adapt each year, chemicals totally outside the limits of biologic experience.

Among them are many that are used in man's war against nature. Since the mid-1940's over 200 basic chemicals have been created for use in killing insects, weeds, rodents, and other organisms described in the modern vernacular as "pests"; and they are sold under several thousand different brand names.

***

Along with the possibility of the extinction of mankind by nuclear war, the central problem of our age has therefore become the contamination of man's total environment with such substances of incredible potential for harm—substances that accumulate in the tissues of plants and animals and even penetrate the germ cells to shatter or alter the very material of heredity upon which the shape of the future depends.

Some would-be architects of our future look toward a time when it will be

Excerpt from Silent Spring *by Rachel Carson (continued)*

possible to alter the human germ plasm by design. But we may easily be doing so now by inadvertence, for many chemicals, like radiation, bring about gene mutations. It is ironic to think that man might determine his own future by something so seemingly trivial as the choice of an insect spray. All this has been risked— for what? Future historians may well be amazed by our distorted sense of proportion. How could intelligent beings seek to control a few unwanted species by a method that contaminated the entire environment and brought the threat of disease and death even to their own kind? Yet this is precisely what we have done. . . .

All this is not to say there is no insect problem and no need of control. I am saying, rather, that control must be geared to realities, not to mythical situations, and that the methods employed must be such that they do not destroy us along with the insects.

***

Questions and Comments for Discussion

1.   Public concern about pesticides was a principal factor in the emergence of the American environmental movement in the late 1960s and early 1970s. Fueled in part by Rachel Carson's 1962 book *Silent Spring,* the Department of Agriculture convinced Congress to revise the existing pesticide registration system in 1964 to permit the Secretary of Agriculture to refuse to register a new product or to cancel an existing pesticide registration. The burden of proof for safety and effectiveness of the pesticide was also placed on the registrant. In 1972, the existing pesticide law was rewritten, resulting in FIFRA. This law, which has been amended five times since 1972, most recently in 1996, is discussed in Chapter 12 of this text.

2.   In the decades following publication of *Silent Spring,* public environmental concerns have continued to mount as populations increase and the ability of humans to modify and despoil the natural environment becomes more obvious. The fact is that the Earth's population is growing rapidly, and even conservative estimates suggest that the "carrying capacity" of the planet may be reached as early as the middle part of the next century. In 1800, the world population was about 957 million people, with 98 percent living in rural areas.

Contrast that with what Joel Cohen, head of the Laboratory of Populations at Rockefeller University and author of the book *How Many People Can the Earth Support?* says: that at 1990 growth rates, the world population could increase 130-fold from about 5.3 billion in 1990 to about 694 billion by 2150. He and many others are concerned that the problems of population explosion are not getting the attention they deserve. In a 1989 article,[1] Arnold Rietze argued that population and human consumption are the most significant causes of environmental degradation. Yet governments tend to focus on pollution problems as more easily addressed than those of population.

***

Some emphasize ethical and religious reasons to protect the natural environment. Consider, for example, the following statement by Bruce Babbitt, U.S. Secretary of the Interior since January 1993, discussing the issue of biodiversity.

Excerpt from "The Future Environmental Agenda for the United States" by Bruce Babbitt

***

The biodiversity issue is very simple. The problem is the mass extinction of species. Around this world, we are exterminating some fifty to one hundred species per day—every day, day in, day out. We are creating the largest mass biological extinction since the Cretaceous Era (which occurred a short time before the Rocky Mountains started coming up out of the earth about sixteen million years ago). This extinction is all the more frightening because of the pace at which it is taking place. There is no indication of where it might stop unless we get serious about taking charge. The difficulty with this issue is that we have not done a very good job of answering the question, why does it matter? How do you persuade a truck driver, a postal worker, or a lawyer, that the loss of species makes any difference?

The intellectual line of attack is to say that there are enormous implications. I will give you some examples. The Madagascar Periwinkle, a tiny, obscure flower, is discovered to be a ninety percent-effective cure for Childhood Leukemia and Hodgkin's Disease. The Pacific yew, which grows in the old growth forests of the Northwest, a trash tree—which the logging companies have been piling non-stop onto bonfires for the last fifty years—turns out to have a substance called Taxol which now appears to be an

extraordinarily potent cancer-fighting drug. There is a cornucopia of such substances out there. Twenty-five percent of the drugs that you take, that are available in drugstores, ultimately have some biological base to them. It might be possible, in theory at least, to independently discover and synthesize these complex substances, but it is not at all clear it would ever happen. The same is true for agriculture. Monocultures like corn and wheat are susceptible to disease and destruction unless they are occasionally hybridized with the wild strains that are still being discovered in many parts of the world.

But there is a much larger issue contained within the biodiversity question. It has to do with the concept of spiritual dominion. It questions whether something is badly wrong in our own philosophy and perception of the world when we recklessly shred the biological fabric of the planet without any regard for the consequences.

Consider the image of Noah and the Ark in Judeo-Christian tradition. My view of that story is that it is an argument for preservation of God's creation, for it says that even in the time of a deluge there is a mandate to preserve every species on earth. Ultimately there is a spiritual or ethical implication in this question: Is it really possible for the human race to live lightly on the land? Or are we simply going to continue to metastasize with our industrial civilization, to the point where we have shredded the tapestry and made ourselves poorer and more lonely in the process?

Bruce Babbitt, The Future Environmental Agenda for the United States, *64* U. Colo. L. Rev. *513 (1993). Reprinted with permission of the University of Colorado Law Review.*

***

In the United States and western European culture, land has traditionally been viewed as a property interest which can and should be capitalized to maximize its utility. Judge Posner summarizes this point in his *Economic Theory of Property Rights,* excerpted in Chapter 3. According to Posner, the legal protection of property rights serves an important economic function by creating incentives to use resources efficiently. The assumption is that an individual owner of land will endeavor to maximize the value of the land.

The notion that land and natural resource use should be maximized through private ownership most certainly assisted land expansion and the economic growth of the United States throughout the nineteenth and early twentieth centuries. While there are many "property rights" advocates who continue to argue this position, there are others who believe that profit maximization through use of private resources will ultimately result in environmental degradation.

In his article, "The Ethical Strands of Environmental Law,"[2] Professor Eric T. Freyfogle assesses the ideological tensions within environmental laws and summarizes some of the moral and ecological claims of environmentalists. According to this author, the question of how to value the earth is not primarily one of dollars and cents, but rather one involving a deep-seated mixture of ecological and ethical values.

Excerpt from "The Ethical Strands of Environmental Law" by Eric T. Freyfogle

To understand the worldview of environmentalists, we must consider the main moral and ecological claims that environmentalists present. . . . A useful place to begin surveying the moral claims of environmentalists is with the noisy challenge that they offer to our anthropocentrism, to our long-held assumption that only humans count in moral terms. In the sixteenth century, Rene Descartes asserted that the painful cries of a tortured animal were the same as noise from a machine's grinding gears: neither machines nor animals had minds or souls, which meant that neither counted for anything morally. Environ-

University of Illinois Law Review *819 (1994).*
© *to the University of Illinois Law Review, held by The Board of Trustees of the University of Illinois.*

mentalists, among others, question this Renaissance wisdom. The more intently we look, the more difficult it is to justify a sharp moral line between humans and the planet's millions of other species. Why is it that humans count and other species do not?

***

Environmentalists today also question our humanly focused utilitarian instincts, our sense that the best way to determine right and wrong when dealing with the land is to look at how an action affects human pleasure or well-being. Because it lacks moral worth, the land is merely an instrument in utilitarian-type ethical schemes, valuable only insofar as it betters human existence. In this moral order, the right way to use the land is the

Excerpt from "The Ethical Strands of Environmental Law" by Eric T. Freyfogle (continued)

way that produces the most human good. The most influential form of utilitarianism today is economic thought, which uses efficiency as its main measure of the good.

The main precepts of utilitarian thought are facing new objections in the modern environmental age. One concern is with the identity of the individuals whose utility is counted. Past practice (particularly free-market economics) considers only the utility of humans now living—or, even more narrowly, the utility of market consumers with dollars to spend. But as environmentalists are prone to ask, what of the interests of the planet's other species, either as individual organisms or as collective entities? What of the wolves of Minnesota and the state-endangered bluebreast darter, resident of the Middle Fork of the Vermillion? Should not our calculations somehow include the utility preferences of the Wyoming mule deer herd, or the health of the high sagebrush biotic community? Then too, there is the matter of future generations of humans, if not future generations of other species. . . .

Who Should Speak for the Environment?

Assuming that protection of the environment is an important goal, then who should represent the environment in the debate over competing values? What environmental goals and perspectives should be represented in that debate and in what forum should that debate be conducted? The answer to these questions clearly affects our final decisions about what we should protect and causes debate about the appropriate balance of competing interests in policy making.

Naturalist Christopher D. Stone once proposed that natural objects such as trees, mountains, rivers, and lakes should, like corporations, have certain legal rights. That position was embraced by Justice Douglas in his dissent in *Sierra Club v. Morton.* If a person or legal entity like the Sierra Club has *standing,* it may obtain judicial review of federal agency action. As you read this case, consider the political and environmental implications of the dispute over whether the Sierra Club had standing to maintain the lawsuit in the case.

SIERRA CLUB v. MORTON
405 U.S. 727 (1972)

STEWART, Justice

I.

The Mineral King Valley is an area of great natural beauty nestled in the Sierra Nevada Mountains in Tulare County, California, adjacent to Sequoia National Park. It has been part of the Sequoia National Forest since 1926, and is designated as a National Game Refuge by special Act of Congress. Though once the site of extensive mining activity, Mineral King is now used almost exclusively for recreational purposes. Its relative inaccessibility and lack of development have limited the number of visitors each year, and at the same time have preserved the valley's quality as a quasi-wilderness area largely uncluttered by the products of civilization.

The United States Forest Service, which is entrusted with the maintenance and administration of national forests, began in the late 1940s to give consideration to Mineral King as a potential site for recreational development. Prodded by a rapidly increasing demand for skiing facilities, the Forest Service published a prospectus in 1965, inviting bids from private developers for the construction and operation of a ski resort that would also serve as a summer recreational area. The proposal of Walt Disney Enterprises, Inc., was chosen from those of six bidders, and Disney received a three-year permit to conduct surveys and explorations in the valley in connection with its preparation of a complete master plan for the resort.

The final Disney plan, approved by the Forest Service in January, 1969, outlines a $35 million complex of motels, restaurants, swimming pools, parking lots, and other structures designed to accommodate 14,000 visitors daily. This complex is to be constructed on 80 acres of the valley floor under a 30-year use permit from the Forest Service. Other facilities, including ski lifts, ski trails, a cog-assisted railway, and utility installations, are to be constructed on the mountain slopes and in other parts of the valley under a revocable special use permit. To provide access to the resort, the State of California proposes to construct a highway 20 miles in length. A section of this road would traverse Sequoia National Park, as would a proposed high-voltage power line needed to provide electricity for the resort. Both the highway and the power line require the approval of the Department of the Interior, which is entrusted with the preservation and maintenance of the national parks.

Representatives of the Sierra Club, who favor maintaining Mineral King largely in its present state, followed the progress of recreational planning for the valley with close attention and increasing dismay. . . . In June of 1969 the Club filed the present suit in the United States District Court for the Northern District of California, seeking a declaratory judgment that various aspects of the proposed development contravene federal laws and regulations governing the preservation of national parks, forests, and game refuges, and also seeking preliminary and permanent injunctions restraining the federal officials involved from granting their approval or issuing permits in connection with the Mineral King project. . . .

[*The District Court had granted the preliminary injunction, rejecting the government's challenge to Sierra Club's standing to sue. The Sierra Club relied on section 10 of the Administrative Procedure Act (APA) which provides:*

"A person suffering legal wrong because of agency action, or adversely affected or aggrieved by agency action within the meaning of a relevant statute, is entitled to judicial review thereof." In earlier cases, the Court had held that persons had standing to obtain judicial review of federal agency action under this section where they alleged that the challenged action had caused them "injury in fact," and the alleged injury was an interest "arguably within the zone of interests to be protected or regulated" by the statutes the agencies were claimed to have violated.

The Court of Appeals for the Ninth Circuit reversed the Trial Court's decision, and the Supreme Court granted Sierra Club's petition for writ of certiorari in the case.]

***

The injury alleged by the Sierra Club will be incurred entirely by reason of the change in the uses to which Mineral King will be put, and the attendant change in the aesthetics and ecology of the area. Thus, in referring to the road to be built through Sequoia National Park, the complaint alleged that the development "would destroy or otherwise affect the scenery, natural and historic objects and wildlife of the park and would impair the enjoyment of the park for future generations." We do not question that this type of harm may amount to an "injury in fact" sufficient to lay the basis for standing under section 10 of the APA.[3] Aesthetic and environmental well-being, like economic well-being, are important ingredients of the quality of life in our society, and the fact that particular environmental interests are shared by the many rather than the few does not make them less deserving of legal protection through the judicial process. But the "injury in fact" test requires more than an injury to a cognizable interest. It requires that the party seeking review be himself among the injured.

The impact of the proposed changes in the environment of Mineral King will not fall indiscriminately upon every citizen. The alleged injury will be felt directly only by those who use Mineral King and Sequoia National Park, and for whom the aesthetic and recreational values of the area will be lessened by the highway and ski resort. The Sierra Club failed to allege that it or its members would be affected in any of their activities or pastimes by the Disney development. Nowhere in the pleading or affidavits did the Club state that its members use Mineral King for any purpose, much less that they use it in any way that would be significantly affected by the proposed actions of the respondents.

***

The requirement that a party seeking review must allege facts showing that he is himself adversely affected does not insulate executive action from judicial review, nor does it prevent any public interests from being protected through the judicial process. It does serve as at least a rough attempt to put the decision as to whether review will be sought in the hands of those who have a direct stake in the outcome. That goal would be undermined were we to construe the APA to authorize judicial review at the behest of organizations or individuals who seek to do no more than vindicate their own value preferences through the judicial process. The principle that the Sierra Club would have us establish in this case would do just that. . . .

The judgment is *affirmed.*

DOUGLAS, Justice, dissenting.

I share the view of my Brother Blackmun and would reverse the judgment below.

The critical question of "standing" would be simplified and also put neatly in focus if we fashioned a federal rule that allowed environmental issues to be litigated before federal agencies or federal courts in the name of the inanimate object about to be despoiled, defaced, or invaded by roads and bulldozers and where injury is the subject of public outrage. Contemporary public concern for protecting nature's ecological equilibrium should lead to the conferral of standing upon environmental objects to sue for their own preservation. . . . This suit would therefore be more properly labeled as *Mineral King v. Morton.*

Inanimate objects are sometimes parties in litigation. A ship has a legal personality, a fiction found useful for maritime purposes. The corporation sole—a creature of ecclesiastical law—is an acceptable adversary and large fortunes ride on its cases. The ordinary corporation is a "person" for purposes of the adjudicatory processes, whether it represents proprietary, spiritual, aesthetic, or charitable causes.

So it should be as respects valleys, alpine meadows, rivers, lakes, estuaries, beaches, ridges, groves of trees, swampland, or even air that feels the destructive pressures of modern technology and modern life. The river, for example, is the living symbol of all the life it sustains or nourishes—fish, aquatic insects, water ouzels, otter, fisher, deer, elk, bear, and all other animals, including man, who are dependent on it or who enjoy it for its sight, its sound, or its life. The river as plaintiff speaks for the ecological unit of life that is part of it. Those people who have a meaningful relation to that body of water—whether it be a fisherman, a canoeist, a zoologist, or a logger—must be able to speak for the values which the river represents and which are threatened with destruction.

I do not know Mineral King. I have never seen it nor travelled it, though I have seen articles describing its proposed "development." . . .

Mineral King is doubtless like other wonders of the Sierra Nevada such as Tuolumne Meadows and the John Muir Trail. Those who hike it, fish it, hunt it, camp in it, or frequent it, or visit it merely to sit in solitude and wonderment are legitimate spokesmen for it, whether they may be a few or many. Those who have that intimate relation with the inanimate object about to be injured, polluted, or otherwise despoiled are its legitimate spokesmen.

. . . [T]he problem is to make certain that the inanimate objects, which are the very core of America's beauty, have spokesmen before they are destroyed. It is, of course, true that most of them are under the control of a federal or state agency. The standards given those agencies are usually expressed in terms of the "public interest." Yet "public interest" has so many differing shades of meaning as to be quite meaningless on the environmental front. . . .

. . . [T]he pressures on agencies for favorable action one way or the other are enormous. The suggestion that Congress can stop action which is undesirable is true in theory; yet even Congress is too remote to give meaningful direction and its machinery is too ponderous to use very often. The federal agencies of which I speak are not venal or corrupt. But they are notoriously under the control of powerful interests who manipulate them through advisory committees,

or friendly working relations, or who have that natural affinity with the agency which in time develops between the regulator and the regulated. . . .

The Forest Service—one of the federal agencies behind the scheme to despoil Mineral King—has been notorious for its alignment with lumber companies, although its mandate from Congress directs it to consider the various aspects of multiple use in its supervision of the national forests.

The voice of the inanimate object, therefore, should not be stilled. That does not mean that the judiciary takes over the managerial functions from the federal agency. It merely means that before these priceless bits of Americana (such as a valley, an alpine meadow, a river, or a lake) are forever lost or are so transformed as to be reduced to the eventual rubble of our urban environment, the void of the existing beneficiaries of these environmental wonders should be heard.

Perhaps they will not win. Perhaps the bulldozers of "progress" will plow under all the aesthetic wonders of this beautiful land. That is not the present question. The sole question is, who has standing to be heard?

Those who hike the Appalachian Trail into Sunfish Pond, New Jersey, and camp or sleep there, or run the Allagash in Maine, or climb the Guadalupes in West Texas, or who canoe and portage the Quetico Superior in Minnesota, certainly should have standing to defend those natural wonders before courts or agencies, though they live 3,000 miles away. Those who merely are caught up in environmental news or propaganda and flock to defend those waters or areas may be treated differently. That is why these environmental issues should be tendered by the inanimate object itself. Then there will be assurances that all of the forms of life which it represents will stand before the court—the pileated woodpecker as well as the coyote and bear, the lemmings as well as the trout in the streams. Those inarticulate members of the ecological group cannot speak. But those people who have so fre-quented the place as to know its values and wonders will be able to speak for the entire ecological community.

Ecology reflects the land ethic; and Aldo Leopold wrote in "A Sand County Almanac 204" (1949), "The land ethic simply enlarges the boundaries of the community to include soils, waters, plants, and animals, or collec-tively, the land."

That, as I see it, is the issue of "standing" in the present case and controversy.

Questions and Comments for Discussion

1.   *Legal standing* requires that in a suit by a citizen against a government officer, the citizen must show that the government's ac-tion invades or will invade a private legally protected interest. The issue of standing in this case raised the important policy ques-tion whether environmental groups should be permitted to utilize the courts in order to challenge such proposed developments.

In earlier cases, the court had defined standing under the Administrative Proce-dure Act as (1) "injury in fact," and (2) re-quired that the injury be an interest "arguably within the zone of interests to be protected or regulated" by the statute the agencies were claimed to have violated.

This case was important because it es-sentially adopted a broad definition of standing. Despite the fact the majority ruled against the Sierra Club, it was not difficult for the club to establish standing under the holding in this case by alleging that it or its members would be affected in any of their activities by the proposed development. In other standing cases, discussed in Chapter 8, the Supreme Court narrowed the test of standing, making it more difficult for envi-ronmental groups to meet this legal require-ment. What are the practical effects of granting or limiting standing in such cases?

2.   Justice Douglas in his dissent noted that one of the political issues in this case is the question, "who should decide—the agency or the courts?" The Forest Service, which is entrusted with the maintenance and adminis-tration of national forests, had approved the Disney plan, and the state of California had proposed construction of a highway to facil-itate its development. Why should private environmental groups then be permitted to challenge the decision of a government agency and elected officials? What is Justice Douglas's response to this question?

3.   What would be the practical results of giving inanimate objects standing so that the object, for example, a tree or a mountain, could sue through a representative, a person, or an environmental group? What are the practical reasons for giving a corporation legal standing? Do you think similar reasons should apply to inanimate objects in envi-ronmental disputes?

4.   Some have urged that animals, such as the dolphin, should be given legal standing. One advantage for doing so, according to those who advocate this position, is that damages for pain and suffering of the ani-mal might be awarded in some cases. What ethical and social policy issues are raised by this controversial proposal?

Economics and Regulation

Today, most agree that protecting and preserving the environment is an important policy goal. The more difficult policy issue is how best to achieve this goal. One important aspect of this debate focuses on whether it is best to regulate pollution through "command and control" legislation, or whether it is best to address the problem through other means such as market incentives.

Those who favor government regulation protecting the environment argue that there are "external costs" to the environment associated with some private actions. (For example, air pollution produced by a manufacturing plant.) These costs are not accounted for because those who bear the external costs, that is, those who breathe air from the plant, are not part of the transaction. In 1968, Garret Hardin argued this point in his essay "The Tragedy of the Commons," part of which is reprinted below.

Excerpt from "The Tragedy of the Commons" by Garret Hardin

The tragedy of the commons develops this way. Picture a pasture open to all. It is to be expected that each herdsman will try to keep as many cattle as possible on the commons. Such an arrangement may work reasonably satisfactorily for centuries because tribal wars, poaching, and disease keep the numbers of both man and beast well below the carrying capacity of the land. Finally, however, comes the day of reckoning, that is, the day when the long-desired goal of social stability becomes a reality. At this point, the inherent logic of the commons remorselessly generates tragedy.

As a rational being, each herdsman seeks to maximize his gain. Explicitly or implicitly, more or less consciously, he asks, "What is the utility to me of adding one more animal to my herd?" This utility has one negative and one positive component.

Reprinted excerpt with permission from Garret Hardin, "The Tragedy of Commons," 162 Science *1243, 1243–1248 (December 18, 1968). Copyright 1968 American Association for the Advancement of Science.*

(1) The positive component is a function of the increment of one animal. Since the herdsman receives all the proceeds from the sale of the additional animal, the positive utility is nearly $+1$.

(2) The negative component is a function of the additional overgrazing created by one more animal. Since, however, the effects of overgrazing are shared by all the herdsmen, the negative utility for any particular decision-making herdsman is only a fraction of -1.

Adding together the component partial utilities, the rational herdsman concludes that the only sensible course for him to pursue is to add another animal to his herd. And another; and another.... But his is the conclusion reached by each and every rational herdsman sharing a commons. Therein is the tragedy. Each man is locked into a system that compels him to increase his herd without limit—in a world that is limited. Ruin is the destination toward which all men rush, each pursuing his own best interest in a society that believes in the freedom of the commons. Freedom in a commons brings ruin to all.

VALUING THE NATURAL ENVIRONMENT

The decision to manage some common resources as "public goods" removes them from traditional market forces. If the market does not operate to determine the value of such goods, how does one assign value to them? As the author of the following article suggests, assigning such value is a complex and controversial problem.

Excerpt from "Valuing Natural Environments: Compensation, Market Norms, and the Idea of Public Goods" by Douglas R. Williams

Current debates in environmental law and policy-making often devolve into questions about whether past and proposed efforts to protect natural environments bear some suitable relation to the community's overall social and economic needs. While these questions are obviously important, it is not at all certain how they can or should be approached, much less resolved. At the heart of such questions lie concerns about the value of natural environments relative to other goods. Accordingly, it is widely acknowledged that valuation of natural environments has been, and will continue to be, a central issue in environmental law.

Valuing natural environments is a complex and controversial undertaking. Political decisions to manage these resources as "commons," or public goods, remove many of them from the play of market forces—forces which otherwise serve as our political community's primary institutional mechanism for allocating goods to particular users, and distributing those goods among individuals. In the market, individuals reveal preferences about the value of various goods by engaging in exchange transactions with others. These preferences are expressed in a common language and measure of value, i.e., the price individuals are willing to pay. In assessing the social value of particular market goods, there is, accordingly, a rough and ready analytic: particular goods may be deemed more valuable than other goods by virtue of their ability to command higher prices; with this price mechanism in place, resources are expected to be allocated in ways that reflect the value of various goods.

Treating natural environments as public goods—and, thus, "blocking" the operation of the market—gives rise to two general sorts of valuation difficulties. The first concerns the manner in which preferences are revealed. When natural environments are managed as public goods, they are not subject to exchange transactions like ordinary market commodities; thus, the common language and measure of value, i.e., prices, is not readily available.

Public decisions concerning the use of natural environments differ from market processes in another, perhaps more fundamental, way. In theory, markets do not discriminate among preferences either by virtue of the reasonableness of the beliefs that inform them or by the intensity with which such preferences are held. The discriminations that do occur in markets are primarily the outcome of offers and acceptances of cash or cash equivalents, which are, in turn, dependent to a considerable degree on the background distribution of wealth. For public goods, three critical differences exist: preferences are not revealed in the same way, not all preferences are considered to be worthy of serious consideration, and the commensurability of the beliefs and values that inform expressed preferences is open to serious question.

27 Connecticut Law Review *366–368 (1995).*

Questions and Comments for Discussion

1.   Determining the value of natural resources is important in deciding whether the "benefit" of a particular course of action is worth the cost of undertaking it. While it may be possible to assign an economic value to the Mineral King development project in *Sierra Club v. Marsh,* for example, how should one determine the value of an unspoiled Mineral King Valley?

2.   One important legal issue which may arise under certain environmental laws is the valuation of natural resources for purposes of "natural resource damages." Where the law mandates payment of money damages for harm to natural resources, should damages be determined based on the cost of restoration only? For example, should damages to Prince William Sound, Alaska, following the *Exxon Valdez* oil spill be based only on the cost of restoration?

MARKET-BASED INCENTIVES v. COMMAND AND CONTROL REGULATION

Future generations and the environment itself pay for the costs of activities which pollute the environment—for example, loss of plant and animal species—but they are not parties to the market creating those costs. These external costs and the failure by private actors to consider the environmental impact of their activites, however, do not automatically lead to the conclusion that regulation and public management are the only way to address this problem.

There are some who challenge whether the regulatory process effectively and efficiently achieves our environmental goals. Many critics argue that past air and water pollution policy, which relies on technology-based command and control regulations, is simply too costly for the benefits received. They point to the economic costs of environmental regulation and question whether the current regulatory approach is the best way to spend scarce resources.

Critics also argue that substituting regulatory bureaucracy for market mechanisms actually perpetuates environmental problems by impeding innovative solutions to environmental problems and punishing the economy. They question the success of current regulatory programs and maintain that many regulations mandate solutions which may actually exacerbate environmental damage, for example, banning some types of packaging when production of substitute goods may result in more air and water pollution.

Defenders of a regulatory approach to environmental policy making, on the other hand, emphasize the successes of national environmental laws. They point out that the first round of environmental laws passed in the 1970s has achieved some obvious success. For example, between 1973 and 1987, 96 percent of total suspended solids (TSS) and 93 percent of biochemical oxygen demand (BOD) of direct industrial discharges to water were eliminated, and the number of people served by a combination of primary and secondary sewage treatment rose from 85 million in 1972 to 1976 million in 1988.[4] Air quality also appears to have improved in most places since 1970, as total emissions of common air pollutants, with the exception of nitrogen dioxide, have declined.[5]

Some "free market environmentalists" argue that providing free market incentives, for example, permitting companies to purchase and sell pollution rights, would be an inexpensive and effective way to reduce pollution. This "free-market" approach was adopted in part in the emissions trading program for SO_2 emissions under the 1990 amendments to the

CAA. Supporters argue that permitting plants to trade emission allowances rather than imposing "command and control" regulations to limit SO_2 emissions ultimately achieves cost reduction by allowing the lowest cost plants to sell their emission permits and reduce overall emissions. Opponents argue that adopting pollution trading essentially grants utilities a "right" to pollute at a certain level and that those who raise the flag of "market incentives" actually want to weaken or avoid environmental requirements altogether.

The debate about whether "free-market" incentives should replace "command and control" regulation of industrial pollution will likely continue as people search for ways to increase efficiency and achieve the greatest benefit for the costs of environmental protection. An important question in this debate is to what extent business should bear the costs of environmental protection. Some argue that industry should bear a substantial amount of the costs of controlling pollution because industry, after all, is a primary source of pollution. Businesses will, presumably, increase the cost of their products to those who purchase them and are, to some extent, responsible for the pollution created by the manufacturing process. Does business itself have any ethical obligations to maintain a clean and safe environment?

PROBLEMS ASSOCIATED WITH RISK ASSESSMENT

In the United States, the system for making choices is essentially a political one, and decision making by agencies as well as elected officials is sometimes subject to direct political pressure. Environmental policy makers should consider the costs as well as the benefits, and not just the politics of environmental protection. Cost-benefit analysis is necessary to determine priorities for protection and to decide the best means for achieving those goals. Cost-benefit analysis is also expressly mandated by some environmental laws.

Risk assessment, a component of cost-benefit analysis, determines whether the cost of regulating a particular risk is acceptable based upon the nature and scope of that risk. While there may be a general awareness of the risks related to a hazardous substance, for example, in many instances it is difficult to assess the actual risks of such exposure. This is in part because of the complexity of factors which may give rise to risk, the fact that the dangers associated with some risks—like exposure to toxic materials—may increase over time, and because of limited scientific knowledge about those effects.

In addition, spending priorities are often dictated at least in part by an often unreliable public perception of environmental risks. So while the public greatly fears abandoned hazardous waste facilities, it is unconcerned about radon in homes. Risk assessment professionals, however, believe radon is a far greater health hazard.[6]

Excerpt from "Coping with Complexity" by Alyson C. Flournoy

A LOOK BACK: THE EMERGENCE OF COMPLEXITY AND UNCERTAINTY

27 Loyola of Los Angeles Law Review 809, 810–823 [1994].

In the earliest days of the modern environmental movement, there was little question about what our problems were: the concrete and perceptible blights of the burning Cuyahoga River, of the Santa

Barbara oil spill and its animal victims, and of human illness caused by air pollution. The causes of these ills seemed equally apparent to many: profitable economic activity, undertaken with insufficient attention to environmental consequences. The solutions to these problems appear straightforward: Eliminate the harmful discharges into air and water, thereby protecting human health and the environment. The Clean Air Act Amendments of 1970, the Clean Water Act of 1972, and other major legislation of the early 1970s charted an ambitious course to achieve these goals.

A number of important statutes enacted during the 1970s and 1980s focused on a single medium or resource and its observable symptoms of environmental stress. Responding to apparent degradation, many statutes directed the executive branch to regulate private conduct to assure some less-than-absolute degree of protection of environmental values. These standards typically mandated agencies to balance technological feasibility and economic impacts on the one hand against concerns for health and environmental quality on the other. The standards were usually only vaguely defined by Congress, their full meaning to be articulated through the regulatory process. Congress contemplated the use of tools such as cost-benefit analysis and risk assessment. But agency decision makers were afforded much discretion to interpret statutory goals and to determine how to use relevant analytic tools in achieving these goals.

By the mid-1970s certain difficulties with this statutory model had become apparent. First, the lack of critical information on feasibility and environmental and economic issues made standard setting an arduous process. Regulatory decisions were in many cases subject to challenge because of inadequate supporting data or analysis. The result was often-lengthy battles challenging agency decisions in the courts.

Second, in part due to Congress's meager direction on policies and priorities, regulators often claimed scientific authority as the basis for regulatory decisions that could not be entirely justified by scientific method. Regulators understandably sought refuge in scientific analysis and conclusions to bolster the controversial policy decisions necessitated by vague statutory directives. But this too facilitated challenges to agency decisions. It also tended to keep certain important policy choices, disguised as scientific conclusions, hidden from public view. Inadequate public understanding of policy choices and the black-and-white picture of environmental problems presented in the media contributed to a distorted public perception of environmental problems and, in some cases, a lack of public support for environmental regulation. Thus, it became clear that ambitious and rigorous statutory goals sometimes entailed unanticipated economic consequences. In response to these problems, statutory deadlines were pushed back, goals were modified, and agencies lumbered on with their herculean task.

Scientific knowledge evolved rapidly over this period, revealing new dimensions of natural systems and our impacts on them. We have become aware of new problems, and of the interrelationship among systems and phenomena previously treated as independent. An ever-increasing body of information has potential relevance to regulatory decisions. Pollution, we have been forced

Excerpt from "Coping with Complexity" by Alyson C. Flournoy (continued)

to realize, is not solely a result of inattention or evil minds and cannot be entirely eliminated without radical change to our society and our economy. Our economy is based on practices that generate enormous environmental impacts, some of which we lack the resources, the know-how, or the will to eliminate. The causes of environmental degradation, direct and indirect, are more numerous than we had realized and less susceptible of complete explanation. Moreover, the natural systems affected are more complex than we earlier realized—or cared to admit. Thus, both the scientific issues and the policy choices involved in regulation are more complex than initially appeared to be the case.

Our growing knowledge base has not meant the elimination of uncertainty. As some gaps in our understanding have been eliminated, they have been replaced by other, sometimes more profound, sources of doubt. Uncertainty often characterizes our understanding of the complex systems and phenomena we have begun to recognize.

As scientific knowledge has advanced and revealed new dimensions of environmental problems, our laws have only partially kept pace. In the area of pollution control, we have continued to work with a medium-specific approach, although the interdependence of natural elements has come to be viewed as central to meaningful analysis of environmental impacts. In resource protection the need for an ecosystemic approach demands that we consider new laws to supplement existing mandates. Our laws regarding public resource and species protection do not adequately respond to the reality of the extinction crisis: that the causes of species extinction are profoundly embedded in long-accepted but unacceptable economic practices, and that preserving species will require economic adjustment for some individuals, industries, and regions. In toxics regulation we have followed the early-adopted strategy of evaluating each candidate substance independently and focusing almost solely on cancer risk, despite growing evidence that cumulative, synergistic, and noncancer effects from these substances may be important. Moreover, in controlling toxics, we have relied on a data-intensive approach that predicates regulation on an often-unattainable volume of information.

Questions and Comments for Discussion

1.   One example of the problem of scientific uncertainty and risk assessment in environmental litigation involves the rules for evaluating the sufficiency of scientific evidence in complex toxic tort litigation. As you will learn in Chapter 4, under traditional tort law, a plaintiff in a civil suit who sues because the defendant's wrongful action harmed the plaintiff must prove that the defendant's action "caused in fact" her injury. Proof of scientific causation in such cases often involves the court's determination of whether scientific evidence introduced at trial supports the verdict in the case.

WHO SHOULD REGULATE?

Whether environmental goals can best be met through regulation at the state or the federal level is another politically charged issue.

In the debate on environmental policy making, the argument can be made that by de-centralizing environmental decision making, local and state governments will be better able to respond to changing circumstances and new information. The risks are in delegating authority to states which lack the resources and political will and expertise to implement environmental programs.

Clearly some environmental problems, like air and water pollution, need decisive action, and most policy makers have embraced a national approach to environmental regulation. But many federal environmental laws, such as the CAA and CWA, have established a state/federal partnership. For example, as you will see in Chapter 10, the Environmental Protection Agency establishes emission standards under the CAA, but states develop proposals for meeting those requirements and undertake monitoring and enforcement responsibilities. In the future, we are likely to see states take on increasing responsibility for administering and enforcing these federal environmental laws.

Excerpt from "Environmental Federalism" by Paul R. Portney

Although . . . the Clean Air and Clean Water acts often serve important responsibilities for state and sometimes local governments, they are all federal laws. Yet there is no reason why environmental policy must be made at the federal level. Over the past decade or so some of the most interesting environmental initiatives have arisen at the state level. This began with the individual states gradually taking over responsibility for the operation and management of air and water pollution programs under the federal laws. . . .

More important, the individual states have become active in passing their own environmental laws. For example, by early 1989 five states (New York, Wisconsin, Massachusetts, Minnesota, and New Hampshire) had passed laws to combat acid rain, and one state (Michigan) had tightened a previous emissions control law because of concern about acid deposition. Similarly, forty states now have their own versions of the federal Superfund law to provide monies to clean up abandoned

"Environmental Federalism" in Public Policies for Environmental Protection, *282–283 [1990].*

hazardous waste disposal sites. Most significant, perhaps, has been the passage in California of the Safe Drinking Water and Toxic Enforcement Act of 1986. . . .

How should one view this resurgence of state regulatory activity? There are good arguments both for and against it. In the case of acid rain, for instance, actions by a handful of individual states are no substitute for a coherent national policy. Interjurisdictional externalities are simply too pervasive in this case for states to effectively act alone. In fact, acid deposition should probably be addressed at the international rather than the national level. This is also true for many water pollution problems.

Also militating against decentralized environmental regulation is the possibility that it would foster an unhealthy competition between states to reduce environmental standards in order to attract new business growth. Although there is little empirical evidence to suggest that this has been so to date, it remains a serious concern to many. Beyond that, environmental standards that differ greatly from state to state would make it very difficult for

Excerpt from "Environmental Federalism" by Paul R. Portney (continued)

companies doing business in many different areas. This is most obvious in the case of motor vehicle emissions standards; automakers simply could not manufacture cars to meet fifty different sets of standards. As in this case, some sort of federal preemption may occasionally be required.

On the other hand, there are reasons to be encouraged about the proliferation of state initiatives. To begin with, while some environmental problems clearly transcend state (or even national) boundaries, others do not. Where they do not, decentralized regulation may reflect local conditions and tastes better than top-down regulation from Washington. There is no reason, for example, why the extent of clean-up activities at each abandoned hazardous waste disposal site should be the same from state to state. If no spill-overs from one area to another exist (and they are unlikely to in the case of such sites), it might make sense to allow states or even local governments the right to decide how far each cleanup should proceed. Similarly, if some communities are willing to tolerate somewhat higher levels of certain contaminants in their drinking water than the federal government feels are advisable, it is not clear why they should be prohibited from doing so. Even if such decentralization in standard-setting were permitted, the federal government would still play the important role of sponsoring research on the adverse health and ecological effects associated with environmental pollutants, the control technologies that could be used to address certain types of problems, and so on. . . .

Questions and Comments for Discussion

1. Some argue that states should be encouraged to become laboratories for experiments in environmental regulation. Daniel P. Selmi, in *Experimentation and the 'New' Environmental Law,*[7] writes: "[I]n the past decade the larger states have shown the capacity to innovate in the environmental law field by undertaking important experiments in risk management, pollution prevention, hazardous waste clean up, information-based disclosure, and marketable permit systems. Moreover, federal environmental law has borrowed heavily from state innovations, at least in recent years.

Most importantly, a couple of practical reasons require that the effort be state-led. First, states are best suited to provide the variety of regulatory settings needed to determine whether economic incentives can viably replace command and control. Furthermore, if economic incentives prove to be a success, states ultimately will be charged with implementing them (unless the current federal-state structure of environmental law is totally discarded). Therefore, gaining experience at the state level seems sensible. . . ."

2. On the other hand, there are those who challenge the proposition that states should be encouraged to act as "laboratories" for social policy making. One author asks: "[W]hat gives the states a special connection to the people, in an era when airlines and interstate highways mean that most Americans cross state borders without thinking about it, whether to pursue their careers or to take a vacation? Are states necessarily wiser? More efficient? More frugal? . . . There are other problems, too. In unbridled competition between the states, for example, what would prevent some states from cutting services and taxes to the bone to lure

businesses, forcing others to do likewise and creating a downward spiral? . . ."[8]

3. One environmental issue with implications for federalism is the extent to which states can regulate the importation of hazardous waste from outside a state for disposal in the state. That question, which raises constitutional issues about the appropriate scope of congressional power under the "commerce clause" of the Constitution, is addressed in Chapter 7 of this text.

LAW AND THE FUTURE: WHERE SHOULD WE GO FROM HERE?

Forty years ago, few people thought much of pouring gasoline down a sewer drain or dumping batteries or paint cans in the trash. Recycling was practically unheard of. Today, many if not most Americans are aware and concerned about the environmental implications of these and other everyday activities, primarily because of the success of federal environmental regulatory policy.

Many believe that global environmental issues will become increasingly important in future environmental policy making. The problems of chemical waste disposal, water pollution, and air pollution do not, after all, stop at national boundaries. And an increasingly global economy will create domestic concerns about the environmental impact of products imported into the American economy—for example, pesticide contamination in imported food. Specific concerns about the effects of global warming, nuclear radiation, and the greenhouse effect are likely to grow as evidence of the harmful effects of human activity on the global environment continues to mount.

Public opinion will continue to play an important role in establishing international environmental policy and determining at what costs society is willing to achieve particular environmental goals. In the following excerpt, the author reviews past American environmental law and policy and considers future themes.

Excerpt from "Evolving Consensus: The Dynamic Future of Environmental Law and Policy" by Ronald H. Rosenberg

As our nation moves towards the threshold of the twenty-first century, it seems an appropriate time for us to take stock of the significant developments our society has produced in the field of environmental protection during the last several decades. Looking back over the past twenty-five years, one would have to be

27 Loyola of Los Angeles Law Review *1048* *[1994].*

impressed by the degree of societal interest and activity in matters of environmental protection. On the most superficial level, the political and popular culture has embraced environmentally protective goals and images. Environmental destruction usually is depicted in a negative light and heroic characterizations often are accorded to those protective of environmental values. This trend even has spilled over into the political sphere, with

Excerpt from "Evolving Consensus: The Dynamic Future of Environmental Law and Policy" by Ronald H. Rosenberg (continued)

at least one recent president describing himself as the "environmental President" and many other congressional leaders emphasizing their support for environmental or "green" issues. Popular culture increasingly reflects pro-environmental images such as the motion pictures *The Pelican Brief, FernGully,* and *Medicine Man,* and the children's cartoon series *Captain Planet.* Popular music and novels also contain many environmental themes. Beyond this, even American consumerism reflects the popular identification with environmental values. Advertising messages increasingly tout the environmentally sensitive characteristics of consumer goods and product packaging. Public opinion polls reflect public attitudes that consistently rank environmental protection as an extremely important and broadly supported public value. . . .

The last quarter century has also revealed great public faith in legal solutions to pressing environmental problems. As unrestrained market forces were perceived to have been responsible for much of the environmental damage in prior years, a legislatively initiated, yet administratively implemented system of environmental regulation was thought to be the best cure. Bureaucratic responses to modern environmental problems were ordered, reflecting the new acceptance of environmental protection as a legitimate government function. During this period Congress enacted at least twenty-five major environmental statutes—some of voluminous proportions and daunting complexity. This surge of congressional action reflected both the success of interest group politics and a naiveté about the complexity and diversity of the problems. It also revealed an exag-

gerated optimism about the regulatory capacity of administrative agencies. The newly created environmental bureaucracy, the Environmental Protection Agency (EPA), was charged with the responsibility of issuing detailed performance-based pollution control rules for a wide range of industrial categories. During this early period environmental legislation occasionally concentrated the EPA's attention and resources upon highly visible, well-publicized environmental issues—often at the expense of problems presenting greater public health and environmental risks. Sometimes major sources of environmental pollution were all but ignored by the EPA and Congress. Nonpoint source water pollution and hazardous air and water pollution control are a few examples.

***

Despite the continuous social development of a national environmental policy during the last quarter century, we must remember that our society and economy constitute a complex system of interrelated parts. Thus, the development of effective and economically feasible environmental regulations is bound to take time. Although we are an impatient people, we must understand that environmental protection is a multifaceted subject with substantial complexities and internal conflicts. Our goals should be to improve our environmental regulation so we may achieve broadly supported environmental goals. Over the next quarter century, I believe that American environmental policy should follow five basic themes.

First, we must recognize the need to adapt to changing conditions both in the natural environment and in the political-legal system. This response to change will be an important measure of the overall success of our environmental policy during this period. We must understand that environmental policies are created on a number of levels: global, national, regional, and finally, local. The environmental rules adopted at each level are important, and each level of action influences the others. . . .

Second, it is important that American environmental policy take a more holistic view of environmental problems. It is important that environmental regulation not be undertaken with a rigid and formalistic rule structure. We must focus on the ultimate goal of achieving environmental improvement. This need to undertake a unified analysis of environmentally damaging activities will require an understanding of the interconnection between various aspects of these activities. . . . Every environmental problem should be assessed in terms of the overall impact of controlling individual aspects of the activity. It may be that different situations will result in different optimal combinations of controls and regulation. . . .

Third, as we move into the next century, it is vitally important to expand our base of knowledge. We need to know more about ecological systems and environmental sciences generally. How are the intricate systems of nature affected by new land development, new products, and new technology? This knowledge will be important to the development of engineering approaches and technology, which hopefully will result in the development of environmentally benign production technologies and development strategies. . . .

Fourth, the next twenty-five years should also see a clarification of pub-

lic values concerning environmental interests. . . . Americans must also decide what their environmental goals are. What is most important to the largest number of people? Establishing our environmental values should help policy makers determine which environmental interests are worthy of protection. However, it is important that we understand that "You can't have it all." It will be necessary to prioritize environmental values and to understand that environmental policy cannot achieve all possible goals designed by all segments of the society. . . .

Finally, we must consider developments in the legal structure of our environmental policy-making apparatus.

Should we continue the existing heavy reliance on regulatory controls to improve environmental conditions? If so, how can the process of environmental regulation be improved, simplified, or streamlined?

. . . [A]nother legal matter worthy of significant consideration is the problem of environmental overregulation. . . . It will be important over the next few years to clarify the parameters of uncompensated regulation for environmental purposes. Uncertainty as to the legitimate boundaries of takings regulation certainly affects both governmental regulators and private property owners adversely. . . .

In addition to regulatory responses to environmental problems, the next quarter century should see an increase in the use of nonregulatory mechanisms. While environmental law has begun to emphasize market alternatives to regulatory controls, the next two-and-a-half decades should see a more sophisticated and blended approach.

Comments and Questions for Discussion

1. What are the five basic themes which this author believes American environmental policy should follow in the future?
2. Do you agree with each of these themes? If so, why? If not, why not?

3. Are there other "themes" which you believe are important for future American environmental policy? If so, what are these other environmental themes and goals which society should strive to meet?

COMMENTS AND CONCLUSION

The purpose of this chapter is to highlight some of the important environmental policy issues, problems, and goals which underlie the environmental laws and policy making, and to encourage you to respond to various points of view expressed by authors in the chapter. Subsequent chapters of this book examine how various environmental laws address particular environmental problems and issues. As you read those chapters, remember that these laws do not spring from a vacuum. Legislators, courts, and agency officers adopt and implement laws and regulations in response to perceived harms and a determination that a particular approach will best address those harms. Ultimately, law making is policy making. As you study environmental law in the following chapters, try to identify the environmental policy-making goals of the law. What environmental concerns does the law attempt to address? How likely is it that the law will achieve those environmental goals? Are there alternative approaches to solving this problem? What are the costs as well as the benefits of this approach to environmental policy making?

GLOSSARY

Clean Air Act (CAA)—The Clean Air Act Amendments of 1970, now known as the Clean Air Act, substantially increased federal authority and responsibility over air pollution. Among other things, the Act directs the EPA to establish national ambient air quality standards which are enforceable by the states through state implementation plans. The Act was amended in 1977 and again in 1990 to address specific problems such as hazardous air pollution and acid rain.

Clean Water Act (CWA)—The 1972 amendments to the Federal Water Pollution Control Act, now known as the Clean Water Act, protect surface water by controlling or preventing discharge of pollutants into those waters. The law was amended in 1987 to address water quality in areas where compliance with minimum discharge standards are insufficient to meet water quality goals.

Comprehensive Environmental Response, Compensation and Liability Act of 1980 (CERCLA)—CERCLA, commonly known as "Superfund," was enacted in 1980 to address the threat to human health and the environment posed by abandoned hazardous waste disposal sites. The law was substantially amended in 1986 by the Superfund Amendments and Reauthorization Act (SARA).

Endangered Species Act (ESA)—This 1973 Act prohibits the import, export, taking, or trading of any endangered species of fish or wildlife. The Act protects both endangered and threatened species. Any person may petition to have a species removed from or added to the endangered or threatened species list.

Environmental Protection Agency (EPA)—This federal agency was created in 1970. The EPA studies environmental problems and establishes and enforces United States environmental standards, including air and water pollution standards, toxic substances regulations, solid and hazardous wastes rules, and pesticide and insecticide registration requirements.

Federal Insecticide, Fungicide, and Rodenticide Act (FIFRA)—First enacted in 1947 and substantially amended in 1972 and again in 1975, 1978, 1980, and 1988, this statute generally provides that a person may not distribute, sell, ship, or deliver a pesticide unless it is registered with the EPA. To be registered under the law, pesticides must be properly labeled and produce no reasonable adverse effects on the environment.

National Environmental Policy Act (NEPA)—NEPA, adopted in 1970, sets forth the general policy of the federal government concerning the environment, establishes the Council on Environmental Quality (CEQ), and requires federal agencies to consider the environmental impact of every major federal action significantly affecting the quality of the human environment.

Oil Pollution Act of 1990 (OPA)—This Act establishes the federal liability scheme for vessels and facilities that spill oil on waters subject to United States jurisdiction.

Resource Conservation and Recovery Act (RCRA)—RCRA was enacted in 1976 to address the problems associated with the generation and disposal of hazardous and solid wastes. RCRA, which applies mainly to active facilities, is designed to provide "cradle-to-grave" control of hazardous waste by imposing management requirements on generators and transporters of hazardous wastes and upon owners and operators of disposal facilities. The law was substantially amended in 1984 by the Hazardous and Solid Waste Amendments (HSWA).

Safe Drinking Water Act (SDWA)—SDWA was enacted in 1974 and amended in 1986 and 1996. Its purpose is to protect the quality of the Nation's drinking water supply by requiring the EPA to establish maximum contaminant level goals and national primary drinking water regulations for certain contaminants found in public water systems.

Superfund—Established by CERCLA; common reference to the provisions of the 1980 act.

Toxic Substances Control Act (TSCA)—Enacted in 1976, TSCA has been amended three times. TSCA places the responsibility on manufacturers to provide data on the health and environmental effects of chemical substances and mixtures, and gives EPA comprehensive authority to regulate the manufacture, use, distribution, and disposal of chemical substances. Other titles in TSCA address specific problems: Title II of TSCA is entitled the Asbestos Hazardous Emergency Response Act, Title III the Indoor Radon Abatement Act, and Title IV the Lead-Based Paint Exposure Reduction Act.

CASES FOR DISCUSSION

1. 1995 legislation passed by the House and expected to prompt a fight in the Senate would require federal agencies to compensate landowners when government actions to protect the

environment cause a decrease in property values. What are the costs and benefits of this proposal? What environmental ethical and economic considerations underlie the debate?

2.   Assume that the Department of the Interior adopts a regulation under the Endangered Species Act which would impose a regulatory moratorium for new listings of endangered species and designation of critical habitat. Whose interests are affected by this regulation? Under Justice Douglas's opinion in *Sierra Club v. Morton,* who should have standing to challenge the regulation? What are the implications of your answer?

3.   One key element of recent proposals to change the course of federal environmental policy is a proposal to impose risk-assessment requirements on federal environmental rule making. One proposal would require that an agency undertake a cost-benefit analysis and adopt a rule only if the benefits outweigh the costs of the rule. What are the practical and policy implications of this requirement? Would you support such an approach to policy making? Why or why not?

ENDNOTES

1. Arnold Rietze, *Environmental Policy—It Is Time for a New Beginning,* 14 Colum. J. Envtl. L. 111 (1989).

2. Eric T. Freyfogle, *The Ethical Strands of Environmental Law,* 1994 U. Ill. L. Rev. 819 (1994).

3. Author's note: Standing under the APA (Administrative Procedure Act) is discussed in Chapter 8 of this textbook.

4. James Lis and Kenneth Chilton, "Clean Water—Murky Policy," Policy Study # 109, Center for the Study of American Business, Washington University, January 1992, p. 8.

5. Paul R. Portney, "Air Pollution Policy," *Public Policies for Environmental Protection* (1990): 50.

6. Kenneth Chilton, "Environmental Dialogue: Setting Priorities for Environmental Protection," Policy Study No. 108, Center for the Study of American Business, Washington University, October 1991.

7. Daniel P. Selmi, *Experimentation and the 'New' Environmental Law,* 27 Loy. L.A.L. Rev. 1061 (1994).

8. R. W. Apple Jr., "You Say You Want a Devolution," *New York Times,* Sunday, 29 January 1995, sec. 4, p. 1.

2

THE AMERICAN LEGAL SYSTEM: SOURCES OF LAW AND RULES OF PROCEDURE

INTRODUCTION

The purpose of this chapter is to provide some general information about the American legal system, and the rules applied by the courts in resolving civil disputes. Knowledge of the American legal system will help you understand how law affects the environment and prepare you to learn from the cases discussed in this text. This chapter examines general sources of law, the American legal system, and rules of civil procedure.

CIVIL CASES IN GENERAL

Civil law describes legal actions brought by an individual against another individual, or in some cases the government, for breach of legal duties owed to that individual. An example of a civil suit is an action by an injured party (the plaintiff) against another person (the defendant) for harm caused to the plaintiff or his property as a result of the defendant's negligence. The *legal remedy* in such cases is generally monetary. In some civil cases a court may order other kinds of relief such as an *injunction,* which is a court order prohibiting the defendant from engaging in certain activity in the future.

Another kind of civil law case is a case where an individual or group challenges a law directly, or challenges an administrative agency's action taken in carrying out a statute or administrative rule. Examples include cases brought by businesses and individuals to challenge agency rule making under environmental laws like the Clean Air and Clean Water acts and cases where a petitioner challenges the legality of the statute itself. For example, in Chapter 7 you will read an excerpt from *Hodel v. Virginia Surface Mining and Reclamation Association* (452 U.S. 264 [1981]) where plaintiffs argued that the Surface Mining Control and Reclamation Act resulted in an unconstitutional taking of their property in violation of the Fifth Amendment. Plaintiffs had filed an action for *declaratory relief,* a legal action challenging the legality of the statute. The Supreme Court ultimately upheld the constitutionality of the statute in that challenge.

In order to obtain review of agency action by the courts (called *judicial review*), a petition is filed in a court under the relevant statute. Various legal doctrines may affect a court's willingness to grant judicial review in cases challenging agency action. These doctrines, including *standing* and *exhaustion of administrative remedies,* are discussed in depth in Chapter 8.

Most statutes permit a petition to be filed for review of federal agency action in a federal court of appeals, although some statutes mandate review in a federal district court. The court reviews the decison of the administrative agency to determine whether the agency violated a provision of law in its interpretation or application.

When special statutory procedures for review are lacking, a party looks to general rules governing jurisdiction and procedure. Instead of challenging an agency rule directly, an individual may choose to wait until an enforcement action is brought against him and challenge the rule in that proceeding.

GENERAL SOURCES OF LAW

The American system of government is a *federal* system with a central government made up of the Congress, the president, and the federal court system and fifty *state* governments made up of a state legislature, a governor, and a state court system. A person in the U.S. is subject to laws passed by both the federal and state governments as well as state political subdivisions within the state, like counties and cities.

In the event of a conflict between state and federal law, which law controls? Under the express language of the "Supremacy Clause" of the U.S. Constitution, the Constitution is the supreme law of the land, so that federal laws enacted by the federal government under its constitutional power take priority over state laws. All powers not given to the federal government are reserved to the states, under the Tenth Amendment to the Constitution.

The scope of federal power is an important question in environmental law issues. Whether federal environmental law "pre-empts" state law, and the federal government's power to enact environmental laws under its "commerce clause" powers, raises important political and social policy questions. These questions are examined in Chapter 7.

Constitutional Law

The first and most important source of law is the *U.S. Constitution.* The Constitution and federal laws enacted in conformance to its provisions take priority over all other laws. Under the principle of *judicial review,* the courts may declare any state or federal law which conflicts with provisions of the U.S. Constitution "unconstitutional" and thus null and void. The states also have adopted *state constitutions,* which take priority over conflicting state laws. Chapter 7 examines some of the constitutional issues which may arise under Congress' power to regulate interstate commerce under the commerce clause.

Another important constitutional issue in environmental law cases is the scope of the Fifth and Fourteenth Amendments' prohibitions against the government's "taking" of private property without just compensation. This issue is explored in Chapter 6. The Bill of Rights, the first ten amendments to the Constitution, is also a basis for constitutional challenges to state and federal environmental laws. The Bill of Rights contains specific language which protects individuals from certain government actions which interfere with individual freedom. In Chapter 14, you will read the *Dow Chemical* case in which the Dow

Chemical Company argued that aerial photographs taken of its property by the EPA without a search warrant violated Dow's Fourth Amendment Constitutional right against unreasonable searches and seizures (476 U.S. 227 [1986]).

A First Amendment Challenge The First Amendment to the Constitution protects freedom of speech. The First Amendment reads as follows:

> Congress shall make no law respecting an establishment of religion, or prohibiting the free exercise thereof; or abridging the freedom of speech, or of the press; or the right of the people peaceably to assemble, and to petition the Government for a redress of grievances.

In the following case, trade associations challenged a California law which prohibited advertising products as "biodegradable" or "recyclable" unless the product met the definition of those terms set out in the statute. Plaintiffs argued that the statute violated plaintiff's First Amendment right of freedom of speech and should be held unconstitutional by the court. In upholding the statute, the majority of the court held that the statute met a four-pronged legal test (the intermediate scrutiny test) established by the Supreme Court for commercial speech. A portion of the court's opinion finding that the statute regulated only commercial speech and applying the "intermediate scrutiny test" to the statute is set out below.

ASSOCIATION OF NATIONAL ADVERTISERS v. LUNGREN
44 F.3d 726 (9th Cir. Cal. 1994)

CHOY, Circuit Judge

Appellants, the Association of National Advertisers, Inc, *et al.* (Trade Associations), appeal the district court's grant of summary judgment upholding the constitutionality of California Business and Professions Code § 17508.5.... We affirm.

I. FACTUAL AND PROCEDURAL BACKGROUND

Section 17508.5 makes it unlawful for a manufacturer or distributor of consumer goods to represent that its products are "ozone friendly," "biodegradable," "photo-degradable," "recyclable," or "recycled" unless their goods meet the statute's definitions of those terms. . . .[1] In 1990, the California legislature enacted this statute in the wake of a report on environmental advertising issued by a ten-state task force of state attorneys general (the Task Force). This report summarized the findings of the Task Force from a public meeting it convened in March 1990 to address the potential for abuse raised by the increasing popularity of what the attorneys general characterized as "[g]reen marketing . . . the marketing craze of the 1990s."

The Task Force found disparities in the usage of these terms by different firms and noted the assertions of environmental groups and business representatives that there was "growing confusion surrounding many environmental marketing claims" creating a "fertile ground for abusive business practices. . . ." The Task Force further discerned a "wide degree of consensus among business and environmental groups" on the need for "development of national standards, guidelines or definitions to guide business in making environmental claims and to help consumers understand the claims made." Section 17508.5 is an attempt to implement these findings at the state level.

In February 1992, the Trade Associations responded to the passage of Section 17508.5 by bringing suit in the Northern District of California against the attorney general of California, Appellee Daniel Lungren (Lungren or California). The Trade Associations sought a declaration that Section 17508.5 impermissibly restricts both commercial and non-commercial speech and is unconstitutionally vague. . . .

II. DISCUSSION

The Trade Associations contend that the district court erred in holding that Section 17508.5 regulates only commercial speech. They further asserted that as a result the district court applied to the statute an unduly deferential standard of review, the intermediate scrutiny [test] governing commercial speech. We disagree. . . .

We agree with the district court that "the messages regulated by Section 17508.5 possess the three characteristics recognized by the court as constitutive of commercial speech" in *Bolger v. Youngs Drug Products Corp.,* 463 U.S. 60 (1983). In *Bolger,* the court struck down a federal statute prohibiting the mailing of unsolicited advertisements for contraceptives under the First Amendment. In doing so, the court set out three characteristics which, in combination, supported its conclusion that the informational pamphlets at issue constituted commercial speech, including (i) their advertising format, (ii) their reference to a spe-

cific product, and (iii) the underlying economic motive of the speaker. . . .

Here, the district court reasonably found all three of these factors present. Judge Patel observed:

> First, by its explicit terms, the statute regulates representations concerning a specific consumer good which take[s] the form of advertisements or product labels. Second, Section 17508.5 specifically requires that the representation be made about a specific consumer good which a firm manufactures or distributes. Third, there is little doubt that by touting the environmental benefits of consumer products, plaintiffs' association members hope to capture a portion of the 'green market.'

Accordingly, the district court correctly settled on the "more relaxed inquiry" applicable to restrictions on commercial speech . . . Under this intermediate scrutiny, the asserted governmental interest must be "substantial," rather than "compelling," and the regulation adopted must "directly advance" this interest, rather than be "precisely drawn." . . .

. . . [W]e conclude that the district court established the basis for intermediate scrutiny by determining correctly that Section 17508.5 is directed only at commercial speech and does not collaterally stifle more privileged speech. . . .

[*Applying this test, the court found that the statute directly advanced the asserted government interest. That governmental interest included increasing consumer knowledge and awareness and discouraging exploitation and deception in the growing green market.*]

Questions and Comments for Discussion

1.   As this case illustrates, the courts have fashioned various tests for determining whether a statute violates First Amendment constitutional principles depending on the

kind of speech at issue. How did the court define *commercial speech* in this case?

2.   Once the court concluded that the speech at issue in this case was commercial speech,

the court applied the *intermediate scrutiny* test, a test less strict than that applied to fully protected political and non-commercial speech. According to the court, the intermediate scrutiny test is a "more relaxed inquiry." What are the characteristics of this test?

3.   Why did the majority of the appeals court agree with the district court that Section 17508.5 withstood the intermediate scrutiny test? What consumer protection interests supported its conclusion?

4.   The constitutionality of a statute like this one raises conflicting First Amendment concerns. As an illustration of those concerns, consider the words of Judge Noonan, who filed a dissent in this case. He said, in part:

> I accept the majority's conclusion that the speech made criminal by this statute is commercial speech. I follow the doctrine of the Supreme Court that commercial speech is, ordinarily, more subject to state regulation than noncommercial speech. I have no doubt at all that untrue or deceptive advertising can be outlawed. I see no problem in the government prescribing precise labels for what cures our bodies or goes into them, or goes into a gas tank. But I have great difficulty in seeing this statute as anything other than a zealous and unconstitutional intrusion by a state government into an area where technologies are developing, the free play of ideas is important, and the free speech of everyone, including manufacturers and distributors, is essential to the development of a healthy environment. Tested by our Bill of Rights, the statute is defective.

Judge Noonan went on to say,

> A variety of words are commonly used in American advertising, all of which are potentially misleading. For example: antique, bargain, economical, environmentally sound, naturally good. A paternalistic government might decide to protect consumers by criminalizing all advertising containing these words if the product advertised failed to conform with the state's own definition. That the terms defined were capable of misleading use would be incontestable. That a criminal law of this character would violate the First Amendment would be equally incontestable.

Treaties

Under the Constitution, treaties made by the president with foreign governments and approved by the U.S. Senate by two-thirds vote are considered "the supreme law of the land." This means that a state or a federal law may be invalid if it conflicts with the provisions of a duly enacted treaty. Chapter 15 examines treaties such as the **North Atlantic Free Trade Agreement** (NAFTA) and **General Agreement on Tariffs and Trade** (GATT) which have important implications for the national and international environment.

State and Federal Statutes

Statutes are laws passed by Congress or the state legislatures which become effective when signed by the executive (the president or a state's governor). An example of a state statute is the California "green marketing" statute at issue in the *Lungren* case above. Federal environmental statutes, for example, the Clean Air and Clean Water acts, and administrative rules properly enacted in conformance to them, take priority over state and local laws.

Local laws, called *ordinances,* are enacted by legislatures like a city council under authority of state law. Most states, for example, have statutes authorizing local governments to adopt a local zoning code. Under zoning ordinances, local governments, such as cities or counties, regulate land use within their jurisdiction. Some local governments have also adopted ordinances to address specific environmental concerns, which may be challenged in court. For example, assume a local government passes an ordinance to regulate pesticide application within its jurisdiction. Possible legal challenges include whether the ordinance falls within the local government's power to protect the health and safety and whether federal law pre-empts or supercedes the ordinance.

Executive Orders

The executive branch generally does not make laws, but executives, like the president and the governors of the states, have the responsibility to enforce the law. In some cases, however, executives may issue *executive orders,* which are legally enforceable if the legislature has delegated that power to the executive or if the order is justified on constitutional grounds. While environmental statutes generally empower administrative agencies to develop and promulgate rules and regulations, the president can also empower an executive agency to promulgate regulations by executive order.

Administrative Law

Most environmental law today consists of federal and state administrative rules and regulations, administrative decisions, and administrative policy implemented in enforcement actions. These administrative rules and regulations comprise a body of law known as *administrative law.* The *Federal Register* and the **Code of Federal Regulations** (CFR) contain these federal administrative rules and regulations, while state administrative agency rules and regulations are codified at the state level.

Agencies have the authority to adopt and implement administrative rules, to adjudicate disputes, and to impose sanctions for violations of their rules in conformance to statutes creating and delegating to them such powers. The influence of agency action and administrative rule making is pervasive in the area of environmental law and regulation. Chapter 8, Administrative Law, examines administrative law principles and issues in more depth.

Common Law

Common law is judge-made law or case law that originated in England in the Middle Ages and continues to evolve as judges write legal opinions on actual cases. In America, England, and other common law countries, judges are required to follow the decisions of other judges in their jurisdiction in similar cases. This doctrine is called the doctrine of *stare decisis,* which means "let the decision stand." However, every case is unique, and for this reason, common law permits a court to "distinguish" prior case law, so that common law evolves.

In cases where public policy no longer supports application of a particular legal rule, courts also may modify the common law rule altogether. An example of the ability of common law to evolve is *Prah v. Maretti* 321 N.W. 2d 182 (Wis. 1982), a nuisance case discussed in Chapter 3. In that case, Prah sued Maretti, alleging that the construction of Maretti's home would constitute a private nuisance because it would substantially obstruct Prah's solar collectors, which supplied energy for heat and hot water.

The district court granted summary judgment for Maretti. Under traditional American common law, a landowner had no legal right in the absence of an easement to unobstructed light and air from the adjoining land. However, the Wisconsin Supreme Court permitted Prah to pursue a nuisance claim in the case. The court based its decision on its conclusion that policies supporting the original rule were no longer applicable. The court said:

Courts should not implement obsolete policies that have lost their vigor over the course of the years. The law of private nuisance is better suited to resolve landowners' disputes about property development in the 1980s than is a rigid rule which does not recognize a landowner's interest in access to sunlight. . . .

And it quoted with approval the following statement:

Inherent in the common law is a dynamic principle which allows it to grow and to tailor itself to meet changing needs within the doctrine of *stare decisis,* which, if correctly understood, was not static and did not forever prevent the courts from reversing themselves or from applying principles of common law to new situations as the need arose. If this were not so, we must succumb to a rule that a judge should let others 'long dead and unaware of the problems of the age in which he lives, do his thinking for him' (quoting Justice Douglas, 49 Columbia Law Review [1949]).

COURT STRUCTURE

State court systems, which include those of the 50 states and the District of Columbia, are established by the state constitutions. They share fundamental common characteristics with variation between the particular structure of the system in each state. The federal court system is established by Article III of the U.S. Constitution.

Appendix A provides graphic depictions of the court systems.

State Court Systems

Inferior Courts   The state court systems generally consist of three levels of courts—inferior courts, trial courts, and appellate courts. *Inferior courts* are minor courts with limited jurisdiction to resolve minor criminal matters and small civil disputes. Examples include municipal courts and small claims courts. In most cases, appeals from these courts of limited jurisdiction require a new trial (or ***trial de novo***) because the minor courts do not keep a formal record of their proceedings.

State Trial Courts   By far, the vast amount of legal business in this country takes place in state trial courts. In most states, there is at least one state trial court for each county, and larger counties may have many more. The state trial court establishes the *facts* in a dispute and *applies the law to the facts* in order to reach a decision. In some cases, such as serious criminal offenses and certain kinds of civil cases, a party is entitled to a jury trial. In these cases, a jury determines the facts and applies the law to those facts as instructed by the trial court judge. In non-jury cases, the judge performs both functions.

What does it mean to "find the facts"? As an example, the plaintiff alleges that runoff from the defendant's goat farm is polluting a pond on her property. The defendant denies that any such pollution is taking place. The fact-finder in this case will hear evidence produced by both sides. This evidence might include testimony of relevant parties, photographic and other evidence, and perhaps expert witnesses. Then the jury will determine whether or not, in fact, such pollution has occurred, and if so, whether it was caused by the defendant's activities.

Assuming it finds these facts to be true, the jury will then apply the law of the state to that finding of fact. Ultimately it may determine that the defendant is legally obligated to pay monetary damages to the plaintiff to compensate her for the damage done to her property.

There is no limit on the amount of civil damages which may be awarded by trial courts, which are courts of *general jurisdiction,* and there is no limit on the kinds of criminal cases which the trial court may hear. Trial courts are known as circuit, superior, district, or county courts in different states. Some courts also have established separate divisions to hear particular matters.

State Appellate Courts   All states have at least one appeals court, which in most states is called the state supreme court. Most states also have an intermediate level of appeals courts that hears appeals from the state trial courts and determines whether there were any legal errors in the trial court proceedings. State appeals courts also hear appeals from state administrative agency decisions.

In general, an appeals court decides only *questions of law,* not questions of fact. In reading appellate court decisions, keep in mind that the appeals court does not make factual findings in the case, but generally takes the facts as found by the trial court to be true.

The state supreme court is the ultimate interpreter of state law. State courts may also hear cases involving federal law, including questions of Constitutional law, unless the federal courts have been given *exclusive* jurisdiction over the matter. For example, bankruptcy cases are heard exclusively in federal bankruptcy courts. The U.S. Supreme Court has the final word in cases where the issues involve federal law.

Function of the Court: Statutory Interpretation   In order to apply the law to particular facts, a court is sometimes required to *interpret* the law. In environmental law cases, courts are often asked to interpret the meaning of ambiguous statutory language. Sometimes the language itself may be inherently ambiguous—for example, when is a person an "operator" for purposes of CERCLA, and thus subject to liability for cleanup costs under the Superfund law? In some cases, legislatures intentionally use ambiguous language in order to give courts the opportunity to flesh out the meaning of the statute through case by case adjudication. In other cases, legislators simply fail to address a particular problem, either because it is controversial, or simply because they failed to foresee that particular issue. For all these reasons, the courts frequently must interpret the language as well as apply statutory law in a given case.

Courts use several techniques to interpret the meaning of particular words in a statute. The most important is the rule of *plain meaning,* which requires a court to apply the statute according to the plain, accepted meaning of the language used. A second technique is for the court to review the *legislative history* of the statute in order to ascertain legislative intent or legislative purpose. In addition, courts may rely on the *general public purpose* of the statute, *prior interpretations* of similar language in other cases, and certain *maxims* of statutory interpretation.

Maxims are rules of logic applied by courts in order to interpret statutory language. In Chapter 9 the Supreme Court, in *Babbitt v. Sweethome,* focused on the meaning of the word "harm" in the Endangered Species Act. In an earlier decision, the court of appeals had limited the meaning of the word harm by applying a statutory maxim—*noscitur et sociis,* which literally means "words are known by the company they keep." The Supreme Court rejected that interpretation, and upheld the Fish and Wildlife Service's definition of the word harm to include significant habitat modification which actually harms an endangered species. The Supreme Court relied on the "plain meaning" of the word harm and legislative history of the act in upholding the agency's interpretation in that case.

Jurisdiction of State Courts   Jurisdiction is defined as the power of the court to hear a case. There are two kinds of jurisdiction: (1) **Subject matter jurisdiction,** meaning that the court has the power to hear that type of case, and (2) either **personal** (*in personam*) **jurisdiction over the defendant** or *in rem* **jurisdiction** which is over property located within the state. Both kinds of jurisdiction must be present in order for a court to issue a decision binding the parties in a case.

Personal jurisdiction, means that the court must be able to exercise jurisdiction over the particular defendant based on the residence, location, or activities of the defendant. State courts have jurisdiction over citizens of the state, those who are residents of the state, and those who are in the state when process is served on them. In addition, a defendant can *consent* to personal jurisdiction. States have also enacted **long-arm statutes** which give courts *in personam* jurisdiction over out-of-state defendants in some cases. Under typical long-arm statutes, acts which may establish personal jurisdiction over nonresidents include the following:

- doing business in the state;
- causing personal injury or property damage by an act or omission within the state;
- causing personal injury or property damage in the state by an occurrence, act, or omission done outside the state if the defendant regularly does or solicits business or derives substantial benefit from goods, materials, or services used, consumed, or rendered in the state;
- supplying or contracting to supply services in the state;
- owning, using, or possessing real property or real property interest within the state;
- contracting to ensure or act as a surety on behalf of any person, property, or risk within the state;
- living in a marital relationship within the state notwithstanding subsequent departure from the state, as to all obligations for alimony, custody, child support, or property settlement, if the other party continues to reside in the state.

A state must also meet minimum constitutional *due process requirements* in order to exercise jurisdiction over the defendant. The courts have held that the requirements of due process mandate there be sufficient "minimum contacts" between the state and the defendant before the state can exercise jurisdiction over the defendant. In addition, the state must properly serve *notice* to the defendant of the action against him.

In the following case, companies which had entered into a consent decree obligating them to finance the cleanup of a Superfund site sued several other companies and individuals who had contributed to contamination at the site in order to recover some of the costs of cleaning the site. The suit was filed in federal court in Florida and involved the Sapp Battery Superfund site near Cottondale, Florida. The defendants included companies who sold batteries to Sapp between 1978 and 1980. One defendant from South Carolina filed a motion to dismiss the plaintiffs' case against him for lack of personal jurisdiction. A portion of the court's discussion of this issue follows.

CHATHAM STEEL CORP. et al. v. BROWN et al.
858 F. Supp. 1130 (N.D. Fla. 1994)

Defendant Charles Cleveland, formerly doing business as Carolina Waste & Salvage, moves the Court to dismiss Plaintiffs' claim against him for lack of personal jurisdiction. Cleveland contends the Court cannot exercise jurisdiction over him under Florida's long-arm statute. Furthermore, Cleveland argues he does not have sufficient "minimum contacts" with the state of Florida to satisfy the dictates of Due Process. The Court, however, finds it has personal jurisdiction over Cleveland in this matter and therefore the motion is DENIED.

In the late 1970s, Cleveland operated Carolina Waste & Salvage as a sole proprietorship. Cleveland currently is a shareholder of Carolina Scrap Processing, Inc., a successor corporation to Carolina Waste & Salvage (both entities will hereinafter be referred to as "Carolina Scrap"). Cleveland is a resident of South Carolina, and Carolina Scrap has always been located in Anderson, South Carolina.

Carolina Scrap sold spent batteries to Sapp Battery on at least five occasions in 1978. In making these purchases, Sapp followed its standard procedure: Sapp contacted Carolina Scrap inquiring whether it had batteries to sell; and if it did, Sapp sent one of its trucks to Anderson, South Carolina, to pick up the batteries. Sapp paid for the batteries by check after they were loaded onto its truck at Carolina Scrap. After Sapp picked up the batteries, Carolina Scrap retained no interest or control over the batteries. . . .

Aside from its dealing with Sapp, Carolina Scrap appears to have no other contacts with the state of Florida. It is uncontested Carolina Scrap owns no property or bank accounts in Florida. Carolina Scrap is not licensed to do business in Florida, and maintains no offices here. Furthermore, the record does not reveal Carolina Scrap has advertised in Florida or generated any revenue from the state. In sum, Cleveland contends that based on this paucity of contacts with Florida, he and Carolina Scrap cannot be subject to personal jurisdiction in a Florida court. . . .

Determining whether the Court may exercise personal jurisdiction over Cleveland requires a two-step analysis. First the Court must ascertain whether Florida's long-arm statute authorizes the Court to exercise jurisdiction. Assuming jurisdiction exists under Florida's statute, the Court must then determine whether or not sufficient "minimum contacts" exist to satisfy the Due Process clause of the Fourteenth Amendment. Only if both steps in this analysis are satisfied may the Court exercise jurisdiction over Cleveland.

Plaintiffs assert two provisions of Florida's long-arm statute permit the Court to exercise jurisdiction in this case. Initially, Plaintiffs contend Carolina Scrap has committed a "tortious act" within Florida and therefore jurisdiction is proper under Florida statute 48.193(1)(b). At the same time, Plaintiffs argue the Court may exercise jurisdiction under 48.193(1)(f)(2). Under this provision, a defendant submits itself to the jurisdiction of Florida court if it:

(f)   Caus[es] injury to persons or property within this state arising out of an act or omission by the defendant outside this state, if, at or about the time of the injury . . .

(2) Products, materials, or things processed, serviced, or manufactured by the defendant anywhere were used or consumed within this state in the ordinary course of commerce, trade, or use. Fla. State. 48.193(1)(f)(2) (1993). . . .

The Court agrees with Cleveland that § (f)(2) does not confer jurisdiction in this case. Although the batteries Carolina Scrap sold to Sapp ultimately "injured" property in Florida, there is no indication Carolina Scrap "processed," "serviced," or "manufactured" the batteries in any fashion. Carolina Scrap did not manufacture the batteries it sold or alter them physically prior to sale. Instead, the record indicates Carolina Scrap collected spent batteries to broker to recyclers like Sapp. The Court does not read § (f)(2) as extending jurisdiction to cases like this where the defendant merely possesses a product before sending it to Florida. . . .

The Court, however, finds Cleveland and Carolina Scrap committed a "tortious act" in Florida thereby triggering jurisdiction under Fla. statute. . . . By selling batteries to Sapp Battery, Carolina Scrap helped create the serious environmental hazard that is now the "Sapp Battery Site" near Cottondale, Florida. . . .

Having found Florida's long-arm statute confers jurisdiction over Cleveland, the Court next ascertains whether the exercise of jurisdiction comports with the Due Process clause of the Fourteenth Amendment. This determination in turn necessitates two inquiries. First, to establish personal jurisdiction, the defendant must have sufficient "minimum contacts" with the forum state. . . . Second, the exercise of jurisdiction must not offend "traditional notions of fair play and substantial justice. . . ." The Eleventh Circuit . . . succinctly stated the Court's inquiry on this issue:

To constitute constitutionally minimum contacts, the defendant's contacts with the applicable forum must satisfy three criteria.

First, the contacts must be related to the plaintiff's cause of action or have given rise to it. . . . Second, the contacts must involve "some act by which the defendant purposely avails itself of the privilege of conducting activities within the forum . . . , thus invoking the benefits and protections of its laws. . . . " Third, the defendant's contacts with the forum must be "such that [the defendant] should reasonably anticipate being haled into court there. . . . "

Here, Carolina Scrap's contacts with Florida are related to Plaintiffs' cause of action. On at least five occasions in 1978, Carolina Scrap sold spent batteries to Sapp. Sapp transported these batteries back to Florida where it broke them open at its Cottondale, Florida, site. In the process, Sapp released lead and acid from these batteries into the environment thereby contributing to the toxic contamination that exists today. . . .

Similarly, the Court concludes that Carolina Scrap "purposely availed" itself of the privilege of doing business in Florida. Carolina Scrap decided to sell batteries to Sapp so the batteries could be broken at Sapp's Florida facility. . . .

Finally, the Court, with some hesitation, concludes Carolina Scrap could have "reasonably anticipated" being haled into a Florida court when it sold batteries to Sapp. . . . [W]hen Carolina Scrap sold batteries to Sapp, RCRA—governing the handling, disposal and treatment of hazardous wastes—was in effect. While this action does not involve a claim under RCRA, Carolina Scrap should have been aware of its obligations under federal law to properly handle and dispose of a hazardous waste. In this respect Carolina Scrap should have been aware that its dealings with Sapp could result in litigation. . . .

[*After finding that the court's exercise of personal jurisdiction comported with "traditional notions of fair play and substantial justice," the Court concluded it had personal jurisdiction over Cleveland in this case.*]

Questions and Comments for Discussion

1. In order to determine whether the court could exercise jurisdiction over the defendant Cleveland and Carolina Scrap in this case, the court undertook a two-step analysis. What are the two parts of this test?

2. What is a "long-arm statute?" What two provisions of the Florida long-arm statute gave the court jurisdiction over defendants in this case in plaintiff's opinion? Why did the court find that the long-arm statute established jurisdiction in this case?

3. What are the two tests required to meet the due process requirements for jurisdiction as articulated by the court? What further policy reasons did the court give for exercising jurisdiction in this case?

4. You may have been somewhat confused by the fact that a federal court was applying a state long-arm statute to determine jurisdiction in this case. Although a federal court may exercise subject matter jurisdiction over cases involving a federal question or diversity of the parties (as discussed in the next section of this chapter), this jurisdiction usually only extends to those defendants who would be subject to the *in personam* jurisdiction of the state where the district court sits. Venue requirements also further limit the plaintiff's choice of federal district court.

5. *Venue,* which differs from jurisdiction, refers to the particular physical location where a court exercises jurisdiction. Under typical venue statutes, a plaintiff can bring an action in either the county where a majority of the defendants reside or in the county where the cause of action arose.

6. Under *in rem* jurisdiction, a state court may determine rights in property located within the state, even though the persons affected by that determination are outside the state's *in personam* jurisdiction. An example of exercise of *in rem* jurisdiction is a "quiet title" case where a state court determines title to land located within the state.

Federal Court System

The District Court   Unlike the state court system, federal courts are courts of limited jurisdiction. This means that a plaintiff must establish a basis for federal court jurisdiction before the court can hear the case. The two most important bases of federal court jurisdiction are **federal question jurisdiction** and **diversity jurisdiction.** As the name suggests, federal question jurisdiction arises when a plaintiff alleges that the case involves a substantial federal question. Examples include constitutional questions like those in the *Lungren* case testing the state's "green marking" statute. Federal laws and treaties also give rise to federal question jurisdiction. Federal jurisdiction is *exclusive* only in those cases where the law so provides. In many cases, federal and state courts have **concurrent jurisdiction** over a case or controversy. This means that a plaintiff may bring a case involving a federal question in either state or federal court, provided she can obtain personal jurisdiction over the defendant. In some cases, a defendant may be entitled to *remove* a case from state to federal district court.

The second important basis of federal jurisdiction is diversity jurisdiction, which arises when a suit is between citizens of different states and the amount in controversy exceeds $50,000. For purposes of diversity, a corporation is considered a citizen of both its state of incorporation and the state of its principal place of business.

The district court functions like a state trial court, that is, it finds the facts and applies the law to those facts to reach a decision. There are other specialized courts within the federal court system. These include the claims court, court of international trade, and tax courts. Generally, decisions by these courts are appealed to a federal appeals court.

Courts of Appeal and the United States Supreme Court   The function of the federal appeals court is similar to that of a state appeals court. These courts do not conduct trials but rather hear appeals from decisions of the federal district courts. There are thirteen federal courts of appeals—twelve circuit courts representing eleven districts and the District of Columbia, plus a federal circuit court of appeals, which hears a variety of specialized appeals.

The U.S. Supreme Court functions primarily as an appeals court, although there are rare circumstances where the Supreme Court may function as a trial court. For example, the Supreme Court has *original and exclusive jurisdiction* over suits between two or more states. And it has original, but not exclusive, jurisdiction over some other specific cases, including controversies between the United States and a state.

Most of the appeals heard by the U.S. Supreme Court come from federal courts of appeals and state supreme courts. By far, most of these cases reach the U.S. Supreme Court on **writ of certiorari,** which is a discretionary writ. This means that the Court is not required to take the case, but decides whether or not it wants to hear the case. The U.S. Supreme Court's *certiorari* jurisdiction for appeals from a state supreme court (or the highest court in the state) exists in cases where a person challenges the validity of a treaty or federal statute, alleges that a state statute conflicts with federal law, or claims a title, right, privilege, or immunity under federal law.

STEPS IN A CIVIL LAWSUIT (CIVIL PROCEDURE)

The Federal Rules of Civil Procedure establish the basic steps in a civil lawsuit in federal court. Most states have adopted similar rules. Familiarity with the terms and concepts from this basic set of rules governing the conduct of civil cases will help in understanding the cases. A basic understanding of the steps in a civil lawsuit is important for all citizens, especially for those who may be involved in a civil lawsuit someday. Exhibit 2.1 on page 43 illustrates the important stages and motions in a civil lawsuit.

The Adversary System

Both civil and criminal proceedings in the United States are based on the *adversary system.* This means each of the parties (plaintiff and defendant in a civil suit, prosecutor and defendant in a criminal suit) aggressively present the facts in a way that is most favorable to its side. The judge, or in some cases a jury, acts as neutral arbiter to resolve the dispute. A basic assumption of the adversary system is that in permitting the parties to present their best case and to criticize the other's arguments, the true facts will emerge.

Critics of the adversary system fear that too often an aggressive advocate can obscure rather than clarify the truth. Another problem is the substantial time and expense associated with pursuing litigation. Some cases take years to reach trial, and even longer to be resolved on appeal. And even if a person wins and is awarded court costs, in most cases this does not include expert witness fees and attorney's fees. One way to avoid this problem is not to litigate, increasing pressure to negotiate and settle claims early in the process. Time and cost considerations also encourage *alternative dispute resolution* (ADR), such as mediation and arbitration. In addition, there are requirements that disputes be brought within a specified time, and legal doctrines which prevent re-litigating an issue which has been judicially decided.

Commencing the Action—The Complaint and Summons

A plaintiff begins a lawsuit by filing a *complaint,* a statement (1) alleging facts sufficient to show that the court has jurisdiction in the case, (2) summarizing the nature of the dispute and stating facts showing that the plaintiff is entitled to legal relief from the defendant, and (3) stating the remedy sought. The complaint is first filed with the court clerk, who assigns it a file and file number. A copy of the complaint, along with the *summons,* is then served on the defendant.

The summons notifies the defendant that he is being sued, and it must be served properly in order for the defendant to be legally notified of the suit. Statutes, court rules, and constitutional due process requirements set the standards for proper service. Personal delivery, service by registered mail, and in some cases service by publication, can constitute proper service under state and federal law.

The Defendant's Answer

Once the defendant is served with a copy of the complaint, the defendant files an *answer,* in which he admits or denies the allegation. He may also file *preliminary objections or motions*—for example, a motion to dismiss for lack of jurisdiction or a motion to dismiss for failure to state a claim. This means that the complaint does not state a legal cause of action against him, even if all of the allegations in the complaint are true. As part of the answer or separately, the defendant may file a *counterclaim,* in effect filing a complaint against the plaintiff.

In a civil lawsuit against a private party, the plaintiff has the burden of proving, *by a preponderance of the evidence,* facts sufficient to establish his case. The "preponderance of the evidence" test is often described as a test requiring the plaintiff to prove that the facts are "more likely than not" true. (This test is a much easier one for the plaintiff to meet in a civil suit than the test of "beyond a reasonable doubt" required in criminal cases.) The defendant has the burden of proving any affirmative defenses by a preponderance of the evidence, and must prove the allegations of any counterclaim against the plaintiff by the same standard.

The complaint, answer, and plaintiff's reply to defendant's counterclaim (if filed) form the *pleadings.* The function of the pleadings is to define and limit the questions before the court in the case. Not only do the pleadings limit the scope of the dispute, they also provide notice of the other party's claims. This is important because the rules provide for broad *discovery* mechanisms, through which parties can discover information relevant to the dispute.

The modern rules of civil procedure substantially reduce the possibility of a surprise at trial because they make it difficult, and in many cases improper, to withhold relevant information from the other party in the litigation. Under modern procedural rules, both parties are to be as fully informed as possible so that both can present their clearest and best cases. The *pretrial conference* between attorneys and judge helps the parties to clarify the issues in controversy and often leads to settlement negotiations.

Even more important are *discovery* mechanisms which help the parties gather information relevant to the issues in dispute. Major discovery techniques include:

1. *interrogatories:* written questions relevant to the dispute;
2. *motions for the production of real evidence* by which a party can inspect and copy documents, books, papers, accounts, etc.;
3. *requests for admissions:* a written request seeking a statement of the truth of a matter or the genuineness of a document;
4. a *motion to submit to medical or physical examination:* relevant when the mental or physical condition of a party is relevant in a controversy; and
5. *depositions:* written statements made out of court under oath which are used to preserve and "freeze" the testimony of the witness.

These discovery methods provide an arsenal of weapons for attorneys to search for the facts of the case. It should be noted that they may also be aggressively used to delay proceedings and to increase the cost of litigation. When parties complain about being "papered to the wall" in civil litigation, they are referring to the voluminous discovery requests which are frequently generated by parties in major lawsuits.

Motion for Summary Judgment

Either party may, at any point in the proceedings, ask the court to grant it summary judgment. A party is entitled to *summary judgment* if there are no questions of fact and one party is entitled to judgment as a matter of law. In such cases, trial is unnecessary. The moving party may satisfy the first part of the test through the pleadings, discovery information, affidavits, and in some cases actual testimony at a hearing on the motion. One of the most important legal questions before the court in determining whether to grant summary judgment is whether or not the facts *are in dispute.* If the facts are in dispute, summary judgment is inappropriate.

Earlier in this chapter you read a portion of the *Chatham Steel* case. In that case, companies which were obligated to finance clean up of the Sapp Battery Superfund site near Cottondale, Florida sought recovery for costs they had incurred from other **potentially responsible parties** (PRPs). Plaintiffs sued a number of individuals and companies identified by the U.S. and plaintiffs as (PRPs) under CERCLA.

The court's opinion in that case was written in response to a motion by plaintiffs for summary judgment and cross-motions by various defendants in the case. The court's discussion on plaintiff's motion for summary judgment in general and in particular defendants Brown and Mandy Sapp, former owners of the site, is set out below.

CHATHAM STEEL CO. et al. v. BROWN et al.
858 F. Supp. 1130 (N.D. Fla. 1994)

DISCUSSION

A motion for summary judgment should be granted when "the pleadings, depositions, answers to interrogatories and admissions on file, together with the affidavits, if any, show that there is no genuine issue of material fact and that the moving party is entitled to summary judgment as a matter of law. . . ." An issue of fact is "genuine" if the record as a whole could lead a rational trier of fact to find for the nonmoving party. . . . An issue is "material" if it might affect the outcome of the case under the governing law. On motion for summary judgment, the Court must take the evidence in a light most favorable to the non-moving party. . . .

To establish a claim under § 107(a) of CERCLA, a plaintiff must prove[:]

1. the site in question is a "facility" as defined in § 101(9) of CERCLA;
2. a release or threatened release of a hazardous substance has occurred;
3. the release or threatened release has caused the plaintiff to incur response costs; and
4. the defendant is a responsible party under § 107(a) of CERCLA.

. . . Here it is uncontested Plaintiffs have established the first three elements of their § 107 claim. The Sapp Battery Site qualifies as a "facility" under CERCLA, . . . and there has been a release of a hazardous substance—principally, lead. Moreover, Plaintiffs have incurred response costs in cleaning up the site and will continue to incur costs in the future.

. . . As former owners of the site, Brown and Mandy Sapp are liable under Section 107(a)(2). This subsection imposes liability on "any person who at the time of disposal of any hazardous substance owned or operated any facility at which such hazardous substances were disposed of. . . ."

The Sapps have not responded to Plaintiffs' motion. The land records of Jackson County, Florida, however, unequivocally establish Brown and Mandy Sapp owned the entire property from 1970 to 1973, and at least some of the property until 1978. The deposition of former Sapp employee Otis Corbin also establishes Brown and Sapp operated the battery breaking business at the time lead and battery acid were released into the environment.

On the basis of this record, there is no genuine issue of material fact as to Brown and Mandy Sapp's liability under Section 107(a)(2) of CERCLA. Accordingly, Plaintiffs' motion for summary judgment against these two defendants is GRANTED.

Questions and Comments for Discussion

1.   What two tests must the moving party meet in order to win a motion for summary judgment?

2.   How did the plaintiff meet this test against defendant Sapp in this case?

3.   The grant of summary judgment is a final judgment which may be appealed by the losing party. In many cases, the issue on appeal of grant of summary judgment is whether the facts were in dispute. This requires the appeals court to consider all the material facts in order to determine whether a reasonable person *could* find for the appealing party.

4.   Assuming that the judge denies preliminary motions and the case is not settled, the parties proceed to *trial*. If the jury finds for the plaintiff, it may award damages, including damages to *compensate* plaintiff for injuries he incurred, and in some cases *punitive* damages, which are designed to punish intentional malicious wrongdoing by the defendant. Other remedies, such as an injunction ordering a party to refrain from some activity, may be ordered by the judge in some cases.

Appeals

The appeals court is not a trial court and it does not re-try the facts. Rather, the court considers whether errors of law at the trial court level require the court to *reverse* the decision, *remand* (return) the case to the trial court for further proceedings, or *affirm* the trial

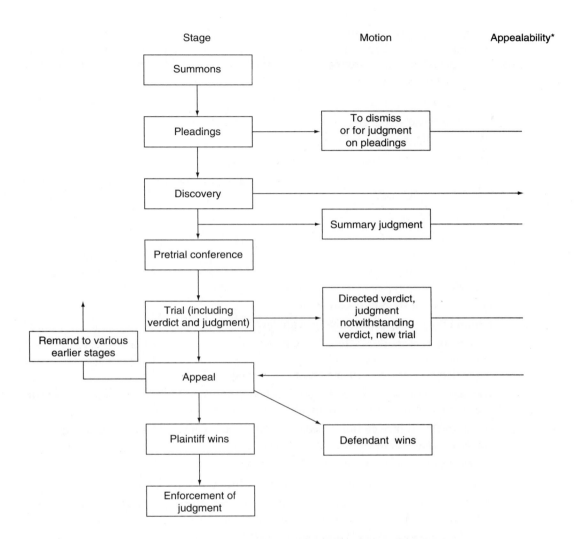

Stage   Motion   Appealability*

*As discussed later in the chapter, many other trial court rulings also are appealable.

Exhibit 2.1   The Most Important Stages and Motions in Civil Litigation (Appeals Assumed)

court's decision. Questions of law raised on appeal include such things as a trial judge's decision to grant or deny a motion to dismiss or motion for summary judgment, trial rulings on jurisdiction and service of process, or rulings on the admissibility of evidence during trial.

CONCLUSION

This chapter has provided some general information about the American legal system and rules of civil procedure. In addition, you have examined general sources of law and the function of courts in interpreting and applying statutory law. Throughout the remaining chapters of this text you will read portions of court decisions addressing various issues of environmental law. Keep in mind that these cases not only contribute to a growing body of environmental law, they also represent the resolution of real disputes between real parties. As you read these cases, ask yourself these questions:

1. What were the facts in this case?

2. Who sued whom and why?

3. How did this case reach this court?

4. What were the legal issues before the court?

5. How did the court resolve those legal issues and what were its reasons for its decision in the case?

GLOSSARY

Civil law—Law involving actions for breach of legal duties owed by private parties to other individuals. A civil lawsuit may be based on a statute or common law.

Code of Federal Regulations (CFR)

Common law—Judge-made law or "case law."

Concurrent jurisdiction—Situation where two or more legal authorities exercise jurisdiction over an individual. For example, both the state and federal courts may have jurisdiction over a particular case or controversy.

Diversity jurisdiction—Federal court jurisdiction based on the fact that the parties are citizens of two different states. Requires at least $50,000 in controversy.

Federal question jurisdiction—Federal court jurisdiction based on a substantial question arising under the laws of the United States.

General Agreement on Tariffs and Trade (GATT)

In rem **jurisdiction**—Jurisdiction over property located within the state.

Long-arm statute—Statute which gives the courts in a state personal jurisdiction over out-of-state defendants for certain acts done within the state.

North Atlantic Free Trade Agreement (NAFTA)

Personal jurisdiction over the defendant—Jurisdiction over the defendant based on residency, consent, presence within the state, or state long-arm statute.

Potentially responsible parties (PRPs)

Subject matter jurisdiction—Jurisdiction over a particular kind of case.

Trial de novo—New trial.

Writ of certiorari—Discretionary writ by which the U.S. Supreme Court reviews lower court decisions from the state and federal appeals courts.

CASES FOR DISCUSSION

1. Plaintiff was the distributor of a mound leveler who claimed that the product, which is used to control fire ants, was not a pesticide subject to registration under FIFRA. The

distributor sued the EPA but failed to serve the government with a copy of the summons and complaint. Should the federal district court dismiss plaintiff's action against the U.S. Environmental Protection Agency? *Turner v. U.S. E.P.A.,* 848 F. Supp. 711 (S.D. Miss. 1994).

2.   Plaintiffs sued defendants for claims for removal costs and damages resulting from an oil spill. The Oil Pollution Act (OPA) requires that plaintiffs present claims to the responsible party prior to bringing suit [OPA § 1013(a)]. Plaintiffs failed to do so. Does the fact defendants moved the claims office and advertised the wrong address after the move, even though it provided notice to the plaintiffs and it did not change its fax and telephone numbers, eliminate the requirement that plaintiffs must first present claims to the defendant? *Boca Ciega Hotel, Inc. v. Bouchard Transportation Co.,* 844 F. Supp. 1512 (M.D. Fla. 1994).

3.   Counter-claim defendants actively participated in an action arising from disputes over insurance coverage for the costs of cleaning up polychlorinated biphenyl (PCB) contamination caused by the insured's operation of a natural gas pipeline. Subsequently, they argued that the district court lacked jurisdiction over them for, among other things, failing to execute service of process as required by the Federal Rules of Civil Procedure. Did defendants effectively waive the defense of lack of personal jurisdiction by actively participating in the action? *In re Texas Eastern Transmission Corp. PCB Contamination Insurance Coverage Litigation,* 15 F.3d 1230 (3d Cir. 1994).

4.   Plaintiffs filed an action in state court against defendants, alleging state common law causes of action arising from the disposal of hazardous materials by defendants. Defendants removed the case to federal court. Plaintiffs then moved to remand the case to state court because there was no diversity of citizenship, and plaintiff's complaint did not allege a substantial question of federal law. One of plaintiff's theories was negligence *per se* under CERCLA and RCRA. Should the federal court exercise jurisdiction in this case? *Polcha v. AT&T Nassau Metals Corp.,* 837 F. Supp. 94 (M.D. Pa. 1993).

5.   Companies constructing and proposing to operate a hazardous waste incinerator in Ohio moved to dismiss claims by West Virginia's citizens under RCRA and common law challenging the incinerator's construction and operation. The case was filed in a West Virginia federal district court. Among other things, the companies argued that the court lacked personal jurisdiction over the companies. The companies had established an office in West Virginia to provide brochures, pamphlets, and similar publications to interested members of the public on the construction and eventual operation of the incinerator. Can the federal court exercise personal jurisdiction over the defendants in this case? *Palumbo v. Waste Technology Industries,* 23 Envtl. L. Rep. 20414 (D.W. Va. 1992).

ENDNOTES

1. For example, the statute defines "biodegradable" to mean that a material has the proven capability to decompose in the most common environment where the material is disposed within one year through natural biological processes into nontoxic carbonaceous soil, water, or carbon dioxide.

3

INTRODUCTION TO THE LAW OF PROPERTY

INTRODUCTION

The sources of environmental law are varied and complex. One area of law which has particular significance for the student of environmental law is the law of property. Fundamental rules of American property law are essentially common law, or judge-made rules, and reflect earlier English common law rules. Some of the traditional rules governing ownership of real and personal property have been superseded by environmental statutes or regulations. For example, a prior owner of contaminated property may be liable for the costs of cleaning up the property under federal Superfund law even though he long ago sold the property to another person.

Why should a student of environmental law be familiar with the common law rules governing property? First, many environmental cases discuss legal theories of property rights and describe ownership interests in property. A knowledge of some principles of property law and common legal terms used to describe ownership interests will help in understanding those cases. Keep in mind, however, property rights are generally defined by state law, and specific property laws may differ from state to state.

Second, much of the debate over "regulatory takings" focuses on the problem of defining the appropriate scope of an owner's rights to develop and use his property for private gain. Under current law, statutes or regulations which restrict an owner's property rights may constitute a "taking" of property, and thus require the government to pay compensation. Environmental laws and regulations which limit the owner's rights to use his property for example, by prohibiting development of property containing "wetlands," may be subject to this legal attack.

Third, principles of American property law reflect common assumptions about the appropriate relationship between humans and their environment—land, water, and other natural resources which support human life. The way in which the law classifies ownership rights in these natural resources reflects society's changing environmental values. The rules of property ownership rights reflect this evolving concept of the value of land, air, and water.

At a fundamental philosophical level, property law consists of a system of legal rules which define the way we think about land and natural resources. As you consider the principles of property law discussed in this chapter, consider the following questions: What are the ethical, political, and social policy assumptions on which these rules are based? Who makes the rules governing the rights of property owners? What are the environmental and economic implications of these rules?

THE NATURE OF PROPERTY

What is **property**? Some might define property by describing it as a "thing"—for example, a tree or a mountain. To the lawyer, however, property is a *legally protected expectation of deriving certain advantages from a thing.*[1] Land (called *real property),* is defined by the relationship between a person and a piece of the earth. A person who is the "owner" of land has legal rights in relation to this real property, such as the right to possess it, to exclude others from it, to use it, and to transfer it by gift or sale to another. He also has certain duties in regard to the property.

A property owner may transfer all or some ownership rights to another. For example, the owner might agree to transfer possession to another for a specified period of time. This contract is called a **lease.** In this arrangement, the tenant buys possession of the property but does not acquire other ownership rights, such as the right to sell the property to another person.

Property rights are protected by the law, but they are not unlimited. Property as a legal concept reflects society's notions of the appropriate relationship between human beings and things of the world. The debate about a private property owner's responsibility for protecting common environmental resources like wetlands or endangered species is essentially a debate about the nature of private ownership rights and duties.

Property is also an *economic* concept, as the following excerpt suggests.

Excerpt from *Economic Analysis of Law* by Richard Posner

Imagine a society in which all property rights have been abolished. A farmer plants corn, fertilizes it, and erects scarecrows, but when the corn is ripe his neighbor reaps and sells it. The farmer has no legal remedy against his neighbor's conduct since he owns neither the land that he sowed nor the crop. After a few such incidents the cultivation of land will be abandoned and the society will shift to methods of subsistence (such as hunting) that involve less preparatory investment.

This example suggests that the legal protection of property rights has an important economic function: to create incentives to use resources efficiently. Although the value of the crop in our example, as measured by consumer willingness to pay, may have greatly exceeded the cost in labor, materials, and foregone alternative uses of the land, without property rights there is no incentive to incur these costs because there is no reasonably assured reward for incurring them. The proper incentives are created by the parceling out among the

Economic Analysis of Law, *Richard Posner (1973).* © *1973 Little, Brown and Company, assigned to Aspen Law & Business, a division of Aspen Publishers, Inc.*

Excerpt from Economic Analysis of Law *by Richard Posner (continued)*

members of society of mutually exclusive rights to the use of particular resources. If every piece of land is owned by someone, in the sense that there is always an individual who can exclude all others from access to any given area, then individuals will endeavor by cultivation or other improvements to maximize the value of land.

The creation of exclusive rights is a necessary rather than a sufficient condition for the efficient use of resources. The rights must be transferable. Suppose the farmer in our example owns the land that he sows but is a bad farmer; his land would be more productive in someone else's hands. The maximization of value requires a mechanism by which the farmer can be induced to transfer rights in the property to someone who can work it more productively. A transferable property right is such a mechanism.

Acquisition of Property

The law recognizes different ways a person may acquire a property right in land or things. These include acquisition by *discovery,* by *creation,* and by *capture.*

Those who settled North America in the last centuries found natural resources that seemed unlimited. As the federal government acquired vast areas of new lands, it adopted the policy of transferring those lands to private owners for private development and settlement. The Homestead Act of 1862 permitted settlers to enter and gain title to public land by building a home and cultivating the land. Most landowners today trace their ownership rights to such early land grants.

Under traditional common law, a person can obtain property rights over wild animals by *capture.* This rule, which evolved in a time when people relied on hunting and fishing for their livelihood, recognizes that a person who captures a wild animal owns it. The capture rule reflects the legal assumption that animals, like other natural resources, should be utilized to improve human welfare.

While society continues to recognize the right of humans to acquire animals as property, there are some in America today who challenge the attitudes about the appropriate relationship between animals and humans. There are protests about the use of animals in experiments, for purposes of fashion, or for entertainment. Some suggest that the law should recognize limited animal legal rights, such as the right to be free from cruel and inhumane treatment.

The following case is an example of application of the traditional rule of capture. As you read the 1881 case, consider how the court's interpretation of the law of capture reflected America's economic, social, and ecological values at that time.

GHEN v. RICH
United States District Court District of Massachusetts, 8 F. 159 (1881)

[*This case was brought by the plaintiff to recover the value of a fin-back whale. The whale was killed by plaintiff, but was found three days later on the beach 17 miles from the spot where it was killed, and was sold by the finder to the respondent.*]

NELSON, J.

The facts, as they appeared at the hearing, are as follows: In the early spring months the easterly part of Massachusetts Bay is frequented by the species of whale known as the fin-back whale. Fishermen from Provincetown pursue them in open boats from the shore and shoot them with bomb-lances fired from guns made expressly for the purpose. When killed they sink at once to the bottom, but in the course of from one to three days they rise and float on the surface. Some of them are picked up by vessels and towed into Provincetown, some float ashore at high water and are left stranded on the beach as the tide recedes. Others float out to sea and are never recovered. The person who happens to find them on the beach usually sends word to Provincetown, and the owner comes to the spot and removes the blubber. The finder usually receives a small salvage for his services. . . . Each boat's crew engaged in the business has its peculiar mark or device on its lances, and in this way it is known by whom a whale is killed.

The usage on Cape Code, for many years, has been that the person who kills a whale in the manner and under the circumstances described, owns it, and this right has never been disputed until this case. . . .

It was decided by Judge Sprague, in Taber v. Jenny, 1 Sprague, 315, that when a whale has been killed, and is anchored and left with marks of appropriation, it is the property of the captors; and if it is afterwards found, still anchored, by another ship, there is no usage or principle of law by which the property of the original captors is diverted, even though the whale may have dragged from its anchorage. . . .

I see no reason why the usage proved in this case is not as reasonable as that sustained in the cases cited. Its application must necessarily be extremely limited, and can affect but a few persons. It has been recognized and acquiesced in for many years. It requires in the first taker the only act of appropriation that is possible in the nature of the case. Unless it is sustained, this branch of industry must necessarily cease, for no person would engage in it if the fruits of his labor could be appropriated by any chance finder. It gives reasonable salvage for securing or reporting the property. That the rule works well in practice is shown by the extent of the industry which has grown up under it, and the general acquiescence of a whole community interested to dispute it. . . . If the fisherman does all that it is possible to do to make the animal his own, that would seem to be sufficient.

[*Judgment entered for plaintiff.*]

Questions and Comments for Discussion

1. To what extent do the business interests of whalers affect the court's decision in this case? How would you balance the economic and environmental considerations raised by this case if it were to be decided today?

2. The law of capture, which provides that the taking of a wild animal vests property rights in the huntsman, was recognized in early Roman law. Although American law still follows the English common law rule of capture, the government today regulates the taking of some wild animals and protects endangered species as discussed in Chapter 9 of this text.

3. To what extent should the federal government be able to regulate the taking of wild animals by an owner on his property? What are the ecological and ethical implications of your answer?

4. Whales occupy a unique political status. Since the signing of the International Con-

vention for the Regulation of Whaling in 1946, whales come under the global jurisdiction of the International Whaling Commission (IWC) established by the treaty to conserve and manage them. In the spring of 1993, both houses of Congress unanimously adopted a resoultion calling for the United States to oppose "any resumption of commercial whaling." At the 1993 meeting of the IWC, the United States and 17 other countries rejected a Revised Management Scheme resolution proposed by Norway and Japan which would have permitted renewed "science-based" commercial whale kill quotas.

Legal Categories of Property

Real v. Personal Property   Traditional property law characterizes property in different ways, and these classifications are not mutually exclusive. One important distinction is that between *real* or *personal* property. The earth's crust and things firmly attached to it (a house, trees) are considered *real property. Personal property* includes all other objects and rights capable of ownership. The distinction between real property and personal property may be important for a number of legal reasons. For example, the rules governing transfer of real property differ from those governing the sale of personal property.

It is not always simple to make the distinction between real and personal property. Property may be characterized differently depending on when that determination is made: trees growing naturally on land will be treated as part of the *real property;* once they are harvested, however, they become movable *personal property.* A stone in the ground is real property until it is quarried; it then becomes personal property. If it is used to build a house, it becomes part of the structure and part of the real property.

A *fixture* is personal property that becomes attached to real property in such a manner that it is treated as real property. Whether a particular item will be treated as real property depends on the intention of the parties, the degree of attachment of the item, and the degree to which the property has been adapted to the use of the item. The distinction may be important in determining whether an item passes with the real property upon sale. Whether an item is a fixture may also determine liability under some environmental laws.

In *U.S.E.P.A. v. New Orleans Public Service, Inc.,* 826 F.2d 361 (5th Cir. 1987), the question of whether an electric transformer containing PCBs became a fixture when installed in a brewery, ultimately determined whether an electric utility was liable for improper storage, marking, and disposal of PCBs under TSCA. In that case, an administrative law judge held that New Orleans Public Service, Inc. (NOPSI) violated TSCA by improperly disposing of electrical transformers containing PCBs. The utility appealed. The evidence was that NOPSI had purchased three 5000-pound 1250 KVA transformers containing PCBs from General Electric. They were installed in the Jackson Brewery Building in New Orleans in 1963, becoming an integral element in the electrical service furnished by NOPSI to the building. The transformers were bolted to the floor and connected with wires to the electrical system of the building.

In 1978, the building was sold to the American Can Company. The transformers were in place and were used until electrical service was discontinued in 1979. In 1982, the building was sold to an investment company for conversion into a retail mall for shops and restaurants. The sale included all attachments, improvements, and components thereof. While a demolishing company was removing the transformers from the building, oil containing PCBs was spilled.

In rejecting NOPSI's argument that it was not responsible for proper disposal of the transformers since they were component parts of the brewery building, the administrative law judge said that the parties themselves regarded the transformers as movables. On appeal, the court disagreed, holding that the transformers were component parts of the building rather than movables. The court determined that NOPSI was not liable for PCB contamination because under state statute, the transformers were "electrical installations."

Property also may be classified as **tangible** or **intangible.** Tangible property has a physical existence, like land or goods. Intangible property has no physical existence. An **easement,** which is a right to use another's property for a certain purpose, or a contract right would be considered intangible.

Public v. Private Property: The Public Trust Doctrine

Property also may be classified as *public* or *private* property. This classification is based on the concept of ownership—property owned by an individual, group of individuals, or a business is considered private property. Public property is property owned by a governmental entity, such as a municipal city hall or park. This distinction may be important in environmental law because public property may be exempt from the application of some environmental laws and regulations.

The distinction may also protect common environmental resources like natural waterways. The *public trust doctrine* recognizes the public's interest in things that are common property—air, running water, the sea, and the shores of the sea. The doctrine was first recognized in classical Rome and found its way into the customs of most European nations in the Middle Ages, including England. Under the doctrine, public trust resources are preserved for the benefit of all. Title to such property vests in the state and is not subject to private ownership.

The most important decision recognizing the public trust doctrine in the United States is an 1882 Supreme Court decision in *Illinois Central Railroad Co. v. Illinois,* 146 U.S. 387 (1882). In that case, the Illinois legislature had granted over 1000 acres of submerged land, essentially the entire commercial waterfront of Chicago, to the Illinois Central Railroad. Four years later the legislature repealed the grant and declared the original grant invalid. The railroad appealed.

The U.S. Supreme Court upheld the state's claim that it could revoke the grant. According to the Court, the state held title to the submerged land "in trust for the people of the state that they might enjoy the navigation of the waters, carry on commerce over them, and have liberty of fishing therein freed from the obstructions or interferences of private parties." Under the public trust doctrine, the Court said the state legislature lacked the power to convey a natural resource like Chicago's harbor into private hands. It said the state can no more abdicate its trust over property in which the whole people are interested than it can abdicate its police power in the administration of government.

The public trust doctrine is traditionally associated with the beds of navigable waters, and the most common application of the doctrine occurs in cases where states have attempted to transfer land under navigable waters within their borders to private parties. Such grants are unenforceable under the public trust doctrine. A private owner cannot acquire rights to trust property under other common law legal doctrines as the *Nascimento* case on page 54 illustrates.

However, the traditional definition of land underlying navigable waters has been challenged by some environmentalists as too narrow. Changing theories of navigability have been used to expand the doctrine to include waters which otherwise might not meet the traditional definition of public trust property. The doctrine may emerge as an important legal doctrine in future environmental cases. There is pressure by some environmentalists to expand the public trust doctrine beyond submerged lands to include resources essential to maintain the general health of natural systems.

Acquisition of Real Property

Origin of Title   *Title* is a legal term which describes ownership rights in real property. As noted previously, private individuals first acquired title to land in the United States from the government or, in some cases, from another country holding the land prior to acquisition by the United States. In 1823, the U.S. Supreme Court in *Johnson v. M'Instosh,* 21 U.S. 543, refused to recognize that plaintiffs' purchase of land from the Piankeshaw Indians conveyed title to the property. The Court said:

> However extravagant the pretension of converting the discovery of an inhabited country into conquest may appear; if the principle has been asserted in the first instance, and afterwards sustained; if a country has been acquired and held under it; if the property of the great mass of the community originates in it, it becomes the law of the land, and cannot be questioned. So, too, with respect to the concomitant principle, that the Indian inhabitants are to be considered merely as occupants, to be protected, indeed, while in peace, in the possession of their lands, but to be deemed incapable of transferring the absolute title to others. However this restriction may be opposed to natural right, and to the usages of civilized nations, yet, if it be indispensable to that system under which the country has been settled, and be adapted to the actual condition of the two people, it may, perhaps, be supported by reason, and certainly cannot be rejected by Courts of justice. . . .

Acquisition of Title by Purchase, Gift, or Will   Most people who own real property have acquired title by purchasing the property from its prior owner. The formal requirements for transfer and recording ownership of real estate vary by state. Real property also may be acquired by gift, when a deed is delivered by the owner to the recipient. The owner of real property, subject to some restrictions, may also dispose of it through a will. To be effective, the will must be drawn and executed in accordance with the statutory requirements of the state in which the real property is located.

How real property has been acquired may be important for purposes of establishing liability under some environmental laws. For example, CERCLA imposes liability for cleanup costs of contaminated property on the owner of the property, but in some circumstances, exempts those who have acquired the property through gift or will.

Acquisition of Real Property by Adverse Possession   State laws also recognize that a person may acquire property by **adverse possession.** Under this doctrine, if a person holds land by open, continuous, and adverse possession for a statutory period of time, he may acquire title to the land. While the actual requirements may differ from state to state, the essential elements of adverse possession are (1) that the possession is hostile and under some claim or right (that is, against the owner's interest), (2) it is actual possession, (3) it is open and notorious (obvious to others), (4) it is continuous, and (5) it is exclusive. In some states, the person claiming title by adverse possession must also pay the taxes on the property.

In the following case, plaintiffs argued that they had acquired title to a shoreline and beach created by fill from dredging along the shore under the doctrine of adverse possession. The court disagreed, holding that the property was subject to the public trust doctrine, and that for policy reasons a person cannot acquire title to real property by adverse possession against the government.

HALL v. NASCIMENTO
594 A.2d 874 (R.I. 1991)

FAY, Chief Justice.

The property in question consists of two adjoining plots of land in the Hummock Point Beach area of Portsmouth known as lot Nos. 25 and 26 and an additional 270 lineal feet of land primarily created by fill from the dredging of Mount Hope Bay that extends from lot Nos. 25 and 26 to the shore of Mount Hope Bay. Prior to the dredge-and-fill operation a ten-foot-wide strip of beach area constituted the shoreline of Mount Hope Bay along the western boundary of lot Nos. 25 and 26. Lot Nos. 25 and 26 were deeded to plaintiffs' predecessors in 1921 and 1922, respectively, by the common grantor Henry A. Brown Corporation (Brown corporation). . . .

In 1926, Brown corporation, the common grantor, deeded to defendants' predecessors, the then-trustees of the [Common Fence Point Improvement] association, "all right, title, and interest of the said grantor in and to all land, marshes, sand bars, causeways, and riparian rights between high and low water marks on the shores of Mount Hope Bay and Sakonnet River, as shown on said Plans No. 1 and No. 2 Hummock Beach Point." The interest conveyed was to be held and maintained by the association in trust for "the sole use and benefit of all property owners, present or future, of all lots shown on said plans."

In 1948 the Army Corps of Engineers dredged a channel in Mount Hope Bay. The association was granted permission by the State of Rhode Island to place the fill from said dredging along the shore of the Common Fence Point area, thereby building up and greatly expanding the ten-foot wide shoreline and beach area abutting lot Nos. 25 and 26. The fill increased the ten-foot strip by 260 feet, creating a 270-foot wide area of shoreline between the waters of

Mount Hope Bay and the original boundaries of lot Nos. 25 and 26 as shown on Plan 1. Following the dredge and fill along the shores of Common Fence Point, the tax assessor for the town of Portsmouth represented the filled area as a public right of way. For taxing purposes lot Nos. 25 and 26 were merged and labeled as lot No. 43. The original ten-foot strip is included in and designated as part of the right of way.

There is no dispute that plaintiffs are the owners of lots No. 25 and 26 as represented on Plan 1. The present challenge concerns the land abutting lot Nos. 25 and 26 to the west, which extends to Mount Hope Bay. It is therefore necessary for this court to examine not only the boundaries of the property as set forth in the deed conveying the title of lot Nos. 25 and 26 to plaintiffs' predecessors but also the nature and history of the parcel of filled land claimed by both plaintiffs and defendants.

***

After examining the deeds pertinent to the property with which we are concerned, in conjunction with the appropriate plat map, we are of the opinion that definite western boundaries to both lot Nos. 25 and 26 are discernable. We conclude that the boundaries do not encompass the ten-foot strip of land that, prior to the dredging and filling of Mount Hope Bay, abutted the waters of the bay and consequently carried with it the littoral rights to that area. Therefore, we find that the trial justice erred in determining that plaintiffs' predecessors, and subsequently plaintiffs, acquired title by deed to the land extending to the high-water mark.

To claim ownership rights in the filled area successfully, plaintiffs must prove that they, through their predecessors, were entitled to littoral rights [ownership rights in the shoreline] to the tidelands that were filled. Such littoral rights could only be claimed if plaintiffs' predecessors had acquired title to the ten-foot strip. Because we have determined that plaintiffs' predecessors did not acquire rights to the ten-foot strip by deed, we conclude that plaintiffs do not hold title to the filled area abutting the ten-foot strip. This determination, however, does not conclude our consideration of the facts presented. We are now compelled to address the trial justice's alternative finding that plaintiffs hold title to the filled area by adverse possession.

Prior to the dredge-and-fill operation, the area, which is now claimed by both plaintiffs and defendants, was submerged land. Because we are dealing with tidelands and littoral rights in this instance, it is necessary to examine the ownership of this property in light of the public trust doctrine. The United States Supreme Court recognizes that in accordance with the public trust doctrine, the state holds title to property that lies below the high-water mark.

It is well settled in Rhode Island that pursuant to the public trust doctrine the state maintains title in fee to all soil within its boundaries that lies below the highwater mark, and it holds such land in trust for the use of the public. The high water mark on the original shoreline that existed prior to the 1948 dredge and fill was located within the bounds of the ten-foot strip of beach area, which, as we have already established, was retained by the association when lot Nos. 25 and 26 were conveyed to plaintiffs' predecessors.

***

Having established the ownership status of the state and rights maintained by the association, we now address the trial justice's decision that the plaintiffs acquired title to the property by adverse possession. We are of the opinion that the trial justice erred in granting the plaintiffs title by adverse possession because a private party cannot adversely possess public property.... As established by the United States Supreme Court, this prohibition on adverse possession applies to all public lands owned by state governments and is not limited to shoreline property.... We therefore conclude that the plaintiffs do not hold title to the ten-foot beach area or the filled area by either deed or adverse possession.

Questions and Comments for Discussion

1. Under the doctrine of *adverse possession,* plaintiffs have to establish that their possession of the disputed property was hostile and under claim of right, actual, open and notorious, continuous, and exclusive. What kinds of proof would plaintiffs need to establish these elements in a case like this?

2. What is the rationale for the doctrine of adverse possession? Should the law permit a person to acquire title to property under this theory? What implications does this theory have for the environment?

3. As the court's holding in this case illustrates, under the common law rule, a person cannot acquire title to property owned by the state under the theory of adverse possession. Why should this be so? A number of states have changed the common law rule, either by legislation or judge-made law. A few permit adverse possession against government land using the same requirements for private lands; others permit it only if possession continues for a period much longer than that in the case of private lands. Under the public trust doctrine, however, such grants may still be subject to legal challenge. See generally, John R. Call, *Adverse Possession of Public Land: A Look at the Recommendation of the Public Land Law Review Commission,* 1971 Law & Soc. Ord. 131; Elmer M. Million, *Adverse Possession Against the United States—A Treasure for Trespassers,* 26 Ark. L. Rev. 467 (1973).

Scope of Interests in Real Property

The owner of real estate not only owns the surface of the earth, but also has rights in the air above the surface and in the soil and minerals below the surface. While the common law rule is a simple one, a number of legal questions may arise in its application.

- What limits should be placed on ownership of air rights in order to accommodate air travel?
- Who owns minerals, like gas and oil, which may migrate under the earth?
- To what extent may one owner block access to the sunlight of another?
- Does an owner of property own geothermal energy beneath the property's surface?

Air Rights   Under traditional common law rule, a person owns property "to the sky," and has the right to exclude others from air space. Invasion of that airspace by another constitutes trespass. Thus, if a person shoots at ducks and other water fowl flying over the plaintiff's land, and the shot lands on plaintiff's land, there is a trespass.[2] In modern life, the courts have had to balance this common law rule against the public necessity for air travel.

In one famous case, *U.S. v. Causby,* 328 U.S. 256 (1946), the U.S. Supreme Court held that there was an unconstitutional taking of plaintiffs' property when airplanes flew close enough over the chicken farm owned by plaintiffs to barely miss the tops of trees. However, the Court acknowledged in that case that a person's air rights are not unlimited. The Court recognized a need to balance competing interests without defining the precise limits of air ownership rights beyond the immediate reaches of the enveloping atmosphere. The Supreme Court said that a landowner owns as least as much of the space above the ground as he can occupy or use in connection with the land.

As society becomes more and more complex, and industry and technology expands, courts rely more on a *nuisance theory* to balance the rights of defendants and plaintiffs in air rights cases. In this case, a court was asked to determine whether an electric utility's use of its airspace for a 600-foot stack could be enjoined (that is, legally prevented) under a nuisance theory because it interfered unreasonably with plaintiff's air rights.

GENERAL AVIATION INC. v. THE CLEVELAND ELECTRIC ILLUMINATING CO.
2 ERC 1328 (N.D. Oh. 1971)

PATTISTI, J.

This suit has been brought to prevent interference with plaintiff's airport operations by a 600-foot stack being constructed by the defendants.

Lost Nation Airport has been maintained by the plaintiff, General Aviation, as a private airport since 1931. Seventeen years later,

in 1948, the Cleveland Electric Illuminating Company (CEI) acquired land nearby, in Eastlake, Ohio, and a few years later built an electric generating plant, whose 307-foot stacks made it necessary to alter approach and landing patterns at the airport. CEI now is constructing an addition to this plant, and air pollution control standards require a 600-foot stack. Despite $72,000 being spent by the defendants for lighting, this stack will have a detrimental impact on the airport, interfering in particular with instrument landings on three of its runways.

The plaintiff, claiming that the height and location of the stack make it a nuisance, that it constitutes an extraordinary structure in the area, and further, that it violates navigable airspace assigned to General Aviation by the Federal Aviation Authority, wants CEI to provide two Localizer-Type Directional Aids (LDAs). These, plaintiff contends, would minimize, but not eliminate the effects of the stack upon instrument approaches to runways 5 and 9.

Superficially, at least, the nuisance argument is a seductive one—but on closer examination is not really relevant to this case. Essentially the law of nuisance will apply when one landowner so uses his property that he interferes with his neighbor's right to the quiet enjoyment of his own land. Here, however, the direct effect of the stack is upon the plaintiff's flights over the defendants' land. Granted that this in turn has a substantial detrimental effect upon the operations at the airport itself, it would seem, nevertheless, that the connection is too remote to give rise to an action for nuisance.

That the stack is extraordinary in the area is, in one sense, uncontrovertible; it will rise to the height, perhaps, of a fifty-story skyscraper. In essence, however, the difference between the 600-foot stack and its 307-foot predecessors will be one merely of degree. The new structure may restrict operations at the airport, as did the construction of the earlier ones, but this inconvenience must not be equated with hazard, since there has been no showing that in this case there will be increased danger resulting from the new stack. Since anyone proposing to use Lost Nation Airport will be guided by maps and charts showing the new stack, it would seem

that plaintiff's specter of danger to the public at large is as intangible as the very air. Thus it is not to this alleged hazard, but rather to questions of possible interference with specific property rights enjoyed by the plaintiff that this court must address itself.

At common law the extent of a landowner's rights in his property was defined as: *"Cujus est solum, ejus est usque and coelum,"*—Ownership of land extends as high as the sky. It has been only with the development of air travel in this century that the blitheness of this maxim has been questioned, and the absurdity of its full implications recognized by the courts. The question of what constitutes the "immediate reaches" of the atmosphere has been the subject of endless legal nit-picking—but perhaps the simplest formula is the one provided by the Court in *Causby:* "The land-owner owns at least as much of the space above the ground as he can occupy or use in connection with the land."

The extent of the defendants' estate in the property, then, is subject to change as dictated by circumstances. Had marshy land or building codes restricted construction to one-story structures, that height would have demarcated the height of CEI's property interest; on the other hand, construction of a skyscraper on previously vacant land may raise the frontier to the very edge of the upper atmosphere. The defendants, then (to repeat) have title not only to the surface of their property, but as much of the airspace above the surface as they actually use.

It is concluded, then, that the plaintiff has no rights in or to defendants' land. Like the airport-respondent in *Griggs v. Allegheny County,* 369 US. 84 (1961), the plaintiff was obligated to purchase the necessary land or to obtain easements from neighboring landowners, and as in *Griggs,* "it did not acquire enough." Accordingly, plaintiff General Aviation's prayer for injunction is hereby denied and its complaint is dismissed.

Questions and Comments for Discussion

1.   Traditional common law theories, such as trespass and nuisance, have prohibited air and water use by a landowner if that use unreasonably harms the interests of a neighboring property owner. However, these theories have generally been found inadequate in dealing with the massive problems of air and water pollution. As a result, Congress has enacted federal legislation to regulate discharge of pollutants into air, land, and water. These laws are examined in detail in subsequent chapters of this text.

2.   What alternatives might the parties have pursued to avoid the problems addressed by this case?

3.   The court discussed in a part of its opinion not reprinted here, the fact that defendants could not have obtained a "prescriptive easement,"which would permit a person to acquire a right to use another's property under a theory similar to that of adverse possession. This doctrine is discussed in a later section of this chapter.

3.   Who owns outer space? More than 300 companies are preparing commercial ventures for outer space. Countries like the United States and Russia have signed treaties to circumvent potential problems which provide that no one owns outer space. But there is no agreement as to where a country's air space ends and outer space begins.

4.   At one time, industry often met requirements under the federal Clean Air Act by building high stacks like the one in this case. High stacks resulted in broader dissemination of pollutants than the shorter stacks. The law changed under a provision added in 1977 so that the degree of emission limitation is not affected by the stack height of any source as exceeds good engineering practice or any other dispersion technique.

Sale of Air Rights   Like mineral rights, air rights may be sold separately from surface rights. Sale of a condominium, for example, may involve the sale of a unit of airspace described as a subdivision of air lots, or may involve a survey showing the dimensions of the unit, or may utilize a floor plan showing the location of each unit. Condominium owners establish their rights and duties in the condominium by agreement, and they should be particularly careful to address their rights if the air lots infringe on others' lots as a result of settling or natural disaster.

Mineral (Subsurface) Rights   Just as an owner owns his property "to the sky," so traditional common law provides that an owner also owns the property "to the depths." Thus a person may sell or lease subsurface mineral rights to his property, and may be entitled to damages if another trespasses on those rights. In one unusual case the opening to an underground cave was located on one person's property, but the cave extended under a considerable portion of a neighboring landowner's property. The owner of the property on which the entrance was located, and who had been conducting tours of the cave for a fee, sued to establish title to all the cave and its cavities under the theory of *adverse possession,* a doctrine discussed earlier in this chapter. But the Indiana Supreme Court held in that case that the elements of adverse possession were not established. Consequently, under common law rule, the court held that the neighboring owner could prohibit others from exploring the caverns under his property, even though the owner had no access to the cave from the surface.[3]

If an owner sells mineral rights to his property, the purchaser may use the surface to tunnel below it to mine the minerals. The provisions of the lease or mineral deed should be carefully drafted to clarify the rights and responsibilities of each of the parties. Strip-mining is of particular environmental concern because this method entails bulldozing, dynamiting, and shovelling off soil and vegetation, with serious damaging consequences.

Both state and federal governments have passed strip-mining controls. In 1977, Congress passed the Surface Mining Control and Reclamation Act.[4] Among other things, the act is designed to assure that surface coal mining operations are conducted to protect the environment and the public interest through effective controls. The act imposes regulatory restrictions on strip-mining and requires that the land be restored to approximately its original state. Despite the detailed provisions of the act, some have suggested that common law remedies are more effective than public law in this area because of enforcement problems.

Oil and natural gas tend to collect in underground reservoirs under land with different ownership. These resources may then migrate, making ownership difficult to determine. *Ownership states* have adopted the position that a landowner owns the oil beneath his land in the same way he owns coal or other minerals.[5] Other states take the position that oil may move when wells are drilled, so that the landowner does not own the oil until he has taken possession of it through pumping. But all oil states follow the rule of *capture,* which provides that a person owns all the oil and gas produced by a well on his land, even if some of it has migrated to his well from a neighbor's property. This rule is subject to regulation, and oil and gas leases vary considerably in their terms and conditions from state to state.

The Mining and Minerals Policy Act of 1970, 30 U.S.C. Sec. 21, declares that it is the policy of the United States to foster and encourage private enterprise in the development of economically stable mining and mineral industries, and the development of methods of disposal, control, and reclamation of mineral waters and mineral land so as to lessen the effects of mining on the environment.

Right to Light   In an earlier agrarian society in a country with vast open spaces, ownership of light rarely became a legal issue. The question of who owns the right to light more frequently arises in a time where many environmentalists promote solar energy as a solution to dwindling energy resources. Under the common law **doctrine of ancient lights,** anyone who used the light for an uninterrupted period of twenty years was entitled to protection for use of that light. Historically, however, American courts rejected that rule, perhaps because of its impact on development.

In *Fountainebleau Hotel Corp. v. Forty-Five Twenty-Five, Inc.,* 114 So.2d 357 (Fla. 1959), the Fountainebleau luxury hotel undertook construction of a 14-story addition which would block the sun for part of the day over the sunbathing areas of a neighboring hotel, the Eden Roc. Eden Roc sued to stop construction of the addition and the trial court found for Eden Roc. However, the Florida Supreme Court held that there was no legal basis for enforcing the neighboring hotel's right to light.

The court said: "No American decision has been cited, and independent research has revealed none, in which it has been held that—in the absence of some contractual or statutory obligation—a landowner has a legal right to the free flow of light and air across the adjoining land of his neighbor."

Parties may avoid the common law rule by contracting for the right to light, and in some states a person may acquire the right by easement or *covenant.* In addition, many states have enacted statutes which change the common law rule and protect the right to light under some circumstances. For example, Wyoming has adopted a statute providing that the first user of light for solar-energy purposes acquires the right to continued use of the light.

Other states have adopted **solar easement laws** and still other states encourage zoning as a means to address solar access considerations. Finally, some state courts have utilized common law nuisance theory to provide protection for solar rights.

In *Prah v. Maretti,* 321 N.W.2d 182 (Wis. 1982), an owner of a solar-heated residence maintained his neighbor's proposed construction of a residence would interfere with his access to light. In holding that the plaintiff could maintain a nuisance action in that case, the Wisconsin Supreme Court said:

> This court's reluctance in the nineteenth and early part of the twentieth century to provide broader protection for a landowner's access to sunlight was premised on three policy considerations. First, the right of landowners to use their property as they wished, as long as they did not cause physical damages to a neighbor, was jealously guarded. Second, sunlight was valued only for aesthetic enjoyment or as illumination. Since artificial light could be used for illumination, loss of sunlight was at most a personal annoyance which was given little, if any, weight by society. Third, society had a significant interest in not restricting or impeding land development. This court repeatedly emphasized that in the growth period of the nineteenth and early twentieth centuries change is to be expected and is essential to property and that recognition of a right to sunlight would hinder property development.
>
> These three policies are no longer fully accepted or applicable. They reflect factual circumstances and social priorities that are now obsolete. First, society has increasingly regulated the use of land by the landowner for the general welfare. Second, access to sunlight has taken on a new significance in recent years. In this case the plaintiff seeks to protect access to sunlight, not for aesthetic reasons or as a source of illumination but as a source of energy. Access to sunlight as an energy source is of significance both to the landowner who invests in solar collectors and to a society which has an interest in developing alternative sources of energy. Third, the policy of favoring unhindered private development in an expanding economy is no longer in harmony with the realities of our society. The need for easy and rapid development is not as great today as it once was, while our perception of the value of sunlight as a source of energy has increased significantly. [For these reasons, the court held that plaintiffs could maintain a nuisance action under these facts.]

Questions and Comments for Discussion

1.   In *Prah v. Maretti,* the court said that the policy of favoring unhindered private development in an expanding economy is "no longer in harmony with the realities of our society." What did the court mean by this statement? What are the policy implications of preventing construction of a neighboring residence which blocks another homeowner's access to sunlight?

2.   What are the advantages and disadvantages of using nuisance law (requiring a fact-specific "balancing of interests" test) as opposed to regulating access to light through zoning or statutory laws? What kinds of problems arise in a government's attempt to legislate a right to light by statute or zoning ordinance?

3.   In another case, plaintiffs argued that the defendant's trees interfered with their solar access and that this constituted a private as well as a public nuisance under the California Solar Shade Control Act. The California court considered the Wisconsin court's policy arguments favoring a change in the law of private nuisance, but took the position that it was "solely within the province of the Legislature to gauge the relative importance of social policies and to decide whether to effect a change in the law." Who should decide the question of right to light—the courts through

common law or the legislature? What are the reasons for your decision and what are the advantages and disadvantages of legislative rather than judicial decision making in such cases? (*Sher v. Leiderman,* 181 Cal. App. 3d 867 [1986])

Water Rights   The right to water is an increasingly valuable part of real estate ownership. Under traditional common law principles, water rights will depend on the type of water body involved and where the water is located. The states have adopted different rules to determine ownership rights in water. Most states west of the Mississippi follow the **prior appropriation doctrine,** characterized by the notion that "first in time is first in right." Most states east of the river follow a **riparian rights doctrine,** characterized by the requirement of reasonable use by riparians. (A *riparian* is a person who owns property adjacent to a waterway.) These common law doctrines reflect different attitudes about an owner's right to exploit water as a resource and the fact that water resources are much less plentiful in the western states.

As a result of the widespread concern over the limits of the basic water supply, and the pressure to protect it from waste and pollution, state and federal laws governing a property owner's right to water continue to grow. The Clean Water Act and other environmental laws addressed in Chapter 11 represent government's attempts to protect public water resources. These environmental laws have affected a water owner's or user's common law rights and obligations.

Several states, particularly in the west, have established state regulations governing private water rights and separate "water courts" to adjudicate those rights.

Ownership Concepts Estates in Land   In this chapter we have examined the nature and scope of real property. This section examines the kinds of ownership rights a person may acquire in real property, and the legal relationship between those who share property interests in land. These basic concepts will help in understanding some of the legal issues in cases involving the rights and responsibilities of property owners under environmental laws.

An **estate** in land is a feudal concept. In the middle ages, people were classified by an estate, such as clergy, nobility, and commoners. Today, the term describes the kind of ownership interests a person has in real property. This is why real property is sometimes called "real estate." Legally, the term is used to describe a kind of interest in real property. The simplest and greatest estate in land is called a **fee simple absolute,** and this is what "owning" real property means to the average person.

A person also may grant some ownership rights to another while retaining an interest in the property. For example, an owner may convey property to another on the condition it is used for a particular purpose. The words "to the City of Bloomington, so long as it uses the property for a public park," is an example of such a conveyance. This grant creates what is called a **fee simple defeasible** because the grantor will recover ownership rights in the property upon breach of the condition.

The nature of ownership rights under such conditional land grants has been the subject of litigation under The National Trails System Act Amendments of 1983. This law represented efforts to preserve shrinking miles of rail track by converting unused rights of way to recreational trails. Several provisions in various laws promote the conversion of abandoned railroad lines to trails (called *"Rails to Trails"* projects). In one case, plaintiffs in

Vermont who claimed under state law a reversionary interest in a railroad right of way adjacent to their land brought a **quiet-title action** (to establish legal title to property), alleging that upon abandonment of the railroad's easement through their property, the right-of-way had reverted to them by operation of state property law. The State of Vermont argued, among other things, that the land could not revert while it was still being used for a public purpose. In *Preseault v. Interstate Commerce Commission,* 494 U.S. 1 (1990), the Supreme Court upheld the constitutionality of the federal "rails to trails" statute, but it avoided deciding whether an unconstitutional taking of petitioner's property had occurred.

Life Estates   A *life estate* arises when one person grants to another an ownership interest in real property which is measured by the life of that (or another) person. "To Davis, for life," creates a life estate, with Davis' life as the "measuring life," and entitles Davis to ownership rights during his life. At Davis' death, the property will automatically revert to the **grantor** or his heirs (the grantor is the person who conveyed the life estate). Like the fee simple absolute and fee simple defeasible, the life estate is a present estate in land, and the grantor retains a future interest (a reversion or remainder interest) in the property.

A life tenant, like a tenant under a lease, has a duty to keep the property in good repair. As a general rule, the life tenant may act as a fee simple owner, but he may not act in such a way that would diminish the market value of the remainder. If he does so, he may be liable for **waste.** Thus a life tenant, like a tenant under a lease, who improperly stores hazardous materials on the property would be liable to the grantor for damages if the property's value were substantially diminished as a result of environmental contamination.

Future Interests in Land   Land interests are not limited to present time, but may be divided into present and future interests. The defeasible fee discussed earlier is an example of an estate in land which contains the possibility that ownership of the property may return to the grantor in the future, an example of a *future interest* in property. In the case of the defeasible fee, that future interest is *only* a possibility—if the **grantee** and her successors comply with the conditions of the grant, the land will not revert to the grantor. Other types of future interests, however, are based on certainties. For example, a *remainder* interest may be given to another living person. "To Davis for life, and then to Beth," creates in Beth (or her heirs) the certainty of future ownership in the property.

Kinds of Ownership

Multiple Ownership of Property   Not infrequently, environmental issues arise in the sale and purchase of real property, especially commercial property. The owner or owners of real property may be liable under state and federal laws for the costs of cleaning up hazardous substances found on the property, even if the owner did not cause or contribute to that contamination. It is not unusual for more than one person to hold an ownership interest in real property. For this reason, it is helpful for the student of environmental law to be familiar with these basic forms of multiple ownership of property.

The **tenancy in common** is the most common type of joint ownership in land. Usually a grant will be construed to be a tenancy in common rather than a joint tenancy. A grant "To Smith and to Jones" creates a tenancy in common. Under a tenancy in common, co-tenants have an equal right to the possession and use of the entire property even though they may hold unequal shares, for example, "⅓ to Smith and ⅔ to Jones." They may also be jointly liable as owners of property under environmental laws regulating the manufacture and storage of hazardous materials.

A tenant in common may sell, lease, or mortgage his undivided interest in the property, and upon his death, his interest passes to his heirs. Whether the parties are tenants in common may be significant in cases determining ownership interests. For example, when two or more persons participate in the location of a mining claim, a tenancy in common arises. Each locator has the same rights (and presumably duties) in respect to his share as a tenant, but he holds his interest independently of the other and may transfer, devise, or encumber it separately without the consent of the other co-tenants.

Unlike the tenancy in common, the **joint tenancy** is characterized by a *right of survivorship*. A grant of land "To Smith and to Jones as joint tenants with rights of survivorship" creates a joint tenancy. Unlike the tenancy in common, under a joint tenancy with rights of survivorship, upon the death of either tenant, ownership automatically vests in the other joint tenant or tenants. Another form of joint tenancy, recognized by about half the states, is called a **tenancy by the entirety.** This tenancy only arises between husband and wife, and can only be terminated by joint action of the husband and wife. The ownership interest of a spouse may become an issue in the determination of liability under some environmental laws.

In some western states, property owned by husband and wife is called **community property.** Community property states classify property in different ways, but generally distinguish between property that was acquired during the marriage and property acquired by gift or inheritance or accumulated prior to marriage.

Some increasingly popular forms of shared ownership of real property include *condominium* arrangements. The purchaser of a condominium purchases the living space (or air space) in a unit. He also purchases an interest in the common areas of the condominium (including the land under the structure) as a tenant in common. The rights and duties of the condominium purchaser are set out in the master deed and the bylaws to the corporation, and states have enacted statutes that also govern those rights and duties. As the *Nascimento* case suggests, an association of condominium or homeowners may, if it is a separate legal entity, acquire an interest in real property.

Landlord and Tenant Law   The relationship between landlord and tenant is determined not only by contract law but also by the law of property. A lease is both a conveyance of a possessory interest in real property by the owner to another (the conveyance of an "estate") and a contract specifying certain particular rights and duties with regard to the property. The estate concept is utilized in property law to define the possessory interest transferred from the owner to the tenant. There are four basic kinds of tenancies:

- the *estate for years,* which has a definite beginning and a definite end;
- the *periodic tenancy,* which lasts for a period of time and is automatically renewed until either party gives notice that it will end;
- the *tenancy at will,* which is characterized by an indefinite duration;
- the *tenancy at sufferance,* which arises when a person in possession refuses to leave after his right to possession has ended

Although a lease may arise from an informal arrangement between the parties, it is always best to state clearly the terms of the lease in writing. The terms are critical in determining the rights and duties of the parties, and these terms may be especially important in the lease of commercial property which becomes subject to a clean-up action under federal or state hazardous waste laws or in a suit for damages under state nuisance law.

Indemnity issues, warranties, and exculpatory clauses in the lease may ultimately determine the liability between the landlord and tenant in such cases. The environmental contract and tort issues arising from the landlord-tenant relationship are addressed in more detail in Chapter 5.

Partition and Waste   If all tenants have the equal right of possession to the property, what happens in a property dispute between co-owners? In such cases, the co-owners may agree upon, or a court may order, a division of the property called a **partition.** Partition is an actual geographical division of the property resulting in former co-owners becoming separate owners of adjoining parcels of land. If it is impossible to physically divide the land, the property may be sold and the proceeds divided.

Waste occurs when a land possessor causes permanent injury to the property which diminishes the value of the property to the permanent owner. A person entitled to property under the terms of a lease is obligated to use the property in such a way that he preserves its value. This would be the case if a tenant of commercial property permits the property to become contaminated with hazardous materials. The tenant may be liable for the owner's loss of value in the real estate under this theory. He may also be liable for the costs of cleaning up the property as an "owner or operator" under federal environmental laws.

Ownership for Investment Purposes

Partnership   Investors often choose to own real property through partnerships and corporations for business purposes, such as to limit liability or to structure assets for tax purposes. The law of partnership is set out in the Uniform Partnership Act, which defines a partnership as an association of two or more persons to carry on as co-owners of a business for profit. Under the act, each partner is a co-owner of partnership property and holds the property as a tenant in partnership, which has the characteristics of a joint tenancy. If a partner dies, the ownership of property of the partnership belongs to the remaining partners. However, a partner's interest in the partnership, which is his share of profits and surplus in the partnership, can pass to his heirs and may be subject to the claims of creditors.

Corporations   Unlike a partnership, a corporation is a legal entity separate and distinct from its shareholders. More complicated than a partnership, a corporation is formed when parties file articles of incorporation and obtain a corporate charter. A corporation's directors must conduct business under procedures set out in its articles and charter, as well as in applicable federal and state statutes. The major advantage of a corporation is that the corporation, as a separate legal entity from its shareholders, is liable for its contracts and torts, and the shareholder's liability is limited to his investment in the corporation.

A corporation may purchase and hold real property in its own name, and a corporation may be liable for harm caused by environmental contamination of its property or for the costs of cleanup. Several important issues involving corporate liability for environmental contamination have emerged in recent years. One issue of debate is the extent to which a person who is a corporate officer or director should be personally liable for the environmental wrongs caused by his actions in that capacity. This debate is addressed in Chapter 14. Another question is the extent to which a corporation should be able to discharge its liability for environmental harm through bankruptcy. Additional questions are whether a corporation may limit its liability by forming subsidiary corporations, and whether a corporate successor may be liable for the environmental harms caused by its corporate predecessor.

The principle of limiting liability through incorporation is vital to capital formation. Otherwise, investors would be unlikely to purchase stock. It is common for corporations to create subsidiaries to engage in different specialized activities, especially if the corporate activity carries with it a high risk of potential liability, such as the generation and disposal of hazardous waste. In the corporate parent/subsidiary relationship, the corporate parent generally controls the actions of the subsidiary. If the subsidiary is found liable for environmental harms, may the parent corporation be held liable as well? The courts are not quick to disregard corporate form, but they have also consistently construed federal hazardous waste laws broadly. As a result of these conflicting policies, the courts' decisions in such cases have not been uniform.

One corporation may purchase the assets of another either directly or through merger. General common law principles establish when a successor corporation is deemed to have purchased the liabilities of its predecessor. In cases involving potential liability under CERCLA, some courts have been willing to extend successor liability beyond that which would arise under traditional common law. Cases illustrating corporate successor liability for environmental harms are discussed in Chapter 13.

Easements and Covenants

A person may acquire other interests in real propery, including non-possessory interests. An *easement* is a non-possessory interest which gives the holder certain rights in the land owned by another. An easement may be valid indefinitely, may have terms, or may end through operation of law. Easements are characterized in different ways. An easement which benefits a particular possessor or tract of land is called an *easement appurtenant*. An easement which belongs to the public regardless of whether the holder owns adjacent property is called an *easement in gross*. An easement may also be characterized as *affirmative* (giving the owner of the easement a right to use another's land) or *negative* (giving the owner of the easement the right to prevent another from using his property—for example, to prevent the blockage of sunlight).

Easements may be created by *express grant,* which must comply with all requirements in the state for conveyance of an interest in land. Easements may also arise by *implication.* An implied easement includes one which arises from necessity. In one case where a court enjoined the use of a lagoon on another's property as part of a final sewage treatment process, the court affirmed a finding that the defendant had not acquired a perpetual easement to use the lagoon. The court said that an implied easement must be continuous, apparent, permanent, and necessary. According to the court, "the necessity should be judged by whether an alternative would involve disproportionate expense and inconvenience, or whether a substitute can be furnished by reasonable labor or expense."[6]

Easements may also arise by *prescription.* Obtaining an easement by prescription is similar to obtaining title to property through adverse possession, discussed in an earlier section of this chapter. The easement must be used for the appropriate period under law (ranging from 5–20 years depending on the state), it must be adverse, it must be open and notorious, and continuous and exclusive. In one case, *McCullough v. Waterfront Park Association, Inc.,* 630 A.2d 1372 (Conn. App. 1993), the Connecticut Court of Appeals held that a homeowner's association had acquired an easement to waterfront property owned by the defendant under this theory.

In the following case, the Oregon Supreme Court held that the public may acquire a right to use property under the English doctrine of "custom," a concept with some similarities to a prescriptive easement.

STATE EX REL THORNTON v. HAY

462 P.2d 671 (Or. 1969)

GOODWIN, J.

William and Georgianna Hay, the owners of a tourist facility at Cannon Beach, appeal from a decree which enjoins them from constructing fences or other improvements in the dry-sand area between the sixteen-foot elevation contour line and the ordinary high tide line of the Pacific Ocean.

The issue is whether the state has the power to prevent the defendant landowners from enclosing the dry-sand area contained within the legal description of their ocean-front property.

The state asserts two theories: (1) the landowners' record title to the disputed area is encumbered by a superior right in the public to go upon and enjoy the land for recreational purposes; and (2) if the disputed area is not encumbered by the asserted public easement, then the state has power to prevent construction under zoning regulations made pursuant to ORS 390.640.

***

The land area in dispute will be called the dry-sand area. This will be assumed to be the land lying between the line of mean high tide and the visible line of vegetation. . . . Below, or seaward of the mean high-tide line is the state owned foreshore, or wet-sand area, in which the landowners in this case concede the public's paramount right, and concerning which there is no justiciable controversy. The only issue in this case, as noted, is the power of the state to limit the record owner's use and enjoyment of the dry-sand area, by whatever boundaries the area may be described.

The trial court found that the public had acquired, over the years, an easement for recreational purposes to go upon and enjoy the dry-sand area, and that this easement was appurtenant to the wet-sand portion of the beach which is admittedly owned by the state and designated as a "state recreation area."

Because we hold that the trial court correctly found in favor of the state on the rights of the public in the dry-sand area, it follows that the state has an equitable right to protect the public in the enjoyment of those rights by causing the removal of fences and other obstacles. . . .

In order to explain our reasons for affirming the trial court's decree, it is necessary to set out in some detail the historical facts which lead to our conclusion. The dry sand area in Oregon has been enjoyed by the general public as a recreational adjunct of the wet-sand or foreshore area since the beginning of the state's political history. The first European settlers on these shores found the aboriginal inhabitants using the foreshore for clam digging and the dry-sand area for their cooking fires. The newcomers continued these customs after statehood. Thus, from the time of the earliest settlement to the present day, the general public has assumed that the dry-sand area was a part of the public beach, and the public has used the dry-sand area for picnics, gathering wood, building warming fires, and generally as a headquarters from which to supervise children or to range out over the foreshore as the tides advance and recede. In the Cannon Beach vicinity, state and local officers have policed the dry sand, and municipal sanitary crews have attempted to keep the area reasonably free from man-made litter.

Perhaps one explanation for the evolution of the custom of the public to use the dry-sand area for recreational purposes is that the area could not be used conveniently by its owners for any other purpose. The dry-sand area is unstable in its seaward boundaries, unsafe during winter storms, and for the most part unfit for the construction of permanent structures. While the vegetation line remains relatively fixed, the western edge of the dry-sand area is subject to dramatic moves eastward or westward in response to erosion and accretion. For example, evidence in the trial below indicated that between April 1966 and August 1967 the seaward edge of the dry-sand area involved in this litigation moved westward 180 feet. At other points along the shore, the evidence showed, the seaward edge of the dry-sand area could move an equal distance to the east in a similar period of time. . . .

The disputed area is *sui generis*. While the foreshore is "owned" by the state, and the upland is "owned" by the patentee or record-title holder, neither can be said to "own" the full bundle of rights normally connoted by the term "estate in fee simple."

In addition to the *sui generis* nature of the land itself, a multitude of complex and sometimes overlapping precedents in the law confronted the trial court. Several early Oregon decisions generally support the trial court's decision, i.e., that the public can acquire easements in private land by long-continued use that is inconsistent with the owner's exclusive possession and enjoyment of his land. . . .

A second group of cases relied upon by the state, but rejected by the trial court, deals with the possibility of a landowner's losing the exclusive possession and enjoyment of his land through the development of prescriptive easements in the public.

In Oregon, as in most common law jurisdictions, an easement can be created in favor of one person in the land of another by uninterrupted use and enjoyment of the land in a particular manner for the statutory period, so long as the use is open, adverse, under claim of right, but without authority of law or consent of the owner. In Oregon, the prescriptive period is ten years. The public use of the disputed land in the case at bar is admitted to be continuous for more than sixty years. There is no suggestion in the record that anyone's permission was sought or given; rather, the public used the land under a claim of right. Therefore, if the public can acquire an easement by prescription, the requirements for such an acquisition have been met in connection with the specific tract of land involved in this case.

The owners argue, however, that the general public, not being subject to actions in trespass and ejectment, cannot acquire rights by prescription, because the statute of limitations is irrelevant when an action does lie. While it may not be feasible for a landowner to sue the general public, it is nonetheless possible by means of signs and fences to prevent or minimize public invasions of private land for recreational purposes. In Oregon, moreover, the courts and the Legislative Assembly have both recognized that the public can acquire prescriptive easements in private land, at least for roads and highways. . . .

Because many elements of prescription are present in this case, the state has relied upon the doctrine in support of the decree below. We believe, however, that there is a better legal basis for affirming the decree. The most cogent basis for the decision in this case is the English doctrine of custom. Strictly construed, prescription applies only to the specific tract of land before the court, and doubtful prescription cases could fill the courts for years with tract by tract litigation. An established custom, on the other hand, can be proven with reference to a larger region. Ocean-front lands from the northern to the southern border of the state ought to be treated uniformly.

The other reason which commends the doctrine of custom over that of prescription as the principal basis for the decision in this case is the unique nature of the lands in question. This case deals solely with the dry-sand area along the Pacific shore, and this land has been used by the public as public recreational land according to an unbroken custom running back in time as long as the land has been inhabited. A custom is defined in Bouvier's Law Dictionary as "such a usage as by common consent and uniform practice has become the law of the place, or of the subject matter to which it relates."

***

The custom of the people of Oregon to use the dry-sand area of the beaches for public recreational purposes meets every one of Blackstone's requisites.[7] While it is not necessary to rely upon precedent from other states, we are not the first state to recognize custom as a source of law. . . .

In support of custom, the record shows that the custom of the inhabitants of Oregon and of visitors in the state to use the dry sand as a public recreation area is so notorious that notice of the custom on the part of persons buying land along the shore must be presumed. In the case at bar, the landowners conceded their actual knowledge of the public's longstanding use of the dry-sand area, and argued that the elements of consent present in the relationship between the land-owners and the public precluded the application of the law of prescription. As noted, we are not resting this decision on prescription, and we leave upon the effect upon prescription of the type of consent that may have been present in this case. Such elements of consent are, however, wholly consistent with the recognition of public rights derived from custom.

Because so much of our law is the product of legislation, we sometimes lose sight of the importance of custom as a source of law in our society. It seems particularly appropriate in the case at bar to look to an ancient and accepted custom in this state as the source of a rule of law. The rule in this case, based upon custom, is salutary in confirming a public right, and at the same time it takes from no man anything which he has had a legitimate reason to regard as exclusively his.

The decree of the trial court is affirmed.

Questions and Comments for Discussion

1.   The court said that to recognize a custom as law it must (1) be ancient; (2) be a right exercised without interruption; (3) be peaceable and free from dispute; (4) be reasonable; (5) be of certain limit; (6) be obligatory (not left to the option of each landowner); and (7) not be repugnant or inconsistent with other customs or laws. Why did the court adopt this as a theory entitling the public to ownership rights in this case rather than that of a prescriptive easement?

Grants of an Express Easement   A property owner may expressly grant to another the right to use his property for a particular purpose. It is not uncommon for a utility or pipeline company to obtain a right of way on another's property for placement of its equipment. In such cases, the rights of the parties will be determined in large part by the actual language in the granting instrument. In *Chevron Pipe Line Co. v. De Roset,* 858 P.2d 164 (Or. App. 1993), for example, the plaintiff was the owner and operator of an interstate petroleum products pipeline that crossed defendant's property. He sought an order enjoining the defendant from placing fill material over the pipeline and requiring defendant to remove fill material and heavy equipment he had placed there, allegedly in violation of plaintiff's easement.

The defendant's predecessors had conveyed a 16.5-foot easement across their land to plaintiff's predecessor, the Salt Lake Pipe Line Company, for purposes of transporting liquid petroleum products from a refinery in Salt Lake City, Utah. The conveyance granted to plaintiff:

The right of way from time to time to lay, construct, reconstruct, replace, renew, repair, maintain, operate, change the size of, increase the number of, and remove pipe lines and appurtenances thereof, for the transportation of oil, petroleum, gas, gasoline, water or other substances, or any thereof, and to erect, install, maintain, operate, repair, renew, power lines and appurtenances thereof on a single line of poles or underground, as Grantee from time to time and place to place may elect, with the right of ingress and egress to and from the same, over and through, under and along that certain parcel of land . . . .

The conveyances reserved to the defendant's predecessor:

the right to use and enjoy said premises, provided that Grantor shall not construct or maintain the whole or any part of any structure on said strip of land or in any manner impair or interfere with the present or prospective exercise of any of the rights therein granted.

The slope of the land made it less than desirable for defendant's proposed use of the property, so over the years he filled the upper portion of his property with fill material of various kind (dirt, concrete, and asphalt) and created two terraces which, at the higher edge, covered plaintiff's pipeline to a depth of 22.55 feet. The plaintiff contended that the presence of the fill and equipment impaired its access to the pipeline and therefore violated the easement's restriction on defendant's use of the property. It asked the court to require the defendant to stop parking equipment on the easement and to remove the fill to a depth of not more than five feet above the pipeline. In plaintiff's view, the placement of fill on the pipeline was *per se* an interference with plaintiff's right to install, replace, and repair the pipe, and thus a violation of the easement.

The court of appeals, however, concluded that the trial court correctly rejected an absolute restriction on the servient tenant's (defendant's) right to use the property. According to the court, "The right of the easement owner, and the right of the land owner, are not absolute, irrelative, and uncontrolled, but are so limited, each by the other, that there may be a due and reasonable enjoyment of both." In view of all the circumstances, the court said the defendant's use of his property did not interfere with plaintiff's use of the easement in a manner not contemplated by the parties at the time the easement was granted.

As this case indicates, the language of the granting instrument determines the relative rights and duties of the parties. In addition, easements in gross (easements which do not belong to any person by virtue of ownership of appurtenant land), granted for commercial or public purposes, are transferrable. The express easement, as an interest in land, should be recorded so that future owners are on notice of its existence.

Restrictive Covenants   A **restrictive covenant** is a voluntary restriction on land use created by contract. The covenant is unique because it not only binds the parties to the contract, but it also binds later owners of the land. Unlike an easement, which is an interest in land, the covenant is a contractual promise that passes with the land. And unlike the defeasible fee, which terminates if the promise is not kept, breach of a restrictive covenant results in damages or an action for injunctive relief.

Covenants are created by a document, usually a deed, which spells out restrictions on land use or refers to another plan containing detailed restrictions on land use. Covenants "run with the land," which means that they apply to subsequent purchasers of the property, and are commonly used in residential development projects to control the physical appearance of property. Some contain specific restrictions based on aesthetics (limiting, for example, the kind of fences or roofs to be constructed in the neighborhood), and may address environmental concerns like the right to light. Even if a restrictive covenant does not mention solar devices, design review requirements, height restrictions, setback and yard requirements, other restrictions may affect residential solar designs.

SUMMARY

This chapter has introduced some fundamental concepts of property law which are useful in a discussion of environmental law issues. The concept of *property* is ultimately a discussion of the relationship between human beings and other things, including plants, animals, the air, the water, and the earth. As such, it is not a static legal concept, but rather reflects economic, social, and political considerations. As those considerations change, so the law of property changes.

The rules governing ownership of property, characterization of property, and estates in land have come down to us from an earlier time. As times have changed, so have these concepts. The evolution of the law of property has been accomplished by the courts to a great extent through common law decision making. As federal and state legislatures become increasingly active in passing laws to protect the environment, property rights are more affected by statutory and administrative regulations.

Some have suggested that society reconsider the legal concept of *ownership*. According to the following author, the traditional common law of property does not promote an ecologically sound perspective on the proper relationship between humans and their environment.

The legal concept of property and the nature of ownership rights have great implications for the environment. From a legal perspective, the proper balance between a government's right to regulate land, air, and water and the individual's right to use and enjoy her property is a constitutional issue of great significance. These questions will be reconsidered and more fully explored in the context of the issue of "takings" in Chapter 6.

Excerpt from "Ownership and Ecology" by Eric T. Freyfogle

What does our law of property have to say to the grain farmer and cattle rancher out on Willa Cather's old Divide? What are the "legal" ways that people relate to the surrounding land, the land that supports and sustains them?

Preeminently, the law sends the message the people are distinct from the land and its component parts. People like our Nebraska farmers are subjects, and the land is merely an object, possessing no moral or legal worth and counting for nothing. There is at work here a distinct dichotomy

43 Case West. Res. L. Rev. *1269 [1993]*

of subject and object, legally worthy and legally worthless. People are the ones who own and dominate, and the land is the thing that is owned and dominated.

A second message we get from the law is that the countryside is something that can be divided distinctly by use of the surveyor's craft and tool. Invisible lines drawn to the fraction of an inch take on somber meaning, first in plats and deeds, and then as fences and in the attitudes and acts of the owner. The division goes still further, as subsurface minerals go to one owner, water to another, and surface rights to still a third. We offer leases and ease-

Excerpt from "Ownership and Ecology" by Eric T. Freyfogle (continued)

ments and covenants and so on, in each instance drawing the land into yet finer particles with an owner, always, for each. Nature is no longer a whole; it is a composite of many differently owned parts.

Each portion of the land, the law suggests, comes under the control and guidance of its owner, and therefore can be managed with little regard for its connections with the surrounding parts of nature. However modest, each land parcel—if not each natural resource—is some owner's bailiwick or castle, undergirded by resonances and echoes of centuries past. To be sure, legal and social restrictions on land use do exist. But such restrictions are mere exceptions to the presumed independence of the law-endorsed one who commands; the rule we fall back on, the rule that provides the cord, is that the owner can, for the most part, do as she likes.

What the law seems to be telling us, from these first legal images, is that property ownership norms are aspects of civil rights and have little to do with the things that most people term property. Property law does not deal with the rights we have in our house or our bicycle; they deal with our rights as against other people with respect to these things. A landowner's right to possess is really his right to keep other people away. An owner, the law suggests, has the right to use, manage, alter, transfer, or destroy as she sees fit—so long as she respects the similar rights of other owners—and these are all rights held against the rest of the world.

At work here is a large and obvious element of abstraction. People count—the owner and those concerned with what the owner does or fails to do—and the thing itself—the field or stream or wetland—fades from the picture. Once the focus shifts from the thing itself we can consider abstractly whether, for example, an owner of property should be able to make a gift of her property, effective upon her death, without complying with the requirements of a valid will. This is the kind of abstract issue that ownership norms take up, and for this kind of work, and in our thinking of property in general, the details of the thing are swept aside.

The sense that arises from the law, in short, is that property law's sole interest is with the relative interests of humans. By important implication, this can also be the owner's only concern. On occasion property law uses an even more restricted vision—that only property-owning humans count—but we need not concern ourselves with this refinement. The point here is that limits on how property can be used are designed principally to divide entitlements among humans. Animals, plants, and other parts of nature all count for nothing. Ecosystems and natural communities, which are the settings for all life, have no independent value or existence.

GLOSSARY

Adverse possession—Means of acquiring title to land by openly taking possession of and using another's property for a certain period of time.

Community property—System of ownership of property by husband and wife that exists in western states (Louisiana, Texas, New Mexico, Arizona, Nevada, California, Idaho, and Washington).

Doctrine of Ancient Lights—A common law doctrine which provided that anyone who used light for an uninterrupted period of twenty years was entitled to protection for use of that light. The doctrine has been rejected by American courts.

Easement—A liberty, privilege, or advantage one holds in another's property.

Estate—A term describing the nature, quality, and quantity of a person's interest in real property.

Fee simple absolute—The fee simple or fee simple absolute is the greatest possible estate in land. The grant of a fee conveys to the grantee complete ownership of the property.

Fee simple defeasible—A fee simple qualified by language that will cause the fee to end when a certain event occurs.

Grantee—Person to whom a legal interest in real property is conveyed or transferred.

Grantor—Person who conveys or transfers an interest in real property to another.

Intangible property—Property which has no physical existence, such as patent rights or stocks and bonds.

Joint tenancy—Form of co-ownership of real property characterized by a right of survivorship.

Lease—A contract between an owner and another for the possession and use of land.

Littoral rights—Belonging to the shore. Littoral proprietors on a sea or lake correspond to riparian proprietors on a stream or pond.

Partition—Physical division of co-owned property whereby co-owners become adjoining landowners or neighbors.

Prior appropriation doctrine—Common law doctrine determining water rights in states primarily west of the Mississippi. Characterized by the doctrine "first in time, first in right."

Property—A legally protected expectation of being able to draw an advantage from a thing.

Quiet title action—Proceeding to establish title to land by bringing into court all who have adverse claims to title to the property.

Restrictive covenant—A contractual promise that passes with the land.

Riparian rights doctrine—Common law doctrine determining water rights in states primarily east of the Mississippi. Characterized by the requirements of "reasonable use." Unlike the prior appropriation doctrine, only riparians (those who own property adjacent to the waterway) may assert these rights.

Solar easement laws—Statutes that permit the execution and recognition of easements for the protection of solar access.

Tangible property—Property which has a physical existence, such as land, furniture, or an automobile.

Tenancy by the entirety—Form of ownership of real property by husband and wife.

Tenancy in common—Form of co-ownership of real property where the parties hold separate undivided interests in the property.

Waste—An unlawful act or omission of duty on the part of a tenant of land which results in permanent injury to the property.

CASES FOR DISCUSSION

1.   Plaintiff, a gravel company, conveyed certain property to a bank which subsequently sold the property to defendants. The property contained three man-made lakes completely within the property and unconnected to any other bodies of water. Plaintiff had operated a "fee fishing and camping" business on the property, and stocked the quarries with fish. The fish also reproduced naturally. Plaintiff sought a declaration from the court that it had a property interest in the fish and therefore had a right to remove the fish from the property. Plaintiff argued that the fish were part of its business inventory and that it did not convey the fish to the bank along with the real property. It claimed that even though defendants owned the property, plaintiff still had a property interest in the fish. Is plaintiff correct? *Tyrrell Gravel Co. v. Carradus,* 619 N.E.2d 1367 (Ill. App. 2 Dist. 1993).

2.   Defendant brought a civil action against her landlords, Gary and Cynthia Friedland, alleging a violation of the Lead Poisoning and Control Act. Ms. Friedland moved to dismiss, claiming that she had been improperly named a defendant because she had no relation to the subject premises and therefore owed no duty to plaintiff. Is the wife of the owner of rental property, who was listed on the lease as a lessor, an owner of the property for purposes of the Massachusetts Lead Poisoning and Control Act? *Roman v. Friedland,* 849 F. Supp. 827 (D. Mass. 1994).

3.   For more than ten years, Smith farmed a section of land in Gaines County, Texas, under agreement with his aunt who owned the property. In 1993, the aunt executed an agreement conveying to plaintiff, Mobil Pipe Line Co., a right of way to "enter at any time and from time to time to lay, repair, maintain, operate and remove a 14-inch pipeline over and through the property." After Smith denied Mobil access across the farm, Mobil sought a court order granting it access to the property. Does the owner of a pipeline right of way easement have the right to enter upon farmland and lay a pipeline when there is no agreement with, but objection from the tenant who farms the land under a lease? *Mobil Pipe Line Co. v. Smith,* 860 S.W. 2d 157 (Tex. App. 1993).

4.   In 1971, the Indiana legislature enacted a statute providing that a severed mineral interest that is not used for a period of twenty years automatically lapses and reverts to the current surface owner of the property, unless the mineral owner files a statement of claim in the local county recorder's office. Does this statute deprive owners of unused mineral interests their property without due process of law? *Texaco Inc. v. Short,* 545 U.S. 516 (1982).

5.   Should geothermal resources (natural steam) be considered in a class with mineral interests rather than as a water resource for purposes of environmental regulation? *Pariani v. State,* 164 Cal. Rptr. 683 (1980).

ENDNOTES

1. Jeremy Bentham, Theory of Legislation, Principles of the Civil Code, n.p., 1864.

2. *Whittaker v. Stangvick,* 100 Minn. 386, 111 N.W. 295 (1907). Trespass and nuisance are discussed in Chapter 4.

3. *Marengo Cave Co. v. Ross,* 10 N.E. 2d 917 (1937).

4. 30 U.S.C., §§ 1201 et seq. (1977).

5. Arkansas, Kansas, Mississippi, Ohio, Pennsylvania, Texas, and West Virginia are ownership states.

6. *Gulf Park Water v. First Ocean Springs Dev.,* 530 So.2d 1325 (Miss. 1988).

7. Author's note: Blackstone was a famous law commentator. His Commentaries on the Laws of England (1765–1769) was the first accessible general statement of English law.

4

COMMON LAW REMEDIES FOR ENVIRONMENTAL HARMS

INTRODUCTION

This chapter addresses common law theories which protect and restrict ownership rights in real property and focuses on four common law tort theories which are used by plaintiffs to recover damages for environmental harm to their property or person: trespass, nuisance, negligence, and strict liability.

A **tort** is a private (civil) wrong against a person or his property. A person injured as a result of the tortious act of another is entitled to a legal remedy, in most cases, money damages. In those cases where money damages are inadequate compensation, the court may issue an *injunction,* which is a court order requiring the defendant to do something or refrain from doing something.

Discussed in this chapter are common law tort theories which have evolved through judicial decision making in individual cases. Tort actions are private civil actions, that is, actions brought by one person against another. Recall that common law is judge-made law. Common law rules tend to be flexible—the courts apply them to particular facts in specific cases.

Common law decision making often depends on the particular facts of each case. Because common law policy is implemented on a case-by-case basis, it has often been criticized as being too slow or too uncertain to resolve the technologically induced problems of environmental pollution. To some extent, this criticism is justified, and as a result both the federal and state governments have adopted laws and administrative rules and regulations to address pollution in a broader legislative/regulatory framework.

Although much public attention is focused on the impact of law on environmental policy making, many federal and state laws do not permit individuals to recover damages for personal injuries or property damages.[1] Consequently, individuals continue to rely on common law tort theories like trespass, nuisance, negligence, and strict liability to recover damages for environmental harms to their property or person.

As courts apply these common law tort principles to the facts in individual cases, they also make environmental policy to meet changes in society. In this way the common law continues to evolve. In the last part of this century, for example, courts have modified traditional trespass theory to define the scope of liability in airborne pollution cases, and have recognized a plaintiff's right to recover damages for emotional distress absent physical injury in pollution and product liability cases.

TORT LAW

Tort liability is based on the concept that a person may be liable for a breach of legal duty owed to another. Tort law differs from criminal law in that it is designed to compensate tort victims rather than to punish the wrongdoer, although in some cases a plaintiff may recover **punitive damages,** money awards designed to deter the defendant from similar actions in the future.

There are different ways to classify torts. One distinction is based on the level of fault by the wrongdoer. *Intentional torts* are where a person acts with desire to cause harm or with knowledge that such harm is substantially certain to follow as a result of his actions. *Recklessness* is conduct by a defendant which demonstrates a conscious disregard for a known risk of probable harm to others.

Negligence defines conduct which falls below established legal standards, with the most common standard being a person's duty to act with reasonable care. Negligence may also be established by proof that a defendant breached other legal duties, such as a duty imposed under state or federal law. Under principles of **strict liability,** a defendant may be liable for some activities which result in harm to others, even though he did not act intentionally or negligently in causing that harm.

TRESPASS

Trespass is an early common law tort which protects a person's right to exclusive possession of property. Trespass is defined as an intrusion on or invasion of the tangible property of another which interferes with the possessor's right of exclusive possession of the property. A wrongful intrusion by a person onto the land of another constitutes trespass. An intrusion can also constitute nuisance if it interferes with the plaintiff's use and enjoyment of his property. For example, gasoline leaks from a service station which contaminate a neighboring property constitute both trespass and nuisance.[2]

A person may be liable for either negligent or intentional trespass. A trespass occurs if a person causes harm by wrongfully entering the land in possession of the other, or wrongfully causes a thing or another person to do so. Thus, if construction work on private property results in a landslide which causes damage to neighboring property, a trespass has occurred.[3] A person may also be liable if he intentionally or negligently remains on the land of another or fails to remove from the land a thing which he is under a duty to remove.

Under traditional common law, if a person intentionally interfered with another's exclusive right of possession of property without a privilege to do so, he was liable for trespass without proof of actual damages. For purposes of trespass law, proof that the defendant knew or should have known that a particular result was substantially certain to follow from his action constitutes intention. If a city closes a sewage overflow valve and knows that the blockage will cause some sewage backup, the city may be liable under the theory of intentional trespass to a homeowner who suffers damages.[4]

Historically, many courts distinguished between trespass and nuisance by applying a "dimensional test." Under the dimensional test, whether an intrusion constituted trespass or nuisance depended on the size of the intruding agent. If the intruding agent could be seen by the naked eye, it was considered trespass. If it could not be seen, it was considered indirect and less substantial, and consequently a nuisance. By limiting liability for trespass to the intrusion of an observable object, the rule limited the scope of a defendant's liability for trespass. But modern courts have modified the rule in airborne pollution cases.

The Oregon Supreme Court first discarded the dimensional test in *Martin v. Reynolds Metals Company.*[5] In that case, the court held that a trespass had occurred when certain fluoride compounds from the manufacturing process of the defendant's aluminum reduction plant became airborne and settled upon the plaintiff's land. Even though the fluoride compounds took the form of gases and particulates invisible to the naked eye, the court said,

> It is quite possible that in an earlier day when science had not yet peered into the molecular and atomic world of small particles, the courts could not fit an invasion through unseen physical instrumentalities into the requirement that a trespass can result only from a *direct* invasion. But in this atomic age even the uneducated know the great and awful force contained in the atom and what it can do to a man's property if it is released.

In the following case, the Washington Supreme Court followed the Oregon court's reasoning in *Martin v. Reynolds Metals* and held that an intentional trespass had occurred in an airborne pollution case. The court also recognized that public policy required modifying traditional common law trespass to incorporate a balancing test like that of nuisance law.

BRADLEY v. AMERICAN SMELTING AND REFINING
709 P.2d 782 (Wash. 1985)

[*This case came before the state court on certification from the U.S. District Court for the Western District of Washington.*]

CALLOW, J.

The parties have stipulated to the facts as follows. Plaintiffs Michael O. Bradley and Marie A. Bradley, husband and wife, are owners and occupiers of real property on the southern end of Vashon Island in King County, Washington. The Bradleys purchased their property in 1978. Defendant ASARCO, a New Jersey corporation doing business in Washington, operates a primary copper smelter on real property it owns in Rushton, which is an incorporated munici-

pality surrounded by the city of Tacoma, Washington. Plaintiffs brought this action against defendant alleging a cause of action for intentional trespass and for nuisance.

Plaintiffs' property is located some 4 miles north of defendant's smelter. Defendant's primary copper smelter (also referred to as the Tacoma smelter) has operated in its present location since 1890. It has operated as a copper smelter since 1902, and in 1905 it was purchased and operated by a corporate entity which is now ASARCO. As a part of the industrial process of smelting copper at the Tacoma smelter, various gases such as sulfur dioxide, and particulate matter, including arsenic, cadmium and other metals, are emitted. Particulate matter is composed of distinct particles of matter other than water, which cannot be detected by the human sense.

[*The court noted that these emissions were subject to regulation under the Federal Clean Air and State statutes, and that the smelter was in compliance with those laws. The parties had stipulated that some particulate emissions of both cadmium and arsenic from the Tacoma smelter continued to be deposited on plaintiff's land, but that there was no proof of actual damages to plaintiffs or their property as a result of the emissions.*]

***

The issues present the conflict in an industrial society between the need of all for the production of goods and the desire of the landowner near the manufacturing plant producing those goods that his use and enjoyment ·of his land not be diminished by the unpleasant side effects of the manufacturing process. A reconciliation must be found between the interest of the many who are unaffected by the possible poisoning and the few who may be affected. . . .

The defendant cannot and does not deny that whenever the smelter was in operation the whim of the winds could bring these deleterious substances to the plaintiffs' premises. We are asked if the defendant, knowing what it had to know from the facts it admits, had the legal intent to commit trespass. . . .

The defendant has known for decades that sulfur dioxide and particulates of arsenic, cadmium and other metals were being emitted from the tall smokestack. It had to know that the solids propelled into the air by the warm gases would settle back to earth somewhere. It had to know that a purpose of the tall stack was to disperse the gas, smoke and minute solids over as large an area as possible and as far away as possible, but that while any resulting contamination would be diminished as to any one area or landowner, that nonetheless contamination, though slight, would follow:

> Intent is broader than a desire to bring about physical results. It must extend not only to those consequences which are desired, but also to those which the actor believes are substantially certain to follow from what he does. . . . The man who fires a bullet into a dense crowd may fervently pray that he will hit no one, but since he must believe and know that he cannot avoid doing so, he intends it. . . .[6]

We find that the defendant had the requisite intent to commit intentional trespass as a matter of law.

***

Trespass is a theory closely related to nuisance and occasionally invoked in environmental cases. The distinction between the two originally was the difference between the old action of trespass and the action on the case: if there was a direct and immediate physical invasion of plaintiff's property, as by casting stones or water on it, it was a trespass; if the invasion was indirect, as by the seepage of water, it was a nuisance.

Today with the abandonment of the old procedural forms, the line between trespass and nuisance has become "wavering and uncertain. . . ." The first and most important proposition about trespass and nuisance principles is that they are largely coextensive. Both concepts are often discussed in the same cases without differentiation between the elements of recovery. . . .

It is also true that in the environmental arena both nuisance and trespass cases typically involve intentional conduct by the defendant who knows that his activities are substantially certain to result in an invasion of plaintiff's interests. The principal difference in theories is that the tort of trespass is complete upon a tangible invasion of plaintiff's property, however, slight, whereas a nuisance requires proof that the interference with use and enjoyment is "substantial and unreasonable. . . ."

We hold that the defendant's conduct in causing chemical substances to be deposited upon the plaintiffs' land fulfilled all of the requirements under the law of trespass.

***

Under the modern theory of trespass, the law presently allows an action to be maintained in trespass for invasions that, at one time, were considered indirect and, hence, only a nuisance. In order to recover in trespass for this type of invasion, a plaintiff must show (1) an invasion affecting an interest in the exclusive possession of his property; (2) an intentional doing of the act which results in the invasion; (3) reasonable foreseeability that the act done could result in an invasion of plaintiff's possessory interest; and (4) substantial damages to the *res* (the property.)

When airborne particles are transitory or quickly dissipated, they do not interfere with a property owner's possessory rights and, therefore, are properly denominated as nuisances. When, however, the particles or substance accumulates on the land and does not pass away, then a trespass has occurred.

While at common law any trespass entitled a landowner to recover nominal or punitive damages for the invasion of his property, such a rule is not appropriate under the circumstances before us. No useful purpose would be served by sanctioning actions in trespass by every landowner within a hundred miles of a manufacturing plant. Manufacturers would be harassed and the litigious few would cause the escalation of costs to the detriment of the many. The elements that we have adopted for an action in trespass requires that a plaintiff has suffered action and substantial damages. Since this is an element of the action, the plaintiff who cannot show that actual and substantial damages have been suffered should be subject to dismissal of his cause upon a motion for summary judgment.

[*Author's note: Following certification, the U.S. District Court found that under the principles articulated by the Washington court in this case, the plaintiffs were not entitled to recover damages for trespass because they could not prove they incurred "substantial damages."*]

Questions and Comments for Discussion

1. The *Bradley* court concluded that the defendant had the requisite intent to commit intentional trespass, and that an intentional deposit of microscopic particulates, undetectable by the human senses, gives rise to a cause of action for trespass as well as a claim of nuisance. But it said that a cause of action under such circumstances also requires proof of actual and substantial damages. How did the court's decision change the traditional common law tort of trespass? What are the policy concerns cited by the court which support this change?

2. As this case suggests, the "intention" of the defendant may be a factor in determining whether trespass has occurred. Under the Restatement, a defendant may be liable in trespass if he intentionally enters land of another, regardless of whether he actually causes harm to the interest of the plaintiff. Actual harm is required for reckless or negligent trespass. How realistic is the distinction between intentional and negligent trespass? Why should a person be liable for intentional trespass if he causes no harm to plaintiff?

3. *Bradley* illustrates some of the limitations of common law adjudication in airborne pollution cases. Suppose that the plaintiffs had been able to prove substantial damages to their property. Should they be entitled to continuing damages or an injunction closing the plant? What would be the impact of permitting individual plaintiffs to sue manufacturers for airborne pollution under a continuing trespass theory? See *Renken v. Harvey Aluminum,* 226 F.Supp.

169 (D.C. Or. 1963), and *Boomer v. Atlantic Cement Company* in the following section.
4.   What are the relative advantages and disadvantages of adopting a regulatory strategy to address the problems of air pollution rather than establishing such policy through common law case adjudication? Do you agree with those who have criticized common law adjudication as too slow and imprecise to be an effective way of establishing environmental policy?

NUISANCE

Nuisance may be defined as an "unreasonable activity or condition on the defendant's land which substantially or unreasonably interferes with the plaintiff's use and enjoyment of his property." Nuisance law protects these rights and does not require a physical invasion of the property. Unlike trespass, a nuisance is a state of affairs, and may be merely a right thing in the wrong place, like a pig in the parlor instead of the barnyard.[7]

To recover damages for nuisance, a plaintiff must prove that the defendant's activities were "unreasonable" and that those activities "substantially interfered" with the plaintiff's enjoyment of his property. This requires the court to engage in a *balancing test* to determine whether a nuisance has occurred. As the court's opinion in *Bradley v. American Smelting and Refining,* above, suggests, nuisance and trespass theories overlap in some cases, and both theories may be utilized by plaintiffs seeking to recover damages for pollution of land, air, and water.

Whether the defendant's activities are unreasonable for purposes of nuisance law depends on whether the activity is customary for the area, whether it causes observable effects most would find unpleasant, whether there are better methods for carrying on the activity, whether there is value to the defendant and society, and whether the defendant's activities began before the plaintiff's occupation of his land.

Like the reasonableness test, the requirement of "substantial harm" to the plaintiff's use and enjoyment of his land in nuisance cases depends upon consideration of a number of factors. These include the value of the plaintiff's loss, whether there is observable damage to the property, and whether the harm is intermittent or unremitting.

Typical nuisance-causing agents include noise, dust, smoke, odors, airborne or waterborne contaminants, and vermin and insects. Nuisance law has been used by plaintiffs seeking to recover damages for environmental harm like the contamination of groundwater from neighboring landfill operations, and for injury caused by noise, dust, and hazardous particulates deposited on land by incinerator and oil refinery operations. As you may recall from the previous chapter, nuisance law has also been utilized by some courts in right-to-light cases.

The successful plaintiff in a nuisance action may recover damages (measured by the loss of the value of the property), or may seek an **injunction** ordering the defendant to cease those activities causing the nuisance. An injunction is subject to the court's discretion and requires the court to balance the plaintiff's hardship if the injunction is not issued against the defendant's hardship if it is. In the following 1970 airborne pollution case, the question of remedy was a central issue. Consider the limitations of the law of nuisance in controlling the general problems of air and water pollution, and the court's view of its role in making policy decisions about how best to address these problems.

BOOMER v. ATLANTIC CEMENT COMPANY
257 N.E.2d 870 (N.Y. 1970)

BERGAN, J.

Defendant operates a large cement plant near Albany. These are actions for injunction and damages by neighboring land owners alleging injury to property from dirt, smoke and vibration emanating from the plant. A nuisance has been found after trial, temporary damages have been allowed; but an injunction has been denied.

The public concern with air pollution arising from many sources in industry and in transportation is currently accorded ever wider recognition accompanied by a growing sense of responsibility in State and Federal Governments to control it. Cement plants are obvious sources of air pollution in the neighborhoods where they operate.

But there is now before the court private litigation in which individual property owners have sought specific relief from a single plant operation. The threshold question raised on this appeal is whether the court should resolve the litigation between the parties now before it as equitably as seems possible; or whether, seeking promotion of the general public welfare, it should channel private litigation into broad public objectives.

A court performs its essential function when it decides the rights of parties before it. Its decision of private controversies may sometimes greatly affect public issues. Large questions of law are often resolved by the manner in which private litigation is decided. But this is normally an incident to the court's main function to settle controversy. It is a rare exercise of judicial power to use a decision in private litigation as a purposeful mechanism to achieve direct public objectives greatly beyond the rights and interests before the court.

Effective control of air pollution is a problem presently far from solution even with the full public and financial powers of government. In a large measure adequate technical procedures are yet to be developed and some that appear possible may be economically impracticable.

It seems apparent that the amelioration of air pollution will depend on technical research in great depth; on a carefully balanced consideration of the economic impact of close regulation; and of the actual effect on public health. It is likely to require massive public expenditure and to demand more than any local community can accomplish and to depend on regional and interstate controls.

A court should not try to do this on its own as a by-product of private litigation and it seems manifest that the judicial establishment is neither equipped in the limited nature of any judgment it can pronounce nor prepared to lay down and implement an effective policy for the elimination of air pollution. This is an area beyond the circumference of one private lawsuit. It is a direct responsibility for government and should not thus be undertaken as an incident to solving a dispute between property owners and a single cement plant—one of many—in the Hudson River valley.

The cement making operations of defendant have been found by the court at Special term to have damaged the nearby properties of plaintiffs in these two actions. . . . The total damage to plaintiff's properties is, however, relatively small in comparison with the value of defendant's operation and with the consequences of the injunction which plaintiffs seek.

***

One alternative is to grant the injunction but postpone its effect to a specified future date to give opportunity for technical advances to permit defendant to eliminate the nuisance; another is to grant the injunction conditioned on the payment of permanent damages to plaintiffs which would compensate them for the total economic losses to their property present and future caused by defendant's operations. For reasons which will be developed the court chooses the latter alternative.

***

[T]echniques to eliminate dust and other annoying by-products of cement making are unlikely to be developed by any research the defendant can undertake within any short period, but will depend on the total resources of the cement industry nationwide and throughout the world. The problem is universal where cement is made.

For obvious reasons the rate of the research is beyond control of defendant. If at the end of 18 months whole industry has not found a technical solution a court would be hard put to close down this one cement plant if due regard be given to equitable principles.

On the other hand, to grant the injunction unless defendant pays plaintiffs such permanent damages as may be fixed by the court seems to do justice between the contending parties. All of the attributions of economic loss to the properties on which plaintiffs' complaints are based will have been redressed.

***

[*The court then held that the injunction should be vacated upon payment by defendant of such amount of permanent damage to the respective plaintiffs as determined by the trial court.*]

JASEN, J. (*dissenting*)

I agree with the majority that a reversal is required here, but I do not subscribe to the newly enunciated doctrine of assessment of permanent damages, in lieu of an injunction, when substantial property rights have been impaired by the creation of a nuisance. . . .

The harmful nature and widespread occurrence of air pollution have been extensively documented. Congressional hearings have revealed that air pollution causes substantial property damage, as well as being a contributing factor to a rising incidence of lung cancer, emphysema, bronchitis and asthma. The specific problem faced here is known as particulate contamination because of the fine dust particles emanating from defendant's cement plant. The particular type of nuisance is not new, having appeared in many cases for at least the past 60 years. It is interesting to note that cement production has recently been identified as a significant source of particular contamination in the Hudson Valley. This type of pollution, wherein very small particles escape and stay in the atmosphere, has been denominated as the type of air pollution which produces the greatest hazard to human health. We have thus a nuisance which not only is damaging to the plaintiffs, but also is decidedly harmful to the general public.

I see grave dangers in overruling our long-established rule of granting an injunction where a nuisance results in substantial continuing damage. In permitting the injunction to become inoperative upon the payment of permanent damages, the majority is, in effect, licensing a continuing wrong. It is the same as saying to the cement company, you may continue to do harm to your neighbors so long as you pay a fee for it. Furthermore, once such permanent damages are assessed and paid, the incentive to alleviate the wrong would be eliminated, thereby continuing air pollution of an area without abatement. . . .

Questions and Comments for Discussion

1.   What do you think of the majority's decision to require payment of "permanent damages" to the plaintiffs in this case in lieu of an injunction? Do you agree with the dissenting judge's statement that this amounts to licensing a continuing wrong? How would you have balanced the equities in this case?

2.   Note that the *Boomer* case was decided in 1970, the year that the modern Clean Air Act was adopted. The Clean Air Act does not necessarily pre-empt common law actions for nuisance like the one in this case. Should plaintiffs be entitled to common law remedies in cases where defendants are in compliance with state and federal air quality regulations? What are the implications of your answer?

3.   In another case, plaintiffs sued a solvent company, alleging contamination and pollution of their well water as a result of defendants' improper handling of toxic chemicals and industrial waste at their facilities. The trial court dismissed the plaintiff's claims for damages under a nuisance theory because no intrusion of contaminated water had occurred and there was no quantifiable damage based on the claim. The plaintiffs maintained that because the defendants had contaminated the groundwater, their property values had diminished, notwithstanding the fact that no contaminants had come or would come onto their property.

Should the court permit that property owners who have only suffered a decrease in property values be entitled to damages under a nuisance theory? For what policy reasons do you think a court might be willing to permit recovery of damages in such cases? *Adkins v. Thomas Solvent Co.,* 487 N.W.2d 715 (Mich. App. 1990).

Public Nuisance

A *public nuisance* affects a large portion of the public. The difference between a public and private nuisance is a matter of degree. The same kind of activity that gives rise to an action for a private nuisance may give rise to an action for public nuisance. But public nuisances cause a pervasive, widespread harm to many while a private nuisance affects a narrower class of individuals. Under various state statutes, the government or private individuals may be authorized to bring an action to abate a public nuisance.

In one California case, *Lincoln Properties, Ltd. v. Higgins,* 23 Envtl. L. Rep. 20665 (E.D. Cal. 1993), Lincoln Center, a shopping center in Stockton, California, asserted a public and private nuisance claim against tenants of Lincoln Center who operated dry cleaning establishments there. Tests conducted in 1985 and 1986 revealed that water in San Joaquin County wells adjacent to the shopping center had been contaminated by several hazardous chemical compounds used by the dry cleaners. Lincoln was statutorily liable for the contamination because it owned the property, and it sued the past and present owners of the dry cleaning facilities in an effort to force them to investigate and remediate the contamination and reimburse Lincoln for costs it had incurred.

The court agreed that the release of man-made carcinogenic chemical compounds in the soil and groundwater under Lincoln Center interfered with Lincoln's free use and comfortable enjoyment of its property and constituted both a public and private nuisance. It said that the nuisance affected a considerable number of persons since it had forced the county to close four water supply wells. It also said that Lincoln had established a nuisance *per se* because actions of the defendants violated the discharge permit requirement of the county code. The court rejected the argument by the dry cleaners because their leases required them to use the premises only for conducting dry cleaning, Lincoln authorized that activity in the lease.

NEGLIGENCE

Negligence imposes liability on a person who breaches a legal duty to another. The *elements* of a negligence action are (1) the defendant had a *legal duty* to the plaintiff; (2) the defendant *breached* that duty; and (3) the defendant's breach of duty was the *actual cause* and (4) *proximate (legal) cause* of (5) a legally recognizable *injury* to plaintiff as a result of the breach.

Unlike intentional torts such as assault, battery, and intentional trespass and nuisance, negligence does not require proof that the defendant intended to bring about a particular result. The essence of a negligence action is breach of legal duty by the defendant. Breach may occur either through defendant's act or failure to act when under a duty to do so.

The basic legal duty that each of us owes to another is the duty to act "with reasonable care." In order to determine whether a person has acted with reasonable care, the finder of fact (either a judge or jury) uses an *objective* standard of conduct—that is, whether the defendant acted or failed to act as a "reasonable person of ordinary prudence in similar circumstances." This is a flexible standard which allows the fact-finder to consider all the circumstances surrounding a particular action.

The law may impose *special duties* on people in some cases. Special duties may arise from a special relationship between the parties. A contractual or agency relationship between the parties may impose a duty to disclose information, and the law has long imposed upon a common carrier or innkeeper a duty to protect passengers and guests against the foreseeable wrongful acts of others. Whether a defendant had a special duty to a plaintiff is a question of law for the judge.

Another important source of legal duties is federal and state laws. Under the theory of **negligence** *per se,* a person may be liable for injuries to another which result from violation of an environmental statute or regulation. Negligence *per se* requires proof that the harm that the statute was designed to prevent occurred to a person whom the statute was intended to protect. To illustrate, assume that there is a law which prohibits the discharge of paint thinner into a public sewer system. If the defendant discharges paint thinner into a public sewer, he can be liable for damages that are foreseeable as a result of his negligence. He may also be subject to a civil or criminal penalty for violating state and federal hazardous waste laws.

Negligence theory may be used by plaintiffs seeking to recover damages from defendants in environmental cases. In most cases, negligence is just one of several different theories argued by plaintiffs in such cases. In some cases parties may be co-defendants in enforcement actions brought against them under various state and federal environmental laws, and one defendant in that action may seek to recover damages from another defendant. In the following case, plaintiffs sought to recover damages from defendants under common law tort theories, as well as under federal and state hazardous waste laws.

JERSEY CITY REDEVELOPMENT AUTHORITY
v. PPG INDUSTRIES
18 Envtl. L. Rep. 20364 (D.N.J. 1987)

SAROKIN, J.:

During the years 1954 through 1964, PPG, either directly or through a subsidiary, owned and operated a plant located on Garfield Avenue in Jersey City, which processed raw chromium ore. During the processing of the chromium ore a residue mud was produced which contained chromium. As a result of the process, large piles of this residue or waste mud existed at the Garfield Avenue property. During the period of January 1958 until July 1963, it is estimated that 73,200 tons of waste mud were produced. During this period the waste mud was routinely removed by various contractors and utilized as fill material in various construction projects including public works projects. Among the contractors who utilized such material for fill purposes was the defendant Lawrence Construction Company.

It is undisputed that as early as 1954 PPG was aware that there were potential health hazards associated with the processing of chromium ore. Employees who were exposed to the process within the plant sustained nasal perforations, skin ulcers, also known as chrome sores, and lung cancer. Those risks were set forth in a detailed report prepared in 1954 by the Industrial Hygiene Foundation of America, and said report was circulated to companies involved in this industry including PPG. . . . In July of 1963 PPG ceased production at the Garfield plant and in 1964 sought purchasers.

Lawrence Construction had acquired fill from the property and utilized it prior to the time the property was available for sale. Clif Associates and Lawrence were related companies and Clif Associates determined to place a bid for the purchase of the premises. Representatives of Lawrence and Clif were aware that the PPG plant had processed chromium ore, but were unaware of any of the specific health hazards as enumerated above. . . .

[*On July 13, 1964, PPG and Clif entered into an agreement for the purchase of the site. After the purchase, in 1973 Lawrence and Clif became aware that chromium ore existed in the soil based upon a report they had received from a testing lab.*]

PPG knew that there were some minor health risks to direct exposure to chromium even in the residue, and knew or should have known, based upon their specialized knowledge, that the chrome might present environmental risks. Furthermore, it was certainly foreseeable that Lawrence would utilize the fill itself and permit others to use it, since that had been the practice while PPG was the owner of the property. . . .

On November 25, 1974, plaintiff (Jersey City Redevelopment Authority, a municipal corporation) and defendant Ambrosio entered into an agreement for demolition and site clearance on the premises owned by the plaintiff, located on Ninth Street in Jersey City. Ambrosio demolished the buildings located at that site. As part of the demolition, it filled the basements of the building which were demolished with brick and other debris, and some fill material from an excavation from a nearby sewer project. The balance of the fill came from the Garfield Avenue property, having been purchased by Ambrosio from Lawrence.

[. . . *In May, 1982, the City advised PPG that there might be contamination at the Garfield site. In August, 1983, the New Jersey Department of Environmental Protection required the plaintiff to take measures necessary to protect the public* *health and environment. The plaintiff incurred $709,864.22 in expenses.*]

NEGLIGENCE

The court concludes that the negligence of both PPG and Lawrence/Clif caused plaintiff's injuries.

PPG acted negligently in conveying Garfield Avenue to Lawrence/Clif without properly advising Lawrence of the potential risks of chromium contamination. The court has found that PPG knew, at the time of the sale, that there were major health risks associated with the inhalation of chromium and some minor health risks from direct exposure to chromium even in the residue. Moreover, PPG knew or should have known, based on their specialized knowledge, that the chromium in the soil might present environmental risks. Furthermore, PPG knew that Lawrence/Clif would use the fill itself and sell it to others—PPG had sold Garfield Avenue fill in the past, including sales to Lawrence itself. Given these facts, PPG was under a duty to advise the purchaser of the property, at a minimum, of the potentiality of such risks even if it was unable to specify it.

PPG's breach of its duty proximately caused plaintiff's injury. As stated above, PPG plainly should have foreseen that Lawrence/Clif would sell chromium-contaminated fill to others. As explained in connection with Count 3, Lawrence/Clif's negligence does not relieve PPG of liability. PPG should not benefit from the fact that Lawrence/Clif gained independent knowledge of the fills' environmental hazards and failed to act thereupon. That Ambrosio actually transported the fill from Garfield Avenue to Ninth Street does not alter this conclusion.

Lawrence/Clif acted negligently in distributing chromium-contaminated fill without warning the purchaser. Lawrence/Clif, at the time it sold fill to Ambrosio, knew that the fill contained chromium and knew that the fill had caused problems with its foundations. Under these circumstances, Lawrence/Clif had a duty to Ambrosio—extending to plaintiff, a foreseeable user of the contaminated soil—to at least notify that the fill contained chromium. Without this knowledge, neither Ambrosio nor plaintiff, its customer, could evaluate whether to risk use of this fill. Furthermore, Lawrence/Clif's breach of this duty was a proximate cause of the contamination at Ninth Street.

The court holds liable PPG and Lawrence/Clif under Count 7 [*Negligence*].

Questions and Comments for Discussion

1.   Summarize the facts in the above case. Who was the plaintiff? Why did the plaintiff sue the defendants? According to the plaintiff, what acts or omissions of the defendants constituted negligence? What might the defendants have done to avoid liability for negligence in this case?

2.   What standard of care were defendants required to meet in this case? Note that in general, a purchase/sale agreement does *not* create a special duty between buyer and seller. Most states, however, have imposed upon the seller of residential property a *duty to disclose* material defects in the property if they are known to the seller and not discoverable by the buyer. Whether this duty to disclose extends to sellers of commercial property is a policy question that is not settled.

Negligent or intentional misrepresentation, including misrepresentation through non-disclosure, may be a basis for recovering damages in tort or for rescinding a contract for the sale or lease of property. *Fraud* is an intentional tort, requiring proof of a false misrepresentation with intent to deceive. What kind of evidence might support such a theory in this case? What kind of evidentiary problems might arise for plaintiffs in attempting to establish fraud under these facts?

3.   The defendants PPG and Lawrence/Cliff were found *joint and severally* liable by the court under a negligence theory. Under joint and several liability, both defendants are liable for the entire amount claimed by plaintiff. This does not mean that the plaintiff can recover damages twice; it may, however, collect the entire amount from either defendant.

4.   Unlike defendants PPG and Lawrence/Cliff, Ambrosio was not held liable under a negligence theory in this case. The court said Ambrosio bought fill from Lawrence/Clif and transported it to Ninth Street without knowledge that the fill contained chromium residue. The court said that Ambrosio's knowledge that Garfield Avenue at one time was a chromium processing plant created no independent duty to test the fill for potential chromium contamination, and that Ambrosio did not act negligently in transporting the fill. Because Ambrosio was under no duty to test the fill, it could not be liable for breach of duty, and could not be liable for negligence. The court's holding as to Ambrosio is an example of the requirement that a party must breach a legal duty to be liable to another under a negligence theory.

CAUSE IN FACT

It is not enough for a plaintiff to prove breach of legal duty in order to recover damages from the defendant under a negligence theory. The plaintiff must also prove that the defendant's breach of duty was a **cause in fact** of her injuries.

The requirement of *cause in fact* requires the plaintiff to prove an actual causal link between the defendant's action and the harm that occurred. Courts frequently employ a *"but-for"* test in determining cause in fact. Under this test, a defendant's conduct is the actual cause of a plaintiff's injury if that injury would not have occurred *but-for* the defendant's breach of duty. In other cases, especially those where the defendant's conduct combined with other circumstances to cause the plaintiff's injury, courts may employ a *substantial factor* test. Under this test, a defendant's conduct is the actual cause if it was a substantial factor in bringing about the plaintiff's injuries.

It may seem that the requirement of cause in fact is fairly simple to meet. However, cause in fact is frequently one of the most difficult requirements for the plaintiff to establish in environmental tort cases. Especially in toxic tort and pollution cases, the requirement of cause in fact may prevent plaintiffs from recovering damages because it is so difficult to prove a causal link between the defendant's activity and the personal injuries that plaintiff alleges occurred to her as a result. The following is a water pollution case illustrating this difficulty.

MEEHAN v. STATE
408 N.Y.S.2d 652 (N.Y. Court of Claims 1978)

WEISBERG, J.

his claim for personal injuries is predicated upon the theory that the State of New York negligently stored rock salt at a Department of Transportation facility known as the Shirley Yard, causing quantities of saltwater to seep into the ground and percolate into claimants' well. It is alleged that as a result of consuming salt-contaminated water from this well, claimant Daniel Meehan's children, Nicole and Robert, became seriously ill.

***

[F]or liability to ensue in the present case, claimants must demonstrate that the State failed to exercise due care and knew, or should have known, that its conduct could result in the contamination of claimants' well. The material facts relative to the issue of negligence are that in May, 1971, the Department of Transportation sent a memorandum to all Regional directors entitled "Minimum Requirements for Salt Storage," which indicated clearly the State's awareness of the potential pollution causing effect of maintaining large stockpiles of rock salt. . . . [*Despite explicit directives, the conditions at the defendant's yard did not comply with the minimum standards set by the Department of Transportation. Consequently, the Court concluded that the state was negligent in failing to operate in accordance with its own standards . . . with relation to a recognized and entirely foreseeable risk of harm.*]

The next link in the causal chain which claimants were obliged to prove was that the negligent operation of the Shirley Yard caused saltwater to enter into the ground and contaminate the well on their property. . . . The Court is cognizant of the practical difficulties involved in tracing the subterranean flow of relatively narrow bands of saltwater. The proof in this case, as in the majority of similar cases, is largely circumstantial. . . .

As the court stated in *Matter of Erin Wine & Liquor Store, Inc. v. O'Connell*, 283 App. Div. 443:

> A conclusion of fact may be legitimately drawn from a preponderance of probabilities in its favor; conversely, the existence of a fact is not established by evidence which does not render its existence more likely than its nonexistence.

When reduced to elementals, the evidence in this case consists of five facts: (1) the existence of large quantities of salt in close proximity to claimants' well, (2) a method of storage which allowed salt to dissolve into the soil, (3) the absence of other sources of salt, (4) a general flow of subterranean waters in the direction of claimant's property relative to the Shirley Yard, and (5) the presence of high sodium and chloride levels in the well.

[*Based on these factors, the Court concluded that a preponderance of probabilities existed in favor of the proposition that the salt which entered claimants' well originated in the State's salt storage facility.*]

The remaining issue is whether the high levels of sodium and chlorides present in the well caused personal injury to Nicole and Robert Meehan.

[*According to facts presented at trial, Nicole suffered from a malrotation of the digestive system at birth but the symptoms disappeared after three or four months. When the Meehan family moved into their present house in Mastic, New York, Nicole was healthy and eating a normal diet. After living in the new house, Nicole started to lose weight, had diarrhea, was lethargic and not retaining fluids. During this time, the Meehans were using well water. Nicole's symptoms improved during hospital stays but returned when she was discharged. She improved when a pediatrician prescribed for her a diet which did not utilize well water. As a baby, Robert was fed a pre-prepared concentrate which was mixed with well water. He also was afflicted with diarrhea, vomiting, rashes and a respiratory infection. After Mrs. Meehan ceased using well water for drinking and cooking, Robert's symptoms disappeared and both children have remained healthy.*]

***

The issue is whether the level of chlorides and sodium in the well water caused the symptoms manifested by the children. This was the subject of conflicting expert testimony. . . .

The circumstantial evidence provided by Mrs. Meehan's testimony to the effect that the children's symptoms began when they drank the water and disappeared when they ceased doing so is unpersuasive. Nicole Meehan exhibited the same symptoms of diarrhea, vomiting and dehydration prior to the family's moving to Mastic. . . . In Robert's case, the diagnosis of pathogenic E Coli was the result of a laboratory test which established the existence of this bacterium. Claimants offered no testimony or other evidence tending to disprove the validity of this diagnosis. Moreover, even assuming that the children's symptoms ceased when use of the well water was discontinued, it was claimants' burden to prove by a preponderance of the evidence that salt was the ingredient causing the trouble. . . .

While a remote possibility exists that the salt did adversely affect the children, mere proof of possibility is insufficient to establish a fact by the preponderance of the evidence. We are of the opinion that the Meehan claim for personal injuries is highly conjectural. Accordingly, this claim is dismissed.

Questions and Comments for Discussion

1.   Under the "but-for" test for this case, plaintiffs were unable to establish cause in fact. Problems of causation raise fundamental questions of risk assessment. Is it ever possible to establish causation beyond doubt using a "but-for" test in these cases? Courts are permitting plaintiffs to prove cause in fact by proving that defendant's act or omission was a "substantial factor" in causing plaintiff's injury.

In many environmental cases, proving that an injury occurred as a result of defendant's activity or product may be extremely difficult. For example, what difficulties would a plaintiff who developed lung cancer after working in an asbestos plant for many years have in proving cause in fact? What kinds of evidence might the defendant introduce to raise doubt about cause in fact in such cases?

2.   Expert witnesses in environmental cases are especially important in helping to establish cause in fact. In *Meehan v. State,* expert testimony by the plaintiffs' medical expert was characterized by the court as "equivocal to a high degree." The plaintiffs' expert was unwilling to state that salt was the cause of the children's illnesses.

In another case, the court held that community members had failed to show that a missile manufacturer had contaminated their drinking water to levels sufficient to cause injury, or that the contaminants caused their health problems. The court held that no reasonable juror could find, based on the expert opinions presented, that it was probable that community members were exposed to the manufacturer's contaminants. The court held that circumstantial evidence only proved a possibility of exposure, and mere possibilities or conjecture cannot establish a probability. Community members' experts presumed exposure and testified that the injuries were consistent with such an exposure, but the court said that the evidence did not prove that community members were exposed to the contaminants. *Renaud v. Martin Marietta Corporation,* 749 F.Supp. 1545 (D. Colo. 1990).

3.   Note that despite explicit directives, the conditions at the defendant's yard did not comply with the minimum standards set by the Department of Transportation for salt storage in this case. Does this help establish negligence *per se* in this case? Why or why not?

PROXIMATE CAUSE

Theoretically, every action by a person sets into motion an infinite chain of events that follow from that action. Like dropping a stone in a pool, effects of the action spread out in all directions. For example, assume that the driver of a truck hauling toxic materials stops for lunch and spends ten minutes longer than necessary at the lunch counter because a waitress arrived at work ten minutes late. Three hours later, the driver's truck collides with another vehicle which suddenly pulls into his path. There is a spill of toxic materials as a result. Should the waitress be liable for negligence in causing the spill? Isn't it true that "but-for" the fact the waitress was late, the accident would not have occurred? If the waitress had been on time, the driver would have been ten minutes farther down the road and would never have had the opportunity to collide with the other car.

No one would seriously suggest that the waitress should be liable for the toxic waste spill in this example. It was simply not within the scope of *foreseeable* possibilities that late arrival at work would result in a toxic waste spill. This is the essence of the legal requirement of **proximate cause** in a negligence case. A defendant's liability is limited to results which were in the *scope of the foreseeable risk* created by his actions. Unlike cause in fact, which is a question of fact, proximate cause is a question of law for the court.

Whether a manufacturer's negligent design and construction of a ship's steering gear system was the proximate cause of an oil spill was an issue in *In re Oil Spill by the Amoco Cadiz,* 954 F.2d 1279 (7th Cir. 1992). In that case, the court ruled that the Amoco Corporation must pay the French government and other parties approximately $204 million in damages for a 1978 oil spill that damaged 180 miles of the Brittany coastline in France. In determining liability under a negligence theory, the court said that the failure of the steering gear system of the *Amoco Cadiz* was proximately caused by the shipbuilder's improper design and construction and Amoco's negligence in failing to make repairs to the ship.

Applying the foreseeability test of proximate cause, one may conclude, as did the court in *Amoco Cadiz,* that it is foreseeable that negligence in the design and construction of a ship's steering gear and failure to repair the gear when it malfunctions could result in an accident that would lead to an oil spill. Another test sometimes used by courts to determine proximate cause is the *reasonable and probable consequences* test, under which a defendant is liable for the reasonable, natural, and probable consequences of his negligent act or omission.

INJURY

A successful plaintiff in a tort case is entitled to recover damages for physical injuries resulting from the defendant's negligent act or omission, and for pain and suffering stemming from those physical injuries. But the law is unsettled on whether a plaintiff should recover damages for purely emotional injuries incurred as a result of defendant's negligence. Part of the court's reluctance to permit recovery of emotional damages is a result of the fear of spurious claims and the difficulty of placing a monetary value on emotional injuries.

This becomes an issue in toxic tort cases where plaintiffs seek to recover damages because they suffered emotional injuries such as severe depression or anxiety as a result of exposure to toxic chemicals. In one such case, *Stites v. Sundstrand Heat Transfer, Inc.,* 660 F. Supp. 1516 (W.D. Mich. 1987), plaintiffs alleged that they suffered severe injuries from exposure to various toxic chemicals leaked from a manufacturing plant defendant operated in Dowagiac, Michigan. One of the chemicals used as a degreasing agent in the manufacturing process was trichloroethylene (TCE).

The Plaintiffs alleged that because of the defendant's failure to properly dispose of used TCE, the chemical entered the plaintiffs' drinking water for many years. They alleged that their prolonged and extensive exposure to the chemical caused them to suffer a depreciation in the market value of their property, loss of the use and enjoyment of the property, severe and permanent injury to their physical health, severe depression over fear of cancer, and humiliation, anxiety, mortification, anguish, emotional distress, outrage, and a loss of society and companionship from fellow family members, all of which was past, present, and future.

On the defendant's motion for summary judgment, the court determined that the plaintiffs failed to demonstrate the existence of sufficient facts to indicate they had a reasonable certainty of acquiring cancer in the future. However, it found the plaintiffs' fear of cancer claim more difficult to resolve. Michigan courts are lenient in finding allegations of physical harm sufficient to satisfy the requirement that plaintiffs' fears manifest themselves in the form of a definite and objective physical injury. The court said that there existed a genuine issue of whether some of the plaintiffs had experienced physical injury as a result of their fear of contracting cancer in the future.

Questions and Comments for Discussion

1.   The issue on appeal in the *Stites* case was whether the trial court should have granted defendant's motion for summary judgment. Recall that a motion for summary judgment requires the court to determine whether there is a dispute of material facts and if not, whether the moving party is entitled to judgment as a matter of law. In this case, the court declined to grant defendant's motion for summary judgment as to the fear of cancer claim. What is the procedural effect of this decision?

2.   Until fairly recently, most courts would not permit plaintiffs to recover for emotional injuries resulting from defendant's negligence absent some physical impact or contact with the plaintiff's person. As this case illustrates, many courts have abandoned this rule and permit recovery for foreseeable emotional injuries alone; however, most still require, as a precondition of recovery, proof that some serious physical injury or symptoms resulted from the plaintiff's emotional distress. What kind of evidence in a case like the *Stites* case could a plaintiff submit to prove physical injury? What are the difficulties in proving such injuries? As a policy matter, should plaintiffs be entitled to recover damages for emotional distress and cancerphobia in toxic tort cases like this one?

MULTIPLE-PARTY TOXIC TORTS CASES

A growing area of environmental litigation involves lawsuits by many persons exposed to toxic materials in the workplace or through the use of certain products or substances. These *toxic tort cases* create some unique problems. As a practical matter, the large number of plaintiffs suing a few defendants may create difficult case management problems. There are usually complex issues of proof in such cases, particularly problems establishing levels of toxicity and proving a causal link between plaintiffs' injuries and exposure to the toxic substance. In some asbestos exposure cases, for example, there are long periods of time between exposure and injury. Apportioning damages among defendants in cases involving multiple defendants also may be difficult.

In response to the complexity of such cases, courts have developed a procedural system to address some of the problems of mass pleadings and multiple lawsuits in such cases. Rule 23 of the Federal Rules of Civil Procedure permits all persons who allege injury to be represented in a *class action* suit. In a class action suit, the class is represented in litigation by one member or small group of the class. Examples of class action in mass tort cases include "agent orange" product liability litigation and asbestos school property damage cases. Innovative procedural devices to facilitate multiple party litigation have been utilized in such cases.

One important development is recognition of *industry-wide liability* in some toxic tort or product liability cases. In cases where it is not possible for a plaintiff to prove which company within an industry produced the particular product causing injury, a court may *apportion* liability among all companies that might have produced the harmful product. This apportionment is usually based on market share throughout the industry at some point in time. Some courts have used this approach in lawsuits based on long-term exposure to asbestos.

DEFENSES TO NEGLIGENCE

There are a number of defenses to tort actions. The defendant can argue that the facts as alleged by plaintiff are not true, or raise affirmative defenses. Under traditional common law, a plaintiff in a negligence case could not recover damages if she was *contributorily negligent* herself or if she *assumed the risk* of injury. The doctrine of *contributory negligence* provides that a plaintiff who fails to exercise reasonable care for his own safety is barred from recovery if his own negligence was a substantial factor in producing his injury. The doctrine of *assumption of the risk* is a defense to liability. It provides that the plaintiff cannot recover damages under negligence if she has *voluntarily* undertaken a *known* risk.

A growing majority of states have discarded the traditional rule that contributory negligence and assumption of the risk are complete bars to recovery of damages by the plaintiff in negligence cases. Most states have adopted a *comparative fault* system which permits the fact-finder to determine the *relative fault* of the parties in a negligence action and to allocate damages to a plaintiff based on that determination.

The doctrines of contributory negligence and assumption of the risk are important in some environmental cases. If a plaintiff's own actions contribute to his exposure to hazardous materials, this may substantially limit his recovery of damages or bar recovery altogether.

In *Hull v. Merck & Co., Inc.,* 758 F.2d 1474 (11th Cir. 1985), a supervisor for a fiberglass coating company was working on a project replacing fiberglass sewer lines at three chemical plants operated by Merck & Co. A year after completing the contract, the employee suffered bone marrow depression and leukemia which he said was caused by exposure to hazardous chemicals during the project. He sued Merck for $2.5 million plus punitive damages, alleging among other things that Merck had negligently failed to disclose the health dangers of the waste chemicals carried in its pipelines and failed to warn of the necessity for wearing protective gear during the replacement work. After being charged that assumption of the risk would bar the employee's recovery under Georgia law, the jury ruled in favor of Merck and the employee appealed.

On appeal, the federal court of appeals said there was ample evidence to support a finding that the employee had assumed the risk of injury in this case. The court said that although the employee might not have had any knowledge of a specific carcinogenic risk posed by toluene (a toxic chemical in the pipeline), he knew from long experience that the handling of waste chemicals warranted protective measures. He also knew that Merck and his own company were supplying adequate safety gear, and despite this fact, and his substantial experience working with chemicals, he quit wearing any of the safety gear after a few days on the job. Under all the circumstances, according to the court, there was more than enough evidence to warrant the jury finding that Hull assumed the risk by working around a continuing flow of waste chemicals during the replacement of the pipes.

STRICT LIABILITY

In the previous discussion you have seen how intentional or negligent behavior may result in liability for environmental harms caused to another. Under the theory of **strict liability,** a person who particpates in certain harm-producing activities may be held liable for harm that results to others, even though he did not intend to cause the harm, and even though he did everything possible to prevent it.

Imposition of liability under the theory of strict liability is a social policy decision. The rationale underlying strict liability is that the risk associated with some activities should be borne by those engaged in that activity rather than by the person who is exposed to the risk. Most courts hold that even if the other person is negligent, contributory negligence is not a bar to recovery under strict liability, although assumption of the risk is generally a good defense in a strict liability action.

The justification for imposing strict liability upon defendants who engage in certain abnormally dangerous or ultrahazardous activities is that the person who voluntarily engages in that activity can ultimately pass the costs of liability on to other consumers, and in this way can "spread the risk" of liability for the activity. You may be aware of one class of activities for which strict liability is imposed—the manufacture or sale of defective and unreasonably dangerous products.

Certain environmentally dangerous activities, such as operating a hazardous waste landfill, may be designated an abnormally dangerous or ultrahazardous activity for which strict liability may be imposed. The decision to designate a particular activity as abnormally dangerous for purposes of this theory is an important policy decision for the courts. Imposing strict liability for certain activities will make conducting that activity riskier and more expensive for the operator. In some cases, people may be reluctant to engage in the activity at all.

Courts generally consider several factors in making the determination that an activity is abnormally dangerous or ultrahazardous for purposes of imposing strict liability. In *Indiana Harbor Belt Railroad Co. v. American Cyanamid Co.,* 916 F.2d 1174 (7th Cir. 1990), the question before the court was whether a railway shipper of hazardous chemicals should be strictly liable for the consequences of a spill or other accident to the shipment en route. In making the determination not to impose strict liability on the shipper of hazardous chemicals, the court reviewed Section 520 of the Restatement (Second) of Torts which lists factors to be considered in making that determination. The court said:

> The roots of section 520 are in nineteenth-century cases. The most famous one is *Rylands v. Fletcher* (1868), but a more illuminating one in the present context is *Guille v. Swan,* 19 Johns (N.Y.) 381 (1822). A man took off in a hot-air balloon and landed, without intending to, in a vegetable garden in New York City. A crowd that had been anxiously watching his involuntary descent trampled the vegetables in their endeavor to rescue him when he landed. The owner of

the garden sued the balloonist for the resulting damage, and won. Yet the balloonist had not been careless. In the then state of balloooning it was impossible to make a pinpoint landing.

Guille was a paradigmatic case for strict liability: (a) The risk (probability) of harm was great and (b) the harm that would ensue if the risk materialized could be, although luckily was not, great (the balloonist could have crashed into the crowd). The confluence of these two factors established the urgency of seeking to prevent such accidents. (c) Yet such accidents could not be prevented by the exercise of due care; the technology of ballooning was insufficiently developed. (d) The activity was not a matter of common usage, so there was no presumption that it was a highly valuable activity despite its unavoidable riskiness. (e) The activity was inappropriate to the place in which it took place—densely populated New York City. (f) Reinforcing (d), the value to the community of the activity of recreational ballooning did not appear to be great enough to offset its unavoidable risks.

In order to determine whether imposing liability under this theory for a shipper of hazardous materials was appropriate, the court in *Indiana Harbor* next examined the circumstances of the case in light of the Restatement factors. The court pointed out that a railroad network is a hub and spoke system and the hubs are in metropolitan areas. It is unlikely that chemicals can be rerouted around all metropolitan areas in the country except at prohibitive cost. Even if it would be feasible to reroute them, a carrier, rather than a shipper, would be better situated to do the rerouting. In any event, according to the court, rerouting is no panacea because it will often increase the length of the journey or compel the use of a poorer track, or both. This in turn increases the probability of an accident and perhaps even the consequences of an accident. After considering these and other factors, the court ultimately concluded that this was not an apt case for strict liability.

Courts have imposed strict liability for a variety of different environmental activities. A Florida appellate court held that fumigation is an ultrahazardous activity for which a fumigation company may be held strictly liable, regardless of any alleged negligence by a third party. In that case, the defendant fumigated two evacuated condominium buildings, but fumes entered a third building through a supposedly impenetrable fire wall. Residents in the third building were injured when they inhaled the fumes, and they sued the fumigator. The court held that because its conduct was an ultrahazradous activity, negligence by third parties (the architect and contractors who allegedly failed to construct a proper fire wall), would not permit the fumigator to avoid liability.[8]

Review the facts in *Jersey City Redevelopment Authority v. PPG Industries* on page 85. You may recall that there were several different theories under which the plaintiff argued it was entitled to recover damages from the defendants in that case. The portion of the court's opinion as to the plaintiff's strict liability theory is set out below.

JERSEY CITY REDEVELOPMENT AUTHORITY
v. PPG INDUSTRIES
18 Envtl. L. Rep. 20364 (D.N.J. 1987)

***

**CLAIM FOR STRICT LIABILITY
AGAINST PPG AND LAWRENCE/CLIF**

The court imposes strict liability upon PPG and Lawrence/Clif for engaging in the abnormally dangerous activity of distributing hazardous substances.

The court's conclusion is based on its application of the standards set forth in the Restatement (Second) of Torts sec. 520, as adopted by the New Jersey Supreme Court in *Department of Environmental Protection v. Ventron,* 94 N.J. 473 (1983). First, it is undisputed that the chromium in the concentrations found constituted a hazardous waste posing a high degree of risk to the environment and a potential although lesser risk to individuals. Second, there is a likelihood that the harm to the environment could be great, particularly if it migrated and entered either ground water or the drinking water supply. Third, the risk could not be eliminated by others subjected to it through the exercise of reasonable care, and only those with specialized knowledge of the risks and of the chromium's existence could protect against it. Fourth, the activity of both defendants was inappropriate to the place where it was carried on—it was foreseeable for both PPG and for Lawrence/Clif to anticipate the utilization of said fill in residential areas. Finally, although the fill served some limited utilitarian purpose, its limited value is far outweighed by its dangerous attributes and the risks that it posed to the environment. Therefore, the court concludes that the distribution of the chromium residue was abnormally dangerous, and that these defendants are strictly liable as a result.

Questions and Comments for Discussion

1. What are the economic implications for industry if strict liability is imposed on an activity? Who ultimately bears the cost of that increased liability?

2. In a portion of the *Jersey City* case not reprinted, the court addressed PPG's argument that it could not be strictly liable because its generation and distribution of the chromium waste was not a **proximate cause** of plaintiff's injuries. The court rejected the defendant's argument, stating: "First, it was foreseeable to PPG when it conveyed Garfield Avenue to Lawrence/Clif that Lawrence would sell chromium-contaminated landfill to other parties. Second, PPG's liability is not relieved by the actions of any intervening parties. As stated, Lawrence/Clif's sale of fill to Ambrosios, though ten years later, was foreseeable. Lawrence's negligence in distributing the fill with its independently gained knowledge of the environmental risks does not relieve PPG of its responsibility. A party engaging in an abnormally dangerous activity should not benefit from the fortuitous negligence of an intervening actor. Additionally, Ambrosio's transportation of the fill to Ninth Street, without knowledge of its chromium content, does not break the cause chain between PPG's actions and plaintiff's injury."

As this statement suggests, whether an "intervening cause" should relieve a defendant of liability under a tort theory is generally a question of proximate cause. As the court indicated, the general rule is that a *foreseeable intervening cause* will not eliminate liability. Can you think of some examples where an intervening cause would be *unforeseeable,* and thus relieve a defendant of liability because his activity did not proximately cause the harm to plaintiff?

3. Keep in mind that even if a court does not impose strict liability upon a defendant's activity, the defendant may still be liable under other theories like negligence, trespass and nuisance, or other tort or contract law theories. In addition, state and federal statutes may entitle a plaintiff to seek reimbursement of costs of cleaning up a contaminated site. In *Jersey City,* for example, the court held that plaintiff was a responsible party under CERCLA, and that CERCLA grants the court the authority to allocate response costs among liable parties using equitable factors as the court determines appropriate. The court, comparing the fault of the plaintiff and defendant, allocated damages equally between Lawrence/Clif and PPG. Even though the plaintiff was a

responsible party under the law, the court believed it would be inequitable to diminish plaintiff's recovery under the circumstances, stating "imposition of CERCLA strict liability upon an unknowing landowner is unnecessary and unfair where knowing generators and distributors are available."

SUMMARY

This chapter focused on several important tort theories used by plaintiffs to recover damages as a result of environmental harm to their person or property. The purpose of tort law is generally to compensate the plaintiff for injuries incurred as a result of the defendant's wrongful act or omission. *Compensatory damages* (that is, money paid to compensate the injured plaintiff) may include sums for property damage, injuries to plaintiff's health, pain and suffering, and other foreseeable losses. Punitive damages may be awarded in cases where defendant's behavior is egregious.

In some cases, plaintiffs also may seek the equitable remedy of an **injunction,** which is a court order requiring the defendant to cease some action. In environmental cases, innovative remedies, such as requiring monitoring or installation of particular control technologies, are sometimes fashioned through the court's power to issue such orders.

Tort law liability ranges from actions to recover damages for *intentional* torts, as in cases of intentional trespass or nuisance, to actions under *negligence* theory based on breach of a legal duty, to **strict liability** actions, which impose liability without fault in cases where the defendant was engaged in an abnormally dangerous or ultrahazardous activity. The elements of these actions differ, and a plaintiff may argue she is entitled to recover damages under many or all of these theories in the same case.

In the following case, residents who lived near a corporation's chemical waste burial site brought a class action against a chemical corporation to recover damages for personal injuries and property damage. The plaintiffs alleged that they were entitled to damages under the legal theories of strict liability, common-law negligence, trespass, and nuisance. The plaintiffs also sought punitive damages from defendants, to *punish* a defendant's wrongful acts and to *deter* a defendant from engaging in wrongful conduct in the future. As you read the facts of this case, review the elements of each of the legal theories discussed.

STERLING v. VELSICOL CHEMICAL CORPORATION
647 F. Supp. 303 (W.D. Tenn. 1986)

HORTON, D.J.

This class action lawsuit was originally filed by plaintiffs against Velsicol Chemical Corporation in the Circuit Court of Hardeman County, Tennesee, on December 4, 1978.

Plaintiffs are a class of persons who owned property or lived within a three mile radius of the northern most boundary line of a 242 acre chemical waste burial site in Hardeman County, Tennessee, owned and operated by Velsicol from late 1964 until it was closed as hazardous in 1973 by order of the State of Tennessee. Plaintiffs in this class action seek damages for personal injury and damages to their property allegedly suffered when water in their home wells became contaminated by hazardous chemicals which escaped from Velsicol's burial site.

***

PLAINTIFF'S CONTENTIONS

The substance of plaintiffs' claims is that they have suffered physical injury, bodily harm, mental and emotional anguish, property damge, and loss and destruction of an entire community and a way of life, all proximately resulting from Velsicol's grossly negligent selection, implementation, operation and burial of more than 300,000 fifty-five gallon drums filled with ultrahazardous chemical waste, and hundreds of boxes of ultrahazardous dry chemical waste on its burial site which adjoined plaintiffs' homes and property. Plaintiffs contend Velsicol was grossly negligent in the selection and implementation of its chemical waste burial site, in the manner in which it containerized chemical waste, in its burial operations, and in allowing ultrahazardous and highly toxic chemical waste to escape from the burial site, infiltrate into and contaminate their underground well water.

Plaintiffs contend that as a result of their drinking, bathing, cooking, canning, cleaning, breathing steam from hot water, and otherwise using their home well water contaminated by hazardous chemicals from Velsicol's burial site, over a period of years, they have suffered severe and permanent physical injuries, mental and emotional anguish, and damage to and loss of their property.

***

STRICT LIABILITY THEORIES

. . . [T]he rule of law from *Rylands v. Fletcher* allows for the imposition of liability for damages proximately caused by the defendant's dangerous, non-natural use of land regardless of the standard of care defendant utilized in conducting that activity.

Generally, modern courts have applied this strict or absolute liability to activities variously characterized as 'perilous,' 'ultra or extra-hazardous,' or 'abnormally dangerous.' "The judicial rationalization seems to be that one who conducts a highly dangerous activity should prepare in advance to bear the financial burden of harm proximately caused to others by such an activity."

[*After reviewing Tennesse cases indicating that strict or absolute liability was an accepted theory of recovery under Tennessee law, the court continued:*]

As noted earlier, no Tennessee cases were found expressly adopting *Ryalnds v. Fletcher.* However, the cases discussed herein lead to the inescapable conclusion that under Tennessee law, Velsicol would be subject to strict or absolute liability for the non-natural, ultrahazardous and abnormally dangerous activities it conducted which gave rise to this action. The facts in the present case align squarely with both the application and the rationale underlying the rule of strict or absolute liability as that doctrine is viewed by Tennessee courts.

The Court holds that the creation, location, operation and closure of the toxic chemical dump site by defendant was and is an inherently and abnormally dangerous activity.

Moreover, the Court concludes that Velsicol's activity on the farm was not only ultrahazardous activity, but also abnormally dangerous activity. This conclusion is made for the following reasons:

1. There was a high degree of risk of some harm to the person, land, or chattels of others . . . ;

2. There was a likelihood that the harm that resulted would be great, such as the increased risk of many diseases including cancer, and the destruction of plaintiffs' quality of life;

3. The inability to eliminate the risk by the exercise of reasonable care;

4. The extent to which the activity at the dump was not a matter of common usage

and as a means of disposal and violated the state of the art;

5. The inappropriateness of the location of the dump where it was carried out; and

6. The extent to which its value to the community (none) was outweighed by its dangerous attributes (great).

NEGLIGENCE

Velsicol is clearly guilty of negligence for the following reasons:

1. There was a standard of conduct imposed by law on Velsicol to protect others from unreasonable harm arising from the dumping of the chemicals on its farm and

2. The defendant breached that duty by its failure to do the following:

— Defendant failed to investigate the geological makeup or strata under the dumpsite prior to its purchase or operation;

— Defendant failed to investigate the hydrological, or water bearing zones under the dumpsite prior to its purchase or operation;

— Defendant failed to hire knowledgeable persons to investigate the area under the dumpsite;

— Defendant failed to install proper monitoring procedures in and around the site;

***

— Defendant failed in the selection, location, operation, and maintenance of the site under the prevailing state of the art for such operation during the entire length of time the dumpsite was open; and

— Defendant failed to take steps in 1967 to halt leakage already occuring from the site. . . .

TRESPASS

Actual trespass is not an issue in this case. Velsicol admits the movement of certain chemicals from its dumpsite through the local aquifer and "onto property owned by various plaintiffs and into the sphere of influence of various wells constitutes a tres-

pass under Tennessee law. . . ." In general, Tennessee law as applied to the present case allows for the recovery of damages caused by admitted "incursion" of Velsicol's chemical waste onto property owned by various plaintiffs within the designated area surrounding Velsicol's Chemical waste burial site.

NUISANCE

The doctrine of nuisance applies to this case. The Court finds Velsicol has interfered with plaintiffs' right to the use and enjoyment of their property—whether owned or leased—by the creation of a nuisance. . . . Occasionally, a nuisance proceeds from a malicious desire to do harm, but usually a nuisance is intentional in the sense that the defendant has created or continued the condition causing the nuisance with full knowledge that the harm to the plaintiffs' interest is substantially bound to follow therefore. A nuisance may also result from conduct which is merely negligence, to-wit: failure to take precautions against a risk apparent to a reasonable man. Finally, a nuisance may occur when a defendant carries on in an inappropriate place an abnormally dangerous or hazardous activity.

PUNITIVE DAMAGES

The principal requirements for the recovery of punitive damages are (1) Proof of an independent cause of action since there is no cause of action for punitive damages; (2) proof of actual or compensatory damages; (3) evidence that the defendant's wrongful act was characterized by either willfulness, wantonness, maliciousness, gross negligence or recklessness, oppression, outrageous conduct, insult, indignity, or fraud. . . .

The Court concludes that Velsicol's actions in creating, maintaining and operating its chemical waste burial site, with superior knowledge of the highly toxic and harmful nature of the chemical contaminants it disposed of therein, and specifically its failure to immediately cease dumping said toxic chemicals after being warned by several state and federal agencies several years prior to the final cessation of such abnormally hazardous and harmful activity, constituted gross, wilful and wanton disregard for the health and well-being of the plaintiffs, and therefore is supportive of an award of punitive and exemplary damages.

***

[*The Court held that five representatives of the class of plaintiffs were entitled to recover compensatory damages totaling $5,273,492.50 and that the corporation was liable to the class as a whole for punitive damages in the amount of $75,000,000. On appeal the appellate court upheld liability but ordered the trial court to recompute the damage award based on its instructions.*]

Questions and Comments for Discussion

1.   *Sterling v. Velsicol* presents an opportunity to review the elements of each common law theory discussed in this chapter and to apply it to the facts of this case. What tests of cause in fact and proximate cause did plaintiffs have to meet in order to be successful in this case? How might plaintiffs in a case like this prove causation at trial?

2.   What are the economic and environmental effects of declaring that the creation, location, operation, and closure of a toxic chemical dumpsite like that of the defendant is an inherently and abnormally dangerous activity? Do you agree that a non-negligent operator should incur liability under this theory even though a plaintiff might be negligent in exposing herself to risks associated with the site?

3.   The court enumerated a number of other reasons why the defendants were liable for negligence under the facts of this case which were omitted from the excerpt of the opinion. Can you think of other reasons a plaintiff might allege an owner or operator of a toxic dump site breached a duty of reasonable care? Should the owner/operator be liable under a theory of negligent or intentional failure to disclose hazardous materials in the dump to adjoining landowners? What are the policy implications of this question?

GLOSSARY

Cause in fact—Requirement in negligence law that the defendant's breach of duty is the actual cause of injury to another person. Tests of cause in fact include the "but-for" test and the "substantial factor" test.

Injunction—An order issued by a court of equity forbidding a party to do some act, or ordering him or his agents to do some act.

Negligence *per se*—Negligence action based on the theory that defendant breached a legal duty under statute, ordinance, or administrative rule or regulation.

Nuisance—A wrong that arises from the unreasonable or unlawful use by a person of his own property which causes substantial interference with the right of another to the use and enjoyment of his property.

Proximate cause—Requirement in negligence law that the defendant's breach of duty is the legal cause of injury to another person. Tests of proximate cause include whether the injury was "foreseeable," or within the scope of foreseeable risk.

Punitive damages—Damages that are designed to punish flagrant wrongdoers and to deter them and others from engaging in similar conduct in the future.

Strict liability—Imposition of liability on an individual or legal entity for the results of his actions regardless of proof of negligence.

Trespass—Intentional, reckless, or negligent entry on another's property, without privilege to do so.

Tort—A private or civil wrong or injury.

CASES FOR DISCUSSION

1.   Henley filed an action against the Ratliff Company, seeking to recover damages for injury to his real property. Ratliff leased the property from Henley in 1972, and began surface mining operations on the property. In 1973, Henley complained to Ratliff's representatives about sand and gravel washing onto his other property as a result of the mining operations. Ratliff's representatives assured Henley they would correct the problem but sand and gravel continued to wash onto Henley's property. Is Henley entitled to recover damages for injury to his property under an intentional trespass theory? *Ratliff Co. Inc. v. Henley,* 405 So.2d 141 (Ala. 1981).

2.   On January 14, 1981, strong odors of gasoline were detected in the basement of a Livingston, Montana, restaurant owned and operated by John and Ruth French. The family home was located on the same lot behind the restaurant. Fire officials investigated and immediately ordered the restaurant closed because of the danger posed by the strong concentration of gasoline fumes. The fumes continued at the restaurant and family home and the Frenches ultimately filed suit against the defendant Ralph E. Moore, d/b/a Interstate Texaco Service, for trespass to real property, negligence, and nuisance. They sought damages for business losses such as loss of income caused by closure of the business, loss of use of the property caused by the gasoline fumes, and diminution of value of the property caused by the presence of gasoline fumes. They also sought damages for pain, discomfort, fears, anxiety, annoyance, inconvenience, and other mental, physical, and emotional distress suffered as a result of the invading gasoline fumes. Are they entitled to recover such damages under any or all of these theories? *French v. Ralph E. Moore, Inc.,* 661 P.2d 844 (Mont. 1983).

3.   An owner of a site contaminated by hazardous substances brought an action against the manufacturers and suppliers of the products containing the hazardous substances to recover cleanup costs and damages under CERCLA and under state law. The plaintiff alleged that it operated a scrap metal business on the site, and that during storage, handling, and dismantling of junk electrical components, PCBs, a hazardous substance, spilled out or leaked at the site. Among other parties, the plaintiff sued General Electric, manufacturer of electrical components containing PCBs, under two theories: strict product liability and negligent failure to warn.

   Liability under product liability or negligent failure to warn only exists if the product was used in a way reasonably foreseeable to the manufacturer. Can General Electric be liable to plaintiffs under either of these theories for damages sustained during plaintiff's dismantling and processing of its electrical components? *Kalik v. Allis Chalmers Corp.*, 658 F.Supp. 631 (W.D. Pa. 1987).

4.   PCBs manufactured by Monsanto were sold for various industrial purposes, including insulation of high voltage electrical equipment like capacitors and transformers. Excessive long-term exposure can cause skin rash and liver disease; consequently, Monsanto confined its sales of PCBs to sealed containers for electrical uses.

One of Monsanto's customers for PCBs was Westinghouse, located in Bloomington, Indiana. Westinghouse waste containing PCBs was hauled to various Bloomington area landfills and small concentrations of PCBs got into the sewer effluent of the plant. Ultimately, the city and Westinghouse entered into an agreement for an environmental cleanup of several landfills and a treatment plant as a result of PCB contamination. The city also filed suit against Monsanto, the manufacturer of the PCBs, for nuisance, abnormally dangerous activity, and trespass for discharging PCBs into the sewer system. Can Monsanto, the *manufacturer* of the PBCs, be liable to the city under any of these theories? Why or why not? *City of Bloomington v. Westinghouse Electric Corp.*, 891 F.2d 611 (7th Cir. 1989).

5.   Plaintiffs contended that defendants, two mining companies, should be strictly liable for causing mine drainage pollution of private water supplies pursuant to statute, and under common law theories of private and public nuisance. As to the public nuisance claims, the court cited Section 821B of the Restatement (Second) of Torts, which defines a public nuisance as follows: (1) A public nuisance is an unreasonable interference with a right common to the general public; (2) circumstances that may sustain a holding that an interference with a public right is unreasonable include the following:

a. whether the conduct involves a significant interference with the public health, the public safety, the public peace, the public comfort, or the public convenience or

b. whether the conduct is proscribed by statute, ordinance, or administrative regulation or

c. whether the conduct is of a continuing nature or has produced a permanent or long-lasting effect and, as the actor knows or has reason to know, has a significant effect upon the public right.

Should defendants be responsible under a public nuisance theory for pollution of water wells on various properties in the village of Petersburg, Pennsylvania, caused by mine drainage unlawfully discharged from its mining operations? *Commonwealth v. PBS Coals, Inc.*, 17 Envtl. L. Rep. 20204 (PA. C.P. 1986).

6. Plaintiffs brought an action against defendant, Georgia-Pacific Corporation, to recover compensatory and punitive damages for injury to their property caused by operation of defendant's paper mill. The complaint alleged that plaintiffs' property was damaged by certain noxious and toxic gases, fumes, and smoke, and particles deposited thereon by defendant's mill, that effluents killed trees and vegetation on their property and otherwise depreciated its value. The trial court withdrew the issue of punitive damages and plaintiffs appealed. Defendant contended that it should not be liable for punitive damages if it did everything reasonably possible to eliminate or minimize the damage caused by its mill. If there was evidence from which a jury could have found that defendant had not done everything reasonably possible to minimize the damage to adjoining properties by its mill, should the case have been submitted to the jury on the issue of punitive damages? *McElwain v. Georgia-Pacific Corporation*, 421 P.2d 957 (Ore. 1966).

ENDNOTES

1. Under the Comprehensive Environmental Response, Compensation, Liability Act (CERCLA) (42 U.S.C. §§ 9601 et seq.), the list of recoverable costs and damages are limited to a broad range of expenses associated with Superfund cleanup activity.

2. *French v. Ralph E. Moore, Inc.,* 203 Mont. 327, 661 P.2d 844 (1983).

3. *County of Allegheny v. Merrit Constr. Co.,* 454 A.2d 1051 (Super. Ct. 1982).

4. *Dial v. City of O'Fallon,* 411 NE.2d 217 (Ill. 1980).

5. *Martin v. Reynolds Metals Company,* 342 P.2d 790 (Or. 1959).

6. W. Prosser, *Torts* § 8, at 31–32 (4th ed. 1971).

7. *Village of Euclid v. Ambler Realty Co.,* 272 U.S. 365 (1926).

8. *Old Island Fumigation Inc. v. Barbee,* 604 So.2d 1246 (Fla. App. 1992).

5

ENVIRONMENTAL LIABILITY IN THE SALE OR LEASE OF PROPERTY, PRODUCT LIABILITY, AND INSURER LIABILITY FOR ENVIRONMENTAL HARM

INTRODUCTION

This chapter examines some contract law issues which may arise in environmental law cases, discusses basic contract and tort principles underlying product liability law, and concludes with a look at issues affecting insurer liability for environmental harm.

Contract issues may be important in allocating liability for environmental harm—for example, in cases where a buyer of real property seeks to recover damages for breach of contract from the seller or seeks to rescind the contract because the property is contaminated with hazardous materials. In such cases, warranties, indemnification clauses, and disclaimers in the contract may determine the liability of the seller or the right of the purchaser to rescind. Similar issues may arise in actions between landlord and tenants based on covenants (promises) in the lease.

The second part of this chapter examines principles utilized by plaintiffs to recover damages arising from the sale of environmentally unsafe products. Under principles of contract law, such as breach of express and implied warranties, as well as principles of negligence and strict liability discussed in the previous chapter, plaintiffs have recovered damages for injuries they received as a result of exposure to products containing toxic and dangerous substances like lead, asbestos, and harmful chemicals.

The chapter ends by examining whether insurers are liable for pollution damages to real property under the terms of a comprehensive general liability insurance policy. One RAND report estimated that the cost of cleaning up the nation's hazardous waste sites will approach $500 billion dollars. According to that report, insurance companies have paid out nearly

$500 million dollars annually for Superfund-related liabilities, but only an average of twelve percent goes for actual cleanup. Legal fees and transaction costs account for eighty-eight percent of the funds expended.[1] Most of these "insurer liability" cases involve questions of interpretation of express contract language in a standard comprehensive general liability insurance contract.

CONTRACT LAW

CERCLA Liability

Because a significant number of environmental contract disputes involve questions of CERCLA liability, it is helpful to first summarize some key provisions of that law. Chapter 13 addresses this law and other hazardous waste laws in more detail.

CERCLA, which stands for Comprehensive Environmental Response, Compensation, and Liability Act, was originally enacted in 1980 to address the problem of abandoned hazardous waste disposal sites. CERCLA mandates cleanup of these sites and allocates responsibility for clean-up costs to various "responsible parties." Responsible parties may also be liable for any necessary response costs incurred by others, damages for injury to natural resources, and the costs of certain health studies.

Most courts have held that liability between responsible parties under CERCLA may be allocated by agreement (although such agreements cannot limit a party's liability to the government); consequently, contract language may be critical in determining responsibility between the parties for cleaning up hazardous waste sites under the act.

General Principles

A **contract** may be defined as "a promise or set of promises for the breach of which the law gives a remedy, or the performance of which the law in some way recognizes as a duty."[2] Another way of defining a contract is *a legally enforceable promise or set of promises.* Contract law principles have evolved through common law decision making, although contracts are increasingly governed by statutes like the Uniform Commercial Code (UCC) which is statutory law governing commercial transactions, environmental disclosure laws, and statutes regulating specific kinds of contracts like insurance contracts.

Under broad principles of contract law, a private party is able to create a private enforceable law which governs its relationship with another party. The law ensures that these private agreements are enforceable in order to preserve stability in contracting and to protect commercial enterprise. Contract law goes back thousands of years—the Egyptians and Mesopotamians recognized and enforced contracts. Modern contract law, however, assumed major importance in our legal system in the nineteenth century when the industrial revolution precipitated a need for planning and certainty in commercial transactions.

Common law courts have developed the basic elements of an enforceable contract. These elements include (1) an *agreement* which is (2) *voluntarily* entered into (3) by parties who have the *capacity* to contract (capacity requires that a contracting party be of legal age and mentally competent); (4) the agreement must meet *legal objectives* and (5) be supported by *legal consideration* (defined as something of legal value given in exchange for an act or a promise). In some cases the agreement must be in *writing* to be enforceable.

In many disputes over liability for environmental contamination of real property, the parties have entered into a written contract, either for the sale or lease of the property, which contains express terms and conditions of their agreement. As a general rule, a contract only binds the parties who entered into the agreement. In the following case, the issue involved the liability of a contracting party to a *third party* who was not a party to the original contract. Generally, only a party to a contract may sue another contracting party for damages as a result of breach of contract.

LINCOLN ALAMEDA CREEK v. COOPER INDUSTRIES, INC.
829 F. Supp. 325 (N.D. Cal. 1992)

This action involves a complaint brought by Mary Orsetti against Beta Associates ("Beta"). Orsetti is seeking indemnification or contribution from Beta for alleged negligence, breach of warranty, and misrepresentation in their preparation of a ground contaminants investigation. The matter is before the court on Beta's motion to dismiss the complaint and for summary judgment. After careful consideration of the parties' submissions and arguments, the court GRANTS Beta's motion for summary judgment.

Mary Orsetti entered into an agreement with Lincoln Alameda Creek ("Lincoln"), for the sale of a piece of property located at 29990 Union City Boulevard, Union City, California. According to the agreement, Lincoln's purchase was conditioned upon its approval of the condition of the soils, sub-soils, and groundwater of the property. In October 1986, Lincoln hired Beta, an environmental consultant, to perform a subsurface solid and groundwater contaminants investigation of the property in order to assist Lincoln in deciding whether to purchase it. This contract between Beta and Lincoln was an oral contract. . . .

The report was completed on November 21, 1986 and was given to Lincoln. Lincoln did not discuss with Beta their intention that the report would be for the benefit of anyone other than Lincoln. Beta was also not informed that Mary Orsetti would review or rely on the report. Beta did not have a contract with Orsetti, and did not give Orsetti any express warranty.

The report stated that Beta's analysis of the land did not reveal any of the "constituents of concern" and therefore they felt the property was clear of contamination. The sale of the land was subsequently completed. Lincoln is presently involved in litigation with Orsetti for the alleged contamination of the property. Orsetti brought this third-party complaint[3] against Beta for its alleged negligence, breach of warranty, and misrepresentation in the preparation of the ground contamination report. Orsetti is seeking indemnification[4] and compensatory damages from Beta.

Beta's motion for summary judgment turns on the following issues: (1) whether Beta owed Orsetti any duty of care in the preparation of the report, (2) whether Orsetti was a third-party beneficiary of the contract between Lincoln and Beta and (3) whether Beta committed any fraud or misrepresentation to the damage of Orsetti.

***

[INTENDED BENEFICIARY ARGUMENT]

In order to recover under a theory of breach of contract and warranty, Orsetti must be an intended beneficiary of the contract between Beta and Lincoln. "For a third party to qualify as a beneficiary under a contract, the contracting parties must have intended to benefit [from] that third party, and their intent must appear from the terms of the contract." The third party beneficiary must show that the contract was made "expressly" for her benefit. Therefore, Orsetti must show that the contract between Beta and Lincoln was clearly intended to inure to her benefit.

. . . The contract [between Beta and Lincoln] was oral and its relevant terms have been provided. According to [the evidence], Orsetti was not an intended beneficiary. Beta and Lincoln never discussed the report being produced for the benefit of Orsetti, nor did they intend it to benefit her.

From the available facts, therefore, it is clear that the contract was not made "ex-

pressly" for her benefit. . . . Even if she now says she relied on the contamination report, she has not presented any facts to prove that Lincoln and Beta intended for her to rely on it.

Orsetti also argues that Beta's agreement to test her property included a "warranty of workmanlike service that is comparable to a manufacturer's warranty." [However,] Beta and Orsetti do not have a contractual relationship. Since there is no contract between Beta and Orsetti, a warranty cannot be implied. Accordingly, Beta's motion for summary judgment regarding the breach of contract and warranty cause of action is GRANTED.

Questions and Comments for Discussion

1. Who were the parties to the original contract? Under what theory did Orsetti, the original defendant, argue she was entitled to damages from Beta for breach of warranty under the contract?
2. There may be circumstances where the performance of a contract is intended to benefit a person not a party to the contract. In such cases, the third party may be entitled to enforce the contract. For example, in an insurance contract the benefit to a third person

may be an essential part of the contract. As the court's decision in *Lincoln Alameda Creek v. Cooper Industries* indicates, whether a third party can enforce a contract depends on whether that party was an intended beneficiary of the contract. In cases where a third party's benefit is merely an unintended by-product of the contract, the third party is called an **incidental beneficiary.** Incidental beneficiaries do not acquire the right to enforce the original contract.

Environmental Audits

Prospective purchasers of industrial or commercial property routinely undertake an investigation to ascertain any environmental hazards which might exist on the property. Such knowledge is essential in determining the value of the property and in assessing potential liabilities for future environmental cleanup costs. Perhaps the strongest incentive for conducting an environmental audit prior to purchase is the "innocent landowner" defense available under CERCLA. One of the few defenses under CERCLA available to an owner or operator of contaminated property is proof that at the time the owner acquired the property, the owner "did not know and had no reason to know" that any hazardous substance was disposed of at the property.[5]

Any purchaser of property suspected of contamination should undertake an environmental site assessment (ESA) prior to purchase. In 1993, the ASTM (American Society for Testing and Materials) adopted its *Standard Practices for Environmental Site Assessments* in order to specify what constitutes good commercial and customary practice in conducting ESAs in commercial real estate transactions. The committee created two standard practices, one for "Phase I" ESAs, and one for performing a simpler "transaction screen." The Phase I document includes a review of real estate and other relevant records; site reconnaissance; interviews with current owners, occupants, and local governmental officials; and an evaluative report. The environmental professional then prepares a report containing an opinion on the effect of "recognized environmental conditions" on the property.

The transaction screen is the initial tool for determining whether a Phase I ESA is required. The transaction screen is designed to "red-flag" circumstances which call for further investigation—for example, the presence of contaminants on adjoining property. CERCLA itself is not specific about what constitutes environmental due diligence, but it does establish a sliding scale depending on what is considered good commercial or customary practice at the time and location, and the status of the parties.

CONTRACT WARRANTIES AND DISCLAIMERS

A **warranty** is a contract promise that a fact stated in the agreement is true. A contracting party may warrant, for example, that there are no federal or state environmental cleanup actions against the property pending at the time of sale. A warranty may be *express* or *implied.* An express warranty is one which is actually expressed in words in the contract. An *implied in fact* warranty is one which is not stated in actual words, but is implied from the intention and conduct of the parties. For example, a court might find that the seller implicitly warranted that the property was in compliance with all local and state environmental laws at the time of sale because this was the intention of the parties, even though the parties did not include an express warranty to that effect in their contract. A warranty may also be *implied in law.* An implied in law warranty is one which was not expressly or implicitly intended by the parties, but is *imposed* on the parties by law for public policy reasons. Later sections of this chapter discuss the court imposed *implied warranty of habitability* in the sale of residential property and the *implied warranty of merchantability* in the sale of goods, both warranties implied in law.

The importance of environmental warranties in the sale of real estate has grown in direct response to the potential liability of landowners under CERCLA. Superfund liability (and liability under state laws modeled after Superfund) is a driving force behind attempts by sellers and buyers to allocate liability for environmental problems in real estate transactions. First, the cost and time required to clean up hazardous waste contamination is significant and in many if not most cases cleanup costs will far exceed the purchase price of the property. Second, under CERCLA, strict liability (that is, liability without proof of fault) may be imposed on the current owner or operator of a contaminated site, as well as on previous owners or operators within the chain of title. Activities by a tenant which result in a release of hazardous substances also expose the tenant and the landlord to potential liability for cleanup costs. Consequently, potential CERCLA liability has significantly affected the previously less complicated transfer of property, land, and building leases.

As a result, purchasers of property with suspected environmental liabilities not only routinely demand an environmental audit of the property before proceeding to closing, they also demand contract warranties that the property is in compliance with current state and federal law, and indemnification agreements protecting the purchaser from liability for specified areas of concern. These agreements, assigning liability and costs associated with cleanup and remediation of a site, are increasingly important for purchasers of commercial real estate.

The courts and the EPA have recognized that the enforcement of such agreements helps facilitate the purchase and sale of commercial property in the face of uncertain environmental liabilities. For this reason, a majority of courts permit private parties to allocate the risk of CERCLA cleanup costs between the parties by contract, although a minority of courts prohibit contractual allocation of environmental liability under any circumstances. Those courts which recognize and enforce such agreements hold that the agreements are only sufficient to allocate liability between parties to the agreement. Contractual warranties and indemnification agreements are *not* enforceable against the government, and would not affect a party's liability to the government under CERCLA.

In the following case, the purchasers of a commercial site brought an action against the seller, alleging damages for breach of express warranties, implied warranties, breach of contract, and fraudulent misrepresentation due to the presence of contamination at the property site.

VERSATILE METALS, INC. v. UNION CORP.
693 F. Supp. 1563 (E.D. Pa. 1988)

JAMES MCGIRR KELLY, D.J.

This action arose from a dispute concerning a contract for the sale of assets [including equipment and inventory] and the lease/purchase of real property located at 6801 State Road in Philadelphia, Pennsylvania, which was discovered to be substantially contaminated with PCBs six months into the tenancy of the plaintiffs-tenants[,] Versatile Metals, Inc. Defendants[,] the Union Corporation and the Metal Bank of America[,] filed their answer and counterclaimed for breach of contract, breach of lease, breach of an indemnification clause, waste, fraud, and an action for cost recovery under the Comprehensive Environmental Response, Compensation, and Liability Act (CERCLA). . . . Pennsylvania contracts for the sale of goods[6] are governed by the Uniform Commercial Code. The sale and lease of real estate is governed by the law of Pennsylvania.

The parties are in agreement that the issue of whether the terms of the subject contracts constitute[s] certain express warranties is a matter for this court. The language of

the contracts is clear and unambiguous. The interpretation of a written contract that is clear and unambiguous is for the court. . . .

In deciding whether the terms of a contract constitute express warranties, the Court must look to [the Uniform Commercial Code]. It is not necessary for the creation of an express warranty that the seller use formal words such as "warrant" or "guarantee" or that he have a specific intention to make a warranty, but an affirmation merely of the value of the goods or a statement purporting to be merely the opinion of the seller or commendation of the goods does not create a warranty.

Three fundamental issues are presented. First, the Court must determine whether the statement constitutes an "affirmation of fact or promise" or "description of the goods." Second, assuming the Court finds the language used susceptible to the creation of a warranty, it must then be determined whether the statement was "part of the basis of the bargain." If it was, an express warranty exists.

Section 4.05 of the Asset Purchase Agreement provides:

4.05 *Environmental Matters.* Seller and Union jointly and severally represent and warrant to Buyer that as of November 26, 1984 the land included in the Leased Premises was free of contamination in violation of any applicable federal, state, or local law or regulation relating to the protection of health, safety, and environment. Seller and Union jointly and severally agree to indemnify and hold Buyer harmless from any and all costs, damages, liabilities and expenses resulting from hazardous waste in the Inventory existing on and the land included in the Leased Premises at November 20, 1984, provided that, with respect to the Inventory, Buyer acts in the following manner:

(a) Buyer shall keep all Inventory purchased hereunder segregated from any other inventories of Buyer;

(b) Buyer shall give seller prompt telephone notice upon discovery of capacitors and other items in such inventory that may contain hazardous waste and shall at the sole expense, risk and liability of Seller cooperate with Seller in Seller's removal and shipment of such items; and

(c) Buyer shall act in a reasonable manner both before and after discovery of items containing hazardous wastes in order to prevent leakage and otherwise minimize contamination or other damage.

A careful reading of this section produces the following understanding of its terms. First, it contains an express warranty that the land included in the "Leased Premises" is free of any contamination which would be violative of applicable laws or regulations. Defendants do not contest the import of this statement. Secondly, the Seller agreed to indemnify and hold Buyer harmless from any damage resulting from the presence of hazardous waste in the Inventory and the land on or before November 20, 1984, providing Buyer complied with the aforementioned conditions.

. . . The jury found that the property at 6801 State Road was substantially contaminated both before and after the plaintiffs took possession of the property on November 20, 1984. The contamination that occurred after November 20, 1984, or while plaintiffs were in possession, resulted from hazardous waste material, including items which contained PCB contaminants, already on the site prior to their tenancy and purchase. The jury did not find that the contamination was due to any additional hazardous waste material which was brought on the site by the plaintiffs after they took possession.

The jury found that Versatile Metals failed to substantially comply with paragraphs (a), (b) and (c) of Section 4.05 of the Asset Purchase Agreement, and this failure to comply substantially prejudiced the defendants. When asked to apportion the fault between the parties, the jury found that Versatile Metals was fifty-five percent responsible and Metal Bank forty-five percent responsible for the contamination. The reasonable cleanup costs incurred by Metal Bank attributable to Versatile Metals' actions was found to be $1,107,489. . . .

Questions and Comments for Discussion

1. In this case, the court found that the seller had breached an express warranty to buyers, but that the buyers' failure to comply with requirements of the contract substantially prejudiced the defendants. As a result, the jury apportioned cleanup costs between the parties. Under CERCLA, both parties could be responsible for the cleanup costs. Note that both principles of real property law and statutory law under the Uniform Commercial Code (which is applicable to the sale of goods) were applied by the court in this case. Why were both kinds of law relevant?

Indemnification Agreements

In *Versatile Metals,* the buyer also contended it was not liable under CERCLA because the seller, Metal Bank, agreed to an **indemnification agreement,** which would reimburse the buyer, Versatile Metals, if any contamination of the land occurred as a result of hazardous waste at the property before the date the buyer took possession. Under CERCLA, a person may by agreement be held harmless or indemnified by another party.

Section 107(e)(1) provides:

> (1) No indemnification, hold harmless, or similar agreement or conveyance shall be effective to transfer from the owner or operator of any vessel or facility or from any person who may be liable for a release or threat of a release under this section, to any other person the liability imposed under this section. Nothing in this subsection shall bar any agreement to insure, hold harmless, or indemnify a party to such agreement for any liability under this section.[7]

The apparent contradictory language of this section has given rise to conflicting interpretations of the enforceability of indemnity clauses in CERCLA cases.

The indemnity clause in Section 4.05 of the Asset Purchase Agreement in *Versatile Metals* provided:

> Seller and Union jointly agree to indemnify and hold Buyer harmless from any and all costs, damages, liabilities, and expenses resulting from hazardous waste in the Inventory existing on and the land included in the lease premises at November 20, 1984, *provided that,* with respect to the *inventory,* Buyer acts in the following manner. . . .

Recall that the indemnity clause contained certain conditions, including the requirement that Versatile Metals was to keep all inventory purchased segregated from any other inventories and to give prompt telephone notice to Metal Bank upon discovery of any items in the inventory which might contain hazardous waste. Because Versatile Metals failed to fulfill those conditions, it was unable to invoke the indemnity provisions in the contract.

Disclaimers of Liability and the "As Is" Clause

Just as a buyer may want to protect himself from potential liability in the purchase of contaminated property, so a seller may attempt to insulate himself from liability in the sale of the property through express contractual **disclaimers.** A disclaimer is a statement in a contract that one party will not be liable for damages to the other for breach of contract under certain circumstances.

Contract disclaimers of environmental liability in the sale of commercial property are generally enforceable as long as they are negotiated by the parties in good faith and as long as the parties have actual notice of their contents. However, courts always retain the power to declare a contract provision unenforceable if they find the clause violates *public policy* or that the clause is unconscionable. Public policy is a broad term which describes a court's or legislator's view of policy which is in the best interests of the public and society in general. It may be manifested by statute or by judicial determination. Some contractual disclaimers, such as disclaimers of implied warranties in the sale of residential property, may be unenforceable because they are not in the best interest of the public. In addition, courts may refuse to enforce a contract provision which is **unconscionable.** Unconscionability is generally defined as a contract provision which is both procedurally and substantively unfair. A court may also set aside a contract if it finds that the parties did not *voluntarily* enter into the agreement. Under this theory, a party who was *mistaken* about an important fact, or who entered into the agreement because of *misrepresentation* by the other party, is entitled to rescind the contract.

In the following case, a plaintiff purchaser sought to enforce a contract for the sale of commercial property after the property was discovered to be contaminated. The seller sought to rescind the contract on the basis that the parties were mutually mistaken about the contamination on the property and because the seller was obligated under state and federal law to bear the cost of cleaning up the property. The buyer relied on an **as is** provision in the contract in arguing that the contract was enforceable.

GARB-KO INC. v. LANSING-LEWIS SERVICES, INC.

423 N.W.2d 355 (Mich. App. 1988)

THOMAS, Judge.

Plaintiff appeals as of right from the trial court's order denying specific performance[8] of a sales contract against defendants. We affirm.

This case presents an anomalous situation in which the seller seeks to rescind a contract for the sale of land based on a defect in the property discovered after the sales agreement was entered into. Garb-Ko and Action Auto, the parent company of Lansing-Lewis Services, Inc., entered into a buy-sell agreement on or about February 11, 1985, by which plaintiff was to purchase a gas station and automotive parts store in East Lansing from defendants for $320,000. The buy-sell agreement contained an "as is" clause. The site was to be used for a 7-Eleven store. The property has seven underground storage tanks which hold four thousand to six thousand gallons of gasoline each.

Garb-Ko did not inquire into the environmental condition of the property or the integrity of the gasoline tanks prior to making the offer to purchase. Action Auto subsequently learned that the gasoline storage tanks on the property might be leaking and contaminating the ground and groundwater. Neither party was aware of any contamination on the property at the time the buy-sell agreement was executed. Garb-Ko was informed of the contamination on the property in a letter dated April 5, 1985, and given the option of terminating the agreement or providing Action Auto with full indemnification for all costs and penalties arising out of any gasoline storage leakage and proceeding with the sale. Garb-Ko did not agree to indemnify the sellers for the costs and expenses arising out of the contamination and did not accept the seller's offer to terminate the agreement. . . .

A bench trial was held on December 23, 1985, to determine whether specific performance of the buy-sell agreement should be ordered. The court found that a mutual mistake affecting a basic, material assumption of the contract had occurred and that it would be unreasonable and unjust to enforce the terms of the buy-sell agreement. . . .

A contract may be rescinded because of a mutual mistake of the parties; however, this equitable remedy is granted only in the sound discretion of the trial court. The determination whether plaintiffs are entitled to rescission involves a bifurcated inquiry: (1) was there a mistaken belief entertained by one or both of the parties to a contract? and (2) if so, what is the legal significance of the mistaken belief?

In its opinion and order, the trial court found that the parties had clearly entered into the buy-sell agreement under a serious mistake of fact since, at the time the agreement was signed, neither party was aware of the gasoline leakage. We agree.

A contractual mistake "is a belief not in accord with the facts." This mistake must relate to a fact in existence at the time the contract is executed. The testimony at trial clearly revealed that there had been a large gasoline leak on the property that could result in contamination of both soil and groundwater. The testimony also indicated that none of the contracting parties were aware of that fact at the time they executed the buy-sell agreement.

***

Here, the mutual mistake relates to a basic assumption of the parties upon which the contract was made. Additionally, this mistake materially affects the agreed performance of the parties. In any commercial real estate sale, the parties assume and desire that the sale will result in a complete transfer of rights, obligations, and responsibilities. The purchaser does not want the seller involved in, or disrupting the new business in any way. Likewise, the seller desires to sever all ties with the property and any obligations. Under the common law, a sale of property resulted in such a transfer of rights and obligations. However, environmental-protection statutes have altered the common law and made previous owners of sites liable for environmental contamination. Under these laws, a previous owner may be required to conduct a site investigation and cleanup and would have a continuing liability after contaminated property is sold. It is this continuing responsibility for the land in question which requires us to affirm the trial court's ruling rescinding the buy-sell agreement and denying plaintiff's request for specific performance of the agreement.

We are not persuaded by plaintiff that the "as is" clause contained in the buy-sell agreement controls and bars rescission of the contract. Paragraph 11 of the buy-sell agreement states:

"PURCHASER HAS PERSONALLY EXAMINED THIS PROPERTY AND AGREES TO ACCEPT SAME IN ITS PRESENT CONDITION EXCEPT AS MAY BE SPECIFIED HEREIN AND AGREES THAT THERE ARE NOT OTHER ADDITIONAL WRITTEN OR ORAL UNDERSTANDINGS."

Under this clause, the risk was clearly allocated to the purchaser. 1 Restatement Contracts, 2nd, sec. 152 states that when a legally significant mutual mistake has occurred, the contract is voidable by the adversely affected party, unless he bears the risk of the mistake. However, the purchaser is not the adversely affected party; thus, the "as is" clause holds no significance. Here, due to the state and federal environmental-protection statutes which impose continuing liability after the sale of the land on defendant sellers for contamination that occurred while defendants owned the property, it is clear that they are the adversely affected party. The "as is" clause of the buy-sell agreement would not operate to relieve defendant sellers of their liability under these statutes. Had plaintiff agreed to indemnify Action Auto for all costs and penalties arising out of any gasoline storage leakage, rescission possibly would not have been granted. However, since plaintiff did not do so, defendant sellers remain the adversely affected party having incurred the "burden" imposed by law of cleaning up the contamination. The contract is voidable under sec. 152(1) of the Restatement.

In this case, equity requires that we affirm the trial court's ruling. Defendants have a continuing obligation and responsibility for the contaminated property. One expert estimated that the cost of cleanup could be anywhere from $100,000 to $1,000,000. In order to contain further cleanup costs and third-party claims arising from use of the contaminated land, defendants need control over the use of the property. Sale to plaintiff would not give them such control.

Indeed, this case is unique since rarely does a purchaser of property, after discovering that the property is contaminated, request that the sale continue and ask the court to order specific performance of the contract. However, due to the continuing nature of the obligation and responsibilities defendants have over the environmental contamination of the property, we conclude that the trial court did not err in ordering rescission of the contract and denying plaintiff's request for specific performance.

Affirmed.

Questions and Comments for Discussion

1. Who sued whom in this case and why? Who wanted to enforce the contract? Generally, if a party breaches a contract, it is obligated to pay damages to the other party. In this case, the buyer sought the equitable remedy of **specific performance.** This remedy is appropriate in cases where contract damages are inadequate to compensate a contracting party for breach. Under this remedy, a court may order the breaching party to actually perform the contract. The remedy is particularly appropriate in cases where the contract involves the sale of unique property like real estate.

2. As the court indicated in this case, a court may set aside a contract on the basis of *mutual mistake* if it finds that (1) both parties were mistaken about a basic assumption on which the contract was made; (2) the mistake had a material effect on the agreed exchange of performance; and (3) the mistaken party did not *bear the risk* of the mistake. A party may "bear the risk" of the mistake if it agrees to accept the property "as is." As in this case, however, a court may refuse to enforce an "as is" clause if it finds that enforcement is inappropriate or that the clause was not intended to apply under the particular circumstances of the case.

3. A party may also rescind a contract if it can show that it entered into the contract because the other party *misrepresented* an important fact about the property. Misrepresentation is defined as a "false assertion of fact." Under this theory, a false assertion of material fact can be the basis of **rescission** if the other party actually and reasonably relied on the misrepresentation. Misrepresentation which is intentionally and knowingly made to deceive another is called *fraud* and may be the basis for contract rescission as well as action for damages for intentional tort. Innocent and negligent misrepresentation may also be the basis for contract rescission if they concern a material fact and the other party actually and justifiably relied on the misrepresentation. A buyer may be entitled to rescind a contract for the purchase of real property if the seller misrepresented the fact that the property was not environmentally contaminated.

Implied Warranties of Habitability

Most states have recognized an **implied warranty of habitability** in the sale of new residential property. Under this theory, a builder-vendor who sells a new home impliedly warrants that the home will be fit and habitable. Similarly, most states recognize an implied warranty of habitability in residential leases. Under these implied warranties, a purchaser or tenant of residential property may be entitled to damages or rescission if the property is uninhabitable because of the presence of environmental hazards like radon gas, asbestos, or formaldehyde.

Residential and Commercial Leases

Historically, a lease agreement between a landlord and a tenant was viewed primarily as a conveyance of real property. This relationship has changed dramatically, and the relationship is more typically characterized as a contractual one. Under modern contract law, doctrines such as unconscionability and the implied warranty of habitability are applied to the sale and lease of residential property. These doctrines are used to protect tenants as well as to ensure that policies underlying the enactment of public health and safety laws, such as environmental laws, are met.

Just as the implied warranty of habitability in the sale of new property is generally limited to sales of new *residential* property, so implied warranties of habitability are generally limited to leases of residential property. However, the same policies that underlie protection of tenants in residential property often apply to the sale and lease of commercial property. For example, an employee who works in a "sick" building (a building with hazards which may affect the health of those working within it) may reasonably argue that the landlord or builder should be liable for damages under the theory that the commercial landlord also impliedly warrants that the building is safe for human habitation. Considering the trend toward expanding liability of the owner or lessor of residential property under these theories, it is certainly possible that courts will expand protection of commercial tenants.

Most cities and states have adopted housing codes which impose duties on the landlord with respect to conditions of the property. These codes commonly require that the property meet minimum standards of cleanliness, safety, and sanitary conditions. Violation of such standards may give rise to an action for breach of an implied warranty of habitability.

Some states have also recognized specific environmental hazards which may pose a risk to tenants and have enacted laws designed to protect tenants from those hazards, such as those posed by lead-based paint. As of October 1995, Title X of the Housing and Community Development Act of 1992 requires sellers of pre-1978 housing units to disclose to prospective buyers or tenants any known lead hazards.

In the following case, a tenant sued her landlord for personal injuries sustained by her child who ingested lead-based paint.

HARDY v. GRIFFIN
569 A.2d 49 (Ct. 1989)

DEMAYO, Judge.

The plaintiff, Patricia Hardy, brought this action on behalf of her six-year-old child, Verron Hardy, claiming that he suffered severe and permanent brain damage from his exposure to, and ingestion of, lead-based paint.

From about November 1, 1984, to August 1, 1986, the plaintiff occupied a housing unit at 18 Arthur Street in New Haven. During this time, Verron was found to have abnormally high levels of lead in his blood. The named defendant and the defendant Leona A. Griffin were the owners of 18 Arthur Street and leased the premises to Patricia Hardy.

In this case of first impression, the plaintiff has claimed damages on a theory of strict liability because of the defendants' alleged violation of both state statutes and a city ordinance. The failure to keep the premises free of lead-based paint is claimed to be the violation and is also the basis for a claim made under the Connecticut Unfair Trade Practices Act (CUTPA).

The defendants have denied any knowledge of the existence of such paint, suggesting that if there were any, it existed prior to their purchase of the property. They further deny the use of any lead-based paint on the premises.

From the evidence the plaintiff presented at trial, the court concludes that Verron suffers from lead paint poisoning and that this condition was a result of his exposure to the lead-based paint present at 18 Arthur Street.

The named defendant admitted that in January, 1987, he received a notice from the city of New Haven advising him of the presence of lead paint at 18 Arthur Street. On prior occasions, he had been put on notice that repairs to this unit were required. The plaintiff testified that she had seen Verron eating paint chips, which prompted her to have him tested for the presence of lead in his blood. She also stated that the apartment was painted by the defendants but that the previous coat of paint was not scraped. This underlying coat was described as "thick, chipped and peeling."

The named defendant's suggestion that someone "set him up" by spraying on lead paint is entitled to no credence. As for the testimony offered by the defendants that Verron was observed eating paint out of a can, their own evidence as to the dates of the termination of the manufacture and sale of lead-based paint in Connecticut renders this event, even if it is accepted by this court as having occurred, to be of dubious significance.

In support of the strict liability theory, the plaintiff cites General Statutes sec. 47a-8 and the New Haven Code of General Ordinances. Section 47a-8 provides as follows: "The presence of paint which does not conform to federal standards as required in accordance with the Lead-Based Paint Poisoning Prevention Act . . . or of cracked, chipped, blistered, flaking, loose or peeling paint which constitutes a health hazard on accessible surfaces in any dwelling unit, tenement or any real property intended for human habitation shall be construed to render such dwelling unit, tenement or real property unfit for human habitation and shall constitute a noncompliance with subdivision (2) of subsection (a) of section

47a-7." Section 47a-7(a)(2) imposes an affirmative duty upon landlords to "make all repairs and do whatever is necessary to put and keep the premises in a fit and habitable condition. . . ." The New Haven Code of General Ordinances sets a stricter standard than the federal standards referred to in sec. 47a-8.

The plaintiff cites *Panoroni v. Johnson,* 158 Conn. 92, 256 A.2d 246 (1969). In that case, the Supreme Court stated: "The violation of an ordinance enacted for the protection of the public is negligence as a matter of law." *Panoroni* also involved the New Haven housing code, and the court found that the plaintiff there was a member of the class for whose protection the New Haven code was enacted. This court similarly concludes that the plaintiff in the present case is a member of the class for whose protection the provision of the housing code referred to above was enacted.

The defendants' breach, therefore, of the duty imposed by the New Haven Code of General Ordinances to maintain rental premises free of lead paint (or not to rent premises containing lead paint) renders them liable for the injuries incurred by Verron Hardy. On the facts here, the court further finds that the defendants are liable for Verron's condition by virtue of their negligent failure to keep the premises free of lead paint and because they rented the premises when they should have known of the presence of lead paint.

***

In view of [experts'] testimony, there is little doubt that Verron is severely and permanently mentally disabled as a result of lead poisoning, causing behavioral and learning abnormalities. He has a marked inability to concentrate and to organize his thoughts. It is unlikely he will be able to graduate from high school.

[Arthur W.] Wright [professor of economics at the University of Connecticut] testified that, assuming total disability, he computed Verron's loss of earning capacity over his life expectancy. The court accepts his lowest computation, which presumes Verron will complete the eighth grade, as the most realistic. The court sees little likelihood that he will enter and complete high school. Wright's computation for the completion of eight grades is $828,626.

In view of the foregoing, judgment may enter for the plaintiff to recover from the defendants the sum of $828,626, plus attorney's fees of $100,000 and costs.

Questions and Comments for Discussion

1. The legal theory utilized in this case negligence *per se,* is discussed in Chapter 4. Under this theory, a defendant is liable for negligence if he breaches a *statutory* duty, and (1) the kind of harm the statute was designed to prevent (2) occurs to a person the statute was designed to protect. This theory provides additional incentives for landlords to comply with laws like those in effect in this case.

2. According to a report by the Centers for Disease Control, some 57 million U.S. homes built before 1980 contain lead-based paint. About four million of those homes have young children who are at special risk because lead can cause mental retardation, learning disabilities, hyperactivity, attention deficit disorder, convulsions, lack of coordination, kidney damage, and even death. Some claim minority communities are the hardest hit by the lead paint situation. Some experts suggest that the best way to rid communities of lead paint poisoning is through education. What policy arguments support holding landlords liable for lead-paint exposure to young children? What policies oppose holding landlords liable under a non-disclosure theory?

3. In other recent lead-abatement cases, plaintiffs have recovered money damages under various legal theories, including negligence, negligence *per se* for violation of state law, and breach of implied warranty of habitability. For a survey of cases, see Note, "Landlord Liability for Lead Poisoning of Tenant Children Caused by Defects in the Premises," 70 U. Det. Mercy L. Rev. 429-450 (1993).

4. Another potential source of lead in residential property is lead pipes. Before the 1920s, lead pipes were commonly used in homes. Lead leaching from copper pipes and soldered with lead is also another major source of water contamination. In 1991, the EPA issued a regulation requiring public water suppliers to monitor lead levels in the water supply by sampling and minimizing the corrosivity of the water's lead levels. Amendments to the 1986 Safe Drinking Water Act banned the use of solder that contained more than 0.2 percent lead and other plumbing materials that contained more than eight percent lead in residential plumbing systems.

Expanding Landlord and Tenant Liability

As the above case illustrates, courts have continued to abrogate the traditional doctrine of *caveat lessee* ("let the tenant beware") in landlord-tenant transactions. Under various statutory and common law theories, modern courts have held landlords liable for harms caused to the tenant as a result of environmental contamination or toxic substances on the property.

Under common law theories like negligence and nuisance, landlords may incur liability for the actions of their tenants. At least one court has held that a landlord may be liable for negligence in the selection of the tenant and for the wrongdoing of the tenant when the landlord continues to exercise control over the premises. In *Rivertone Corp. v. General Thermo-*

forming, 456 N.Y.S.2d 869 (A.D. 1982), the State of New York, Town of Vestal, and three of its water districts brought an action to abate a nuisance caused by contamination of the soil and groundwater under premises owned by the defendant Knowles and leased by the defendant Monarch Chemicals. The government alleged that the tenant handled and stored dangerous chemicals on the site, and these seeped into the public water supply.

The owner moved to dismiss the complaint, claiming that he had engaged in no affirmative misconduct at the site. However, the court said that the record reflected the possibility that the owner knew of possible contamination at the site. The landlord's failure to take any precautions to prevent contamination of the groundwater was sufficient to support liability under a nuisance theory. According to the court, at the very least the plaintiffs had stated a valid cause of action against the owner respecting negligent maintenance of a nuisance.

The adoption of CERCLA has also had a substantial impact on the leasing of commercial industrial property. Under CERCLA, both the landlord and tenant (as owner and operator) may be liable for the cleanup costs associated with disposal of hazardous substances on the property. Just as in disputes between buyers and sellers of contaminated property, in allocating responsibilities between the landlord and tenant the court will consider express contractual agreements by the parties, and factors such as the amount of hazardous substances involved, the degree of involvement by the parties in the transportation, treatment, and storage of the substances, and the degree of care exercised by the parties with respect to the substances involved.

Avoiding Environmental Liability

As the previous discussion suggests, purchasers and sellers of real property, as well as lessors and lessees, should consider and address potential liability that may result from noncompliance with environmental laws or from environmental contamination of the property. This is especially true for those involved in the sale or lease of commercial property which may have been contaminated as a result of prior manufacturing or industrial activity at the site or which may become contaminated through such activity. It is especially important for these commercial parties to consider and address all the potentially relevant environmental issues that may arise at such sites.

A prospective purchaser should make appropriate inquiry into past ownership and use of the facility prior to purchase in order to exercise "due diligence" in determining whether the property has been contaminated. The seller and buyer should also attempt to limit their respective liabilities through various contractual provisions. Typical contract representations, warranties, and indemnities include:

1. Warranties that the property and operations on the site comply with applicable environmental laws, regulations, and court or administrative orders

2. Warranties that there are no pending private or governmental claims relating to environmental conditions on the property

3. Warranties that necessary permits, licenses, and government approvals are in existence or may be obtained

4. A provision that the seller has made all relevant disclosures and exercised due care in discovering the existence of any environmental liabilities at the site

The seller may refuse to provide such warranties based on lack of knowledge of prior activity at the site, but may agree to give the buyer a reasonable period of time to evaluate potential liability before the buyer is obligated to proceed with the purchase. A seller may choose to provide that any representations or warranties are based solely upon the "seller's actual knowledge" and may wish to limit his representations to those activities occurring during his ownership of the property. The seller may also limit the time period for those representations and warranties, or limit the extent of his liability for breach of warranties or misrepresentation to a certain dollar amount.

The seller should also seek a promise from the buyer that the buyer will use his best efforts to maintain and operate the premises in compliance with all applicable environmental laws.

Indemnification agreements often include promises to reimburse the other party for environmental liabilities as well as attorneys' fees and litigation expenses. Indemnity agreements should include:

1. the length of time the agreement is in effect;
2. provisions for notice of claims subject to the indemnity;
3. monetary limits on liability; and
4. applicability of the indemnity agreement to acts of a seller's predecessors.

The contract also may provide a **right of termination** if an environmental audit reveals problems. This right of termination may be triggered by the discovery by either party of environmental problems within a specified time. In some cases, a right of termination may be more narrowly defined to arise in the event of triggering conditions such as a certain cost to correct, a certain length of time to remedy, or a particular kind of problem.

The concerns of the landlord and tenant are similar to those of buyers and sellers. Just as a purchaser should investigate the property prior to purchase, so a tenant should ensure that he is not leasing property with environmental liabilities. The tenant should seek a guarantee from the landlord that the property is free from environmental liabilities prior to executing the lease and a promise to indemnify the tenant for liability incurred as a result of pre-existing contamination at the site.

The landlord should include lease provisions requiring the tenant to comply with all applicable laws and regulations, and failure to comply would constitute a material breach of the lease. The landlord who leases commercial property should review activity or equipment on the property which may result in contamination or violation of applicable environmental laws. The landlord may require a security deposit to offset pollution cleanup expenses.

The landlord should retain the right to enter and inspect the property for contamination. The tenant should be required to notify the landlord of any significant release, environmental problems, or receipt of any notices of environmental liability. Finally, at lease termination, the tenant should be required to clean up any contamination and to return the property in a condition that complies with all laws.

The value of these contractual provisions is somewhat limited, as warranties and indemnification agreements are only as good as the ability of the contracting party to pay. The protection afforded by these contractual devices is often limited in time, and there may be a long latency period before environmental problems are discovered at the site. These contractual devices do not necessarily insulate the buyer from most federal and state claims for clean-up response costs.

PRODUCT LIABILITY LAW

Product liability law is concerned with compensating for personal injury or property damage from *defective products*. There is no single theory used by plaintiffs, who often rely on both contract and tort theories to recover damages. A person injured by a defective product may argue that the defect constituted a breach of *express* or *implied warranty*. All states have adopted the Uniform Commercial Code, which contains provisions recognizing an *implied warranty of merchantability* in the sale of goods. This implied warranty is created by operation of law and permits a plaintiff to recover **damages** if the product was sold by a merchant and is not fit for commnon, ordinary use.

A plaintiff may also rely on common law tort theories like *negligence* in maintaining an action against the seller or manufacturer of a defective product. Negligence theory applies in cases where the plaintiff claims that the manufacturer/seller failed to use reasonable care in the design, manufacture, inspection, or packaging of the product. A product may also be defective because the seller or manufacturer negligently failed to warn of dangers associated with the product.

The theory that most exemplifies product liability actions today is **strict liability.** Chapter 4 examined cases where courts imposed strict liability for ultrahazardous or abnormally dangerous activities by a defendant—for example, operation of a hazardous waste landfill. Strict liability theory in defective product cases is based on the Restatement (Second) of Torts, Section 402(a), which states:

> A seller engaged in the business of selling a particular product is liable for physical harm or property damage suffered by the ultimate user or consumer, if the product was in a defective condition unreasonably dangerous to the user or consumer or to his property.

Under this theory, a merchant-seller may be liable to a consumer injured by a defective product even though the seller exercised all possible care in the preparation and sale of the product.

Product liability actions have been brought by plaintiffs who allege they were injured by toxic or environmentally unsafe products. The courts have held asbestos insulation manufacturers strictly liable for damages for asbestosis and mesothelioma contracted by industrial workers. In *Borel v. Fibreboard Paper Products Corp.,*[9] evidence showed that the manufacturers failed not only to test their products for adverse affects, they also failed to avail themselves of scientific knowledge regarding the dangers of asbestos. According to the court of appeals, these dangers made the defendants' asbestos products unreasonably dangerous to the ultimate user and thus defective under the Restatement of Torts, Section 402(a).

In the following case, a farmer who suffered crop loss after using a pesticide manufactured by the defendant brought an action to recover damages for harm that occurred to his corn. He argued that the product was defective and that the seller had negligently misrepresented facts about the product. One issue before the court was whether the Federal Insecticide, Fungicide, and Rodenticide Act pre-empted plaintiff's state common law tort claims against the pesticide manufacturer.

GORTON v. AMERICAN CYANAMID CO.
533 N.W.2d 746 (Wis. 1995)

WILCOX, Justice.

During the 1980s, American Cyanamid developed an herbicide known as SCEPTER. The herbicide is designed to control weeds in soybean crops. SCEPTER was first sold for use in Wisconsin in 1987. SCEPTER has been marketed through American Cyanamid sales personnel and technical representatives, and is sold by agricultural dealers chosen by American Cyanamid.

In May of 1987 and 1988, Gorton Farms bought SCEPTER for their soybean fields. Gorton Farms purchased SCEPTER from the Delong Company, an authorized American Cyanamid agricultural dealer. . . . There is no dispute that the herbicide provided excellent weed control for the soybean plants.

In the spring of 1988, Gorton Farms planted field corn as a follow crop to the soybeans. Thus, the corn was planted into fields that had eleven months earlier been sprayed with SCEPTER. In June 1988, there was evidence that the field corn was not growing properly. Gorton farms asked Ronald Doersch of the University of Wisconsin Agronomy department to examine the fields. Doersch indicated that the corn could have been adversely affected by the previous application of SCEPTER.

On February 9, 1990, Gorton Farms filed a complaint against American Cyanamid alleging theories of breach of warranty, defective product based on failure to provide adequate instructions for use, and negligent misrepresentation concerning SCEPTER's use in follow corn crops. . . .

***

The threshold issue on review is whether the circuit court properly concluded that FIFRA does not preempt Gorton Farms' state common law tort claims. American Cyanamid asserts that all of Gorton Farms' claims are predicated on a theory of failure to warn and, as such, as preempted by Sec. 136v(b) of FIFRA. Gorton Farms responds that "FIFRA does not preempt common law damage liability based on negligent and outrageous conduct and testing and in misrepresenting SCEPTER's safety to follow corn, which conduct was part of [American Cyanamid's] marketing and sales activity and not based on SCEPTER's labeling or packaging."

[After discussing the doctrine of federal preemption and legal precedents in the case, the court continued:] In the present case, Gorton Farms brought claims based on defective product, breach of warranty and negligent misrepresentation. There is no dispute that each claim is a viable action under Wisconsin state law. American Cyanamid, however, asserts that each of these claims is derivative to the labeling and packaging of SCEPTER and therefore, should be preempted by FIFRA. Gorton Farms counters that its proof at trial never touched on or attacked SCEPTER's labeling or packaging; rather, it centered on American Cyanamid's field tests, lack of scientific testing, and false and misleading statements in the promotion of SCEPTER.

In its amended complaint . . , Gorton Farms alleges the following:

13. SCEPTER as labeled for use in Wisconsin is a defective product since its application interferes with the normal crop rotation and causes a loss in crop yield.

14. American Cyanamid Company failed to adequately warn Gorton Farms of the dangerous nature of the product and provided defective instructions for use.

15. As a result of American Cyanamid Company's manufacture and sale of this de-

fective product and its defective warnings and instructions in use, Gorton Farms suffered pecuniary losses in its corn yield in 1988 and 1989.

These allegations provide two distinct claims: (1) strict liability—defective design or manufacture, and (2) strict liability—failure to warn. . . .

Gorton Farms' third and final cause of action asserts a claim for negligent misrepresentation:

17. American Cyanamid Company formulated or manufactured and sold its product known as SCEPTER and negligently held out and represented to Wisconsin farmers that the product was a safe and effective means of controlling weeds in soybean crops . . . without harm to subsequent crops.

***

We follow the [U.S. Supreme Court's reasoning in] *Cipollone v. Liggett Group, Inc.*, 112 S.Ct. 2608 (1992), on this point and hold that Gorton Farms' claim based on misrepresentation survives preemption under FIFRA. We see nothing in FIFRA that seeks to overturn the long-standing rules governing misrepresentation. On the contrary, FIFRA simply seeks uniformity in labeling and packaging and mandates that states shall not impose labeling or packaging requirements other than those prescribed by the statute itself. . . .

Here, Gorton Farms presented evidence that American Cyanamid made presentations that SCEPTER was safe to follow corn. These representations were made through written product such as promotional materials, advertisements, technical reports, as well through oral statements made by American Cyanamid's technical service representatives. All of the statements assuring that SCEPTER was "safe" and "extremely safe" had no relation to the labeling or packaging of the herbicide. Gorton Farms also presented evidence that American Cyanamid internal documents unequivocally showed that SCEPTER caused damage to follow corn crops in a variety of circumstances and yet, the company failed to disclose any information other than assertions that SCEPTER was safe to follow corn. As noted by Gorton Farms in its brief to this court: "Having heard rumors of SCEPTER carry over to follow corn in the fall of 1987, John Gorton asked an [American Cyanamid] technical service representation about it in February 1988, and [American Cyanamid's] representative assured him it was safe to plant corn following soybeans treated with SCEPTER. Thereafter, Gorton Farms again purchased SCEPTER for use in 1988."

We conclude that not only does the Gorton Farms' misrepresentation claim survive preemption under FIFRA, the evidence adduced at trial was credible and sufficient to sustain the jury's finding that American Cyanamid made negligent misrepresentations of facts as to the safety of SCEPTER and that this conduct was outrageous. . . .

Order of the circuit court is affirmed.

Questions and Comments for Discussion

1. As this case suggests, an important question in "failure to warn" cases involving pesticides is the extent to which FIFRA pre-empts state tort law actions against pesticide manufacturers based on design defect, failure to warn, and negligence theories. In contrast to this case, consider *Shaw v. Dow Brands Inc.*, 944 F.2d. 364 (7th Cir. 1993). In that case, a consumer's lungs were permanently damaged from the fumes that resulted from his mixture of two bathroom cleaning products. He sued the manufacturers in state court and the case was removed to federal court. The district court

determined that the consumer's state law of strict liability and negligence claims for failure to warn were pre-empted by FIFRA.

The federal court of appeals agreed, saying that whether federal law pre-empts state law turns on congressional intent. In this instance, that intent is explicit in the statute which states: "Such state shall not impose or continue in effect any requirements for labeling or packaging in addition to or different from those required under this subchapter."

The consumer had argued that there is still room for common law tort actions for defective labels. While the court said the consumer's argument was appealing, it said it would be silly to pretend that federal lawmakers, seeking to occupy a whole field of regulation, would not also be concerned about the distorting effects of tort actions.

Relying on *Cipollone v. Liggett Group Inc.*, which held that sweeping congressional efforts to pre-empt state regulation also bar state damages claims, the court said that "If common law actions cannot survive under the 1969 Cigarette Act, then common law actions for labeling and packaging defects cannot survive under FIFRA." Chapter 7 of this text includes an extended discussion of the pre-emption doctrine.

Defenses in Product Liability Actions

States have placed limits on the time within which a product liability action may be brought, stated in the **statute of limitations.** Time limits in product liability cases involving environmental hazards like asbestos may be critical in determining whether a plaintiff is entitled to recover damages for injuries caused by exposure to a toxic substance over a long period. In most states, the statute of limitations for negligence and strict liability is shorter than the UCC statute of limitations for express and implied warranty claims. However, the statute generally begins to run only after the defect is or should have been discovered. Consequently, the tort statute of limitations may be more advantageous to the plaintiff in some product liability cases than the longer contractual statute of limitations.

Some states have enacted specific statutes which address time limits on product liability suits. Some also have special time limits for delayed manifestation injuries such as those resulting from exposure to asbestos. Finally, some states have adopted statutes which establish a *useful safe life* defense. Such statutes prevent the plaintiff from suing where the harm occurs after the product's "useful safe life" has passed.

Whether a particular defense to a product liability action will be permitted depends in part on the legal theory underlying plaintiff's action. Traditional defenses include *misuse of the product* by the plaintiff, *assumption of the risk* by the plaintiff, or *contributory negligence.*

The traditional defenses of assumption of the risk and contributory negligence are discussed in Chapter 4. *Product misuse* occurs when a plaintiff uses the product in an unusual, unforeseeable way. In some cases, however, if the defendant should have foreseen the misuse and failed to take reasonable steps to prevent it, he still may be liable. The defense of product misuse is generally applicable under all product liability theories.

The Problem of Causation   In product liability cases, as well as other toxic tort actions where a plaintiff seeks to recover damages for injuries from a toxic substance, causation is often difficult to prove. Claims for injuries from exposure may include existing illnesses, increased risks of future illness, and costs for future medical surveillance. Causation is often difficult to prove because of the difficulty in establishing a correlation between the physical injury and exposure to the substance. The plaintiff may have been exposed once or several times over an extended period of time. And often there is a long latency period between the exposure and the disease. As the *Meehan* case in Chapter 4 illustrates, the testimony of medical experts is often necessary to establish a causal connection between exposure to a toxic substance and resulting injury or disease.

Summary of Product Liability Law   Product liability law refers to the body of legal rules which governs damages resulting from the sale of defective goods. These include negligence, breach of warranty, and strict liability theories. Breach of warranty is essentially a *contract* theory, while negligence and strict liability are *tort* theories. Under traditional common law negligence theory, a plaintiff is entitled to recover damages for injuries from exposure to a toxic substance if she can prove that the defendant breached a legal duty to her which resulted in her injuries. In addition, she must prove that the defendant's negligence actually caused her injuries, and that it was foreseeable such injuries would result.

In some product liability cases where the product has many component parts and a long chain of distribution, it may be difficult for the plaintiff to prove that the manufacturer was negligent. Under traditional common law doctrine, defenses such as contributory negligence and assumption of the risk also act as a complete bar to recovery.

Beginning in the early 1960s, courts began to compensate those injured by defective products under a strict liability theory. The states' adoption of this theory most symbolizes the product liability explosion. This theory is based on the assumption that sellers, manufacturers, and their insurers should bear the economic costs of defective products, and pass on those costs. Strict liability is characterized as liability without fault. The injured consumer does not need to establish that the manufacturer or seller breached a duty of reasonable care in the manufacture, design, or sale of the product.

Strict liability also recognizes that contract and negligence law are often inadequate protection from defective products. As the economy of society has moved toward a corporate based system, it is less likely that consumers can deal directly with a manufacturer, protect themselves through contracts, or inspect the manufacturing process. Product liability law has thus shifted toward a **caveat venditor** approach ("let the seller beware"). Strict liability is based on the perception that sellers and manufacturers are better able to bear the economic costs associated with defective products than the injured consumer.

Product liability theories entitle a person to recover damages for injuries or property damage caused by toxic or hazardous products. By recognizing the right to sue under product liability theories, courts have permitted common law remedies to supplement federal laws regulating the manufacture, transportation, and disposal of toxic chemicals. Consequently, state common law and statutory product liability law act as additional incentives for manufacturers and sellers to ensure that products are environmentally safe.

INSURER LIABILITY FOR ENVIRONMENTAL DAMAGES

Passage of comprehensive federal and state environmental legislation like CERCLA has significantly expanded the potential liability of corporate defendants for hazardous waste contamination at company-owned sites. In response, corporate defendants have turned to their insurance carriers for defense and reimbursement costs of their cleanup and liability costs under the terms of their general liability insurance policies. Considering the enormous costs involved in cleaning up hazardous waste sites and the often substantial tort liability in toxic torts cases, it is not surprising that parties who may be liable for those costs are willing to invest substantial sums in litigation to avoid or minimize that liability. This is also true in insurer liability cases.

Most cases challenging insurer liability have involved comprehensive general liability **(CGL) insurance policies.** Standard language contained in the CGL policy has been the subject of much litigation, especially in cases concerning the environmental contamination of real property. In these cases, insurers have often aggressively fought liability under the theory that environmental cleanup costs are not covered under the express language of the CGL policy.

Standard CGL Policy Language

The standard CGL policy provides coverage for *bodily injury* and *property damage* which occurs during the policy period. Generally, the insurer's duty to indemnify the insured is triggered by a determination that bodily injury or property damage occurred during the policy period.

Prior to 1966, most CGL policies generally covered liability of an insured if it was caused by an "accident." The term "accident" was not defined in the policy. In 1966, standard CGL policy language was changed to substitute the word "occurrence" for "accident." Thus after 1966, standard CGL language generally read:

> The company will pay on behalf of the insured all sums which the insured shall become legally obligated to pay as damages because of bodily injury or property damage to which this insurance applied, caused by an occurrence, and the Company shall have the right and duty to defend any suit against the insured seeking damages on account of such bodily injury or property damage, even if any of the allegations of the suit are groundless, false or fraudulent. . . .

After 1973, the word "occurrence" was defined in the standard policy to mean "an accident, including continuous or repeated exposure to conditions which results in personal injury or property damage neither expected nor intended from the standpoint of the insured." In the mid-1970s, the CGL standard policy was further changed by the insertion of a standard "pollution exclusion" clause. This standard exclusion clause was used between the 1970s and mid-1980s. It was subsequently replaced by a clause which attempts to exclude *any* liability for pollution-related occurrences.

The standard "pollution exclusion" clause used by the insurance industry between the mid-1970s and mid-1980s read as follows:

> This policy does not apply to bodily injury or property damage arising out of the discharge, dispersal, release or escape of smoke, vapors, soot, fumes, acids, alkalines, toxic chemicals, liquids or gases, waste materials or other irritants, contaminants or pollutants into or upon land, the atmosphere or any water course or body of water, but this exclusion does not apply if such discharge, dispersal, release or escape is sudden and accidental.

Techniques of Contract Interpretation

Contract interpretation is a process by which a court determines the meaning of the language used by the parties in the contract. Courts are often required to interpret contract language. Words are vague in the sense that they rarely describe a "neatly bounded class," and contract language, like all language, may contain ambiguities. Contracts may be ambiguous because of inconsistent language within the contract itself or because the circumstances which occurred were outside the contemplation of the parties. As a result, courts are frequently called upon to give meaning to contract language within the context of a specific dispute.

Courts attempt to interpret language in light of the *intention* of the parties. Courts rely on the *express* language of the contract, or give effect to a term *implied* by the parties. In determining intention, a court may look at all the relevant circumstances surrounding the transaction. It may also rely on dictionary definitions under the theory that the parties should be bound by the common or "plain meaning" of the words they use. Courts also sometimes employ rules and legal maxims as an aid to contract interpretation. One rule of contract interpretation, especially important in insurer liability cases, is that in interpreting *standardized form contracts,* courts generally construe ambiguity of language *against* the drafter. This means that ambiguities in standardized CGL insurance contracts could be construed against the insurer. In addition, if language is reasonably susceptible to two interpretations, the interpretation which favors public interest is preferred.

CGL Policy Language

The meaning of particular words used in the standard CGL insurance contract has been the subject of much litigation. The meaning of words like "occurrence," "damages," and "sudden and accidental" in the standard pollution exclusion clause may ultimately determine insurer liability for environmental damages incurred by the insured. Insurer liability cases focus on several questions: For example, when does an event "occur" for purposes of the CGL policy? Does the term "damages" in standard policy language include environmental cleanup costs mandated under federal law, or is the term limited to money damages like those which may be recovered in a civil law tort action? Is an event "expected or intended" for purposes of the policy if the insured should have expected the event (as, for example, where toxic chemicals gradually leak from a site)? What is the meaning of "sudden and accidental" in the standard pollution exclusion?

Contract interpretation is generally a question of state law, and courts have reached different conclusions about the meaning of these words in standard CGL policy language. The meaning of the word "damages" has frequently been litigated by insured and insurers in environmental insurance cases, with some courts holding that the word "damages" does not include CERCLA cleanup costs, but a majority ruling that CERCLA costs can be covered as "damages" under CGL policy.

Most insurer liability cases involve CGL policies written before the mid-1980s, as most later policies contain absolute pollution liability exclusion clauses. An insurer may be liable under the terms of an earlier policy for events which occurred during the applicable policy period, even though the event, like leaking hazardous waste at a site, may not be discovered until later. In the following case, plaintiffs sued their liability insurer seeking costs of cleaning up groundwater and soil contaminated by paint sludge. The district court ruled in favor of the plaintiffs and the insurance company appealed. On appeal, the appellate court was required to interpret a pollution exclusion clause included in many standard liability insurance policies.

PATZ v. ST. PAUL FIRE & MARINE INS. CO.
15 F.3d 699 (7th Cir. 1994)

POSNER, Chief Judge.

St. Paul Fire & Marine Insurance Company appeals from a judgment in favor of its insureds (the Patz family and their corporation) rendered after a jury trial. The appeal requires us to interpret a pollution-exclusion clause found in many liability insurance policies. Federal jurisdiction is based on diversity of citizenship, and the substantive issues are governed by the law of Wisconsin.

In the northern Wisconsin town of Pound, the family Patz has a substantial although not sophisticated business of manufacturing farm equipment. Founded by a Patz whose formal education had ended in the third grade, the business is now managed by his three sons and one son-in-law, none of whom—as their counsel has emphasized to us—has a college education. No employees of the business are college-educated, either. In 1971, the Patzes decided that before selling the farm equipment they manufacture they would paint it. Two consulting firms, paid "alot of bucks" by the Patzes for their expertise in the paint business, not only set up a production line for painting the equipment but also advised the Patzes on how to dispose of the wastes generated as a by-product of the painting. One of these wastes is water contaminated by phosphate. The consultants suggested that the Patzes dig an open pit for the water. The idea, well accepted in the waste-disposal community at the time, was that the water would evaporate, leaving a deposit of phosphate solids that would rest at the bottom of the pit and could be easily removed and used as fertilizer. Because the soil where the pit was to be dug was highly compacted clay soil, the water was expected to evaporate before it could permeate the soil, and so the soil beneath the pit would not be contaminated. Another waste by-product of the painting process, paint sludge, the con-

sultant advised the Patzes to shovel into barrels which could be carted off to the town dump to be burned or buried there.

All this was done as recommended by the consultants until 1980, when Wisconsin's Department of Natural Resources [(the Department)] began nosing around the Patzes' operation. The Department advised the Patzes that although the barrels of sludge were not hazardous to the environment, the town dump was not licensed to receive them. The Department told them to remove the barrels, 27 in number, that the dump had not as yet either buried or burned. Rather than taking the barrels to a licensed dump, as the Department suggested but did not order, the Patzes took the barrels back to their property, buried them, and paved them over to make an extension of the factory's parking lot. As additional sludge accumulated, the Patzes burned it on their premises. Although the Department's focus was on the barrels, not the evaporation pit, the Patzes discontinued the use of the pit in 1980 and filled it in the following year.

The Patzes' homes are located on the same premises as their factory, and to the south of the pit and the parking lot. Water in the area runs from north to south.

In 1986 the Department returned and conducted an environmental audit which discovered groundwater contamination from the pit and soil contamination from the buried barrels, though in neither case had the contamination spread beyond the Patzes' premises. The Department ordered the removal of the barrels together with some of the soil beneath it, and the removal of a good deal of soil beneath the pit. It cost the Patzes $400,000 to clean up the two sites, and that is the amount they sought to recover from the insurance company.

St. Paul resisted on the basis of two clauses in the liability insurance policy. The first, the pollution-exclusion clause, excludes coverage for "bodily injury or property damage arising out of the discharge, dispersal, release or escape of smoke, vapors, soot, fumes, acids, alkalis, toxic chemicals, liquids or gases, waste materials or other irritants, contaminants, or pollutants into or upon land, the atmosphere, or any water course or body of water; but this exclusion does not apply if such discharge, dispersal, release or escape is sudden and accidental." St. Paul's position is that the deposit of the phosphate-contaminated water in the evaporation pit, and of the barrels of paint sludge in the ground beneath the parking lot, constituted a "discharge" of waste materials into the land. This discharge, though not the resulting contamination, was intentional, not accidental, and therefore does not come within the exclusion from the exclusion. The Patzes counter that all that is excluded from the exclusion is discharges by which the insured intends to cause damage, in this case damage in the form of pollution or contamination of soil and groundwater. . . .

***

At first and even second glance, the insurance company's interpretation of the pollution-exclusion clause has a great deal to recommend it. Excluded from coverage, on the most natural reading of the clause, are all discharges (etc.) of waste materials, except those that are sudden and accidental. Although it is exceedingly unlikely that the Patzes intended to foul their own nest by disposing of the paint wastes in the way they did, there was nothing sudden and accidental about the deposit of the phosphate-contaminated water in the evaporation pit or about the burying of the barrels of paint sludge to extend the parking lot. What is more, as enterprises in this day and age generally do not pollute intentionally, the pollution-exclusion clause would have a very limited domain if inter-

preted as excluding only deliberate pollution. And another clause in the insurance policy excludes intentional harms, making the pollution-exclusion clause redundant if interpreted as narrowly as the Patzes would like.

Yet there are cases that read the pollution-exclusion clause just that narrowly. We are drawn to an intermediate interpretation, in which the clause is read to distinguish between deliberately discharging waste materials into land, air, or water, whether or not "harm" is intended, and placing those materials in a container that is buried in land or water and subsequently leaks or breaks, discharging waste materials into the land or water surrounding the container. The distinction is easy to see with regard to the barrels of paint sludge. The Patzes might just have dumped the sludge on the ground; if so, whether or not they intended to pollute the land or even knew it might pollute the land, any liability resulting from this dumping would, on the interpretation we are exploring, have been excluded. That is not what they did. They put the sludge in barrels and buried them. As the barrels themselves were not contaminants, no discharge of contaminants into the soil occurred until the barrels leaked or broke. The discharge that occurred then—the discharge from the barrels—was "sudden and accidental" in the sense of unintended and unexpected, which is the meaning that Wisconsin's highest court impressed upon those words.

***

This reading of the pollution-exclusion clause, which distinguishes between an intentional act not intended to discharge wastes into the environment and an intentional such discharge, is not inevitable, but it is plausible, and it is consistent with a number (possibly the majority, though this is unclear) of the cases—signally including Wisconsin's highest court and therefore binding on us in this diversity suit. . . .

***

St. Paul's alternative ground is that the policy excludes coverage for property damage to property owned by the insured, and to date the only contamination from the waste materials generated by the painting operation is to soil and groundwater within the boundaries of the Patzes' own land. But the Patzes are not attempting to obtain an insurance award for a reduction in the value of, or other damage to, their land. How could they? It is a policy of liability insurance, not casualty insurance, on which they have sued. They seek to recover the cost of complying with a government order to clean up a nuisance. The fact that the cleanup occurred on their land is irrelevant. For all we know, the damage to the land was much less than the cost of cleaning it up.

[*The district court's decision in favor of the insured must therefore be AFFIRMED.*]

Questions and Comments for Discussion

1.   The insurance industry is built on risk assessment. Until insurers can better identify and predict their potential liability for environmental damages under CGL policies, it is likely that insurer/insured litigation will continue in environmental contamination cases. Costs of insurance premiums will rise as a result. The industry may refuse to insure any potential environmental liability, with the result that environmentally risky businesses will be more expensive, or in some cases eliminated.

On the other hand, holding insurers liable under the terms of CGL policies may further public policy goals by providing more funds for cleanup costs. And holding insurers liable provides a powerful incentive for insurers to monitor the activities of their insured. Higher premiums also may provide a disincentive for insured industries to pollute. Should these public policy concerns be a factor in the courts' interpretation of standard CGL policy language in these cases?

2.   The insurance industry has proposed changes in the Superfund program. The American International Group (AIG), for example, suggests replacing the retroactive liability system for old sites with a national environmental trust fund (NETF). The NETF would be financed across all economic sectors without regard to site-specific liability and used to finance the cleanup of old Superfund sites. The Superfund liability system would not be abolished for present and future waste sites. This proposal will surely become part of the Superfund reauthorization debate. What are the advantages of a "no fault" system for cleaning up old contaminated sites? What are the disadvantages of such a proposal?

SUMMARY AND CONCLUSION

This chapter has focused on some important issues of liability in environmental cases. Many liability issues arise in contracts for the sale or lease of real property where the property subsequently turns out to be contaminated with toxic or hazardous materials. In these cases, contractual devices such as disclaimer clauses, warranties, and indemnification agreements may determine the liability of the parties for cleanup costs mandated by federal and state governments.

Changing concepts of contract law in society have led courts to abandon traditional notions of **caveat emptor** in favor of *caveat venditor* in the sale and lease of residential property. Under this changing policy, courts have recognized implied warranties of habitability in the sale and lease of residential property. A landlord or seller also may be liable to a purchaser for failing to disclose an environmental liability on the property or for negligently or innocently misrepresenting the environmental condition of the property. Breach of environmental laws like lead-abatement laws may be the basis for tort liability of a landlord or a seller under the theory of *negligence per se*.

In product liability cases–actions to recover damages for injuries to person or property caused by a defective product–plaintiffs may employ contract law and tort law, including negligence law and principles of strict liability. Product liability law is important in environmental cases where consumers or employees sue the seller or manufacturer of products which contain toxic or hazardous materials, for example, insecticides or pesticides.

This chapter also addressed disputes about insurer liability for environmental damage or cleanup costs under the terms of a standard comprehensive general liability insurance policy. Insurer liability cases not only provide a good example of the court's responsibility for interpreting and applying specific contract language in an environmental cleanup dispute, they also exemplify the court's application of public policy principles in contract interpretation cases involving environmental damages.

GLOSSARY

As is—Contract provision which implies that a buyer is taking delivery of goods or property which may be defective and that he is purchasing the property upon the express condition that he must trust to his own examination.

Caveat emptor—Traditional doctrine "let the buyer beware."

Caveat venditor—More modern doctrine "let the seller beware."

CGL insurance policy—Comprehensive general liability policy.

Consideration—Something of legal value given in exchange for an act or a promise.

Contract—A legally enforceable promise.

Covenant—Contract promise or agreement.

Damages—Compensation in money for a loss or damage.

Disclaimer—Contract provision whereby one party denies responsibility for certain events or occurrences.

Implied warranty of habitability—Warranty implied in law that a new structure will be habitable and fit for occupation.

Implied warranty of merchantability—Warranty imposed by law in contracts for the sale of goods that the goods are "merchantable."

Incidental beneficiary—Third party who does not acquire the right to enforce a contract because the contract was not designed to benefit the third party even though benefit to the third party is a by-product of the contract.

Indemnification agreement—An agreement by which one person promises to reimburse another person, or hold him harmless, for loss of damage.

Product liability—Theories used in cases where plaintiffs seek to recover damages for personal injury or property damage as a result of a defective product.

Right of termination—Express contractual provision giving a party the right to cancel a contract upon the occurrence of some event.

Specific performance—Performance of a contract compelled by the court.

Statute of limitations—Statute which prescribes time limits on the right to bring certain legal actions.

Strict liability—Product liability theory which holds the manufacturer of a defective product liable for physical harm or property damage suffered by the purchaser even though the seller exercised all reasonable care in the preparation and sale of the product.

Unconscionable contract—A contract or contract term which is procedurally and substantively unfair; a contract which "no man in his senses would make and no fair and honest man would accept."

Warranty—A contractual promise that a fact is true.

CASES FOR DISCUSSION

1.   Hazardous materials were discharged into the environment during a tenant's lease of an industrial site. In determining whether the tenant may be liable as an operator of the site under CERCLA, is the government required to prove that the tenant was responsible for the contamination at the site, or may the tenant be liable for cleanup costs if the tenant merely had authority to control the facility, including parts of the facility that it did not lease? *Northwestern Mut. Life Ins. Co. v. Atlantic Research Corp,* 847 F.Supp. 389 (E.D. Va. 1994).

2.   Does a developer-seller of residential housing and its broker have a duty to disclose to potential buyers the existence of a nearby closed landfill, which was known or should have been known to the seller and/or its broker? *Strawn v. Canuso,* 638 A.2d 141 (N.J. Super. A.D. 1994).

3.   The state of New York and town of Vestal brought suit to abate a nuisance allegedly caused by contamination of the soil and groundwater under premises owned by defendant. The state charged that defendant's tenant handled and stored dangerous chemicals on the site which seeped into the public water supply. Defendant moved to dismiss, claiming that absence of affirmative misconduct on its part relieved it of any potential liability. Can the landlord be liable for negligence in the selection of a tenant, and for the wrongdoing of the tenant when the landlord continues to exercise control over the premises? *State v. Monarch Chemicals, Inc.,* 456 N.Y.S.2d 867 (A.D. 1982).

4.   Does the seller of a trucking company have to indemnify the buyer for its potential liability under CERCLA arising out of dioxin contamination of the trucking company's terminal? The indemnity clause of the sales contract provided that the seller would indemnify the buyer for all liabilities, damages, and claims arising out of any misrepresentation or breach of the agreement. The agreement also required the buyer to assert its claims for indemnity within three years of the closing date. The contamination was discovered within three years after the sale, but the EPA did not classify the terminal as a confirmed dioxin site until after the three-year limit. *Jones v. Sun Carriers, Inc.,* 856 F.2d 1091 (8th Cir. 1988).

5.   A purchaser of a hazardous waste site sued the seller for contribution for cleanup costs incurred by the purchaser. The seller filed an action seeking a determination whether it was contractually obligated to indemnify the purchaser under the terms of the sales contract.

Can an indemnity and release provision in a sales agreement executed *before* the enactment of CERCLA encompass liability for CERCLA-incurred costs? *Olin Corp. v. Consolidated Aluminum Corp.*, 5 F.3d 10 (2d Cir. 1993).

6.   A sale of assets agreement provided that claims would be determined by arbitration under the Commercial Arbitration Rules of the American Arbitration Association. Can claims concerning Superfund liability at an industrial site be arbitrated along with other common law claims under the sales agreement for the site? *Disston Co. v. Sandvik, Inc.*, 750 F.Supp. 745 (W.D. Va. 1990).

ENDNOTES

1. *Insurers Spending Hundreds of Millions, But Most Goes for Legal Fees, Not Cleanups*, 23 Envtl. L. Rep. (Envtl. L. Inst.) No. 1, at 9 (May 1, 1992).

2. Restatement (Second) of Contracts Section 1 (1981).

3. Author's note: A third party complaint is one filed by a defendant against a third party.

4. Author's note: Reimbursement for costs or damages incurred.

5. CERCLA, 42 U.S.C. §9601(35)(A). See discussion of this defense in Chapter 13.

6. Under the UCC, "goods" are defined as "tangible, moveable personal property." UCC Section 2-105.

7. 42 U.S.C. Section 9607(e) (1980).

8. Author's note: Under the remedy of specific performance, the defendant is ordered to perform the contract according to its terms.

9. *Borel v. Fibreboard Paper Prod. Corp.*, 493 F.2d 1076 (5th Cir. Tex. 1973).

6

LAND USE REGULATION AND REGULATORY TAKINGS

INTRODUCTION

Local and regional land use regulations such as local zoning laws often have an impact on the environment. This chapter examines land use regulations and some of the legal issues that may arise in controlling land use to protect the environment.

Land use restrictions have prohibited construction and development in environmentally sensitive areas like beachfronts, mountainsides, and flood plains. Owners and developers argue that the regulations are beyond the scope of the government's police power, that the regulations deprive the owner of all economic use of his property and thus constitute a "taking" of his property, or that the regulation was imposed by a procedurally flawed process.

ZONING

The term **zoning** describes local and regional regulations which control the use of land within a particular jurisdiction. Zoning laws usually take the form of ordinances, that is, laws passed by local governments like a city, town, or county. Zoning ordinances generally divide a community into different districts or zones, and designate types of structures and activities which may be permitted or prohibited in certain zones according to this classification. Zoning regulations also address such matters as building height, landscaping, set-back requirements, and types of construction permitted within a particular zone. Some communities also address aesthetic issues, such as building exteriors, in the zoning code.

Zoning is a principal tool of urban planning. Soon after the first comprehensive zoning ordinance in the United States was adopted in 1916 by New York City, it was attacked in the courts under the theory that it encroached on constitutionally protected property rights. In 1926, the U.S. Supreme Court upheld comprehensive zoning in *Euclid v. Ambler Realty Co.*[1] In that case, the Supreme Court recognized that the zoning process is a permissible exercise of the government's police power and that a decrease in land value as a result of zoning legislation does not necessarily constitute a taking of property requiring compensation under the Fifth and Fourteenth Amendments of the Constitution. The *Euclid* landmark case upheld the basic validity of comprehensive zoning ordinances. After *Euclid,* a validly enacted ordinance may still be unconstitutional as applied to a particular tract of land, but this determination is made on a case-by-case basis.

Authority to Zone Under Police Power

Euclid v. Amber Realty Co. established the principle that regulating the use of property is valid and will be upheld so long as the regulation is justified under the government's *police power.* Police power is generally defined as the power to legislate for the health, morals, safety, and welfare of the community. The power of the government to protect the public health, safety, and welfare is found in the U.S. and state constitutions, and is generally construed very broadly by the courts. But a land use regulation which bears no rational relationship to the police power to protect general public health, safety, and welfare will be held unconstitutional and unenforceable.

In the following case, plaintiffs wanted to operate a landfill on a site in West Virginia's panhandle country near North Mountain. Geo-Tech Reclamation Industries (GRI) had obtained an option to purchase a 331-acre site and subsequently filed an application for a landfill operating permit. Its application was denied by the director of the Department of Natural Resources on the ground that the proposed landfill had engendered "adverse public sentiment." A second plaintiff, LCS, acquired an option to purchase the site in 1987, and its application to operate a solid waste disposal facility was also rejected. The West Virginia Water Resources Board affirmed the director's decision on the basis of adverse public sentiment. Plaintiffs brought a declaratory judgment challenging the constitutionality of the state statute, arguing that it violated due process by impermissibly delegating legislative authority to local citizens and that the statute exceeded the state's police power. The district court found the statute unconstitutional, and the state appealed.

GEO-TECH RECLAMATION INDUSTRIES, INC. v. HAMRICK

886 F.2d 662 (4th Cir. 1989)

ERVIN, C.J.:

In this consolidated appeal, several West Virginia state environmental officials (collectively "West Virginia") and an organization known as "Citizens to Fight North Mountain Waste Site" appeal from determinations on summary judgment that a provision of West Virginia's Solid Waste Management Act is facially unconstitutional. Because we find that the statutory language in question bears no rational rela-

tion "to the public health, safety, morals or general welfare," we must affirm the decision below.

I.

West Virginia, like many other states, has enacted a statutory scheme governing solid waste disposal. . . . The Act flatly prohibits the operation of open dumps and requires landfill operators to obtain a permit from the Department before construction, operating, or abandoning any solid waste disposal facility.... Among the various reasons for which a permit may be denied,

> the director may deny the issuance of a permit on the basis of information in the application or from other sources including public comment, if the solid waste facility may cause adverse impacts on the natural resources and environmental concerns under the director's purview in chapter twenty of the Code, destruction of aesthetic values, destruction or endangerment of the property of others or is significantly adverse to the public sentiment of the area where the solid waste facility is or will be located.

It is the final clause of this section—giving the Director authority to deny a permit solely because it is "significantly adverse to the public sentiment"—which is at issue in this case.

***

We see no reasons to decide whether [the statute] works an impermissible delegation of power to local residents because the statute suffers from a more profound constitutional infirmity. It is well settled that land-use regulations "must find their justification in some aspect of the police power, asserted for the public welfare." *Euclid v. Ambler Realty Co.,* 272 U.S. 365 (1926). West Virginia strenuously argues that it acts well within the broad confines of its police power in regulating the development of solid waste disposal facilities. With this we certainly agree. No one would question the state's power to impose a broad array of restrictions on an activity, such as the operation of a landfill, which was recognized as a nuisance even by the early common law.

West Virginia also argues that within this broad array of restrictions, the state may legislate to protect its communities against not only such tangible effects as increased traffic, noise, odors, and health concerns, but also against the possibility of decreased community pride and fracturing of community spirit that may accompany large waste disposal operations. Here again, we do not quarrel with the state's position. "The concept of the public welfare is broad and inclusive. The values represented are spiritual as well as physical, aesthetic as well as monetary." (Citations omitted.) West Virginia may undoubtedly regulate the siting and operation of solid waste disposal facilities so as to eliminate or at least alleviate the deleterious effects of such facilities on more inchoate community values.

The question raised in this case, however, is whether sec. 20-5F-4(b) does in fact further this laudable purpose or whether it is instead "arbitrary and capricious, having no substantial relation" to its purported goal. The state argues that the statute's adverse public sentiment clause promotes its stated purpose by allowing citizens to comment upon a proposed landfill's impact on community pride, spirit, and quality of life. But, with commendable candor, the state also recognizes that many who may speak out against a landfill will do so because of self-interest, bias, or ignorance. These are but a few of the less than noble motivations commonly referred to as the "Not-in-My Backyard" syndrome....

"Where property interests are adversely affected by zoning, the courts generally have emphasized the breadth of municipal power to control land use and have sustained the regulation if it is rationally related to legitimate state concerns.... But an ordinance may fail even under that limited standard of review." Nothing in the record suggests, nor can we conceive, how unreflective and unseasoned public sentiment that "a dump is still a dump" is in any way rationally related to the otherwise legitimate goal of protecting community spirit and pride.

***

[W]e find that sec.20-5F-4(b)'s clause authorizing the director to reject permits that are "significantly adverse to the public sentiment" bears no substantial or rational relationship to the state's interest in promoting the general public welfare. The district court's decision is therefore AFFIRMED.

Establishing Planning Authority

Zoning involves the legitimate exercise of the government's police power to regulate land use. A plan for development is a first step in the zoning process. The municipality first undertakes a study of the area to be regulated to project future growth and public needs. This study results in the adoption of a **master plan,** a planning "constitution" in the sense that zoning ordinances and rezoning decisions must conform to it. The local government's authority to adopt a master plan derives from state laws. In adopting its master plan and local zoning ordinance, the municipality must comply with these state zoning enabling statutes based in most cases on a *standard state zoning enabling act.* The following case illustrates the importance of a properly adopted master plan.

TRIPLE G LANDFILLS, INC. v. BOARD OF COMMISSIONERS OF FOUNTAIN COUNTY, INDIANA
977 F.2d 287 (7th Cir. 1992)

FLAUM, Circuit Judge.

In July 1989, Triple G Landfills, Inc. (Triple G) acquired an option to purchase a 189-acre tract in Fountain County, Indiana, on which it hoped to build a sanitary landfill. Subsequently geological tests and engineering work performed by Triple G, at a cost of approximately $175,000, confirmed that the site was suitable for use as a landfill. Local residents soon caught wind of Triple G's plans and, as is often the case, were less than thrilled. On July 31, the Fountain County Board of Commissioners (Board) convened a special meeting to address the issue, and over the next six months enacted a series of measures designed to restrict landfill construction in the county. The final measure, an ordinance, is the subject of this case.

For a number of years, the State of Indiana has required prospective landfill operators to submit a permit application to the Indiana Department of Environmental Management (IDEM), the state agency charged with regulating the siting, design, operation and closure of sanitary landfills. The ordinance adds a second layer of regulations, at the county level, requiring prospective operators who have already obtained a state permit to submit another permit application to the county, and forbidding the construction or operation of landfills without a county permit. The siting standards imposed under the ordinance are far more stringent than those imposed by the State, and here effectively preclude Triple G from developing its tract—or any other tract in the County, for that matter—as a landfill.

Triple G brought suit, seeking a declaration that the ordinance was invalid under the federal constitution and state law, and a permanent injunction against its enforcement. The district court overruled the County's motion to dismiss and subsequently granted summary judgment to Triple G, resting its decision entirely on state law. The County appeals both decisions, and we affirm.

***

[W]e deem it necessary to address only one (issue.) Indiana law prohibits local governmental bodies from enacting zoning ordinances in the absence of a comprehensive zoning plan. Ind. Code sec. 36-7-4-601(a). The parties stipulate that the county has not enacted a comprehensive plan, and that the ordinance is invalid if classified as a zoning ordinance. Hence, the only issue remaining is whether the ordinance is a zoning ordinance under Indiana law. The district court held that it was, and we review that decision *de novo*. . . .[2]

We limit our attention to two matters. The first regards the County's contention that the ordinance is not a zoning ordinance because it does not partition the county into two or more distinct districts. While it is true that in some states there is no such thing as a single-district zoning ordinance, that is not the case in Indiana. The state enabling statute authorizes zoning bodies "having jurisdiction over the geographic area described in the zoning ordinance [to] establish *one (1) or more* districts, which may be for agricultural, commercial, industrial, residential, special or unrestricted uses." Accordingly, Indiana law clearly recognizes that an ordinance can be a zoning ordinance even if it creates only a single district. . . .

The County contends that its ordinance . . . does not impose a *moratorium* upon landfill construction, but merely establishes a *regulatory regime* governing landfill permitting and operations. As we discussed above, however, the ordinance has the practical effect of foreclosing all landfill development in Fountain County; any alleged distinction between it and a formal moratorium is illusory. . . .

We conclude that the ordinance is a zoning ordinance, and therefore, due to the absence of a comprehensive zoning plan in Fountain County, is invalid under Indiana law.

AFFIRMED.

Regulating Land Use under the Zoning Code

Once the government entity has adopted a master plan and an **official map** detailing existing and planned streets, sewers, water lines, parks, etc., the governmental body adopts ordinances establishing various districts and providing for rules and regulations to enforce the code. Zoning is generally categorized as residential, commercial, industrial, or agricultural. The Standard State Zoning Enabling Act provides that the local government may establish an administrative board that can make exceptions to the zoning regulations in particular areas, so long as those exceptions are in keeping with the master plan. These exceptions are called **variances.**

Exceptions from Zoning Regulations

An application for a variance requires that the petitioner show (1) he would suffer an undue hardship if the ordinance is enforced, and (2) that the granting of the variance will not be excessively disruptive of the surrounding land or the master plan. A *special permit,* may grant an exception to the zoning code provided certain requirements are met. The decision to grant a variance or special permit rests with the administrative board, such as a *Board of Zoning Appeals.* Denial of a variance or special permit may be challenged on the grounds that the decision was arbitrary, procedurally flawed, or amounted to an unconstitutional taking of property without just compensation.

A **nonconforming use** is an activity or structure on the property that is prohibited by a zoning ordinance passed *after* the use existed. These uses are generally immune from new zoning ordinances. However, the nonconforming activity or structure cannot be expanded, and may be lost if the activity is abandoned or the building is destroyed. Courts have also declared some nonconforming uses to be *nuisances,* and have eliminated them under that theory. For example, a nonconforming use landfill in a residential area might be enjoined as a nuisance under this theory.

In the following case, the operator of an asphalt company brought action against the city to determine whether its property was a valid nonconforming use. The Land Court Department held that it was, and the city appealed.

DERBY REFINING COMPANY v. CITY OF CHELSEA
555 N.E.2d 534 (Mass. 1990)

GREANY, J.

The question in this case is whether Belcher New England, Inc. (Belcher), may operate a liquid asphalt storage facility on waterfront property at 99 Marginal Street in Chelsea. Belcher maintains that its use of the property is protected as a prior nonconforming use, from the application of a new Chelsea zoning ordinance which purports to prohibit the use. . . . We conclude, as did the Land Court, that the use is protected. Consequently, we need not address the arguments pertaining to the validity of the new zoning ordinance. . . .

The property lies on the bank of the Chelsea Creek in Chelsea, in a highly industrialized neighborhood formerly designated as an industrial waterfront district. . . . "[T]he district is generally old and unattractive and is composed largely of oil tank farms, warehouses, junkyards, and a shipyard. Abutting the district is an industrial district which contains a junkyard, a truck sales office, a fruit and produce warehouse, and land owned by the Quincy and Sun Oil Companies. The banks of the creek in East Boston across from the site are lined with oil tank farms and a salvage yard. . . .

Sometime around 1960, Texaco constructed a petroleum storage facility on the property by installing seven large storage tanks, a dock, "breasting dolphins," and a truck-loading ramp. . . . The facility also includes two brick buildings, which housed Texaco's offices, warehouses, and physical plant, and a separate garage to house and service delivery trucks.

Texaco continued to operate the petroleum storage facility on the property until 1983, when, in response to a change in economic conditions in the industry, it proceeded to "mothball" the Marginal Street facility. . . . The business office was closed, and its contents removed. However, Texaco continued to heat the building, and hired a security firm to check the premises.

After "mothballing" the property, Texaco tried to sell it. . . . After one proposed sale fell through, Texaco succeeded in selling the facility to Derby Refining Company (Derby) on January 15, 1986. On that same date, Derby leased the facility to Belcher. The Chelsea zoning ordinance in effect when Derby took title to the premises from Texaco provided for an industrial waterfront district. Permitted uses in this district included "oil and gas tank farms including distributive facilities." The use of the property as a petroleum storage facility was thus a conforming use at the time of Derby's acquisition of the property.

Belcher . . . ultimately decided to operate a liquid asphalt storage facility on the premises. . . . On March 14, 1986, after Derby had purchased the property but before

Belcher had begun work to prepare it for asphalt storage, notice appeared in the Chelsea *Record,* a newspaper of general circulation in Chelsea, of a public hearing to be held on proposed amendments to the zoning ordinance. The new zoning ordinance passed pursuant to that notice radically changed the permitted uses in the new waterfront district which was no longer zoned as an *industrial* waterfront district. . . . Belcher's intended use of the property as an asphalt storage facility was rendered a nonconforming use by this new zoning ordinance.

***

Under Massachusetts law, the right to continue a non-conforming use is not confined to the existing user, but runs with the land. However, that right can be lost if a predecessor in title has abandoned the use. . . . To constitute an abandonment, the discontinuance of a nonconforming use must result from "the concurrence of two factors: (1) the intent to abandon and (2) voluntary conduct, whether affirmative or negative, which carries the implication of abandonment."

Mere nonuse or sale of property does not, by itself, constitute an abandonment. . . . The fact that Texaco "mothballed" the facility constitutes evidence of nonuse, but is not enough by itself to require a finding of abandonment. We agree with the judge that the reasonable inference to be drawn from the manner in which Texaco shut down the facility is precisely the opposite of abandonment—that Texaco intended to preserve the facility in good condition for a profitable resale. . . .

Chelsea next argues that the asphalt storage facility was not lawfully in existence at the time of the change to the zoning ordinance because Belcher at that time did not have a letter of intent to operate its facility on file with the Coast Guard. A valid nonconforming use is not rendered unlawful by failure to possess requisite government approval, provided that such approval can be easily obtained. . . .

To be protected as a preexisting, nonconforming use, Belcher's use of the property must not constitute a "change or substantial extension" of Texaco's previous use. . . . We agree with the judge that Belcher's current use "is nearly identical in nature to that of Texaco: bulk deliveries by ocean-going vessels, bulk tank storage and wholesale distribution. . . . Chelsea argues that the character of the storage activities occurring on the property has changed due to the fact that liquid asphalt must be kept heated. We [have] held that "a valid nonconforming use does not lose that status merely because it is improved and made more efficient," provided, however, that the changes are "ordinarily and reasonably adapted to the original use and do not constitute a change in the original nature and purpose of the undertaking." Having concluded above that the original use of the property as a tank farm for petroleum products has not changed, we ask whether the modifications cited by Chelsea are "ordinarily and reasonably adapted" to that use. We conclude that they are.

***

JUDGMENT AFFIRMED.

Subdivision Regulations

A **subdivision** is a parcel of land that has been divided into two or more units. A **planned unit development** (PUD) is a development project which permits mixed uses or different types of housing within the same development. The developer needs local planning board approval of the subdivision or PUD at the beginning of the project, which usually contains on-site plans for streets, sidewalks, and sewers.

Deteriorating public infrastructure and explosive suburban growth have created tremendous fiscal problems for cities. Local governments must continue to maintain existing streets, water and sewage facilities, parks, and schools, and must provide for expanding development. Taxpayers expect the municipality to provide these services, yet they resist property tax increases to fund these projects. For this reason, many municipalities rely on municipal **exactions** to fund off-site capital improvements and services. An exaction is a traditional construction, dedication, or in-lieu fee payment for site-specific needs such as streets, sidewalks, and drainage.

STATE CONTROLS OF LAND DEVELOPMENT

Historically, land use regulation has been a matter of local control. However, the environmental implications of land development are not limited to one small jurisdictional unit. As a result, regional, state, and federal agencies are more involved in the approval of environmentally sensitive projects. Some states have adopted acts establishing environmental commissions. In Maine, commercial or industrial developments in excess of twenty acres must be approved by an environmental improvement commission. In Washington, a developer must meet the requirements of the state environmental act in addition to local zoning requirements.[3]

Some states, like Minnesota, have provided for regional development commissions, and intrastate regional planning occurs in some large metropolitan areas. Interstate agreements, like the Lake Tahoe Regional Planning Compact, are undertaken to address environmental concerns for an entire region touching more than one state. The constitutional validity of these agreements may be tested in court under a variety of theories, including a "takings" argument, equal protection argument, due process, and separation of powers. Despite the fact that there is a trend toward regional or state planning, however, most planning and land use controls are still essentially local matters.

WETLANDS REGULATIONS

An example of federal regulation of land use is wetlands protection under the federal Clean Water Act. A developer is required to obtain a permit to dredge and fill wetlands governed by the act.

Wetlands is a general term which describes a variety of ecosystems. It may include marshes, fens, bogs, wet meadows, and swamps. Because wetlands are transitional zones between water and dry land, they are unique habitats for a variety of fish and wildlife. Under regulation of the EPA, wetlands are

> those areas that are inundated or saturated by surface or ground water a frequency and duration sufficient to support, and under normal circumstances do support, a prevalence of vegetation typically adapted for life in saturated soil conditions.

In the past, wetlands were often considered nuisances because they were sources of insects and unpleasant odors. People drained and converted wetlands to farm land, or filled them to support residential and industrial development. As a result, more than half of

America's original wetlands have been destroyed. Increased understanding of the importance of wetlands to ecological processes has led to protection of wetlands. The Environmental Protection Agency is responsible for restoring and maintaining the integrity of the nation's waters.

Section 404 of the Clean Water Act establishes a permit program which regulates the discharge of dredged or fill materials into waters of the United States, including most wetlands. The U.S. Fish and Wildlife Service and National Marine Fisheries Service have important advisory roles in the permit review process, which is jointly administered by the U.S. Army Corps of Engineers and the EPA.

Under Section 404, any individual, company, corporation, or government entity planning construction or fill activities in wetlands must first obtain a permit from the Corps. These activities include:

- place of fill (rock, soil, or sand) necessary for the construction of structures or impoundments;
- site development fills;
- fills for causeways, roads, dams, dikes, etc.;
- fills for construction of ponds, intake or outlet pipes.

Some have called federal regulation of wetlands "national zoning."[4] The permit requirements of the Clean Water Act may delay, and in some cases halt, development of private property. Projects for the construction of refineries, highways, and shopping centers have been halted by the act. Jurisdiction has also been expanded from coastal and riparian waters to inland isolated areas.

No Net Loss Policy

In 1977 amendments to the Clean Water Act, Congress authorized the states to establish a permit program for dredge and fill activities in non-navigable waters. The amendments also authorized the Corps of Engineers (or the state with an approved program) to issue "general" permits for certain activities which have minimal adverse affects. The general permit program is designed to reduce the regulatory burden for activities involving incidental dredge or fill work. Section 404(f) provides for exemptions from the regulation if the operator avoids specific effects on navigable waters.

In 1989, the Corps and EPA signed a Memorandum of Agreement (MOA) endorsing a "no net loss" policy for the nation's wetlands. Under the memorandum, the Corps is to avoid adverse impacts in permit decisions whenever possible and is required to choose the least environmentally damaging alternative. Off-site mitigation is to be used as a last resort. In November 1992, the oil industry obtained a clarification that the policy does not apply to wetlands in Alaska. Under the MOA, the EPA and the Corps are developing guidelines for establishing and operating a wetlands mitigation bank.

Mitigation policy under the MOA endorses a national goal of no overall net loss of the nation's remaining wetlands base. In most cases, a minimum of one-to-one acreage replacement of wetlands is required to achieve this goal. The concept of "mitigation banking" is a controversial one, and likely to be the focus of some debate during future reauthorization hearings on the Clean Water Act.

State Wetlands Protection

State and local laws also protect wetlands. For example, in Indiana, the U.S. Army Corps of Engineers, the EPA, the Indiana Department of Environmental Management (IDEM), and the Indiana Department of Natural Resources (IDNR) all regulate wetlands and administer various permit programs.

The Indiana Water Pollution Control Law gives IDEM the authority to protect wetlands. The Federal Clean Water Act also authorizes the IDEM's water quality certification program. The state agency thus reviews all the Corps' dredge and fill applications to ensure that the proposed activities will not adversely affect water quality. The Corps cannot grant a Section 404 dredge and fill permit without first obtaining a water quality certification or wavier from IDEM.

The Indiana Flood Control Act requires a permit from the IDNR in order to construct within the floodway of a river or stream and adjacent wetlands.

Finally, the Indiana Preservation of Lakes Statute requires a lake permit from IDNR when construction activities are likely to occur in or immediately adjacent to a freshwater lake.

The permits necessary to undertake development in a wetlands depend on the work planned and on both state and federal laws and regulations. The applicant has the responsibility to obtain all necessary permits. Appropriate agencies review and evaluate applications and consider whether the project poses hazards to life and property; whether the project will result in unreasonable, detrimental effects on fish and wildlife, botanical resources, and the natural beauty of the area; and whether the project will adversely affect water quality.

Flood Plain Regulation

The average annual costs of floods in the United States has risen dramatically, in part a result of the increasing number of dwelling units that are located in flood hazard areas. Problems of flooding are addressed through regulation by a municipality and state and federal governments. Comprehensive land use zoning by municipalities is designed to help ensure proper use of land within the entire community. The problem is defining "community." Each unit of local government can plan and zone only for its own territory. Most local governments have been slow to address problems of flood plain management, as flooding was not generally perceived as a land use problem, and because the size and shape of local governments often bear little relation to watercourses except when used as political boundaries.

In some states, *Regional Special Districts* have been created to enforce regional flood plain regulations. Such districts are a class of substate governmental units. They are created by the state legislature and generally possess the right to sue and be sued, to own property, and enter into contracts. Their functions are limited to responsibilities defined by state law.

Flood plain regulation may dramatically limit the development of property. For this reason, such regulations are sometimes challenged as an unconstitutional "taking" of property, a topic discussed in following sections.

STANDARDS OF REVIEW

The government is required to apply zoning and other land use regulations in a fair and nondiscriminatory manner. At a minimum, *due process* requires that a property owner be given notice of action affecting his property, that the owner have an opportunity to be heard at the hearing, and that the decision be a rational one based on the evidence. However, courts do not re-weigh the evidence on appeal. If there is *substantial evidence* to support the agency's decision, the court will defer to the agency's determination on appeal.

IN RE QUECHEE LAKES CORP.
580 A.2d 957 (Vt. 1990)

ALLEN, Chief Justice.

Quechee Lakes Corporation appeals from an Environmental Board decision requiring substantial modifications in its already-constructed Ridge condominium project. We affirm.

In 1981, Quechee Lakes Corporation (Quechee) obtained a land-use permit to build a twenty-eight unit condominium project on a high ridge overlooking the Quechee valley. During the course of construction, a number of revisions to the architectural plans were made without additional permit procedures. The external changes included the addition of skylights, the enlargement of sliding glass doors, the addition of clerestory and other windows, a fourteen-foot increase in the depth of three of the six buildings, the addition of four-foot overhangs and wraparound decks, a reduction of roof pitches, and the relocation of some buildings.

Only after construction had been completed did Quechee file an application for an amended land use permit, seeking to bring its original permit into conformity with the project as built. By this time, most of the condominium units had been sold.

The District Environmental Commission held hearings on the alterations and approved them in many respects. Certain of the changes were found to be objectionable, however, and the Commission conditioned the amended permit on four mitigating actions: the removal of the skylights, the installation of nonglare glass, the addition of tree plantings, and the installation of a barrier on the access road.

Quechee appealed to the Environmental Board, objecting only to the skylight removal condition and the Commission's denial of its motion for reconsideration. . . . After a *de novo* hearing and two site visits, the Board found that the condominium buildings are "one of the most visually prominent features in the valley." The Board found further that, taking the skylights and additional glazing together, approximately two-thirds more glass was visible than was approved under the original plans; that light from the windows and skylights is visible from many points in the valley at night; and that reflective glare from these sources results in a significant visual impact even during cloudy days. The Board also found that some of the other construction changes increased the perceived mass of the project. . . .

***

Quechee asks this Court to disregard the evidence produced through its own witnesses and from the Board's site visits and instead to focus upon the evidence actually introduced by the parties opposing the application. Quechee argues that this latter evidence, taken alone, was insufficient to establish that the project would have an adverse aesthetic impact. Since [the statute] places the Burden of Proof on the parties opposed to the permit where aesthetic impact is at issue, Quechee contends that the Board erred in concluding that the project would have such an impact. . . .

Where the sufficiency of the evidence is questioned on appeal from a decision of the Board, this Court employs a deferential standard of review. The legislature has mandated that "the findings of the board with respect to questions of fact, if supported by substantial evidence on the record as a whole, shall be conclusive. This Court has defined "substantial evidence" to mean "such relevant evidence as a reasonable mind might accept as adequate to support a conclusion." After reviewing the record as a whole, we conclude that the Board's findings and conclusions are supported by substantial evidence. . . .

Where a conflict in the evidence develops, its resolution falls within the Board's jurisdiction, for the Board is the proper trier of fact. The trier of fact has the right to believe all of the testimony of any witness, or to believe it in part and disbelieve it in part, or to reject it altogether. Thus, it is not for this Court to reweigh conflicting evidence, reassess the credibility or weight to be given certain testimony, or determine on its own whether the factual decision is mistaken. Instead, our focus is upon the evidence supporting the Board's findings and the question whether that evidence is adequate. . . .

[*Judgment affirmed.*]

Questions and Comments for Discussion

1. In *In Re Quechee,* the developer argued that the board erred in making two site visits to the Quechee Valley during the course of the proceedings, and that its findings of fact and conclusions of law were based in part on observations made during these visits. The developer argued that the board's personal observations are not evidence and that, in any event, the board failed to put the observations on the record. The court disagreed. This was a question of first impression in Vermont. What are the arguments in favor of permitting site visits? What are some arguments against permitting this kind of evidence in administrative hearings?

2. This case may also be viewed as an example of "aesthetic zoning." What are the public policy reasons supporting a board's authority to regulate as in this case? Describe a case where aesthetic issues also have economic implications for the developer and the community.

CONSTITUTIONAL ISSUES IN LAND USE REGULATION

Zoning and Discrimination

Zoning ordinances are by definition discriminatory because they create distinctions based on classifications. A zoning ordinance may specify that certain uses require a minimum area, such as a one-acre lot in certain residential zones. Courts have looked to factors such as minimizing overcrowding, reducing the burden on public facilities like schools and water and sewer systems, and preserving the rural character of the area to support such classifications. If, however, there is no relationship between the area requirements and a reasonable exercise of the police power, a court will find that the zoning is exclusionary and serves only private interests.

A difficult legal issue arises in cases where a zoning ordinance excludes certain kinds of uses altogether, such as commercial and industrial uses. Some courts have upheld such ordinances, but others have held that the local government unit must provide adequately for all types of uses within its confines. In Pennsylvania, the courts have taken the position that a township may not refuse to permit waste disposal facilities and quarrying operations altogether.[5]

An owner may also challenge a zoning ordinance on the grounds that the zoning ordinance was discriminatory as applied to that particular owner. In *Anderson v. Douglas County,*[6] a landowner brought suit against the county and zoning administrator, under federal civil rights statutes, claiming that their denial of permission to "thin spread" petroleum-contaminated soil violated his equal protection and due process rights.[7] The district court granted the county's motion for summary judgment, and the landowner appealed.

The agency's approval of thin-spreading in *Anderson* had been contingent on compliance with applicable zoning ordinances and approval by local authorities. The county planning and zoning commission had refused to issue a conditional use permit for the defendant. In upholding the commission's decision, the appeals court said:

> A party claiming a violation of equal protection must establish that he or she is 'similarly situated' to other applicants for the license, permit, or other benefit being sought, particularly with respect to the same time period. Anderson failed to establish that similarly situated persons did not have to obtain conditional use permits.

The court also found that the county's decision to require a conditional use permit for thin-spreading was not irrational because it was clearly related to public health, safety, or welfare concerns.

LAND USE REGULATION AND THE "TAKINGS" ISSUE

One important legal issue in property law is the appropriate relationship between the rights of private property owners and the obligation of government to regulate land use for the protection of the public good. This is an important matter to environmentalists, property owners, public officials, and society in general.

Protecting environmentally sensitive areas like wetlands, flood plains, and beachfront property has led to the adoption of state and federal regulations to limit development in such areas. Private property owners sometimes challenge such environmental laws by arguing an unconstitutional *taking* of their property in violation of the Fifth Amendment to the United States Constitution. The Fifth Amendment applies to the states through the Fourteenth Amendment.

The word *takings* comes from the Fifth Amendment, which states: [*"No person shall be . . .*] *deprived of life, liberty, or property, without due process of law; nor shall private property be taken for public use, without just compensation."*

Fifth Amendment Requirements

The Fifth Amendment recognizes that a basic characteristic of government is its power to protect the health, safety, and general welfare of its citizens. Under the language of the amendment, a government can take title to private property in order to use it for a public purpose, for example, a park or a school. This power, which is called the power of **eminent domain,** is also established in various state constitutions. Legal actions brought under this power of eminent domain are called *condemnation proceedings.*

The government must meet the requirements of the Fifth Amendment in order to exercise its power of eminent domain. First, the government must establish that the taking is necessary for a *public purpose*. In general, the public purpose requirement is rarely a problem in takings cases because it has consistently been interpreted broadly by the courts, and "[t]he role of the judiciary in determining whether that power [eminent domain] is being exercised for a public purpose is an extremely narrow one."[8] As the *Nollan* case set out later in this section illustrates, the government's action must also be rationally related to a legitimate public purpose.

In addition, in order to exercise its power of eminent domain under the Fifth Amendment, the government must pay *just compensation* for the property. In cases where the government takes title to the property under its power of eminent domain, courts usually use a test of *fair market value* at the time of the taking to determine just compensation. (Fair market value has been defined as "what a willing buyer would pay in cash to a willing seller.") If the courts find a taking has occurred in a regulatory takings case, the question of just compensation may raise difficult valuation problems. Should courts consider the diminished value of the regulated portion of the property only, or consider the value of the parcel as a whole? Should ecological values to the public be considered in determining just compensation to the private landowner in such cases?

"Regulatory" Takings

The requirements of the Fifth Amendment only apply in cases where there has been a taking of property. This requirement is not at issue in cases where a government exercises its traditional power of eminent domain and takes title to private property. In some cases, however, a property owner may argue that the government's regulation so deprives the owner of the use and value of the property that it constitutes a taking for purposes of the Fifth Amendment.

The idea that government regulation could constitute a compensable taking developed in the twentieth century. In 1922, the Supreme Court considered the problem in *Pennsylvania Coal Co. v. Mahon,* 260 U.S. 393. In that case, a coal company challenged a state law forbidding the mining of anthracite coal in such a way as to cause the subsidence of surface structures. In that case, Justice Holmes stated the often-cited maxim: "The general rule at least is that while property may be regulated to a certain extent, if regulation goes too far it will be recognized as a taking."

The difficulty, and one which has not been satisfactorily resolved by the courts, is how to establish rules to identify when a regulation has "gone too far." In *Village of Euclid,* the landmark zoning case discussed previously, the Supreme Court held that "mere regulation" of property does not constitute a taking for purposes of the Fifth Amendment. On the other hand, some regulations may effectively deprive an owner of all economic value of his property and thus constitute a taking.

The courts have continued to struggle to establish standards for determining when a taking, as opposed to "mere regulation" has occurred. It seems settled that a regulation may cause substantial diminution in the value of land, and still not constitute a taking if the land can be used for some economic benefit by the owner. However, a regulation which totally deprives the owner of any economic use of his property will likely constitute a taking. At what point does government's regulation of private property so deprive an owner of the value and use of his property that it constitutes a taking of property under the Fifth Amendment?

The question arises in challenges to land use regulations (either on their face or as applied to a particular landowner) which substantially diminish the value of property by limiting or prohibiting use or development. Zoning and flood plain regulations, permit requirements for wetlands development, and flood plain restrictions are but a few examples of the kinds of restrictions which may give rise to a takings challenge.

In the following case, property owners challenged a decision of the California Coastal Commission because it had imposed a condition that the owners grant public access to the beachfront before it would grant permission for the owners to rebuild their beach house. The owners, the Nollans, appealed the commission's ruling, and the California Court of Appeals rejected their claim that the condition violated the takings clause. The U.S. Supreme Court agreed to review the case.

NOLLAN v. CALIFORNIA COASTAL COMMISSION
483 U.S. 825 (1987)

JUSTICE SCALIA delivered the opinion of the court.

The Nollans own a beachfront lot in Ventura County, California. A quarter-mile north of their property is Faria County Park, an oceanside public park with a public beach and recreation area. Another public beach area, known locally as "the Cove," lies 1,800 feet south of their lot. A concrete seawall approximately eight feet high separates the beach portion of the Nollans' property from the rest of the lot. The historic mean high tide line determines the lot's oceanside boundary.

The Nollans originally leased their property with an option to buy. The building on the lot was a small bungalow, totaling 504 square feet, which for a time they rented to summer vacationers. After years of rental use, however, the building had fallen into disrepair, and could no longer be rented out.

The Nollans' option to purchase was conditioned on their promise to demolish the bungalow and replace it. In order to do so, they were required to obtain a coastal development permit from the California Coastal Commission. On February 25, 1982, they submitted a permit application to the Commission in which they proposed to demolish the existing structure and replace it with a three-bedroom house in keeping with the rest of the neighborhood.

The Nollans were informed that . . . the Commission staff had recommended that the permit be granted subject to the condition that they allow the public an easement to pass across a portion of their property bounded by the mean high tide line on one side, and their seawall on the other side. This would make it easier for the public to get to Faria County Park and the cove. The Nollans protested imposition of the condition, but the Commission overruled their objections and granted the permit subject to their recordation of a deed restriction granting the easement.

***

Had California simply required the Nollans to make an easement across their beachfront available to the public on a permanent basis in order to increase public access to the beach, rather than conditioning their permit to rebuild their house on their agreeing to do so, we have no doubt there would have been a taking. To say that the appropriation of a public easement across a landowner's premises does not constitute the taking of a property interest but rather (as Justice Brennan contends) "a mere restriction on its use," is to use words in a manner that deprives them of all their ordinary meaning. Indeed, one of the principal uses of the eminent domain power is to assure that the government be able to require conveyance of just such interests, so long as it pays for them. . . .

Given, then, that requiring uncompensated conveyance of the easement outright would violate the Fourteenth Amendment, the question becomes whether requiring it to be conveyed as a condition for issuing a land use permit alters the outcome. We have long recognized that land use regulation does not effect a taking if it "substantially advance[s] legitimate state interests" and does not "den[y] an owner economically viable use of his land. . . ." Our cases have not elaborated on the standards for determining what constitutes a "legitimate state interest" or what type of connection between the regulation and the state interest satisfies the requirement that the former "substantially advance" the latter. They have made clear, however, that a broad range of governmental purposes and regulations satisfies these requirements. The Commission argues that among these permissible purposes are protecting the public's ability to see the beach, assisting the public in overcoming the "psychological barrier" to using the beach created by a developed shorefront, and preventing congestion on the public beaches. We assume, without deciding, that this is so, in which case the Commission unquestionably would be able to deny the Nollans their permit outright if their new house (alone, or by reason of the cumulative impact produced in conjunction with other construction) would substantially impede these purposes, unless the denial would interfere so drastically with the Nollans' use of their property as to constitute a taking.

The Commission argues that a permit condition that serves the same legitimate police-power purpose as a refusal to issue the permit should not be found to be a tak-

ing if the refusal to issue the permit would not constitute a taking. We agree. Thus, if the Commission attached to the permit some condition that would have protected the public's ability to see the beach notwithstanding construction of the new house—for example, a height limitation, a width restriction, or a ban on fences—so long as the Commission could have exercised its police power (as we have assumed it could) to forbid construction of the house altogether, imposition of the condition would also be constitutional. Moreover (and here we come closer to the facts of the present case), the condition would be constitutional even if it consisted of the requirement that the Nollans provide a viewing spot on their property for passersby with whose sighting of the ocean their new house would interfere. Although such a requirement, constituting a permanent grant of continuous access to the property, would have to be considered a taking if it were not attached to a development permit, the Commission's assumed power to forbid construction of the house in order to protect the public's view of the beach must surely include the power to condition construction upon some concession by the owner, even a concession of property rights, that serves the same end. If a prohibition designed to accomplish that purpose would be a legitimate exercise of the police power rather than a taking, it would be strange to conclude that providing the owner an alternative to that prohibition which accomplishes the same purpose is not.

The evident constitutional propriety disappears, however, if the condition substituted for the prohibition utterly fails to further the end advanced as the justification for the prohibition. When that essential nexus is eliminated, the situation becomes the same as if California law forbade shouting fire in a crowded theater, but granted dispensations to those willing to contribute $100 to the state treasury. . . . [T]he lack of nexus between the condition and the original purpose of the building restriction converts that purpose to something other than what it was. The purpose then becomes, quite simply, the obtaining of an easement to serve some valid governmental purpose, but without payment of compensation. Whatever may be the outer limits of "legitimate state interests" in the takings and land use context, this is not one of them. In short, unless the permit condition serves the same governmental purpose as the development ban, the building restriction is not a valid regulation of land use but "an out and out plan of extortion."

The Commission claims that it concedes as much, and that we may sustain the condition at issue here by finding that it is reasonably related to the public need or burden that the Nollans' new house creates or to which it contributes. We can accept, for purposes of discussion, the Commission's proposed test as to how close a "fit" between the condition and the burden is required, because we find that this case does not meet even the most untailored standards. The Commission's principal contention to the contrary essentially turns on a play on the word "access." The Nollans' new house, the Commission found, will interfere with "visual access" to the beach. That in turn (along with other shorefront development)

will interfere with the desire of people who drive past the Nollans' house to use the beach, thus creating a "psychological barrier" to "access." The Nollans' new house will also, by a process not altogether clear from the Commissions' opinion but presumably potent enough to more than offset the effects of the psychological barrier, increase the use of the public beaches, thus creating the need for more "access." These burdens on "access" would be alleviated by a requirement that the Nollans provide "lateral access" to the beach.

Rewriting the argument to eliminate the play on words makes clear that there is nothing to it. It is quite impossible to understand how a requirement that people already on the public beaches be able to walk across the Nollans' property reduces any obstacles to viewing the beach created by the new house. It is also impossible to understand how it lowers any "psychological barrier" to using the public beaches, or how it helps to remedy any additional congestion on them caused by construction of the Nollans' new house. We therefore find that the Commission's imposition of the permit condition cannot be treated as an exercise of its land use power for any of these purposes. . . .

[The Judgment Is] Reversed.

Questions and Comments for Discussion

1.   In this case the Court said that there must be an "essential nexus" between a regulation and its purpose. Was that essential nexus met in this case? Why or why not?

2.   In his dissent in *Nollan,* Justice Brennan wrote:

The Commission's determination that certain types of development jeopardize public access to the ocean, and that such development should be conditioned on preservation of access, is the essence of responsible land use planning. The

Court's use of an unreasonably demanding standard for determining the rationality of state regulation in this area thus could hamper innovative efforts to preserve an increasingly fragile national resource.

What are the public policy concerns which underlie the debate between the majority and dissent in this case? Do you agree that the Nollans should be compensated in this case under a "takings" theory? What are the implications of your answer?

Takings Analysis: When Does a Taking Occur?

Rather than formulating precise rules determining when a regulatory taking occurs, the courts have chosen to address each case on an *ad hoc* factual inquiry. The Supreme Court has identified the following factors to be used in determining whether a regulation is a taking:

1. The *economic impact* of the regulation, with particular regard to the extent to which the regulation "has interfered with distinct investment backed expectation"

2. The *character of the public activity,* for example, a *physical invasion* will more readily be identified as a taking than a regulation which merely adjusts "the benefits and burden of economic life to promote the common good"

3. The *history of sustaining reasonable police power regulations* that destroyed or adversely affected recognized real property interests, and which have been viewed as permissible government action (for example, zoning cases)[9]

Temporary Takings   In 1987, in *First English Evangelical Lutheran Church of Glendale v. County of Los Angeles,*[10] a majority of the Supreme Court held that the church was entitled to damages for a temporary taking when Los Angeles County adopted an ordinance prohibiting the church's camp site structures within a flood protection area. The Court held that an ordinance which denied the church of "all use of its property" for a period of years would require compensation by the government. Several justices dissented in this case on the grounds that the decision was a "loose cannon" which would ignite a litigation explosion. The Court remanded the case to the California Court of Appeals, which subsequently found that the ordinance did not deny appellant all use of its property and was a "reasonable moratorium for a reasonable period of time."

Lucas v. South Carolina Coastal Council   A majority of the U.S. Supreme Court appears to have reaffirmed its holding in *First Evangelical Church* in a subsequent takings case, *Lucas v. South Carolina Coastal Council,* 112 S. Ct. 2886 (1991). In *Lucas,* the South Carolina legislature had enacted a law requiring a landowner to obtain a permit before developing any coastal land located within a "critical area" designated by the act. Lucas purchased two residential lots in 1986 which he intended to develop. He paid $975,000 for the lots. At that time, neither was located in the "critical area" and so no permit was required. In 1988, however, the state legislature enacted the Beachfront Management Act which expanded the "critical area" for purposes of the act; the act prohibited construction of any occupiable improvements on Lucas's lots.

In his lawsuit, Lucas claimed that the act denied him all economically viable use of his property and thus constituted a taking. The trial court agreed, and awarded him compensation in the amount of $1,232,387.50. The government appealed and the South Carolina Supreme Court reversed, because in its opinion there was no compensation required for a land use regulation designed to prevent serious public harm. Lucas, the landowner, appealed to the U.S. Supreme Court.

LUCAS v. SOUTH CAROLINA COASTAL COUNCIL
505 U.S. 1003 (1992)

Prior to Justice Holmes' exposition in *Pennsylvania Coal Co. v. Mahon,* 260 U.S. 393 (1922), it was generally thought that the Takings Clause reached only a "direct appropriation" of property, or the functional equivalent of a "practical ouster of [the owner's] possession." Justice Holmes recognized in *Mahon,* however, that if the protection against physical appropriations of private property was to be meaningfully enforced, the government's power to redefine the range of interests included in the ownership of property was necessarily constrained by constitutional limits. If, instead, the uses of private property were subject to unbridled, uncompensated qualification under the police power, "the natural tendency of human nature [would be] to extend the qualification more and more until at last private property disappear[ed]." These considerations gave birth in that case to the oft-cited maxim that, "while property may be regulated to a certain extent, if regulation goes too far it will be recognized as taking."

Nevertheless, our decision in *Mahon* offered little insight into when, and under what circumstances, a given regulation would be seen as going "too far" for purposes of the Fifth Amendment. In 70-odd years of succeeding "regulatory takings" jurisprudence, we have generally eschewed any "'set formula'" for determining how far is too far, preferring to "engage in . . . essentially ad hoc, factual inquiries." We have, however, described at least two discrete categories of regulatory action as compensable without case-specific inquiry into the public interest advanced in support of the restraint. The first encompasses regulations that compel the property owner to suffer a physical "invasion" of his property. In general (at

least with regard to permanent invasion), no matter how minute the intrusion, and no matter how weighty the public purpose behind it, we have required compensation. . . .

The second situation in which we have found categorical treatment appropriate is where regulation denies all economically beneficial or productive use of land. As we have said on numerous occasions, the Fifth Amendment is violated when land-use regulation "does not substantially advance legitimate state interests *or denies an owner economically viable use of his land.*" (Emphasis added by the Court.)

***

The trial court found Lucas's two beachfront lots to have been rendered valueless by respondent's enforcement of the coastal-zone construction ban. Under Lucas's theory of the case, which rested upon our "no economically viable use" statements, that finding entitled him to compensation. Lucas believed it unnecessary to take issue with either the purposes behind the Beachfront Management Act, or the means chosen by the South Carolina Legislature to effectuate those purposes. The South Carolina Supreme Court, however, thought otherwise. In its view, the Beachfront Management Act was no ordinary enactment, but involved the exercise of South Carolina's "police powers" to mitigate the harm to the public interest that petitioner's use of his land might occasion. . . .

It is correct that many of our prior opinions have suggested that "harmful or noxious uses" of property may be proscribed by government regulation without the requirement of compensation. For a number of reasons, however, we think the South

Carolina Supreme Court was too quick to conclude that that principle decides the present case. . . .

Where the State seeks to sustain regulation that deprives land of all economically beneficial use, we think it may resist compensation only if the logically antecedent inquiry into the nature of the owner's estate shows that the proscribed use interests were not part of his title to begin with. This accords, we think, with our "takings" jurisprudence, which has traditionally been guided by the understandings of our citizens regarding the content of, and the State's power over, the "bundle of rights" that they acquire when they obtain title to property. It seems to us that the property owner necessarily expects the uses of his property to be restricted, from time to time, by various measures newly enacted by the State in legitimate exercise of its police powers; "[a]s long recognized, some values are enjoyed under an implied limitation and must yield to the police power. . . ." In the case of land . . . we think the notion pressed by the council that title is somehow held subject to the "implied limitation" that the State may subsequently eliminate all economically valuable use is inconsistent with the historical compact recorded in the Takings Clause that has become part of our constitutional culture. . . .

The "total taking" inquiry we require today will ordinarily entail (as the application of state nuisance law ordinarily entails) analysis of, among other things, the degree of harm to public lands and resources, or adjacent private property, posed by the claimant's proposed activities, the social value of the claimant's activities and their suitability of the locality in question, and the relative ease with which the alleged harm can be avoided through measures taken by the claimant and the government. . . .

It seems unlikely that common-law principles would have prevented the erection of any habitable or productive improvements on petitioner's land; they rarely support prohibition of the "essential use" of land. The question, however, is one of state law to be dealt with on remand. . . . South Carolina must identify background principles of nuisance and property law that prohibit the uses he now intends in the circumstances in which the property is presently found. Only on this showing can the State fairly claim that, in proscribing all such beneficial uses, the Beachfront Management Act is taking nothing.

[*The judgment is reversed and the cause remanded.*]

Questions and Comments for Discussion

1. What are two categories of takings identified by the Supreme Court in *Lucas?* Can you give a hypothetical example of each?

2. How would you identify the "public purpose" in *Lucas?* Did the Supreme Court challenge the state's power to pass the Beachfront Management Act under its police power? Why or why not?

3. Police power regulations are presumably valid if they leave the owner with some "economically viable" use of the land.

Couldn't Lucas put a cart on his property and sell hotdogs? How should "economic viability" be defined?

4. In some cases, the question of economic viability depends on whether the loss is measured by determining the loss for the entire parcel of property, or only the regulated portion. For example, in *Keystone Bituminous Coal Association v. Pennsylvania,* 480 U.S. 470 (1987) (another case involving a Pennsylvania statute requiring coal companies to provide underground support for the

surface), the Supreme Court said the takings test should be based on an entire coal field owned by petitioners and not just the coal pillars the companies couldn't mine.

5.   One very important aspect of the *Lucas* case is its acceptance of a "nuisance exception." This is presumably an exception which permits the government to prevent a misuse or illegal use of property without the government action constituting a taking. How should nuisance be defined? If this is purely a matter of state law, does nuisance only refer to acts recognized as nuisances in the past? Would a law which prohibited a person from killing all wildlife and flora and fauna on his land constitute a taking or would it fall under a "nuisance" exception? Should it?

6.   On remand, the South Carolina State Supreme Court concluded that there was no common law basis on which to restrain Lucas' desired use, and therefore it remanded the case to the trial court for the purpose of determining damages as a result of the state's temporary taking of the property.

Challenges to Land Use Regulations: Summary and Conclusion

Cases like *Lucas* affirm that land use regulations must be fair and reasonable, be applied in a nondiscriminatory fashion, and not deprive an owner of all economic use of his property. A land use regulation is more likely to survive a takings challenge if the regulation:

- incorporates a "performance standard" rather than prohibits specific activities;
- includes special permit and variance procedures to avoid prohibiting all possible uses of the entire property;
- is reasonable and fair in provisions for administrative enforcement;
- documents nuisance reduction objectives;
- and, if totally prohibitory, is limited to narrow areas and provides, where appropriate, transferrable development rights.

The courts have struggled to clarify the law governing regulatory takings, but the test is ultimately a fact-sensitive one. The implications of the *Lucas* decision are still somewhat unclear. Justice Scalia, writing for the majority in *Lucas,* reaffirmed that a regulatory taking occurs when a regulation results in a physical invasion of an owner's property, and that a taking occurs when the owner is deprived of all economically beneficial use of his property. The court also recognized that nuisance law may be used to prohibit all economically viable uses of land only when a property owner could have had no reasonable expectation to use the property productively at the time of acquisition.

This *nuisance exception* poses an important issue for environmental law and policymakers: Under what circumstances may nuisance law, which is a matter of state law, sustain an environmental regulation which amounts to a total taking of all economic use of the property? The answer to this question is far from clear. Some view the *Lucas* decision as a narrow ruling while others see the case affording greater protection for private property rights in future regulatory takings cases. Ultimately, the takings cases raise fundamental policy questions about the appropriate balance between private property rights and the government's power to regulate the land use to protect the environment.

GLOSSARY

Eminent domain—The power of the government to take property for public use but requiring the payment of just compensation.

Exaction—A construction or dedication requirement, or in-lieu fee payment for site-specific needs such as streets, sidewalks, and drainage as a condition of approval of a development plan.

Master plan—Community plan for land use required by state zoning enabling legislation.

Nonconforming use—Use of property which is permitted, even though it does not conform to the zoning ordinance, because the zoning ordinance was adopted *after* the use existed.

Official map—Map setting out existing and planned improvements required by state zoning enabling legislation.

PUD—Planned unit development, which is a development project that permits mixed land uses within the development.

Subdivision—Parcel of land divided into units.

Variance—Exception to a requirement of the zoning code requiring petitioner to show (1) he would suffer undue hardship if the ordinance is enforced and (2) the granting of the variance will not be excessively disruptive of the surrounding land or master plan.

Zoning—Term which describes local and regional land use regulations controlling the use of land within a particular jurisdiction.

CASES FOR DISCUSSION

1.   The Town of Indialantic, Florida, enacted a zoning regulation imposing setback requirements on oceanfront property to protect the sand dunes. An affected landowner challenged the regulation as an unconstitutional taking of his property. When purchased, the owner's lots were not represented on the town's zoning map—this required the owner to get the town's permission before building any structure. The lots first appeared on the zoning maps in 1967 and since that time had been classified Tourist, which permitted residential, multiple living units, professional, hotel, motel, clubs, and lodges. In March 1973, the town adopted an ordinance requiring beachfront structures to be set back 50 feet from the mean high water line or 25 feet from the bluff line of the dunes, whichever distance was greater; in 1973, the town adopted an ordinance establishing front setbacks for coastal construction. When the owner applied for a variance to allow construction of a single family dwelling on his property, the Board of Adjustment denied his application. Is the setback requirement on oceanfront property constitutional, or does it constitute a taking of private property without just compensation in this case? *McNulty v. Town of Indiatlantic,* 727 F.Supp. 604 (M.D. Fla. 1989).

2.   The Army Corps of Engineers denied a request from a large scale miner of limestone to fill wetlands purchased before enactment of the Corps' Section 404 restrictions, and the owner appealed. In 1972, shortly before the enactment of the Clean Water Act, the owner had purchased 1560-acre wetlands in Dade County, Florida, for $2,964,000. In 1977, the Army Corps of Engineers enacted regulations requiring owners of wetlands parcels to ob-

tain permits under Section 404 of the Clean Water Act. In 1980, the Corps concluded that the proposed mining would cause irremediable loss of an ecologically valuable wetland parcel and denied the owner's application for a permit. Does the denial of a dredge and fill permit constitute an unconstitutional taking under these circumstances? *Florida Rock Industries, Inc. v. U.S.,* 18 F.3d 1560 (Fed. Cir. 1994).

3.   A city planning commission conditioned approval of petitioner's application to expand her store and pave her parking lot upon her compliance (1) with dedication of land for a public greenway along a nearby creek to minimize flooding that would be exacerbated by her development and (2) for a pedestrian/bicycle pathway intended to relieve traffic congestion in the central business district. Petitioner appealed, alleging that the land dedication requirements were not related to the proposed development and therefore constituted an uncompensated taking of her property under the Fifth Amendment. Is the petitioner correct? *Dolan v. City of Tigard,* 512 U.S. 374 (1994).

4.   The Outdoor Advertising Control Act of 1971 prohibited outdoor advertising within 660 feet of interstate and primary highways where visible from the road. The Department of Transportation ordered the removal of plaintiff's signs and plaintiff claimed the act unconstitutionally violated his freedom of expression. Is the act constitutional? *Department of Transp. v. Shiflett,* 310 S.E.2d 509 (Ga., 1984).

5.   Pursuant to a 1986 ordinance, the city council of the city of Virginia Beach downgraded some 403 acres of land from a planned unit development status to agricultural status. Earlier ordinances had allowed development of this land for single- and multi-family residential, commercial, and recreational uses. Is the 1986 ordinance enforceable? *City of Va. Beach v. Virginia Land Investment Ass'n No. 1,* 389 S.E.2d 312 (Va. 1990).

6.   A landowner argued that state law permitting the Ohio Hazardous Waste Facilities Board to bypass local zoning ordinances when siting hazardous waste facilities was unconstitutional, and that the siting of a facility near her property constituted a "taking" for which compensation had to be provided. Is the waste-siting statute constitutional? *Miller v. PPG Inds.,* 547 N.E.2d 1216 (Oh. Ct. App. 1988).

7.   A landowner challenged the Virgin Islands Coastal Zone Management committee's grant of a building permit on the ground that it breached a restrictive deed covenant. The Board of Land Use held a meeting that was attended by an attorney for the builder, but the landowner was not invited. At the meeting, material was submitted and arguments and comments made by various representatives of the builder. At the conclusion of the meeting, the board affirmed the permit. Was the grant of the permit supported by substantial evidence? *Maitland v. Pelican Beach Properties, Inc.,* 892 F.2d 245 (3d Cir. V.I. 1989).

8.   In 1978, Congress passed the Boundary Waters Canoe Area Wilderness Act, which regulated conduct on over a million acres of northern wilderness, of which the United States owned 792,000 acres. The act barred the use of motorboats and snowmobiles in almost all of the area. The state of Minnesota, which owned over 280,000 acres of land and water in the region, filed a suit challenging the authority of the federal government to regulate nonfederally owned land use. Is Minnesota correct that the federal government exceeded its authority? *Minnesota ex rel. Alexander v. Block,* 660 F.2d 1240 (8th Cir. 1981).

9.   Landowners owned riverfront acreage within a flood plain. The property was zoned for commercial use when purchased; however, the city later changed it to a more restrictive riverfront classification. The owners did not receive written notice of the change; rather, notification of the change was published in several newspaper articles. The parties learned of the change after the statute of limitations had run out to appeal the rezoning. They filed suit, alleging that the zoning ordinance was unconstitutional as applied to their property. Are they correct? *Karches v. City of Cincinnati,* 526 N.E.2d 1350 (Oh. 1988).

ENDNOTES

1. 272 U.S. 365 (1926).

2. Author's note: a new hearing.

3. See *Polygon Corp. v. City of Seattle,* 578 P.2d 1309 (1978).

4. William L. Want, *Expanding Wetlands Jurisdiction Affects Property Transactions,* NAT'L. L. J., Nov. 13, 1989, at 19.

5. See, e.g., *Exton Quarries v. Zoning Board of Adjustment,* 228 A.2d. 169 (1966).

6. 4 F.3d. 574 (8th Cir. 1993).

7. Thin-spreading is a method of soil treatment by which petroleum-contaminated soil is incorporated into healthy, native soil to biodegrade the petroleum.

8. *United States ex rel. T.V.A. v. Welch,* 327 U.S. 546 (1946).

9. *Penn Central Transportation Co. v. City of New York,* 438 U.S. 104 (1978).

10. 482 U.S. 304 (1987).

7

FEDERALISM AND THE ENVIRONMENT

INTRODUCTION

Federalism describes the relationship between the national (federal) government and the governments of the fifty states. Under a federal system, individual states form a union and subordinate their power to that of the central government. In the United States, both the federal government and the states possess certain powers, including the power to make and enforce laws. The powers of the federal government are those expressly granted by the U. S. Constitution. Those powers not expressly (or impliedly) granted to the federal government by the Constitution are reserved to the states.

The relationship between the powers and responsibilities of the state and federal governments is complex, and it is probably inevitable that conflicts would arise in environmental cases. In cases where states have attempted to regulate the importation of hazardous waste, for example, a significant legal question is the extent to which one state may effectively protect its own environment without unconstitutionally interfering with other states' rights to engage in **interstate commerce.** Another important issue is the extent to which federal laws supersede or **pre-empt** state environmental laws. This chapter examines some of these issues.

The final section of this chapter examines the federal government's power to regulate government property under the **property clause** of the U.S. Constitution. The federal government owns a vast amount of property within the United States, and the Constitution gives Congress the power to enact rules and regulations governing this property. In 1989, these public lands were estimated at nearly 690 million acres, an area about the size of India. These tracts contain much of the remaining national wilderness lands, and some federal laws have been enacted to protect and preserve these areas.

THE COMMERCE CLAUSE

A basic premise of American law is that the federal government is a government of *limited, delegated* powers. The main source of the enumerated powers of Congress is Article I of the Constitution. It gives to Congress the power to coin and borrow money, regulate commerce with foreign nations, create post offices, and regulate copyrights and patents. The Constitution does not specifically set out the powers of the states (although state constitutions sometimes list the powers that state legislatures may exercise), but the **Tenth Amendment** specifically reserves those powers not delegated to the United States by the Constitution, nor prohibited by it, to the States or to the people. The U.S. Constitution does place limits on the powers of the states. Most significantly, Article VI of the Constitution establishes the principle of federal supremacy. Under this principle, the Constitution and all laws made under it are the "supreme law of the land." State laws which conflict with federal laws are void and unenforceable under this principle.

One of the powers expressly delegated to Congress in Article I of the Constitution is the power to regulate interstate commerce (commerce among the states). This power is called the *commerce power.* Section 8 of Article I states: "Congress shall have power . . . to regulate Commerce . . . among the several States." The drafters of the Constitution apparently believed that this power was necessary to limit protectionist state restrictions on interstate trade which were common after the American Revolution.

The meaning and scope of the **commerce clause** have been refined by the courts in a series of cases. As a result, two different and important legal doctrines have emerged. First, the commerce clause is a *source of congressional regulatory power.* Second, the commerce clause acts as an *independent check on state regulation* which unduly restricts interstate commerce.

The Commerce Clause as a Source of Federal Regulatory Power

The literal language of the commerce clause gives Congress the power to regulate commerce among the states. This power has been very broadly construed by the courts. The courts have also interpreted the commerce clause to apply to **intrastate** activities which have any appreciable effect on interstate commerce. Thus the commerce clause permits Congress to regulate both interstate matters and intrastate matters which may impact interstate commerce. The Supreme Court has upheld federal legislation advancing noncommercial police power purposes. From the power to regulate interstate commerce, the courts have recognized broad congressional power to regulate for the public health, safety, and welfare.

In a complex interdependent society, there are few activities which do not affect interstate commerce. This is especially true of activities affecting the environment, as environmental problems do not follow geographic lines. The federal government's power to pass laws protecting the environment and regulating land use within the states has been consistently affirmed by the courts under its power to regulate interstate commerce. In the following case the Supreme Court considered the extent of congressional power under the commerce clause to enact environmental legislation affecting private property.

In *Hodel v. Virginia Surface Mining and Reclamation Association,* plaintiffs challenged the constitutionality of the Surface Mining Control and Reclamation Act of 1977. The district court rejected plaintiff's challenge that the law violated the commerce clause, but it held that the act violated the Tenth Amendment because it "displaced the States' freedom to structure operations in areas of traditional function." The district court also held that various provisions of the act effected an uncompensated taking of private property in violation of the Fifth Amendment. The government appealed.

HODEL v. VIRGINIA SURFACE MINING AND RECLAMATION ASSOCIATION, INC.

452 U.S. 264 (1981)

JUSTICE MARSHALL delivered the opinion of the Court.

The Surface Mining Act is a comprehensive statute designed to "establish a nationwide program to protect society and the environment from the adverse effects of surface coal mining operations. [The law] establishes a two-stage program for the regulation of surface coal mining. . . . Under the permanent phase, a regulatory program is to be adopted for each state, mandating compliance with the full panoply of federal performance standards, with enforcement responsibility lying with either the State or Federal Government. . . .

On October 23, 1978, the Virginia Surface Mining and Reclamation Association, Inc., an association of coal producers engaged in surface coal mining operations in Virginia, 63 of its member coal companies, and four individual landowners filed suit in federal district court seeking declaratory and injunctive relief against various provisions of the Act. Plaintiffs' challenge was primarily directed at (the Act's) performance standards. . . .

***

On cross-appeal, appellees (plaintiffs below) argue that the District Court erred in rejecting their challenge to the Act as beyond the scope of congressional power under the Commerce Clause. They insist that the Act's principal goal is regulating the use of private lands within the borders of the States and not, as the District Court found, regulating the interstate commerce effects of surface coal mining. Consequently, appellees contend that the ultimate issue presented is "whether land *as such* is subject to regulation under the Commerce Clause, i.e.,

whether land can be regarded as being 'in commerce.'" In urging us to answer "no" to this question, appellees emphasize that the Court has recognized that land-use regulation is within the inherent police powers of the States and their political subdivision and argue that Congress may regulate land-use only insofar as the Property Clause grants it control over federal lands.

We do not accept either appellees' framing of the question or the answer they would have us supply. The task of a court that is asked to determine whether a particular exercise of congressional power is valid under the Commerce Clause is relatively narrow. The Court must defer to a congressional finding that a regulated activity affects interstate commerce, if there is any rational basis for such a finding. . . .

Judicial review in this area is influenced above all by the fact that the Commerce Clause is a grant of plenary authority to Congress. This power is complete in itself, may be exercised to its utmost extent, and acknowledges no limitations, other than are prescribed in the constitution. Moreover, this Court has made clear that the commerce power extends not only to "the use of channels of interstate or foreign commerce" and to "protection of the instrumentalities of interstate commerce . . . or persons or things in commerce," but also to "activities affecting commerce." As we explained in *Fry v. United States,* 421 U.S. 542, 547 (1975), "[e]ven activity that is purely intrastate in character may be regulated by Congress, where the activity, combined with like conduct by others similarly situated, affects commerce among the States or with foreign nations."

Thus, when Congress has determined that an activity affects interstate commerce, the Courts need inquire only whether the finding is rational. Here, the District Court properly deferred to Congress' express findings, set out in the Act itself, about the effects of surface coal mining on interstate commerce. Section 101(c), 30 U.S.C. sec. 1201(c) recites the congressional finding that

> many surface mining operations result in disturbances of surface areas that burden and adversely affect commerce and the public welfare by destroying or diminishing the utility of land for commercial, industrial, residential, recreational, agricultural, and forestry purposes, by causing erosion and landslides, by contributing to floods, by polluting the water, by destroying fish and wildlife habitats, by impairing natural beauty, by damaging the property of citizens, by creating hazards dangerous to life and property, by degrading the quality of life in local communities, and by counteracting governmental programs and efforts to conserve soil, water, and other natural resources.

The legislative record provides ample support for these statutory findings. . . .

***

The denomination of an activity as a "local" or "intrastate" activity does not resolve the question whether Congress may regulate it under the Commerce Clause. As previously noted, the commerce power "extends to those activities intrastate which so affect interstate commerce, or the exertion of the power of Congress over it, as to make regulation of them appropriate means to the attainment of a legitimate end, the effective execution of the granted power to regulate interstate commerce." This Court has long held that Congress may regulate the conditions under which goods shipped in interstate commerce are produced where the "local" activity of producing these goods itself affects interstate commerce. . . . Appellees do not dispute that coal is a commodity that moves in interstate commerce. Here, Congress rationally determined that regulation of surface coal mining is necessary to protect interstate commerce from adverse effects that may result from that activity. This congressional finding is sufficient to sustain the Act as a valid exercise of Congress' power under the Commerce Clause.

[*Accordingly, the Court affirmed the judgment of the District Court upholding the Act against the Commerce Clause attack, and it reversed the judgment below insofar as the District Court held various provisions of the Act unconstitutional.*]

Questions and Comments for Discussion

1. The Supreme Court in *Hodel v. Virginia Surface Mining and Reclamation Association* rejected the argument that the surface coal mining act violated the constitutional *limitation* on the commerce power imposed by the Tenth Amendment. The district court had relied on an earlier Supreme Court decision (*National League of Cities v. Usury,* 426 U.S. 833 [1976]) in concluding that the act contravened the Tenth Amendment because it interfered with the states' "traditional governmental function" of regulating land use. The Supreme Court in *Hodel* reexamined *National League of Cities* and said that the Tenth Amendment challenge must fail. According to the Court, nothing in *National League of Cities* suggested that the Tenth Amendment shields the states from pre-emptive federal regulation of *private* activities affecting interstate commerce.

The Tenth Amendment served as a basis of important federalism rulings before Roosevelt's New Deal, but it has subsequently been considered to be nothing more that a truism stating that "all is retained which has not been surrendered." After *National League of Cities,* there was some confusion about the limits of congressional power under the Tenth Amendment. Later Supreme Court cases, however, have rejected Tenth Amendment challenges to other important environmental laws.

2.   In *Hodel v. Virginia Surface Mining and Reclamation Association,* the Court also held that the act did not result in an uncompensated taking of private property in violation of the Fifth Amendment's "just compensation" clause. Neither appellees nor the court identified any property in which appellees had an interest that had allegedly been taken by operation of the act. Review the test of regulatory takings in Chapter 6. What must a land owner prove in order to mount a successful takings challenge in a case like this?

3.   In *Hodel v. Indiana,* 452 U.S. 314 (1981), a companion case, the Supreme Court rejected another attack on the same statute. In the Indiana case, the district court had held unconstitutional certain provisions of the Surface Mining Control and Reclamation Act which attempted to protect prime farm land. (Provisions included a requirement that an applicant obtain a permit for mining on prime farm land to show that he had the capacity to restore the land, and a provision requiring surface mine operators to remove topsoil separately and preserve it for use during reclamation.) The district court found that only 0.006 percent of the total prime farm land in the nation was affected annually by mining and mining on farm land had only an "infinitesimal" impact on interstate commerce. However, the Supreme Court rejected this argument, noting that the grain production from the land affected would still be in the neighborhood of $56 million per year.

4.   In a concurring opinion in *Hodel v. Virginia Surface Mining,* Justice Rehnquist warned:

> [I]t would be a mistake to conclude that Congress' power to regulate pursuant to the Commerce Clause is unlimited. Some activities may be so private or local in nature that they simply may not be *in* commerce. Nor is it sufficient that the person or activity reached had *some* nexus with interstate commerce. Our cases have consistently held that the regulated activity must have a *substantial* effect on interstate commerce.

In light of the majority decisions in *Hodel v. Virginia Surface Mining and Reclamation Association,* and *Hodel v. State of Indiana,* how "substantial" must the effect on interstate commerce be? How likely is it that a court would find a local activity which even minimally affects the environment can be regulated by Congress under the commerce clause?

***

United States v. Lopez   To some, the 1995 U.S. Supreme Court's opinion in *United States v. Lopez,* 514 U.S. 549, signals an important shift in commerce clause cases. In *Lopez,* the Supreme Court ruled that Congress had overstepped its powers under the commerce clause when it banned gun possession near public schools. The petitioner in that case had challenged the federal Gun-Free School Zones Act of 1990, which made it a federal offense "for any individual knowingly to possess a firearm at a place that the individual knows, or has reasonable cause to believe, is a school zone."

Justice Rehnquist, writing for the majority of the Supreme Court in the case, began with what he called "first principles":

> The Constitution creates a Federal Government of enumerated powers. As James Madison wrote, '[t]he powers delegated by the proposed Constitution to the federal government are few and defined. Those which are to remain in the State governments are numerous and indefinite.'

He continued,

> The commerce power 'is the power to regulate; that is, to prescribe the rule by which commerce is to be governed. This power, like all others vested in Congress, is complete, in itself, may be exercised to its utmost extent, and acknowledges no limitations, other than are prescribed in the Constitution.'

The majority opinion then reviewed three broad categories that Congress may regulate under its commerce power: regulation of the use of the channels of interstate commerce; regulation of the instrumentalities of interstate commerce; and regulation of those activities having a substantial relation to interstate commerce.

According to the majority opinion, the difficulty in the final category is that case law has not clearly delineated whether an activity must "affect" or "substantially affect" interstate commerce in order to fall within Congress' power to regulate it under the commerce clause. Turning to the criminal statute at issue in the case, the Court said that by its terms the statute had nothing to do with "commerce" or any sort of economic enterprise, nor was it an essential part of a larger regulation of economic activity. Further, the Court said the law contained no jurisdictional element which would ensure, through case-by-case inquiry, that the firearm possession affected interstate commerce. According to the majority opinion in *Lopez,* the determination of congressional power under the commerce clause is ultimately one of degree. The Court admitted that determining whether an intrastate activity is commercial or noncommercial may in some cases result in legal uncertainty. But in this case, the majority said:

> To uphold the Government's contentions here, we would have to pile inference upon inference in a manner that would bid fair to convert congressional authority under the Commerce Clause to a general police power of the sort retained by the States. Admittedly, some of our prior cases have taken long steps down that road, giving great deference to congressional action. The broad language in these opinions has suggested the possibility of additional expansion, but we decline here to proceed any further. To do so would require us to conclude that the Constitution's enumeration of powers does not presuppose something not enumerated, and that there never will be a distinction between what is truly national and what is truly local. This we are unwilling to do.

At the least, the Supreme Court's opinion in *U.S. v. Lopez,* suggests that a majority of the Court is willing to take another look at the appropriate balance between federal and state powers in commerce clause cases. This decision, coupled with rhetoric in Congress suggesting the need to rethink the nature of federalism, has garnered a great deal of attention.

The extent to which *Lopez* signals a real shift in commerce clause inquiry by the Supreme Court is unclear. Some commentators see the case as an important step in reevaluating the federal government's exercise of control over traditional state functions. Others do not think it will have much effect, in part because four justices dissented and there were clear differences among the five justices forming the majority opinion in *Lopez.*

Although it is unlikely that the courts would strike down major existing federal environmental laws under a commerce clause challenge based on the *Lopez* decision, environmental cases based on the reasoning in *Lopez* will make their way through the courts.[1] The debate about the appropriate role of federal regulation to protect the environment as a matter of public policy will surely continue.

The "Dormant Commerce Clause" and State Regulation of Out-of-State Waste

On its face, the commerce clause is a grant of power to Congress, not a restriction on the state's power to legislate. Since the early nineteenth century, however, the Supreme Court has also construed the commerce clause to *prevent* certain kinds of state legislation which discriminate against interstate commerce. Under this theory, courts invalidate state laws which unduly burden interstate commerce on the ground that they are *inconsistent with* the power to regulate interstate commerce granted to the federal government. Courts have used the commerce clause to invalidate such state laws even in cases where Congress itself has failed to legislate. Such cases utilize the **dormant commerce clause** theory so called because the commerce clause prohibits certain state actions even in cases where Congress has failed to act.

There are two tests used by courts to invalidate state laws which unconstitutionally impede the flow of commerce. The first test governs state laws which discriminate against interstate commerce on their face. Such legislation is virtually *per se* unconstitutional. The second test subjects nondiscriminatory state legislation to a *balancing test,* weighing the impact of a statute on interstate commerce against the state's justification for the statute.

Under both tests, state laws discriminating against the importation of hazardous waste from outside the state have been held invalid by the Supreme Court. The problem of out-of-state waste is a significant one for many states. States on the eastern and western seaboards are running out of room to dispose of waste products within their borders, and the cost of dumping such waste has increased to the point that it is often cheaper to transport it hundreds of miles away to states where dumping is cheaper. Several states have attempted to minimize, restrict, or completely ban the flow of such waste from other states. Almost all such attempts have been defeated under the dormant commerce clause theory.

In the first Supreme Court decision addressing this issue, *City of Philadelphia v. New Jersey,* 437 U.S. 617 (1978), the Supreme Court struck down a New Jersey statute which prohibited the importation of most solid or liquid waste into the state which originated or was collected outside its territorial limits. The parties in the case disagreed about the purpose of the legislation. Plaintiffs who challenged the law argued that the statute was cloaked "in the currently fashionable garb of environmental protection," but that it was actually a legislative effort to suppress competition and stabilize the cost of solid waste disposal for New Jersey residents. The state, however, cited the purpose of the statute as set out in the statute itself:

> The Legislature finds and determines that . . . the volume of solid and liquid waste continues to rapidly increase, that the treatment and disposal of these wastes continues to pose an even greater threat to the quality of the environment of New Jersey, that the available and appropriate landfill sites within the State are being diminished, that the environment continues to be threatened by the treatment and disposal of waste which originated or was collected outside the State, and that the public health, safety and welfare require that the treatment and disposal within this State of all wastes generated outside of the State be prohibited.

The U.S. Supreme Court said that it was not necessary to resolve the dispute about the ultimate legislative purpose of the act. The Court said, "Contrary to the evident assumption of the state court and the parties, the evil of protectionism can reside in legislative means as well as legislative ends. Thus it does not matter whether the ultimate aim of (the statute) is to reduce the waste disposal costs of New Jersey residents or to save remaining open lands from pollution, for we assume New Jersey has every right to protect its residents' pocketbooks as well as their environment. . . ." However, according to the Court, whatever New

Jersey's ultimate purpose in enacting the law, that purpose could not be accomplished by discriminating against articles of commerce coming from outside the state unless there was some reason, apart from their origin, to treat them differently. The Court held that both on its face and in its effect, the act violated the commerce clause. The Court said:

> The New Jersey law at issue in this case falls squarely within the area that the Commerce Clause puts off limits to state regulation. On its face, it imposes on out-of-state commercial interests the full burden of conserving the State's remaining landfill space. It is true that in our previous cases the scarce natural resource was itself the article of commerce, whereas here the scarce resource and the article of commerce are distinct. But that difference is without consequence. In both instances, the State has overtly moved to slow or freeze the flow of commerce for protectionist reasons. It does not matter that the State has shut the article of commerce inside the State in one case and outside the State in the other. What is crucial is the attempt by one State to isolate itself from a problem common to many by erecting a barrier against the movement of interstate trade. . . .

The Supreme Court in *City of Philadelphia* said there was a difference between laws banning the importation of hazardous waste and state quarantine laws which have been upheld in the face of commerce clause challenges. The Court distinguished cases upholding quarantine laws on the basis that in these cases, the "very movement" of the articles risked contagion and other evils. According to the Court, in quarantine cases the state does not discriminate against interstate commerce as such, but simply prevents the traffic of noxious articles, whatever their origin.

Since its decision in *City of Philadelphia,* the Court has consistently refused to permit states to discriminate against out-of-state waste in order to protect state landfill space. Not only is this a significant environmental issue, it also raises important policy questions about a state's ability to control other resources within its boundaries.

States like Indiana and Alabama have continued to try to slow the receipt of out-of-state hazardous and solid waste by indirect methods, but the courts have generally relied on the holding in *City of Philadelphia* to strike down such attempts. In the following case, petitioners challenged an Alabama law which imposed a hazardous waste disposal fee on hazardous wastes generated outside the state and disposed of at a commercial facility in Alabama. The fee did not apply to such waste having a source in Alabama. The Alabama State Supreme Court held that the fee advanced legitimate local purposes which could not be adequately served by reasonable nondiscriminatory alternatives and was therefore valid under the commerce clause. Petitioners appealed to the U.S. Supreme Court.

CHEMICAL WASTE MANAGEMENT, INC. v. HUNT
504 U.S. 334 (1992)

JUSTICE WHITE delivered the opinion of the Court.

Petitioner, Chemical Waste Management, Inc., a Delaware corporation with its principal place of business in Oak Brook, Illinois, owns and operates one of the nation's oldest commercial hazardous waste land disposal facilities, located in Emelle, Alabama. Opened in 1977 and acquired by petitioner in 1978, the Emelle facility is a hazardous waste treatment, storage, and disposal facility operating pursuant to permits issued by the Environmental Protection Agency (EPA) under the Resource Conservation and Recovery Act of 1976 (RCRA), and by the State of Alabama. Alabama is 1 of only 16 states that have commercial hazardous waste landfills, and the Emelle facility is the largest of the 21 landfills of this kind located in these 16 States.

The parties do not dispute that the wastes and substances being landfilled at the Emelle facility include substances that are inherently dangerous to human health and safety and to the environment. Such waste consists of ignitable, corrosive, toxic and reactive wastes which contain poisonous and cancer causing chemicals and which can cause birth defects, genetic damage, blindness, crippling and death. Increasing amounts of out of state hazardous wastes are shipped to the Emelle facility for permanent storage each year. From 1985 through 1989, the tonnage of hazardous waste received per year has more than doubled, increasing from 341,000 tons in 1985 to 788,000 tons by 1989. Of this, up to 90% of the tonnage permanently buried each year is shipped in from other States.

Against this backdrop Alabama enacted Act No. 90-326 (the Act.) Among other provisions, the Act . . . imposes the "additional fee" at issue here which states in full:

> For waste and substances which are generated outside of Alabama and disposed of at a commercial site for the disposal of hazardous waste or hazardous substances in Alabama, an additional fee shall be levied at the rate of $72.00 per ton.

II.

No State may attempt to isolate itself from a problem common to the several States by raising barriers to the free flow of interstate trade. . . .

The Act's additional fee facially discriminates against hazardous waste generated in States other than Alabama, and the Act overall has plainly discouraged the full operation of petitioner's Emelle facility. Such burden-

some taxes imposed on interstate commerce alone are generally forbidden.

The State, however, argues that the additional fee imposed on out of state hazardous waste serves legitimate local purposes related to its citizens' health and safety. Because the additional fee discriminates both on its face and in practical effect, the burden falls on the State "to justify it both in terms of the local benefits flowing from the statute and the unavailability of nondiscriminatory alternative adequate to preserve the local interests at stake." At a minimum such facial discrimination invokes the strictest scrutiny of any purported legitimate local purpose and of the absence of nondiscriminatory alternatives.

The State's argument here does not significantly differ from the Alabama Supreme Court's conclusions on the legitimate local purposes of the additional fee imposed, which were: (1) protection of the health and safety of the citizens of Alabama from toxic substances; (2) conservation of the environment and the state's natural resources; (3) provision for compensatory revenue for the costs and burdens that out of state waste generators impose by dumping their hazardous waste in Alabama; (4) reduction of the overall flow of wastes traveling on the state's highways, which flow creates a great risk to the health and safety of the state's citizens.

These may all be legitimate local interests, and petitioner has not attacked them. But only rhetoric, and not explanation, emerges as to why Alabama targets *only* interstate hazardous waste to meet these goals. . . .

Ultimately, the State's concern focuses on the volume of the waste entering the Emelle facility. Less discriminatory alternatives, however, are available to alleviate this concern, not the least of which are a generally applicable per-ton additional fee on *all hazardous waste disposed of within Alabama,* or a per-mile tax on *all* vehicles transporting hazardous waste across Alabama roads, or an evenhanded cap on the total tonnage landfilled at Emelle, which would curtail volume from all sources. To the extent Alabama's concern touches environmental conservation and the health and safety of its citizens, such concern does not vary with the point of origin of the waste, and it remains within the State's power to monitor and regulate more closely the transportation and disposal of all hazardous waste within its borders. Even with the possible future financial and environmental risks to be borne by Alabama, such risks likewise do not vary with the waste's state of origin in a way allowing foreign, but not local waste to be burdened. In sum, we find the additional fee to be "an obvious effort to saddle those outside the State" with most of the burden of slowing the flow of waste into the Emelle facility. That legislative effort is clearly impermissible under the Commerce Clause of the Constitution.

Questions and Comments for Discussion

1.   The majority in *Chemical Waste Management v. Hunt* distinguished other court decisions holding that state quarantine laws do not violate the commerce clause. (A quarantine law is one which bans the importation or sale of articles which risk contagion or other evils.) The Court in *Hunt* said the additional fee in the Alabama act could not legitimately be deemed a quarantine law because Alabama permitted both the generation and landfilling of hazardous waste within its borders and the importation of still more hazardous waste subject to payment of the additional fee. The Court specifically distinguished *Maine v. Taylor,* 477 U.S. 131 (1986), where the Supreme Court upheld a Maine statute banning the importation of out-of-state baitfish into the state of Maine. According to the Court, "Maine there demonstrated that the out-of-state baitfish were subject to parasites foreign to in-state baitfish. This difference posed a threat to the state's natural resources, and absent a less discriminatory means of protecting the environment—and none was available—the import of baitfish could properly be banned. To the contrary, the record establishes that the hazardous waste at issue in this case is the same regardless of its point of origin."

The Supreme Court has thus conceded that some quarantine laws are not forbidden by the commerce clause even though they discriminate against out-of-state commerce. But it has distinguished state quarantine laws like that in *Maine v. Taylor* from those banning the importation of hazardous waste into the state. Are there any similarities in the issues posed by these two cases? In what way do they differ? Do different policies underly the Alabama and Maine legislation?

2.   Congress has expressly not authorized states to enact legislation like that in *Chemical Management v. Hunt* and *City of Philadelphia.* Should it do so? What are the political, environmental, and legal implications of your answer?

3.   Justice Rehnquist dissented in *Chemical Management v. Hunt.* According to his dissent, "taxes are a recognized and effective means of discouraging the consumption of scarce commodities—in this case the safe environment that attends appropriate disposal of hazardous wastes. I therefore see nothing unconstitutional in Alabama's use of a tax to discourage the export of this commodity to other states." What is the *commodity* at issue in this case? Is it landfill space or is it hazardous waste? What difference does or should this distinction make?

The Balancing Test

As the earlier out-of-state waste cases illustrate, state laws which discriminate on their face against out-of-state commerce rarely survive a challenge under the commerce clause. Generally, challenges attack laws which are not discriminatory *on their face* but have the *effect* of burdening out-of-state commerce. Most state legislation challenged under the dormant commerce clause falls within this category. In these cases, courts use a *balancing test* between the burden imposed on interstate commerce and the state's interests in passing the legislation. State legislation attacked as a burden on commerce must be *rationally related to a legitimate* state purpose. Courts consider a wide range of factors in determining whether the state's interest outweighs the federal interest in the free flow of interstate trade including the *importance* of the state interest, the degree to which it *restricts the federal interest,* and the degree to which the state regulatory scheme actually *advances the purpose of the federal legislation.*

An example of application of this balancing test is the case of *Proctor & Gamble Co. v. Chicago,* 509 F.2d 69 (7th Cir. 1975). In that case, plaintiffs, who manufactured phosphate detergents, challenged an ordinance of the City of Chicago which banned the use of detergents containing phosphates. The plaintiffs demonstrated that the ordinance had an adverse effect upon their businesses, which were national in scope. Because of warehousing methods used in the industry, the Chicago ordinance would effectively restrict sales of plaintiff's product in a wide geographic area including Wisconsin, Indiana, and Michigan.

The City of Chicago introduced evidence of the harmful effect of phosphates in contributing to the eutrophication of rivers and lakes. (Eutrophication is a process whereby a body of water becomes overnourished in nutrient elements which results in the overgrowth of green plants or algae.) The ordinance was designed to counteract eutrophication on the Illinois Waterway, which contained a high percentage of phosphorous, and Lake Michigan, which is the source of Chicago's water supply.

The trial court had held that the ordinance was unconstitutional, finding that the ordinance resulted in increased manufacture and distribution costs to plaintiffs and that the ordinance burdened interstate commerce. The trial court also found that the city's justifications for the ordinance were not sufficient to outweigh its interference on interstate commerce.

The Seventh Circuit, however, reversed the trial court and decided that the ordinance was constitutional under the balancing test. The court said:

> Where the statute regulates evenhandedly to effectuate a legitimate local public interest, and its effects on interstate commerce are only incidental, it will be upheld unless the burden imposed on such commerce is clearly excessive in relation to the putative local benefits.

Under the balancing test applied in *Proctor & Gamble Co. v. Chicago,* the court considered the *burden* imposed on interstate commerce by the ordinance, and found that the ordinance was not a burden on interstate commerce but merely a "burden" on a company with interstate distribution facilities. According to the court, there was no impairment of the company's ultimate ability to transport its product in interstate commerce. There was also no evidence of actual conflict between the Chicago ordinance and other jurisdictions which might inhibit the uniformity necessary for national manufacture and distribution of detergents. Even though the ordinance had the effect of preventing potential purchasers in other states from obtaining a detergent formula that manufacturers might legally sell in those states, it was an incidental burden on commerce, and one which the City Council could not control. The court concluded that under the balancing test, the burden imposed by the ordinance was slight compared to the important purpose of the ordinance. Under this analysis, the ordinance was constitutional.

Some judges and scholars have criticized the use of a balancing test in cases like *P&G v. Chicago*. First, balancing tests are often unpredictable in their application. Second, critics argue that courts should not second-guess state legislatures about the balance between a statute's costs and benefits. They argue that those decisions should properly be made within the political process and unwise or unsound decisions can be addressed in that process. Despite these criticisms, however, the balancing test has so far prevailed, and courts have upheld state environmental laws, like container laws, under this balancing test.[2]

State laws which restrict the importation of certain items of commerce into the state have also been upheld under a balancing test. In *Maine v. Taylor,* 477 U.S. 131 (1986) (discussed in the notes following the *Chemical Waste Management* case), the Supreme Court upheld the constitutionality of a state law which banned the importation of baitfish into the state. Experts had testified that live baitfish imported into the state posed two significant threats to Maine's unique and fragile fishers. First, Maine's pollution of wild fish—including its own indigenous gold shiners—would be placed at risk by parasites prevalent on out-of-state baitfish. Second, non-native species inadvertently included in shipments of baitfish could disturb Maine's aquatic ecology. There was no satisfactory way to inspect shipments of live baitfish for parasites or commingled species.

A majority of the Supreme Court said that the state merely needed to demonstrate that the statute served a legitimate local purpose and that this purpose could not be served as well by available nondiscriminatory means. In holding that the statute did not violate the commerce clause, the Court said, "As long as a State does not needlessly obstruct interstate trade or attempt to place itself in a position of economic isolation, it retains broad regulatory authority to protect the health and safety of its citizens and the integrity of its natural resources." According to the Court, this was not a case of arbitrary discrimination against interstate commerce. The record suggested that Maine had legitimate reasons apart from their origin, to treat out-of-state baitfish differently.

The State as a "Market Participant"

The courts have held that state regulation may be insulated from regulation under the commerce clause if the state acts as a "market participant." Under this theory, if a state is not exercising a regulatory function but has itself entered the market, traditional concerns underlying the dormant commerce clause theory do not apply. For example, in *Swin Resource System, Inc. v. Lycoming County,*[3] the operator of a solid waste processing facility sued a county which operated a landfill. Swin challenged regulations which gave the county residents preference in the use of the landfill. The court of appeals, however, said that the county was acting as a *market participant* rather than a *market regulator* in deciding the conditions under which Swin could use its landfill. The Court said:

> No court, to our knowledge, has ever suggested that the commerce clause requires city-operated garbage trucks to cross state lines in order to pick up the garbage generated by residents of other states. If a city may constitutionally limit its trucks to collecting garbage generated by city residents, we see no constitutional reason why a city cannot also limit a city-operated dump to garbage generated by city residents. With respect to municipal garbage trucks

and municipal garbage dumps, application of the market participant doctrine enables 'the people [acting through their local government] to determine as conditions demand . . . what services and functions the public welfare requires.'[4]

FEDERAL PRE-EMPTION OF STATE LAWS AFFECTING THE ENVIRONMENT

If a state law conflicts with a federal law enacted by Congress under its constitutional powers, the federal law takes priority and the state law is unenforceable. In such cases, state law is said to be *pre-empted* by federal law. The doctrine of pre-emption is based on the **supremacy clause** of Article VI of the U.S. Constitution, which provides:

> This Constitution, and the Laws of the United States which shall be made in Pursuance thereof; and all Treaties made, or which shall be made, under the authority of the United States, shall be the supreme Law of the Land; and the Judges in every State shall be bound thereby, any Thing in the Constitution or Laws of any State to the Contrary notwithstanding.

On the other hand, the Tenth Amendment protects the power of states. The potential conflict between federal supremacy and state authority is reconciled by a presumption that regulation by both the federal and state governments is valid. However, Congress can forbid states from regulating in a particular area of national interest, and may do so either by *expressly* pre-empting state authority, or by *implying* pre-emption from the scope and range of its action.

In cases where state law clearly conflicts with federal law, and it is impossible to follow both, federal law will control. However, the presence of a conflict between federal and state law is not always so clear. In cases where state law does not expressly conflict with federal law, but is "incompatible" with federal law, federal law also controls.

The courts have recognized four circumstances where federal law will pre-empt state action:

1. *Express pre-emption* by Congress
2. Congressionally *implied pre-emption*
3. Cases where *dual compliance is impossible*
4. Cases where state law *interferes with the policy objectives* of federal law

Every pre-emption case is unique and usually raises questions of statutory interpretation because the courts must determine whether Congress *intended* to pre-empt state law in adopting particular laws. Consequently, whether state law is pre-empted by federal law or regulation is an issue which is decided on a case-by-case basis.

Express (Manifest) Intention to Pre-Empt State Law

If it wishes to do so, Congress can *expressly* forbid the states from legislating in an area Congress has been given the power to regulate. In some cases, congressional intention to occupy a particular field is stated expressly in federal legislation. In the following case, the plaintiff sought to invalidate a state statute regulating the transportation of hazardous liquids by pipeline within the state. A federal trial court held that the state law was expressly pre-empted by federal law, and the state appealed.

KINLEY CORP v. IOWA UTILITIES BD.
999 F.2d 354 (8th Cir. 1993)

McMILLIAN, Circuit Judge.

The underlying facts are not disputed. Appellee Kinley Corp. owns and operates an interstate hazardous liquid pipeline extending some 13 miles from an Amoco Oil Co. terminal facility located near Council Bluffs, Nebraska. The pipeline is 4 inches in diameter and transports aviation jet fuel. Aviation jet fuel is a petroleum product and thus a "hazardous liquid" for purposes of the Hazardous Liquid Pipeline Safety Act of 1979 (HLPSA), 49 U.S.C. app. sec. 2001(2)(A). The pipeline was constructed in April 1968 and was purchased by Kinley after construction had begun but before it was completed. Neither the company that constructed the pipeline nor Kinley ever applied for a Chapter 479 state pipeline permit until 1988. Chapter 479 establishes a comprehensive state program supervising the intrastate and interstate transportation by pipeline of solid, liquid or gaseous substances, with the exception of water and interstate natural gas, in order to protect the safety and welfare of the public. In July 1987, IUB (Iowa Utilities Board) formerly the Iowa State Commerce Commission, became aware of the existence of the pipeline . . . and in August 1987 inspected the pipeline. . . .

In June 1989 IUB issued an administrative order directing Kinley to show cause why civil penalties should not be assessed for noncompliance with Chapter 279 and IUB's administrative regulations. In April 1990 IUB denied Kinley's application for a state pipeline permit and ordered Kinley

not to operate the pipeline in Iowa or to replace portions thereof, and assessed civil penalties.

***

Appellants acknowledge that the safety provisions of Chapter 479 were preempted by the HLPSA. However, they argue that the non-safety provisions, specifically the financial responsibility provisions designed to protect the state's farmland and topsoil from damage due to construction, operation and maintenance of pipelines and to guarantee payment of property and environmental damages were not preempted. . . .

The Supremacy Clause, U.S. Const. Art. VI, cl. 2, invalidates state laws that "interfere with, or are contrary to," federal law. Congressional intent is the critical question in any preemption analysis.

Under the Supremacy Clause, federal law may supersede state law in several different ways. First when acting within constitutional limits, Congress is empowered to pre-empt state law by so stating in express terms. In the absence of express preemptive language, Congress' intent to pre-empt all state law in a particular area may be inferred where the scheme of federal regulation is sufficiently comprehensive to make reasonable the inference that Congress "left no room" for supplementary state regulation. Pre-emption of a whole field also will be inferred where the field is one in which "the federal interest is so dominant that the federal system will be assumed to preclude enforcement of state laws on the same subject."

Even where Congress has not completely displaced state regulation in a specific area, state law is nullified to the extent that it actually conflicts with federal law. Such a conflict arises when "compliance with both federal and state regulation is a physical impossibility," or when state law "stands as an obstacle to the accomplishment and execution of the full purposes and objectives of Congress." *Hillsborough County v. Automated Medical Laboratories, Inc.,* 471 U.S. at 713.

In the present case, we need look no further than the express statutory language. The HLPSA contains the following express pre-emption provision: "No state agency may adopt or continue in force any safety standards applicable to *interstate* pipeline facilities or the transportation of hazardous liquids associated with such facilities." We agree with the district court that this is a case involving express pre-emption and that Congress has expressly stated its intent to pre-empt the states from regulating in the

area of safety in connection with interstate hazardous liquid pipelines. For this reason, the state cannot regulate in this area and Chapter 479 is invalid to the extent it purports to do so. . . .

[W]e note that the legislative history of the HLPSA, especially when considered with the Natural Gas Pipeline Safety Act (NGPSA) further demonstrates Congress's intent to pre-empt state safety regulation of interstate hazardous liquid pipelines. In 1979, at the same time the NGPSA was amended to cover liquified natural gas, Congress also enacted the HLPSA. The HLPSA established federal safety regulation over the transportation of hazardous liquids by pipeline and defined "hazardous liquid" to include petroleum and petroleum products. In enacting the HLPSA, Congress intended to "establish a statutory framework similar to the NGPSA to regulate transportation of hazardous liquids by pipeline. . . ."

Accordingly, we affirm the judgment of the district court.

***

Questions and Comments for Discussion

1.   In *Kinley v. Iowa Utilities Bd.,* the state also argued that Chapter 479 was valid because it was a gap-filling state regulation. The state argued that transportation of a hazardous liquid through pipelines that operate at a stress level of 20 percent or less of the specified minimum yield strength of the line pipe is exempt from federal safety and accident reporting requirements, and that Chapter 479 permissibly fills this gap in the federal regulatory scheme. The court of appeals disagreed. The court said that the decision of the Department of Transportation to exempt certain pipelines from federal regulation did not necessarily mean that the state can step in and

impose its own regulations. "[A] federal decision to forego regulation in a given area may imply an authoritative federal determination that the area is best left *unregulated,* and in that event would have as much pre-emptive force as a decision to regulate." According to the court, Congress granted exclusive authority to regulate interstate hazardous liquid pipelines to the secretary of the Department of Transportation. This congressional grant of authority precluded state decision making in this area altogether and left no regulatory room for the state to either establish its own safety standards or supplement the federal safety standards.

Pre-Emption of State Law by Congressional Intent

In cases where Congress has expressly stated its intent to pre-empt state regulation in a field, that intention will control. However, in cases where Congress has not *expressly* stated such intention, intention to pre-empt may be *implied* from the scope and range of federal regulation in the area. Courts faced with the question of pre-emption in such cases may examine legislative history to make the determination of legislative intent. Courts may also determine that federal regulation is so pervasive that it manifests congressional intent to pre-empt the field. Congressional *purpose* in enacting regulation may also be relevant to the determination of pre-emption.

There are important constitutional implications underlying whether federal law pre-empts state law in a given field. In implied pre-emption cases courts sometimes *balance* state and federal interests in a way similar to commerce theory analysis. Some pre-emption cases also raise burden-on-commerce issues. The difference is that in burden-on-commerce cases, courts are concerned with the policy implications of the commerce clause. In pre-emption cases, courts rely on the supremacy clause and focus on whether Congress intended to dominate an area of regulation.

Field pre-emption occurs when Congress has intended to dominate an entire area or field, and state laws regulating the same area are impliedly pre-empted. An example of field pre-emption is the federal nuclear power regulatory scheme. In a number of cases challenging state regulation of nuclear materials and nuclear power plants, courts have upheld claims that Congress intended to pre-empt the field of radiation safety and power plant construction.

There are arguably strong policy reasons why there should be uniformity in setting nuclear radiation standards. Variation in radiological emissions, standards and design, and licensing requirements would result in expensive and unique designs for each plant. State governments argue that the health, safety, and welfare of their residents are essentially matters of state concern. However, state attempts to require safer and lower levels of radiation emissions have not met with success. Even in this area, however, the states retain some latitude to act.

In *Silkwood v. Kerr-McGee Corp.*, 464 U.S. 238 (1984), Karen Silkwood was a laboratory analyst at a Kerr-McGee plant that fabricated plutonium fuel pins for use in nuclear power plants. After she was contaminated by plutonium from the plant, she died in an automobile accident. Karen's father sued Kerr-McGee as administrator of her estate to recover for the contamination to Karen's person and property under Oklahoma tort law. The jury awarded Mr. Silkwood $505,000 in actual damages and $10 million in punitive damages. The court of appeals reversed the punitive damages award and other portions of the trial court decision, finding that the award was pre-empted by federal law. Silkwood appealed to the U.S. Supreme Court.

The Supreme Court recognized that the statutory scheme and legislative history of the federal Atomic Energy Act had convinced the court that Congress intended that the federal government regulate the radiological safety aspects in the construction and operation of a nuclear plant. Kerr-McGee argued that because the state-authorized award of punitive damages punished and deterred conduct related to radiation hazards in this case, the punitive damage award was pre-empted. The Court, however, said that a review of the legislative history of the federal law, coupled with an examination of Congress' actions with respect to other portions of the act, convinced it that the pre-empted field did not extend as far as Kerr-McGee maintained. It said:

No doubt there is tension between the conclusion that safety regulation is the exclusive concern of federal law and the conclusion that a state may nevertheless award damages based on its own law. But Congress [apparently] intended to stand by both concepts and to tolerate whatever tension there was between them. It may be that the award of damages based on the state law of negligence or strict liability is regulatory in the sense that a nuclear plant will be threatened with damages if it does not conform to state standards, but that consequence was something that Congress was quite willing to accept.

The Supreme Court reversed the court of appeals judgment with respect to punitive damages and returned the case to the court of appeals for proceedings consistent with its opinion. Subsequently, the court's opinion was superceded by federal statute.[5]

State Law Incompatible with Congressional Intent

Federal regulations generally are national in scope and do not vary with local concerns. State and local laws often address matters of more limited concern. If compliance with both state and federal law is impossible, or if state law obstructs federal regulations, courts will hold that federal law pre-empts state law.

However, some states may want to enact more stringent environmental standards than federal standards, and Congress may permit states to do so. For example, the Resource Conservation and Recovery Act (RCRA) expressly provides:

> [N]o State or political subdivision may impose any requirements less stringent than those authorized under this subchapter respecting the same matter. . . . [However, n]othing in this chapter shall be construed to prohibit any State or political subdivision thereof from imposing *any requirements, including those for site selection, which are more stringent than those imposed by such regulations.*

Relying on this section, in *LaFarge Corporation v. Campbell*, 813 F. Supp. 501 (W.D. Tex. 1993), a federal district court held that RCRA did not pre-empt a state statute which prohibited the burning of hazardous waste-derived fuel within one-half mile of an established residence. The court said that Congress obviously did not intend RCRA to pre-empt all state law governing the disposal of hazardous waste.

The court in *LaFarge* also pointed out that state laws and regulations concerning health and safety are historically a matter of local concern, and it noted that other courts have reached the same conclusion: if application of the law or regulation does not result in an absolute prohibition of a type of technology or prohibit importation of hazardous waste, federal law does not pre-empt it. The court noted that ordinances prohibiting the storage, treatment or disposal of "acute hazardous waste" within its jurisdiction are pre-empted by RCRA, but that siting prohibitions have been upheld. In the case of the siting ordinance at issue in *LaFarge*, the court said that the purposes of the statute were rational and within the purview of the legislature's authority to regulate hazardous waste management as anticipated by Congress.

As noted earlier, challenges to state laws under a pre-emption theory frequently involve commerce clause challenges as well. In *LaFarge*, the plaintiff also argued that the siting prohibition was invalid under the commerce clause because it did not regulate "evenhandedly." However, the court said that the state statute applied evenhandedly to in-state and out-of-state companies and had only an incidental impact on interstate commerce.

According to the court, the relevant inquiry was whether or not the siting prohibition effected a legitimate public interest, and if so, where the burden on interstate commerce was clearly excessive in relation to the local benefits of the act. Under this test, the siting prohibition did not violate the commerce clause.

State Laws Interfering with Policy Objectives of Federal Law

A final category of pre-emption includes cases where plaintiffs claim that state law interferes with the accomplishment of the purposes of federal laws. If a federal agency licenses a private activity as part of a resource management program, for example, it may be argued that the federal government has authorized that activity. Thus a state law that restricts that activity conflicts with federal law.

In one such case, the Federal Energy Regulatory Commission (FERC), as a part of its licensing process, granted an applicant a license for a hydroelectric facility in California. The license prescribed minimum stream flows from the plant, but the minimum flow standard under the FERC standard permitted stream flows to decline to less than a third of the state's proposed minimum requirements. The State of California sought to impose its own more environmentally protective stream flow requirements, but FERC concluded that the task of setting such rates rested within its exclusive jurisdiction. The court of appeals affirmed FERC's decision. On appeal the Supreme Court held that FERC's minimal standards controlled. Justice O'Connor, writing for the majority, summarized as follows:

> A state measure is 'pre-empted to the extent it actually conflicts with federal law, that is, when it is impossible to comply with both state and federal law, or where the state law stands as an obstacle to the accomplishment of the full purposes and objectives of Congress.' As Congress directed in FPA (The Federal Power Act) sec.10(a), FERC set the conditions of the license, including the minimum stream flow, after considering which requirements would best protect wildlife and ensure that the project would be economically feasible, and thus further power development. Allowing California to impose significantly higher minimum stream flow requirements would disturb and conflict with the balance embodied in that considered federal agency determination.'[6]

Summary of the Pre-Emption Doctrine

Despite the fact that the courts have articulated several tests to determine whether federal law pre-empts state law, every pre-emption case is unique. In each case, courts focus on the question whether Congress *intended* to pre-empt state power to regulate in the same area. This is generally a question of statutory construction and requires the courts to interpret the language of the federal statute, its legislative history, and its purpose. In the absence of an express intention to pre-empt, the courts may *infer* pre-emption in cases where Congress has comprehensively regulated a field, when its interest is so dominant that the federal scheme is presumed to preclude enforcement of state laws, when the purpose of the federal law is obstructed by state law, or when state law actually conflicts with federal law. These rules are not precise guidelines, however, and each case turns on the specific facts and peculiarities of the case.

FEDERAL PUBLIC LAND LAWS

Another important federal power arises from the property clause of the U.S. Constitution. Article IV, Section 3 provides that "Congress shall have the Power to dispose of and make all needful Rules and Regulations respecting the Territory or other property belonging to the United States." This power expressly vests in Congress regulation of federal land.

Of the nearly 690 million acres of public land owned by the federal government in 1989, almost 260 million acres were reserved for national forests and parks, and vast tracts of public land contain many of the nation's resources. The Bureau of Land Statistics estimated in 1989 that federal lands produced 14 percent of the nation's oil and 30 percent of its natural gas. In addition, the federal government owns approximately 20 percent of commercial forest land, 40 percent of merchantable timber, and over 60 percent of softwood saw timber.[7]

Historically, the federal government tried to divest itself of public lands by transferring ownership to private parties. However, increasing interest in preserving national areas, especially wilderness and coastal areas, has led Congress to enact laws designed to both preserve and protect public lands while capitalizing upon those resources. The property clause of the Constitution gives Congress the power to protect these lands. In the following case the Supreme Court addressed the scope of congressional power to regulate federal property under the property clause. In this case, the State of New Mexico challenged the constitutionality of the Wild Free-Roaming Horses and Burros Act. The district court held the act was unconstitutional and enjoined its enforcement, and the federal government appealed.

KLEPPE v. STATE OF NEW MEXICO
426 U.S. 529 (1976)

MR. JUSTICE MARSHALL delivered the opinion of the Court.

At issue in this case is whether Congress exceeded its powers under the Constitution in enacting the Wild Free-Roaming Horses and Burros Act.

The Wild Free-Roaming Horses and Burros Act (Act) was enacted to protect "all unbranded and unclaimed horses and burros on public lands of the United States" from "capture, branding, harassment, or death." To accomplish this, "they are to be considered in the area where presently found, as an integral part of the natural system of the public lands." The Act provides that all such animals on the public lands administered by the Secretary of the Interior through the Bureau of Land Management (BLM) or by the Secretary of Agriculture through the Forest Service are committed to their jurisdiction, who are "directed to protect and manage [the animals] as components of the lands . . . in a manner that is designed to achieve and maintain a thriving natural ecological balance on the public lands." If the animals stray from those lands onto privately owned land, the private landowners may inform federal officials, who shall arrange to have the animals removed.

The State of New Mexico, its Livestock Board and director, and the purchaser of three unbranded burros seized by the Board (pursuant to state law) on federal lands and sold at public auction, brought this suit for declaratory judgment that the Act is unconstitutional.

***

The Property Clause of the Constitution provides that "Congress shall have Power to dispose of and make all needful Rules and Regulations respecting the Territory or other Property belonging to the United States." In passing the Wild Free-Roaming Horses and Burros Act, Congress deemed the regulated animals "an integral part of the natural system of the public lands" of the United States, and found that their management was necessary "for achievement of an ecological balance on the public lands." According to Congress, these animals, if preserved in their native habitats, "contribute to the diversity of life forms within the Nation and enrich the lives of the American people." Indeed, Congress concluded the wild free-roaming horses and burros "are living symbols of the historic and pioneer spirit of the West." Despite their importance, the Senate Committee found that these animals

> have been cruelly captured and slain and their carcasses used in the production of pet food and fertilizer. They have been used for target practice and harassed for 'sport' and profit. In spite of public outrage, this bloody traffic continues unabated, and it is the firm belief of the committee that this senseless slaughter must be brought to an end.

For these reasons, Congress determined to preserve and protect the wild free-roaming horses and burros on the public lands of the United States. The question under the Property Clause is whether this determination can be sustained as a "needful" regulation "respecting" the public lands. In answering this question, we must remain mindful that, while courts must eventually pass upon them, determinations under the Property Clause are entrusted primarily to the judgment of Congress.

Appellees argue that the Act cannot be supported by the Property Clause. They contend that the Clause grants Congress essentially two kinds of power: (1) the power to dispose of and make incidental rules regarding the use of federal property; and

(2) the power to protect federal property. According to appellees, the first power is not broad enough to support legislation protecting wild animals that live on federal property; and the second power is not implicated since the Act is designed to protect the animals, which are not themselves federal property, and not the public lands. As an initial matter, it is far from clear that the Act was not passed in part to protect the public lands of the United States or that Congress cannot assert a property interest in the regulated horses and burros superior to that of the State. But we need not consider whether the Act can be upheld on either of these grounds, for we reject appellees' narrow reading of the Property Clause. . . .

[A]ppellees have presented no support for their position that the Clause grants Congress only the power to dispose of, to make incidental rules regarding the use of, and to protect federal property. This failure is hardly surprising for the Clause, in broad terms, gives Congress the power to determine what are "needful" rules "respecting" the public lands. And while the furthest reaches of the power granted by the Property Clause have not yet been definitively resolved, we have repeatedly observed that "[t]he power over the public lands thus entrusted to Congress is without limitations."

The decided cases have supported this expansive reading. It is the Property Clause, for instance, that provides the basis for governing the territories of the United States. And even over public land within the States, "[t]he general Government doubtless has a power over its own property analogous to the police power of the several States, and the extent to which it may go in the exercise of such power is measured by the exigencies of the particular case." *Camfield v. United States,* 167 U.S. 518, 525 (1897). We have noted, for example, that the Property Clause gives Congress the power over the public lands "to control their occupancy and use, to protect them from trespass and injury and to prescribe the conditions upon which others may obtain rights in them. . . ." And we have approved legislation respecting the public lands "[i]f it be found necessary for the protection of the public, or of intending settlers [on the public lands]." In short, Congress exercises the powers both of a proprietor and of a legislature over the public domain. Although the Property Clause does not authorize "an exercise of a general control over public policy in a State," it does permit "an exercise of the complete power which Congress has over particular public property entrusted to it." In our view, the "complete power" that Congress has over public lands necessarily includes the power to regulate and protect the wildlife living there."

[*For this and other reasons discussed in the opinion*] *the judgment of the district court is reversed and the case is remanded for further proceedings consistent with this opinion.*

Questions and Comments for Discussion

1.   In *Kleppe v. New Mexico,* The State of New Mexico argued that if the Court approved the Wild Free-Roaming Horses and Burros Act as a valid exercise of Congress' power under the property clause, then it would sanction "an impermissible intrusion on the sovereignty, legislative authority and police power of the State and have wrongly infringed upon the State's traditional trustee powers over wild animals." The Supreme Court rejected this argument. The Court said, "Absent consent or cession a State undoubtedly retains jurisdiction over federal lands within its territory, but Congress equally surely retains the power to enact legislation respecting those lands pursuant to the property clause. And when Congress so acts, the federal legislation necessarily overrides conflicting state laws under the supremacy clause." According to the Court, "a different rule would place the public domain of the United States completely at the mercy of state legislation."

2.   The State's concern expressed above is another example of the tension between the powers of the state and federal government to regulate land use within a federal system. In *Kleppe v. New Mexico,* the State also expressed concern that the act violated traditional state power over wild animals. The Court agreed that the states have "broad trustee and police powers over wild animals within their jurisdictions." But the Court said, "[T]hose powers exist only in so far as their exercise may not be incompatible with, or restrained by, the rights conveyed to the Federal government by the Constitution."

3.   Reconsider the traditional common law property rule regarding capture of wild animals discussed in Chapter 3. How does the federal law in this case and the Court's opinion upholding its provisions reflect a change from traditional common law principles? What are the policy reasons underlying congressional action in this case? Would it make a difference if Congress were to enact a law to permit hunting and killing of wild burros and horses on public lands rather than a law protecting them from such activities?

While the property clause gives Congress the power to make rules and regulations governing property belonging to the United States, the Supreme Court has held that this is not necessarily an *exclusive* power. For example, the Supreme Court has upheld a state law requiring a permit for mining on public lands.[8]

An important question is the extent to which the property clause gives the federal government regulatory power over private lands adjoining public lands. Some courts have interpreted the property clause to give Congress the power to prevent activities on private lands which would interfere with congressional purpose in protecting public lands.

In *Cappaert v. United States,* 426 U.S. 128 (1976), the question before the Supreme Court was whether the reservation of Devil's Hole (a deep limestone cavern in Nevada) as a national monument also reserved federal water rights in unappropriated water at the site. (Recall from Chapter 3 that water rights in the Western states are based on a doctrine called the "prior appropriation" doctrine. Under this doctrine, "first to use the water in time is first in right.")

In this case, the Cappaert petitioners owned a 12,000-acre ranch near Devil's Hole, 4,000 acres of which were used for growing crops and grazing over 1700 head of cattle. The federal proclamation designating Devil's Hole a national monument was made in January, 1952. In 1968, the Cappaerts began pumping groundwater on their ranch and were the first to appropriate groundwater from an aquifer which was also the source of the water in Devil's Hole.

The question before the Supreme Court was whether the federal government intended to reserve unappropriated and available water in its federal reservation of public land. The Court said that the district court had correctly determined that the level of the pool (within the cave) could be permitted to drop to the extent that the drop did not impair the scientific value of the pool as the natural habitat of the species sought to be preserved. Under the implied-reservation of water doctrine, the Court said an amount of water necessary to fulfill the purpose of the monument reservation was impliedly reserved by the government.

Federal Land Management Legislation

Although the federal government's power to regulate federal lands is grounded in the property clause, there is no comprehensive statutory scheme regulating federal lands. Rather, there is a patchwork of statutes governing different kinds of land and resource use. Many of these statutes are complex, technical, and have been refined in judicial decisions. This final section of the chapter reviews some of the more significant federal acts governing public lands and wildlife.

In 1976, Congress enacted comprehensive legislation governing public lands entitled the *Federal Land Policy and Management Act* (FLPMA), 43 U.S.C. 1701. FLPMA states that the policy of the United States is that public lands will be managed to:

- protect scientific, scenic, historical, ecological, and environmental values;
- preserve certain public lands in their natural condition;
- provide wildlife habitats and outdoor recreation for humans.

FLPMA promotes the concept of *multiple use* and *sustained yield* on public lands. *Multiple use* means a combination of balanced and diverse uses that will best meet the needs of present and future generations of Americans, including recreational, range, timber, mineral, watershed, fish and wildlife, and natural, scenic, or scientific values. *Sustained yield* means the maintenance of a high-level output of various renewable resources on public lands, consistent with the principle of multiple use.

The *Bureau of Land Management (BLM)* within the *Department of the Interior* has authority to manage public lands under the act. The BLM develops and maintains land use plans for public lands. It is authorized to acquire public lands and may sell a tract of public land (except for designated wilderness areas, wild and scenic rivers, or national trails) if it makes certain statutory findings. The FLPMA also authorizes the BLM to withdraw public lands from sale or disposition and directs it to review certain areas within the public domain for their suitability as wilderness.

The *National Forest Management Act* (NFMA)[9] establishes procedures for management of the national forests. Authority to manage national forests is vested in the *U.S. Forest Service* (USFS) within the *Department of Agriculture*. The USFS maintains a Renewable Resource Program for the protection, management, and development of the National Forest System, and it must manage the renewable resources in a way that is consistent with the concepts of multiple use and sustained yield. Under the NFMA, the USFS develops and maintains land and resource management plans within the National Forest System. Among other things, these plans must:

- consider the environment;
- provide for plant and animal diversity;
- ensure that watershed conditions will not be irreversibly damaged and that harvested lands can be restored within five years;
- ensure that water resources will be protected;
- restrict clear-cutting and similar management practices.

In the NFMA, Congress recognized the complexity of managing the nation's renewable forest resources by mandating a continuous analysis of the Renewable Resource Program. It also required the Secretary of Agriculture to "develop, maintain, and, as appropriate, revise land and resource management plans for units . . . coordinated with the land and resource management planning process of state and local governments and other Federal agencies."[10]

The National Environmental Policy Act and Endangered Species Act

The National Environmental Policy Act (NEPA) and the Endangered Species Act (ESA) are laws that apply to actions by a federal agency which significantly affect the human environment or threaten an endangered species. Using these laws, plaintiffs have challenged decisions by the Bureau of Land Management under FLPMA or the National Forest Service under NFMA as violations of NEPA or the ESA. In a series of cases filed to protect the spotted owl and limit logging in the old growth forests of the Pacific Northwest, NEPA and the ESA were used to challenge logging plans approved by federal agencies on national forest lands. The Clean Water Act and Clean Air Act also have provisions designed to protect national resources from air and water pollution.

The Surface Mining Control and Reclamation Act of 1977[11]

Congress enacted the Surface Mining Control and Reclamation Act in 1977. Congress recognized that coal mining operations contributed "significantly to the nation's energy requirements" but simultaneously underscored concern over surface mining operations which, for example:

destroy[ed] or diminish[ed] the utility of land for commercial, industrial, residential, recreational, agricultural, and forestry purposes, by causing erosion and landslides, by contributing to floods, by polluting the water, by destroying fish and wildlife habitats, by impairing natural beauty, by damaging the property of citizens, by creating hazards dangerous to life and property, by degrading the quality of life in local communities, and by counteracting governmental programs and efforts to conserve soil, water, and other natural resources.

The act regulates the environmental effects of strip mining and the surface effects of underground mining. It is administered by the *Office of Surface Mining* (OSM) within the *U.S. Department of the Interior.* The law provides minimum environmental performance standards for strip mining, and establishes an Abandoned Mine Land Reclamation Fund to, among other things,

- reclaim and restore land and water resources affected by past mining;
- seal and fill abandoned deep mine entries and voids;
- control water pollution and prevent coal mine subsidence.

The act also encourages states to regulate strip mining within their borders, and directs the OSM to establish a federal program in any state that does not have an approved strip mining regulatory program.

Earlier in this chapter you read portions of *Hodel v. Virginia Surface Mining and Reclamation Ass'n.* In that case plaintiffs brought a pre-enforcement challenge to the constitutionality of the Surface Mining Control and Reclamation Act of 1977. In *Hodel,* the U.S. Supreme Court upheld the constitutionality of the act against a number of different constitutional challenges.

The Coastal Zone Management Act

In 1972, Congress adopted the Coastal Zone Management Act (CZMA).[12] In adopting the act, Congress recognized the "increasing and competing demands upon the lands and waters of our coastal zone occasioned by population growth and economic development," and found a "national interest in the effective management, beneficial use, protection, and development of the coastal zone." The act establishes a structure providing for the active involvement of coastal states, the development of coastal zone management plans, a process for state input into the development of federally approved plans, and an ultimate decision by the Secretary of Commerce whether a proposed activity deemed inconsistent by the states is permissible. The Outer Continental Shelf Lands Act (OCSLA), 43 U.S.C. 1331, also establishes policies and procedures for managing the oil and natural gas resources of the Outer Continental Shelf (OCS).

Federal Wildlife Protection Acts

In addition to the Endangered Species Act and the Wild Free-Roaming Horses and Burros Act there are a number of acts designed to protect specific species. These are briefly summarized as follows:

1. *The Marine Mammal Protection Act* (MMPA), 16 U.S.C. 1361, makes it unlawful except as specifically permitted under statute or treaty, to take, possess, or trade a marine mammal or marine mammal product, or to use a method of commercial fishing that violates MMPA regulations.

2. *The Bald and Golden Eagle Protection Act,* 16 U.S.C. 668, makes it a criminal offense to possess, take, or trade a bald or golden eagle.

3. *The National Wildlife Refuge System (NWRS) Administration Act,* 16 U.S.C. 668dd-ee, establishes a National Wildlife Refuge System and limits the transfer or disposal of such lands. The law makes it illegal to knowingly disturb, remove, or destroy property in the NWRS.

4. *The Migratory Bird Treaty Act,* 16 U.S.C. 703, makes it unlawful to pursue, hunt, take, capture, kill, possess, trade, or transport any migratory bird or bird part, nest, or egg included in the terms of international agreements between the United States and Mexico, Japan, and the Soviet Union.

Wilderness Protection Laws

The *Wild and Scenic Rivers Act,* 16 U.S.C. 1271, preserves U.S. rivers which have outstanding scenic, recreational, geologic, fish and wildlife, historic, cultural, or other important values.

The *Wilderness Act of 1964,* 16 U.S.C. 1131, establishes the national Wilderness Preservation System, consisting of wilderness lands designated by Congress. Such areas are to be administered in a way that leaves them unimpaired for future generations. No commercial enterprises or permanent roads in such areas are permitted except in specific instances.

Summary of Federal Land Management Laws

Perhaps no other topic better illustrates society's changing perspective on the natural environment than the series of laws enacted to protect and preserve national lands, wilderness areas, and wildlife. With few exceptions, most of the federal laws designed to protect and limit exploitation of public lands and protect endangered or threatened species have been adopted in the last quarter of this century. For state and local governments, much has changed in that time as well. Informed land management has become an issue of importance at all levels of government.

Reviewing land management developments, one writer has observed:

1. An increasingly complex response to increasingly disturbing health, safety, environmental, and land management problems

2. A growing reliance on administrative expertise and land planning evaluations

3. A struggle to balance environmental and land planning goals with other governmental program responsibilities

4. Efforts to broaden decision input and to require meaningful and timely participation of those affected by the decision

5. Efforts to encourage coordination among state and federal officials, and an expanding role for appropriate enforcement including mechanisms for citizen suits and judicial remedies[13]

Federal and state land management issues are complex and it is often difficult to bring together diverse groups and interests. But in order to preserve land and resources for future generations it is essential that natural resources be managed in an intelligent and environmentally sensitive manner. Because of these concerns, it is likely that comprehensive land management, perhaps in coordinated state-federal schemes, will increasingly dominate future land management policies in the United States.

GLOSSARY

Commerce Clause—Section 8 of Article I of the U.S. Constitution which gives Congress the power to regulate commerce among the states.

Dormant commerce clause—Constitutional theory that the commerce clause also prevents state legislation that discriminates against interstate commerce.

Federalism—Union of states subordinated to a central (federal) government.

Interstate commerce—Commerce between states.

Intrastate commerce—Commerce within a state.

Pre-emption—Term which refers to the question whether federal law will take priority over state law.

Property clause—Article IV, Section 3, of the U.S. Constitution which gives Congress the power to make rules and regulations for property belonging to the United States.

Supremacy clause—Article VI of the U.S. Constitution which makes the Constitution and laws of the United States the "supreme law of the land."

Tenth Amendment—U.S. Constitution amendment which reserves those powers not delegated to the federal government to the states.

CASES FOR DISCUSSION

1.   Plaintiffs were brokers of municipal solid waste who arranged for trucks to haul waste from temporary storage sites in New York, New Jersey, and Pennsylvania to landfills in Indiana. They challenged the constitutionality of several Indiana statutes which regulated the trucking of municipal waste. These included a statutory ban on "backhauling" of municipal waste, which limited types of other items that could be carried in trucks used to haul municipal waste to landfills; a statute imposing registration and stickering requirements on transportation vehicles; a statute providing an additional statutory fee for municipal waste originating outside the state; and a statutory provision requiring only out-of-state haulers of solid waste to post surety bonds. Do these statutes violate the commerce clause? *Government Suppliers Consolidating Services, Inc. v. Bayh,* 975 F.2d 1267 (7th Cir. 1992), *cert. denied* 113 S.Ct. 977 (1973).

2.   A landfill operator brought an action challenging the constitutionality of county ordinances which required that all compostable solid waste generated in a county be delivered to a county waste facility. The trial court held that the ordinances impermissibly discriminated against interstate commerce, and the counties appealed. Do county ordinances providing that compostable solid waste cannot be transported out of the county but must be delivered to a local solid waste composting facility violate the commerce clause? *Waste Systems Corp. v. County of Martin, Minn.,* 985 F.2d 1381 (8th Cir. 1993).

3.   In 1991, the Illinois General Assembly passed the Coal Act, which amended state law by adding a new section concerning Illinois' implementation of and compliance with the 1990 Clean Air Act. Under the Coal Act, public utilities were required to devise clean air compliance plans and present the plans to the utility commission for approval. In devising and approving those plans, public utilities and the commission were required to take into account . . . "the need to use coal mined in Illinois in an environmentally responsible manner in the production of electricity, and the need to preserve as a valuable state resource the mining of coal in Illinois." Under another provision of the act, every generator of a certain capacity was required to "include in its Clean Air Act compliance plan the installation of pollution control devices (i.e., scrubbers) . . . to enable [the units] to continue to burn Illinois coal." Plaintiffs contended the Coal Act impermissibly favored in-state interests by requiring the commission to base compliance decisions on the use of Illinois coal and by requiring public utilities to consider building scrubbers designed to use Illinois coal in their operations. Does the Coal Act violate the commerce clause? *Alliance for Clean Coal v. Craig,* 840 F. Supp. 554 (N.D. Ill. 1993).

4.   Plaintiffs, who were neighboring property owners, filed a state court action against oil companies who owned, controlled, and operated a large multitank storage facility for gasoline, petroleum, and other fuel products. The plaintiffs alleged the defendants were negligent in permitting toxic substances to escape from the facility and contaminate the plaintiffs' properties. The defendants argued that the plaintiffs' common law negligence claims were pre-empted by the Clean Air Act. The court was required to resolve the question whether the case should be brought in state court or in federal court under federal question jurisdiction.

The 1990 Clean Air Act states:

> Nothing in this subsection shall preclude, deny or limit any right of a State or political subdivision thereof to adopt or enforce any regulation, requirement, limitation or standard (including any procedural requirement) that is more stringent than a regulation, requirement, limitation or standard in effect under this subsection or that applies to a substance not subject to this subsection.

Is the plaintiff's action for negligence under state common law tort theory pre-empted in this case? *Gutirrez v. Mobil Oil Corp.,* 798 F. Supp. 1280 (W.D. Tex. 1992).

5.   The Hazardous Materials Transportation Act (HMTA) provides that:

> (a) In general
> Except as provided, in subsection (d) of this section and unless otherwise authorized by federal law, any requirement of a State or political subdivision thereof or Indian tribe is pre-empted if—
> (1) compliance with both the State or political subdivision or Indian tribe requirement and any requirement of this chapter or of a regulation issued under this chapter is not possible,
> (2) the State or political subdivision or Indian tribe requirement as applied or enforced creates an obstacle to the accomplishment and execution of this chapter or the regulations issued under this chapter. . . .

In adopting these pre-emption rules, Congress specifically found that "many states and localities have enacted laws and regulations which vary from federal laws and regulations . . . thereby creating the potential for unreasonable hazards in other jurisdictions and confounding shippers and carriers which attempt to comply with multiple and conflicting registration, permitting, routing, notification, and other regulatory requirements."

The Prairie Island Mdewakanton Sioux Trial Council enacted an ordinance which regulated the transportation of nuclear materials on reservation land, requiring that transporters obtain a separate tribal license for each shipment of nuclear material. The ordinance also required that license applications be filed 180 days in advance of each shipment and be accompanied by an application fee of $1,000. The ordinance also gave the Tribal Council authority to determine whether to issue a license, and to impose a $1,000,000 civil fine for willful violations of the ordinance.

The ordinance varied from the federal law in that the federal act did not require a transportation license for individual shipments of radioactive materials. The Northern States Power Company brought an action seeking a declaratory judgment that the ordinance was pre-empted by the Hazardous Materials Transporation Act. Was the federal district court correct in issuing a preliminary injunction against the enforcement of the ordinance? *Northern States Power Company v. Prairie Island Mdewakanton Sioux Indian Community,* 991 F.2d 458 (8th Cir. 1993).

ENDNOTES

1. For example, in *Cargill Inc. v. U.S.,* 116 S.Ct. 407 (1995), the Supreme Court declined to review a decision that land adjacent to the San Francisco Bay National Wildlife Refuge is a wetlands subject to regulation under the Clean Water Act. Citing *Lopez,* the petitioner argued that the use of seasonably wet areas by migratory birds creates too tenuous a connection to interstate commerce to bring the areas within the sweep of the commerce clause.

2. *Minnesota v. Clover Leaf Creamery Co.,* 449 U.S. 456 (1981).

3. 883 F.2d 245 (3d Cir. 1989).

4. *Swin Resource Systems, Inc. v. Lycoming County,* 883 F.2d 245 (3d Cir. 1989).

5. *O'Conner v. Commonwealth Edison Co.,* 13 F.3d 1090 (7th Cir. 1994).

6. *California v. Federal Energy Regulatory Commission,* 495 U.S. 490 (1990).

7. BLM, *Public Land Statistics,* 1, 5 (1989).

8. *California Coastal Commission v. Granite Rock Co.,* 480 U.S. 572 (1987).

9. 43 U.S.C. § 1701–1702, 1732 (1993).

10. 16 U.S.C. § 1604 (a).

11. 30 U.S.C. § 1201–1328 (1988 & Supp. IV 1992).

12. 16 U.S.C. § 1451–1464 (1993).

13. James E. Brookshire, *Engaging the Future; A Survey of Federal Environmental and Land Management Developments,* 26 URB. LAW. 293 (1994).

8

PRINCIPLES OF
ADMINISTRATIVE LAW

INTRODUCTION

The concept of environmental law as defined in this book includes local, state, and national laws used to prevent, deter, or punish actions which damage or threaten the environment. Previous chapters have reviewed common law rules and constitutional issues which arise in environmental cases. This chapter focuses on one of the most significant areas of law affecting the environment—**administrative law.** Administrative law encompasses the legal rules governing the powers, duties, and procedures of administrative agencies.

Concern for the environment is not new in America, as the writings of Henry David Thoreau in the mid-nineteenth century illustrate. However, the decision to address environmental issues through regulatory policy administered by government agencies is a fairly recent concept. Beginning in the 1960s, public concern for the environment began to build, sparked by publication of Rachel Carson's *Silent Spring* and fueled by a counter-culture movement embracing a "back to nature" perspective. American environmental concerns built throughout the decade, culminating in the first "Earth Day" in 1970, and significantly, the creation of the Environmental Protection Agency (EPA) by President Nixon's executive order in 1970.

Throughout the 1970s and into the 1980s, Congress enacted major pieces of environmental legislation. These include the National Environmental Policy Act and Endangered Species Act, the Clean Air Act, the Clean Water Act, the Toxic Substances Control Act and Federal Insecticde, Fungicide, and Rodenticide Act and the Resource Conservation and Recovery Act and Comprehensive Environmental Response, Compensation and Liability Act.

The responsibility for administering these and other important environmental laws falls to various federal agencies, most importantly, the Environmental Protection Agency (EPA). With jurisdiction over air pollution, water pollution, drinking water, hazardous waste disposal, pesticides, and toxic substances, the EPA is one of the most powerful regulatory agencies in the federal government. Furthermore, all the states have enacted state environmental protection laws, in some cases more stringent than those at the federal level, and have created state agencies with the power to administer and enforce those state and federal environmental laws within their jurisdiction.

Federal and state agencies play a central role in rule making, adjudication, and enforcement of the various provisions of federal and state environmental laws. In many cases, principles of administrative law are critical in resolving environmental disputes. In cases where there is scientific data supporting both sides of an issue, the important issue may be the question of the burden of proof on the issue, whether the administrative agency's decision was within the scope of its authority, or whether the agency's procedure was consistent with legal requirements.

It has been estimated that administrative law issues are at or close to the heart of somewhere between eighty and ninety percent of all disputes concerning federal environmental laws and regulations.[1]

THE "DELEGATION DOCTRINE": SCOPE OF AGENCY AUTHORITY

There is nothing in the federal or most state constitutions providing for the creation of administrative agencies. However, as government's role in protecting the environment has increased, the legislative and executive branches of government have increasingly *delegated* some of their powers to administrative agencies. In the vast majority of cases, the legislative body delegates power to an agency by *statute,* and it is placed into the *executive branch* of government. The statutes creating an administrative agency are called **enabling legislation.**

Agencies typically are given powers with characteristics of each of the three branches of government. For example, many agencies have the *legislative power* to issue rules and regulations which may impose civil or criminal penalites for violation. In addition, most agencies have *executive power* to enforce provisions of the statute and agency rules and regulations. Finally, agencies often have *judicial power* to hold hearings and adjudicate individual disputes involving questions of compliance. In addition, the agency is responsible for analyzing issues and performing the day-to-day tasks of enforcing and administering laws passed by the legislative body.

A fundamental principle of administrative law is that the powers and duties of the administrative agencies are derived from the statutes which create those powers, and an agency only has such power and authority as the legislature expressly or impliedly delegates through the enabling legislation. Under the **delegation doctrine,** the courts examine such questions as whether the legislature and chief executive could constitutionally delegate a particular power to the agency or whether the statutory language in the enabling legislation is too broad or vague to adequately define the agency's power.

In the first part of this century, the courts took a narrow view of the ability of Congress to delegate constitutional powers to administrative agencies. However, following a series of cases challenging Franklin D. Roosevelt's "New Deal" legislation in the 1930s, courts have generally recognized that Congress and the executive branch can constitutionally delegate some of their powers to administrative agencies. As a result, delegation of legislative authority to administrative agencies has led to increasing government regulation through agency rule making.

Because an agency's powers are limited to those powers expressly and impliedly authorized by its enabling legislation, if a court determines that the agency action exceeded agency authority under its enabling legislation, the action is illegal and unenforceable.[2]

THE ADMINISTRATIVE PROCEDURE ACT

If its enabling legislation specifically requires the agency to follow certain procedures in decision making, the agency must act in accordance with those procedures. Absent specific requirements in its enabling legislation, a federal agency's actions are governed by the provisions of the **Administrative Procedure Act** (APA).[3] Passed in 1946, the APA establishes the basic framework governing federal agency action. Congress has enacted other regulatory statutes which may supplement or supersede provisions of the APA, and judicial interpretation of enabling legislation and APA provisions in the context of specific statutes has refined general principles. Presidents have also imposed procedural requirements on agency rule making by executive order.

The APA provides a blueprint of modern administrative law. It establishes minimum procedural requirements for many types of agency actions, specifically rule making and adjudication. Adjudication refers to case-by-case decision making by the agency in a hearing with trial-like procedures. The APA also provides a framework for judicial review of administrative decision making. It addresses the availability of review of agency action, the scope of judicial review, and court review of agency inaction. Because states have generally modeled state administrative procedure legislation on the APA, its principles also govern judicial decision making at the state level.

General Framework of the APA

An administrative agency may exercise different kinds of powers as long as its enabling legislation expressly or impliedly authorizes it to do so. Two important powers addressed by the APA are policy making through *rule making* and policy making through *adjudication.* An agency makes policy through rule making by issuing legislative rules and regulations. Policy making through adjudication occurs when the agency acts like a judicial body and applies legal standards set out by statute or regulation to the facts of a particular case in a hearing.

In addition, most agencies have the power to enforce rules or findings through sanctions like civil and criminal penalties. Most agencies have other important powers, including the power to investigate complaints, to advise businesses and individuals on matters of concern to the agency, to conduct studies, and to issue permits and licenses when authorized to do so by statute. The courts have recognized that an agency may formulate policy through different means as long as it is authorized to do so by its enabling legislation.[4]

Rule Making vs. Adjudication

There are benefits in implementing environmental policy by rule making rather than adjudication. Commentators have suggested that rule making is fairer to the class of persons affected by a rule because of the wider notice provisions and opportunity for participation under APA provisions. Rule making is *prospective* rather than *retroactive,* that is, it imposes consequences for future conduct rather than past conduct or present status. Creation and application of a rule provide greater clarity and greater likelihood of uniform enforcement than creating policy through adjudication. Rule making also is more efficient because it eliminates the need for a case-by-case adjudication of the issue.

On the other hand, there are some advantages to policy making through adjudication. First, the increasing procedural complexity of rule making, as a result of additional and new requirements on the rule-making process–like paperwork reduction provisions, impact statements, etc. may make case adjudication more efficient in some situations. Second, it is easier to modify specific rules through adjudication; therefore, changing agency policy may be simpler and thus more efficient through adjudication. And because adjudicatory decisions are specific to the particular circumstances of the case, the rule that emerges through adjudication is also less likely to be over- or under-inclusive in its impact.

In general, however, courts and commentators prefer agencies to establish and implement policy through administrative rule rather than adjudication, and most agencies use rule making to develop legislative policy rules. Most major pieces of environmental legislation adopted by Congress since the 1960s delegate to federal agencies (usually the EPA) the power to implement the legislation through rule making. A number of environmental statutes explicitly authorize the agency to promulgate legislative rules, and some agencies are required by their enabling legislation to issue rules on certain issues. For example, the EPA was required to promulgate performance standards for the treatment, storage, or disposal of certain hazardous wastes within eighteen months of the enactment of RCRA in 1976.

Rule Making Under the APA

Under the APA, a "rule" is defined as:

> The whole or a part of an agency statement of general or particular applicability and future effect designed to implement, interpret, or prescribe law or policy or describing the organization, procedure, or practice requirements of an agency. . . (5 U.S.C. sec. 551[4]).

Types of administrative rules include:

1. *Substantive rules.* These rules prescribe law or policy and are legally enforceable in court. A rule which prescribes safety requirements for certain kinds of activities is an example of a substantive rule. Substantive rules must meet the rule making requirements of the APA.

2. *Procedural rules.* An agency may create rules governing agency organization, procedure, or practice. These are exempt from some of the rule-making requirements of the APA.

3. *Interpretive rules.* These are statements issued by agencies which present the agency's understanding of the meaning of the language in the regulations or the statutes it administers. An example of an interpretive rule is the EPA's interpretation of the meaning of "stationary source" under the Clean Air Act which was at issue in *Chevron v. NRDC,* a case that follows.

Deference to Agency Opinion

In cases where persons challenge agency action in court, one important question is the extent to which courts should defer to the agency's interpretation of the statutes it administers. This is not only a legal question but also a public policy question of substantial importance. As a practical matter, the language in enabling legislation is often broad and subject to interpretation. The question "who should decide" the meaning of the statutory language is a significant one because it goes to the scope of the agency's power and the relationship between the powers of the agency and those of the three branches of government.

In the following case, the U.S. Supreme Court addressed the standard of review of an agency's interpretation of a statute. This case involved interpretation of the Clean Air Act Amendments of 1977, which required "non-attainment" states (states which had not met earlier requirements of the Clean Air Act) to establish a permit program for certain new sources of air pollution within the states. The question in the case centered on the appropriate definition of the term "stationary source" used in the Clean Air Act. The EPA by administrative rule permitted the states to adopt a plant-wide definition of the term "stationary source." Under the EPA definition, an existing plant which contained several pollution-emitting devices could install or modify one piece of equipment without meeting permit conditions, if the alteration would not increase the *total* emissions from the plant.

Environmental groups filed a petition for review of the EPA regulation in the D.C. Circuit Court of Appeals, and the court of appeals set aside the regulations. Chevron U.S.A. and others appealed to the Supreme Court. The question before the court was whether the EPA's rule permitting states to treat all pollution-emitting devices within the same industrial grouping as though they were encased within a single "bubble" was based on a reasonable construction of the term "stationary source" in the act.

CHEVRON U.S.A. INC. v. NATURAL RESOURCES DEFENSE COUNCIL
467 U.S. 837 (1984)

JUSTICE STEVENS delivered the opinion of the Court.

***

When a court reviews an agency's construction of the statute which it administers, it is confronted with two questions. First, always, is the question whether Congress has directly spoken to the precise question at issue. If the intent of Congress is clear, that is the end of the matter; for the court, as well as the agency, must give effect to the unambiguously expressed intent of Congress. If, however, the court determines Congress has not directly addressed the precise question at issue, the court does not simply impose its own construction on the statute, as would be necessary in the absence of an administrative interpretation. Rather, if the statute is silent or ambiguous with respect to the specific issue, the question for the court is whether the agency's answer is based on a permissible construction of the statute.

"The power of an administrative agency to administer a congressionally created program necessarily requires the formulation of policy and the making of rules to fill any gap left, implicitly or explicitly, by Congress." If Congress has explicitly left a gap for the agency to fill, there is an express delegation of authority to the agency to elucidate a specific provision of the statute by regulation. Such legislative regulations are given controlling weight unless they are arbitrary, capricious, or manifestly contrary to the statute. Sometimes the legislative delegation to an agency on a particular question is implicit rather than explicit. In such a case, a court may not substitute its own construction of a statutory provision for a reasonable interpretation made by the administrator of an agency.

We have long recognized that considerable weight should be accorded to an executive department's construction of a statutory scheme it is entrusted to administer, and the principle of deference to administrative interpretations "has been consistently followed by this Court whenever a decision as to the meaning or reach of a statute has involved reconciling conflicting policies, and a full understanding of the force of the statutory policy in the given situation has depended upon more than ordinary knowledge respecting the matters subject to agency regulations. . . . If this choice represents a reasonable accommodation of conflicting policies that were committed to the agency's care by the statute, we should not disturb it unless it appears from the statute or its legislative history that the accommodation is not one that Congress would have sanctioned."

In light of these well-settled principles it is clear that the Court of Appeals misconceived the nature of its role in reviewing the regulations at issue. Once it determined, after its own examination of the legislation, that Congress did not actually have an intent regarding the applicability of the bubble concept to the permit program, the question before it was not whether in its view the concept is "inappropriate" in the general context of a program designed to improve air quality, but whether the Administrator's view that it is appropriate in the context of this particular program is a reasonable one. Based on the examination of the legislation and its history . . . , we agree with the Court of appeals that Congress did not have a specific intention on the applicability of the bubble concept in these cases, and conclude that the EPA's use of that concept here is a reasonable policy choice for the agency to make.

***

. . . [T]he Administrator's interpretation represents a reasonable accommodation of manifestly competing interests and is entitled to deference: the regulatory scheme is technical and complex, the agency considered the matter in a detailed and reasoned fashion, and the decision involves reconciling conflicting policies. Congress intended to accommodate both interests, but did not do so itself on the level of specificity presented by these cases. Perhaps that body consciously desired the Administrator to strike the balance at this level, thinking that those with great expertise and charged with responsibility for administering the provision would be in a better position to do so; perhaps it simply did not consider the question at this level; and perhaps Congress was unable to forge a coalition on either side of the question, and those on each side decided to take their chances with the scheme devised by the agency. For judicial purposes, it matters not which of these things occurred.

Judges are not experts in the field, and are not part of either political branch of the Government. Courts must, in some cases, reconcile competing political interests, but not on the basis of the judges' personal policy preferences. In contrast, an agency to which Congress has delegated policymaking responsibilities may, within the limits of that delegation, properly rely upon the incumbent administration's views of wise policy to inform its judgments. While agencies are not directly accountable to the people, the Chief Executive is, and it is entirely appropriate for this political branch of the Government to make such policy choices—resolving the competing interests which Congress itself either inadvertently did not resolve, or intentionally left to be resolved by the agency charged with the administration of the statute in light of everyday realities.

When a challenge to an agency construction of a statutory provision, fairly conceptualized, really centers on the wisdom of the agency's policy, rather than whether it is a reasonable choice within a gap left open by Congress, the challenge must fail. In such a case, federal judges—who have no constituency—have a duty to respect legitimate policy choices made by those who do. The responsibilities for assessing the wisdom of such policy choices and resolving the struggle between competing views of the public interest are not judicial ones: "Our Constitution vests such responsibilities in the political branches."

We hold that the EPA's definition of the term "source" is a permissible construction of the statute which seeks to accommodate progress in reducing air pollution with economic growth. "The Regulations which the Administrator has adopted provide what the agency could allowably view as . . . [an] effective reconciliation of these twofold ends. . . ."

The judgment of the Court of Appeals is reversed.

Questions and Comments for Discussion

1.   What two-part test was used by the Court to determine whether agency interpretation of its statutory language should be upheld in this case?

2.   Under the holding in this case, courts are required to determine whether congressional *intention* was clearly stated in the agency's enabling legislation. Doesn't this require the courts to *first* interpret the statute before deciding whether to defer to agency interpretation? As a practical matter, the line between deference to agency interpretation and the court's primary responsibility to interpret statutory law is a hazy one.

3.   This case involved the "bubble" concept in the interpretation of "stationary source" of air pollution under the Clean Air Act. What is the "bubble" concept? How might a bubble result in cleaner air despite lowering air quality standards in some cases?

4.   Despite the principle of deference stated in this case, courts may avoid deferring to agency interpretations of law in cases where they find the "plain meaning" of the statute differs from the agency's opinion.[5] As a general rule, courts appear more likely to defer to agency interpretation when the legislative scheme is very technical and implementation details are delegated to the agency's expertise.

5.   There are important public policy issues underlying the *Chevron* decision. Some argue that courts should defer to administrative agencies like the EPA because of its scientific expertise in determining how best to implement public policy. But there are those who argue that in many cases, the regulatory agency entrusted with environmental protection is "captured" by the industry it regulates. Consequently, they say, agency rule making too often defers to the concerns of business and industry. To what extent do you think courts should defer to agency expertise? What are the implications of your answer?

Application of the Delegation Doctrine

The *Chevron* decision requires courts to defer to an agency's interpretation of the statutory language it is authorized to administer. But agency rule making which exceeds the agency's authority violates the delegation doctrine and will be unenforceable. A court of appeals decision striking down the EPA's "lender liability" rule under CERCLA illustrates this point.

In this case, petitioners challenged an EPA rule limiting the liability of lenders for CERCLA cleanup costs. As potential litigants, petitioners did not want to be foreclosed from recovering costs from lenders exempted from CERCLA liability. Following a series of conflicting court decisions interpreting the scope of a CERCLA exemption, the EPA adopted a final administrative rule specifying the range of activities that might be undertaken by secured lenders without incurring CERCLA liability. Following is a portion of the court of appeals' opinion holding that the EPA lacked the authority to define lender liability under CERCLA by administrative rule.

KELLEY v. UNITED STATES EPA
15 F.3d 1100 (D.C. Cir. 1994)

OPINION: SILBERMAN, *Circuit Judge:*

Petitioners challenge an EPA regulation limiting lender liability under CERCLA. We hold that EPA lacks statutory authority to restrict by regulation private rights of action arising under the statute and therefore grant the petition for review.

***

CERCLA . . . authorizes private parties and EPA to bring civil actions independently to recover their costs associated with the cleanup of hazardous wastes from those responsible for the contamination. Section 107 of CERCLA generally imposes strict liability on, among others, all prior and present "owners and operators" of hazardous waste sites. Congress created a safe harbor provision for secured creditors, however, in the definition of "owner or operator," providing that "such term does not include a person, who, without participating in the management of a vessel or facility, holds indicia of ownership primarily to protect his security interest in the vessel or facility."

Conflicting judicial interpretations as to the scope of this secured creditor exemption opened the possibility that lenders would be held liable for the cost of cleaning up contaminated property that they hold merely as collateral. Lenders lacked clear guidance as to the extent to which they could involve themselves in the affairs of a facility without incurring liability and also as to whether they would forfeit the exemption by exercising their right of foreclosure, which could be thought to convert their "indicia of ownership"—the security interest—into ac-

tual ownership. In *United States v. Fleet Factors Corp.,* 901 F.2d 1550 (11th Cir. 1990), the court, although adhering to the settled view that Congress intended to protect the commercial practices of secured creditors "in their normal course of business," nevertheless stated that "a secured creditor will be liable if its involvement with the management of the facility is sufficiently broad to support the inference that it could affect hazardous waste disposal decisions if it so chose."

This language, portending as it did an expansion in the scope of secured creditor liability, caused considerable discomfort in financial circles. . . . EPA, responding to the understandable clamor from the banking community and in light of the federal government's increasing role as a secured creditor after taking over failed savings and loans, instituted a rulemaking proceeding to define the secured creditor exemption when legislative efforts to amend CERCLA failed. In April 1992, EPA issued the final regulation, which employs a framework of specific tests to provide clearer articulation of a lender's scope of liability under CERCLA.

[*The Court first analyzed and then rejected EPA's argument that various specific sections of CERCLA expressly or impliedly delegated authority to the agency to define lender liability by rule.*]

***

There remains the question of whether the regulation can be sustained as an interpretative rule. The preamble to the final regulation suggests that EPA attempted to straddle two horses—issuing the rule as a legislative regulation but asserting in the alternative that as an interpretative rule, it would still be entitled to judicial deference and therefore affect private party litigation. Although we have admitted that the distinction between legislative and interpretative rules is "enshrouded in considerable smog," it is commonly understood that a rule is legislative if it is "based on an agency's power to exercise its judgment as to how best to implement a general statutory mandate," and has the binding force of law. By contrast, an interpretative rule "is based on specific statutory provisions, and represents the agency's construction of the statute that is—while not binding—entitled to substantial judicial deference under *Chevron U.S.A. Inc. v. Natural Resources Defense Council, Inc.*

The rule bears little resemblance to what we have traditionally found to be an interpretative regulation. EPA does not really define specific statutory terms, but rather takes off from those terms and devises a comprehensive regulatory regimen to address the liability problems facing secured creditors. This extensive quasi-legislative effort to implement the statute does not strike us as merely a construction of statutory phrases. . . . In any event, the same reason that prevents the agency from issuing the rule as a substantive regulation precludes judicial deference to EPA's offered "interpretation." If Congress meant the judiciary, not EPA, to determine liability issues—and we believe Congress did—EPA's view of statutory liability may not be given deference. "A precondition to deference under *Chevron* is a

congressional delegation of administrative authority." *Chevron,* which sets forth the reigning rationale for judicial deference to agency interpretation of statutes, is premised on the notion that Congress implicitly delegated to the agency the authority to reconcile reasonably statutory ambiguities or to fill reasonably statutory interstices. Where Congress does not give an agency authority to determine (usually formally) the interpretation of a statute in the first instance and instead gives the agency authority only to bring the question to a federal court as the "prosecutor," deference to the agency's interpretation is inappropriate. As we have explained, that is all that EPA can do regarding liability issues. Moreover, even if an agency enjoys authority to determine such a legal issue administratively, deference is withheld if a private party can bring the issue independently to federal court under a private right of action. . . . Petitioners . . . wish to preserve the right to sue lenders when, in petitioners' view, a lender's behavior transgresses the statutory test—whether or not EPA would regard the lender as liable. As we read the statute, Congress intended that petitioners' claim in such an event should be evaluated by the federal courts independent of EPA's institutional view. . . .

We well recognize the difficulties that lenders face in the absence of the clarity EPA's regulation would have provided. Before turning to this rulemaking, EPA sought congressional relief and was rebuffed. We see no alternative but that EPA try again. The petition for review is granted and the regulation is hereby vacated.

Questions and Comments for Discussion

1. What concerns by lenders prompted the EPA's "lender liability" rule?

2. According to the court, what is the difference between an interpretative rule and legislative rule? According to the court, who

should clarify the issue of lender liability under CERLCA?

3. CERCLA subjects four classes of parties to potential liability for hazardous waste cleanup costs, including a current owner or

operator of the site. Under what circumstances might a lender become an "owner or operator" for the purposes of CERCLA? What is the "secured lender exemption" under CERLCA which was the subject of the EPA's rule?

4.   Congress has clarified the "secured lender exemption" by essentially codifying the EPA lender liability rule in the Asset Conservation, Lender Liability and Deposit Insurance Protection Act of 1996. What concerns of lenders prompted this change?

Procedures for Rule Making Under the APA

The APA does not require that all administrative rule making follow a single fixed approach. Rather, there are three basic procedures for rule making under the APA. These are informal rule making, formal rule making, and hybrid rule making.

Formal rule-making procedures are only required when a statute other than the APA requires a rule to be made "on the record after opportunity for an agency hearing." Formal ("on the record") rule making is governed by Sections 556 and 557 of the APA. These sections require that the agency support its rule with substantial evidence in an exclusive rule-making record, and that there be an oral hearing presided over by agency members or an administrative law judge. In formal rule making, the parties are granted certain trial-like procedural rights including the right to conduct cross-examination and the right to submit proposed findings and conclusions for agency consideration. Formal rule making is the exception in agency rule making, and except in rate making and food additive cases, formal rule-making procedures are seldom used by agencies.

Most agency rule making is *informal rule making,* sometimes called "notice and comment" rule making. Informal rule making is governed by Section 553 of the APA. Unless exempted by another provision of the act, rule making under this section requires:

1.   *Notice* of the proposed rule making published in the *Federal Register.* (The *Federal Register* is the official government publication in which agency statements of organization, procedural rules, and public notices must be printed.) The notice must include a statement of time, place, and nature of the proceedings, a reference to the legal authority under which the rule is proposed, and terms or a description of the issues to be addressed by the proposed rule.

2.   *Opportunity to interested persons* to submit written data, view, or arguments on the proposal, with or without opportunity for oral presentation.

3.   A *concise general statement of the basis and purpose of the final rule.*

4.   *Publication* of the final rule not less than 30 days before its effective date.

Some agency rules are exempt from these requirements, and the APA authorizes agencies to dispense with notice and comment requirements for "good cause." However, these exemptions are narrowly construed by the courts.

An agency undertakes rule making in order to fulfill its statutory responsibilities, and Congress may require by statute that the agency undertake specific rule-making actions within a particular time. Congress may also precipitate agency rule making by "recommending" or "urging" action by the agency. Under Section 553 (e) of the APA, the public may also generate rule making by the agency. Agencies are required under this section to give interested persons "the right to petition for the issuance, amendment, or repeal of a rule." The president and Office of Management and Budget also play an important role in reviewing agency rule-making decisions and setting priorities for agency rule making.

In some environmental statutes, Congress has required a "hybrid" form of rule-making procedure. **Hybrid rule making** describes rule-making requirements contained in specific pieces of legislation which combine both "notice and comment" procedures with formal rule-making requirements. Statutes like the Occupational Safety and Health Act[6] and the Mine Safety and Health Act,[7] for example, are called "hybrid" rule-making statutes because they combine elements of both formal and informal rule making. In some statutes, Congress may mandate requirements like a public hearing prior to rule making, cross-examination of witnesses appearing at the hearing, and more extensive statements of justification for the agency rule. Congress may also seek to control agency rule making by imposing statutory deadlines for completion of rule making. For example, the Asbestos Hazard Emergency Response Act of 1986 required the EPA to publish final rules within 360 days.

OTHER STATUTES AFFECTING RULE MAKING

Congress has imposed additional requirements on agency rule making through other legislation. Examples of laws affecting administrative agency rule making include:

1. *The Regulatory Flexibility Act,* 5 U.S.C. Sections 601-12, which requires agencies to consider the potential impact of regulations on small business.
2. *The Paperwork Reduction Act of 1980,* 44 U.S.C. Sections 3501-3520, which assigns to the Office of Management and Budget (OMB) the responsibility for coordinating federal information policy.
3. *The National Environmental Policy Act,* (NEPA), 42 U.S.C. Sections 4321-47, which directs agencies to consider the potential environmental impact of major federal actions significantly affecting the quality of the human environment. NEPA requirements are discussed in Chapter 9 of this textbook.
4. *The Federal Advisory Committee Act,* 5 U.S.C. App., Pub. L. No. 92-463, 86 stat. 770, which regulates the formation and operation of advisory committees by federal agencies.
5. *The Negotiated Rulemaking Act of 1990,* 5 US. C. Section 561 *et seq.,* which establishes a statutory framework for negotiated rule making to formulate proposed regulations. Under negotiated rule making, representatives of the agency and various affected interest groups negotiate the text of a proposed rule.
6. *The Federal Register Act,* 44 U.S.C. Section 1501 *et seq.* The APA requires publication in the *Federal Register* of agency statements of organization, procedural rules, and public notices mandated for formal and informal rule making.

JUDICIAL REVIEW OF AGENCY DECISION MAKING

Judicial review occurs when a court reviews an agency's final action. Issues which may arise during judicial review include (1) whether court review of agency action is available at all; (2) if so, what is the appropriate standard of judicial review; and (3) what remedies, if any, are available in cases where the agency has failed to initiate or to complete rule making. Many of these questions require the courts to consider principles of constitutional law as well as administrative law because they raise fundamental concerns about the appropriate relationship between the courts, the legislative and executive branches of government, and the agency.

Is Agency Action Subject to Review?

Section 701 of the APA provides that the action of "each authority of the Government of the United States" is subject to judicial review, except where "statutes preclude judicial review" or "where agency action is committed to agency discretion by law."

In the following case, the Supreme Court considered this presumption of reviewability in determining whether petitioners were entitled to judicial review of the Secretary of Transportation's approval of federal funds to build a road through a park.

CITIZENS TO PRESERVE OVERTON PARK v. VOLPE
401 U.S. 402 (1971)

Mr. JUSTICE MARSHALL delivered the opinion of the court.

The growing public concern about the quality of our natural environment has prompted Congress in recent years to enact legislation designed to curb the accelerated destruction of our country's natural beauty. We are concerned in this case with the Department of Transportation Act of 1966 and the Federal-Aid to Highway Act of 1968. These statutes prohibit the Secretary of Transportation from authorizing the use of federal funds to finance the construction of highways through public parks if a "feasible and prudent" alternative route exists. If no such route is available, the statutes allow him to approve construction through parks only if there has been "all possible planning to minimize harm" to the park.

Petitioners, private citizens as well as local and national conservation organizations, contend that the secretary has violated these statutes by authorizing the expenditure of federal funds for the construction of a six-lane interstate highway through a public park in Memphis, Tennessee. Their claim was rejected by the District Court and the Court of Appeals for the Sixth Circuit af-

firmed. . . . We now reverse the judgment below and remand for further proceedings in the District Court.

Overton Park is a 342-acre city park located near the center of Memphis. The park contains a zoo, a nine-hole municipal golf course, an outdoor theater, nature trails, a bridle path, an art academy, picnic areas, and 170 acres of forest. The proposed highway, which is to be six-lane, high-speed, expressway, will sever the zoo from the rest of the park. Although the roadway will be depressed below ground level except where it crosses a small creek, 26 acres of the park will be destroyed. . . .

[*The Court noted that the highway project had been approved by various federal agencies, including approval by the Secretary of Transportation of the route and design. Neither announcement approving the route and design was accompanied by a statement of the secretary's factual findings, and he did not indicate why he believed there were no feasible and prudent alternative routes or why design changes could not be made to reduce the harm to the park.*]

***

A threshold question—whether petitioners are entitled to any judicial review—is easily answered. Section 701 of the Administrative Procedure Act provides that the action of "each authority of the Government of the United States," which includes the Department of Transportation, is subject to judicial review except where there is a statutory prohibition on review or where "agency action is committed to agency discretion by law." In this case, there is no indication that Congress sought to prohibit judicial review and there is most certainly no "showing of 'clear and convincing evidence' of a . . . legislative intent" to restrict access to judicial review.

Similarly, the Secretary's decision here does not fall within the exception for action "committed to agency discretion." This is a very narrow exception. The legislative history of the Administrative Procedure Act indicates that it is applicable in those rare instances where "statutes are drawn in such broad terms that in a given case there is no law to apply."

Section 4(f) of the Department of Transportation Act and sec. 138 of the Federal-Aid Highway Act are clear and specific directives. Both the Department of Trans-

portation Act and the Federal-Aid to Highway Act provide that the Secretary "shall not approve any program or project" that requires the use of any public parkland "unless (1) there is no feasible and prudent alternative to the use of such land, and (2) such program includes all possible planning to minimize harm to such park. . . ." This language is a plain and explicit bar to the use of federal funds for construction of highways through parks—only the most unusual situations are exempted. . . .

Congress clearly did not intend that cost and disruption of the community were to be ignored by the secretary. But the very existence of the statute indicates that protection of parkland was to be given paramount importance. The few green havens that are public parks were not to be lost unless there were truly unusual factors present in a particular case or the cost or community disruption resulting from alternative routes reached extraordinary magnitudes. If the statutes are to have any meaning, the Secretary cannot approve the destruction of parkland unless he finds that alternative routes present unique problems.

Plainly there is "law to apply" and thus the exemption for action "committed to agency discretion" is inapplicable. . . .

The Issue of "Standing"

Standing is the legal status conferring on a person or legal entity the right to challenge agency action in the courts. The decision to grant judicial review of an agency decision upon the petition of an aggrieved citizen raises important questions: Who should be the final decision maker in determining environmental policy—the courts or the administrative agency? What role should the public play in environmental policy making? To what extent should agency decision making be protected from judicial review because it is legislative power protected from court review by the separation of powers doctrine of the U.S. Constitution?

Under Article III of the Constitution, federal court jurisdiction is limited to "cases or controversies." The courts have held that Article III requires a person seeking judicial review to demonstrate some actual or threatened injury. The issue of standing in environmental cases has become important because challenges to agency rules and decisions are often brought by environmental organizations like the Environmental Defense Fund and National Wildlife Federation.

In the first chapter of this text you read excerpts from *Sierra Club v. Morton.*[8] In that case, the Supreme Court first addressed the important issue of "standing" in environmental cases and controversies. In *Sierra Club v. Morton,* environmental groups had challenged the Forest Service's appproval of a $35 million development project in the Mineral King Valley of California. The issue before the Court was whether plaintiff environmental groups had standing to challenge the agency's approval. Sierra Club relied on Section 702 of the APA, which reads:

> A person suffering legal wrong because of agency action, or adversely affected or aggrieved by agency action within the meaning of a relevant statute, is entitled to judicial review thereof. . . .

In *Sierra Club v. Morton,* the Supreme Court stated the rule that a person has standing to obtain judicial review of federal agency action under this section if the action had caused him "injury in fact," and the alleged injury was an interest "arguably within the zone of interests to be protected or regulated" by the statute. The Court recognized that injury to aesthetics or ecology could constitute legal injury, but it said that the party seeking review must allege facts showing that he himself was adversely affected by the agency action.

Subsequently, the Court clarified these requirements in an expansive interpretation of standing. In *United States v. Students Challenging Regulatory Agency Procedures,* 412 U.S. 669 (1973) (SCRAP I), students challenged the federal agency's approval of a railroad rate increase because it would discriminate against recycled goods. In SCRAP I, the court held that the students had standing, even though the injury alleged by plaintiffs was minimal.

The Supreme Court appears to have retreated from its earlier expansive interpretations of the standing requirement since 1990, limiting standing for such organizations. For example, in 1990 in *Lujan v. National Wildlife Federation,*[9] the Court denied the National Wildlife Federation standing to obtain review of the Bureau of Land Management's administration of the Federal Land Policy and Management of Act of 1976. The issue in that case was whether the Bureau had properly fulfilled its duties under the act in deciding to permit previously withdrawn federal lands to be opened up to mining activities.

Justice Scalia, writing for the majority, found that the Federation was a proper representative of individual members' interests and that those interests were within the zone of interests of the statute. However, because the facts alleged in the affidavits of individual members did not establish that their interests would be affected by the government action, the court held that the plaintiff lacked standing.

In 1992, Justice Scalia, again writing for the majority, concluded that an environmental organization lacked standing to challenge an agency decision even though the environmental statute at issue contained a provision authorizing citizen suits.

The Endangered Species Act requires federal agencies, in consultation with the Secretary of the Interior, to insure that agency action is not likely to jeopardize a threatened or endangered species. In *Lujan v. Defenders of Wildlife,*[10] plaintiffs challenged a joint regulation by the Fish and Wildlife Service and National Marine Fisheries which provided that consultation was only required for actions taken in the United States or on the high seas. Plaintiffs' concern was that international development projects funded in part by the U.S. government posed a threat to endangered species abroad.

The initial question before the Court was whether plaintiff environmental groups had standing to challenge the agency rule. The court of appeals had held that the environmental groups had standing under a specific citizen-suit provision of the statute. The

Supreme Court disagreed. It held that plaintiffs lacked standing because they had suffered no concrete injury as required by Article III of the Constitution. A portion of the Court's opinion in that case follows.

LUJAN v. DEFENDERS OF WILDLIFE ET AL.
504 U.S. 555 (1992)

JUSTICE SCALIA delivered the opinion of the Court.

This case involves a challenge to a rule promulgated by the Secretary of the Interior interpreting sec. 7 of the Endangered Species Act of 1973 in such fashion as to render it applicable only to actions within the United States or on the high seas. The preliminary issue, and the only one we reach, is whether the respondents here, plaintiffs below, have standing to seek judicial review of the rule.

***

Respondents' claim to injury is that the lack of consultation with respect to certain funded activities abroad "increas[es] the rate of extinction of endangered and threatened species." Of course, the desire to use or observe an animal species, even for purely aesthetic purposes, is undeniably a cognizable interest for purpose of standing. But the 'injury in fact' test requires more than injury to a cognizable interest. It requires that the party seeking review be himself among the injured. To survive the Secretary's summary judgment motion, respondents had to submit affidavits or other evidence showing, through specific facts, not only that listed species were in fact being threatened by funded activities abroad, but also that one or more of respondents' members would thereby be "directly" affected apart from their "special interest" in th[e] subject."

With respect to this aspect of the case, the Court of Appeals focused on the affidavits of two Defenders' members—Joyce Kelly and Amy Skilbred. Ms. Kelly stated that she traveled to Egypt in 1986 and "observed the traditional habitat of the endangered Nile crocodile there and intend[s] to do so again, and hope[s] to observe the crocodile direct," and that she "will suffer harm in fact as a result of the American role in overseeing the rehabilitation of the Aswan High Dam on the Nile and [in] develop[ing] Egypt's Master Water Plan." Ms. Skilbred averred that she traveled to Sri Lanka in 1981 and "observed th[e] habitat" of "endangered species such as the Asian elephant and the leopard" at what is now the site of the Mahaweli Project funded by the Agency for International Development (AID), although she "was unable to see any of the endangered species;" . . . "[T]his development project," she continued, "will seriously reduce endangered, threatened, and endemic species habitat including areas that I visited . . . "[which] may severely shorten the future of these species;" that threat, she concluded, harmed her because she "intend[s] to return to Sri Lanka in the future and hope[s] to be more fortunate in spotting at least the endangered elephant and leopard. . . ."

We shall assume for the sake of argument that these affidavits contain facts showing that certain agency-funded projects threaten listed species—though that is questionable. They plainly contain no facts, however, showing how damage to the species will produce "imminent" injury to Mss. Kelly and Skilbred. That the women "had visited" the areas of the projects before the projects commenced proves nothing. . . . And the affiants' profession of an "inten[t]" to return to the places they had visited before—where they will presumably, this time, be deprived of the opportunity to observe animals of the endangered species—is simply not enough. Such "some day" intentions—without any description of concrete plans, or indeed even any specification of when the some day will be—do not support a finding of the "actual or imminent" injury that our cases require.

Besides relying upon the Kelly and Skilbred affidavits, respondents propose a series of novel standing theories. The first, inelegantly styled "ecosystem nexus," proposes that any person who uses *any part* of a "contiguous ecosystem" adversely affected by a funded activity has standing even if the activity is located a great distance away. This approach, as the Court of Appeals correctly observed, is inconsistent with our opinion in *National Wildlife Federation,* which held that a plaintiff claiming injury from environmental damage must use the area affected by the challenged activity and not an area roughly "in the vicinity" of it. . . .

Respondent's other theories are called, alas, the "animal nexus" approach, whereby anyone who has an interest in studying or seeing the endangered animals anywhere on the globe has standing; and the "vocational nexus" approach, under which anyone with a professional interest in such animals can sue.

Under these theories, anyone who goes to see Asian elephants in the Bronx Zoo, and anyone who is a keeper of Asian elephants in the Bronx Zoo, has standing to sue because the Director of AID did not consult with the Secretary regarding the AID-funded project in Sri Lanka. This is beyond all reason. Standing is not "an ingenious academic exercise in the conceivable," but as we have said requires, at the summary judgment stage, a factual showing of perceptible harm. It is clear that the person who observes or works with a particular animal threatened by a federal decision is facing perceptible harm, since the very subject of his interest will no longer exist. It is even plausible—though it goes to the outermost limit of plausibility—to think that a person who observes or works with animals of a particular species in the very area of the world where that species is threatened by a federal decision is facing such harm, since some animals that might have been the subject of his interest will no longer exist. It goes beyond the limit, however, and into pure speculation and fantasy, to say that anyone who observes or works with an endangered species, anywhere in the world, is appreciably harmed by a single project affecting some portion of that species with which he has no more specific connection.

Questions and Comments for Discussion

1.   Standing is an important threshold question in many environmental cases. The doctrine determines the kinds of challenges which courts will entertain in environmental rule-making cases. Do you think that environmental groups like the plaintiffs in *Lujan v. Defenders of Wildlife* should be able to challenge an agency rule under the facts in this case? To what extent does your answer depend on whether you think the courts, the administrative agency, or the legislative branch should determine the appropriate geographic scope of the ESA?

2.   The standing doctrine in environmental litigation has undergone vast changes since the Court's opinion in *Sierra Club v. Morton.* Of particular importance to environmentalists in *Lujan v. Defenders of Wildlife* was the Supreme Court's rejection of the plaintiff's argument for procedural standing based on the express "citizen suit" provision of the Endangered Species Act. Citizen suit provisions permit members of the public to bring suit against government agencies to enforce provisions of the act. These provisions originated with the Clean Air Act Amendments of 1970 and have been a component of environmental enforcement ever since.

The ESA citizen suit provision provided "[A]ny person may commence a civil suit on his own behalf . . . to enjoin any person, including the United States and any other governmental instrumentality or agency . . . who is alleged to be in violation of any provision of this chapter." However, the majority of the Supreme Court in *Defenders* concluded that this citizen suit provision did not create an automatic procedural right in *all* citizens to challenge the secretary's inaction. It said that plaintiff's "raising only a generally available grievance about government, claiming harm that is indistinguishable from the public at large," did not satisfy the Article III requirement for a case or controversy.

For a critical discussion of the implications of this decision for future environmental litigation, see Roberta J. Borchardt, "*Lujan v. Defenders of Wildlife:* Unwarranted Judicial Interference with Congressional Power and Environmental Protection," 1992 Wisc. Law Rev. 1337, and "Standing on Shaky Ground: The Supreme Court Curbs Standing for Environmental Plaintiffs in *Lujan v. Defenders of Wildlife,*" 38 St. Louis Univ. Law J. 199 (1993).

"Timing" Issues in Judicial Review

There are other legal doctrines which may be relevant in determining whether the courts will grant judicial review in a particular case. Agency action must be *final* to be reviewable by the courts. The requirement of finality derives from Section 704 of the APA, which provides that "agency action made reviewable by statute and *final* agency action for which there is no other adequate remedy in a court are subject to judicial review." The requirement of finality prevents waste of judicial resources in considering an agency position which may be changed. However, it is not always a simple matter to determine whether the action of the agency is final, especially in cases where the agency's *failure* to act is challenged. The requirement of finality may also be an issue in cases where the enabling legislation requires final action by an entity other than the agency itself. In *Public Citizen v. U.S. Trade Representative,*[11] a federal court of appeals held that the Office of Trade Representative's failure to prepare an environmental impact statement for the North Atlantic Free Trade Agreement (NAFTA) was not subject to judicial review because the president and not the agency was required to submit the final trade agreement to Congress for approval. This case is discussed in Chapter 15.

A party must also *exhaust* all administrative remedies, seeking all possible relief from the agency itself before seeking review by the courts. Like the requirement of finality, the requirement of exhaustion also preserves judicial resources by giving the agency the opportunity to correct any errors which may have occurred at an earlier stage in the proceedings. Exhaustion of administrative remedies is not frequently an issue in rule-making cases because administrative procedures are generally completed upon issuance of the final rule under the APA.

In addition, judicial review is only appropriate when the issues are "fit for judicial decision" and when delaying review will cause hardship for the challenging party. These requirements are generally treated under the judicial doctrine of **ripeness.** The doctrines of finality, ripeness, and **exhaustion of administrative remedies** are closely interrelated, and are used to limit court review of agency action in cases where such review is premature.

The Scope of Judicial Review

Assuming that agency rule making is subject to judicial review, the next important question is the standard which should be used by courts to judge the validity of that action. In some regulatory acts, an enabling statute may specify the standard of review. In most cases, however, there is no specific review standard in the enabling legislation, and review is governed by provisions of the APA.

Section 706 of the APA governs the scope of judicial review. It provides:

> To the extent necessary to decision and when presented, the reviewing court shall decide all relevant questions of law, interpret constitutional and statutory provisions, and determine the meaning or applicability of the terms of an agency action. The reviewing court shall:
>
> 1. compel agency action unlawfully withheld or unreasonably delayed; and
>
> 2. hold unlawful and set aside agency action, findings, and conclusions found to be:
>   A. arbitrary, capricious, an abuse of discretion, or otherwise not in accordance with law;
>   B. contrary to constitutional right, power, privilege, or immunity;
>   C. in excess of statutory jurisdiction, authority, or limitations, or short of statutory right;
>   D. without observance of procedure required by law;
>   E. unsupported by substantial evidence in a case subject to sections 556 and 557 of this title or otherwise reviewed on the record of an agency hearing provided by statute; or
>   F. unwarranted by the facts to the extent that the facts are subject to trial de novo by the reviewing court.[12]
>
> In making the foregoing determinations, the court shall review the whole record or those parts of it cited by a party, and due account shall be taken of the rule of prejudicial error.

The subsections most applied in informal rule-making cases are (2)(A), (B), (C), and (D). The standard of review traditionally applied by the courts in reviewing agency action is the *"arbitrary or capricious"* test of Section 706(2)(A). In determining whether agency action meets this requirement, courts generally examine whether the rule-making record supports the agency's conclusions, whether the agency met procedural requirements imposed by law or public policy, and whether the agency's conclusions were reasonable in light of the evidence before it.

At this point, we return to the *Overton Park* case discussed in the previous section of this chapter. You may recall that in that case, environmental groups challenged the Secretary of Transportation's approval of federal funds for construction of a highway through a park. The Supreme Court first determined that the secretary's decision was subject to review. In a portion of the case set out below, the Supreme Court addressed the question of the appropriate scope of judicial review of the secretary's decision. (You may want to review the facts of *Overton Park v. Volpe* set out earlier in this chapter before proceeding with this portion of the opinion.)

OVERTON PARK v. VOLPE
401 U.S. 402 (1971)

***

[T]he existence of judicial review is only the start: the standard for review must also be determined. For that we must look to sec. 706 of the Administrative Procedure Act, which provides that a "reviewing court shall . . . hold unlawful and set aside agency action, findings and conclusions found" not to meet six separate standards. In all cases agency action must be set aside if the action was "arbitrary, capricious, an abuse of discretion, or otherwise not in accordance with law" or if the action failed to meet statutory, procedural, or constitutional requirements. In certain narrow, specifically limited situations, the agency action is to be set aside if the action was not supported by "substantial evidence." And in other equally narrow circumstances the reviewing court is to engage in a *de novo* review of the action and set it aside if it was "unwarranted by the facts. . . ."

Even though there is no *de novo* review in this case and the Secretary's approval of the route of I-40 does not have ultimately to meet the substantial evidence test, the generally applicable standards of sec. 706 require the reviewing court to engage in a substantial inquiry. Certainly, the Secretary's decision is entitled to a presumption of regularity. But that presumption is not to shield his action from a thorough, probing, in-depth review.

The court is first required to decide whether the Secretary acted within the scope of his authority. . . . Congress has specified only a small range of choices that the Secretary can make. Also involved in this initial inquiry is a determination of whether on the facts the Secretary's decision can reasonably be said to be within that range. The reviewing court must consider whether the secretary properly construed his authority to approve the use of parkland as limited to situations where there are no feasible alternative routes or where feasible alternative routes involve uniquely difficult problems. And the reviewing court must be able to find that the Secretary could have reasonably believed that in this case there are no feasible alternatives or that alternatives do involve unique problems.

Scrutiny of the facts does not end, however, with the determination that the Secretary has acted within the scope of his statutory authority. Section 706 (2)(A) requires a finding that the actual choice made was not "arbitrary, capricious, an abuse of discretion, or otherwise not in accordance with law." To make this finding the court must consider whether the decision was based on a consideration of the relevant factors and whether there has been a clear error of judgment. Although this inquiry into the facts is to be searching and careful, the ultimate standard of review is a narrow one. The court is not empowered to substitute its judgment for that of the agency.

The final inquiry is whether the Secretary's action followed the necessary procedural requirements. Here the only procedural error alleged is the failure of the Secretary to make formal findings and state his reason for allowing the highway to be built through the park.

Undoubtedly, review of the Secretary's action is hampered by his failure to make such findings, but the absence of formal findings does not necessarily require that the case be remanded to the Secretary. Neither the Department of Transportation Act nor Federal-Aid Highway Act requires such formal findings. Moreover, the Administrative Procedure Act requirements that there be formal findings in certain rule-making and adjudicatory proceedings do not apply to the Secretary's action here. And, although formal findings may be required in some cases in the absence of statutory directives when the nature of the agency action is ambiguous, those situations are rare. Plainly, there is no ambiguity here; the Secretary has approved the construction of I-40 through Overton Park and has approved a specific design for the project.

***

. . . [W]e do not believe that (prior case law) compels us to remand for the Secretary to make formal findings. . . . [T]here is an administrative record that allows the full, prompt review of the secretary's action that is sought without additional delay which would result from having a remand to the Secretary.

That administrative record is not, however, before us. The lower courts based their review on the litigation affidavits that were presented. These affidavits were merely *"post hoc"* rationalizations, which have traditionally been found to be an inadequate basis for review. And they clearly do not constitute the "whole record" compiled by the agency: the basis for review required by sec. 706 of the Administrative Procedure Act.

Thus it is necessary to remand this case to the District Court for plenary review of the Secretary's decisions. That review is to be based on the full administrative record that was before the Secretary at the time he made his decision. But since the bare record may not disclose the factors that were considered or the Secretary's construction of the evidence it may be necessary for the District Court to require some explanation in order to determine if the Secretary acted within the scope of his authority and if the Secretary's action was justifiable under the applicable standard.

The court may require the administrative officials who participated in the decision to give testimony explaining their action. Of course, such inquiry into the mental processes of administrative decisionmakers is usually to be avoided. And where there are administrative findings that were made at the same time as the decision, there must be a strong showing of bad faith or improper behavior before such inquiry may be made. But here there are no such formal findings and it may be that the only way there can be effective judicial review is by examining the decisionmakers themselves.

The District Court is not, however, required to make such an inquiry. It may be that the Secretary can prepare formal findings . . . that will provide an adequate explanation for his action. Such an explanation will, to some extent, be a "post hoc rationalization" and thus must be viewed critically. If the District Court decides that additional explanation is necessary, that court should consider which method will prove the most expeditious so that full review may be had as soon as possible.

Questions and Comments for Discussion

1. What standard of review did the Court apply in this case? What tests did the Court apply to determine whether the secretary's action should be upheld?

2. Why did the Court send this case back to the district court for further proceedings?

3. *Overton Park* is an important case not only for its discussion of the appropriate scope of judicial review of agency action under the APA, but also because of its emphasis on the need for the agency to compile a *record for review*. Although this case involved an adjudicatory decision rather than rule making, it has prompted agencies to develop adequate and sometimes extensive records in informal rule-making cases.

4. To what extent does the Court appear to defer to agency decision making in this case? To what extent does the Court's language in this case intrude on agency expertise in decision making? How would you strike the appropriate balance in this case?

5. Following the Court's ruling in this case, it returned to the lower courts. The agency held new hearings and prepared an environmental impact statement. Secretary Volpe announced in 1973 that he could find no feasible and prudent alternative to going through the park, and in a challenge by the Tennessee Department of Transportation, the court of appeals upheld the secretary's ruling. Today the original interstate highway corridor abruptly ends at the edge of the park and a bypass to the north carries I-40 traffic.

The "Arbitrary and Capricious" Test   In cases subsequent to *Overton Park,* the Supreme Court has continued to refine the arbitrary and capricious test. For example, in *Baltimore Gas & Electric Co. v. NRDC,* 462 U.S. 87 (1983), the Supreme Court upheld a series of rules issued by the Nuclear Regulatory Commission which evaluated the environmental effects of a nuclear power plant's fuel cycle. The Court said that a reviewing court "must generally be at its most deferential" when examining agency predictions which are "within its area of special expertise, at the frontiers of science." According to the Court, the NRC's conclusions were within the bounds of "reasoned decisionmaking" and the agency had considered the relevant factors and articulated a rational connection between the facts found and the choice made. Once the agency meets those requirements, the Court said, "it is not our task to determine what decision we, as Commissioners, would have reached."

"In Excess" Cases of Statutory Jurisdiction   Under Section 706(2)(C) of the APA, an agency action which exceeds the authority delegated to it by statute is illegal and unenforceable. As the *Chevron* decision illustrates, cases challenging agency action under this theory raise important questions about the appropriate scope of the agency's power to determine how best to implement its legislative mandate.

This policy question is especially important in environmental rule-making cases. Most environmental laws contain language which mandates agency action under circumstances defined in general terms—for example, when "reasonably necessary to protect the public health or safety." While the enabling language of major environmental acts may be broad and indefinite, the agency often must resolve precise and technical issues in order to issue a particular regulation, as in setting limits on the amount of a particular pollutant which may be expelled into the air or water.

Legal, factual, and policy issues are often entangled in such cases. For example, in *Industrial Union Dep't, AFL-CIO v. American Petroleum Inst.,*[13] the Occupational Safety and Health Administration (OSHA) had issued a rule regulating the level of the carcinogen benzene in the workplace to a level of one part benzene per million parts of air. OSHA had set its standard on the basis of a policy judgment that in regulating carcinogens, no exposure level could be considered safe. Thus it set the standard at the lowest technologically feasible level that would not impair the viability of regulated industries.

Several industries challenged the rule. The court of appeals held that in setting the 1 ppm exposure limit, OSHA had exceeded its standard-setting authority because it had not been shown that the 1 ppm exposure limit was "reasonably necessary or appropriate to provide safe and healthful employment" as required by the statute. According to the court, the statute did not give OSHA unbridled discretion to adopt standards designed to create absolutely risk-free workplaces regardless of cost.

On appeal, the Supreme Court in a plurality opinion agreed with the court of appeals and vacated the OSHA standard. According to Justice Sevens, OSHA had failed to show by substantial evidence that benzene constituted a "significant risk" at the current level of exposure. The Court relied on the statutory definition of "occupational safety and health standard" as a standard that was "reasonably necessary or appropriate to provide safe or healthful employment." The Court interpreted this provision as requiring a finding of *significant health risk* before OSHA was authorized to regulate. Justice Stevens wrote:

> By empowering the Secretary to promulgate standards that are 'reasonably necessary or appropriate to provide safe or healthful employment and places of employment' as required by section 3 (B), the act implies that, before promulgating any standard, the secretary must

make a finding that the workplaces in question are not safe. But 'safe' is not the equivalent of 'risk-free.'

Failure to Observe Procedure   Under Section 706(2)(D) of the APA, a court will set aside an agency rule if the agency failed to follow procedures required by law. Rules in such challenges are generally informal requirements under the APA or other statutes which contain rule-making procedures.

In the 1970s, some courts began to impose procedures beyond those required by the APA, either to improve the record of the proceeding or to ensure an added degree of fairness in agency decision making. The question of the courts' authority to impose additional requirements on agency procedures ultimately reached the Supreme Court in *Vermont Yankee Nuclear Power Corp v. N.R.D.C.*[14] The controversy in that case involved the procedures used in a rule-making hearing by the Atomic Energy Commission. The Commission had broad regulatory authority over the development of nuclear energy under the Atomic Energy Act of 1954. Under the act, a utility seeking to construct and operate a nuclear power plant was required to obtain a separate permit or license at both the construction and operation stage of the project. Vermont Yankee was granted a permit to build a nuclear power plant in Vernon, Vt., and applied for an operating license. Following a hearing on Vermont Yankee's application to the licensing board, the Commission instituted proceedings and adopted a rule addressing the hazards of fuel reprocessing or disposal.

Plaintiff environmental groups challenged the Commission's rule and its decision to grant Vermont Yankee an operating license. The court of appeals for the district circuit determined that the rule-making procedures used by the agency were inadequate and overturned the rule. Vermont Yankee appealed.

VERMONT YANKEE NUCLEAR POWER CORP.
v. NATURAL RES. D. C.
435 U.S. 519 (1978)

Mr. Justice REHNQUIST delivered the opinion of the Court.

In 1946, Congress enacted the Administrative Procedure Act, which as we have noted elsewhere was not only "a new, basic and comprehensive regulation of procedures in many agencies," but was also a legislative enactment which settled long-continued and hard-fought contentions, and enacted a formula upon which opposing social and political forces have come to rest. Interpreting [section 4 of the Act] . . . , we held that generally speaking this section of the Act established the maximum procedural requirements which Congress was willing to have the courts impose upon agencies in conducting rulemaking proce-

dures. Agencies are free to grant additional procedural rights in the exercise of their discretion, but reviewing courts are generally not free to impose them if the agencies have not chosen to grant them. This is not to say necessarily that there are no circumstances which would ever justify a court in overturning agency action because of a failure to employ procedures beyond those required by the statute. But such circumstances, if they exist, are extremely rare. . . .

It is in the light of this background of statutory and decisional law that we granted certiorari to review two judgments of the Court of Appeals for the District of Columbia Circuit because of our concern that they had seriously misread or misapplied this statutory and decisional law cautioning reviewing courts against engrafting their own notions of proper procedures upon agencies entrusted with substantive functions by Congress. We conclude that the Court of Appeals has done just that in these cases, and we therefore remand them to it for further proceedings.

***

In prior opinions we have intimated that even in a rulemaking proceeding when an agency is making a "quasi-judicial" determination by which a very small number of persons are "exceptionally affected, in each case upon individual grounds," in some circumstances additional [trial-type] procedures may be required in order to afford the aggrieved individuals due process. It might also be true, although we do not think the issue is presented in this case and accordingly do not decide it, that a totally unjustified departure from well-settled agency procedures of long standing might require judicial correction.

But this much is absolutely clear. Absent constitutional constraints or extremely compelling circumstances the administrative agencies should be free to fashion their own rules of procedure and to pursue methods of inquiry capable of permitting them to discharge their multitudinous duties. . . .

Respondent NRDC argues that sec. [553] of the Administrative Procedure Act merely establishes lower procedural bounds and that a court may routinely require more than the minimum when an agency's proposed rule addresses complex or technical factual issues or "Issues of Great Public Import." We have, however, previously shown that our decisions reject this view. . . . We also think the legislative history . . . does not bear out its contention. . . . [C]ongress intended that the discretion of the *agencies* and not that of the courts be exercised in de-

termining when extra procedural devices should be employed.

There are compelling reasons for construing sec. [553] in this manner. In the first place, if courts continually review agency proceedings to determine whether the agency employed procedures which were, in the court's opinion, perfectly tailored to reach what the court perceives to be the "best" or "correct" result, judicial review would be totally unpredictable. And the agencies, operating under this vague injunction to employ the "best" procedures and facing the threat of reversal if they did not, would undoubtedly adopt full adjudicatory procedures in every instance. Not only would this totally disrupt the statutory scheme, through which Congress enacted "a formula upon which opposing social and political forces have come to rest," but all the inherent advantages of informal rulemaking would be totally lost.

Secondly, it is obvious that the court in these cases reviewed the agency's choice of procedures on the basis of the record actually produced at the hearing, and not on the basis of the information available to the agency when it made the decision to structure the proceedings in a certain way. This sort of Monday morning quarterbacking not only encourages but almost compels the agency to conduct all rulemaking proceedings with the full panoply of procedural devices normally associated only with adjudicatory hearings.

Finally, and perhaps most importantly, this sort of review fundamentally misconceives the nature of the standard for judicial review of an agency rule. The court below uncritically assumed that additional procedures will automatically result in a more adequate record because it will give interested parties more of an opportunity to participate and contribute to the proceedings. But informal rulemaking need not be based solely on the transcript of a hearing held before an agency. Indeed the agency need not even hold a formal hearing. Thus the adequacy of the "record" in this type of proceeding is not correlated directly to the type of procedural devices employed, but rather turns on whether the agency has followed the statutory mandate of the Administrative Procedure Act or other relevant statutes. If the agency is compelled to support the rule which it ultimately adopts with the type of record produced only after a full adjudicatory hearing, it simply will have no choice but to conduct a full adjudicatory hearing prior to promulgating every rule. In sum, this sort of unwarranted judicial examination of perceived procedural shortcomings of a rulemaking proceeding can do nothing but seriously interfere with that process prescribed by Congress. . . .

In short, nothing in the APA, . . . the circumstances of this case, the nature of the issues being considered, past agency practice, or the statutory mandate under which the commission operates, permitted the court to review and overturn the rulemaking proceeding on the basis of the procedural devices employed (or not employed) by the Commission so long as the Commission employed at least the statutory *minima,* a matter about which there is no doubt in this case.

Questions and Comments for Discussion

1.   Since this case, federal courts have followed the Supreme Court's ruling in *Vermont Yankee* and not imposed procedural requirements on agencies beyond those required by the APA. But *Vermont Yankee* has not displaced case law concerning the requirements of notice, opportunity to comment, and adequacy of the agency's statement for the rule under the APA.

2.   There were advantages for the commission to resolve safety and radiation waste disposal questions by rule making rather than adjudication in this particular case. Once the rule was published as a regulation, it could be incorporated by reference in future licensing hearings without the need to re-litigate the issue. What are the disadvantages of resolving such issues by rule rather than adjudication? Should environmental groups be able to challenge an agency's decisions on safety requirements on a case-by-case basis, or is rule making the more efficient and better decision-making device?

Judicial Review of an Agency's Failure to Act   Challenges to an administrative agency's failure to act are also authorized under the APA. Section 706(1) provides that a reviewing court may "compel agency action unlawfully withheld or unreasonably delayed." Section (559b) of the APA also provides that "within a reasonable time, each agency shall proceed to conclude a matter presented to it."

The courts have generally applied a highly deferential standard of review in such cases, recognizing that the agency is in the best position to determine its priorities. In one case, *Heckler v. Chaney,*[15] the Supreme Court said that the Food and Drug Administration's decision not to initiate an enforcement action against a party was not reviewable, in part because the agency had to evaluate factors within its expertise in setting priorities, and because the agency's failure to act provided no "focus for judicial review."

Cases where plaintiffs have challenged an agency's failure to initiate rule making or unreasonable delay in initiating such proceedings often raise issues of ripeness and finality. In *Sierra Club v. Thomas,*[16] the D.C. Circuit Court of Appeals held that EPA's delay in concluding rule making concerning whether to place strip mines on its list of pollutant sources under the Clean Air Act was not unreasonable. The court said, "Because a court is in general ill-suited to review the order in which an agency conducts its business, we are properly hesitant to upset an agency's priorities by ordering it to expedite one specific action, and thus to give it precedence over others."

Courts are especially reluctant to order environmental agencies to expedite rule making in cases where the rule involves the evaluation of highly technical and scientific data.[17]

SUMMARY AND REVIEW

Basic principles of administrative law underlie the legal and policy issues in environmental cases and controversies. Environmental regulatory policies are increasingly set, administered, and enforced by agencies like the EPA.

The administrative state has continued to grow since the late nineteenth century. In the 1930s, Congress passed laws to ensure fairness and minimal due process protections in agency proceedings. These include the Federal Register Act, which provided for a daily record of administrative activities, and the Administrative Procedure Act (APA).

Absent requirements in the agency's enabling legislation or other relevant statutes, the APA establishes minimum requirements for agency proceedings. The APA recognizes different kinds of agency procedures, including "formal adjudication," "formal rule making," informal adjudication," and "informal rule making." Formal rule making is seldom used and most rule making is "informal rule making" (also called "**notice and comment rule making**") governed by Section 553 of the APA. The APA also addresses adjudication, which varies from relatively informal oral hearings to structured proceedings resembling formal trials.

This chapter has reviewed some of the basic principles of administrative law, focused on informal rule making under the APA, and examined some of the legal issues which may arise in judicial review of agency action and inaction. Cases challenging environmental rule making and adjudication question the appropriate balance between agency expertise and political accountability: To what extent should the courts defer to an agency's interpretation of its own enabling legislation? When is agency action "final" for purposes of judicial review? What constitutes an "arbitrary and capricious" action or "abuse of discretion" by an administrative agency?

These issues are present in many of the environmental cases arising under the major environmental laws of the last three decades, and all of these issues question the role of the courts in reviewing agency action. In later chapters of this text we will examine specific federal environmental laws regulating the manufacture and disposal of toxic substances, the disposal of hazardous wastes, and regulating discharge of substances into the air and water. Administrative law issues are often at the heart of cases and controversies involving the appropriate interpretation and enforcement of statutory mandates under these major environmental acts.

GLOSSARY

Administrative law—That area of law which encompasses rules governing the powers, duties, and procedures of administrative agencies.

Administrative Procedure Act—Passed in 1946, the APA establishes the basic framework of administrative law governing agency action, including rule making.

Delegation doctrine—Legal doctrine which addresses the question whether a branch of government may constitutionally assign some of its powers or duties to an administrative agency.

Enabling legislation—Those statutes establishing an administrative agency.

Exhaustion of administrative remedies—Legal doctrine which provides that a party must seek all possible legal relief from an administrative body before courts will grant review.

Hybrid rule making—Rule-making requirements contained in some legislation which combine formal and informal rule-making procedures.

Interpretive rules—Statements issued by agencies which present the agency's understanding of the meaning of language in its regulations or statutes.

Judicial review—Court review of an agency's final decision.

"Notice and comment" rule making—Informal rule making under the APA.

Procedural rules—Rules governing organization, procedure, or practice of an agency or organization.

Ripeness—Legal doctrine which provides that before judicial review is granted, there must be legal issues presented by the case which are appropriate for judicial decision making.

Standing—The legal question whether a person or legal entity has the right to challenge agency action in court.

Substantive rules—Rules prescribing law or policy.

CASES FOR DISCUSSION

1.   Tobacco trade groups and companies challenged a U.S. Environmental Protection Agency report that classified environmental tobacco smoke as a known human carcinogen. The Radon Gas and Indoor Air Quality Research Act required the EPA Administrator to conduct research on the identification and characterization of sources of indoor air pollution and the effects of that pollution on human health. The EPA used notice and comment procedures in adopting the report. Does the report and classification by the EPA constitute final agency action subject to court review? *Flue-Cured Tobacco Cooperative Stabilization Corp. v. U.S. E.P.A.,* 857 F.Supp. 1137 (D.C. Ct. Mid. No. Car. 1994).

2.   The U.S. Army Corps of Engineers asserted jurisdiction over property it claimed contained wetlands pursuant to the Federal Water Pollution Control Act (FWPCA). A provision of the FWPCA provides that a court has jurisdiction to review enforcement actions only if the government seeks administrative penalties or judicial enforcement of a compliance order. The Corps had yet to take such action against plaintiffs. Is the Corps' assertion of jurisdiction reviewable under APA Section 704? Why or why not? *Child v. United States,* 851 F.Supp. 1527 (D. Utah, 1994).

3.   The U.S. EPA interpreted RCRA's definition of "solid waste" to include slag produced as a by-product of steel production. Plaintiff challenged the interpretation, arguing that the EPA abused its discretion in concluding that slag is part of the waste disposal problem subject to the requirements of RCRA. Should the court uphold the EPA's interpretation of "solid waste" as including slag? What standard should a court apply in determining whether the

EPA's interpretation of RCRA's definition of "solid waste" to include slag is a permissible one? *Owen Electric Steel Co. of South Carolina v. Browner,* 37 F.3d 146 (4th Cir. 1994).

4.   Three conservation groups brought an action under the Administrative Procedure Act, claiming that the U.S. Forest Service violated various environmental statutes and regulations by failing to consider basic principles of ecology in developing a management plan for a national forest. They argued that the service ignored important scientific principles in developing the plan, and as a result, failed to consider its effect on biological diversity in violation of various federal statutes and regulations. What is the appropriate standard of review of the agency's decision to base the management plant on principles other than those proposed by the plaintiffs' theories of conservation biology? If there is uncertainty about how those principles should be applied, to what extent should the court defer to the agency's decision? *Sierra Club v. Marita,* 845 F.Supp. 1317 (E.D. Wisc, 1994).

ENDNOTES

1. Government Institutes, Inc., Environmental Law Handbook 35 (1993).

2. See, e.g., Justice Rehnquist's concurring opinion in *Industrial Union Dept., AFL-CIO v. American Petroleum Institute,* 448 U.S. 607 (1980).

3. 5 U.S.C. §§ 551–59, 701–06, 1305, 3105, 3344, 5372, 7521. For a discussion of the history and contemporary impact of the APA, see generally, *Administrative Law Symposium,* 72 Va. L. Rev. 215 (1986).

4. *SEC v. Chenery Corp.* 332 U.S. 194 (1947).

5. See, e.g., *Hercules v. EPA,* 938 F.2d 276 (D.C. Cir. 1991).

6. 29 U.S.C. § 651 *et seq.*

7. 30 U.S.C. § 801 *et seq.*

8. 405 U.S. 727 (1972).

9. 497 U.S. 871 (1990).

10. Manuel Lujan, Jr. was the Secretary of the Interior who promulgated the agency rule at issue in this case.

11. 5 F.3d 549 (D.C. Cir. 1993).

12. Author's note: A trial *de novo* is a new trial before the court.

13. 448 U.S. 607 (1980).

14. 435 US. 519 (1978).

15. 470 U.S. 821 (1985).

16. 828 F.2d 783 (D.C. Cir. 1987).

17. For example, *U.S. Steelworkers of America v. Rubber Manufacturing Ass'n,* 783 F.2d 1117 (D.C. Cir. 1986) where the court refused to order OSHA to expedite its rule making on benzene.

9

THE NATIONAL ENVIRONMENTAL POLICY ACT AND THE ENDANGERED SPECIES ACT: ENVIRONMENTAL LAWS REGULATING GOVERNMENT ACTIONS

INTRODUCTION

This chapter focuses on two federal acts which have transformed the way agencies undertake projects affecting the environment. The first section examines the **National Environmental Policy Act** (NEPA). An essential purpose of NEPA is to ensure that federal agencies give the same consideration to environmental factors as to other factors in making decisions. NEPA compels the federal government to administer federal programs in the most environmentally sound fashion. To effect that policy, an agency must consider the impact of any action significantly affecting the human environment. NEPA established the Council on Environmental Quality (CEQ) in the executive office of the president. The CEQ's duties include advising the president on environmental issues and interpreting NEPA provisions for agencies and the public.

The second part of this chapter examines provisions of the **Endangered Species Act** (ESA). The ESA contains both substantive and procedural requirements protecting endangered species from government and, in some cases, private actions. Some cases have raised the question of the meaning of "taking" an endangered species, which is prohibited by ESA.

NEPA was passed in 1970; ESA in 1973. Since their adoption, environmental groups have used these laws to challenge such actions as the granting of an airport operating certificate,[1] the operation of a nuclear power plant,[2] and a plan to incinerate food wastes in

Antarctica.[3] As a result of lawsuits brought under NEPA and ESA, proposed government projects have been delayed, modified, and in some cases permanently halted. Inevitably, many of the courts' decisions under NEPA and the ESA are controversial. At the heart of many of these cases are frequently conflicting opinions about the appropriate balance between environmental protection policies and policies favoring land development and utilization of natural resources.

THE NATIONAL ENVIRONMENTAL POLICY ACT (NEPA)

The National Environmental Policy Act of 1969 (NEPA), signed into law on January 1, 1970, has been called the "Magna Carta" of the country's environmental movement. At the time it was passed, NEPA was considered the most important and far-reaching environmental and conservation measure ever enacted by Congress.[4] NEPA contains three important elements. Section One of the act contains a lofty declaration of national environmental policies and goals. Section Two contains several "action-forcing" provisions requiring federal agencies to implement those policies and goals. And Title II of the act establishes a Council on Environmental Quality (CEQ) in the executive office of the president.

Section 101

In Section 101 of NEPA, Congress declared that the federal government has the continuing responsibility

> to use all practicable means, consistent with other essential considerations of national policy, to improve and coordinate federal plans, functions, programs, and resources to the end that the nation may:
>
> 1. fulfill the responsibilities of each generation as trustee of the environment for succeeding generations;
>
> 2. assure for all Americans safe, healthful, productive, and aesthetically and culturally pleasing surroundings;
>
> 3. attain the widest range of beneficial uses of the environment without degradation, risk to health or safety, or other undesirable and unintended consequences;
>
> 4. preserve important historic, cultural and natural aspects of our national heritage, and maintain, wherever possible, an environment which supports diversity and variety of individual choice;
>
> 5. achieve a balance between population and resource use which will permit high standards of living and a wide sharing of life's amenities; and
>
> 6. enhance the quality of renewable resources and approach the maximum attainable recycling of depletable resources.

Note that Section 101 of NEPA requires the federal government to use *all practicable means* to administer federal programs in the most environmentally sound fashion. NEPA does not give the environment greater priority than other national goals, but it does commit to protecting and promoting environmental quality. It also requires federal agencies to consider the environmental consequences of their actions.

The Council on Environmental Quality

Title II of NEPA created the **Council on Environmental Quality** (CEQ) in the executive office of the president. It is composed of three members appointed by the president and confirmed by the Senate. The CEQ is required by statute to assist and advise the president in the preparation of an annual environmental quality report. Under Executive Order No. 11512, the CEQ also issues guidelines to federal agencies for the preparation of environmental impact statements and for coordinating federal programs relating to environmental quality.

Under CEQ regulations, NEPA and other planning requirements are integrated by the agencies as early as possible to ensure that those plans reflect environmental values.[5] CEQ regulations also define key words in Section 102(2)(C) which mandates agencies to prepare a formal environmental impact statement under certain circumstances.

In 1993 President Clinton created the *Office of Environmental Policy* (OEP). As part of a proposal to elevate the Environmental Protection Agency to Cabinet status, Clinton proposed abolishing the CEQ and shifting its function to the OEP. However, opposition from the 103rd Congress compelled the White House to merge the OEP into the CEQ.

"Action-Forcing Provisions" of NEPA

Section 102 of NEPA contains provisions intended to force agencies of the federal government to consider the environmental consequences of their actions in light of the broad policy goals of Section 101. Section 102(1) contains a broad directive that "to the fullest extent possible" federal policies, public laws, and regulations should be *interpreted and administered in accordance with the policies set forth in NEPA.*

Section 102(2) of NEPA contains a mandate to perform certain procedures to ensure that agencies *utilize a systematic, interdisciplinary approach in planning and in decision-making which may have an impact on man's environment.*

This section contains provisions which may form a basis for judicial intervention, the most significant of which is Section 102(2)(C). The crucial language of this section reads:

> [All agencies of the federal government shall—]
> (C) include in every recommendation or report on proposals for legislation and other major federal actions significantly affecting the quality of the human environment, a detailed statement by the responsible official on—
>
> i. the environmental impact of the proposed action,
>
> ii. any adverse environmental effects which cannot be avoided should the proposal be implemented,
>
> iii. alternatives to the proposed action,
>
> iv. the relationship between local short-term uses of man's environment and the maintenance and enhancement of long-term productivity, and
>
> v. any irreversible and irretrievable commitments of resources which would be involved in the proposed action should it be implemented. . . .

The requirement of an **environmental impact statement** (EIS) for proposals for legislation and federal actions significantly affecting the quality of the human environment has been the focus of most of the litigation surrounding NEPA. The meaning of nearly every word in this section ("major," "federal," "significantly affecting," "human environment") has been litigated extensively. This chapter examines some of these issues in the section entitled "Threshold Requirements for the EIS."

Shortly after NEPA was passed, a lawsuit was brought to clarify the fundamental compliance requirements of the act. In one of the most important decisions interpreting NEPA to date, Judge Skelly Wright of the D.C. Circuit Court of Appeals wrote a crucial opinion where the court made it clear that the language of the statute established a "strict standard of compliance."

Petitioners in that case argued that the rules adopted by the **Atomic Energy Commission** (AEC) to govern consideration of environmental matters in agency decision making failed to satisfy the requirements of NEPA. The AEC, on the other hand, contended that the NEPA mandate was vague and gave agencies much discretion in complying with the broad scope of the act. But the court held that NEPA was a "good deal clearer and more demanding" than the commission contended and that Section 102(2)(C) of NEPA created "judicially enforceable duties." As a result of the court's decision in this case, preparation of an EIS is a formal legal requirement which has significantly influenced federal agency decision making. Further, an agency's failure to comply with the requirements of NEPA is subject to judicial review by the courts. A portion of the court's opinion in that case follows.

CALVERT CLIFFS' COORD. COM.
v. UNITED STATES AEC
449 F.2d 1109 (1971)

The sort of consideration of environmental values which NEPA compels is clarified in Section 102(2)(A) and (B). In general, all agencies must use a "systematic, interdisciplinary approach" to environmental planning and evaluation "in decision-making which may have an impact on man's environment." In order to include all possible environmental factors in the decisional equation, agencies must "identify and develop methods and procedures . . . which will insure that presently unquantified environmental amenities and values may be given appropriate consideration in decision making along with economic and technical considerations." "Environmental amenities" will often be in conflict with "economic and technical considerations." To "consider" the former "along with" the latter must involve a balancing process. In some instances environmental costs may outweigh economic and technical benefits and in other instances

they may not. But NEPA mandates a rather finely tuned and "systematic" balancing analysis in each instance.

To ensure that the balancing analysis is carried out and given full effect, Section 102(2)(C) requires that responsible officials of all agencies prepare a "detailed statement" covering the impact of particular actions on the environment, the environmental costs which might be avoided, and alternative measures which might alter the cost-benefit equation. The apparent purpose of the "detailed statement" is to aid the agencies' own decision making process and to advise other interested agencies and the public of the environmental consequences of planned federal action. Beyond the "detailed statement," Section 102(2)(D) requires all agencies specifically to "study, develop, and describe appropriate alternatives to recommended courses of action in any proposal which involves unresolved conflicts concerning alternative uses of available resources." This requirement, like the "detailed statement" requirement, seeks to ensure that each agency decisionmaker has before him and takes into proper account all possible approaches to a particular project (including total abandonment of the project) which would alter the environmental impact and the cost-benefit balance. Only in that fashion is it likely that the most intelligent, optimally beneficial decision will ultimately be made. Moreover, by compelling a formal "detailed statement" and a description of alternatives, NEPA provides evidence that the mandated decision-making process has in fact taken place and, most importantly, allows those removed from the initial process to evaluate and balance the factors on their own.

Of course, all of these Section 102 duties are qualified by the phrase "to the fullest extent possible." We must stress as forcefully as possible that this language does not provide an escape hatch for footdragging agencies; it does not make NEPA's procedural requirements somehow "discretionary." Congress did not intend the act to be such a paper tiger. Indeed, the requirement of environmental consideration "to the fullest extent possible" sets a high standard for the agencies, a standard which must be rigorously enforced by the reviewing courts.

Unlike the substantive duties of Section 101(b) which require agencies to "use all practicable means consistent with other essential considerations," the procedural duties of Section 102 must be fulfilled to the "fullest extent possible."

***

[T]he Section 102 duties are not inherently flexible. They must be complied with to the fullest extent, unless there is a clear conflict of *statutory* authority. Considerations of administrative difficulty, delay or economic cost will not suffice to strip the section of its fundamental importance.

We conclude, then, that Section 102 of NEPA mandates a particular sort of careful and informed decision-making process and creates judicially enforceable duties. The reviewing courts probably cannot reverse a substantive decision on its merits, under Section 101, unless it be shown that the actual balance of costs and benefits that was struck was arbitrary or clearly gave insufficient weight to environmental values. But if the decision was reached procedurally without individualized consideration and balancing of environmental factors—conducted fully and in good faith—it is the responsibility of the courts to reverse. As one district court has said of Section 102 requirements: "It is hard to imagine a clearer or stronger mandate to the courts."

***

Questions and Comments for Discussion

1. In the beginning of his opinion, Judge Wright wrote: "These cases are only the beginning of what promises to become a flood of new litigation—litigation seeking judicial assistance in protecting our natural environment. Several recently enacted statutes attest to the commitment of the government to control, at long last, the destructive engine of material 'progress.' But it remains to be seen whether the promise of this legislation will become a reality. Therein lies the judicial role."

Judge Wright believed that it was the court's duty to "see that important legislative purposes, heralded in the halls of Congress, are not lost or misdirected in the vast hallways of the federal bureaucracy." How did the court interpret legislative purpose in this case? Should it matter that NEPA's legislative history is sparse and that there were several versions of NEPA, and that after minimal debate, the Senate agreed to a conference report on the bill by voice vote?

2. Consistent with the court's opinion in this case, most consider NEPA to be a "procedural statute." Compliance with its provisions calls for planning and analysis that demonstrate that environmental considerations and alternatives to the proposed action have been fully considered and documented. As the court says, NEPA requires that the agency fully consider the environmental impact of its proposed action and alternatives to that action. However, if the agency meets those procedural requirements, it should be able to proceed with the proposed action. Only under circumstances where the agency's decision to proceed with a proposed action is "arbitrary and capricious" will the court intervene. Under what circumstances might an agency's decision to proceed be considered "arbitrary and capricious" under the holding in *Overton Park,* discussed in Chapter 2?

Threshold Requirements for the EIS

Section 102(2)(C) requires an environmental impact statement in every recommendation or report on proposals for legislation and other major federal actions significantly affecting the quality of the human environment. The language of this section is critical in determining whether a federal agency must prepare an EIS. Is the agency's plan a "proposal"? Is the proposal for a "major" federal action? Will it "significantly affect the human environment?" Key terms in this statement are defined in the CEQ regulations and have been the subject of much litigation.

These are called "threshold" requirements because they determine whether an agency must prepare an EIS for a project. An EIS is often costly and time-consuming, and failure to prepare an EIS is an action subject to judicial review by the courts. Thus the agency's decision to prepare an EIS is an important one.

Under CEQ regulations, an **environmental assessment** (EA) is used as a screening device to determine whether an agency must prepare an EIS or make a **"Finding of No Significant Impact"** (FONSI). The EA is a public document which discusses the need for the proposal and alternatives as required by Section 102(2)(E) of NEPA. If the agency determines no environmental impact statement is required, it prepares a FONSI. The FONSI briefly presents the reasons why an action will not have a significant effect on the human environment, and it must include a summary of the EA. Under some limited circumstances, the agency must make the FONSI determination available for public review. The decision not to prepare an EIS is reviewable by the courts.

Three requirements must be met under the statute before an EIS is required: The action must be federal, qualify as "major," and have a significant environmental impact. In many cases, the "federal" requirement does not pose much difficulty, because policies, plans, programs, and projects proposed by federal agencies meet this definition. State and local actions which are regulated, licensed, permitted, or approved by federal agencies are also considered "federal" for the purposes of NEPA. Whether federal assistance to a non-federal project also triggers the requirements of NEPA generally depends on the extent of control that the federal agency may assert over the project.

The requirements that the project be "major" and that it "significantly" affect the environment, have been the subject of some discussion. A substantial commitment of resources qualifies the project as "major," and CEQ regulations have defined "significantly" by requiring consideration of both the "context" and "intensity" (the severity of impact) of the action.

The requirement of "environmental impact" raises another important question. How broadly should the term environment be defined? To define "environmental impact," the statute speaks of the need to assure all Americans "safe, healthful, productive, and aesthetically and culturally pleasing surroundings." Courts have agreed that NEPA is not limited to the natural environment (wilderness, rivers, etc.), but may include impact on the urban environment.

In *Hanley v. Mitchell,* 460 F.2d 640 (2d Cir. 1972), the General Services Administration (GSA) had decided to build a correction center in lower Manhattan. The question before the court in that case was whether the GSA was required to prepare a detailed EIS for the project under NEPA. The court held that the construction of a new jail in Manhattan potentially involved significant environmental effects including not only air and water pollution but also "the quality of life for city residents. Noise, traffic, burdened mass transportation systems, crime, congestion, and even availability of drugs all affect the urban environment. . . ." Some courts in subsequent cases have concurred with this broad definition, but others have concluded that pure economic impacts without accompanying physical impacts do not trigger NEPA.[6]

The CEQ regulations define the "human environment" as the natural and physical environment and the relationship of people with that environment. Under the CEQ definition, economic or social effects by themselves do not require preparation of an environmental impact statement. When an environmental impact statement is prepared and economic or social and natural or physical environmental effects are interrelated, then the environmental impact should discuss all of those effects on the human environment.[7]

The problem of defining the meaning of "environmental impact" first reached the Supreme Court in a case questioning whether the **Nuclear Regulatory Commission** (NRC) was required to prepare an EIS before allowing Metropolitan Edison to resume operation of one of the nuclear reactors at Three Mile Island. The court of appeals had held that the NRC improperly failed to consider whether the risk of an accident at Three Mile Island might cause harm to the psychological health and community well-being of residents of the surrounding area. In reversing the court of appeals decision, Justice Rehnquist, writing for the majority of the Supreme Court, considered the meaning of "environmental impact" under NEPA. A portion of the Supreme Court's opinion in that case is set out below.

METROPOLITAN EDISON CO. et al.
v. PEOPLE AGAINST NUCLEAR ENERGY
460 U.S. 766 (1983)

All the parties agree that effects on human health can be cognizable under NEPA, and that human health may include psychological health. The Court of Appeals thought these propositions were enough to complete a syllogism that disposes of the case: NEPA requires agencies to consider effects on health. An effect on psychological health is an effect on health. Therefore, NEPA requires agencies to consider the effects on psychological health asserted by PANE [People Against Nuclear Energy, (plaintiff in the case)]. . . .

To paraphrase the statutory language [of Section 102(C)] in light of the facts of this case, where an agency action significantly affects the quality of the human environment, the agency must evaluate the "environmental impact" and any unavoidable adverse environmental effects of its proposal. The theme of Section 102 is sounded by the adjective "environmental": NEPA does not require the agency to assess *every* impact or effect of its proposed action, but only the impact or effect on the environment. If we were to seize the word "environmental" out of its context and give it the broadest possible definition, the words "adverse environmental effects" might embrace virtually any consequence of a governmental action that someone thought "adverse." But we think the context of the statute shows that Congress was talking about the physical environment—the world around us, so to speak. NEPA was designed to promote human welfare by alerting governmental actors to the effect of their proposed actions on the physical environment.

***

Our understanding of the congressional concerns that led to the enactment of NEPA suggests that the terms "environmental effect" and "environmental impact" in Section 102 be read to include a requirement of a reasonably close causal relationship between a change in the physical environment and the effect at issue. This requirement is like the familiar doctrine of proximate cause from tort law. The issue before us, then, is how to give content to this requirement. This is a question of first impression in this court. . . .

PANE argues that the psychological health damage it alleges "will flow directly from the risk of [a nuclear] accident." But a *risk* of an accident is not an effect on the physical environment. A risk is, by definition, unrealized in the physical world. In a causal chain from renewed operation of TMI-1 to psychological health damage, the element of risk and its perception by PANE's members are necessary middle links. We believe that the element of risk lengthens the causal chain beyond the reach of NEPA.

Risk is a pervasive element of modern life; to say more would belabor the obvious. Many of the risks we face are generated by modern technology, which brings both the possibility of major accidents and opportunities for tremendous achievements. Medical experts apparently agree that risk can generate stress in human beings, which in turn may rise to the level of serious health damage. For this reason, among many others, the question whether the gains from any technological advance are worth its attendant risks may be an important public policy issue. Nonetheless, it is quite different from the question whether the same gains are worth a given level of alteration of our physical environment or depletion of our natural resources. The latter question rather than the former is the central concern of NEPA.

Time and resources are simply too limited for us to believe that Congress intended to extend NEPA as far as the Court of Appeals has taken it. . . . The scope of the agency's inquiries must remain manageable if NEPA's goal of "insuring a fully informed and well-considered decision," is to be accomplished.

[*The Court ultimately concluded that, for these and other reasons discussed in the opinion, the NRC was not required to consider PANE's contentions, and judgment of the Court of Appeals was reversed.*]

***

Questions and Comments for Discussion

1. The Supreme Court apparently agreed with the lower court that "effects on human health can be cognizable under NEPA, and that human health may include psychological health." But according to the court, an effect qualifies as environmental only if it

has a "reasonably close causal relation" to a change in the physical environment. The holding of this case suggests that a psychological effect can only qualify as environmental if it is "proximately caused" by a physical event. Consider the requirement of proximate cause discussed in Chapter 4. What policy reasons support applying that requirement in a case like this one? Are there reasons why applying such a test might have negative policy ramifications?

2. Agencies must determine the significance of actions by classifying actions into three general categories: those with significant effects (automatically requiring preparation of an EIS); actions with no significant effects (thus "categorically excluded" from NEPA requirements); and all other actions for which a determination must be made on a case-by-case basis.

Between the two extremes of significant and insignificant lies a gray area in which Environmental Assessments (EAs) aid decisionmakers. Factors considered include the impact on public health, unique features of the geographic area, the precedential effect of the action, and whether the action is highly controversial. Ultimately, a decision has to be made about the magnitude of those concerns in every proposal—in close cases, courts seem to tend toward requiring the preparation of an EIS.

Scope and Timing of the EIS

The EIS and the EIS process is the focal point of NEPA. The EIS ensures that the agency will have available and carefully consider detailed information concerning significant environmental impacts of the proposed action, and guarantees that relevant information will be made available to the public so that the public can play a role in the decision-making process. The EIS is not only a "full disclosure law," it also provides a record for a court to review in determining whether the agency has made a good faith effort to take environmental values into account.[8]

Once the decision has been made to prepare an EIS, there are a number of legal issues which may arise concerning its preparation. The questions of its *scope* (what it must address) and *timing* (when it must be prepared) become critical because failure to analyze the required environmental effects or include alternatives may result in a court declaring the EIS inadequate. The questions of scope and timing have been addressed by the courts in a number of cases.

The CEQ regulations contain detailed procedural requirements for the entire EIS process. The process begins with an environmental assessment, (EA) which is a brief analysis of the need for an EIS. If the agency decides to prepare an EIS, the first step in the process is called *scoping*. The agency must publish a notice of intent to prepare the EIS in the *Federal Register,* a daily publication of agencies' proposed regulations. In the scoping process, the agency invites participation by the public and affected agencies, determines the scope of the EIS, and decides which issues are significant and should be examined in depth. It may also determine, as lead agency, to prepare the entire EIS or allocate responsibility to other agencies.

Determining the proper scope of the EIS is very important. One way to defeat the purposes of NEPA is to "segment" a project so that each stage of the project is considered separately. By segmenting a project, an agency may avoid addressing the overall environmental costs and countervailing benefits of the project as a whole.

Determining the proper scope of the EIS also may be difficult. In a 1973 opinion involving the Atomic Energy Commission's nuclear breeder reactor program, Judge Skelly

Wright, who also authored the *Calvert Cliffs* decision discussed earlier, considered this problem. Judge Wright, writing for the majority of the court, said that two factors should be considered in determining whether an EIS was required for the agency's proposal to build a particular nuclear plant or whether an EIS was required for the agency's nuclear reactor program as a whole: (1) the extent to which meaningful information was presently available on the proposed technology and its alternatives, and (2) to what extent irretrievable commitments were being made and other options precluded as the program progressed.[9]

The question of timing of the EIS may also be significant. NEPA requires that the EIS be included in "every recommendation or report on proposals for legislation and other major federal actions." Under the language of this section, an agency is not required to comply with NEPA until a proposal exists. But an agency may not recommend a proposal or proceed with a major action until an EIS and record of decision have been prepared. The CEQ regulations require agencies to begin preparation of an EIS early in the proposal process. Once the proposal is made, the EIS must accompany the proposal through the decision-making process. In a 1975 decision, the Supreme Court used a relatively mechanical test in determining the scope and timing of the EIS. It said, " . . . [T]he time at which the agency must prepare the final "statement" is the time at which it makes a recommendation or report on a *proposal* for federal action."[10]

Subsequently, the Supreme Court more fully addressed the scope and timing issues of the EIS. In the following case, several environmental groups brought a lawsuit against officials of the Department of the Interior and other federal agencies responsible for issuing coal leases, approving mining plans, granting rights of way, and taking other actions necessary to enable private companies and public utilities to develop coal reserves on land owned or controlled by the federal government. The plaintiffs claimed that the federal officials could not allow further development of individual reserves of the region identified as the "Northern Great Plains Region" without preparing a comprehensive environmental impact statement for the entire region. The district court held that the complaint failed to state a claim for relief and granted the government's motion for summary judgment. The court of appeals, on request of the plaintiff environmental groups, issued an injunction against the department's approval of four mining plans in one small section of the region. Federal officials petitioned the Supreme Court for review.

KLEPPE v. SIERRA CLUB
427 U.S. 390 (1976)

MR. JUSTICE POWELL delivered the opinion of the Court.

Section 102(2)(C) of the National Environmental Policy Act of 1969 (NEPA) requires that all federal agencies include a detailed statement of environmental consequences—known as an environmental impact statement—"in every recommendation or report on proposals for legislation and other major Federal actions significantly affecting the quality of the human environment." 42 U.S.C. Sec. 4332(2)(C). The United States Court of Appeals for the District of Columbia Circuit held that officials of the Department of the Interior (Department) and certain other federal agencies must take additional steps under this section, beyond those already taken, before allowing further development of federal coal reserves in a specific area of the country. For the reasons set forth, we reverse.

***

The Northern Great Plains region identified in respondents' complaint encompasses portions of four States—northeastern Wyoming, eastern Montana, western North Dakota, and western South Dakota. There is no dispute about its richness in coal, nor about the waxing interest in developing that coal, nor about the crucial role the federal petitions will play due to the significant percentage of the coal to which they control access. The Department has initiated, in this decade, three studies in areas either inclusive of or included within this region.

[*The government had issued a "Coal Programmatic EIS" shortly before the petitions for certiorari were filed in the case.*]

***

The major issue remains the one with which the suit began: whether NEPA requires petitioners [government agencies] to prepare an environmental impact statement on the entire Northern Great Plains region. Petitioners, arguing the negative, rely squarely upon the facts of the case and the language of Sec. 102(2)(C) of NEPA. We find their reliance well placed.

As noted in the first sentence of this opinion, Sec. 102(2)(C) requires an impact statement "in every recommendation or report on proposals for legislation and other major Federal actions significantly affecting the quality of the human environment." Since no one has suggested that petitioners have proposed legislation on respondents' region, the controlling phrase in this section of the Act, for this case, is "major federal actions." Respondents can prevail only if there has been a report or recommendation on a proposal for major federal action with respect to the Northern Great Plains region. Our statement of the relevant facts shows there has been none; instead, all proposals are for actions of either local or national scope.

***

[*The Court rejected the Court of Appeals ruling that the petitioners "contemplated" a regional plan or program. It then continued:*]

Even had the record justified a finding that a regional program was contemplated by the petitioners, the legal conclusion drawn by the Court of Appeals cannot be squared with the Act. The court recognized that the mere "contemplation" of certain action is not sufficient to require an impact statement. But it believed the statute nevertheless empowers a court to require the preparation of an impact statement to begin at some point prior to the formal recommendation or report on a proposal. The Court of Appeals accordingly devised its own four-part "balancing" test for determining when during the contemplation of a plan or other type of federal action, an agency must begin a statement. The factors to be considered were identified as the likelihood and imminence of the program's coming to fruition, the extent to which information is available on the effects of implementing the expected program and on alternatives thereto, the extent to which irretrievable commitments are being made and option precluded "as refinement of the proposal progresses," and the severity of the environmental effects should the action be implemented.

***

The Court [*of Appeal's*] reasoning and action find no support in the language or legislative history of NEPA. The statute clearly states when an impact statement is required, and mentions nothing about a balancing of factors. Rather, as we noted last Term, under the first sentence of Sec. 102(2)(C) the moment at which an agency must have a final statement ready "is the time at which it makes a recommendation or report on a *proposal* for federal action." The procedural duty imposed upon agencies by this section is quite precise, and the role of the courts in enforcing that duty is similarly precise. A court has no authority to depart from the statutory language and, by a balancing of court-devised factors, determine a point during the germination process of a potential proposal at which an impact statement *should be prepared.* Such an assertion of judicial authority would leave the agencies uncertain as to their procedural duties under NEPA, would invite judicial involvement in the day-to-day decision-making process of the agencies, and would invite litigation. As the contemplation of a project and the accompanying study thereof do not necessarily result in a proposal for a major federal action, it may be assumed that the balancing process devised by the Court of Appeals also would result in the preparation of a good many unnecessary impact statements.

***

Questions and Comments for Discussion

1. The Court deferred to the agency's expertise in determining whether a comprehensive EIS for the entire region was necessary. The Court said: *"Respondents conceded at oral argument that to prevail they must show that petitioners have acted arbitrarily in refusing to prepare one comprehensive statement on this entire region, and we agree. The determination of the region, if any, with respect to which a comprehensive statement is necessary requires the weighing of a number of relevant factors, including the extent of the interrelationship among proposed actions and practical considerations of feasibility. Resolving these issues requires a high level of technical expertise and is properly left to the informed discretion of the responsible federal agencies. Absent a showing of arbitrary action, we must assume that the agencies have exercised this discretion appropriately."*

Judicial review of agency decision making under NEPA is governed by the Administrative Procedure Act, 5 U.S.C. The "arbitrary and capricious" test applied under this section is more fully discussed in Chapter 8.

2. Justices Marshall and Brennan dissented in part in the *Kleppe* decision. In their opinion, the majority held that the federal courts may not remedy violations of NEPA "until it is too late for an adequate remedy to be formulated." Their concern was that NEPA litigation is primarily brought at the end of the agency process to challenge agency decisions made without adequate environmental impact statements or without any statements at all. The dissenting justices believed that in this case, where federal agencies were violating NEPA prior to their basic decision to act, the Court of Appeals correctly devised a different and effective remedy: Essentially in circumstances where both the likelihood of eventual agency action and the danger posed by non-preparation of an environmental impact statement were great, judicial intervention should be allowed prior to the time at which an impact statement must be ready.

The problem focused on by the dissenting justices is essentially a *timing* problem. If courts have to wait until a federal action is proposed in order to issue an order to prepare an adequate impact statement, this will do little to further consideration of environmental factors. What is the majority's response to this concern? How would you strike the balance on the question of timing?

3. The CEQ guideline on timing reads in part:

"An agency shall commence preparation of an environmental impact statement as close as possible to the time the agency is developing or is presented with a proposal so that preparation can be completed in time for the final statement to be included in any recommendation or report on the proposal. The statement shall be prepared early enough so that it can serve practically as an important contribution to the decision-making process and will not be used to rationalize or justify decisions already made.

Does this guideline comply with the majority decision in *Kleppe?*

4.   The cost of preparing an EIS is usually substantial. For example, studies released in 1985 indicated that typical permit application and mining plan processing costs for the Office of Surface Mining for western mines ranged from $37,000 to $100,000. If an EIS was required, the processing cost increased by an amount ranging from $75,000 to $200,000. With few exceptions, however, the courts have held that the agency's cost of preparing an EIS may be recovered from an applicant or other recipient of a service.

Contents of the EIS

Section 102(2)(C) of NEPA requires that an EIS describe (i) the environmental impacts of the proposed action; (ii) any adverse environmental impacts which cannot be avoided should the proposal be implemented; (iii) the reasonable alternatives to the proposed action; (iv) the relationship between local short-term uses of man's environment and the maintenance and enhancement of long-term productivity; and (v) any irreversible and irretrievable commitments of resources which would be involved in the proposed action should it be implemented. CEQ regulations provide a recommended format for EIS preparation.

Agencies generally prepare two EISs: a draft EIS and a final EIS. These statements may be *supplemented* if the agency makes substantial changes in its proposed action or if significant new circumstances or information exist that are relevant to the environmental concerns of the proposed action. An agency decision not to prepare a supplemental EIS may be challenged in the courts. For example, several challenges to agency action in the battle over protecting the northern spotted owl in the Pacific Northwest were based on failure to prepare and file a **supplemental EIS** in light of new information available to the federal agency. The Supreme Court has held that the appropriate standard of review in cases where agencies have failed to prepare a supplemental EIS is whether the agency acted "arbitrarily or capriciously" in deciding not to prepare the supplemental statement.[11]

The agency files the draft EIS with the EPA and announces its availability to the public in the *Federal Register.* A waiting period is mandated by law which provides all interested persons, organizations, and agencies time to comment on the agency's compliance. The final EIS is subsequently circulated to all interested parties. The final action in the process is preparation of a **record of decision** (ROD), which identifies and explains the decision, identifies the alternatives considered by the agency, and specifies the alternatives which were environmentally preferable. The record must state whether the agency has taken "all practicable" means to avoid or minimize environmental harm from the selected alternative.

The public comment procedures mandated by NEPA are an essential part of the NEPA review process. Agencies with jurisdiction over a proposed action or agencies with relevant special expertise must comment on relevant EISs. The purpose of the EIS is to ensure that agency decisions are based on an understanding of environmental consequences and the reasonable alternatives available. The alternatives section is the heart of the EIS. The agency must consider a reasonable range of alternatives, but is not required to consider every possibility that might be conjectured. And as a general rule, the agency must discuss the alternative of "no action" to provide a basis for comparing the environmental effects of the alternatives. In addition, the EIS must discuss the environmental effects of the alternatives.

A leading case on the question of what alternatives must be included in the EIS is *NRDC v. Morton,* 458 F.2d 827 (D.C. Cir. 1972). In that case, involving the lease sale of 80 tracts of submerged lands off the Louisiana coast for oil and gas development, plaintiffs attacked the Interior Department's EIS for failing to consider a number of alternative approaches to the energy problem. The district court found that the agency's EIS failed to provide the "detailed statement" of environmental impact and alternatives, and it granted a preliminary injunction enjoining the sale of leases pending compliance with NEPA. The Government appealed and the court of appeals denied the government's motion for summary reversal of the district court's decision.

In its opinion in that case, the court of appeals announced a "rule of reason" regarding an agency's duty to discuss alternative courses of action. The court held that the Interior Department must discuss all *reasonable* alternatives to action by any part of the federal government. It also held that the agency must discuss in the EIS the environmental effects of those alternatives. The "rule of reason" test was subsequently approved by the Supreme Court.[12] Portions of the appellate court's opinion follow.

NATURAL RESOURCES DEFENSE COUNCIL, INC. v. MORTON
458 F.2d 827 (D.C. Cir. 1972)

Paragraph (iii) of Sec. 102(2)(C) [of NEPA] is a terse notation for: 'The alternative ways of accomplishing the objectives of the proposed action and the results of not accomplishing the proposed action.'

Congress contemplated that the Impact Statement would constitute the environmental source material for the information of the Congress as well as the executive, in connection with the making of relevant decisions, and would be available to enhance enlightenment of—and by—the public. The impact statement provides a basis for (a) evaluation of the benefits of the proposed project in light of its environmental risks, and (b) comparison of the net balance for the proposed project with the environmental risks presented by alternative courses of action.

***

We reject the implication of one of the Government's submissions which began by stating that while the Act requires a detailed statement of alternatives, it 'does not require a discussion of the environmental con-sequences of the suggested alternative.' A sound construction of NEPA, which takes into account both the legislative history and contemporaneous executive construction, requires a presentation of the environmental risks incident to reasonable alternative courses of action. The agency may limit its discussion of environmental impact to a brief statement, when that is the case, that the alternative course involves no effect on the environment, or that their effect, briefly described, is simply nonsignificant. A rule of reason is implicit in this aspect of the law as it is in the requirement that the agency provide a statement concerning those opposing views that are responsible.

***

What NEPA infused into the decision-making process in 1969 was a directive as to environmental impact statements that was meant to implement the congressional objectives of government coordination, a comprehensive approach to environmental management, and a determination to face problems of pollution 'while they are still of manageable proportions and while alternative solutions are still available' rather than persist in environmental decision-making wherein 'policy is established by default and inaction' and environmental decisions 'continue to be made in small but steady increments' that perpetuate the mistakes of the past without being dealt with until 'they reach crisis proportions.'

We reiterate that the discussion of environmental effects of alternatives need not be exhaustive. What is required is information sufficient to permit a reasoned choice of alternatives so far as environmental as-

pects are concerned. As to alternatives not within the scope of authority of the responsible official, reference may of course be made to studies of other agencies—including other impact statements. Nor is it appropriate, as government counsel argues, to disregard alternatives merely because they do not offer a complete solution to the problem. If an alternative would result in supplying only part of the energy that the lease sale would yield, then its use might possibly reduce the scope of the lease sale program and thus alleviate a significant portion of the environmental harm attendant on offshore drilling. . . .

Questions and Comments for Discussion

While the appeals court said that it could not grant the government's motion for summary reversal of the district court's injunction, it did say that the NEPA requirement of discussion of reasonable alternatives does not require a "crystal ball" inquiry. According to the court: "Where the environmental aspects of alternatives are readily identifiable by the agency, it is reasonable to state them." However, the court said, "There is reason to conclude that NEPA was not meant to require detailed discussion of the environmental effects of alternatives when those effects cannot be readily ascertained and the alternatives are remote and speculative." The court concluded:

A final word. In this as in other areas, the functions of courts and agencies, rightly understood, are not in opposition but in collaboration, toward achievement of the end prescribed by Congress. So long as the officials and agencies have taken the 'hard look' at environmental consequences mandated by Congress, the court does not seek to impose unreasonable extremes or to interject itself within the area of discretion of the executive as to the choice of the action to be taken.

Informed by our judgment that discussion of alternatives may be required even

though the action required lies outside the Interior Department, the secretary will, we have no doubt, be able without undue delay to provide the kind of reasonable discussion of alternatives and their environmental consequences that Congress contemplated.

Contents of the EIS: The requirements of an EIS can be briefly summarized as follows, based on statutory language and CEQ regulations interpreting NEPA:

1. *Alternatives requiring discussion:* NEPA requires agencies to consider and discuss two types of alternatives in the EIS. The agency must consider alternatives to the proposed action, and the agency must study, develop, and describe appropriate alternatives to recommended courses of action in any proposal which involves unresolved conflicts concerning alternative uses of available resources.

2. *Range of alternatives:* As discussed in the *Kleppe* decision, an agency must consider reasonable alternatives, but the range is subject to a rule of reason, and depends on the nature and timing of the proposed action. As a general rule, the agency must discuss the alternative

of no action, or maintaining the status quo. This provides a basis for comparing environmental effects of the alternative courses of action.

3. *Environmental effects:* NEPA requires federal agencies to discuss in the EIS the environmental impact of the proposed action, any adverse environmental effects which cannot be avoided if the proposal is implemented, the relationship between local short-term uses of man's environment and the maintenance and enhancement of long-term productivity, and any irreversible and irretrievable commitments of resources which would be involved in the proposed action should it be implemented. All significant environmental effects must be considered, and cumulative effects must also be considered.

4. *Mitigation:* Mitigation measures must be discussed in sufficient detail to ensure that environmental consequences have been fairly evaluated, but the Supreme Court has held that NEPA does not require a complete mitigation plan to be formulated and adopted by the agency. *Robertson v. Methow Valley Citizens' Council,* 490 U.S. 332 (1989).

5. *Cost-benefit:* An EIS must contain some form of balancing or informal cost-benefit analysis. The analysis must be sufficient to provide the public and decisionmaker sufficient information to permit a reasoned evaluation and decision. However, under NEPA, environmental costs are not entitled to more weight than other costs and benefits.

Evaluation of NEPA

The preceding discussion has focused on some of the requirements of NEPA and some of the issues that may arise in court cases brought under provisions of the act. A more important policy question is whether NEPA is successful in achieving its stated purpose "to improve and coordinate federal plans, functions, programs, and resources to preserve and maintain the environment." What is the act's impact on decision making by federal agencies? Does NEPA impose any *substantive* requirements on federal agency decision making or is it merely a procedural statute which adds bureaucratic cost and delay without achieving any significant and substantive changes in agency decisions? Is there any judicial remedy under NEPA if a project is clearly environmentally unsound but the EIS is perfect and the agency meets all the procedural requirements of the act?

The Supreme Court has taken the view that NEPA is purely procedural and that the statement of environmental policies in Section 101 of the act is "prefatory." According to the Supreme Court, "[I]f the adverse environmental effects of the proposed action are adequately identified and evaluated, the agency is not constrained by NEPA from deciding that other values outweigh the environmental costs. . . . NEPA merely prohibits uninformed—rather than unwise—agency action."[13]

But this does not mean that NEPA is unsuccessful in compelling agencies to achieve its stated goals. Some have suggested that as a practical matter, substantive review of an agency decision and review of the EIS amounts to the same thing because it would be extremely difficult for an agency to prepare an adequate EIS for a proposal that was clearly "arbitrary and capricious." Even more important, the EIS process not only ensures that an agency, in reaching its decision, will carefully consider the significant environmental impacts of the proposal, the EIS requirement also ensures that all relevant information will be made available to the public so that the public (including environmental "watch dog" groups) may also play a role in both the decision-making process and the implementation of that decision.

The importance of the EIS as a means for disseminating information to the public about the environmental impacts of agency decision making should not be underestimated. The courts have recognized that publication of the EIS gives the public the assurance that the agency has indeed considered environmental concerns in its decision-making process, and perhaps more significantly, it provides a springboard for public comment.[14]

Very few federal projects have been halted by permanent injunction under NEPA. However, NEPA litigation has caused substantial delays in a number of federal projects and modification or abandonment of others. Certainly there are cases where agencies have avoided taking controversial actions because of potential NEPA litigation. Whether the benefits attained under NEPA outweigh the expense and delay to federal projects depends to some extent on one's point of view about the project in dispute.

Likewise, whether NEPA has made a major contribution to preserving the environment depends on one's point of view. Some have suggested that the Supreme Court, which has never upheld a NEPA claim on the merits, has evidenced little support for the statute, and this attitude has diminished NEPA's effectiveness. Others see NEPA as a cornerstone of environmental law whose mandates are becoming more fully integrated into the decision-making process of federal agencies. Whatever the ultimate verdict on NEPA may be, it is clear that in some cases it is a potent device for focusing the public's attention on environmental concerns.

THE ENDANGERED SPECIES ACT

The **Endangered Species Act** (ESA) was enacted almost unanimously in 1973. The ESA is a powerful statute that places the highest priority on the protection of endangered species. It is also one of America's most controversial environmental laws. The ESA prohibits government agencies from authorizing, funding, or carrying out any activities that might harm an endangered species or its habitat. The Act also prohibits private individuals from *taking* an endangered species. The meaning of the word *taking* has been the subject of much litigation, and is the source of much controversy. *Taking* may be so broadly defined that it may be construed to prohibit virtually any activity that might result in harm to a protected species.

History and Purposes

The ESA followed an earlier species protection act, the 1916 National Park Service Act. The National Park Service Act declared as a fundamental purpose, "conserving scenery and natural and historical objects and the wild life therein. . . ." Subsequently, two species protection acts, passed in 1966 and 1969, authorized the federal government to purchase land for the conservation of species threatened with extinction. These acts also directed federal agencies to preserve the habitats of such species "insofar as practicable." The language in these acts required agencies to consider and weigh the costs of preservation against the benefits of protection.

In adopting the ESA, Congress continued a land acquisition program to protect endangered species. Significantly, however, Congress abandoned the practicability criteria of earlier acts in affording legal protection to endangered species. Determination that a species is endangered or threatened is, under the ESA, to be made "solely on the basis of the best scientific and commercial data available to [the Secretary]. . . ."[15] Section 7 of the act protects endangered species from federal agency action without regard to the economic consequences of protection and Section 9 prohibits any person from taking an endangered species. As a result, the ESA has been called a "roadblock" statute. Except in limited circumstances, it contains substantive, specific, and mandatory provisions protecting an endangered species and its habitat regardless of cost.

One of the most important and famous cases interpreting the ESA was decided in 1978 in *Tennessee Valley Authority v. Hill.* That case, interpreting Section 7 of the ESA, involved a classic environmental conflict arising from the federal agency's decision to build a dam, called the Tellico Dam, on a last remaining segment of the Little Tennessee River. A citizens' coalition had sought to block the project and had obtained an injunction under NEPA. The NEPA injunction lasted two years but was subsequently dissolved in 1973 when the **Tennessee Valley Authority** (TVA) produced an adequate EIS. That same year, an ichthyologist at the University of Tennessee discovered a small endangered fish, the snail darter, living in the project area. The plaintiffs filed another lawsuit, arguing that the dam project would destroy the habitat of the snail darter in violation of the ESA. The trial court agreed with plaintiffs but declined to issue an injunction in the case. The court of appeals granted the injunction and the U.S. Supreme Court granted a petition for review.

TENNESSEE VALLEY AUTHORITY v. HILL
437 U.S. 153 (1978)

MR. CHIEF JUSTICE BURGER delivered the opinion of the Court.

The questions presented in this case are (a) whether the Endangered Species Act of 1973 requires a court to enjoin the operation of a virtually completed federal dam—which had been authorized prior to 1973—when, pursuant to authority vested in him by Congress, the Secretary of the Interior has determined that operation of the dam would eradicate an endangered species; and (b) whether continued congressional appropriations for the dam after 1973 constituted an implied repeal of the Endangered Species Act, at least as to the particular dam.

***

Until recently the finding of a new species of animal life would hardly generate a cause celebre. This is particularly so in the case of darters, of which there are approximately 130 known species, 8 to 10 of these having

been identified only in the last five years. The moving force behind the snail darter's sudden fame came some four months after its discovery, when the Congress passed the Endangered Species Act of 1973. This legislation, among other things, authorizes the Secretary of the Interior to declare species of animal life "endangered" and to identify the "critical habitat" of these creatures.

[*The Court focused on Section 7 of the Act which requires federal departments and agencies to "take such action necessary to insure that actions authorized, funded, or carried out by them do not jeopardize the continued existence of such endangered species and threatened species or result in the destruction or modification of habitat of such species. . . ."*]

***

II

We begin with the premise that operation of the Tellico Dam will either eradicate the known population of snail darters or destroy their critical habitat. Petitioner does not now seriously dispute this fact. . . . [T]he Secretary (of Interior) promulgated regulations which declared the snail darter an endangered species whose critical habitat would be destroyed by creation of the Tellico Reservoir. Doubtless petitioner would prefer not to have these regulations on the books, but there is no suggestion that the Secretary exceeded his authority or abused his discretion in issuing the regulations. . . .

It may seem curious to some that the survival of a relatively small number of three-inch fish among all the countless millions of species extant would require the permanent halting of a virtually completed dam for which Congress has expended more than $100 million. . . . We conclude, however, that the explicit provisions of the Endangered Species Act require precisely that result.

One would be hard pressed to find a statutory provision whose terms were any plainer than those in Section 7 of the Endangered Species Act. Its very words affirmatively command all federal agencies "to *insure* that actions *authorized, funded, or carried out* by them do not *jeopardize* the continued existence" of an endangered species or *result* in the destruction or modification of habitat of such species. . . . This language admits of no exception. Nonetheless, petitioner urges, as do the dissenters, that the Act cannot reasonably be interpreted as applying to a federal project which was well underway when Congress passed the Endangered Species Act of 1973. To sustain that position, however, we would be forced to ignore the ordinary meaning of plain language. It has not been shown, for example, how TVA can close the gates of the Tellico Dam without 'carrying out' an action that has been "authorized" and "funded" by a federal agency. Nor can we understand how such action will "*insure*" that the snail darter's habitat is not disrupted. Accepting the Secretary's determinations, as we must, it is clear that TVA's proposed operation of the dam will have precisely the opposite effect, namely the *eradication* of an endangered species.

Concededly, this view of the act will produce results requiring the sacrifice of the anticipated benefits of the project and of many millions of dollars in public funds. But examination of the language, history, and structure of the legislation under review here indicates beyond doubt that Congress intended endangered species to be afforded the highest of priorities.

***

As it was finally passed, the Endangered Species Act of 1973 represented the most comprehensive legislation for the preservation of endangered species ever enacted by any nation. Its stated purposes were "to provide a means whereby the ecosystems upon which endangered species and threatened species depend may be conserved," and "to provide a program for the conservation of such . . . species. . . ." In furtherance of these goals, Congress expressly stated in Sec. 2(c) that "all Federal departments and agencies *shall* seek *to conserve endangered species* or threatened species to the point at which the measures provided pursuant to this chapter are no longer necessary. Aside from Section 7, other provisions indicated the seriousness with which Congress viewed this issue: Virtually all dealings with endangered species including taking, possession, transportation, and sale were prohibited, except in extremely narrow circumstances. . . .

[*After further discussion the court affirmed the decision of the Court of Appeals that the project should be enjoined under the ESA.*]

Questions and Comments for Discussion

1.   Justices Powell and Blackmun filed a dissent in *TVA v. Hill*. They argued that the opinion of the majority "adopts a reading of section 7 of the Act that gives it a retro-active effect and disregards 12 years of consistently expressed congressional intent to complete the Tellico Project. . . . More-over, it ignores established canons of statu-tory construction." The dissenters expected Congress to amend the Endangered Species Act to "prevent the grave consequences made possible by today's decision." Ac-cording to the dissenters, "[F]ew, if any, Members of that body will wish to defend an interpretation of the Act that requires the waste of at least $53 million, and denies the people of the Tennessee Valley area the benefits of the reservoir that Congress intended to confer. There will be little sen-timent to leave this dam standing before an empty reservoir, serving no purpose other than a conversation piece of incredu-lous tourists. . . ."

The dissenters were right in this regard. In 1978, Congress amended the Endan-gered Species Act to provide flexibility by creating a Cabinet-level review board (called the "**God Committee**") which could grant an exemption if it found by special majority that:

a.   the federal project is of regional or na-tional significance;

b.   there is no "reasonable and prudent al-ternative;" and

c.   the project as proposed "clearly out-weighs the alternatives."

The amendment creating this exemption was passed following a torrent of criticism leveled against the act following the snail darter decision in the Tellico Dam case. However, on January 23, 1979, the "God Committee" unanimously denied an exemp-tion for Tellico on economic grounds. Ac-cording to the committee, the project was ill-conceived and uneconomic in the first place and deserved to be killed on its own merits.

The project ultimately went forward when Senator Baker and Congressman Duncan of Tennessee added a rider to a House appropriations bill which explicitly overrode the decision as it applied to the Tellico project.

2.   Many argued in the Tellico Dam case that a statute should not be applied if it would lead to an "absurd" or "extreme" re-sult. The Supreme Court held in this case that even when a statute leads to what a court might think was an absurd result, the statute was to be applied as it is written. Do you agree that it is the function of a court to apply the law "as written" regard-less of the consequences in a particular case? Why or why not?

3.   Unlike earlier species protection acts, the ESA does not permit the Secretary of the Interior to consider the economic impact of listing a species as endangered under the act. Should economic costs be considered in making that determination? In considering your answer to this policy question, con-sider the reasons *why* species protection may have value. Many have argued that the environment has instrumental value to hu-mans—be it aesthetic, religious, or eco-nomic, and thus there is value in preserving species for present and future human be-ings. But should endangered species be pro-tected on a biocentric or non-human level? Does a species like the snail darter have in-herent value even if human beings do not recognize its value? As the snail darter con-troversy suggests, whether economic costs should be considered in protecting endan-gered species (the "cost-benefit" contro-versy) is tied to an ethical, ecological, and political debate about how, when, and what environmental values human beings should protect, and at what cost.

Key Provisions: The Listing Procedures of Section 4

The ESA contains several important sections designed to implement the species protection policies of the act. Section 4 sets out the procedure for listing of an endangered or threatened species under the act. This is perhaps the most important section of the act because the ESA's protections are contingent upon the listing process. The Secretary of the Interior (and in some cases Secretary of Commerce) has authority to list an endangered or threatened species under the act.

> Section 4 provides that the secretary shall by regulation *determine whether any species is an endangered species or a threatened species because of any of the following factors:*
>
> A. the present or threatened destruction, modification, or curtailment of its habitat or range;
>
> B. over-utilization for commercial, recreational, scientific, or educational purposes;
>
> C. disease or predation;
>
> D. the inadequacy of existing regulatory mechanisms; or
>
> E. other natural or manmade factors affecting its continued existence.

The determination that a species is endangered excludes consideration of economic impact of that decision. Section 7(b)(1)(a) states:

> The Secretary shall make determinations required by subsection (a)(1) of this section solely on the basis of the best scientific and commercial data available to him after conducting a review of the status of the species. . . .[16]

Once a species is listed as endangered or threatened, it is protected at all costs. The rule that "all federal departments and agencies shall seek to conserve all endangered and threatened species" is strictly construed. When the species is listed, the secretary must designate the *critical habitat* within a year of the listing. This is defined as the *geographical area with the physical or biological features essential to the species survival.* In designating critical habitat, the secretary is required to take into consideration the economic impact, and any other relevant impact of specifying any particular area as critical habitat. The secretary may exclude an area if the benefits of exclusion outweigh the benefits of designating an area as critical habitat, unless the secretary determines, based on the best scientific and commercial data available, that the failure to designate an area as critical habitat will result in the extinction of the species.[17] *Recovery plans,* biological blueprints for actions needed to bring about species' recovery, also must be created under this section.

The definition of species under the ESA is very broad. "Species" includes any subspecies of fish, wildlife, or plants. An *endangered species* is further defined as "any species in danger of extinction throughout all or a significant portion of its range other than a species of the Class Insecta determined to constitute a pest. . . ." A *threatened* species is defined as a species that while not yet endangered, is likely to become so in the foreseeable future.

The endangered species program is administered by the U.S. **Fish and Wildlife Services** (FWS) and the National Marine Fisheries Services (NMFS). A state or federal agency, individual, or any other entity may petition either of these two agencies to list a species. If there is sufficient biological data, the species is named an official candidate, and after notification in the *Federal Register,* the species is added to the list of endangered or threatened species.

The determination to list or not list a species is subject to judicial review. Despite prompting from various groups, only a fraction of endangered and threatened species known to be eligible have been listed. As of 1991, a total of 651 domestic species were listed as threatened or endangered under the ESA, with an additional 600 considered serious candidates and 3000 identified as potentially eligible.[18]

Section 7: Application to Federal Agencies

Section 7 of the act is entitled "Interagency Cooperation." Like NEPA, this section is directed at federal agencies. Section 7 contains the following mandate:

> Each Federal agency shall, in consultation with and with the assistance of the Secretary, insure that any action authorized, funded, or carried out by such agency . . . is not likely to jeopardize the continued existence of any endangered species or threatened species or result in the destruction or adverse modification of habitat of such species which is determined by the Secretary, after consultation as appropriate with affected States, to be critical. . . .

This section was the focus of the Supreme Court's discussion and opinion in *TVA V. Hill* (the "Tellico Dam case"). Section 7 also establishes the Endangered Species Committee. This "God Committee" may grant an exemption from the requirements of the section. This committee's function was discussed after the Tellico Dam case in the text.

Section 9: The "Takings" Prohibition

The application of Section 9 of the act is much broader than Section 7 because it applies to "any person," not just actions of federal agencies. Section (1) applies to any endangered species of fish or wildlife listed under the act. It makes it unlawful for any person to:

A. import any such species into, or export any such species from the United States;

B. take any such species within the United States or the territorial sea of the United States;

C. take any such species upon the high seas;

D. possess, sell, deliver, carry, transport, or ship, by any means whatsoever, any such species taken in violation of subparagraphs (B) and (C);

E. deliver, receive, carry, transport, or ship in interstate or foreign commerce, by any means whatsoever and in the course of a commercial activity, any such species;

F. sell or offer for sale in interstate or foreign commerce any such species; or

G. violate any regulation pertaining to such species or to any threatened species of fish or wildlife listed pursuant to Section 1533 of this title and promulgated by the Secretary pursuant to authority provided by this chapter.

A separate provision of this section addresses endangered plants.

Section 9(a)(B) and (C) prohibit taking any endangered species, and imposes heavy criminal sanctions to the act of killing or capturing endangered animals. In the context of the ESA, the word *taking* should be distinquished from the concept of taking under the Fifth Amendment as discussed in Chapter 6. *Taking* an endangered species in violation of the ESA is defined in the act as *"harass, harm, pursue, hunt, shoot, wound, kill, trap, capture, or collect, or attempt to engage in any such conduct."* The meaning of the word "take" as used in the act has been the subject of much litigation, and it raises substantial questions about the appropriate balance between the rights of a property owner to develop his property and the government's interest in protecting endangered species' habitats.

Many have criticized the ESA because the potential sweep of the act is so broad. Some argue that an expansive definition of the takings prohibitions of the ESA will effectively prevent activities on public or private lands that would otherwise be considered a reasonable economic use of the property. The ESA has generated controversy because it can halt development projects if that project potentially threatens a listed species.

In a recent series of cases, landowners, logging companies, and families dependent on the forest products industries in the Pacific Northwest and in the Southeast, challenged the Fish and Wildlife Service definition of the word "harm" in the ESA.

The agency had defined the word "harm" in the statutory definition of "take" as follows:

Harm in the definition of 'take' in the Act means an act which actually kills or injures wildlife. Such act may include significant habitat modification or degradation where it actually kills or injures wildlife by significantly impairing essential behavioral patterns, including breeding, feeding or sheltering.[19]

Two federal appeals courts were divided on whether the agency's definition of "harm" in the takings prohibition of the ESA was a permissible one. In *Sweet Home Chapter of Communities for a Great Oregon v. Babbitt,*[20] the D.C. Circuit Court of Appeals had determined that the FWS definition exceeded the scope of Section 9's takings prohibition. The Ninth Circuit Court of Appeals, however, had upheld the definition in another case.[21] In 1995, the Supreme Court agreed to address the issue. A portion of the Court's analysis upholding the agency definition of "harm" is set out below.

BABBIT v. SWEET HOME CHAPTER OF COMMUNITIES FOR A GREAT OREGON
115 S.Ct. 2407 (1995)

JUSTICE STEVENS delivered the opinion of the Court.

***

Because this case was decided on motions for summary judgment, we may appropriately make certain factual assumptions in order to frame the legal issue. First, we assume respondents have no desire to harm either the red-cockaded woodpecker or the spotted owl; they merely wish to continue logging activities that would be entirely proper if not prohibited by the ESA. On the other hand, we must assume *arguendo* that those activities will have the effect, even though unintended, of detrimentally changing the natural habitat of both listed species and that, as a consequence, members of those species will be killed or injured. . . . The Secretary . . . submits that the sec. 9 prohibition of takings, which Congress defined to include "harm," places on respondents a duty to avoid harm that habitat alteration will cause the birds unless respondents first obtain a permit pursuant to section 10.

The text of the [Endangered Species] Act provides three reasons for concluding that the Secretary's interpretation is reasonable.

First, an ordinary understanding of the word "harm" supports it. The dictionary definition of the verb form of "harm" is "to cause hurt or damage to: injure. . . ." In the context of the ESA, that definition naturally encompasses habitat modification that results in actual injury or death to members of an endangered or threatened species.

Respondents argue that the Secretary should have limited the purview of "harm" to direct applications of force against protected species, but the dictionary definition does not include the word "directly" or suggest in any way that only direct or willful action that leads to injury constitutes "harm." Moreover, unless the statutory term "harm" encompasses indirect as well as direct injuries, the word has no meaning that does not duplicate the meaning of other words that sec. 3 uses to define "take." A reluctance to treat statutory terms as surplusage supports the reasonableness of the Secretary's interpretation . . .

Second, the broad purpose of the ESA supports the Secretary's decision to extend protection against activities that cause the precise harms Congress enacted in statute to avoid. . . . As stated in sec. 2 of the Act, among its central purposes is "to provide a means whereby the ecosystems upon which endangered species and threatened species depend may be conserved. . . ."

***

Third, the fact that Congress in 1982 authorized the Secretary to issue permits for takings that sec. 9 would otherwise prohibit, "if such taking is incidental to, and not the purpose of, the carrying out of an otherwise lawful activity," . . . strongly suggests that Congress understood sec. 9(1)(1)(B) to prohibit indirect as well as deliberate takings. . . . Congress' addition of the sec. 10 permit provision supports the Secretary's conclusion that activities not intended to harm an endangered species, such as habitat modification, may constitute unlawful takings under the ESA unless the Secretary permits them.

***

When it enacted the ESA, Congress delegated broad administrative and interpretive power to the Secretary. . . . The task of defining and listing endangered and threatened species requires an expertise and attention to detail that exceeds the normal province of Congress. Fashioning appropriate standards for issuing permits under sec. 10 for takings that would otherwise violate sec. 9 necessarily requires the exercise of broad discretion. The proper interpretation of a term such as "harm" involves a complex policy choice. When Congress has entrusted the Secretary with broad discretion, we are especially reluctant to substitute our views of wise policy for his. . . .

The judgment of the Court of Appeals is reversed.

Questions and Comments for Discussion

1. What techniques of statutory interpretation did the court use in determining whether the agency's interpretation of the word "harm" was a reasonable one?

2. Whether habitat modification constitutes a "taking" of a protected species under the act is a question of significance to environmentalists and to landowners. Section 7's prohibition against jeopardizing a species or modifying critical habitat only applies to federal agencies. Section 9, however, applies to all persons. If this includes intentional disruption of habitat, as occurs during land development, the statute's prohibitions of "harm" as interpreted by the Fish and Wildlife Service may have a significant effect on private property rights.

3. *Incidental Takings:* As discussed in this case, in 1982 Congress authorized the secretary to issue permits for takings that would otherwise be prohibited under Section 9. Section 10 of the ESA provides that the sec-

retary may permit, under terms and conditions he prescribes, a taking otherwise prohibited by Section 9 if the taking is "incidental to, and not the purpose of, the carrying out of an otherwise lawful activity." This section permitting "incidental takings" requires that the applicant submit a conservation plan, including steps for minimizing and mitigating such impacts. If the secretary finds, after opportunity for public comment, that the taking will be incidental, and will not appreciably reduce the likelihood of the survival and recovery of the species in the wild, the secretary may issue a permit for the activity. This section is presumably designed to minimize the economic impact of the ESA on private property development which may affect habitat of an endangered or threatened species.

4. The Endangered Species Act also closes down the United States market to endangered wildlife. The market for endangered species actually encourages species extinction by raising the value of an animal as it approaches extinction. The ESA attempts to eliminate the pressures on endangered animals in other parts of the world by closing down the lucrative and major U.S. market for such species. Foreign species protected under the act include leopards, turtles, rare birds for feathers, and elephants for ivory. Reconsider the *Ghen v. Rich* case set out in Chapter 3. Do you think the purposes of species protection acts like the ESA and Eagle Protection Act should outweigh individual rights to purchase and sell personal property and to develop real property? What are the political, economic, and environmental implications of your answer?

Evaluation of the Endangered Species Act

Many critics of the ESA target the Supreme Court's decision in *TVA v. Hill* for making species protection a "trump card" which takes priority over all other government objectives. Because the Supreme Court ruled out a cost-benefit analysis in that case, some believe that the ESA has become the "ultimate environmental statute." In this view, species protection "whatever the cost" implies an obligation to forego all other opportunities and responsibilities to protect threatened and endangered species.[22]

Critics also suggest that the ESA has been ineffective in actually saving species. A study published in 1994 asserted that of all species listed by the Fish and Wildlife Service and National Marine Fisheries Service since 1966, only four species had actually recovered to a point allowing their delisting, and of these four, three are birds native to an island in the western Pacific. According to this study, over 80 percent of all listed species were declining despite protection under the ESA.[23] And the costs of saving species is great. In 1990, the Department of the Interior estimated the cost of recovering all presently known species at $4.6 billion, and some suggest this is an extremely low estimate.

Many consider the most controversial aspect of the ESA to be its power to take private property through extensive regulation of land use. *Regulatory takings,* discussed in Chapter 6, may occur if the government regulates the use of private property in such a way as to deprive the owner of all of its economic value. In some cases, an owner who is prohibited from developing his property because it may destroy the critical habitat of an endangered species may argue that the law has deprived him of the use and value of the property without just compensation in violation of the Fifth Amendment.

When Congress considers reauthorization of the ESA, the argument will be made that the law should allow consideration of the costs and benefits of saving species and to involve the private sector in recovery plan development.

Others, however, counter with the assertion that despite the reputation for inflexibility and stringent application, the facts are otherwise. According to one researcher, despite what appears to be a mandatory blueprint established by the ESA to preserve endangered species, over the years the agencies primarily responsible for its implementation have been able to convert the act from command legislation to a species permit system in which the permitting is done largely at the agency's discretion. According to this view, the ESA has accommodated the overwhelming majority of human activity without impediment.[24]

The controversy surrounding the ESA and NEPA is not likely to abate. First, in many if not most cases, plaintiffs have employed these statutes as a means to an end—the end being their desire to halt major government projects which they see as a threat to the environment. Frequently, NEPA and the ESA provide the only way for environmentalists to challenge such projects. For example, in *TVA v. Hill,* the discovery of the snail darter led to a lawsuit under the ESA seeking to halt a development project threatening an entire river valley. The snail darter was a "canary in a coal mine," and environmental groups used NEPA and the ESA to try to halt the dam project and to preserve the last remaining stretch of the Tennessee River.

Consider also the case of the northern spotted owl. Environmental groups have used the EIS requirements of the NEPA (specifically challenging the necessity for and adequacy of the EIS), the ESA, and provisions of federal forestry management laws in a series of lawsuits designed to halt logging in the old-growth forests of the Pacific Northwest. Once the spotted owl was listed as an endangered species, plaintiffs argued that agreements between the National Forest Service and the timber industry which permitted logging in the forests of Olympic National Park and Forest threatened the critical habitat of the owl and must be halted under provisions of the ESA. It is primarily the ancient old-growth forests of the Pacific Northwest that the plaintiffs have sought to preserve. The owl became a way to protect the forests by providing a legal basis on which environmental groups could challenge the forest service's management plans. For many, the spotted owl has also become a symbol of conflicting points of view between loggers, environmentalists, the timber industry, the government, and members of the scientific community.

In his book *The Final Forest,* William Dietrich, a Pulitzer prize-winning science correspondent for the *Seattle Times,* provides a fascinating account of the conflicting perspectives raised by the spotted owl controversy. We conclude this chapter with a look at some of those perspectives.

Excerpts from *The Final Forest* by William Dietrich

The spotted owl came to illustrate two enormously significant trends: the increasing importance people are placing on preserving a diversity of species, and the growing political power of science.

Abridged with the permission of Simon & Schuster from THE FINAL FOREST *by William Dietrich. Copyright © 1992 by William Dietrich.*

The first trend is marked by the value humans have begun to place on species that have neither obvious utility—such as cattle or deer or dogs—or a particular striking nobility—such as lions or whales or eagles. Since the 1970s biologists have been well aware of the growing tendency of Americans, especially those who lived in cities, to anthropomorphize animals, to attribute to them human and cuddly aspects they don't really have. Bob Moorhead, a biologist in Olympic National Park, has a theory about this. He believes that as urban society becomes more technical and impersonal, there is a corresponding increase of yearning for what he calls "touchy-feely" things. . . .

With the stage thus set, perhaps it is not surprising there was an immediate concern for the owl, particularly among bird watchers. Yet the spotted owl's very obscurity and nondescript nature took human attitudes toward the natural world another step. It made the calls for the owl's preservation a challenge to an older, more human centered view of the world, where the kinds of animals people cared about were the kind they were familiar with. Here was an animal few people had ever seen, and yet many people were willing to assert it mattered. . . (p. 52).

***

Robert Lee, the sociologist at the University of Washington who is sympathetic to the plight of logging communities, has argued that loggers can be just as upset at a clearcut as a hiker. . . . Loggers have what he thinks is a more realistic view of nature, a willingness to use it as well as enjoy it. "They accept the rules of life," he said. "They know somebody has to cut it, so let's do the best job possible."

In a speech on this theme, Lee said that, "Unlike advocates for old growth preservation and reform in forest management practices, rural woods workers tend to romanticize people and view nature pragmatically. . . . People are humanized and nature is a morally neutral object that is readily converted into a commodity. . . ."

Forest preservation, Lee said, has for some environmentalists taken the place of traditional religion by enabling them to deny the terrifying historical and ecological realities of contemporary human existence. . . . It is the symbolic importance of these forests as enduring symbols of undisturbed nature, not their biological functions, that has such broad public appeal. . . (pp. 139–140).

***

[Matthew] Carroll (an assistant professor of natural resource sociology at Washington State University) theorizes that there are at least three principal philosophies found in the woods. The Forest Service and similar government agencies tend to be utilitarian, he said, measuring the forest by how it can provide the most good for the most people. Gifford Pinchot, the first chief of the Forest Service, spelled this out in 1905, writing that, "Where conflicting interests must be reconciled, the question will always be decided from the standpoint of the greatest good of the greatest number in the long run." If the majority wants wood products, the Forest Service responds to that. If the majority wants preservation instead, the Forest Service will eventually shift in response.

Environmentalists, Carrol said, tend to be transcendentalist in approach. They find a spiritual, almost religious experience in nature and tend to stress the values of scenery, wildlife, and ecology, the fabric of natural life that offers contrasts and lessons to human civilization.

The third philosophy, Carroll suggests, is a market philosophy. The forest's value is set by the price society puts

Excerpt from The Final Forest *by William Dietrich (continued)*

on its tangible products. This is the philosophy of the big timber companies, he said, and it tends to be the philosophy of most timber communities. . . (pp. 140–41).

***

[Mitch Friedman (founder of the Greater Ecosystem Alliance) estimated] existing parks and wilderness areas . . . represented at best perhaps half the original natural ecosystems in the United States. "That's not radical anymore," he said of wilderness designation. What American society needed to do, he was concluding, was not just set aside more preserves but manage all land in an ecosystem—including cities, farms, and commercial forest land—to preserve ecological values. Essentially, Friedman said, people had to discover the correct rate of "sustainable extraction" and modify civilization to fit. . . . Environmentalists had to persuade Congress, he said, that "Congress can't mandate the survival of species by law." The nation was going at its goals backward. It was waiting for species to reach a crisis point and then trying to protect them individually, instead of modifying human development to coexist with the natural world. (p. 160).

***

Mason (a timber mill owner) said he understands the origins of the old-growth conflict. "For the first time, Americans are aware resources are finite," he said. "I agree it is very appropriate that areas be set aside."

"But on the other hand, it is also very appropriate some of the land be farmed. An inappropriate way is to file a court injunction and make a town die." Mason shook his head. "There are three and four generations of people here who haven't done anything wrong."

The world will cut just as many trees, Mason predicted. They will just cut them elsewhere and probably in places that recover more poorly, such as the tropical rain forest or the slow-growing taiga of the north. Since 1960, worldwide wood consumption has nearly tripled. Mason simply isn't convinced by the environmentalists' arguments. He thinks they have a manipulative leadership and a naive rank and file. "They've got this sense of guilt that it is wrong their lifestyle is gobbling up the earth," he said. "The way they address this guilt is instead of curbing their consumer use and conserving resources they continue their life-style and send a check to the Audubon Society. That's the tragedy of this whole thing. What they're doing doesn't curb world demand. All it does is restrict supply." (pp. 246–47).

Questions and Comments for Discussion

1. To what extent do you think the tendency of Americans to anthropomorphize animals affects the likelihood that some animals rather than others will be *selected* for protection under the endangered species act? Are some species "more deserving" of protection than others? What are the implications of your answer?

2. Some of the controversy in the spotted owl cases derives from lack of scientific certainty. It is very difficult to determine the number of endangered species, like owls,

within a certain geographical area, and the impact of a particular activity like logging on a particular species. To what extent does science have the ability to offer a research-based "truth" in such cases? Who should bear the cost of such scientific studies?

3.   Some environmental activists have taken the law into their own hands by implanting nails and pieces of steel in trees scheduled to be cut by loggers. Are such protests and active sabotage ever justified? What are the ethical implications of your answer?

4.   If Mason is correct (in the last excerpt), what are the ethical and ecological ramifications of closing down timber harvest in the Pacific Northwest only to drive harvesting to other poorer countries?

SUMMARY

This chapter has focused on two laws which have substantially changed the way federal agencies make decisions affecting the environment. The National Environmental Policy Act and the Endangered Species Act provide a basis on which government proposals may be challenged because the agency has not adequately considered the environmental impact or harm to a threatened or endangered species. NEPA and the ESA have been used to attack significant government proposals and costly development projects in a number of important lawsuits. These laws may in some cases apply to private property developers as well.

As the Tellico Dam and the spotted owl controversy illustrate, there are no easy answers to the problem of striking an appropriate balance between land development and conservation of natural resources. NEPA and the ESA require administrative agencies to consider the implications and alternatives of their actions and to comply with the substantive mandates of the acts. The courts ultimately become involved in resolving many of these disputes because it is their function to interpret and apply the language of the statutes, and to ensure that decision making by federal agencies meets the requirements of these laws.

GLOSSARY

AEC—Atomic Energy Commission.

CEQ—Council on Environmental Quality (created by the National Environmental Policy Act).

EA—Environmental assessment. Used to analyze whether an EIS is required under NEPA.

EIS—Environmental impact statement (a requirement of the National Environmental Policy Act).

ESA—Endangered Species Act.

Federal Register—Daily government publication of federal agency actions and proposed actions.

FONSI—"Finding of No Significant Impact" (and therefore a finding that no EIS is required) under NEPA.

FWS—Fish and Wildlife Service, which administers the ESA.

"God Committee"—Cabinet-level review board created by the Endangered Species Act to provide flexibility under the act. The committee has the power to grant exemptions under the act.

laches—An equitable theory barring recovery when a party seeking relief has failed to enforce a right at the appropriate time.

NEPA—National Environmental Policy Act.

NRC—Nuclear Regulatory Commission.

ROD—Record of decision. Formal statement identifying and explaining an agency decision.

SEIS—Supplemental EIS which may be required under NEPA if the agency makes substantial changes in a proposed action or if significant new circumstances or information arise.

TVA—Tennessee Valley Authority (defendant federal agency in *TVA v. Hill,* the "snail darter" case).

CASES FOR DISCUSSION

1.   The United States Forest Service prepared an environmental impact statement for a project to build seven telescopes on Emerald Peak of Mount Graham in Arizona. It notified the Coalition of the San Carlos Apache Tribe of its decision. The agency had first asked the tribe for input in 1985. In 1986, the tribe failed to respond to a request for comment to the agency's draft EIS. In 1988, the tribe asked to be removed from the agency's mailing list. In 1991, however, the tribe brought suit against the agency, seeking to halt the project. Is the tribe's action challenging the agency decision and its environmental impact statement barred by **laches,** an equitable theory barring recovery when the party seeking relief has failed to enforce a right at the proper time? *Appache Survival Coalition v. U.S.,* 21 F.3d 895 (9th Cir. 1994).

2.   The U.S. Forest Service changed its management plan for the Bighorn National Forest in Wyoming by changing its regeneration standard from 7 to 5 years. Plaintiff Sierra Club argued that this affected a significant change in the agency's land resource management plan prompting the need for a new environmental impact statement. The agency had prepared an Environmental Assessment (EA) in which it had concluded that the change was not significant. Is the plaintiff correct that a new EIS is required? *Sierra Club v. Cargill,* 11 F.3d 1545 (10th Cir. Colo. 1993).

3.   Is the U.S. Forest Service required by NEPA to consider the connected and cumulative environmental impacts of a timber company's proposed timber management project? The Forest Service decided not to consider the connected and cumulative impact of a timber company's applications for seven road access permits into the forest along with its timber management activities, but assessed the impact of the roads separately. The agency subsequently determined it was not required to prepare an EIS for one of the access roads. Was the Forest Service correct? *Alpin Lakes Protection Society v. U.S.F.S.,* 838 F. Supp. 478 (W.D. Wash. 1993).

4.   Is the United States Trade Representative required to prepare an environmental impact statement for the North Atlantic Free Trade Agreement (NAFTA)? *Public Citizen v. OTR,* 5 F.3d 549 (D.C. Cir. 1993).

5.   May the U.S. Forest Service reasonably regulate the use of an unpaved forest development road by private landowners used to access their lands within a national forest? The owners argued that the regulation interfered with their constitutional right to travel. The Forest Service maintained that its regulations, requiring limited closure and special methods of snow removal, were necessary to protect the amount of run-off into the Salmon River, habitat of the Chinook salmon, an endangered species. Is the Forest Service correct? *Mountain States Legal Foundation v. Espy,* 833 F. Supp. 808 (D. Idaho 1993).

6.   Was the General Service Administration required to prepare an EIS for its proposal to build a federal courthouse in Portland, Oregon? The General Service Administration had prepared an Environmental Assessment and subsequently issued a FONSI. Plaintiffs argued that an EIS was required and that the project would impact low-income housing and affect homelessness in the community. *Morris v. Myers,* 845 F. Supp. 750 (D. Or. 1993).

7.   Plaintiff environmental group alleged that the National Science Foundation violated NEPA by failing to prepare an environmental impact statement before going forward with plans to incinerate food wastes in Antarctica. NSF argued that there is a presumption against extraterritorial application of statutes, and that the plain language of 102(2)(C) of NEPA precluded its application in Antarctica. Does NEPA apply in this case? *Environmental Defense Fund v. Massey,* 986 F.2d. 528 (D.C. Cir. 1993).

8.   Should the court issue an injunction ordering a railroad to reduce speed at the site of a train derailment because spilled corn from the derailment attracts grizzly bears? A derailment had spilled 10,000 tons of corn and attracted the bears along the tracks of the Burlington Railroad. By October 1990, defendant's train had collided with and killed at least five bears in the immediate vicinity of the spills. Plaintiffs sought the injunction, arguing that the killings of the bears were a "taking" under the Endangered Species Act. *National Wildlife Federation v. Burlington No. Railroad,* 852 F. Supp. 32 (D.C. 1994).

9.   Petitioners sought to set aside a listing by the Fish and Wildlife Service (FWS) of the Bruneau Hot Springs snail as an endangered species because the FWS waited seven-and-one-half years between the proposal to list the snail and actually promulgating the final rule. Are petitioners correct? *Idaho Farm Bureau Federation v. Babbitt,* 58 F.3d 1392 (9th Cir. 1993).

10.   Does limited deer hunting authorized by the Massachusetts Division of Fisheries and Wildlife on the Quablein Reservation in eastern Massachusetts constitute a prohibited "taking" of bald eagles? Plaintiffs argued that eagles would be harmed by ingesting lead pellets from carcasses not claimed by hunters. *American Bald Eagle v. Babbitt,* 9 F.3d 163 (1st Cir. 1993).

11.   Defendant was convicted of violating the Marine Mammal Protection Act by "taking" a protected animal, which is defined in part in the act as "harass, hunt, capture, or kill." The defendant had fired shots behind a porpoise which was eating tuna from his fishing lines. Is the defendant guilty of violating the act? *U.S. v. Hayashi,* 22 F.3d 859 (9th Cir. 1994).

ENDNOTES

1.   *West Houston Air Committee v. FAA,* 784 F.2d 702 (5th Cir. 1986).

2.   *Metropolitan Edison v. People vs. Nuclear Energy,* 460 U.S. 766 (1983).

3.   *Environmental Defense Fund v. Massey,* 986 F.2d 528 (1993).

4. 115 Cong. Rec. 40, 416 (1969) (Statement of Sen. Jackson).

5. 40 C.F.R. Section 1501.2 (1978).

6. *Breckinridge v. Rumsfeld,* 57 F.2d 864 (6th Cir. 1976), *cert. denied* 429 U.S. 1061 (1977).

7. 40 C.F.R. Section 1508.14.

8. "Publication of an EIS . . . serves a larger information role. It gives the public the assurance that the agency 'has indeed considered environmental concerns in its decision making process,' and perhaps more significantly, provides a springboard for public comment." *Robertson v. Methow Valley Citizens Council,* 490 U.S. 332 (1989).

9. Under this criteria, the court concluded that an EIS for the whole program was required. *Scientists' Institute for Public Information, Inc. v. AEC,* 481 F.2d 1079 (D.C. Cir. 1973) (commonly called the "SIPI" decision).

10. *Aberdeen & Rockfish Railroad Co. v. Students Challenging Regulatory Agency Procedures,* 422 U.S. 289 (1975)[Scrap II].

11. *Marsh v. Oregon Natural Resources Council,* 490 U.S. 360 (1989).

12. *Vermont Yankee Nuclear Power Corp. v. NRDC,* 435 U.S. 519 (1978).

13. *Robertson v. Methow Valley Citizens Council,* 490 U.S. 332 (1989).

14. *Id.* at 349.

15. 16 U.S.C.A. Section 1533(b)(1)(A).

16. *Id.*

17. 16 U.S.C.A. Section 1533 (b)(1)(B)(2).

18. U.S. Fish and Wildlife Service, Department of the Interior, Endangered Species Technical Bulletin 16 (1991).

19. 50 CFR Section 17.3 (1994).

20. 17 F.3d 1463 (D.C. Cir. 1994).

21. The Ninth Circuit Court of Appeals has stated in dicta that the FWS regulation defining "harm" was consistent with the ESA. *Palila v. Hawaii Dept. of Land & Nat. Resources* (Palila II), 649 F. Supp. 1077 (D. Haw. 1986), aff'd, 852 F.2d 1106 (9th Cir. 1988).

22. Thomas Lambert and Robert J. Smith, "The Endangered Species Act: Time for a Change," (Center for the Study of American Business 1994).

23. *Id.* at 11–12.

24. Oliver A. Houck, *The Endangered Species Act and its Implementation by the U.S. Departments of Interior and Commerce,* 64 Colo L. Rev. 227 (1993).

10

CONTROLLING AIR POLLUTION

INTRODUCTION

Air, essential to life, consists of a thin band of gases (mostly nitrogen and oxygen) which shields the earth from the sun's radiation, supports the process by which green plants convert water and carbon dioxide into oxygen (photosynthesis), and provides water in the form of precipitation. Polluted or "dirty" air harms natural resources and may cause sickness or even death in humans, plants, and animals. In addition to the costs in human sickness and stunted or blighted crops, long-term exposure to air pollution corrodes bridges and buildings and may ultimately devastate entire ecosystems.

Air pollution is not a recent phenomenon. Natural decomposition of organic matter, volcanic eruptions, and forest fires all contaminate the air. However, one of the major changes caused by the industrial revolution was a dramatic increase in air pollution. In fact, the popular vision of a nineteenth century industrialized city is one obscured by smog and plumes of smoke. In the twentieth century, the expansion of the chemical and petroleum industries and the widespread domination of the automobile have added to air pollution and increased concerns about the risks of dirty air.

In the United States, the problem of air pollution was first addressed through common law nuisance or trespass suits brought by injured plaintiffs against polluters. As Chapter 4 discussed, these common law remedies were generally inadequate to address the broader problems of air pollution. Damages for common law torts are only awarded after the injury has occurred. Furthermore, because decision making occurs case by case in common law, it does not lend itself to a comprehensive regulatory scheme to address the problem of air pollution across a broad geographic area or industry.

The first air pollution ordinances in the United States were passed in 1881 by the cities of Chicago and Cincinnati to control smoke and soot from furnaces and locomotives. Federal clean air legislation was first enacted in 1955. In 1963, Congress enacted the Clean Air Act, which included the first federal regulation of motor vehicles and fuels. 1965 saw the passage of the Motor Vehicle Pollution Control Act, which permitted the secretary of Health, Education, and Welfare (HEW) to set emissions standards for new motor vehicles. In 1967, Congress passed the Air Quality Act, which required states to establish air quality control regions and directed HEW to identify viable pollution control techniques which states could use to attain air quality standards. When it became clear that the states had made little progress toward clean air attainment standards, Congress enacted the Clean Air Act Amendments of 1970.

THE CLEAN AIR ACT OF 1970

The Clean Air Act Amendments of 1970, now simply referred to as the Clean Air Act, substantially increased federal authority and responsibility for controlling air pollution. The 1970 act was passed in the year of the first "Earth Day," and although it established a federal/state partnership in regulating the sources of air pollutants, the Clean Air Act ultimately resulted in federal dominance of air pollution regulation. The 1970 Clean Air Act created the basic statutory framework of the law, and the act has been significantly amended twice since its passage in 1970. The 1977 amendments to the act constituted a "mid-course" correction of the law. In 1990, Congress dramatically expanded regulatory requirements for both stationary and mobile sources, and addressed problems like acid rain and toxic pollutants.

Overview of the Clean Air Act

The Clean Air Act, 42 U.S.C. 7401 *et seq.,* as adopted in 1970 and amended in 1977 and 1990 creates an extensive and detailed set of laws to address the problem of air pollution throughout the nation. In general, these requirements are established by the federal government (by the EPA) and administered by the states. There are three general categories of regulatory programs under the Clean Air Act.

First, the newly created Environmental Protection Agency (EPA) was required to establish primary and secondary **national ambient air quality standards** (NAAQSs) for air pollutants which endanger public health and/or welfare and which result from numerous and diverse sources. Congress determined that these federal primary standards for common air pollutants should be uniform throughout the nation for each air quality control region established under earlier clean air law. These standards were minimum standards and no state could choose to impose less strict standards, though they could choose stricter standards. Each state has primary responsibility for ensuring that air quality within its borders meets those standards by submitting to the EPA **state implementation plans** (SIPs) which specify the manner in which those standards will be achieved and maintained. The 1970 Clean Air Act required the state plan to meet the primary NAAQSs standards no later than three years from the date of the approval of the plan. New and modified sources were subject to a permit program, and existing sources were regulated under a program established by the SIP. The 1990 amendments required states to develop and implement an operating permit program for all major sources of air pollution.

The Clean Air Act as amended also requires the EPA to establish uniform national emission standards for *new* sources of air pollution. The EPA must set such standards for new vehicles, new stationary sources of air pollution (including modified sources) and hazardous air pollutants from both new and existing sources. New stationary sources are subject to the technology-forcing requirement that they install the **best available control technology** (or BACT) to meet a specified limit on pounds of pollutants which can be emitted per unit of plant input or output.

In addition to regulating hazardous air pollution, the Clean Air Act contains requirements for specific pollutants like ozone and carbon monoxide in areas that have failed to meet the NAAQSs requirements for those substances. Other provisions address visibility impairment and stratospheric ozone protection. The 1990 amendments establish an **emissions trading policy** and allowance program for sulfur dioxide, a precursor of acid rain. The 1990 amendments also tightened mobile source emissions standards and established new fuel-related programs designed to reduce motor vehicle emissions.

The following sections examine these and other provisions of the Clean Air Act in more depth. The final section of the chapter considers some of the policy implications of the act.

Sources of Air Pollution

The Clean Air Act regulates **stationary sources** of pollutants, such as industrial facilities and power plants, as well as *mobile sources* like automobiles and trucks. The definition of a stationary source within the act is broad and includes "any building, structure, facility, or installation which emits or may emit any air pollutant."

In *Chevron v. NRDC,* 467 U.S. 837 (1984), discussed in Chapter 5, the Supreme Court addressed whether the EPA could permit a state to adopt a plant-wide definition of the term "stationary source" as used in the Clean Air Act. This definition, called the **bubble** theory, treats various components of an industrial complex as a single source for regulatory purposes. Under the bubble theory, increases in emissions from one component may be offset by decreases in emissions from another component, so long as the net effect does not increase total emissions. In *Chevron,* the Supreme Court upheld the EPA's decision to permit states to treat all of the pollution-emitting devices within the same industrial grouping as though they were encased within a single "bubble."

National Ambient Air Quality Standards (NAAQSs)

Sections 108 and 109 of the Clean Air Act direct the EPA to establish primary and secondary national ambient air quality standards (NAAQSs) for any air pollutant which has an adverse impact on the public health or welfare. *Primary standards* are those necessary to protect human health; *secondary standards* are those required "to protect the public welfare from any known or anticipated adverse effects associated with the presence of such air pollutant in the **ambient air.**" This latter standard extends protection to such things as wildlife, soil, water, vegetation, climate, and property.

EPA has promulgated NAAQSs for six **criteria pollutants:** sulfur dioxide (SO_2), ozone (O_3), carbon monoxide (CO), lead (Pb), nitrogen dioxide (NO_2), and **particulate matter** (PM_{10}). With the exception of sulfur dioxide, the EPA has established the same levels for both primary and secondary standards of these pollutants.

Sulfur dioxide, a poisonous gas which comes from burning coal and oil, is highly corrosive and may bond to particles of smoke and dust, traveling long distances. The primary danger to health from SO_2 is lung and respiratory damage. Sulfur dixoide also is an ingredient in acid rain, discussed later.

Ozone is a principal ingredient in smog, and can severely affect people with heart and lung diseases. It causes eye irritation and reduces resistance to infection. At low altitudes, ozone is a pollutant which is formed when nitrogen oxides react with oxygen in the presence of sunlight. Because ozone is not emitted, ozone is measured by determining the concentration of ozone in the air. Ozone is a widespread and stubborn problem in many if not most major cities in the United States. The 1990 Clean Air Act amendments specifically address ozone nonattainment areas by adopting five categories of nonattainment—marginal, moderate, serious, severe, and extreme—and impose stringent controls on sources within those areas.

Carbon monoxide (CO) is a deadly colorless and odorless gas given off by cars and trucks. Wood stoves, incinerators, and some industrial processes also contribute to carbon monoxide pollution. In addition to presenting health risks to human, carbon monoxide contributes to the **greenhouse effect** and the formation of ozone.

Airborne lead poses a serious health risk, especially to neurological systems and kidneys of children and the unborn. A principal source of airborne lead was leaded gasoline used in cars and trucks.

Nitrogen oxides (NO_x) include nitric oxide (NO) and nitrogen dioxide (NO_2). Nitric oxide is converted into nitrogen dioxide on its release into the air. Nitrogen oxides are emitted from natural sources, such as decomposing organic matter. Nitrogen oxides are also emitted as a gas when burning fuel reacts with nitrogen in the air. NO_x is a key ingredient in smog and discolors the sky brown; it is also an element in acid rain and depletion of the ozone layer. Its primary health effects are lung and respiratory tract damage.

Particulates are solid or liquid particles suspended in the air which carry poison into the lungs. Many industrial processes contribute particulate matter to the air—these include steel mills, power plants, smelters, and cement plants. Other activites, such as industrial and construction work and wood-burning fireplaces, also produce particulates. Depending on the size and shape of the matter, particulates can damage lungs and lead to respiratory damage. Some particulates are carcinogenic. The original standard for regulating particulates was PM30 (30 microns or smaller). The EPA subsequently reduced the standard to the current standard of PM10, the respirable fraction. Particulates that are very small are of particular concern because they can be breathed into the lungs.

The EPA is required to fix the NAAQSs at levels necessary to protect the public health with an "adequate margin of safety" and to protect the public welfare, and NAAQSs must be reviewed and revised every five years by the EPA. In the following case, several lead and minerals industries challenged the EPA's NAAQS for lead. The question raised in the case was whether, in setting the NAAQS for lead emissions, the EPA could also consider the economic or technological feasibility of attaining those standards, or whether it was to be guided solely by public health or welfare concerns. In this case, the court made it clear that in establishing national ambient air quality standards, the EPA administrator is not permitted to consider the economic or technological feasibility of attaining those standards. The court also took the position that it had a limited role in reviewing the agency's decision. As long as the decision was based on a "consideration of the relevant factors," the court said it should defer to the administrator's decision.

LEAD INDUSTRIES ASSOCIATION, INC. v. EPA
647 F.2d 1130 (D.C. Cir. 1980)

WRIGHT, C.J.

Man's ability to alter his environment to achieve perceived goals has undoubtedly made an enormous contribution to his economic and social well-being. This undertaking is not, however, without attendant costs. One of these costs is the toll that these alterations may exact on the environment itself and, in turn, the dangers that this may pose for the public health and welfare. Unfortunately, man's ability to alter the environment often far outstrips his ability to foresee with any degree of certainty what untoward effects these changes may bring. The issues presented by these cases illustrate this sad fact.

Lead's environmental significance is a consequence of both its abundance and its utility. The relative abundance of lead in the earth's crust makes it unique among the toxic heavy metals. And centuries of mining and smelting, and the use of lead in a variety of human activities, have increased the natural background concentration of lead in the environment. But it is only since the industrial age and the use of lead as a gasoline additive that lead has become pervasive. Today lead is ubiquitous. It is found in almost every medium with which we come into contact—food, water, air, soil, dust, and paint, each of which represents a potential pathway for human lead exposure through ingestion or inhalation.

The widespread presence of this toxic metal in the environment poses a significant health risk. Lead is a poison which has no known beneficial function in the body, but when present in the body in sufficient concentrations lead attacks the blood, kidneys, and central nervous and other systems and can cause anemia, kidney damage, severe brain damage, and death.

There are three major sources of the body's lead burden. In most people the largest source is diet. Another source, particularly in children, is the habit of placing hands, objects, and materials in the mouth. The third major source is the ambient air; airborne lead is deposited in the respiratory tract as a person breathes lead-contaminated air and is subsequently absorbed into the bloodstream. Once the lead is in the bloodstream its source is immaterial; total lead intake is the sum of the intake from all these sources. The multiplicity of sources of lead intake increases the difficulty of controlling human lead exposure. Much of the protective activity in this area has focused on limiting the amount of lead in the ambient air, the most controllable source of lead exposure. In this country, by far the largest source of lead emissions accounting for 88 percent of total lead emissions according to EPA estimates is the exhaust of motor vehicles powered by gasoline containing lead additives. Another eight percent of lead emissions is the result of solid waste incineration and combustion of waste oil. Industrial facilities account for the remaining four percent of total lead emissions.

Acting pursuant to authority conferred on it by Congress in the Clean Air Act, as amended, EPA has been involved in regulation of lead emissions almost since the Agency's inception. . . .

***

STATUTORY AUTHORITY

The petitioner's first claim is that the administrator exceeded his authority under the statute by promulgating a primary air quality standard for lead which is more stringent than is necessary to protect the public health because it is designed to protect the public against "sub-clinical" effects which are not harmful to health. According to petitioners, Congress only authorized the administrator to set primary air quality standards that are aimed at protecting the public against health effects which are known to be clearly harmful. They argue that Congress so limited the administrator's authority because it was concerned that excessively stringent air quality standards could cause massive economic dislocation.

In developing this argument petitioner St. Joe Minerals Corporation contends that EPA erred by refusing to consider the issues of economic and technological feasibility in setting the air quality standards for lead. St. Joe's claim that the administrator should have considered these issues is based on the statutory provision directing him to allow an "adequate margin of safety" in setting primary air quality standards. In petitioner's view, the administrator must consider the economic impact of the proposed standard on industry and the technological feasibility of compliance by emission sources in determining the appropriate allowance for a margin of safety. St. Joe argues that the administrator abused his discretion by refusing to consider these factors in determining the appropriate margin of safety for the lead standards, and maintains that the lead air quality standards will have a disastrous economic impact on industrial sources of lead emissions.

This argument is totally without merit. [Petitioner] is unable to point to anything in either the language of the act or its legislative history that offers any support for its claim that Congress, by specifying that the administrator is to allow an "adequate margin of safety" in setting primary air quality standards, thereby required the administrator to consider economic or technological feasibility. To the contrary, the statute and its legislative history make clear that economic considerations play no part in the promulgation of ambient air quality standards under Section 109.

Where Congress intended the administrator to be concerned about economic and technological feasibility, it expressly so provided. . . . Section 109(b) speaks only of protecting the public health and welfare. Nothing in its language suggests that the administrator is to consider economic or technological feasibility in setting ambient air quality standards.

The legislative history of the act also shows the administrator may not consider economic and technological feasibility in setting air quality standards; the absence of any provision requiring consideration of these factors was no accident; it was the result of a deliberate decision by Congress to subordinate such concerns to the achievement of health goals. Exasperated by the lack of significant progress toward dealing with the problem of air pollution under the Air Quality Act of 1967 and prior legislation, Congress abandoned the approach of offering suggestions and setting goals in favor of "taking a stick to the States in the form of the Clean Air Amendments of 1970." Congress was well aware that, together with Sections 108 and 110, Section 109 imposes requirements of a "technology-forcing" character.

. . . The "technology-forcing" requirements of the act "are expressly designed to force regulated sources to develop pollution control devices that might at the time appear to be economically or technologically infeasible."

Questions and Comments for Discussion

1. What are the three chief sources of lead exposure to humans? According to the EPA in this case, what is the largest source of lead emissions?
2. What is the appropriate standard of judicial review of the agency's rule making in this case? (Hint—under the Clean Air Act, the standard of review is the same standard of review as that contained in the Administrative Procedure Act and applied by the court in *Overton Park v. Volpe,* discussed in Chapter 8.)
3. What techniques of statutory interpretation did the court utilize in determining that the EPA had not exceeded statutory authority under the Clean Air Act in setting the NAAQS for lead?

State Implementation Plans

The health-based national ambient air quality standards are a fundamental part of the Clean Air Act. As you saw in *Lead Industries v. EPA,* the courts have held that cost and technological capability must be subordinated to protection of the public health in setting NAAQSs under the act. The NAAQSs establish minimum national standards for ambient air quality. In imposing *national* standards for ambient air quality in the Clean Air Act, Congress recognized that air quality in one area will ultimately affect air quality in other regions. By establishing national standards, Congress also helped ensure that no state can gain a competitive edge over another by setting less stringent air quality controls.

The Clean Air Act also creates a federal/state partnership by giving states the primary responsibility for meeting the NAAQSs within the state. After the NAAQSs are established for pollutants, states are required to develop a plan for implementation, **attainment,** maintenance, and enforcement of those standards. These plans are called *state implementation plans* (SIPs). In the SIP, the states establish source-specific requirements for addressing primary and secondary air quality standards under the act.

The state must meet NAAQSs within three years after approval of the SIP. While the state is required to meet the minimum standards for regulated pollutants, it may also adopt an implementation plan which is designed to exceed those national ambient standards. In approving the SIP, the administrator is not permitted to consider claims of economic and technological infeasibility. In the following case, *Union Electric Co. v. EPA,* 427 U.S. 246 (1976), a utility company argued that the EPA should disapprove Missouri's SIP on the ground that SO_2 emission limitations were economically and technologically infeasible. The Supreme Court, however, agreed with the EPA that economic and technological feasibility were not relevant to the EPA administrator's approval of the state plan. The Court said that claims of economic and technological infeasibility should be raised before the state agency formulating the implementation plan.

UNION ELECTRIC COMPANY v. ENVIRONMENTAL PROTECTION AGENCY
427 U.S. 246 (1976)

MR. JUSTICE MARSHALL *delivered the opinion of the Court.*

We must decide whether the operator of a regulated emission source, in a petition for review of an EPA-approved state plan . . . can raise the claim that it is economically or technologically infeasible to comply with the plan.

. . . The heart of the [Clean Air Act Amendments of 1970] is the requirement that each State formulate, subject to EPA approval, an implementation plan designed to achieve national primary ambient air quality standards—those necessary to protect the public health—"as expeditiously as practicable but . . . in no case later than three years from the date of approval of such plan." The plan must also provide for the attainment of national secondary ambient air quality standards—those necessary to protect the public welfare—within a "reasonable time." Each state is given wide discretion in formulating its plan, and the act provides that the administrator "shall approve" the proposed plan if it has been adopted after public notice and hearing and if it meets eight specified criteria.

On April 30, 1971, the administrator promulgated national primary and secondary standards for six air pollutants he found to have an adverse effect on the public health and welfare. Included among them was sulfur dioxide, at issue here. After the promulgation of the national standards, the State of Missouri formulated its implementation plan and submitted it for approval. Since sulfur dioxide levels exceeded national primary standards in only one of the state's five air quality regions—the Metropolitan St. Louis Interstate region—the Missouri plan concentrated on a control strategy and regulations to lower emissions in that area. . . .

Petitioner is an electric utility company servicing the St. Louis metropolitan area, large portions of Missouri, and parts of Illinois and Iowa. Its three coal-fired generating plants in the metropolitan St. Louis area are subject to the sulfur dioxide restrictions in the Missouri implementation plan. . . .

***

The administrator's position is that he has no power whatsoever to reject a state implementation plan on the ground that it is economically or technologically infeasible, and we have previously accorded great deference to the administrator's construction of the Clean Air Act. After surveying the relevant provisions of the Clean Air amendments of 1970 and their legislative history, we agree that Congress intended claims of economic and technological infeasibility to be wholly foreign to the administrator's consideration of a state implementation plan. As we have previously recognized, the 1970 amendments to the Clean Air Act were a drastic remedy to what was perceived as a serious and otherwise uncheckable problem of air pollution. The amendments place the primary responsibility for formulating pollution control strategies on the states, but nonetheless subject the states to strict minimum compliance requirements. These requirements are of a "technology-forcing character," and are expressly designed to force regulated sources to develop pollution control devices that might at the time appear to be economically or technologically infeasible.

***

Our conclusion is bolstered by recognition that the amendments do allow claims of technological and economic infeasibility to be raised in situations where considera-

tion of such claims will not substantially interfere with the primary congressional purpose of prompt attainment of the national air quality standards. Thus, we do not hold that claims of infeasibility are never relevant in the formulation of an implementation plan or that sources unable to comply with emission limitations must inevitably be shut down.

Perhaps the most important forum for consideration of claims of economic and technological infeasibility is before the state agency formulating the implementation plan. So long as the national standards are met, the state may select whatever mix of control devices it desires, and industries with particular economic or technological problems may seek special treatment in the plan itself. Moreover, if the industry is not exempted from, or accommodated by, the original plan, it may obtain a variance, as petitioner did in this case; and the variance, if granted after notice and a hearing, may be submitted to the EPA as a revision of the plan. Lastly, an industry denied an exemption from the implementation plan, or denied a subsequent variance, may be able to take its claims of economic or technological infeasibility to the state courts.

[*The Court noted that there are also ways a state can secure relief from the EPA for individual emission sources, or classes of sources, that cannot meet the national standards.*]

In short, the amendments offer ample opportunity for consideration of claims of technological and economic infeasibility. Always, however, care is taken that consideration of such claims will not interfere substantially with the primary goal of prompt attainment of the national standards. Allowing such claims to be raised by appealing the administrator's approval of an implementation plan, as petitioner suggests, would frustrate congressional intent. It would permit a proposed plan to be struck down as infeasible before it is given a chance to work, even though Congress clearly contemplated that some plans would be infeasible when proposed. And it would permit the administrator or a federal court to reject a state's legislative choices in regulating air pollution, even though Congress plainly left with the states, so long as the national standards were met, the power to determine which sources would be burdened by regulation and to what extent. Technology forcing is a concept somewhat new to our national experience and it necessarily entails certain risks. But Congress considered those risks in passing the 1970 amendments and decided that the dangers posed by uncontrolled air pollution made them worth taking. Petitioner's theory would render that considered legislative judgment a nullity, and that is a result we refuse to reach.

Questions and Comments for Discussion

1.   Who was petitioner? Why did the petitioner sue the EPA?
2.   Does the EPA have the power to reject a State Implementation Plan on the ground it is economically or technologically infeasible? Why or why not?

The SIP is a document that must be continually updated in order to meet federal requirements. Although it must be submitted to the EPA for approval, the states are generally free to choose from various control methods as long as those are sufficient to meet EPA standards. Among other things, the SIP:

1.   ensures that the NAAQSs are attained "as expeditiously as practical" but at most not later than three years after approval of the SIP;

2.   may include emissions limitations for stationary pollution sources, with additional controls as necessary;

3.   may require installation and operation of monitoring devices on ambient air quality;

4.   must provide for an enforcement and regulation program;

5.   provides for inspection and testing of motor vehicles if necessary and practicable;

6.   contains provisions to prevent interstate pollution and to provide for prevention of significant deterioration of air quality in areas where the NAAQSs have been attained.

SIPs must be revised within three years of the issuance of any new or revised NAAQSs, or in the event the administrator finds the SIP is "substantially inadequate" or that revision is necessary to comply with any other requirement of the act. If the administrator disapproves a SIP, the state must correct the deficiency or the EPA must promulgate a Federal Implementation Plan within two years.

The Clean Air Act contains severe sanctions for a state's failure to develop an approved SIP. These include a cutoff of federal highway funds and additional emissions offsets for new or modified sources seeking new source permits.

Nonattainment Areas

The 1970 Clean Air Act established target dates for states to attain the applicable NAAQS. It soon became clear that many states would fail to meet the applicable NAAQS within the time period established. In 1977 Congress adopted additional requirements for **nonattainment areas,** which had failed to meet applicable NAAQSs.

A substantial number of major cities in the United States still do not meet one or more of the NAAQSs. The most widespread and difficult problem is **ozone,** which is formed when volatile organic compounds and nitrogen oxides react in the presence of sunlight. The 1990 Clean Air Act amendments contain additional requirements for SIPs in nonattainment areas, and include specific requirements for CO, fine particles, **volatile organic compounds** (VOCs), and NO_x (precursors of ozone.) Ozone nonattainment areas are required to meet ozone NAAQS within a set period of years, depending on the severity of the ozone problem. Southern California, which suffers from the most serious ozone problem, is required to meet the ozone NAAQSs within 20 years of the enactment of the 1990 Clean Air Act amendments. State implementation plans within ozone nonattainment areas also must address mobile source emissions through vehicle inspection and maintenance problems, gasoline vapor recovery rules, clean fuel vehicle programs, transportation control measures, and work-related vehicle trip reduction programs.

Nonattainment area SIPs must also provide for **reasonably available control technology** (RACT) for existing sources of pollution and must require permits for the construction and operation of new or modified major stationary sources anywhere within the nonattainment area. Such sources are required to meet the **lowest achievable emission rate** (LAER).

There are serious sanctions for those nonattainment areas. Failure to submit a SIP meeting the requirements of the law can lead to a complete construction ban in the affected area and withholding of clean air grant funds.

New Source Performance Standards

The costs of retrofitting existing sources with state-of-the-art technology are often prohibitive. Consequently, in the Clean Air Act, Congress required the highest levels of technological performance for new sources, which have more flexibility in design and location. The EPA is required to establish **New Source Performance Standards** (NSPSs) intended to limit emissions from a new stationary source if it causes or contributes significantly to air pollution which may reasonably be anticipated to endanger public health or welfare. Under the 1970 act, new source performance standards for stationary sources are to reflect the "degree of emission reduction available" through technology "adequately demonstrated" to be the best, taking into consideration "non-air quality health and environmental impacts and energy requirements."

The 1977 amendments expressly required the EPA to reduce emissions for three pollutants (sulfur dioxide, nitrogen dioxide, and particulates, arising from combustion of fossil fuels) by a specific percentage below what they would be in the absence of technological control.

The EPA has set NSPSs for approximately sixty source categories, including most major industrial processes. These standards serve as a minimum level of control required at new or modified sources through the permitting program. Under the 1990 amendments, major pollution sources (both existing and new sources) are required to obtain an operating permit, which specifies compliance requirements.

The NSPS applies to a facility on which construction is begun after the date of proposal of the NSPS. The NSPS serves as a minimum level of control that can be required at such new or modified sources. NSPSs are to be reviewed by the EPA every four years, although the review has actually been much less frequent. In response to this problem, the 1990 amendments mandated the EPA to review and revise several specific NSPSs.

The Permit Program

Title V of the 1990 Clean Air Act amendments requires each state to develop and implement an operating permit program for seven sources of air pollution. These include:

- Power plants covered by acid rain control provisions of the 1990 Clean Air Act amendments
- Major sources of pollution, which are those sources which emit or may emit more than 100 tons per year of any air pollutant
- New or modified sources subject to New Source Performance Standards
- Sources of hazardous air pollutants regulated by the act
- New or modified sources subject to PSD (Prevention of Significant Deterioration permits, discussed in the next section) permitting requirements
- New or modified sources in nonattainment areas (areas that do not meet National Ambient Air Quality Standards)
- Any other source which the EPA decides should be required to obtain a permit

The EPA has issued final regulations setting minimum requirements for the permitting program. Facilities which are major sources of pollution must submit a complete application to the state permitting authority. The applications must contain identification of emissions of pollutants, points of emissions, emission rates, description of air pollution control equipment, and identification of air pollution control requirements.

The permitting depends on whether the source is located in an area that has attained the NAAQSs for the pollutant in question. For example, in nonattainment areas, the state program must require that a proposed new or modified source offset its potential to emit nonattainment pollutants through reductions from other facilities in the area.

States implement the permit program. Within eighteen months after receiving the permit application, the permitting authority must take final action. The permits are for a fixed term which cannot exceed five years, and states collect fees from permittees to cover the costs of operating the program. The permit system should give sources more flexibility than the SIP system because permitted facilities may change their operations and emissions without revision to the permit or SIP, as long as these changes do not result in an increase of emissions above the permit limitations.

The permit program should also provide more certainty to facilities because compliance with the terms and conditions of the permit will be considered compliance with the act and EPA regulations in effect at the time the permit is issued. The Clean Air Act amendments also recognize the public's right to participate in the permitting process at the state level and to seek EPA action to oppose issuance of a permit. Under the law, the public also has access to periodic reports of emissions monitoring results, including evidence of noncompliance by a source.

The PSD Program

One of the major goals of the Clean Air Act is to protect and enhance the quality of the nation's air. To that end, Part C contains provisions to ensure that air quality in areas which meet or exceed federal standards does not deteriorate. An important function of the PSD program (**Prevention of Significant Deterioriation**) is to protect and improve the quality of air that is already "clean," that is, air that already meets NAAQSs.

A new pollution source (including a "major modification" of an existing **major stationary source**) in an area which has attained the NAAQSs must obtain a permit under the PSD program. Under the program, major emitting sources must undergo a preconstruction review before beginning operations in attainment areas. The PSD program also sets ceilings for certain pollutants in those areas.

The 1977 amendments to the Clean Air Act established three kinds of PSD areas and increment standards for sulfur dioxide and particulate matter levels for each area. Class I includes most large national parks and wilderness areas and has the most stringent increment levels. Class II includes areas where deterioration occurring through moderate and controlled growth is insignificant. In Class III areas, the increment standard is the least stringent because a greater amount of deterioration is considered insignificant. Most PSD areas are Class II areas.

Under the 1977 amendments, in an area classified under the PSD program, any major emitting facility under construction must obtain a permit mandating that it utilize the best available control technology for each pollutant subject to regulation. In the following case, plaintiff environmental groups challenged the EPA's definition of "major emitting facility" for purposes of the PSD program.

NATURAL RESOURCES DEFENSE COUNCIL v. ENVIRONMENTAL PROTECTION AGENCY

937 F.2d 641 (D.C. Cir. 1991)

WRIGHT, C.J.

Surface coal mining operations throw up "fugitive dust," which primarily comes from traffic on unpaved haul roads and from wind erosion. This dust accounts for virtually all of the air pollution generated at surface coal mines. The Environmental Protection Agency concluded that such fugitive emissions should not count in identifying facilities that are so "major" as to trigger application of the Clean Air Act's provisions on prevention of significant deterioration.

The PSD provisions impose stringent permit requirements on construction of any new "major emitting facility" in an area that has attained compliance with national ambient air quality standards. "Construction" includes modification of an existing source. The act defines such facilities as plants of certain listed types that produce 100 tons or more of any air pollutant per year, together with "any other source with the potential to emit 250 tons per year or more of any air pollutant." Section 169(1).

In *Alabama Power Co. v. Costle,* 636 F 2d 323 (CA DC 1979), we held that Section 169(1)'s definition of "major emitting facility" was limited by the act's generic definition, (Section 302(j)) which reads: "Except as otherwise expressly provided, the terms 'major stationary source' and 'major emitting facility' mean any stationary facility or source of air pollutants which directly emits, or has the potential to emit, one hundred tons per year or more of any air pollutant (including any major emitting facility or source of fugitive emissions of any such pollutant, as determined by rule by the administrator [of EPA]." The result, we held in *Alabama Power,* is that calculation of Section 169(1)'s 250-ton threshold may include fugitive emissions only as determined by rule by the EPA administrator. The primary issue here is the scope of the administrator's authority in making that determination.

In 1984 EPA promulgated a list of 27 categories of industrial stationary sources for which fugitive emissions are to be included in determining whether a source is "major." It declined to add surface coal mines to the list, relying primarily on a finding that the socioeconomic costs of regulating the mines would outweigh any environmental benefits. The petitioners argue that cost-benefit is not the right standard, and that in any event, it would, if correctly applied, require EPA to count coal mines' fugitive emissions when identifying major emitting facilities, at least in some circumstances. We find EPA's construction permissible, and uphold its application of cost-benefit analysis.

The petitioners claim that Congress clearly expressed an intent in Section 302(j) to impose a non-discretionary duty on the administrator to subject all sources of fugitive emissions to the full panoply of PSD and non-attainment requirements. In their view, the provision's "by rule" requirement contemplates nothing more than the simple ministerial task of determining which sources have the potential to emit more than the threshold limit. As surface coal mines concededly fall within this category, they claim the agency must subject them to the permit requirements of the PSD rules.

***

We must now decide whether the agency's construction is a permissible one. EPA concluded that Congress intended it to make two findings before requiring inclu-

sion of fugitive emissions in the threshold applicability determinations for sources in a particular category: "(1) That the sources have the potential to degrade air quality significantly and (2) that no unreasonable socioeconomic impacts relative to the benefit would result from subjecting the sources to [PSD requirements]."

Congress placed no explicit restraints on the rulemaking discretion of EPA; it is to act as it determines. Nor is the issue addressed in the legislative history. So long as the agency construction represents a reasonable accommodation of conflicting congressional policies, we must defer.

The purposes of the PSD include: [T]o insure that economic growth will occur in a manner consistent with the preservation of existing clean air resources . . . [and] to assure that any decision to permit increased air pollution in any area to which this section applies is made only after careful evaluation of all the consequences of such a decision. . . ." 42 USC 7470. Nothing in the legislative history undermines the inference that Congress believed that its PSD provision should balance the values of clean air, on the one hand, and economic development and productivity, on the other, and much confirms it. In *Alabama Power* we said Section 302(j) may be welcomed as serendipitous, for it gives EPA flexibility to provide industry-by-industry consideration and the appropriate tailoring of coverage. The EPA construction of Section 302(j) thus fits the statutory language, the over congressional purposes, and our prior understanding of its role.

Questions and Comments for Discussion

1.   What are **"fugitive emissions"** in this case and how might they pose a threat to human health? What is a "major emitting facility" for purposes of the PSD requirements? What is the significance of that definition?

2.   Why did the EPA determine that fugitive emissions in this case were not "major?" What legal test did the court use in determining to uphold the EPA rule in this case?

3.   The court noted that the EPA's approach in defining fugitive emissions in this

case seemed especially appropriate for extractive industries. It said, "The idea of special rules for prevention of significant deterioration was born from a fear that polluters might avoid air quality regulations by relocating their plants to pristine areas where ambient pollution levels were well below statutory ceilings. The extractive industries pose such a fear only indirectly, as one may extract a mineral deposit only where one finds it." Do you agree with this analysis? What are the environmental policy implications of your answer?

***

Hazardous Air Toxics

Before the 1990 amendments, the EPA controlled emissions of hazardous air pollutants through the promulgation of *National Emissions Standards for Hazardous Air Pollutants* (NESHAPs). NESHAPs were to be set at a level adequate to protect the public health with an ample margin of safety. However, in instances where there was no safe level of exposure for a particular toxic air pollutant, an important question was whether the law mandated a complete prohibition of such emissions. If so, businesses that could not meet the NESHAP standard would have to close down. And developing adequate data to protect a NESHAP with that result from judicial challenge proved very difficult for the agency. For these reasons, EPA took the position that industries must develop the best available control technology for regulated toxic pollutants in cases where complete emissions prohibition would result in widespread industry closings.

In the following case, environmental groups challenged the EPA's decision to apply the BACT standard to emissions of the toxic air pollutant vinyl chloride.

NATURAL RESOURCES DEFENSE COUNCIL, INC. v. U.S. ENVIRONMENTAL PROTECTION AGENCY

824 F.2d. 1146 (D.C. Cir. 1987)

BORK, *Circuit Judge:*

Current scientific knowledge does not permit a finding that there is a completely safe level of human exposure to carcinogenic agents. The administrator of the Environmental Protection Agency, however, is charged with regulating hazardous pollutants, including carcinogens, under section 112 of the Clean Air Act by setting emission standards "at the level which in his judgment provides an ample margin of safety to protect the public health."

Petitioner Natural Resources Defense Council ("NRDC") contends that the administrator must base a decision under section 112 exclusively on health-related factors and, therefore, that the uncertainty about the effects of carcinogenic agents requires the administrator to prohibit all emissions. The administrator argues that in the face of this uncertainty he is authorized to set standards that require emission reduction to the lowest level attainable by best available control technology whenever that level is below that at which harm to humans has been demonstrated. We find no support for either position in the language or legislative history of the Clean Air Act. We therefore grant the petition for review and remand to the administrator for reconsideration in light of this opinion.

. . . The statute directs the administrator to set an emission standard promulgated under section 112 "at the level which in his judgment provides an ample margin of safety to protect the public health."

This case concerns vinyl chloride regulations. Vinyl chloride is a gaseous synthetic chemical used in the manufacture of plastics and is a strong carcinogen. In late 1975, the administrator issued a notice of proposed rulemaking to establish an emission standard for vinyl chloride. In the notice, the EPA asserted that available data linked vinyl chloride to carcinogenic, as well as some noncarcinogenic, disorders and that "[r]easonable extrapolations" from this data suggested "that present ambient levels of vinyl chloride may cause or contribute to . . . [such] disorders." The EPA also noted that vinyl chloride is "an apparent non-threshold pollutant," which means that it appears to create a risk to health at all non-zero levels of emission. . . .

[*The EPA had concluded it was faced with two alternative interpretations of its duty under the law. It could determine that the law required a complete prohibition of emissions of non-threshold pollutants, which could require the closure of an entire industry, or it could interpret Section 112 to authorize setting emissions standards requiring emission reduction to the lowest level achievable by use of the best available control technology, in cases where complete emission prohibition would result in widespread industry closure. The EPA adopted the latter alternative on the belief that it would "produce the most stringent regulation of hazardous air pollutants short of requiring a complete prohibition in all cases."*]

***

We find no support in the text or legislative history for the proposition that Congress intended to require a complete prohibition of emissions whenever the EPA

cannot determine a threshold level for a hazardous pollutant. Instead, there is strong evidence that Congress considered such a requirement and rejected it. . . . Congress' use of the term "ample margin of safety" is inconsistent with the NRDC's position that the administrator has no discretion in the face of uncertainty. The statute nowhere defines "ample margin of safety."

Congress' use of the word "safety," moreover, is significant evidence that it did not intend to require the administrator to prohibit all emissions of non-threshold pollutants. As the Supreme Court has recently held, "safe" does not mean "risk-free." Instead, something is "unsafe" only when it threatens humans with "a significant risk of harm."

. . . [T]he NRDC's position would eliminate any discretion and would render the standard "ample margin of safety" meaningless as applied to carcinogenic pollutants. Where *any* scientific uncertainty existed about the ill effects of a nonzero level of hazardous air pollutants—and we think it unlikely that science will ever yield *absolute* certainty of safety in any area so complicated and rife with problems of measurement, modeling, long latency, and the like—the administrator would have no discretion but would be required to prohibit all emissions. Had Congress intended that result, it could very easily have said so by writing a statute that states that no level of emissions shall be allowed as to which there is any uncertainty."

***

[*The Court distinguished the holding in* Union Electric, *and . . .* Lead Industries, *(discussed previously in this chapter). . . . The Court next restated the* Chevron *rule requiring it to uphold the administrator's construction if it represents "a reasonable policy choice for the agency to make."*]

Despite this deferential (*Chevron*) standard, we find that the administrator has ventured into a zone of impermissible action. The administrator has not exercised his expertise to determine an acceptable risk to health. To the contrary, in the face of uncertainty about risks to health, he has simply substituted technological feasibility for health as the primary consideration under this Section. . . . In setting an emission standard for vinyl chloride, the administrator has made no finding with respect to the effect of the chosen level of emissions on health. . . .

We find that the congressional mandate to provide "an ample margin of safety" "to protect the public health" requires the administrator to make an initial determination of what is "safe." This determination must be based exclusively upon the administrator's determination of the risk to health at a particular emission level. Because the administrator in this case did not make any

finding of the risk to health, the question of how that determination is to be made is not before us. We do wish to note, however, the administrator's decision does not require a finding that "safe" means "risk-free," or a finding that the determination is free from uncertainty. . . .

[*The court held that the administrator could not consider cost and technological feasibility in determining what is "safe," which must be based solely upon the risk to health; but it said that it was not the court's intention to bind the administrator to any specific method of determining what is "safe" or what constitutes an "ample margin." The Court thus vacated the rule and remanded the case for reconsideration in light of its opinion.*]

Questions and Comments for Discussion

1.   The EPA had concluded that it was faced with two alternative interpretations of its duty under Section 112 of the Clean Air Act. What were those two alternatives? How did it interpret its duty under the statutory language at issue in this case?

2.   According to the Court, what are the problems in defining "safety" for purposes of regulating hazardous air pollutants under Section 112? What does this word mean in the court's opinion?

3.   In his opinion in this case, Judge Bork distinguished Sections 109 and 110 of the Clean Air Act where prior cases (such as the *Lead Industries* case summarized earlier in this chapter) had limited consideration of cost and technological feasibility. He held that Section 112 of the act allowed EPA to consider cost and technological feasibility in setting emissions standards, after determining what is "safe" based solely on the risk to health.

Prior to the 1990 amendments, the EPA had designated only eight hazardous air pollutants and proposed only seven NESHAPs—for arsenic, asbestos, benzene, beryllium, mercury, radionuclides, and vinyl chloride. In the 1990 amendments Congress lists 189 hazardous air pollutants which must be controlled through the application of technological standards based on the **maximum achievable control technology** (MACT). If those controls fail to reduce the risks to public health or the environment, further health-based standards are required. Under the 1990 amendments, the EPA is also to establish regulations to control and prevent accidental releases of regulated hazardous pollutants or other hazardous substances. Owners and operators of facilities where substances are present must prepare risk management plans for each substance which exceeds a threshold level. The act also establishes a Chemical Safety and Hazard Investigation Board to investigate accidental releases and make recommendations to avoid such releases.

Acid Rain Provisions

Acid rain refers to increased acidity as measured in reduced pH levels in ambient moisture or precipitation. Acid rain harms fish and other aquatic life, trees, man-made structures, and human lungs. The acid rain control program is a result of a long and sometimes contentious political debate about whether and how to address this problem. In the 1990 Clean Air Act amendments, proponents of controlling acid rain prevailed by limiting the scope of the legislation to steam electric generating units.

The 1990 amendments mandate permanent capping of electric utility emissions of sulfur dioxide (SO_2) and a reduction in nitrogen oxide (NO_x), both of which are precursors of acid rain. Under the acid rain program, electric utility sources of SO_2 are assigned SO_2 allowances under a statutory formula. An *allowance* is an authorization to emit one ton of SO_2. A plant's annual SO_2 emissions cannot exceed the allowances allocated to it, or otherwise acquired by it, for a given calendar year. The allowances are not a property right, and they can be limited, revoked, or modified.

The program will grant 8.9 million electric utility allowances when the program is fully implemented in the year 2000. Allowances may be saved (also called **banking**) to be used at a later date, and are fully transferable. The EPA is required to auction allowances annually. Those eligible to hold allowances may purchase them at the auction, and holders of allowances can contribute to the auction and receive a pro-rata share of the proceeds. The EPA is required to establish an allowance tracking system to facilitate the creation of a market for allowance trading.

Title IV of the Clean Air Act as amended also addresses nitrogen oxide (NO_x) emissions. The amendments established a goal of reducing annual NO_x emissions to a level approximately two million tons below 1980 levels. The act provides utilities some flexibility in meeting NO_x requirements. However, development of NO_x regulations has proven controversial. For example, industry representatives and environmentalists have disagreed about whether the act mandates the use of low NO_x burner technology for certain kinds of boilers and whether the EPA has discretion under the act to impose NO_x emission limits stricter than those established by statute.

Stratospheric Ozone Protection

The stratospheric ozone layer is a thin layer of triatomic oxygen above the earth which blocks the sun's ultraviolet radiation. Ozone-depleting chemicals like **chlorofluorocarbons** (CFCs) and **halons** do not break down in the atmosphere, but rather they slowly migrate into the stratosphere. When they finally break apart, they free chlorine and bromine radicals which react with stratospheric ozone molecules, thereby depleting stratospheric ozone concentrations. Scientists fear that a decrease in the stratospheric ozone layer will lead to more ultraviolet radiation at the surface of the earth with an increased incidence of skin cancer, cataracts, and harm to crops and aquatic life.

The Clean Air Act Amendments of 1990 provide for a phase-out of the production and importation of ozone-depleting chemicals. They also establish a comprehensive regulatory program for these chemicals and for products containing these chemicals. The law establishing the program for phaseout of ozone-depleting substances is based on the *Montreal Protocol,* an international agreement which was signed in 1987 by the United States and most other industrial nations. This agreement is discussed in Chapter 15.

Parties to the Montreal Protocol were required to freeze production of CFCs at 1986 levels until 1993, and to produce no more than 80 percent of their 1986 levels from 1993 through 1998, and no more than 50 percent of those levels after 1998. Halon production was frozen at the 1986 levels. Parties to the agreement were also required to limit consumption of controlled substances. The Montreal Protocol was amended in 1990 to provide more stringent phaseout for CFCs and halons and to include methyl chloroform and carbon tetrachloride. In 1989, Congress amended the Internal Revenue Code to impose excise taxes on the sale or use of ozone-depleting chemicals listed in the Montreal Protocol.

Provisions addressing stratospheric ozone in the Clean Air Act contain a production phase-out schedule which is, in some respects, more stringent than the Montreal Protocol schedule. The law also directs the EPA to establish transferable "allowances" for regulated substances, and to issue rules regulating the use, recycling, disposal, and release of these substances, as well as rules for servicing motor vehicle air conditioners, and for labeling products containing these substances.

Mobile Source Fuels and Fuel Additives

The Clean Air Act also addresses mobile sources of air pollution. To that end, the act authorizes the EPA to regulate motor fuels and fuel additives used in automobiles, trucks, marine vessels, and other mobile sources of pollution.

Distillation, cracking, and reforming of crude oil produces a number of fuel products, including gasoline, diesel and kerosene fuel oil, and liquefied propane gas. **Coal liquefaction** also produces a number of fuel products like those derived from crude oil, but it is mostly associated with methanol production. Fermentation of corn or other grain produces liquid ethanol.

Fuels like gasoline and diesel fuel are actually a complex blend of many components. Because of their diversity in composition and use, these fuels and fuel additives pose special problems for regulators. In 1992, the EPA had required registration of over 6,300 motor fuels and fuel additives.[1]

Additives are chemicals added to base fuel in small quantities, generally to improve engine performance. These include detergents, dispersants, fluidizer oils, anti-icers, and flow improvers. Additives can be blended at various points, sometimes even after consumer purchase.

The EPA designates fuels and fuel additives that must be registered under the act. Prior to the 1990 amendments, EPA's designation regulations included only the most common motor vehicle fuels—gasoline and diesel fuel. The 1990 amendments made it clear that fuel or fuel additives used exclusively in non-road engines or non-road vehicles are also within the scope of the EPA's designation authority. Consequently, fuel for a wide range of vehicles and engines, including fuel for marine vessels, is within the scope of the act. Regulation of aviation fuel is the responsibility of the Federal Aviation Administration (FAA).

Once designated, a fuel or fuel additive may not be marketed unless it is registered. In order to register a fuel, the manufacturer must notify the administrator of any additive in the fuel, specify its concentration, and identify its purpose. EPA may regulate certain fuels and additives by imposing registration requirements. Under Section 211 of the act, the EPA may control or prohibit the manufacture and sale of any fuel or fuel additive if the emissions product: (a) "causes or contributes to air pollution that may reasonably be anticipated to endanger the public health or welfare; or (b) will impair to a significant degree the performance of any emission control device or system which is in or is likely to be in general use."

The EPA has regulated the lead content in gasoline by promoting unleaded gasoline and phasing out leaded gasoline. The EPA has regulated phosphorus content of gasoline and gasoline volatility in order to reduce hydrocarbon emissions. In 1990 the EPA also issued a regulation requiring an 80 percent reduction of sulfur in diesel fuel.

The 1990 amendments did not disturb the EPA's broad authority to regulate fuels and fuel additives, but they added three new programs—a nationwide program requiring detergents in gasoline, an oxygenated gasoline program designed to curb CO emissions in the nation's worst CO nonattainment areas, and a reformulated gasoline program designed to limit emissions of **air toxics** and ozone precursors in the worst ozone nonattainment areas.

One of Congress's most ambitious fuel requirements in the 1990 Amendments was for the use of unconventional fuel for unconventional vehicles in certain geographical areas. The clean fuel vehicle program establishes a California pilot test program requiring the production and sale of 300,000 clean fuel vehicles annually by 1999, and it requires operators of centrally fueled fleets of ten or more vehicles in certain CO and ozone nonattainment areas to purchase and use clean fuel vehicles.

Motor Vehicle Provisions

Motor vehicle emissions standards and control requirements apply to manufacturers of new motor vehicles and new motor vehicle engines. Compliance with emission standards is enforced by the EPA through a certification program, production and in-use testing, inspection and maintenance programs, and onboard emissions diagnostic systems. Under the Clean Air Act, motor vehicle provisions have evolved by generally following precedents set under the California motor vehicle emissions control program. Over the years Congress has gradually moved toward a scheme of prescribing control requirements by statute rather than delegating the determination of standards to the EPA. The scheme focuses on environmental concerns with little consideration of cost effectiveness and technological feasibility.

The 1990 amendments substantially tightened mobile source emissions standards and required automobile manufacturers to gradually reduce tailpipe emissions. **Hydrocarbons** had to be reduced by 35 percent and NO_x by 60 percent in all vehicles sold in 1996. The law also requires an additional 50 percent reduction by 2003, unless the EPA finds those standards are not necessary, technologically feasible, or cost effective.

Indoor Air Pollution

The problem of indoor air quality, and how much of a threat it poses to workers, is a serious concern to many, but the health effects of many suspected pollutants and inadequate ventilation are not well understood. While the Clean Air Act does not regulate indoor air pollution, the Occupational Health and Safety Administration (OSHA) has estimated that 21 million of the 70 million Americans who work indoors are subjected to poor air quality. OSHA has considered adopting a rule addressing indoor air quality issues, including tobacco smoke and ventilation issues. These proposals have proved controversial, particularly a provision requiring employers to provide separately ventilated smoking rooms.

Potential sources of indoor air pollution include chemicals from office materials and mechanical equipment, tobacco smoke, microbiological contaminants, and outside air pollutants. Dust from wood, carpets and paper, chemicals from carbonless forms, molds in ventilation systems, formaldehyde in carpet adhesives, ozone, and particulate from copy machines all contribute to unhealthy indoor air.

Radon Gas and Indoor Air Quality Research Act

In 1986 Congress passed the Radon Gas and Indoor Air Quality Research Act, 42 U.S.C. 7401. The act requires the EPA administrator to conduct research on the identification and characterization of sources of indoor air pollution and its effects on human health and to report its findings to Congress. In January 1993, under the authority of the Radon Act, EPA released a report classifying environmental tobacco smoke as a known human carcinogen.

The EPA's general finding in the report was that "the widespread exposure to environmental tobacco smoke in the United States presents a serious and substantial public health impact." The report also demonstrated that the smoke increases the risk of lung cancer in healthy nonsmokers.

Tobacco trade groups and companies have challenged the EPA report in court. Among other things, plaintiffs alleged that the EPA manipulated and "cherry-picked" data, ignored critical statistical studies and chemical analyses, and failed to account for confounding factors and sources of bias. According to plaintiffs, the report has had a substantial regulatory impact, evidenced by, for example, the U.S. Postmaster's order of a nationwide ban on smoking in postal facilities and the introduction in Congress of legislation that would prohibit smoking in all buildings owned or leased by federal agencies.

Noise Pollution and Abatement Act

In 1970, Congress amended the Clean Air Act by adopting the Noise Pollution and Abatement Act, 42 U.S.C. 1857. The act directed EPA to establish an Office of Noise Abatement and Control. The office, which does not have regulatory authority, is responsible for investigating the effects of noise on the public health and welfare and for identifying major sources of noise and their effects. These include the effects of noise at different volumes, projected growth of noise levels in urban areas, the psychological and physiological effects of noise on humans, and effects of noise on wildlife and property. The noise program was dismantled in the early 1980s. The EPA's primary role for noise issues is to ensure that agencies carry out programs in a manner that promotes an environment free from hazardous noise levels. Workplace noise is regulated by the Occupational Safety and Health Administration within the Department of Labor, and airport noise by the Federal Aviation Administration.

POLICY IMPLICATIONS OF THE CLEAN AIR ACT

A first step in developing a policy to address the problem of air pollution is recognizing its harmful effects. Today there is a general consensus that air pollution poses a significant risk to the health of humans and other life as well as to natural resources. However, there is continuing debate about how best to address those problems, such as, to what extent should the government intervene to limit pollution discharge through "command and control" regulation rather than to discourage pollution through market incentive devices? To what extent should air pollution control decisions be centralized and to what extent should those decisions be left to the states? What threshold limits of various pollutants should be imposed to protect the public health? What are the costs and benefits of controlling air pollution through command and control regulatory policy? To what extent should those costs and benefits be balanced in determining regulatory policy?

A fundamental policy question facing Congress in 1970 was how best to address these and other issues. Prior to passage of the Clean Air Act amendments of 1970, attempts to address the problems of air pollution through local ordinances and nuisance laws had been less than successful. State permitting systems operating prior to that date had also encountered problems. These included the difficulty of setting and enforcing pollution standards and the difficulty in interpreting and applying technical scientific and engineering data. The determination of the amount of a pollutant that can be assimilated into the air without causing harm is a difficult and complex scientific question which understaffed state agencies lacked the funds and expertise to address. In addition, political and economic issues at the state level, especially concern by the states over industrial flight (that is, losing industry to other states with less stringent pollution requirements), made it difficult for states to adopt and enforce strict pollution control standards.

In the 1970 Clean Air Act, Congress addressed some of these problems by establishing a state-federal partnership for controlling air pollution. Under this partnership the EPA establishes maximum permissible concentrations of criteria air pollutants. The federal agency sets primary standards protecting human health and secondary standards if health-based standards are insufficient to protect non-health values such as agricultural products and exposed materials. The EPA must set those standards at levels that provide an adequate margin of safety.

By establishing NAAQSs which all areas of the country must meet, the 1970 Clean Air Act made it more difficult for industries to avoid locating in states with stricter pollution standards than in other states. But the decision to impose national uniform standards also means that all areas of the country are locked into the same national standards, regardless of the costs of control, the quality of air, or geographic or climatic conditions of the particular area. Further, as the court held in *Lead Industries Association, Inc. v. EPA,* the law requires the EPA to set primary air quality standards to allow an "adequate margin of safety" without consideration of economic or technological feasibility. In doing so, Congress apparently took the position that there were indeed "safe" levels for common air pollutants; however, there is debate about whether that is indeed true—that is, whether there are *any* safe levels for such pollutants. On the other hand, adopting a zero emissions policy would have substantially affected businesses, and it is unlikely that Congress envisioned that kind of economic disruption. Despite the fact the courts have held that NAAQSs must be set without regard to economic or technological feasibility, in fact the EPA does have some flexibility in setting standards in light of scientific and economic uncertainties.

As a part of the federal-state partnership, the states have primary responsibility for ensuring that these national standards are met. They do so by adopting SIPs which must be approved by the EPA. In SIPs, states set performance standards for existing sources while the EPA imposes strict standards for new plants. These latter requirements are called *new source performance standards* (NSPSs) and are based on the state of the art in pollution control at the time the standards are set, but the requirement does introduce some economic considerations into the standard setting process.

By permitting the states in SIPs to determine how best to achieve the national standards imposed by the act, the 1970 law implicitly recognized that the states are subject to differing political and economic realities, and that they are in the best position to determine within their jurisdiction how best to achieve national goals. The law also recognized that controlling pollution is a traditional function of the state's authority to protect public health and safety. But the 1970 Clean Air Act also recognized that air pollution does not stop at state boundaries and that there are political and economic limits on the states' willingness to impose strict pollution controls within their jurisdiction.

STANDARD SETTING UNDER THE CLEAN AIR ACT

In the 1970 act, Congress made the decision to regulate air pollution by imposing emission standards on certain kinds of polluters—thus adopting a "command and control" regulatory system. Under this system, an important policy question is the *kind* of standard which should be imposed. Congress adopted at least two different kinds of standards in order to achieve the goals of the act. These include *technology-based* standards and *performance* standards. An example of a performance standard is the NAAQS, which establishes minimum national ambient air quality standards for conventional pollutants (although the law does require health to be considered for nonconventional pollutants). A performance standard is set for motor vehicle emissions in Title II of the act.

Technology-based standards are based on achievable emission rates using technology, for example, the requirement that new stationary sources must install the "best available control technology" (BACT) to meet a specified limit on pollution emissions.

Technology standards are generally easier to administer than performance standards and more equitable in that all sources are subject to the same requirements regardless of particular circumstances (such as geographic or climatic circumstances which may unfairly affect the ability of industries to meet performance standards). On the other hand, technology-based standards may be economically inefficient, and they also permnently fix technological standards at a particular level. A chief problem with the technology-standard approach is the concern that the law provides no incentive for future technological innovation and improvement beyond the standard set.

One possible way to encourage the development of future pollution control technology is to impose technology-forcing requirements. In Title II of the Clean Air Act Congress mandated numerical performance standards for motor vehicle exhaust emissions that could not be met by existing technology (although the law did include provisions which would allow postponement of compliance mandates.) Presumably, by setting emission standards beyond the reach of conventional control methods, Congress can encourage the development and commercialization of new technologies. Development of the catalytic converter, which controls automotive tail-pipe emissions, was spurred by the 1970 Clean Air Act. Under the 1990 amendments, fuel providers are subject to technology-forcing requirements because the law mandates the development and sale of reformulated gasoline in seriously polluted areas. These and other requirements of the act suggest that Congress believes new technologies must be developed in order to protect the public health and environment. Technology-forcing provisions may give American industry a competitive edge over other countries.

Problems also were encountered in setting standards for hazardous air pollutants. Earlier versions of the Clean Air Act had required the EPA to promulgate standards for hazardous pollutants which would provide "an ample margin of safety." Setting such standards, however, proved difficult because scientific data was insufficient to identify the standard which should be imposed, and in many cases strict application of the standard would have prohibited emissions altogether. Attempts to establish levels were frequently met with costly and time-consuming challenges from industries fearing substantial economic costs or closure. On the other hand, when the EPA attempted to avoid industry disruption by adopting a technology-based standard for vinyl chloride, environmental groups successfully challenged this approach. By 1990 the EPA had set standards for only eight pollutants.

In the 1990 amendments to the act, Congress abandoned the harm-based standard for hazardous air pollutants and adopted a technology-based standard for 180 specific substances

(NESHAPs). The law also retained a harm-based standard for hazardous air pollutants in that it requires the EPA to enact further measures if necessary to avoid unacceptable risks.

As the NESHAP regulations illustrate, the 1990 amendments contained a number of specific and mandatory directives rather than broad authority which would permit the EPA latitude. For example, the acid rain program in Title IV is so detailed it specifies the level of emissions permitted at each power plant in the nation. There are also various "hammers" to mandate agency action. The 1990 amendments provide that after January 1, 1995, no gasoline can be sold in covered areas unless the fuel has been certified to comply with EPA regulations. It was thus very important for fuel refiners and suppliers that the EPA promulgated necessary regulations for the industry in a timely fashion.

One of the difficulties state and federal regulatory agencies encounter in administering the complex and detailed provisions of the Clean Air Act is collecting and interpreting the data necessary to support standard setting and implementation and enforcement decisions. For example, regulators often have difficulty in predicting whether a particular set of emission standards will meet air quality standards.

The problem of scientific uncertainty is one which permeates environmental regulatory policy in general. In the context of standard setting under the Clean Air Act, industries often challenge the data supporting the agency's standard and its choice of scientific models. Because courts tend to defer to agency expertise in such cases, these challenges are often won or lost at the agency level rather than in court. Challenges by industry illustrate problems common to environmental law and regulatory policy making in general, such as scientific uncertainty, the cost and time required to research and defend standard setting, and the extent to which courts should defer to agency expertise in implementation.

One of the more important themes in the 1990 amendments was the utilization of market-based control strategies to reduce air pollution. Most illustrative is the acid rain program, which includes a marketable emission allowances trading program to achieve SO_x reductions. The 1990 amendments also establish a marketable permit system to implement the phase-out program for ozone-depleting chemicals and utilized other market approaches to achieve emission reductions. Those who support emissions trading and the concept of offsets in general argue that this approach best reduces net pollution at the lowest possible cost to industry.

Citizens have the power to enforce virtually all of the regulatory mandates and deadlines for EPA and state action under Section 304(c). In light of the detailed and mandatory nature of many of the act's directives, the citizen suit provision is an important enforcement mechanism of the Clean Air Act.

Clearly, the EPA will be faced with enormous responsibilities in implementing the requirements of the Clean Air Act. The 1990 amendments impose additional responsibilities on the EPA by including programs which focus on previously unregulated pollution sources. Smaller sources will be increasingly regulated in more polluted areas in order to control ozone air pollution, and smaller sources are also governed under the air toxics control program of the 1990 amendments. Studies show that surface coatings and solvent evaporation from paint, solvents, and coatings are responsible for more than 30 percent of urban hydrocarbon emissions. Consumer and commercial products like paints and solvents must be reformulated to reduce such emissions under the 1990 amendments.

The agency's agenda will likely be heavily influenced by these and other requirements into the foreseeable future. However, the agency's responsibilities appear to be increasing while its funding has diminished. While some attempts in Congress to repeal or amend major environmental laws have been unsuccessful, diminished funding will presumably have the effect of slowing the administration and enforcement of environmental regulatory policy in general.

What kinds of conclusions can we draw from regulatory policy controlling air pollution? First, the Clean Air Act as written is a tremendously complex and technical law with broad and sweeping goals. It represents a federal-state partnership with increasing responsibilities delegated to the EPA. Since the adoption of the act in 1970, air quality in the United States appears to have improved in most places, but there are some who question whether there is a clear correlation between this improvement and passage of the act.[2]

There are and will continue to be substantial difficulties in standard setting under the act because of the problems of scientific and technological uncertainties, and the difficulty in determining costs and benefits of regulatory policy. For the same reasons, it is often difficult to assess the success of various provisions, including the degree of industry compliance in meeting performance standards. Critics of the act point to these and other policy concerns in arguing that there are cheaper and more efficient ways to achieve existing limits on pollutant emissions and air quality goals. One critic argues that the Clean Air Act should be rewritten to permit the EPA to take costs and other factors into account when issuing national ambient air quality standards.[3] In addition, many argue that the "new source bias" under the act should be reduced. The new source bias is a result of the fact that the tougher pollution regulations applying to new sources discourage the construction of new plants and the retirement of older plants.

Whether Congress will address these or other recommendations in future amendments remains to be seen. What is clear is that the act will continue to change. Improved data inventory and expanded and improved ambient monitoring would strengthen the act. Finally, many advocate expanded emissions trading among existing sources and consideration of costs as well as benefits in standard setting as a way to reduce net air pollution in the most cost-effective manner. Others, however, strongly oppose integrating cost-benefit analysis into the Clean Air Act because they fear this would substantially weaken the protection of public health and the environment.

GLOSSARY

Acid rain—Precipitation containing a high concentration of acids produced by sulfur dioxide, nitrogen oxide, and other substances emitted during the combustion of fossil fuels.

Air toxics—Any pollutant for which a national ambient air quality standard does not exist, and which may reasonably be anticipated to cause cancer, developmental effects, reproductive dysfunctions, neurological disorders, or other serious or irreversible chronic or acute health effects in humans.

Ambient air—Outdoor air.

Attainment—Designation indicating whether a particular area meets a national ambient air quality standard for a pollutant.

Banking—Under the 1990 amendments, an emission source may save or "bank" SO_2 emission reductions that are in excess of regulatory requirements.

Best Available Control Technology (BACT)—Technology standard determined on a case-by-case basis, required of major sources in PSD areas.

Bubble—Theory under which an imaginary structure is placed over existing and/or neighboring plants in determining the source of emissions for purposes of the Clean Air Act.

Carbon monoxide—(CO), a colorless, odorless gas. One of six criteria pollutants under the Clean Air Act.

Chlorofluorocarbons (CFCs)—Chemical compounds containing carbon, fluorine, and chlorine atoms; these are easily liquified chemicals used in refrigeration, air conditioning, packaging, aerosol propellants and insulating. CFCs are linked to the depletion of the stratospheric ozone layer.

Coal liquefaction—Processes which convert coal to partially liquid form.

Criteria pollutant—A pollutant for which a national ambient air quality standard has been set by the EPA. Criteria pollutants include suspended particulates, sulfur dioxide, nitrogen oxides, ozone, hydrocarbons, and lead.

Emissions trading policy—Policy adding flexibility to emissions control by utilizing bubbles, offsets, and banking of emission reduction credits. Generally, permits a source to emit more pollutants than is allowed if another source reduces its level of emissions by that amount.

Fugitive emissions—Emissions that do not pass through a stack, chimney, vent, or other equivalent opening.

Greenhouse effect—Occurs when the sun's energy passes through the air and is absorbed by the earth; the earth then radiates the energy as heat waves absorbed in the air. The air permits the passage of light but not of heat, creating an effect similar to a greenhouse. Absorption of radiated heat energy is due to pollutants or contaminants in the atmosphere, such as increased levels of CO_2, not because of the air itself.

Halons—Chemical compounds containing bromine, iodine, chlorine, and fluorine; halons are linked to the depletion of the stratospheric ozone layer.

Hydrocarbons—A group of organic compounds containing hydrogen and carbon which contribute to photochemical pollution.

Lowest Achievable Emission Rate (LAER)—Strictest possible limits on emissions from new or existing major stationary sources; applies in nonattainment areas.

Major stationary source—Source which emits or has the potential to emit a specified quantity of pollutants under the Clean Air Act.

Maximum Achievable Control Technology (MACT)—Emission rate based on best demonstrated control technology or practices; applies to air toxics under the Clean Air Act.

National Ambient Air Quality Standards (NAAQSs)—Includes national primary and national secondary standards. National primary standards are set at a level of air quality necessary to protect the public health, allowing for an adequate margin of safety; national secondary standards are set at a standard necessary to protect the public welfare from any known or anticipated adverse effects associated with the presence of such pollutant in the ambient air.

New Source Performance Standards (NSPSs)—Emission limitations for specific new or modified sources based on the best available control technology.

Nonattainment—Area shown by air quality modeling to exceed any national ambient air quality standard for a pollutant. Monitoring of nonattainment areas is required under the Clean Air Act.

Ozone—Photochemical oxidant significantly contributing to the formation of smog. Ozone is regulated as a criteria pollutant.

Particulate matter (PM)—Broad class of diverse substances existing as discrete particles in the air, including liquid droplets or solids. Particulate matter is regulated as PM10, that is, particulates of 10 microns or less, the respirable fraction.

Prevention of Significant Deterioration (PSD)—Program for attainment areas which requires preconstruction review and application of BACT for all firms within an industry category planning to construct or modify facilities within the area.

Reasonably Available Control Technology (RACT)—Control equipment reasonably available and economically feasible for achieving the lowest emission limit applicable to a given source in nonattainment areas.

State Implementation Plan (SIP)—Plan submitted by a state providing for attaining and maintaining established air quality standards. If the state does not submit an approvable plan, EPA must issue one for the state.

Stationary source—Includes a building, structure, facility, or installation which emits or may emit an air pollutant.

Volatile organic compounds (VOCs)—Petroleum-based organic compounds which mix with other substances in the air to form ozone.

CASES FOR DISCUSSION

1.   A district court dismissed a citizen suit challenge under the Federal Water Pollution Control Act and the Clean Air Act against a company which possessed necessary state and local permits to construct a distribution center. The state had classified the center as a minor source of pollution under the acts. Plaintiffs challenged that designation, arguing that emissions of motor vehicles traveling to and from the center should be attributable to the center. Can emissions of motor vehicles traveling to and from a distribution center be attributable to the center itself for purposes of designating it as a major source of air pollution under the Clean Air Act? *Village of Oconomowoc Lake v. Dayton Hudson Corp.*, 24 F.3d 962 (7th Cir. 1994), cert. denied, 115 S. Ct. 322 (1994).

2.   Does the Illinois Coal Act violate the commerce clause of the U.S. Constitution? The act required public utilities to devise Clean Air Act compliance plans and to present them to the Illinois Commerce Commission for approval. Under the act, utilities and the commission were required to take into account the need to use coal mined in Illinois and the need to preserve as a valuable state resource the mining of coal in Illinois. The act also directed the four largest public utility plants in Illinois to include in their compliance plans the installation of devices to control sulfur dioxide emissions to enable them to continue to burn Illinois coal. *Alliance for Clean Coal v. Craig*, 840 F. Supp. 554 (N.D. Ill. 1993), aff'd 44 F.3d 591 (7th Cir. 1995).

3.   Can the president of a company that imports and resells foreign automobiles be liable for violations of the Clean Air Act, which prohibits the importation of new motor vehicles not covered by a certificate of conformity issued by the EPA? The facts showed that the president was actively involved in the violations that occurred. *U.S. v. JBA Motorcars, Inc.*, 839 F. Supp. 1572 (S.D. Fla. 1993).

4.   Does the Clean Air Act preempt Michigan's Solid Waste Management Act's express limitation on the authority of local communities to restrict the location of a waste-to-energy solid waste incinerator? *Southeastern Oakland County Resource Recovery Authority v. City of Madison Heights,* 5 F.3d 166 (6th Cir. 1993).

5.   Are ventilation buildings in plans for Boston's central artery/tunnel project which will vent underground highway and tunnel automobile emissions, indirect sources under the Clean Air Act, or are they stationary sources subject to the act's preconstruction permit requirements? *Sierra Club v. Larson,* 2 F.3d 462 (1st Cir. 1993).

6.   Do the Clean Air Act Amendments of 1990 eliminate a state's obligation to comply with its pre-1990 state implementation plan? *American Lung Ass'n v. Kean,* 856 F. Supp. 903 (D.N.J. 1994).

ENDNOTES

1. 57 Fed. Reg. 13,168 (1992).

2. Paul R. Portney, *Air Pollution Policy,* in Public Policies for Environmental Protection 51 (Paul R. Portney, ed. 1993).

3. *Id.*

11

THE CLEAN WATER ACT

INTRODUCTION

Water, which covers 72 percent of the surface of the earth, is essential to life. An adequate water supply is also essential for the economic, industrial, and agricultural development of human society. In the United States today, irrigation has transformed deserts like the Imperial Valley in California into fertile land which generates billions of dollars in livestock, grain, and produce. In the western United States, aggressive programs to divert and dam rivers and tap into groundwater have allowed cities to grow and thrive on essentially arid land.

Despite its value, water is often taken for granted, especially in parts of the world where it is a common resource. In the early development of the eastern part of this country, there was little concern about excessive water use or water pollution. In the latter part of this century, however, alarm over shrinking water resources and water health and safety has led to demands for laws to protect this valuable resource.

This chapter focuses on laws protecting the nation's water from water pollution. These laws include the Clean Water Act (CWA), the **Safe Drinking Water Act** (SDWA), and the **Oil Pollution Act** (OPA). Water resource management, not directly addressed here, has historically been a matter of state, rather than federal law. State laws (both statutory and common) generally regulate the use of water within the state by treating the water rights of individuals as property rights, a topic addressed in Chapter 3. As one might expect, laws establishing water rights have evolved differently in states where water is a plentiful resource from those where water resources are scarce. Although federal law generally governs water pollution and state law generally regulates water management, it is important to note that the policy issues involved in protecting water quality and managing water resources are interrelated.

HISTORY OF FEDERAL WATER POLLUTION CONTROL

Federal water pollution control law protects the nation's navigable waters by controlling the discharge of pollutants into rivers, streams, and other waterways. The first federal law regulating discharge of pollutants into the nation's waterways was the *Rivers and Harbors Appropriations Act of 1899,* designed to protect navigation. In the 1940s, public concern over drinking water contamination led to federal programs to assist states in constructing waste treatment plants. In 1948, Congress passed the **Federal Water Pollution Control Act** (FWPCA), which permitted courts to order pollution abatement after considering the practicability and economic feasibility of such abatement.

In 1965, Congress passed *The Water Quality Act,* under which the federal government assisted states in establishing and enforcing water quality standards. Prior to 1972, standards were generally set by the states. The laws usually established permissible concentrations of pollutants which were to be used to formulate individualized permit limitations for dischargers.

The 1965 act was generally considered ineffective because of its limited scope, awkward enforcement mechanisms, and state inaction. In addition, establishing pollutant parameters for a body of water created problems in determining when a particular discharge violated applicable standards. In response to these problems, Congress (in 1972) passed a comprehensive revision and recodification of the FWPCA, which became known as the *Clean Water Act* (CWA). In its 1977 amendments to the act, Congress specifically addressed the problem of toxic pollutants. In 1987, Congress amended the act to establish new water quality requirements in areas where compliance was insufficient to meet national goals and to address the problem of stormwater discharges. Almost certainly, the act will be amended further when next reauthorized. Environmental taxes and fees, pollution prevention, nonpoint source control, regional water quality issues, and wetlands regulation are among those issues likely to generate heated debate. It is not surprising that proposals to regulate and control water use engender controversy. These issues directly affect the health, welfare, and economic resources of every person within the United States.

OVERVIEW OF THE CLEAN WATER ACT

The CWA establishes the basic framework of current federal water pollution control law. The act requires the EPA to set nationwide effluent standards on an industrywide basis for discharge of pollutants into waters of the United States. "New source" direct dischargers are subject to even more stringent standards of performance. To implement these requirements, the act establishes the **National Pollutant Discharge Elimination System** (NPDES). Under this system, the EPA issues permits for the discharge of any pollutant or contamination of pollutants into public waterways based on technology and water quality-based standards of the act. Discharge from a point source without a permit or in violation of permit requirements can result in criminal and/or civil liability.

The act contains specific provisions governing federal and state coordination in administering the act. States can administer the permit program if the states meet the legal requirements for doing so. The EPA, however, continues to play an important role in state programs, and it provides technical support and guidance to the states. Most states have assumed the responsibility for permitting under these provisions, but federal rules and interpretations continue to dominate application of the law at the state and local level.

The CWA also requires that industries which discharge indirectly to publicly owned water treatment works (POTWs) meet **pretreatment standards** under the act. The law also contains specific provisions governing oil spills and discharge of toxic substances. Section 404 of the CWA gives the Army Corps of Engineers the authority to issue permits for the discharge of dredged or fill material to waters of the United States.

Pollution Discharge Prohibition

Section 101(a) of the CWA states: "The objective of this act is to restore and maintain the chemical, physical, and biological integrity of the Nation's waters." National goals include achievement of a level of water quality which "provides for the protection and propagation of fish, shellfish and wildlife" and "for recreation in and on the water," and the elimination of discharge of **pollutants** into surface waters and prohibition of discharge of toxic pollutants. Section 301(a) of the CWA prohibits the discharge of any pollutant by any person into navigable waters, except in compliance with the act's permit requirements. The discharger bears the burden of proving compliance.

The act defines *discharge of a pollutant* to mean "any addition of any pollutant to navigable waters from any point source. . . ." The wording used in this section has generated much litigation because it defines the scope of application of the act.

Section 502(14) of the act specifies the following list of materials considered to be pollutants for purposes of the NPDES regulation:

> dredged spoil, solid waste, incinerator residue, sewage, garbage, sewage sludge, munitions, chemical wastes, biological materials, radioactive materials (except those regulated under the Atomic Energy Act of 1954), heat, wrecked or discarded equipment, rock, sand, cellar dirt, and industrial, municipal, and agricultural waste discharged into water.

This definition of pollutant has been broadly interpreted to include virtually all waste material whether or not it has value at the time it is discharged.[1] For example, in *Hudson River Fishermen's Ass'n v. Arcuri,*[2] the court held that owners and developers of an abandoned construction site were liable under the FWPCA for discharging pollutants without a permit. The court said that solid waste, including wrecked, discarded equipment, garbage, rock, sand, and dirt which was discharged from the site into a tributary of the Hudson River constituted pollutants under the act. Bombs dropped on a naval target range[3] and dead fish and fish parts discharged by a power plant[4] have also been held to be pollutants under this definition.

One of the more difficult issues under the act is the meaning of the term **point source,** which is defined to include "any discernible, confined and discrete conveyance . . . from which pollutants are or may be discharged."[5] The courts have tended to interpret the definition of point source very broadly in order to achieve the policies underlying the CWA. There are, however, some discharges which are expressly exempted as point sources under the act. These include irrigation return flows, discharge of sewage from vessels regulated under other sections of the act, and certain agricultural and silvicultural discharges.

In the following case, citizens brought suit under the CWA, alleging that pollution from the liquid manure spreading operations of a large dairy farm violated provisions of the act. A central issue in the case was whether the animal feeding lot operation was a point source, and if so, whether it fell within the "agricultural stormwater discharges" exception to point source discharges under the act.

CONCERNED AREA RESIDENTS FOR THE ENVIRONMENT v. SOUTHVIEW FARM
34 F.3d 114 (2d Cir. 1994)

OAKES, Senior Circuit Judge:

***

BACKGROUND

Plaintiffs, who refer to themselves collectively as Concerned Area Residents For the Environment ("CARE"), are a group of landowners who live near Southview Farms, a dairy farm in the town of Castile, in Wyoming County, New York. Defendants are the farm itself, and Richard H. Popp, an individual. Southview Farm is one of the largest dairy farms in the state of New York. It employs twenty-eight full-time and nine part-time employees. As of 1992, it owned 1,100 crop acres and had an animal population of 1,290 head of mature cows with over 900 head of young cattle, heifers, and calves, making a total of 2,200 animals.

Unlike old-fashioned dairy farms, Southview's operations do not involve pasturing the cows. Instead, the cows remain in their barns except during the three times per day milking procedures. Also unlike old-fashioned dairy farms where the accumulated manure was spread by a manure spreader, Southview's rather enormous manure operations are largely performed through the use of storage lagoons and liquid cow manure. The storage lagoons number five on the main farm property ("A Farm"). One four-acre manure storage lagoon has a capacity of approximately six to eight million gallons of liquid cow manure.

In connection with this particular manure storage lagoon, Southview has installed a separator which pumps the cow manure over a mechanical device which drains off the liquid and passes the solids out through a compressing process. The solids that remain are dropped into bins for transport while the liquid runs by gravity through a pipe to the four-acre manure storage lagoon. This separated liquid was apparently used for the purpose of washing down the barns where the cows are housed.

Insofar as application of the manure as fertilizer to the land is concerned, there is a center pivot irrigation system for spreading liquid manure over the fields. . . . Southview also spreads its manure with a hard hose traveler which is a long piece of plastic tubing on a large reel. . . . Southview also uses conventional manure spreading equipment including spreaders pulled by tractors and self-propelled vehicles which, generally speaking, have a 5,000-gallon capacity for liquid manure. These vehicles were used to spread manure from the smaller lagoons on the "A Farm" which do not receive liquid manure processed through the separation system. Southview's manure spreading record reflects the application of millions of gallons of manure to its fields.

***

DISCUSSION

The CWA provides that, absent a permit and subject to certain limitations, "the discharge of any pollutant by any person shall be unlawful." A pollutant includes solid waste, . . . sewage, . . . biological materials, . . . and agricultural waste discharged into water" and thus includes the manure in this case. A "discharge" is "any addition of any pollutant to navigable waters from any point source." The term "point source" includes "any discernible, confined and discrete conveyance, including but not limited to any . . . concentrated animal feeding operation. . . . This term does not include agricultural stormwater discharges and return flows from irrigated agriculture." Our basic questions on review then are whether the defendants discharged the manure pollutant from any point source into navigable waters and whether the agricultural stormwater exemption or any other limitation applies.

The plaintiff-appellant's contentions relate to five specific CWA violations which the jury found but the district court overturned on the defendant's motion for judgment [as a matter of law.]

[*One of these violations was liquid manure flowing into and through a swale on field 104 and through a drain tile leading directly into a stream which ultimately flowed into the Genesee River on July 13, 1989.*]

. . . It is significant to note, as previously stated, that the cows are not put out to pasture. The fields to which the manure is applied, as above indicated, are used for crops. The United States appears as amicus curiae in support of the appellants on the basis that, because the Southview operations involve more than 700 cattle, it is a facility which is defined in the regulations under the Act as a CAFO [concentrated animal feeding operation], and therefore one type of "point source" under the Act, thereby requiring a permit for discharges which was not obtained in this instance. As we have stated, the Act defines the term "point source" as including "any . . . concentrated animal feeding operation." In this connection, the district court concluded that, as a matter of law, Southview was not a CAFO [that is, a "concentrated animal feeding operation" treated as a point source under EPA regulations] because crops are grown on a portion of the farm. The United States contends that Southview is a CAFO as a matter of law because crops are not grown in the feed lot in which the milking cows are confined. . . .

JULY 13, 1989, VIOLATION OF FIELD 104

The July 13 violation, found by the jury but overturned by the district court, as we have said, occurred on field 104 on the Wyant property which shares the boundary line with Letchworth State Park. Field 104 contains a slew or swale which tends to collect liquid manure spread by Southview's tankers and conveys it through a pipe in a stone wall and through the stone wall itself into a ditch which runs from some length on the Southview property before it reaches the boundary of the state park.

On July 13, 1989, appellants Kirk Bly and Philip Karcheski observed the manure collecting in the slew or swale and flowing into the ditch which in turn flowed off of the Southview property into Letchworth State Park property, and, in turn, joined a stream which ultimately flowed into the Genesee River.

The district court held and appellees contend that the July 13 discharge was not a point source discharge because the liquid simply and quite naturally flowed to and through the lowest areas of the field, and that the pollutants reached the stream that flows into the Genesee "in too diffuse a manner to create a point source discharge." The district court also suggested that the pollutants were not "collected" by human activity but in fact the opposite occurred in that the manure was dispersed over the ground.

The appellants argue that . . . even if the liquid manure flowing from field 104 into the swale could be characterized as "diffuse run-off," as the district court characterized it, the manure pollutant was nevertheless thereafter channelled or collected sufficiently to constitute a discharge by a point source. Alternatively, the appellants contend that the appellees' liquid manure-spreading vehicles themselves may be treated as point sources because [the law] defines a point source to include a "container" or "rolling stock." They point out that a number of district court cases have found vehicles to be within the definition of point sources. They urge that by pumping the liquid manure from Southview's various lagoons into manure spreading tankers and other vehicles before discharging the liquid manure on to its various fields, Southview has "collected by human effort" the pollutant discharged into the navigable waters.

We agree with the appellants on both counts. We believe that the swale coupled with the pipe under the stone wall leading into the ditch that leads into the stream was in and of itself a point source. As this court has previously noted, the definition of a point source is to be broadly interpreted. . . . Here, the liquid manure was collected and channelized through the ditch or depression in the swale of field 104 and thence into the ditch leading to the stream on the boundary of the Southview property as it adjoins Letchworth State Park. . . .

Moreover, we agree with the appellants that, alternatively, the manure spreading vehicles themselves were point sources. The collection of liquid manure into tankers and their discharge on fields from which the manure directly flows into navigable waters

are point source discharges under the case law. . . . The district court also believed that the defendant's actions were "the kind of activity that Congress wanted to keep beyond the reach of the Act," like irrigation return flows or storm-water runoffs. Again, we disagree, for reasons that appear below in our discussion of the position of the United States.

***

We conclude with the United States . . . that Southview has an animal feeding lot operation with a tremendous number of cattle in a concentrated feeding facility in which no vegetation is grown; that operation in and of itself is a point source within the Clean Water Act and not subject to any agricultural exemption thereto.

Accordingly the judgment of the district court, setting aside the jury's verdict, is reversed and the cause remanded for further proceedings in accordance with this opinion.

Questions and Comments for Discussion

1. Who sued the defendants in this case? Why did the United States join the suit with plaintiffs?
2. What is the definition of "point source" under the CWA? Did it include liquid manure runoff in this case? Why or why not?
3. One of the issues addressed by the court in this case was whether the defendants' operation was a **Concentrated Animal Feeding Operation** (CAFO). A CAFO is treated as a point source under the law, and it differs from an operation which grazes dairy cattle on land. In contrast, agricultural storm water runoff is a nonpoint source pollution exempt from the CWA.

The court in this case noted that under CWA regulations, a CAFO is an animal feeding operation (AFO) which contains more than 700 mature dairy cattle. The court said, "There appears to be no doubt that Southview's feed lot meets the criteria of [the regulation defining a CAFO]."

4. Critics of the CWA argue that while it includes enforceable requirements to control point sources of pollution, such as factories and sewage plants, more than half of the water pollution today is caused by runoff that forms when rain or snow washes toxins and pollutants into the surface waters from farms, logging and mining operations, and roads. How to control nonpoint source pollution is an emerging regulatory issue which will likely generate controversy. Should Congress amend the CWA to regulate agricultural runoff as a point source? What are the practical and policy implications of your answer?
5. The 1996 Farm Bill established a new Environmental Quality Incentives Program to improve water quality and to address other environmental issues in agricultural production. Half of the $200 million in annual funds are to be used to improve management practices relating to livestock.

The bill also reauthorized the Conservation Reserve Program to combat soil erosion and to protect water quality, and extended authorization for the Wetlands Reserve Program, which offers incentives for protection of wetlands.

The term **navigable waters** is defined in the act as "waters of the United States, including the territorial seas." The meaning of these words has been expanded by EPA regulation to include navigable waters, tributaries, interstate waters, and intrastate lakes, rivers, and streams used in interstate commerce.[6] The courts have interpreted this definition to include all waters over which the federal government can exercise jurisdiction, and the term includes wetlands under Section 404 of the act. In some recent cases challenging the jurisdiction of the federal government to regulate dredging and filling of wetlands, the interpretation of the term "navigable waters" has been critical. Two of those cases, *United States v. Riverside Bayview Homes, Inc.,* and *Hoffman Homes, Inc. v. EPA,* are discussed later in this chapter.

The term **person** is also broadly construed under the act. The word is defined by the law to include an individual, corporation, partnership, association, state, municipality, commission, or other political subdivision of a state. Consequently, an officer of a corporation, as an individual, may be a "person" subject to criminal liability under the act.

NPDES Exclusions

As the *Southview Farms* case illustrates, there are statutory and regulatory exceptions under the NPDES program. These include the following:

1. Discharges of sewage from vessels (not including trash, garbage, or other materials discharged overboard. Discharges of refuse matter into navigable waters is prohibited under the **Refuse Act,** 33 U.S.C. 407).
2. Discharge of pollutants to a POTW by an indirect discharger. (Pretreatment standards for industries discharging into a POTW are included in a separate section of the CWA.)
3. Any discharge in compliance with CERCLA.
4. Nonpoint source agricultural or silvicultural activities unless otherwise explicitly covered in NPDES regulations.
5. Return flows from irrigation.
6. Discharges to privately owned treatment works unless required to be permitted under regulation.
7. Discharges of dredged or fill material regulated under Section 404 of the CWA.

An important issue in defining of navigable waters is whether the CWA's prohibition against "discharge into navigable waters of the United States" includes underground waters. The act does not clearly include underground aquifers as a class of water, although states must "control the discharge of pollutants into wells" as a precondition to operating the NPDES program. The EPA lacks direct authority under the CWA to regulate subsurface injection as a means of disposal. However, as the following case suggests, the agency may exercise its authority under the act to regulate underground discharges which flow into navigable waters. Even though the EPA may lack the authority to regulate underground injection which does not migrate into navigable waters, it does have the authority to regulate the underground injection of hazardous wastes under the Resource Conservation and Recovery Act and the Safe Drinking Water Act.

SIERRA CLUB v. COLORADO REFINING COMPANY
838 F. Supp. 1428 (D. Colo. 1993)

Kane, Senior District Judge.

This case is before me on a motion to dismiss filed by defendant Colorado Refining Company. Plaintiff Sierra Club asserts three causes of action. The first is for unpermitted discharges into Sand Creek in violation of Section 301 of the Clean Water Act, the second for discharges to Sand Creek in violation of CRC's NPDES Permits and the Clean Water Act, and the third for failure to determine the impact to Sand Creek of its noncomplying discharges in violation of the Clean Water Act. . . .

This complaint was filed on August 12, 1993. . . . Sierra Club brings this "citizen suit" alleging that CRC has illegally discharged pollutants, in excess of permit limits, into Sand Creek from its refinery located in Adams County, Colorado, immediately to the south of the creek. Sierra Club further alleges that such discharge has and continues to degrade the water quality of Sand Creek and to diminish the fish populations downstream from the refinery. . . .

***

The Clean Water Act provides that "[e]xcept as in compliance with this section . . . , the discharge of any pollutant by any person shall be unlawful. . . ." The term "discharge of a pollutant" is defined as "any addition of any pollutant to navigable waters from any point source. . . ." "Point source" is defined as "any discernible, confined and discrete conveyance, including but not limited to any pipe, ditch, channel, tunnel, conduit, well, discrete fissure, container . . . from which pollutants may be discharged. . . ." For the purpose of the Clean Water Act, the term "navigable waters" has been defined broadly as "the waters of the United States, including the territorial seas." Federal Courts have interpreted this directive broadly to include waters tributary to those which are navigable in fact.

CRC argues that while the term "navigable waters" is construed broadly, Congress did not intend to include groundwater within its definition. CRC maintains that certain allegations in the complaint indicate that Sierra Club's first cause of action is totally founded on the discharge of pollutants by CRC into the soil and groundwater which then make their way into Sand Creek.

***

A review of the case law addressing the regulation of groundwater under the Clean Water Act reveals that "isolated/nontributary groundwater," such as confined wells, has been unequivocally excluded from the Act by some courts. However, these cases and others do not preclude the act from applying to the regulation of "tributary groundwater," such as in the present case, which migrate from groundwater back into surface waters. . . .

. . . [C]ase law conflicts as to whether "navigable waters" in the Clean Water Act encompass groundwater. Although there is little direct Tenth Circuit authority in this regard, the Sierra Club has cited two opinions which indicate that that circuit has placed a broad interpretation on the scope of the Clean Water Act. In *United States v. Earth Sciences, Inc.,*[7] the court ruled that unpermitted leach mining waste escaping into the Rito Seco Creek through overflow of a reserve sump and through groundwater seeps violated the Clean Water Act which "was designed to regulate to the fullest extent possible those sources emitting pollution into rivers, streams and lakes." Although the court was chiefly addressing the issue of whether "navigable waters" include waters such as the Rito Seco Creek, which are not navigable in fact, the observations made are nevertheless pertinent. As the court in *Earth Sciences* noted, "[i]t seems clear Congress intended to regulate discharges into every creek, stream, river or body of water that in any way may affect interstate commerce. Every court to discuss the issue has used a commerce power approach and agreed upon that interpretation. . . ."

These decisions leave little doubt that the Tenth Circuit has chosen to interpret the terminology of the Clean Water Act broadly to give full effect to Congress' declared goal and policy "to restore and maintain the chemical, physical and biological integrity of the Nation's waters." With this in mind, I conclude that the Clean Water Act's preclusion of the discharge of any pollutant into "navigable waters" includes such discharge which releases "navigable waters" through groundwater. I therefore find that Sierra Club's allegations that CRC has and continues to discharge pollutants into the soils and groundwater beneath the refinery which then make their way to Sand Creek through the groundwater state a cause of action under the Clean Water Act.

Questions and Comments for Discussion

1.   A significant gap in the CWA is the fact its provisions do not apply to groundwater. For a discussion of groundwater issues, see Wood, *Regulating Dischargers Into Groundwater: The Crucial Link in Pollution Control Under the Clean Water Act,* 12 Harv. Envtl L. Rev. 569 (1988).

Citizen Suit Provision

The *Sierra Club* case was brought as a "citizen suit" under Section 505 of the CWA. This section authorizes any person having an interest "which is or may be adversely affected" to bring a civil action either against a discharger for violation of the act or against the EPA for failing to enforce the act's provisions. The act encourages citizen suits by specifically providing for the payment of attorney and expert witness fees when appropriate. National environmental groups like the Sierra Club have utilized this section to enforce provisions of the act. Courts have generally held that members of these environmental groups have standing under the language of this section.

Most major federal environmental protection laws contain citizen suit provisions (important exceptions are FIFRA and NEPA). Because the NPDES program under the CWA requires that dischargers file routine discharge monitoring reports, it is relatively easy for citizens to discover and prove violations under the NPDES program. For this reason, there have been more citizen suits filed under the CWA than any other federal environmental law.[8]

Permit Program Conditions

The (NPDES) permit system serves two primary functions: First, the NPDES permit establishes specific levels of performance each discharger is required to meet; second, the law requires the discharger to monitor and report compliance to the appropriate agency. Effluent limitations include technology-based limitations on discharge and water quality-based limitations on discharge. Technology-based limitations are industry-specific and based upon technological and economic capability. Water quality-based limitations are more stringent limitations imposed to protect the quality of the receiving water. Technological and economic capability are not factors in developing these latter effluent standards.

Monitoring and Reporting Requirements

The self-monitoring requirements of the NPDES program are critical in assuring compliance with requirements of the CWA. Under Section 308, the EPA may require the owner or operator of any point source to maintain specific records, install, use, maintain monitoring equipment, identify pollutant parameters which must be sampled, and impose other requirements necessary to assure accurate sampling and reporting of effluent discharge. Records must be maintained for three years, or longer if required by the authority issuing the permit, and annual reporting is required at a minimum. The data are open to the public (information protected as trade secrets is excluded).

In the past, NPDES permits usually targeted four or five pollutants. Today, the number of pollutants regulated is generally much larger because the agency is required to address specific toxins and heavy metal substances in industrial point-source discharges. In addition to site-specific conditions, the following "boilerplate" conditions must be included in all NPDES permits:

1. The duty to minimize or prevent permit violations with a reasonable likelihood of adversely affecting human health or the environment
2. The duty to properly operate and maintain the facility and treatment equipment
3. The duty to permit authorities to enter and inspect the premises and records
4. The duty to report facility changes or changes in operation or ownership to permitting authorities
5. The prohibition of a "by-pass" of treatment by the facility unless necessary for essential maintenance.

Technology-Based Limitations

One issue in the NPDES regulatory process is the determination of effluent discharge limitations. The CWA uses three methods for establishing discharge limitations. These include (1) *technology-based effluent limitations,* which establish the baseline for treatment requirements; (2) *water quality-based effluent limitations,* which are more stringent requirements imposed to achieve water quality standards; and (3) *limits on toxic discharges* when necessary to protect public health.

Technology-based limitations are based on the performance of pollution control technologies. These limitations consider several factors, including the technological and economic feasibility of the pollution control technology. The law does not, however, require a discharger to use a specific pollution control technology—the discharger can choose any technology as long as it can satisfy the applicable discharge limits.

The CWA provided for the establishment of technology-based effluent limitations on an industry-by-industry basis. Technology standards were to be phased in so that by July 1, 1977, effluent limitations would be governed by **best practicable control technology** (BPT) standards and by 1983, effluent limitations would be governed by **best available technology economically achievable** (BAT) standards. Generally, BPT limitations represent "the average of the best" treatment technology in an industrial category. In setting BPT standards, the EPA considers the total cost of the technology in relation to effluent benefits, the age of equipment, engineering aspects, nonwater quality environmental impact, and other relevant factors. *Rybachek v. EPA,* 904 F.2d 1276 (9th Cir. 1990).

BAT was originally based on the single best performer within an industry, rather than on an average of exemplary plants. Under the original act, the EPA was to consider factors similar to BPT factors, except BAT involved consideration of the cost of achieving the pollution reduction rather than a comparative benefit and cost analysis. The BAT definition was essentially unchanged by 1977 and 1987 amendments, but its date for attainment was extended. The 1977 amendments created a new standard—**the best conventional pollutant control technology** (BCT), which applies to conventional pollutants, discussed later in this chapter.

In implementing the act, the EPA set technology-based effluent limitations by categories. Industrial categories were based on products manufactured and subcategories of the processes or raw materials used in the production process. BPT and BAT criteria were applied to these categories and subcategories, and contained maximum daily and monthly average limitations. Following lawsuits by industry and confusion in the courts, the Supreme Court upheld this approach, but required the EPA to develop a variance procedure for plants which do not fit into a particular subcategory. Congress subsequently amended the act to incorporate this fundamentally different factors (FDF) variance. The FDF variance is discussed later in this chapter.

Much of the dramatic improvement in water quality in recent decades has been credited to reductions in discharges of some pollutants from these technology-based limits. This approach has also been credited for helping to ensure a market for the development of water pollution control technology. However, a technology-based approach to regulating effluent discharge has also been criticized as being costly to industry, because the standards are set without reference to the receiving waters. Critics also argue that this approach actually stifles innovation. They argue that industries will be reluctant to install controls more stringent than that required because improved technology will mean more stringent requirements in the future.

CONTROL OF CONVENTIONAL POLLUTANTS

Conventional pollutants are defined as BOD (biochemical oxygen demand), TSS (total suspended solids), oil and grease, pH (acidity and alkalinity), and fecal coliform. BOD is a measure of the amount of oxygen needed for organic material to decompose. The higher the BOD, the more conventional organics are in the water.

Suspended solids in water are soil sediment and other particles which can carry nutrients, bacteria, and harmful material. Natural erosion as well as development, forestry, and farming activities cause increased suspended solids in waterways. A very low (acidic) or very high (alkaline) pH is unfavorable to most aquatic life. Concentrations of fecal coliform and other bacteria from human and animal waste create a risk of infection and disease.

BPT and BCT are two technology-based standards which apply to discharges of conventional pollutants directly into surface water. As mentioned earlier, the EPA generally establishes BPT limitations based on model technology used by the best performers in an industry. In setting this standard, the EPA must also consider the total cost in relation to the benefits, called a "limited cost-benefit analysis."

The BCT standard was added by the 1977 CWA amendments. It was designed to be less stringent than the BAT standard but as or more stringent than the BPT standard for the discharge of conventional pollutants. Today the BAT standard is identical to the BPT standard. Congress presumably adopted the BCT standard because the improvement in conventional pollutant loads between 1972 and 1977 was significant and because the cost of moving to BAT for conventional pollutants was too high. BCT may be imposed only if found cost effective in two areas: (1) a comparison between costs of reducing discharges and resulting water quality benefits and (2) a comparison between industrial and municipal costs for treating conventional pollutants.

Best Available Technology (BAT)

BAT is defined by the EPA as the "very best control and treatment measures that have been or are capable of being achieved." Toxic and nonconventional pollutants, identified in the act and listed at 40 C.F.R. Section 401.15, must meet this stricter technology-imposed standard. By definition, BAT limitations must be both technologically available and economically achievable.

In setting BAT standards, the EPA considers factors similar to those for BPT and BCT, but cost is a less important factor. While the EPA is required to consider whether the BAT limitation is economically achievable, it is not required to balance cost with benefit as required under BPT standards. The BAT effluent limitations primarily focus on priority toxic pollutants while "conventional" pollutants are governed by standards established in the 1977 amendments.

The formal, detailed regulatory process envisioned by the CWA is ongoing, and in some cases the EPA may not have yet established applicable effluent limits or performance standards for a discharge permit. In such cases, the regulations authorize discharge limits based on best professional or engineering judgment.

Water Quality Standards

Water quality standards, unlike technology-based standards, are performance standards based upon the impact of a discharge on receiving waters. Water quality requirements are designed to achieve a certain level of quality and to ensure that the level of quality is consistent with public water supply, recreation, industrial, or agricultural uses, and the protection of fish and wildlife. These goals are summarized by the phrase "fishable/swimmable waters." Water quality standards are adopted by the states and approved by the EPA and include (1) the designated use or uses of a water body, (2) the water quality criteria necessary to protect those uses, and (3) an antidegradation statement.

Water quality goals for a particular body of water serve as a basis for imposing treatment controls beyond the minimum required by the CWA. While the act relies on a technology-based standard approach, water quality limitations are to be imposed when achievement of technology-based standards will not result in reaching water quality goals. Other harm-based provisions in the CWA include variances based on receiving water quality available to dischargers of heat, nonconventional pollutants, and alternative water quality-based ocean discharge criteria.

Many states as well as the EPA have avoided some of the problems inherent in setting and administering water quality performance standards by relying on technology-based standards, which are easier to implement. In fact, it has been suggested that environmental standard setting in general is moving away from harm-based regulation toward a technology-based approach for this reason.[9]

Toxicants and Nonconventional Pollutants

The EPA's toxicant strategy developed following failure to establish a workable program to control the discharge of toxic pollutants. As a result of a lawsuit filed by the Natural Resources Defense Council (NRDC) against the EPA, *NRDC v. Train,*[10] the EPA and NRDC developed a policy for identifying the pollutants which would be the primary subject of regulation, the industries to be regulated, and the methods of regulating toxic discharges. The agreement was approved by the court in a settlement decree and incorporated into subsequent amendments of the CWA.

The fact that the EPA decided to regulate toxic pollutants primarily through BAT-based effluent limitations, and that Congress codified this methodology into the 1977 amendments, is evidence that the CWA's original toxic pollutant control mechanism was cumbersome and ineffective. The consent decree and subsequent amendments to the CWA have focused attention away from a few conventional pollutants to effluent toxicity, which may include over a hundred dangerous pollutants. As a result of the increasing focus on toxic pollutants, water quality standards may become increasingly important because they impose more stringent limitations on the discharger.

In 1977, Congress also created a third class of pollutants—"nonconventional" pollutants—which include nontoxic, nonconventional pollutants such as ammonia, chlorine, colors and dyes, iron, and total phenols. These substances are subject to the BAT effluent limits, but dischargers are entitled to cost-based and harm-based variances.

New Source Performance Standards (NSPS)

The CWA requires all new pollution sources in an industry (including major modifications of existing sources) to meet standards reflecting "the greatest degree of effluent reduction . . . achievable through application of the best available demonstrated control technology." These new source performance standards (NSPSs) are as stringent or more as the BAT standard, although in most cases they are equivalent to BAT. In setting these requirements, the EPA considers not only pollution control techniques, but also alternative production processes and methods. In addition, costs are less important in establishing an NSPS than in establishing BAT, in part because new sources can incorporate the most efficient processes and treatment systems in new plant designs.

Variances

The CWA permits a facility that is "fundamentally different" from those on which effluent guidelines are based to seek a variance from a BAT, BCT, or pre-treatment standard for existing sources (PSES) technology-based effluent limitation. The FDF variance must be submitted within 180 days of establishing the guideline, and the cost of controlling pollutants by the industry may not be considered. The law also recognizes a few other instances where the EPA may grant variances from BAT limitations, but in general these instances are rare and the variances almost never granted.

In 1980, the Supreme Court issued an opinion in which it discussed the difference between the BPT and BAT technology-based standards and reviewed the EPA's regulations providing for variances from the 1977 BPT limitation. In that case, the National Crushed Stone Association, Consolidation Coal Co., and others challenged both the BPT standards and the variance provision applicable to their industries. The Court granted *certiorari* to resolve conflicting decisions in the lower courts concerning these issues. In the following case, the Court held that the EPA was not required to consider economic capability in granting variances from BPT standards under the CWA.

EPA v. NATIONAL CRUSHED STONE ASSOCIATION
449 U.S. 64 (1980)

JUSTICE WHITE delivered the opinion of the court.

***

Section 301(c) of the [Clean Water] Act explicitly provides for modifying the 1987 (BAT) effluent limitations with respect to individual point sources. A variance under section 301(c) may be obtained upon a showing "that such codified requirements (1) will represent the maximum use of technology within the economic capability of the owner or operation; and (2) will result in reasonable further progress toward elimination of the discharge of pollutants." Thus, the economic ability of the individual operator to meet the costs of effluent reductions may in some circumstances justify granting a variance from the 1987 limitations.

No such explicit variance provision exists with respect to BPT standards, but in *E.I.du Pont de Nemours v. Train,* 430 U.S. 112 (1977), we indicated that a variance provision was a necessary aspect of BPT limitations applicable by regulations to classes and categories of point sources. The issue in this case is whether the BPT variance provision must allow consideration of the economic capability of an individual

discharger to afford the costs of the BPT limitation. For the reasons that follow, our answer is in the negative.

***

The Administrator's present interpretation of the language of the statute is amply supported by the legislative history, which persuades us that Congress understood that the economic capability provision of sec. 301(c) was limited to BAT variances; that Congress foresaw and accepted the economic hardship, including the closing of some plants, that effluent limitations would cause; and that Congress took certain steps to alleviate this hardship, steps which did not include allowing a BPT variance based on economic capability. . . .

. . . Congress [did not] restrict the reach of section 301(c) [to BAT variances] without understanding the economic hardships that uniform standards would impose. Prior to passage of the Act, Congress had before it a report jointly prepared by EPA, the Commerce Dept., and the council on Environmental Quality on the impact of the pollution control measures on industry. That report estimated that there would be 200 to 300 plant closings caused by the first set of pollution limitations. Comments in the Senate debate were explicit: "There is no doubt that we will suffer some disruptions in our economy because of our efforts; many marginal plants may be forced to close. . . ."

Congress did not respond to this foreseen economic impact by making room for variances based on economic impact. In fact, this possibility was specifically considered and rejected. . . . Instead of economic variances, Congress specifically added two other provisions to address the problem of economic hardship.

First, provision was made for low-cost loans to small businesses to help them meet the cost of technological improvements. . . . Second, an employee protection provision was added, giving EPA authority to investigate any plant's claim that it must cut back production or close down because of pollution control regulations. . . .

***

. . . The statute itself does not provide for BPT variances in connection with permits for individual point sources . . . In the face of sec. 301(c)'s explicit limitation and in the absence of any other specific direction to provide for variances in connection with permits for individual point sources, we believe that the Administrator has adopted a reasonable construction of the statutory mandate.

In rejecting EPA's interpretation of the BPT variance provision, the Court of Appeals relied on a mistaken conception of the relation between BPT and BAT standards. The court erroneously believed that since BAT limitations are to be more stringent than BPT limitations, the variance provision for the latter must be at least as flexible as that for the former with respect to affordability. The variances permitted by sec. 301(c) from the 1987 limitations, however, can reasonably be understood to represent a cost in decreased effluent reductions that can only be afforded once the minimal standard expressed in the BPT limitation has been reached.

We conclude, therefore, that the Court of Appeals erred in not accepting EPA's interpretation of the Act. EPA is not required by the Act to consider economic capability in granting variances from its uniform BPT regulations.

The judgment of the Court of Appeals is reversed.

Questions and Comments for Discussion

1. What was the legal issue in this case? How did the Court resolve this issue?
2. What is the difference between BPT and BAT standards? According to the Court, what is a significant difference between variances for individual point sources?
3. According to the Court, how did Congress respond to the foreseen economic impact of the CWA? Why might Congress have decided to provide for individual variances for BAT standards under the CWA but not for BPT?
4. As noted, Section 301 of the CWA as amended expressly provides for variance from BAT limits to dischargers that can demonstrate that proposed alternative limits "(1) will represent the maximum use of technology within the economic capability of the owner or operator; and (2) will result in reasonable further progress toward the elimination of the discharge of pollutants."

In *Chemical Manufacturers Assoc. v. NRDC*, 470 U.S. 116 (1985), the Supreme Court held that the EPA's issuance of FDF variances from toxic pollutant effluent limitations were permissible under Section 301(l) of the CWA.

Pretreatment and Indirect Dischargers

In many cases, industrial facilities do not discharge directly into surface water but rather into **publicly owned treatment works** (POTWs), owned by a state or municipality.

Discharges by industry into POTWs are not regulated as direct discharges under the NPDES system but rather are regulated by *pretreatment standards* adopted under Section 307(b) of the CWA. The CWA requires the EPA to promulgate pretreatment standards which will (1) protect the POTW operation and (2) prevent discharge from the POTW without adequate treatment. Discharges by POTWs into U.S. waters must meet the requirements of the NPDES system.

General pretreatment regulations prohibit discharge into a POTW of any pollutant causing a "pass-through," which is defined as a discharge that exits the POTW in quantities or concentrations which would cause a violation of the POTW's NPDES permit. General pretreatment regulations also prohibit specific discharges, including pollutants that create a fire or explosion hazard; cause corrosive structural damage to the POTW; obstruct the flow; heat the water inhibiting biological activity in the POTW; contain oil, or produce toxic gases. The 1990 amendments to pretreatment regulations also require the discharger to notify the POTW of any discharge of hazardous waste.

"Categorical" pretreatment regulations are established by the EPA for specific quantities or concentrations of pollutants, focusing on industries and toxic pollutant categories specified in the NRDC consent decree. Generally, the facility must meet the same requirements for pretreatment as for discharge into surface water.

Pretreatment requirements are enforced by the EPA and the states which have the authority to issue such permits. Pretreatment regulations also include reporting and monitoring requirements to ensure compliance.

Effluent Limitations for Publicly Owned Treatment Works

The CWA contains specific requirements applicable to POTWs which are required to obtain an NPDES permit. The majority of POTWs use biological wastewater treatment technology to meet permit limitations. These systems are designed to address organic loads such as BODs found in domestic wastewater, but they are often unable to address nonorganic substances discharged into the system by industrial users. The CWA also requires POTWs to meet regulations designed to address issues specific to these systems. These include requirements for developing and enforcing pretreatment requirements and requirements for managing and disposing of sewage sludge.

A POTW with a total design flow of greater than five million gallons per day, and which receives pollutants from nondomestic sources regulated under the CWA, must establish a pretreatment program. The program must include legal authority to control indirect dischargers, procedures to ensure compliance with the POTW's pretreatment program, funding and adequate personnel to ensure compliance, the ability to limit discharge of pollutants, and procedures to ensure that the POTW will respond to noncompliance. After approval, the pretreatment program conditions are incorporated into the POTW's NPDES permit.

The CWA requires that effluent limitations for POTWs be based on *secondary treatment,* which specifies the minimum level of effluent quality obtainable for conventional pollutants, BOD, TSS, and pH. Primary treatment includes screening, sedimentation, and/or skimming, while secondary treatment mechanisms include biological processes (such as activated sludge), followed by clarification, filter, or oxidation ponds.[11] POTWs are also required to meet more stringent standards to maintain state water quality standards.

An important part of the act is the construction grants program under Title II. This program provided over $50 billion to municipalities and wastewater treatment authorities for matching grants for construction and land acquisition between 1972 and 1990.

PROTECTING WETLANDS

Section 404 Permit Program

Section 404 of the CWA controls dredging or disposing filling material into navigable water. Section 404 extends to all U.S. waters, including **wetlands,** the collective term for marshes, swamps, bogs, and similar areas between open water and dry land.

Wetlands were once considered valueless. Many were drained for use as farmland, industrial facilities, and residential development. More recently, however, studies of ecological processes have illustrated the value of these natural resources. Wetlands help improve water quality, reduce flood and storm damage, and provide essential habitats for many species.

Section 404 authorizes the Army Corps of Engineers to designate disposal areas and issue permits to discharge dredged and fill material. Section 404 permits are not subject to the general permit program under the CWA and differ both substantively and procedurally from the NPDES program.

Jurisdiction of the Section 404 permit program depends on the definition of "waters of the United States." In 1977, the corps issued regulations extending Section 404 jurisdiction to all "wetlands" that are "adjacent" to traditionally navigable waters, all tributaries of traditionally navigable waters, and all interstate waters and adjacent wetlands.

In the following case, a developer challenged the corps' definition that "waters of the United States" under Section 404 of the act includes "adjacent wetlands." The district court had enjoined the developer from filling a portion of his property for development, and the developer appealed. On appeal, the sixth circuit reversed, construing the corps' regulations to exclude from the category of adjacent wetlands, wetlands that were not subject to flooding by adjacent navigable waters at a frequency sufficient to support the growth of aquatic vegetation. In the view of the court of appeals, a broader definition of wetlands might result in the taking of private property without just compensation. The U.S. Supreme Court granted review in the case.

UNITED STATES v. RIVERSIDE BAYVIEW HOMES, INC.
474 U.S. 121 (1985)

JUSTICE WHITE delivered the opinion of the Court.

This case presents the question whether the Clean Water Act, together with certain regulations promulgated under its authority by the Army Corps of Engineers, authorizes the Corps to require landowners to obtain permits from the Corps before discharging fill materials into wetlands adjacent to navigable bodies of water and their tributaries.

I.

The relevant provisions of the Clean Water Act originated in the Federal Water Pollution Control Act Amendments of 1972, and have remained essentially unchanged since that time. Under sections 301 and 502 of the Act, any discharge of dredged or fill materials into "navigable waters"—defined as the "waters of the United States"—is forbidden unless authorized by a permit issued by the Corps of Engineers pursuant to sec. 404. After initially construing the Act to cover only waters navigable in fact, in 1975 the Corps issued interim final regulations redefining "the waters of the United States" to include not only actually navigable waters but also tributaries of such waters, interstate waters and their tributaries, and nonnavigable intrastate waters whose use or misuse could affect interstate commerce. More importantly for present purposes, the Corps construed the Act to cover all "freshwater wetlands" that were adjacent to other covered waters. A "freshwater wetland" was defined as an area that is "periodically inundated" and is "normally characterized by the prevalence of vegetation that requires saturated soil conditions for growth and reproduction." In 1977, the Corps redefined its definition of wetlands . . . [to] read as follows:

> "The term "wetlands" means those areas that are inundated or saturated by surface or ground water at a frequency and duration sufficient to support, and that under normal circumstances do support, a prevalence of vegetation typically adapted for life in saturated soil conditions. Wetlands generally include swamps, marshes, bogs and similar areas."

In 1982, the 1977 regulations were replaced by substantively identical regulations that remain in force today.

Respondent Riverside Bayview Homes, Inc. (hereafter respondent) owns 80 acres of low-lying, marshy land near the shores of Lake St. Clair in Macomb County, Michigan. In 1976, respondent began to place fill materials on its property as part of its preparations for construction of a housing development. The Corps of Engineers, believing that the property was an "adjacent wetland" under the 1975 regulation defining "waters of the United States," filed suit . . . seeking to enjoin respondent from filling the property without permission of the Corps.

[*In a portion of the opinion not printed here, the Court first concluded that the possibility that application of the regulatory program might in some instances result in the taking of property was no justification for narrowly construing the act to curtail the program. The Supreme Court expressly recognized in* Bayview Homes, *that wetlands designation may in some cases give rise to a "takings" claim if it renders the property unsuitable for development. The "takings" issue is discussed in Chapter 6.*]

***

An agency's construction of a statute it is charged with enforcing is entitled to deference if it is reasonable and not in conflict with the expressed intent of Congress. . . . Accordingly, our review is limited to the question whether it is reasonable, in light of the language, policies, and legislative history of the Act for the Corps to exercise jurisdiction over wetlands adjacent to but not regularly flooded by rivers, streams, and other hydrographic features more conventionally identifiable as "waters."

On a purely linguistic level, it may appear unreasonable to classify "lands," wet or otherwise, as "waters." Such a simplistic response, however, does justice neither to the problem faced by the Corps in defining the scope of its authority under section 404(a) nor to the realities of the problem of water pollution that the Clean Water Act was intended to combat. In determining the limits of its power to regulate discharges under the Act, the Corps must necessarily choose some point at which water ends and land begins. Our common experience tells us that this is often no easy task: the transition from water to solid ground is not necessarily or even typically an abrupt one. Rather, between open waters and dry land may lie shallows, marshes, mudflats, swamps, bogs—in short, a huge array of areas that are not wholly aquatic but nevertheless fall far short of being dry land. Where on this continuum to find the limit of "waters" is far from obvious.

Faced with such a problem of defining the bounds of its regulatory authority, an agency may appropriately look to the legislative history and underlying policies of its statutory grants of authority. Neither of these sources provides unambiguous guidance for the Corps in this case, but together they do support the reasonableness of the Corps' approach of defining adjacent wetlands as "waters" within the meaning of section 404(a). Section 404 originated as part of the Federal Water Pollution Control Act Amendments of 1972, which constituted a comprehensive legislative attempt "to restore and maintain the chemical, physical, and biological integrity of the Nation's waters." This objective incorporated a broad, systemic view of the goal of maintaining and improving water quality: as the House Report on the legislation put it, "the word 'integrity' . . . refers to a condition in which the natural structure and function of ecosystems is maintained. Protection of aquatic ecosystems, Congress recognized, demanded broad federal authority to control pollution, for "[w]ater moves in hydrologic cycles and it is essential that discharge of pollutants be controlled at the source."

In keeping with these views, Congress chose to define the waters covered by the Act broadly. Although the Act prohibits discharges into "navigable waters," the Act's definition of "navigable waters" as "the waters of the United States" makes it clear that the term "navigable" as used in the Act is of limited import. In adopting this definition of "navigable waters," Congress evidently intended to repudiate limits that had been placed on federal regulation by earlier water pollution control statutes and to exercise its powers under the [C]ommerce Clause to regulate at least some waters that would not be deemed "navigable" under the classical understanding of that term.

Of course, it is one thing to recognize that Congress intended to allow regulation of waters that might not satisfy traditional tests of navigability; it is another to assert that Congress intended to abandon traditional notions of "waters" and include in that term "wetlands" as well. Nonetheless, the evident breadth of congressional concern for protection of water quality and aquatic ecosystems suggests that it is reasonable for the Corps to interpret the term "waters" to encompass wetlands adjacent to waters as more conventionally defined. . . .

We cannot say that the Corps' conclusion that adjacent wetlands are inseparably bound up with the "waters" of the United States—based as it is on the Corps' and EPA's technical expertise—is unreasonable. In view of the breadth of the federal regulatory authority contemplated by the Act itself and the inherent difficulties of defining precise bounds to regulable waters, the Corps' ecological judgment about the relationship between waters and their adjacent wetlands provides an adequate basis for a legal judgment that adjacent wetlands may be defined as waters under the Act. . . .

***

We are thus persuaded that the language, policies, and history of the Clean Water Act compel a finding that the Corps has acted reasonably in interpreting the Act to require permits for the discharge of fill material into wetlands adjacent to the "waters of the United States." The regulation in which the Corps has embodied this interpretation by its terms includes the wetlands on respondent's property within the class of waters that may not be filled without a permit; and, as we have seen, there is no reason to interpret the regulation more narrowly than its terms would indicate. Accordingly, the judgment of the Court of Appeals is Reversed.

Questions and Comments for Discussion

1. Although the Supreme Court upheld the corps' definition of wetlands in this case, property owners continue to challenge wetlands designation *as applied*—that is, to challenge the factual determination that property constitutes a wetlands in a given case. In *Hoffman Homes, Inc. v. EPA,* 999 F.2d 256 (7th Cir. 1993), a developer petitioned for review of an EPA order imposing a penalty for discharging dredged or fill material into an intrastate wetland. The Court found that evidence did not support the EPA's conclusion that the water partially filled by the developer had an effect on interstate commerce, and therefore vacated the EPA's order. The EPA's chief judicial officer had ruled in that case that the regulation extended to the area (Area A). The agency's finding was based on the conclusion that Area A, before being filled, was a suitable or potential habitat for migratory birds. The Court found that the chief judicial officers finding was not supported by "substantial evidence."

2. As *Hoffman Homes* suggests, the corps regulates intrastate waters or isolated waters and their adjacent wetlands if their use, degradation, or destruction *could affect* interstate or foreign commerce. Activities affecting interstate commerce include use of water by interstate or foreign travelers for recreational purposes, waters from which fish or shellfish are taken and later sold in interstate commerce, and waters that are used or could be used for industrial purposes in interstate commerce. Under corps and EPA policy, the actual or possible use of wetlands by migratory birds is a sufficient nexus to interstate commerce to support jurisdiction, although *Hoffman Homes* implies that something more than *possible* use may be necessary to support Section 404 jurisdiction.

In the 1977 amendments to the act, Congress authorized the states to establish a permit program for dredge and fill activities in non-navigable waters. The amendments also authorized the corps (or the state with an approved program) to issue "general" permits for certain activities which have minimal adverse affects, designed to reduce the regulatory burden for activities involving incidental dredge or fill work. Section 404(f) provides for exemptions from the regulation if the operator avoids specific effects on navigable waters.

In 1989, the corps and EPA signed a Memorandum of Agreement endorsing a "no net loss" policy for the nation's wetlands. Under the memorandum, the corps is to avoid adverse impacts in permit decisions whenever possible and is required to choose the least environmentally damaging alternative. Off-site mitigation is to be used as a last resort. In November 1992, the oil industry obtained a clarification that the policy does not apply to wetlands in Alaska. Under the memorandum, the EPA and corps are developing guidelines for establishing and operating a wetlands mitigation bank.

Mitigation policy under the memorandum endorses a national goal of no overall net loss of the nation's remaining wetlands base. In most cases, a minimum of one-to-one acreage replacement of wetlands is required. The concept of *mitigation banking* is a controversial one, and likely to be the focus of some debate during reauthorization hearings on the CWA.

Wetlands designation has become an important issue for many in the environmental and business communities for ecological, economic, and political reasons. Perhaps no issue other than habitat protection more clearly questions the extent to which private property owners should be entitled to use and develop their property if such development results in harm to the environment.

Other Government Mechanisms for Wetlands Protection

Governmental wetlands protection other than regulation includes land acquisition and utilizing economic incentives and disincentives. Both government and private conservation organizations can purchase wetlands or easements for the purpose of establishing conservation areas. Government can also provide incentives to private industries and landowners who sell or donate wetlands to government agencies or qualified conservation organizations as a charitable contribution (with a corresponding tax deduction). Congress has also passed laws that create economic disincentives to wetland destruction. The "Swampbuster" provision of the Food Security Act of 1985 attempts to discourage further conversion of wetlands to farm land by eliminating farm program benefits for those who produce crops on wetlands converted after December 1985.

Numerous states have also enacted laws to protect wetlands, and some have local wetlands protection ordinances. In addition, most coastal states protect coastal wetlands under state statute.

NONPOINT SOURCE POLLUTION

The NPDES permit system, which is a cornerstone of the CWA, only addresses point source pollution. In fact, a substantial source of pollution of the nation's waterways is a result of nonpoint source pollution. **Nonpoint source pollution** is caused by diffuse sources normally associated with agricultural, silvicultural, and urban runoff, precipitation, atmospheric deposition, or percolation. As in the *Southview Farm* case discussed earlier, conveyance of runoff through a mechanism such as a pipe or a trench may be treated as a point source.

Nonpoint source pollution is most easily addressed through land use planning. This approach was adopted by the 1972 CWA amendments which established a planning and regulatory program for controlling nonpoint source pollution. Under this section, states must identify and address nonpoint source pollution through an area-wide planning process. Unfortunately, this politically unpopular program has not met with great success.

In 1987, Congress amended the act to further address the problem, authorizing funding for nonpoint source pollution programs and requiring states to prepare a management program for controlling it. States must also identify water bodies which fail to meet standards for toxic pollutants. Congress also created the voluntary *National Estuary Program,* under which states plan and implement additional controls on sources of pollutants to estuaries. More recently, in the 1996 Farm Bill, Congress established an Environmental Quality Incentives Program to improve water quality and address some environmental issues posed by agricultural production.

Stormwater Discharge

The question of how and when to regulate stormwater runoff is a difficult one. Most runoff cannot be controlled easily or monitored using point source or "end of pipe" technology. On the other hand, in many instances stormwater runoff is discharged through storm sewers or other conveyances, and thus can be considered a point source. The 1987 CWA amendments required the EPA to regulate five categories of municipal or stormwater discharges. These include discharges which have NPDES permits (as of February 1987), discharges associated with industrial activity, discharges from municipal storm sewers meeting criteria under the act, and other discharges that "contribute to a violation of a water quality standard or [are] a significant contributor of pollutants to waters of the United States."[12]

Stormwater regulations do not apply to all discharges by industry, only those associated with industrial activity. The EPA defines stormwater to include stormwater runoff, snow melt runoff, and surface runoff and drainage. Agricultural stormwater discharges are specifically excluded by statute.

OIL AND HAZARDOUS SUBSTANCES SPILLS

Section 311 of the CWA addresses water pollutant discharges resulting from accidental releases and spills. This section addresses spill planning and prevention, reporting responsibilities, and response authorities. Discharges in compliance with an NPDES permit are not considered spills for purposes of this section. Releases of hazardous substances into water are also addressed under CERCLA, which is examined in more detail in Chapter 13.

The CWA specifically prohibits the discharge of oil or hazardous substances into or upon *designated waters,* defined to include navigable waters, adjoining shorelines, the contiguous zone, and waters beyond the contiguous zone containing or supporting natural resources. Section 311 requires the person in charge of the vessel or facility to report the discharge to the appropriate agency as soon as he has knowledge of the spill. Reports filed according to this provision cannot be the basis for any criminal action against the person reporting (see, for example, the prosecution of Captain Hazelwood, captain of the *Exxon Valdez,* discussed in Chapter 15).

The Oil Pollution Act (OPA) was adopted in 1990 in response to the damage caused by the *Exxon Valdez* oil spill in Alaska. Among other things, the OPA expanded the law's requirements for prevention and preparedness requirements, imposed legal liability on shippers and oil companies for the cost of spills, and established a liability trust fund. The law also extensively amended Section 311 of the CWA.

OPA authorizes the president to arrange for the removal of the actual or threatened discharge of oil or a hazardous substance and requires such removal to be done in accordance with the *National Contingency Plan* (established by the EPA under CERCLA.) The owner and operator is liable for the actual costs of removal, but Section 311 limits that liability based on the type of vessel or facility involved.

The CWA as amended also provides for the development and implementation of **spill prevention, control and countermeasure plans** (SPCC) for owners and operators of nontransportation-related onshore facilities that store in excess of 1,320 gallons of oil above ground or 42,000 gallons below ground. The plan must describe previous spills and response and prevention measures to be taken in future spills. Containment equipment and structures and other physical plant requirements may be included.

OCEAN DUMPING

Except for oil spills and ocean outfalls, ocean dumping is regulated under the **Marine Protection, Research, and Sanctuaries Act** (MPRSA) of 1972.[13] EPA regulations prohibit the issuance of a permit for ocean discharge unless the discharge will not cause unreasonable degradation of the environment. The MPRSA imposes conditions on the issuance of ocean dumping permits and prohibits the dumping of radiological, chemical, and biological warfare agents or high-level radioactive waste. It also specifically prohibits the dumping of sewage sludge and industrial wastes after 1991, except in emergencies as defined by the act. The secretary of the Army may issue permits for dumping of dredged material into ocean waters if findings made are similar to those required of the EPA. Ocean incineration is considered ocean dumping and consequently requires a permit.

Enforcement of the Clean Water Act

The 1987 amendments to the CWA substantially strengthened criminal penalty provisions, and the 1990 OPA extended those penalties to oil and hazardous waste spills. Negligent and "knowing" violations are subject to criminal penalties, including fines and imprisonment. The law created the offense of "knowing endangerment," which imposes substantial fines and imprisonment on a person who knowingly violates a permit requirement and knowingly places another person in imminent danger of death or serious bodily injury as a result. The law also strengthened penalties for filing false reports or tampering with any monitoring device or method. Criminal and civil liability enforcement issues under environmental laws in general are examined in Chapter 14.

THE SAFE DRINKING WATER ACT

The Safe Drinking Water Act (SDWA) was passed by Congress in 1974 and substantially amended in 1986, and again in 1996. The purpose of the act is to protect the nation's drinking water supply. Its goals are two-fold: first, to ensure that tap water is fit to drink, and second, to prevent the contamination of groundwater. Other laws which play a role in protecting the quality of drinking water include the Resource Conservation and Recovery Act (RCRA), and the Comprehensive Environmental Response, Compensation and Liability Act (CERCLA) which are designed to help prevent and clean up groundwater contamination. Drinking water standards established under SDWA are significant standards in RCRA and CERCLA actions ordering cleanup of groundwater contamination.

The act applies to public water systems (PWS). The law defines a "public water system" as any system "for the provision of piped water for human consumption," with at least fifteen service connections or which serves at least twenty-five individuals and does not have to be publicly owned. "Water for human consumption" includes not only drinking water but also water for bathing and showering, cooking and dishwashing, and maintaining oral hygiene.

There are two types of PWSs: community and noncommunity. The distinction is based on the assumption that systems serving residential populations should be designed to protect against long-term adverse effects of chronic exposure to contaminants. SDWA requires the EPA to establish national primary and secondary drinking water regulations for particular contaminants. Primary drinking water standards are designed to protect against adverse health effects, while secondary standards address contaminants that may adversely affect the odor or appearance of water. Primary standards are based on **maximum contaminant level goals** (MCLG). Once that standard is set, the EPA must specify a **maximum contaminant level** (MCL) for drinking water that is as close as feasible to the MCLG. For some contaminants like lead, the MCL measured at the water source will not protect public health, because levels of lead often depend more on the condition of indoor plumbing than on the lead content of the water source. In these circumstances, the EPA has prescribed treatment techniques (such as additives) to control lead in drinking water. The SDWA also requires any pipe, solder, or flux used in installation or repairs to be lead free. The SDWA specifically addresses lead hazards by requiring states to test for lead contamination in their schools' drinking water.

The SDWA also requires the EPA to establish and regulate state underground injection programs. The EPA estimates that there are almost 400,000 injection wells subject to underground injection control (UIC) requirements.[14] This program most affects wells used for the disposal of hazardous waste, and the injection or reinjection of fluids to aid in extracting certain minerals in oil and gas production.

The act also protects aquifers that are the sole or principal source of drinking water. Most of New Jersey, all of Staten Island, Cape Cod and Nantucket Island are examples of designated sole-source aquifers (SSAs.) The law bars federal assistance for projects which might contaminate an SSA. Local governments can seek federal assistance in designing "comprehensive management plans" for protection of an aquifer.

The SDWA also encourages states to establish programs to protect wellhead areas, surrounding waters, wells or well fields, and it establishes minimum requirements and authorizes federal assistance for such programs.

1996 Amendments

The 1996 amendments to the SDWA seek to improve water quality by giving regulators more flexibility in monitoring of contaminants and creating a grant and loan fund to pay for water system improvements. The law contains a "right to know" provision, under which large water systems will be required to provide customers with annual reports on water contaminants and the health effects of those contaminants.

The law requires the EPA to use risk assessment and cost-benefit analysis in setting new standards for contaminants, but the analysis cannot be used to weaken existing standards or to set standards for certain contaminants.

SUMMARY AND DISCUSSION

In a 1992 hearing before the Senate Committee on the Environment and Public Works, various speakers assessed the CWA on its twentieth anniversary. Representatives of environmental groups, the Chemical Manufacturers Association, and state and federal officials pointed out the progress made in the past twenty years in reducing the amount of pollution released into the nation's waters. According to EPA estimates, the amount of key pollutants in sewage had been reduced by half, and the release of toxic industrial pollutants had been reduced by about one billion pounds per year.

Despite the successes of the program, environmentalists continue to argue that there is still much work to be done to address the problems of waste water and toxic pollutant discharges, and to reduce the amount of water pollution caused by runoff from farms, factories, and city streets.

Industry spokespersons, while proud of contributions from industries to the success of the regulatory program, point out that the successes have not come cheaply. The chemical industry, for example, estimates that the additional costs of EPA compliance approached $6 billion over the decade between 1987 and 1997. Many in industry urge that sounder scientific and risk assessment principles be utilized, and they argue that additional controls for point source pollution would be very expensive. Those with this view urge Congress to focus on the significant remaining sources of water quality impairment, such as agricultural and urban runoff, rather than on imposing increasingly more stringent point source limitations on industry.

As Congress considers reauthorization of the CWA, among the significant issues are regulatory reform, which would impose upon the EPA additional procedural rulemaking requirements, and the call for changes to clarify compensable regulatory "takings" as may occur in wetlands disputes. It remains to be seen whether Congress, in its zeal for regulatory reform, will substantially rewrite the CWA.

Much of the criticism of the CWA, like that of the Clean Air Act discussed in the previous chapter, focuses on the effectiveness of a "command-and-control" approach to pollution control, the relative effectiveness of harm-based and technology-based approaches, and the economic implications of current water and air pollution control policy. Today's CWA is predominantly a technology-based command-and-control program.

While there is little doubt that the command-and-control approach adopted by the Clean Air and Clean Water acts has been successful in improving the quality of the nation's air and water, there are also substantial policy concerns about the command-and-control approach. This chapter concludes with a critique of command-and-control regulation in general.

From "Reflexive Environmental Law" By Eric W. Orts

Environmental regulation remains relatively new. The first major environmental statutes adopted in the early 1970s in the United States and Europe were command-and-control. This form of regulation is top-down. It seeks to control pollution in one of two ways. First, the government can establish performance standards for polluters, commonly enforced through a system of permits. Issued through a bureaucratic process, pollution permits allow industrial firms and other identifiable sources to continue emitting pollutants, but only at regulated rates. Pollution in excess of the technical limits specified in the permits is prohibited.

Reprinted by special permission of Northwestern University School of Law, *Northwestern University Law Review,* Volume 83, Issue 1, pp. 1235–1240 (1995).

Second, the government can require uniform technology-based controls for certain types of activities that cause pollution. Examples include requiring catalytic converters on automobiles and requiring installation of "best available technologies" for sources of air or water pollution. Violations of both performance-based and technology-based command-and-control regulations are remedied by civil fines and, increasingly, criminal prosecutions.

Command-and-control approaches to environmental regulation have been heavily criticized. Economic studies have repeatedly demonstrated that command-and-control methods are often wildly inefficient and even "irrational." Although most critics recognize that command-and-control has achieved significant success in some cases, they emphasize that it is a blunt instrument for achieving environ-

From "Reflexive Environmental Law" by Eric W. Orts (continued)

mental goals. The command-and-control method often sets environmental policy goals without fully considering the economic costs involved. It also often works ineffectively. Even at great cost, command-and-control often fails to achieve the environmental results hoped for.

Because command-and-control relies heavily on active governmental oversight, its effectiveness depends also on the enthusiasm and competence of regulators. Administrations less interested in the goals of environmental policy than other objectives—such as economic growth—can relax command-and-control regulations. For example, many believe that the Reagan and Bush administrations accomplished an environmental slow-down for macroeconomic purposes. Most notorious was the regulation of the regulators accomplished by former Vice President Quayle's Council on Competitiveness. The Council routinely and secretly pruned environmental regulations it judged to have deleterious effects on economic growth.

Two other problems with command-and-control regulation are perennial. First, administrative agencies responsible for issuing regulations are vulnerable to "capture" by the very industries they are supposed to regulate. Second, administrative bureaucracy betrays a tendency to build itself up independently and to perpetuate itself through the self-seeking behavior of employee-bureaucrats—or what economists call "rent-seeking." The problem of capture raises questions about the fairness and effectiveness of command-and-control. . . . The very fact of an administrative "command center" presents an obvious moral hazard: those commanded may improperly attempt to influence the commands given. The

problem of bureaucratic rent-seeking follows whenever a centralized power is set up. Those given power may work to hinder sound public policy. Rather than advancing the interests of society-at-large, bureaucrats may prefer to help themselves. Administrative capture and bureaucratic rent-seeking thus supply another level of criticism of command-and-control.

Command-and-control regulations have also been criticized as too static. Statutes enacted at a particular time in history are limited by the available knowledge of the time, especially scientific and technical knowledge. Because command-and-control statutes cannot "learn" easily from changing circumstances and developing knowledge, they often fall short of achieving their objectives in a rapidly changing world. Experience with automobile emissions control under the Clean Air Act in the past twenty years provides a good example. Strict technology-forcing legislation mandated significantly improved emission controls for new cars. But vehicle miles traveled (VMT) doubled during the same time period due to increasing suburbanization, the advent of hour-long commuting habits, and the appearance of many more cars on the road. Rapidly increasing VMT more than offset the gains of newer, cleaner vehicles replacing older, dirtier ones. Technological controls on new automobiles prevented the current air pollution problem from being much worse, but it failed to account for the "behavioral treadmill" of automobile use that undermined the basic strategy. . . .

Yet another difficulty with command-and-control regulation is *environmental juridification.* The word "juridification" means "proliferation of law." It was

From "Reflexive Environmental Law" by Eric W. Orts (continued)

coined to describe modern regulatory approaches to industrial labor organizations, and the word was first used in the context of labor, corporate, antitrust, and welfare law. However, juridification applies more broadly to any area of social life that the regulation impulse of modern states deems worthy of "controlling" through enactment of highly technical and specific laws. Increasingly, juridification extends to the natural environment, a phenomenon some commentators refer to ironically as "legal pollution."

The amount of environmental law and regulation in the United States alone is staggering. Not counting state statutes and common law, there are over one hundred separate environmental statues at the federal level. The texts of seven major federal environmental statutes run to several thousand pages. Accompanying regulations stretch for several feet on the library shelf. The myriad provisions of the Clean Air Act alone, according to Chief Justice Rehnquist, "virtually swim before one's eyes." Another judge describes the statute as "prolix" and "larded with definitions." It is fair to say that no single individual can possibly "know" all of the environmental law out there, even if one's attention is limited only to United States Law. . . .

Environmental juridification significantly increases the burden of compliance for businesses. By the year 2000, EPA estimates that expenditures made in the United States under environmental programs to control pollution will amount to approximately *two percent* of GNP. Moreover, a recent survey of corporate general counsels found that less than a third of them believed fully complying with applicable environmental laws was even possible. The burden becomes even greater for many multinational businesses when the laws of several countries, as well as international environmental law, are added to the equation.

Environmental juridification points to a critical weakness of the command-and-control approach. There are cognitive limits to protecting the environment through detailed orders. As new laws are passed to regulate critical areas and old laws are revised to close or open loopholes, the legal system's capacity actually to process the material becomes impaired. Eventually, traditional command-and-control regulation breaks down under its own weight.

Questions and Comments for Discussion

Despite this author's criticisms of "command-and-control" regulation, many regard portions of the Clean Water and Clean Air acts to be the most effective of federal environmental statutes. Former EPA Administrator William Ruckelshaus, for example, believes that the regulation of pollution from mobile sources—vehicles—in the CAA has been a major success, and that municipal sewage treatment controls in the CWA have greatly improved the water quality in the United States. (Statement made before the Senate Environment and Public Works Committee, July 16, 1993.) What are the arguments in defense of command-and-control legislation? What short-comings do you recognize in this approach to environmental regulation?

An alternative to command-and-control regulation is market-based environmental regulation. This includes taxes or charges on environmentally harmful regulations and the concept of tradeable pollution rights as exemplified by the acid rain permit trading program under the Clean Air Act. There are problems with this approach: In some cases it would be prohibitively expensive to set up a permit market system to address some environmental problems affecting large numbers of people—for example, automobile pollution. Some strongly object to the idea of "licensing" pollution at all, as the effects on human health and the environment may be unclear.

GLOSSARY

BAT—Best available technology economically achievable.

BCT—Best conventional pollutant control technology.

BPT—Best practicable control technology.

CAFO—Concentrated animal feeding operation, treated as a "point source" under EPA CWA regulations.

FWPCA—Federal Water Pollution Control Act, which as amended in 1972, became known as the Clean Water Act.

MCL—Maximum contaminant level for drinking water set as close as feasible to the MCLG.

MCLG—Maximum contaminant level goals for contaminants under the Safe Drinking Water Act.

MPRSA—Marine Protection, Research, and Sanctuaries Act of 1972.

Navigable waters—Under the CWA, "waters of the United States, including the territorial seas."

Nonpoint source pollution—Water pollution resulting from runoff, precipitation, atmospheric deposition, or percolation.

NPDES—National Pollutant Discharge Elimination System under the CWA.

OPA—The Oil Pollution Act of 1990.

Person—Under the CWA, an individual, corporation, partnership, association, state, municipality, commission, or political subdivision of a state, or any interstate body.

Point source—Under the CWA, "any discernible, confined and discrete conveyance . . . from which pollutants are or may be discharged." The term does not include agricultural stormwater discharges and return flows from irrigated agriculture.

Pollutant—Under the CWA, "dredged spoil, solid waste, incinerator residue, sewage, garbage, sewage sludge, munitions, chemical wastes, biological materials, radioactive materials (except those regulated under the Atomic Energy Act of 1954), heat, wrecked or discarded equipment, rock, sand, cellar dirt, and industrial, municipal, and agricultural waste discharged into water."

POTW—Publicly owned treatment works.

Pretreatment standards—Standards for treating industrial discharges into a publicly owned treatment works (POTW).

Refuse Act—33 U.S.C. 407 makes it unlawful to throw, discharge, or deposit any refuse matter, other than that flowing from streets and sewers and passing into a liquid state, into navigable waters.

SDWA—Safe Drinking Water Act of 1974, and amended in 1986.

SPCC plans—Spill Prevention, Control and Countermeasure plans for owners and operators of non-transportation-related onshore facilities storing in excess of 1320 gallons of oil above ground or 42,000 gallons below ground.

Wetlands—A collective term for marshes, swamps, bogs, and similar areas where land meets water.

CASES FOR DISCUSSION

1.   A county passed an ordinance completely banning land application of sewage sludge as a method of sludge disposal. A group of farmers challenged the ordinance on the basis that it was pre-empted by the CWA and that it conflicted with the act. Is the ordinance enforceable? *Welch v. Rappahannock County Board of Supervisors,* 860 F. Supp. 328 (W.D. Va. 1994).

2.   A district court held that a farmer's clearing and draining of a thirty-acre wetland constituted "normal farming activities" exempt under Section 404 of the CWA. The district court held that the farmer's activities constituted part of an "established farming operation," and thus were exempt as normal farming activities. Is the exemption for farming activities available if it is necessary to modify the hydrological regime at the site to make it suitable for farming? *U.S. v. Brace,* 41 F.3d 117 (3d Cir. 1994).

3.   Two individuals were convicted of discharging dirt and sand on the wetlands area of their property in violation of the CWA. They were each sentenced to twenty-one-month prison terms and ordered to pay $5,250 fines and comply with a site restoration plan. After losing on direct appeal, the men raised the claim that Congress unconstitutionally delegated to the U.S. Army Corps of Engineers its duty to define "waters of the United States." Did the FWPCA unconstitutionally delegate authority to the corps by allowing the agency to define "waters of the United States?" *Mills v. United States,* 36 F.3d 1052 (11th Cir. 1994).

4.   May the State of Washington include minimum stream flow requirements intended to protect migrating salmon and trout in a hydroelectric project's certification under the general permitting sections of the CWA insofar as necessary to enforce state water quality standards adopted under authority of the act? *PUD No. 1 of Jefferson County v. Washington Dept. of Ecology,* 114 S.Ct. 1900 (1994).

5.   The EPA vetoed a FWPCA Section 404 permit issued by the U.S. Army Corps of Engineers for the construction of a dam and reservoir. The EPA based its veto solely on a finding of the "unacceptable environmental effects" of the project. Does the EPA need to consider the affected area's need for water in reaching its decision, or may it veto the project solely on the basis of unacceptable environmental effects? *James City County v. U.S. EPA,* 12 F.3d 1330 (4th Cir. 1993).

6.   Does the Pueblo Native American tribe have authority as a state under the CWA to develop water quality standards that are more stringent than federal standards for part of the Rio Grande River? *City of Albuquerque v. Browner,* 865 F. Supp. 733 (D.N.M. 1994).

9.   Is an artificial retention pond that discharges only to groundwater and is unconnected to any navigable water subject to the requirements of the CWA? Plaintiffs argued that the possibility that pollutants might seep into groundwater leading to navigable waters was sufficient to subject it to CWA claims in the suit. *Oconomowoc Lake, Wis. v. Dayton Hudson Corp.,* 24 F.3d 962 (7th Cir. 1994).

ENDNOTES

1. 33 U.S.C.A § 1362 (6).

2. 862 F. Supp. 73, (S.D.N.Y. 1994).

3. *Weinberger v. Romero-Barcelo,* 456 U.S. 305 (1982).

4. *National Wildlife Fed'n v. Consumers Power Co.,* 675 F. Supp. 989 (W.D. Mich. 1987) rev'd on other grounds, 862 F.2d 580 (6th Cir. 1988).

5. 33 U.S.C.A. § 1362 (14).

6. 40 C.F.R. § 122.2.

7. 599 F.2d 368 (10th Cir. 1979).

8. Zygmunt Plater, Robert Abrams, William Goldfarb, *Environmental Law and Policy: Nature, Law, and Society* at 856 (1992).

9. *Ibid.,* 846.

10. 8 E.R.C. 2120 (D.D.C. 1976), 6 Envtl. L. Rep. 20588 (DC 1976), modified sub nom. *NRDC v. Castle,* 12 E.R.C. 1833 (D.D.C. 1969).

11. Parthenia B. Evans, *Clean Water Act Handbook* at 109 (Sonreel, American Bar Assoc., 1994).

12. 33 U.S.C.A. § 1342 (2).

13. 33 U.S.C. § 1401 *et seq.*

14. Environmental Law Handbook at 259 (Government Institutes, Inc., 1993).

12

REGULATING TOXIC SUBSTANCES AND PESTICIDES

INTRODUCTION

The production and use of chemicals in manufacturing and agricultural industries in the United States has expanded dramatically since the last part of the twentieth century, and chemicals, especially man-made chemicals, have made important contributions to improvements in industrial and consumer materials and agricultural productivity. However, as the development and use of man-made chemicals has increased, people have become increasingly concerned about the environmental and human health risks associated with pesticides and other synthetic and natural chemical substances. This chapter examines federal laws regulating the manufacture and sale of toxic chemicals and pesticides. Major federal laws which address these concerns are the Toxic Substances Control Act (TSCA), the Federal Insecticide, Fungicide, and Rodenticide Act (FIFRA), and the Federal Food, Drug, and Cosmetic Act (FFDCA), as amended by the Food Quality Protection Act of 1996.

In 1972, Congress established the basic framework of the **Federal Insecticide, Fungicide, and Rodenticide Act** (FIFRA) through major amendments to the existing act. FIFRA gives the EPA the authority to regulate the use and safety of pesticides, which includes insecticides, rodenticides, and herbicides, produced and used in the United States.

The EPA has the authority to set tolerance levels for pesticide residues in food under the **Federal Food, Drug, and Cosmetic Act** (FFDCA). This function was transferred to the EPA from the Food and Drug Administration (FDA) when the agency was established in 1970. The *Food Quality Protection Act of 1996* (P.L. 104-170) amended both the FFDCA and FIFRA to provide a more comprehensive and coordinated protective regulatory scheme for pesticides.

The **Toxic Substances Control Act** (TSCA) was adopted in 1976 to fill a void left by other environmental statutes and regulations. Unlike other federal laws regulating chemical pollutants which have already entered the environment, TSCA provides the EPA the authority to review and regulate the manufacture, use, and distribution of chemical substances *before* they are introduced into commerce.

Other pollution laws adopted in the 1970s, especially the Clean Air Act and the Federal Water Pollution Control Act (Clean Water Act), are also chemical control laws. In addressing such air and water toxicants through technology-based "command-and-control" legislation, these federal anti-pollution laws prohibit or severely limit the use or discharge of certain chemicals and toxic substances used in the industrial process, especially affecting the manufacturing processes of the steel, auto, and chemical industries.

The Clean Air and Clean Water acts require regulatory decisions to be based upon technological availability or margins of safety, and they limit agency consideration of economic factors in setting regulatory policy. TSCA and FIFRA differ from the Clean Air and Clean Water acts in that they adopt a risk-cost balancing approach to the regulation and use of toxic substances. TSCA and FIFRA also differ from these laws because they address the way chemicals and pesticide products are manufactured and used, rather than focusing primarily on the residual problems to human health and the environment which result from their use.

THE FEDERAL INSECTICIDE, FUNGICIDE, AND RODENTICIDE ACT (FIFRA)

Our ability to understand the relative costs and benefits of pesticide use is complicated by our lack of understanding of the environmental side effects and cost to human health of the widespread use of chemicals. The issue of pesticides is a particularly environmentally sensitive one because it directly affects the safety of the human food supply and the health of agricultural workers. Alarms over the use of the pesticide Alar on apples and concerns in California about spraying pesticides to eradicate the medfly, for example, illustrate how public attention can become riveted on such issues.

The issue of chemical pesticides was one of the earliest toxic chemical problems to gain widespread public attention. In 1962, Rachel Carson's *Silent Spring* sparked enormous public concern about the potential environmental and health effects of chemical pesticides. In her book, Carson contended that humans "have allowed these chemicals to be used with little or no advance investigation of their effect on soil, water, wildlife, and man himself," and, according to Carson, "[F]uture generations are unlikely to condone our lack of prudent concern for the integrity of the natural world that supports all life."[1]

The first pesticide law, adopted in 1910, was a labeling law which prohibited the manufacture of insecticides or fungicides which were adulterated or misbranded. In 1947, Congress enacted the original version of FIFRA, which was still primarily a labeling statute. In 1954, Congress gave the FDA the authority to establish pesticide residue tolerances for food and animal feed. In 1964, FIFRA was amended to strengthen the act, but in practice cancellation of pesticide registration was seldom invoked, and there were no sanctions for a consumer's application of chemicals.

Amid growing concern about the effects of pesticides and other chemicals, Congress adopted major amendments to FIFRA in 1972 which established the basic structure of the present law. FIFRA has since been amended in 1975, 1978, 1980, 1988, and 1996. Under FIFRA, the EPA has expanded authority over the use of pesticides and more flexibility in controlling their use. This law requires that all pesticides be registered with the EPA before shipment, delivery, or sale in the United States can be made. Before registering a pesticide under FIFRA, the EPA must evaluate the risks to the environment.

FIFRA: An Overview

FIFRA has the following purposes:

1. *Section 3* establishes a *registration system* by which the EPA evaluates the risks posed by pesticides. Under this system, pesticides are also *classified and certified for specific uses* in order to control exposure.
2. *Section 6* permits the EPA to *suspend, cancel, or restrict* pesticides which pose a risk to the environment.
3. *Sections 12, 14, and 16* authorize the EPA to enforce the requirements of FIFRA through inspections, labeling notices, and regulations by state authorities.

A pesticide cannot be legally shipped or sold in the United States unless it is registered under the act. The EPA can refuse to register a pesticide determined to be unreasonably hazardous. The EPA can also impose conditions or restrictions to control or reduce the hazard, and it may only permit the use of toxic or carcinogenic pesticides under certain conditions. FIFRA, like TSCA, authorizes the EPA to require manufacturers to submit test data that will be used to determine whether to register a particular pesticide. This is an important provision because testing of a new active ingredient in a pesticide can cost millions of dollars.

Cost-Benefit Analysis under FIFRA

Under the system established by FIFRA, the EPA may not approve a pesticide's introduction into commerce unless the EPA administrator finds that the pesticide will not generally cause *unreasonable adverse effects* on the environment. Unreasonable adverse effects include "any unreasonable risk to man or the environment, taking into account the economic, social, and environmental costs and benefits of the use of any pesticide."[2] Thus, FIFRA, like TSCA, requires the EPA not only to consider the risks posed by a pesticide, but also its economic, social, health, and environmental benefits.

Pesticide Registration

A company that wants to manufacture, formulate, import, or distribute a pesticide in the United States must *register* it under Section 3 of FIFRA. This requirement applies to newly discovered chemicals and to new combinations or mixtures of already registered pesticides. In order to register a new pesticide, the registrant must submit the complete formula, a proposed label, and a description of the tests made and the results of those tests.

The administrator must approve the registration if the following requirements are met:

1. Its composition is such to warrant the proposed claim for it
2. Its labeling and other materials comply with the requirements of the act
3. It will perform its intended function without unreasonable adverse effects on the environment
4. When used in accordance with widespread and commonly recognized practice, it will not generally cause unreasonable adverse effects on the environment

The phrase *unreasonable adverse effects on the environment* was added in 1972 and also appears in the language of Section 6, the cancellation-suspension section of the act.

Registration of pesticides under the act is very specific, by designating the crops and insects on which they may be applied. Registrations are limited to a five-year period, and automatically expire at the end of that period unless a party petitions the agency for renewal. The EPA may require the party to provide additional data supporting the safety of the product.

After 1972, new, more stringent EPA health and safety testing requirements created a double standard, because older pesticides (those registered by the FDA under prior law) could continue to be marketed even though test data demonstrated they did not meet current standards. Consequently, in its 1978 amendments to FIFRA, Congress directed the EPA to review and reregister all older pesticides as quickly as possible, to ensure that all pesticides were subject to the new product testing requirements. In 1988, FIFRA was amended to speed up this reregistration process. To help pay for the testing required for the reregistration program, a *maintenance fee* is assessed on manufacturers of each active ingredient during the reregistration program. In 1992, the EPA said it expected to complete this reregistration process by 2002.[3] The Food Quality Protection Act of 1996 reauthorized and increased user fees for the pesticide reregistration program. The new law also requires the EPA to periodically review pesticide registration with the goal of establishing a fifteen-year cycle of review.

Trade Secrets and Use of Data

Generating and submitting pesticide test data is a major cost in the development and marketing of a new pesticide. To minimize this cost, FIFRA permits the EPA to use test data supplied by one manufacturer to register the product of another manufacturer if the new product contains all or some of the same ingredients. However, the later registrant must compensate the earlier producer for use of its data to minimize one company's taking financial advantage of another.

Another controversial provision of FIFRA permits the release of scientific data generated in the registration process to the public under some circumstances. Section 10 of FIFRA provides that

> when necessary to carry out the provisions of this act, information relating to formulas of products acquired by authorization of this act may be revealed to any federal agency consulted and may be revealed at a public hearing or in findings of fact issued by the administrator.

The question of how the EPA may use data which may constitute a trade secret has become a major issue in the pesticide regulatory process.

In 1984, the Supreme Court held that a company could have a property interest in such data under state law.[4] The key question, according to the Court, was whether the company "could reasonably expect" that secrets would not be disclosed or used by other companies, even with adequate compensation. The Court said that a company could meet this test for data submitted between the 1972 FIFRA amendments and 1978 amendments because a change in Section 10 of the act had promised strict confidentiality to generators of the data.

Pesticide Tolerances in Food: The Federal Food, Drug, and Cosmetic Act (FFDCA)

Under the Federal Food, Drug, and Cosmetic Act (FFDCA), the EPA establishes tolerances (maximum legally permissible levels) for pesticide residues in food or animal feed. This includes residues in processed food or on animal products such as meat, milk, or eggs, as well as on food or crops such as apples, corn, or wheat.

In order to register a pesticide, an applicant must obtain a tolerance for that pesticide. This requires the applicant to provide evidence showing the level of residues likely to result and data necessary to establish safe residue levels.

The FFDCA ensures the safety of food by prohibiting the sale of food that is *adulterated*. Adulterated food is defined as food containing any unsafe food *additive,* which is broadly defined as "any substance that intended use of which results or may reasonably be expected to result . . . in its becoming a component . . . of any food." Prior to 1996, a specific clause in the FFDCA called the **Delaney clause** prohibited the use of any food additive in processed foods that was found to induce cancer.

Prior to 1988, EPA regulations permitted the use of benomyl, mancozeb, phosmet, and trifluralin as food additives. In 1988, however, the EPA found these pesticides to be carcinogens. In *Les v. Reilly,* 968 F.2d 985 (9th Cit. 1992), petitioners sought judicial review of a final order of the EPA and challenged on the ground that the order violated the Delaney clause, 21 U.S.C. Section 834(c)(3). Notwithstanding the Delaney clause, the EPA refused to revoke the earlier regulations, reasoning that, although the chemicals posed a measurable risk of causing cancer, that risk was *de minimis.*

The court in *Les v. Reilly* disagreed with the EPA's refusal to revoke regulations permitting the use of the four pesticides as food additives, finding them contrary to the provisions of the Delaney clause prohibiting food additives that induce cancer. For this reason, the court set aside the EPA's final order in that case.

The Food Quality Protection Act of 1996 and Repeal of the Delaney Clause

The Food Quality Protection Act of 1996 (P.L. 104-1700) amended both the FFDCA and FIFRA to establish a health-based safety standard for pesticide residues in all foods, and to establish a more consistent, protective regulatory scheme for pesticides.

The new law repealed the Delaney clause and substituted the standard of "a reasonable certainty of no harm" for both processed foods and raw agricultural commodities. The standard applies to all risks, not just cancer risks. In setting the standard, the EPA must consider all nonoccupational sources of exposure to pesticides, including drinking water, and exposure to similar pesticides.

The 1996 act contains a special provision requiring an explicit determination that tolerances are safe for children, and places specific limits on the considerations of pesticide benefits when setting tolerances. It also incorporates provisions for endocrine testing, and enhances enforcement of standards by permitting the FDA to impose civil penalties for tolerance violations, and contains a "right to know" provision requiring distribution of a brochure on the health effects of pesticides.

1996 Amendments to FIFRA

The 1996 Food Quality Protection Act reauthorized the reregistration program under FIFRA and increased user fees necessary to complete the review of older pesticides to ensure they meet current standards. The law requires the EPA to periodically review pesticide registrations with the goal of establishing a fifteen-year cycle. The law also contains a provision designed to expedite review of safer pesticides so that they can reach the market sooner and replace older, more dangerous chemicals, and it establishes new requirements to expedite review and registration of antimicrobial pesticides.

Under previous law, the EPA could not suspend a pesticide's registration unless a proposed notice of intent to cancel had been issued. This could delay suspensions in emergency situations. Under the new law, the EPA may suspend a pesticide registration immediately, allowing the EPA to move more quickly in such situations.

Special Registrations

FIFRA also provides for a number of limited registration or exemption mechanisms. For example, the agency has used *conditional registration* under the 1978 amendments to reduce the regulatory advantage enjoyed by older products. If a product is substantially similar in ingredients and proposed use to an already registered pesticide, the agency may conditionally reregister the product and not require the submission of a full set of test data until registrants of older products are required to submit such data under the reregistration program. Another controversial use of conditional registration occurs in cases where an applicant has not had time to complete the long-term toxicological studies required for new products. In some cases, where a product contains new active ingredients, the EPA may register the product on the condition that the registrant complete the testing and submit data within a reasonable period of time.

Under FIFRA, a state government may permit additional uses of a pesticide to combat a pest limited to a specific area or crop. This is called *special local need* registration. The EPA also has authority to exempt federal or state agencies from provisions of FIFRA under emergency situations. The agency may grant an *emergency registration exemption* allowing the use of pesticides for unregistered uses when there is no alternative means to control a serious outbreak or to prevent the introduction or spread of a foreign pest. As of 1991, state governments had obtained 3,026 active special local need registrations, and the EPA had granted 237 emergency exemptions. These provisions are used most heavily in states like California where specialty crops are grown.[5] The agency also may permit *experimental use* of pesticides for the development of data needed for registration of a new product or a new use.

Classification and Certification under Section 3

Under FIFRA, the EPA may classify a pesticide either for *general use* or *restricted use*. The latter group is available only to "certified applicators," and federal and state programs train and certify pesticide applicators. In 1975, Congress amended the law to exempt farmers and their employees who apply pesticides to their own land from the examination requirement for certification.

Criteria for classification of pesticides vary, depending on the type of use, for example, domestic, nondomestic, indoor, or outdoor use. Most pesticides receive general use classification. If a pesticide is unusually toxic or presents a special hazard to human health or the environment, it is classified for restricted use. The EPA establishes the specific requirements that apply to such products by regulations, and other types of use restrictions are imposed through *labeling requirements*. Using a product in a way that violates its labeling restrictions is a violation of FIFRA.

Minor Use Registrations

Minor use registrations of pesticides are those for which product sales do not justify the costs of developing and maintaining EPA registrations. The Food Quality Protection Act increases incentives for the development and maintenance of minor use registrations. But these provisions do not apply if the minor use may pose unreasonable risks or the lack of data would significantly delay EPA decision making.

Removal of Pesticides from the Market

Under Section 6 of FIFRA, the EPA may suspend, cancel, or restrict a pesticide registration to prevent an unreasonable risk to humans or to the environment. *Suspension* is an emergency procedure which permits the EPA to suspend the registration of a pesticide immediately. Under FIFRA, the EPA is required to suspend registration of a pesticide when a product constitutes an "imminent hazard" to humans or the environment. Suspension permits the agency to suspend registration of a pesticide while cancellation proceedings continue.

A *cancellation action* is initiated if a substance is suspected of posing a substantial question of safety to humans or the environment. The cancellation order is final if not challenged within thirty days, but the process is often protracted, sometimes for years. The process typically includes public hearings, a decision from an administrative law judge, review by the administrator, and judicial review.

The complicated procedural requirements and criteria applied by the EPA in cancellation and suspension proceedings under FIFRA are illustrated by the EPA's decision to cancel the registration for the pesticides aldrin and dieldren. In *Environmental Defense Fund, Inc. v. Environmental Protection Agency,* 46 F.2d 528 (D.C. Cir. 1972), environmental groups challenged the failure of the EPA to suspend registrations for these pesticides after initiating proceedings to cancel their registration. In a lengthy opinion, the court determined that EPA findings as to the benefits of the pesticides were deficient and returned the case for further EPA proceedings. The court also distinguished a suspension order from cancellation of registration; according to the court, the function of the suspension decision is to make a preliminary assessment of evidence and probabilities, not to ultimately resolve the difficult issues addressed in the cancellation proceeding.

Because of the cumbersome and lengthy cancellation procedure, the EPA has not frequently used the process. Cancellation has been initiated for DDT, aldrin/dieldrin, 2,4,5–T/Silvex, Kepone, mirex, ethylene dibromide, and Compound 1080. In general, however, the agency tends to address the problems of hazardous pesticides through the review process, which may end in cancellation of some registered uses or reclassification of the product to impose regulatory restrictions on its use.

In the following case, a manufacturer challenged the decision of the EPA to cancel registration of the pesticide diazinon for use on golf courses and sod farms on the ground that it "generally causes unreasonable adverse effects on the environment."

CIBA-GEIGY CORP. v. UNITED STATES EPA
874 F.2d 277 (5th Cir. 1989)

ALVIN B. RUBIN, Circuit Judge:

***

The EPA issued a Notice of Intent to cancel the registrations of pesticide products containing diazinon for use on golf courses and sod farms because of concern about the effects of diazinon on birds. After extensive public hearings, the EPA's Chief

Administrative Law Judge concluded that diazinon should be classified for "restricted use" by licensed applicators only and that its label should be amended, but that its registration for use on golf courses and sod farms should not be canceled. The EPA staff appealed to the Administrator, who, after a careful analysis of the record, ordered diazinon banned from use on golf courses and sod farms. The Administrator accepted many of the Administrative Law Judge's findings and conclusions, but rejected his balancing of the risks and benefits of diazinon use. The Administrator also specifically rejected Ciba-Geigy's argument that, because FIFRA sec. 6(b) authorizes cancellation of the registration of products that "generally cause unreasonable adverse effects on the environment," cancellation is justified only if a product causes unreasonable adverse effects most of the time it is used. The Administrator stated:

FIFRA sec. 6(b) requires compliance with all other provisions of the statute, including FIFRA sec. 3(c)(5)(C) which prohibits unreasonable adverse effects on the environment without regard to whether such effects are caused "generally." Moreover, Ciba-Geigy's reading of the word "generally" as meaning "most of the time" is unnatural. In light of the basic statutory standard in FIFRA sec. 2(bb), which requires consideration of a broad range of factors, "generally" is more appropriately read as meaning "with regard to an overall picture". . . . It is simply untenable to suggest that FIFRA requires continued registration where a pesticide causes unreasonable adverse effects in less than 51 percent of the cases in which it is used.

In the Administrator's view, FIFRA authorizes him to cancel registration of a pesticide whenever he finds that it causes any unreasonable risk, irrespective of the frequency with which that risk occurs.

Once again urging that FIFRA requires the EPA to conclude that diazinon kills birds more than fifty percent of the time before it

can cancel its registration, Ciba-Geigy petitions this court to set aside the Administrator's order.

II.

The Administrative Law Judge concluded that bird kills due to diazinon may be an "unusual occurrence." Ciba-Geigy asserts, therefore, that even if diazinon sometimes causes adverse environmental effects, it does not do so "generally" as the statute requires.

Ciba-Geigy's argument focuses on a single word in the statutory phrase, ignoring the meaning of the phrase as a whole. FIFRA provides that the Administrator may cancel the registration of a pesticide if it appears to him that, "when used in accordance with widespread and commonly recognized practice, [it] generally causes unreasonable adverse effects on the environment." The statute defines "unreasonable adverse effects on the environment" to mean "any unreasonable risk to man or the environment, taking into account the . . . costs and benefits."

Neither the statute nor its legislative history explains the word "generally," but, as the numerous dictionary definitions that the parties have quoted to us make clear, it means "usually," "commonly," or "with considerable frequency," though not necessarily "more likely than not." Interpreting the statutory standard as a whole, therefore, the Administrator may cancel a registration if it appears to him that the pesticide commonly causes unreasonable risks.

Because FIFRA defines "adverse effects" as "unreasonable risks," the Administrator need not find that use of a pesticide commonly causes undesirable consequences, but only that it creates a significant probability that such consequences may occur. FIFRA therefore does not oblige the Administrator to maintain the registration of a pesticide that might not generally have adverse effects but, say, killed children on

50% of the occasions on which it was used. A 50% risk that children might be killed is plainly an "unreasonable risk" more than sufficient to justify cancellation of the noxious pesticide. Similarly, a significant risk of bird kills, even if birds are actually killed infrequently, may justify the Administrator's decision to ban or restrict diazinon use.

Nevertheless, the Administrator improperly read the word "generally" out of FIFRA sec. 6(b). The word is not superfluous: it requires the Administrator to determine that the use of a pesticide in a particular application creates unreasonable risks, though not necessarily actual adverse consequences, with considerable frequency, and thus requires the Administrator to consider whether he has defined the application he intends

to prohibit sufficiently narrowly. If the use of diazinon creates an unreasonable risk of killing birds on only 10% of the golf courses on which it is used, for example, the Administrator should define the class of golf courses on which its use is to be prohibited more narrowly. Without attempting to interpret the vast administrative record ourselves, therefore, we grant Ciba-Geigy's petition to the extent of remanding this case to the Administrator for application of the correct legal standard.

***

[T]he order canceling the registration of diazinon for use on golf courses and sod farms is set aside, and the case is REMANDED to the Administrator for further proceedings consistent with this opinion.

Questions and Comments for Discussion

1. Section 136d(b), entitled *Cancellation and change in classification,* reads in part as follows:

> If it appears to the Administrator that a pesticide or its labeling or other material required to be submitted does not comply with the provisions of this subchapter or, when used in accordance with widespread and commonly recognized practice, generally causes unreasonable adverse effects on the environment, the Administrator may issue a notice of the Administrator's intent either—
> (1) to cancel its registration or to change its classification together with the

reasons (including the factual bases) for the Administrator's action, or
> (2) to hold a hearing to determine whether or not its registration should be canceled or its classification changed.

2. Why did the EPA cancel the registration of the pesticide diazinon for use on golf courses and sod farms?
3. Based on the language of this section, why did the manufacturer argue that the EPA had improperly canceled the registration of the pesticide?
4. How did the court interpret the meaning of the word "generally" as used in this section? What was the court's ruling in this case?

Effect of Cancellation of Registration

What happens to those products already in commercial use if the product's registration is canceled or suspended? In several cases, the EPA has ordered product recalls. For practical reasons, the EPA has usually permitted banned pesticides to be used until supplies are exhausted. Challenges to this policy by environmental groups have generally been unsuccessful.

EPA regulations also establish approved methods for storage and disposal of pesticides under FIFRA, including incineration, soil injection, and other means of disposal. One of the more controversial sections of FIFRA provides compensation to registrants and applicators who are unable to use pesticides they own because of cancellation or suspension of registration. Under this provision, the EPA paid out $20 million to manufacturers of two pesticides, 2,4,5–T and ethylene dibromide (EDB), and indemnification is estimated to be $40 million for the canceled pesticide dinoseb.[6] In the 1988 FIFRA amendments, the indemnity requirement was deleted except for end users such as farmers and applicators.

State Authority to Regulate Pesticides

Another issue which has generated a substantial amount of litigation under FIFRA is the extent to which states and local governments may adopt laws regulating the use of pesticides. In other words, to what extent does FIFRA *pre-empt* state regulatory authority? This question is addressed more fully in Chapter 7.

FIFRA pre-empts state authority to regulate those issues already regulated by FIFRA, although enforcement of the federal law is primarily carried out by the states. States may not permit the sale or use of pesticides prohibited under FIFRA, and they may not impose different labeling or packaging requirements. However, FIFRA generally permits the states to administer pesticide applicator certification programs, issue experimental use permits, register pesticides to meet special local needs, enforce federal pesticide laws, and regulate pesticides in ways not *specifically prohibited* by FIFRA.

The question of whether FIFRA pre-empts the regulation of pesticides by local governments reached the U.S. Supreme Court in *Wisconsin Public Intervenor v. Mortier,* 501 U.S. 597 (1991). In that case the Court held that FIFRA did not pre-empt the regulation of pesticides by a local government which had by ordinance required a permit for the application of pesticide to public lands, private lands subject to public use, or for the aerial application of any pesticide to private lands. While previous law permitted states to set tolerances for pesticides in foods that were stricter than EPA tolerances, the 1996 Food Quality Protection Act generally pre-empts states from doing so.

Enforcement and Penalties

Sale of unregistered, adulterated, or misbranded pesticides, use of a registered pesticide in a manner inconsistent with its labeling, and production of pesticides in an unregistered facility are all violations of FIFRA. Under FIFRA, the EPA may inspect production facilities and examine and test pesticides, impose fines or criminal penalties for violation of the act, and stop the sale of and seize products in violation of the law. FIFRA gives state governments primary authority to enforce the law, and authorizes funding assistance to state enforcement programs. Penalties for violation include civil fines up to $5,000 for each violation of FIFRA, and criminal penalties of up to $25,000 and one year in prison.

FIFRA and Other Laws

As noted earlier, the setting of tolerances for pesticide residues in food is derived from the FFDCA. The EPA sets tolerances "to protect the public health" and to give appropriate consideration "to the necessity for the production of an adequate, wholesome and economical food supply." The Food Quality Protection Act of 1996 sets the standard as "a reasonable certainty of no harm."

Under limited circumstances, the new FFDCA law permits tolerances to remain in effect which would not otherwise meet the standard. This provision, however, is subject to a number of limitations on risk and all tolerances must be consistent with the special provisions for infants and children. The law requires the EPA to consider specific factors in setting tolerances in addition to special provisions for infants and children, and requires that all existing tolerances be reviewed within ten years.

Pesticides in the air may be regulated under the Clean Air Act as hazardous air pollutants, and may be regulated under the Clean Water Act when released as effluents into a body of water. In addition, the EPA and the Department of Labor share responsibility under FIFRA and the **Occupational Safety and Health Act** (OSHA) for protecting agricultural workers from hazardous pesticides. The agencies have cooperated to develop a federal cancer policy, growing out of the EPA's suspension of the pesticides aldrin and dieldrin. In 1990, they concluded a memorandum which facilitates joint enforcement of their laws.

The Coordinated Framework for Regulation of Biotechnology, signed by President Reagan in 1986, set agency rules and statutory authority for ensuring the environmental safety and economic viability of biotechnology industries; legislation regulating the safety of genetically engineered products under TSCA has also been proposed. In 1980, the Supreme Court ruled that genetically altered organisms may be patented.[7] This ruling encourages biotechnology research by assuring and protecting the products derived from that research.

In 1995 in a precedent-setting action, the EPA registered Monsanto's NewLeaf potato, one of the first generation of food crops genetically engineered to resist pests, as a plant pesticide for commercial use under the FIFRA.

THE TOXIC SUBSTANCES CONTROL ACT

Fueled by an overall expansion of the economy and a demand for new products, the United States chemical industry grew rapidly after World War II. In the decades following the war, however, concerns about the effects of particular chemicals led to increased concern about the health risks and environmental effects of the production and dispersion of natural and synthetic materials in general. In the 1950s, association between exposure to asbestos and cancer first began to be reported, and further studies only heightened public concern about asbestos exposure. *Silent Spring* generated great public concern about the adverse effects of synthetic pesticides, such as DDT, and the ability of these chemicals to persist and accumulate in the fatty tissues of higher organisms. Vinyl chloride, organic mercury compounds, and PCBs are other substances which have generated public concern as evidence of their toxic effects on the environment and public health continue to be documented.

In response to mounting concern about the toxic effects of PCBs and other chemical substances, in 1976 Congress passed TSCA. TSCA is a gap-filling statute which permits the EPA to control or ban substances which cause harm to health or the environment, and which are not regulated by other federal environmental laws. Before the passage of TSCA there was no way to ban the manufacture of PCBs or control their use, even though PCB molecules were found to contaminate river and lake sediment. In response to this concern, TSCA specifically includes a ban on the manufacture of PCBs.

TSCA gives the Environmental Protection Agency the authority to:

1. *Screen new chemicals* (Section 5)
2. *Require testing of chemicals* which may present a significant risk to human health or the environment (Section 4)

3. *Gather information* about the adverse health or environmental effects of existing chemicals (Section 8)

4. *Limit or prohibit the manufacture, use, distribution, and disposal of chemicals* posing such risks (Section 6)

Title I of TSCA establishes the basic framework under the act for the control of toxic substances. Subsequent amendments to the law have added Title II, the Asbestos Hazard Emergency Response Act; Title III, the Indoor Radon Abatement Act; and, in 1972, Title IV, the Lead-Based Paint Exposure Reduction Act.

Title I of TSCA gives the EPA broad authority to regulate chemicals, but it requires the agency to balance the risks and costs of doing so. In deciding whether to regulate a particular chemical, the EPA must consider the benefits of the substance to society's economic and social welfare, the risks from alternative substances, and the health or economic risks resulting from the regulation of the substance. Thus, TSCA does not mandate regulation of all chemicals which present a risk to human health or the environment; it only regulates those chemicals which present an unreasonable risk.

Another important part of the act makes industry responsible for providing information about the chemicals it manufactures and distributes. Under TSCA, a manufacturer, which is defined broadly to include importers and extractors of chemical substances, has the responsibility for providing data to the EPA on the health and environmental effects of new and existing substances and mixtures.

Screening New Chemicals

Section 5 of TSCA establishes a Premanufacture Notification Program. Under this program, the EPA assesses the safety of new chemicals *before* they are manufactured. Any person who intends to manufacture or import a new chemical substance must file a **Premanufacture notice** (PMN) with the EPA before undertaking manufacture or importation. Existing chemicals, chemicals used solely for research and development, and chemicals regulated under other laws, for example, pesticides regulated under FIFRA are exempt from the PMN review. The EPA receives nearly 2,000 such notifications every year from manufacturers who want to make or import new chemicals into the U.S. market.[8]

The question whether manufacturers of chemical substances are required to file a PMN calls on the distinction between "new" chemicals (and "significant new uses of existing chemicals" for which a premanufacture notification is required) and "existing" chemicals. Under TSCA Section 8, the EPA keeps and publishes a current list of all chemical substances manufactured or processed for commercial purposes in the United States. This inventory is known as the **TSCA inventory,** and it is the basis for distinguishing between existing and new chemicals which require a premanufacture notification. The EPA continuously adds new chemicals to the inventory which have cleared the TSCA premanufacture notice review, and it also periodically removes or "delists" chemicals not currently manufactured or imported for commercial purposes.

If a chemical is not already listed on the TSCA inventory, or does not fall within an exemption, a company must submit a PMN to the EPA for review before beginning manufacture of the chemical. The PMN must include:

1. The common or trade name of the substance
2. The chemical identity and molecular structure of the substance
3. The estimated production levels for the substance
4. The proposed use of the chemical and method of disposal
5. The estimated levels of exposure in the workplace and number of workers involved
6. The by-products, impurities, and other related products
7. The available test data on health and environmental effects related to manufacture if the data are within the manufacturer's possession and control
8. A description of known or reasonably ascertainable test data

It is important to note that, under TSCA, a manufacturer is *not* expressly required to produce specific tests for a PMN. Unlike comparable laws in other countries, TSCA does not require the manufacturer to provide a minimum set of premarket data on a new chemical as part of the premanufacture review process.

Approval of the PMN

TSCA requires the EPA to review the PMN within ninety days of its submission. After reviewing the notice, the agency publishes a notice in the *Federal Register* advertising the date the PMN was received and the date the ninety-day review period ends. During the review period, the EPA evaluates the risks posed by the new chemical. If the EPA takes no regulatory action within the ninety day period, the company may begin commercial manufacture or importation without further agency approval. The manufacturer or importer, however, must file a Notice of Commencement (NOC) of Manufacture or Import within thirty days of beginning such action. After it receives the NOC, the EPA adds the PMN substance to the TSCA inventory, and it then becomes an existing chemical under TSCA.

If the EPA has questions about a substance submitted for premanufacture review, TSCA allows the EPA to prevent, delay, or limit the manufacture of a new chemical after the ninety-day period expires. Under Section 5, the agency may delay manufacture for an additional ninety days for "good cause." It may also issue a proposed order to limit or prohibit manufacture of the chemical if the agency determines that available information is "insufficient to permit a reasoned evaluation." The agency may approve a new chemical but condition that approval on the manufacturer's providing further data on its uses and effects by adding it to a list of existing substances.

The EPA may also act immediately under Section 5 to limit or delay the manufacture of a chemical substance if the agency concludes that such manufacture "presents or will present an unreasonable risk of injury to health or the environment." Under Section 6, the EPA is permitted to take immediate action to ban the chemical from commercial manufacture, distribution, processing, and use while it undertakes a rule-making action. The scope of judicial review of the EPA's orders depends upon the kind of action taken.

In many cases, rather than issuing orders under Section 5, the agency chooses to enter into a consent agreement with the manufacturer. Under this legally binding agreement, the manufacturer agrees to restrict the new chemical's production, use, disposal, or exposure. The agency then issues a **significant new use rule** (SNUR) which extends those restrictions to all subsequent manufacturers or importers of the substance.

Testing Requirements

TSCA also authorizes the EPA to require manufacturers and processors to develop data about the health and environmental effects of their products. Under Section 4, the EPA may require manufacturers and processors to test chemical substances which are already on the market or about to be produced. The EPA may require the development of such data if it finds that the chemical or mixture may present an "unreasonable risk of injury to human health or the environment, and existing data on and experience with the chemical or mixture are insufficient and testing is necessary to obtain such data."

The language of this section requires the EPA to make a risk determination of both toxicity and exposure before it can order testing. There are several factors used by the agency in determining the possible unreasonable risk of a substance. These include:

- Knowledge of a chemical's physical and chemical properties
- Structural relationships to other chemicals with demonstrated adverse effects
- Data from inconclusive tests
- Case history data

Testing required by the act must be specific with respect to the type of effects to be evaluated, and the agency must specify the standards to be used and the time period for submitting test results to the EPA. TSCA requires the EPA administrator to undertake formal rule making in order to require the manufacturer of the chemical or mixture to conduct testing.

Under Section 4, the **Interagency Testing Committee (ITC),** composed of representatives of eight federal agencies, makes recommendations to the EPA administrator in respect to the chemical substances and mixtures to which the Administrator should give priority consideration. TSCA requires the ITC to give priority to substances suspected of causing or contributing to cancer, gene mutations, or birth defects. Within one year after the ITC designates a chemical, the EPA must propose a test rule or publish reasons why testing is not required.

In the early years of TSCA, the EPA consistently failed to meet the one-year time limit for responding to ITC testing. In 1979, the Natural Resources Defense Council sued the EPA to force it to respond to the backlog of testing recommendations. In *Natural Resources Defense Council v. Costle,*[9] a federal district court held that the EPA had failed to comply with the requirements of Section 4 of TSCA. In January 1981, the court established a timetable for answering the recommendations in order to force the agency to clear up the backlog of testing recommendations.

The agency then began a program whereby it encouraged voluntary testing by industry. This permitted the agency to avoid the delays accompanying formal regulatory rule making. In *Natural Resources Defense Council v. EPA,*[10] the U.S. District Court ruled these voluntary agreements illegal because they were not specifically authorized under TSCA. In 1986, following a proposal by environmental groups and the chemical industry, the EPA issued an interim rule authorizing consent testing agreements negotiated under Section 4 of TSCA. While a formal test rule procedure can take two years, EPA estimates that a consent order can reduce the time period by half.[11] Under TSCA, private citizens can also request testing. The agency must respond to such a petition within ninety days.

In reviewing the agency's rule-making decision to require testing under Section 4 of TSCA, a court reviews the rule-making record to determine whether the factual findings of the agency were supported by substantial evidence. In the following case, petitioners Chemical Manufacturers Association and four companies that manufactured chemicals sought to set aside a rule promulgated by the EPA which required toxicological testing to determine the health effects of the chemical 2-ethyhexanoic acid (EHA), and which placed on exporters of EHA a duty to file certain notices with the agency. An important issue in the case was EPA's determination that the substance presented an "unreasonable risk of injury to human health or the environment" under Section 4 of TSCA.

CHEMICAL MFRS. ASS'N. v. U.S. EPA
859 F.2d 977 (D.C. Cir. 1988)

WALD, C.J.

Petitioners, Chemical Manufacturers Association and four companies that manufacture chemicals seek to set aside a rule promulgated by the Environmental Protection Agency. This Final Test Rule was promulgated under section 4 of the Toxic Substances Control Act ("TSCA"). The Final Test Rule required toxicological testing to determine the health effects of the chemical 2-ethylhexanoic acid ("EHA") and it continues to impose on exporters of EHA a duty to file certain notices with EPA.

We uphold EPA's interpretation of TSCA as empowering the Agency to issue a test rule on health grounds where it finds a more-than-theoretical basis for suspecting that the chemical substance in question presents an "unreasonable risk of injury to health." This, in turn, requires the Agency to find a more-than-theoretical basis for concluding that the substance is sufficiently toxic, and human exposure to it is sufficient in amount, to generate an "unreasonable risk of injury to health." We hold, further, that EPA can establish the existence and amount of human exposure on the basis of inferences drawn from the circumstances under which the substance is manufactured and used. EPA must rebut industry-supplied evidence attacking those inferences only if the industry evidence succeeds in rendering the probability of exposure in the amount found by EPA no more than theoretical or speculative.

The probability of infrequent or even one-time exposure to individuals can warrant a test rule, so long as there is a more-than-theoretical basis for determining that exposure in such doses presents an "unreasonable risk of injury to health." Finally, we hold that the Agency correctly applied these standards in this case and that its findings are supported by substantial evidence. Consequently, we affirm the Final Test Rule.

BACKGROUND

A. Statutory Structure

TSCA provides for a two-tier system for evaluating and regulating chemical substances to protect against unreasonable risks to human health and to the environment. Section 6 of the Act permits EPA to regulate a substance that the Agency has found "presents or will present an unreasonable risk of injury to health or the environment." Section 4 of the Act empowers EPA to require testing of a suspect substance in order to obtain the toxicological data necessary to make a decision whether or not to regulate the substance under section 6. The Act provides, not surprisingly, that the level of certainty of risk warranting a section 4 test rule is lower than that warranting a section 6 regulatory rule. EPA is empowered to require testing where it finds that the manufacture, distribution, processing, use or disposal of a particular chemical substance "may present an unreasonable risk of injury to human health or the environment." The Agency's interpretation of this statutory standard for testing is the central issue in this case.

One of the chief policies underlying the Act is that—

> adequate data should be developed with respect to the effect of chemical substances and mixtures on health and the environment and that the development of such data should be the responsibility of those who manufacture and those who process such chemical substances and mixtures. § 2601(b)(1).

The statute establishes an Interagency Testing Committee, comprised of scientists from various federal agencies, to recommend that EPA give certain chemicals "priority consideration" for testing. Under section 4, the Agency "shall by rule require that testing [of a particular chemical]be conducted" if three factors are present: (i) activities involving the chemical "may present an unreasonable risk of injury to health or the environment"; (ii) "insufficient data and experience" exist upon which to determine the effects of the chemical on health or environment; and (iii) testing is necessary to develop such data. The companies that manufacture and process the substance are to conduct the tests and submit the data to the Agency. Costs of testing are to be shared among the companies, either by agreement or by EPA order in the absence of agreement.

A test rule promulgated under section 4 is subject to judicial review in a court of appeals, pursuant to section 19(a) of TSCA. A test rule may be set aside if it is not "supported by substantial evidence in the rulemaking record . . . taken as a whole."

***

STATUTORY INTERPRETATION

The Toxic Substances Control Act requires EPA to promulgate a test rule under section 4 if a chemical substance, inter alia,

"may present an unreasonable risk of injury to health or the environment." The parties both accept the proposition that the degree to which a particular substance presents a risk to health is a function of two factors: (a) human exposure to the substance, and (b) the toxicity of the substance. . . . They also agree that EPA must make some sort of threshold finding as to the existence of an "unreasonable risk of injury to health." The parties differ, however, as to the manner in which this finding must be made. Specifically, three issues are presented.

The first issue is whether, under section 4 of TSCA, EPA must find that the existence of an "unreasonable risk of injury to health" is more probable than not in order to issue a test rule. CMA argues that the statute requires a more-probable-than-not finding. EPA disagrees, contending that the statute is satisfied where the existence of an "unreasonable risk of injury to health" is a substantial probability—that is, a probability that is more than merely theoretical, speculative or conjectural. . . .

The second issue is whether, once industry has presented evidence tending to show an absence of human exposure, EPA must rebut it by producing direct evidence of exposure. . . . The Third issue is whether the Agency has authority to issue a test rule where any individual's exposure to a substance is an isolated, non-recurrent event. CMA argues that, even if EPA presents direct evidence of exposure, the Act precludes issuance of a test rule where exposure consists only of rare instances involving brief exposure. EPA contends, on the other hand that the Act does not require in all circumstances a risk of recurrent exposure. . . .

***

A. Required Finding of "Unreasonable Risk."

As to the first issue in this case, the standard of probability of an unreasonable risk to health, we find that Congress did not address the precise question in issue.

Examining the EPA interpretation . . . we find it to be reasonable and consistent with the statutory scheme and legislative history. Consequently, we uphold the Agency's construction of TSCA as authorizing a test rule where EPA's basis for suspecting the existence of an "unreasonable risk of injury to health" is substantial—i.e., when there is a more-than-theoretical basis for suspecting that some amount of exposure takes place and that the substance is sufficiently toxic at that level of exposure to present an "unreasonable risk of injury to health."

***

B. Use of Inferences versus Direct
    Evidence of Exposure

The second issue in the case is whether EPA must produce direct evidence documenting human exposure in order to rebut industry-submitted evidence casting doubt on the existence of exposure. EPA contends that it need not provide direct evidence of exposure, even in response to industry evidence rebutting its initial circumstantial case on exposure, so long as the evidence on exposure as a whole provides a more-than-theoretical basis for discerning the presence of an "unreasonable risk of injury to health." EPA concedes that exposure is a necessary component of "unreasonable risk of injury to health." The Agency argues, however, that it can issue a test rule where the existence of exposure is inferred from the circumstances under which the substance is manufactured and used. So long as industry evidence attacking those inferences fails to negate the Agency's more-than-theoretical

basis for inferring the existence of exposure, EPA claims, a test rule is warranted. After a careful search of the legislative materials, we conclude that Congress did not address this particular issue. Applying the second prong of *Chevron,* however, we conclude that the Agency's construction of section 4 is a reasonable one and therefore uphold it.

***

C. Recurrent versus Rare Exposure

The third statutory issue is whether section 4 of TSCA authorizes EPA to issue a test rule where any individual's exposure to a chemical is likely to be a rare, brief event. CMA contends that only recurrent exposure warrants a test rule. EPA maintains that it can issue a test rule in the absence of recurrent exposure, where there is a more-than-theoretical basis for suspecting that infrequent or single-dose exposure presents an "unreasonable risk of injury to health." We find no indication in the statute or its history that Congress addressed this particular issue, but once again turning to the second prong of *Chevron,* we deem reasonable the Agency's construction of section 4 as permitting a test rule even where exposure is not recurrent.

[*The Court concluded that EPA had presented substantial relevant evidence of exposure and toxicity so as to justify the promulgation of a test rule and that its findings as to exposure, subchronic toxicity, and developmental toxicity were supported by substantial evidence on the record viewed as a whole. It therefore denied the petition for review.*]

Questions and Comments for Discussion

1. Who sued whom in this case? Why?
2. What three issues did the court address in this case? How did the court resolve those issues?

3. The court relied on the holding in *Chevron* in reviewing the EPA's interpretation of the statutory language of TSCA. (*Chevron* is discussed more fully in Chapter 8.) What

is the Chevron test of statutory interpretation as set out by the court in this case?

4.   This case provides a good example of the importance of burden of proof in rule making. According to the court, who has the burden of proof in this case? What is the standard of proof?

TSCA Section 4(a)(1)(B) establishes an alternative "exposure trigger" as a basis for requiring testing. Under the language of this section, the EPA can require testing if a chemical substance is produced in substantial quantities, it is reasonably expected to be released into the environment in substantial quantities, or there is or may be significant or substantial human exposure or data are insufficient and testing is necessary to develop the data.

Another provision of Section 4 of TSCA covers cost sharing for testing. When the agency requires a chemical to be tested, all manufacturers and processors participate, but the law permits them to agree to have one laboratory perform the tests and all share the costs of testing.

Section 4(f) of TSCA also contains a provision mandating that the EPA take regulatory action when a chemical poses "a significant risk of serious or widespread harm to human beings." The finding of significant risk has a higher risk threshold than a finding of unreasonable risk under TSCA Section 6. This provision has been triggered for 4,4'-methylenedianiline in 1983, formaldehyde in 1984, and methylene chloride in 1985.

Information Gathering and Reporting

Section 8 of TSCA establishes requirements for the collection, recording, and submission of information by chemical manufacturers and processors to the EPA. Such information includes data on chemical production, use, exposure, and disposal and records of allegations of significant adverse reactions to human health or the environment and unpublished health and safety studies.

Section 8 contains four parts. Section 8(a) is a general reporting section which authorizes the EPA to collect general information on chemicals the EPA may regulate. The EPA designates chemicals included in this section's general reporting list through formal rule making. The list includes both specific chemicals and chemicals listed as part of categories.

Section 8(c) requires manufacturers, processors, and distributors to keep records of significant adverse reactions to health and the environment alleged to have been caused by a chemical substance or mixture they manufacture, process, or distribute. Reports of consumer allegations of personal injury, reports of occupational disease or injury, and reports of damage to the environment are the types of records that EPA may request. After industry expressed concern that they would be overwhelmed with record-keeping requirements under EPA regulations, the EPA reduced the number and types of records which must be kept. For example, the EPA has limited adverse effect allegations that must be recorded to those that substantially impair activity, are long-lasting, or are irreversible.

Under Section 8(d), a person who manufactures, processes, or distributes a chemical substance or mixture is required to submit to the EPA lists and copies of health and safety studies conducted by, known to, or ascertainable by that person. This includes unpublished studies.

Section 8(e) requires chemical manufacturers, processors, and distributors to report substantial risks associated with chemicals. Data required include toxicology tests or results of animal studies indicating adverse health effects. The TSCA Compliance Audit Program (CAP), instituted by the EPA in 1991, has dramatically increased the number of notification reports. Under the CAP program, possible penalties which can be imposed on manufacturers who voluntarily report risks are limited.

Trade Secrets and Data Disclosure   The purpose of TSCA's reporting requirements is to provide the EPA with information so that it can make reasoned judgments about the safety or hazards of chemicals it regulates. Section 8 authorizes the collection of a variety of data which industry is required to maintain, collect, and submit to the EPA. Failure to submit requested information to the EPA may result in either civil or criminal penalties.

Some of the information collected under TSCA includes trade secrets and commercial or financial information which may be confidential. TSCA does not prohibit the disclosure of health and safety studies nor the release of information to federal officials, but TSCA does provide that the EPA may not release any information which is exempt from mandatory disclosure under the Freedom of Information Act. EPA regulations under TSCA are designed to permit industry to submit information to the agency without the fear that confidential trade information will be released to competitors.

Regulation of Existing Chemicals

Section 6 of the TSCA authorizes the EPA to regulate existing chemicals that present an "unreasonable risk to health or the environment." The EPA may control, restrict, or ban the manufacture, use, processing, disposal, or distribution of such chemicals under this section. To determine whether a risk is unreasonable, the EPA must conduct a risk assessment and is required to consider:

1. The effects on health and the environment
2. The magnitude of exposure to humans and the environment
3. The benefits of the substance and the availability of substitutes
4. The reasonably ascertainable economic consequences of the rule

Once the EPA has found an unreasonable risk, it must import the least burdensome restrictions necessary to control the risk.

To date the EPA has attempted to regulate only a few chemical substances under this section. They include asbestos, chlorofluorocarbons, dioxins, hexavalent chromium, certain metalworking fluids, and polychlorinated biphenyls (PCBs.)

In 1989, after more than ten years of effort, the EPA issued a final rule under Section 6 of TSCA to ban the manufacture, import, processing, and distribution of asbestos products. Exposure to asbestos fibers has been associated with pulmonary fibrosis (asbestosis), lung cancer, and other cancers and diseases. In a hard-fought case, industry challenged the EPA's asbestos regulations on a number of grounds. They claimed that the EPA's rule-making procedure was flawed and that the rule was not promulgated based upon substantial evidence. Others contended that the rule was invalid because it conflicted with international trade agreements.

In 1991, the case reached the U.S. Court of Appeals for the Fifth Circuit. Portions of the opinion in which the court discusses Section 6's "substantial evidence" standard and its requirement that the agency adopt the "least burdensome alternative" appear in the case below.

CORROSION PROOF FITTINGS v. EPA
947 F.2d 1201 (1991)

SMITH, *Circuit Judge*

The Environmental Protection Agency (EPA) issued a final rule under section 6 of the Toxic Substances Control Act (TSCA) to prohibit the future manufacture, importation, processing, and distribution of asbestos in almost all products. Petitioners claim that the EPA's rulemaking procedure was flawed and that the rule was not promulgated on the basis of substantial evidence. . . . Because the EPA failed to muster substantial evidence to support its rule, we remand this matter to the EPA for further consideration in light of this opinion.

I. FACTS AND PROCEDURAL HISTORY

Asbestos is a naturally occurring fibrous material that resists fire and most solvents. Its major uses include heat-resistant insulators, cements, building materials, fireproof gloves and clothing, and motor vehicle brake linings. Asbestos is a toxic material, and occupational exposure to asbestos dust can result in mesothelioma, asbestosis, and lung cancer.

The EPA began these proceedings in 1979, when it issued an Advanced Notice of Proposed Rulemaking announcing its intent to explore the use of TSCA "to reduce the risk to human health posed by exposure to asbestos. . . ." An EPA-appointed panel reviewed over one hundred studies of asbestos and conducted several public meetings. Based upon its studies and the public comments, the EPA concluded that asbestos is a potential carcinogen at all levels of exposure, regardless of the type of asbestos or the size of the fiber. The EPA concluded in 1986 that exposure to asbestos "poses an unreasonable risk to human health" and thus proposed at least four regulatory options of prohibiting or restricting the use of asbestos. . . .

Over the next two years, the EPA updated its data, received further comments, and allowed cross-examination on the updated documents. In 1989, the EPA issued a final rule prohibiting the manufacture, importation, processing and distribution in commerce of most asbestos-containing products. Finding that asbestos constituted an unreasonable risk to health and the environment, the EPA promulgated a staged ban of most commercial uses of asbestos. The EPA estimates that this rule will save either 202 or 148 lives, depending upon whether the benefits are discounted, at a cost of approximately \$450-800 million, depending upon the price of substitutes. . . .

***

THE LANGUAGE OF TSCA

A. Standard of Review

Our inquiry into the legitimacy of the EPA rulemaking begins with a discussion of the standard of review governing this case. EPA's phase-out ban of most commercial uses of asbestos is a TSCA Sec. 6(a) rulemaking. TSCA provides that a reviewing court "shall hold unlawful and set aside" a final rule promulgated under section 6(a) "if the court finds that the rule is not supported by substantial evidence in the rulemaking record . . . taken as a whole."

Substantial evidence requires "something less than the weight of the evidence, and the possibility of drawing two inconsistent conclusions from the evidence does not prevent an administrative agency's finding from being supported by substantial evidence." This standard requires (1) that the agency's decision be based upon the entire record, taking into account whatever in the record detracts from the weight of the agency's decision; and (2) that the agency's decision be what "a reasonable mind might accept as adequate to support [its] conclusion." Thus, even if there is enough evidence in the record to support the petitioners' assertions, we will not reverse if there is substantial evidence to support the agency's decision.

Contrary to the EPA's assertions, the arbitrary and capricious standard found in the APA[12] and the substantial evidence standard found in TSCA are different standards, even in the context of an informal rulemaking. Congress specifically went out of its way to provide that "the standard of review prescribed by paragraph (2)(E) of section 7806 [of the APA] shall not apply and the court shall hold unlawful and set aside such rule if the court finds that the rule is not supported by substantial evidence in the rulemaking. "The substantial evidence standard mandated by [TSCA] is generally considered to be more rigorous than the arbitrary and capricious standard normally applied to informal rulemaking," and "afford[s] a considerably more generous judicial review" than the arbitrary and capricious test. The test "imposes a considerable burden on the agency and limits its discretion in arriving at a factual predicate. . . ."

The recent case of *Chemical Mfrs. Ass'n v. EPA*, 899 F.2d 344 (5th Cir. 1990) provides our basic framework for reviewing the EPA's actions. In evaluating whether the EPA has presented substantial evidence, we examine (1) whether the quantities of the regulated chemical entering into the environment are "substantial" and (2) whether human exposure to the chemical is "substantial" or "significant." An agency may exercise its judgment without strictly relying upon quantifiable risks, costs, and benefits, but it must "cogently explain why it has exercised its discretion in a given manner" and "must offer a rational connection between the facts found and the choice made."

We note that in undertaking our review, we give all agency rules a presumption of

validity, and it is up to the challenger to any rule to show that the agency action is invalid. The burden remains on the EPA, however, to justify that the products it bans present an unreasonable risk, no matter how regulated. . . . Finally, as we discuss in detail infra, because TSCA instructs the EPA to undertake the least burdensome regulation sufficient to regulate the substance at issue, the agency bears a heavier burden when it seeks a partial or total ban of a substance than when it merely seeks to regulate that product.

B. The EPA's Burden Under TSCA

TSCA provides, in pertinent part, as follows:

> (a) Scope of regulation—If the Administrator finds that there is a reasonable basis to conclude that the manufacture, processing, distribution in commerce, use, or disposal of a chemical substance or mixture, or that any combination of such activities, presents or will present an unreasonable risk of injury to health or the environment, the Administrator shall by rule apply one or more of the following requirements to such substance or mixture to the extent necessary to protect adequately against such risk using the least burdensome requirements.

As the highlighted language shows, Congress did not enact TSCA as a zero-risk statute. The EPA, rather, was required to consider both alternatives to a ban and the costs of any proposed actions and to "carry out this chapter in a reasonable and prudent manner [after considering] the environmental, economic, and social impact of any action.

We conclude that the EPA has presented insufficient evidence to justify its asbestos ban. We base this conclusion upon two grounds: the failure of the EPA to consider all necessary evidence and its failure to give adequate weight to statutory language requiring it to promulgate the least burdensome, reasonable regulation required to protect the environment adequately. Because the EPA failed to address these concerns, and because the EPA is required to articulate a "reasoned basis" for its rules, we are compelled to return the regulation to the agency for reconsideration.

1. Least Burdensome and Reasonable

TSCA requires that the EPA use the least burdensome regulation to achieve its goal of minimum reasonable risk. This statutory requirement can create problems in evaluating just what is a "reasonable risk." Congress's rejection of a no-risk policy, however, also means that in certain cases, the least burdensome yet still adequate solution may entail somewhat more risk than would other, known regulations that are far more burdensome on the industry and the economy. The very language of TSCA requires that the EPA, once it has determined what an acceptable level of non-zero risk is, choose the least burdensome method of reaching that level.

In this case, the EPA banned, for all practical purposes, all present and future uses of asbestos—a position the petitioners characterize as the "death penalty alternative," as this is the most burdensome of all possible alternatives listed as open to the EPA under TSCA.... By choosing the harshest remedy given to it under TSCA, the EPA assigned to itself the toughest burden in satisfying TSCA's requirement that its alternative be the least burdensome of all those offered to it. Since, both by definition and by the terms of TSCA, the complete ban of manufacturing is the most burdensome alternative—for even stringent regulation at least allows a manufacturer the chance to invest and meet the new, higher standard—the EPA's regulation cannot stand if there is any other regulation that would achieve an acceptable level of risk as mandated by TSCA....

[W]hile the EPA may have shown that a world with a complete ban of asbestos might be preferable to one in which there is only the current amount of regulation, the EPA has failed to show that there is not some intermediate state of regulation that would be superior to both the currently-regulated and the completely-banned world. Without showing that asbestos regulation would be ineffective, the EPA cannot discharge its TSCA burden of showing that its regulation is the least burdensome available to it.

[*The Court remanded the case to EPA for further consideration in light of this opinion.*]

Questions and Comments for Discussion

1. The court discussed petitioners' procedural challenge to the agency's rule making in this case. The petitioners had argued, among other things, that the EPA's rule-making procedure was flawed because it did not cross-examine petitioner's witnesses, it did not assemble a panel of experts on asbestos disease risks, it designated a hearing officer rather than an administrative law judge to preside at the hearing, and it did not swear in witnesses who testified. While the court did not agree with all of these procedural challenges, it did find that the EPA's failure to give notice to the public, before the conclusion of the hearings, that it intended to use "analogous exposure" data to calculate the expected benefits of certain product bans, was an abuse of discretion by the agency. According to the court, "failure to seek public comment on such an important part of the EPA's analysis deprived its rule of the substantial evidence required to survive judicial scrutiny." This case also illustrates the procedural hurdles facing the EPA in a Section 6 rule-making case, and it may explain why the EPA has initiated few Section 6 cases.

2. After the court denied the EPA's petition for rehearing in this case, the Justice Department chose not to appeal the decision

to the Supreme Court. In 1991, the EPA announced it would follow OSHA in promulgating any new regulations regarding inspection of commercial buildings for friable (airborne) asbestos.

The Asbestos Hazard Emergency Response Act (AHERA)

The EPA regulates asbestos under several federal environmental statutes including the Clean Air Act, the Clean Water Act, TSCA's Section 8 reporting requirements, and CERCLA. In 1986, Congress amended TSCA by adding a new Title III, the *Asbestos Hazard Emergency Response Act of 1986* (AHERA). The law requires the EPA to establish regulations for inspecting, managing, planning, and operations and maintenance activities for controlling asbestos-containing materials in schools. In February 1988, as required by AHERA, the EPA sent Congress a study recommending a four-part program to address the existing asbestos hazard in public and commercial buildings. Almost all states have enacted some form of asbestos-related legislation.

In 1986, OSHA established a permissible abestos exposure limit for employees who may be exposed to asbestos-containing material in the workplace. This limit was challenged by several industrial organizations, but the U.S. Court of Appeals for the D.C. circuit upheld the exposure limit although it directed OSHA to reexamine certain aspects of its regulations. The Department of Transportation (DOT) also regulates the transportation of asbestos under the Hazardous Materials Transportation Act (HMTA) of 1975, which is discussed in Chapter 13.

Regulating PCBs

PCB regulations are specifically mandated by TSCA Section 6, which establishes a legal presumption that PCBs pose an unreasonable risk. Manufacturing, processing, or distributing PCBs in commerce in the United States is prohibited by law unless totally enclosed or in an otherwise specifically authorized manner. The law mandates standardized PCB warning labels and limits PCB disposal methods. EPA regulations include those governing the reporting and cleanup of spills containing PCBs and those establishing a nationwide PCB manifesting system. Violation of these regulations can be costly for industry. In 1988, the EPA assessed a $15 million fine against a pipeline company for leaking and spilling PCBs; the required cleanup was estimated to cost the company $400 million.[13]

Radon and Lead-Based Paint

Title III of TSCA directs the EPA to develop model construction standards and techniques for controlling radon levels within new buildings. Radon is an odorless, and colorless gas which has been associated with an increased risk in human lung cancer. TSCA also establishes a radon information clearinghouse and provides for training and grants to states to assist in the development of state radon programs.

Title IV of TSCA, entitled the Lead-Based Paint Exposure Reduction Act, was signed into law by President Bush in 1992. It requires the EPA and OSHA to develop lead paint abatement training and certification programs for contractors, and to identify lead-based paint hazards and safe levels of lead in various media.

Biotechnology

The EPA has also asserted authority under TSCA to regulate genetically engineered micro-organisms. The agency has not yet proposed comprehensive biotechnology regulations but is requiring researchers, manufacturers, processors, distributors, and importers to comply with some TSCA reporting requirements. According to a 1986 policy statement, the EPA requires compliance with PMN requirements for "new" microorganisms and reporting requirements for all microorganisms.

Importers and Exporters

Under TSCA Section 13, importers of chemical substances also must comply with TSCA certification requirements. The importer is responsible for determining whether a chemical substance is on the TSCA inventory, and a manufacturer of any new chemical substance imported into the United States for commercial purposes must file a PMN unless it is imported as "part of an article." Imported wastes are also subject to TSCA because they are chemical substances. Even if accompanied by a hazardous waste manifest under RCRA, imported wastes must meet the certification requirements of TSCA.

Exporters of chemicals may also be subject to notification requirements under TSCA Section 12. However, TSCA requirements do *not* apply to toxic substances distributed for export unless such activities pose an unreasonable risk of harm within the United States. Critics of this provision argue that the United States should not condone the export to other countries of substances it finds dangerous to its own citizens.

OTHER FEDERAL LAWS REGULATING CHEMICALS

While it is not possible to cover all other laws affecting chemicals, one should note that the Consumer Product Safety Act (CPSA), Federal Hazardous Substances Act (FHSA), Flammable Fabrics Act (FFA), and Poison Prevention Packaging Act (PPPA), as well as chemical transport laws and chemical waste and disposal laws discussed in other chapters of this text, all contain provisions affecting the production and use of chemical substances in the United States.

Under provisions of the CPSA, the Consumer Product Safety Commission (CPSC) promulgates safety standards for consumer products, bans unsafe products, and requires recalls or corrective action for unsafe products. Under the act, the Commission has regulated the consumer uses of asbestos and formaldehyde and imposed labeling requirements for paints and solvents.

The FHSA permits the CPSC to regulate hazardous substances produced for use by consumers. Under this act, the commission has labeling authority over products that are toxic, corrosive, flammable, irritant, or radioactive, and it may require the removal of hazardous household substances from the consumer market. Substances covered include turpentine, cleaning fluids, alcohols, and other hazardous substances.

The FFA authorizes the CPSC to set flammability standards for fabrics, and to establish guidelines for testing and rating fabrics. The PPPH also authorizes the CPSC to establish packaging standards for household substances, including child-resistant containers for substances like turpentine, prescription drugs, furniture polish, and charcoal and cigarette lighter fluids.

COMPARISON OF FIFRA AND TSCA

Unlike many major environmental laws regulating the emission of toxicants and pollutants from a production process, TSCA and FIFRA regulate the chemical products themselves. Both FIFRA and TSCA mandate a risk-cost-benefit criteria for agency decision making regarding regulation of chemicals and pesticides, and both TSCA and FIFRA provide for review of new chemicals. These laws also give the EPA authority to address hazardous chemicals already in commerce, including authority to ban the manufacture or use of dangerous chemicals.

There are, however, significant differences between FIFRA and TSCA. TSCA, for example, does not impose up-front testing requirements for new chemicals, although the proposal must identify the chemical and its use as well as its alleged safety. After notification to the EPA, manufacture of a new chemical can begin unless the agency takes affirmative action to prevent it. In contrast, FIFRA prohibits introduction of new chemical pesticides *unless* the EPA registers it. Some suggest the greater probability of adverse consequences from pesticides explains these different approval requirements.

Because the approval processes differ, the costs borne by manufacturers under the two programs also differ. Tests for a major new pesticide ingredient may cost from $5 to $7 million, while a new chemical can be introduced at a cost of between $1,300 and $7,500.[14] It is also easier for the EPA to gather information under FIFRA than TSCA because failure to provide pesticide data may result in loss of registration. Under TSCA, the EPA must issue a rule to gather such data.

In adopting TSCA and FIFRA, Congress incorporated the notion of "unreasonable risk." Thus Congress made the policy decision to adopt cost-risk criteria for regulation of toxic chemicals under these laws, which raises several important questions: To what extent can the risks associated with toxic chemicals be quantitatively evaluated? How effective is the agency's program for gathering and evaluating information about the chemicals it regulates? Considering the long time periods associated with development of disease from exposure to toxic chemicals, can the long-term environmental effects for new chemicals and pesticides be effectively determined?

THE PROBLEM OF RISK ASSESSMENT IN CONTROLLING TOXIC SUBSTANCES

Any discussion of regulatory schemes designed to control toxic substances must include the complicated topic of the problems of risk assessment, which is only briefly examined here. While many of the statutes addressed in this and preceding chapters contain general standards of risk (for example, regulation of hazardous air pollutants under the Clean Air Act), agencies like the EPA and OSHA must determine specific requirements necessary to meet general risk standards under these environmental statutes. They do so by utilizing risk assessment and risk management processes.

Risk assessment may be defined as the process of characterizing the potentially adverse consequences of human exposure to an environmental hazard. *Risk management* is the process by which policy choices are made once those risks have been determined. One of the risks a potentially toxic substance may pose is risk of carcinogenicity (or risk of causing cancer). The following four-step risk assessment process was first described and recommended by a committee of the National Research Council:[15]

1. Hazard Identification: Information used at this stage includes comparisons of molecular structures, short-term studies, animal bioassay data, and epidemiological studies.

2. Dose-Response Assessment: After a hazardous substance is defined, this step determines the response of humans to various levels of exposure. Dose-response assessment usually requires assessments of animal studies.

3. Exposure Assessment: This step determines which populations would be exposed to the chemical and the dosages to which they would be exposed.

4. Risk Characterization: This final step involves estimating the magnitude of the risk to public health. The conclusions drawn by the assessor (that is, the EPA or other agency) are most likely to involve value judgments at this stage.

The courts' willingness to defer to agency decision making in characterizing risk means that if the agency follows an appropriate risk assessment model, the agency's decision has a stronger likelihood of being upheld.

A Critical Analysis of TSCA and FIFRA

FIFRA creates a licensing system for pesticides, which must be registered before they can be sold. The registrant has the initial and continuing burden to demonstrate a pesticide's safety; however, the EPA has the burden in a cancellation proceeding. Critics have pointed to some serious disadvantages, including the fact that approval of a product at the premarket phase of production occurs when little information may be available about long-term effects of the chemical, and the fact that the scheme focuses on new products and risks, although FIFRA's reregistration requirements do address retroactive licensing requirements.

TSCA has been called the most complex, confusing, and ineffective of all federal environmental protection laws.[16] A chief criticism is that TSCA does not permit the EPA to require testing of every chemical but must first find the possibility of a risk of extensive exposure detrimental to humans or the environment, and then require testing because more information is needed. TSCA also requires that the EPA promulgate and support test rules through notice and comment rule making. This cumbersome and difficult procedure means that historically the EPA has rarely imposed a testing rule.[17] Some suggest that in fact TSCA actually discourages manufacturers from premarket testing in order to avoid creating toxic risk data.

Under TSCA, manufacture and distribution may begin if the EPA does not act to require testing before expiration of the 90-day PMN period. While FIFRA presumes a pesticide is unsafe unless the manufacturer proves otherwise, TSCA presumes safety unless the EPA can prove that it is unsafe, and TSCA's use of strict rule-making procedures inhibits the production of health and safety data. The real problem, according to some, is a political one:

> The dilemma that besets TSCA has not changed since its congressional evolution during the 1970s: as a nation we have been, and still are, unwilling to institutionalize a fully preventive approach to pollution control in the face of the pervasive uncertainty that characterizes environmental decision-making.[18]

Critics of imposing a more complex, lengthy approval process for new chemicals and pesticides argue that, in the long run, this would result in higher costs and increased risks because it would deter the production of new and safer products which could replace existing ones that are inherently more dangerous. Others have suggested that the EPA's focus on individual chemicals and narrow categories, combined with the expensive and time-consuming regulatory process, has greatly limited the number of existing chemicals that have been tested. Rather, they argue, testing and assessment strategies should be developed for broad categories of related chemicals.

Because of the uncertainties of risk and the enormous economic implications of chemical regulations, the question of how best to regulate existing and new chemicals and pesticides is a policy question of substantial importance to all involved. This issue will continue to fuel debate and generate litigation and legislation well into the future. Chemical technology has made our modern lifestyle possible; the challenge is to find an appropriate balance between the benefits of chemical production and its use while addressing its possible adverse consequences.

GLOSSARY

Delaney Clause—Provision of the Federal Food, Drug, and Cosmetic Act which banned the intentional addition to food of substances known to cause cancer in animals. Repealed in 1996.

FFDCA—Federal Food, Drug, and Cosmetic Act.

FIFRA—The Federal Insecticide, Fungicide, and Rodenticide Act.

Interagency Testing Committee—Agency set up under TSCA which sets priorities for testing chemical substances and mixtures.

OSHA—The Occupational Safety and Health Administration.

PMN—Premanufacture notice under the Toxic Substances Control Act.

SNUR—Significant new use rule issued under the Toxic Substances Control Act.

TSCA—The Toxic Substances Control Act.

TSCA inventory—An inventory of all existing chemicals under the Toxic Substances Control Act.

CASES FOR DISCUSSION

1. Merrell sued to enjoin the EPA from continuing to register seven herbicides which his local road department sprayed along the road leading to his wife's farm. Merrell argued that the registrations were invalid because the EPA and its predecessor agency had not made public the information on which they were based, and therefore EPA violated the National Environmental Policy Act (NEPA) and its implementing regulations. Merrell argued that the EPA violated NEPA because the EPA failed either to prepare a site-specific environmental impact statement (EIS) for each right of way use registration or to explain why no EIS was necessary. Is the EPA required to prepare an EIS under NEPA when it registers pesticides under FIFRA? *Merrell v. Thomas,* 807 F.2d 776 (9th Cir. 1986).

2.   Plaintiff Deborah Ryan, on her own behalf and her son, Kevin, sued Chemlawn Corporation for injuries allegedly caused by her and her son's exposure to defendant's pesticide products. She sued based on negligence and strict liability, and requested compensatory and punitive damages, as well as injunctive relief. The district court dismissed her claim determining that the facts contained in her complaint were highly technical and would be better resolved by the EPA. The district court had dismissed her suit holding that the plaintiff was required to exhaust all available administrative remedies before having her claim adjudicated in the courts. Did the district court properly dismiss plaintiff's state law claims for compensation and punitive damages? *Ryan v. Chemlawn,* 935 F.2d 129 (7th Cir. 1991).

3.   A consumer's lungs were permanently damaged from the fumes that resulted from his mixture of two bathroom cleaning products. He sued the manufacturers in state court and the case was removed to federal court. The district court determined that the consumer's state law had strict liability and negligence claims for failure to warn which were pre-empted by the FIFRA. Is the consumer's failure to warn theory pre-empted by FIFRA? *Shaw v. Dow Brands Inc.,* 994 F.2d 364 (7th Cir. 1993).

4.   The EPA sought to impose a fine of $25,000 on the General Electric Company (GE) for violating TSCA PCB disposal regulations. The company argued it did not have "fair warning of its [the EPA's] interpretation of the regulations." The dispute turned on whether a process utilized by GE in draining and rinsing PCB-contaminated transformers complied with EPA regulations. After draining the transformers, GE used freon as a solvent/rinse to remove residual PCBs before the transformers were sent to be landfilled. According to the EPA's interpretation, the company was required to send the contaminated solvent for incineration. The EPA argued that the company's intermediate distillation violated applicable requirements because the contaminated solvent was not incinerated immediately. GE claimed that the intermediate processing was permitted under another section of the regulations. Should GE be fined under TSCA for violating PCB disposal regulations if the company was not put on notice concerning the EPA's interpretation of those regulations? *General Electric Co. v. EPA,* 53 F.3d 1324 (D.C. Cir. 1995).

5.   Plaintiffs sued to enforce the Endangered Species Act (ESA) following the EPA's decision to continue registration of strychnine for above-ground use as a rodenticide pending the outcome of the administrative review process under FIFRA. Plaintiffs argued that the EPA's decision resulted in an unauthorized taking of protected species under the ESA. Did the EPA's registration of strychnine for above-ground use result in an unauthorized taking of a protected species under the ESA? *Defenders of Wildlife v. EPA,* 882 F.2d 1294 (8th Cir. 1989).

ENDNOTES

   1. Rachel Carson, *Silent Spring* at 13 (Houghton Mifflin Company, 1962).

   2. 7 U.S.C.A § 136(bb).

   3. Mary Devine Worobec and Cheryl Hogue, *Toxic Substances Control Guide* 2nd ed, at 50–51 (Bureau of National Affairs, 1992).

   4. *Ruckelshaus v. Monsanto,* 467 U.S. 986 (1984).

   5. Worobec and Hogue, 55–56.

6. *Environmental Law Handbook* at 433 (Government Institutes, Inc., 1993).

7. *Diamond v. Chakrobatry,* 447 U.S. 303 (1980).

8. Worobec and Hogue, 18.

9. 14 ERC 1858, *10 Envtl. L. Rep.* 20202 (S.D.N.Y. 1980).

10. 595 F. Supp. 1255 (S.D.N.Y. 1984).

11. Worobec and Hogue, 27.

12. Author's note: The APA "arbitrary and capricious" standard is discussed in Chapter 8 of this text.

13. Worobec and Hogue, 36.

14. Michael Shapiro, "Toxic Substances Policy" in *Public Policies for Environmental Protection,* Paul R. Portney, ed. at 213–215 (Resouce for the Future, 1992).

15. Joseph V. Rodricks, *Calculated Risks: Understanding the Toxicity and Human Health Risks of Chemicals in Our Environment* (Cambridge, 1992).

16. Zygmunt Plater, Robert Abrams, William Goldfarb, *Environmental Law and Policy; Nature, Law, and Society* at 748 (West Publishing Company, 1992).

17. *Ibid.,* 755.

18. *Ibid.,* 759.

13

REGULATING SOLID
AND HAZARDOUS WASTE

INTRODUCTION

Previous chapters examined major federal environmental legislation designed to address the problems of air and water pollution and toxic substances regulation. This chapter focuses on another important area of federal regulation—laws governing the generation, transportation, and disposal of hazardous waste and mandating the cleanup of inactive hazardous waste sites.

The EPA has estimated that 265 million tons of hazardous wastes were produced in the United States in 1984. More recently, agency officials estimate that number to be between 240 and 275 million tons per year.[1] According to the EPA, there are between 30,000 and 50,000 inactive disposal sites containing hazardous wastes throughout the country, and between 1500 to 2500 of these sites pose serious health problems, including possible contamination of public drinking supplies through groundwater contamination. (See Appendix B for an explanation of the pathways of contamination.)

The average life of a hazardous waste disposal site is twenty years, and ownership and operation often change hands during that period of time, making it difficult to identify disposal sites and the hazardous materials contained at the site.[2] Complicating the problems of identifying disposal sites is the fact that, in many cases, generators of waste have hired independent transporters to dispose of wastes away from the site of generation. In response to these concerns and the serious risks associated with hazardous waste generation and disposal, Congress adopted the **Resource Conservation and Recovery Act** (RCRA) in 1976, and in 1980, the **Comprehensive Environmental Response, Compensation, and Liability Act** (CERCLA), known as the "Superfund" law. Since enacting these laws, Congress has passed major amendments to both acts. RCRA has been amended several times, with major changes made to the law in 1984, and CERCLA was revised by the **Superfund Amendments and Reauthorization Act of 1986** (SARA).

RCRA was passed the same year Congress enacted the Toxic Substances Control Act (TSCA). RCRA replaced the language of the Resource Recovery Act and ordered the EPA to create a regulatory program designed to provide "cradle-to-grave" control of hazardous waste. RCRA also required the EPA to set standards for hazardous waste treatment, storage, and disposal facilities.

Between 1976 and 1978, under pressure from the public and Congress, the EPA focused on revising and issuing regulations under the Clean Air and Clean Water Acts. In 1978, however, that focus changed when buried chemicals near Love Canal, New York, began to bubble to the surface and seep into homes. This event alarmed the public and mobilized the EPA and Congress. In 1980, the EPA issued the first two portions of hazardous waste rules mandated by RCRA. Also in 1980, Congress adopted CERCLA, which is designed to address the problem of abandoned, inactive hazardous waste sites.

There is no clear line distinguishing when Superfund or RCRA applies in a particular case because many of the statutes' provisions overlap. Generally, CERCLA addresses past activities and RCRA governs current activities. Another important distinction is that RCRA encourages states to develop and operate their own hazardous waste regulatory programs in lieu of EPA implementation and enforcement. For a state to exercise such jurisdiction, it must receive EPA approval, and in many states the state and federal programs are identical. CERCLA, on the other hand, cannot be delegated to the states, but it does not pre-empt states from adopting an equivalent state Superfund law.

AN OVERVIEW OF RCRA

RCRA is primarily concerned with active waste sites, while CERCLA is designed to address the problem of abandoned hazardous waste sites. As first passed in 1976, RCRA was enacted to address recycling and waste disposal issues.

RCRA was significantly amended in 1984 by the **Hazardous and Solid Waste Amendments** (HSWA). Today, over 500,000 companies and individuals, generating over 172 million metric tons of hazardous waste each year, are required to meet RCRA requirements regulating the generation, transportation, and storage of hazardous waste.[3] HSWA makes it clear that Congress intended to address the special health risks presented by the problems of hazardous waste. In its amendments to the act, Congress made the following policy statement:

> Congress hereby declares it to be the national policy of the United States that, wherever feasible, the generation of hazardous waste is to be reduced or eliminated as expeditiously as possible. Waste that is nevertheless generated should be treated, stored, or disposed of so as to minimize the present and future threat to the environment.

RCRA contains ten subtitles. Significant among these are Subtitle C, which establishes a national hazardous waste management program; Subtitle D, providing for state or regional solid waste plans; and Subtitle I, regulating underground storage tanks.

Structure of the Act

As originally enacted, RCRA was designed not only to address the problems of hazardous waste, but also to control the disposal of solid wastes and promote the recovery of usable materials and the recycling of wastes. RCRA Subtitle C provisions have often overshadowed other goals of the act.

Subtitle D addresses nonhazardous solid waste, and it directs most of the responsibility for active municipal solid waste management to state and local governments. Under the 1984 RCRA amendments, the EPA was required to revise its disposal criteria for sanitary (nonhazardous waste) landfills. The EPA's final rule added landfill construction, operations, monitoring, and closure requirements. The requirements for municipal solid waste landfills are still less stringent than those for hazardous waste landfills, which require standards "necessary for protection of human health and the environment."

Subtitle C imposes management and record-keeping requirements on generators and transporters of hazardous wastes as well as owners and operators of treatment, storage, and disposal facilities. The provisions of Subtitle C are implemented through extensive regulations enacted by the EPA, which cover several hundred pages in the **Code of Federal Regulations** (CFR), located at 40 CFR 260-271 and 40 CFR 124.

The following outline identifies Subtitle C RCRA sections and titles more fully discussed in this chapter:

3001:   Identification of hazardous waste

3002:   Generators of hazardous waste

3003:   Transporters of hazardous waste

3004:   Standards for TSD (treatment, storage and disposal) facilities

3005:   Permit requirements for TSD facilities

3006:   Guidelines for state programs

7002:   Citizen enforcement provisions

7003:   EPA authority to seek injunctive relief

Section 3001: What is Hazardous Waste?

Under RCRA, hazardous waste is a subset of "solid waste." That pivotal term is defined by RCRA as any

garbage, refuse, sludge from a waste treatment plant, water supply treatment plant or air pollution control facility and other discarded material, including solid, liquid, semisolid, or contained gaseous materials resulting from industrial, commercial, mining and agriculture activities and from community activities. . . .

Subtitle C covers those solid wastes deemed hazardous. *Hazardous waste* under RCRA is a solid waste, or combination of solid wastes, which because of its quantity, concentration, or physical, chemical, or infectious characteristics may:

A.   cause, or significantly contribute to an increase in mortality or an increase in serious irreversible, or incapacitating reversible illness;

B.   pose a substantial present or potential hazard to human health or the environment when improperly treated, stored, transported, or disposed of, or otherwise managed.

Under the statute, solid waste includes any *discarded material,* which includes material that is abandoned, recycled, or "inherently waste-like." In *American Mining Congress v. EPA,* 824 F.2d 1177 (D.C. Cir. 1987), trade associations representing mining and oil refining interests challenged RCRA regulations promulgated by the EPA. The EPA regulations amended the definition of "solid waste" to include some secondary materials reused within an industry's ongoing production process. Petitioners maintained that the EPA had exceeded its regulatory authority in seeking to bring materials that are not discarded or otherwise disposed of within the definition of "waste." A portion of the court's opinion can be found in the case that follows.

AMERICAN MINING CONGRESS
v. UNITED STATES EPA
824 F.2d 1177 (D.C. Cir., 1987)

RCRA is a comprehensive environmental statute under which EPA is granted authority to regulate solid and hazardous wastes. Congress' "overriding concern" in enacting RCRA was to establish the framework for a national system to insure the safe management of hazardous waste. In passing RCRA, Congress expressed concern over the "rising tide" in scrap, discarded, and waste materials. As the statute itself puts it, Congress was concerned with the need "to reduce the amount of waste and unsalvageable materials and to provide for proper and economical solid waste disposal practices." Congress thus crafted RCRA "to promote the protection of health and the environment and to conserve valuable material and energy resources."

RCRA includes two major parts: one deals with non-hazardous solid waste management and the other with hazardous waste management. Under the latter, EPA is directed to promulgate regulations establishing a comprehensive management system. EPA's authority, however, extends only to the regulation of "hazardous waste." Because "hazardous waste" is defined as a subset of "solid waste," the scope of EPA's jurisdiction is limited to those materials that constitute "solid waste." That pivotal term is defined by RCRA as any garbage, refuse, sludge from a waste treatment plant, water supply treatment plant, or air pollution control facility and other discarded material, including solid, liquid, semisolid or contained gaseous material, resulting from industrial, commercial, mining, and agricultural operations, and from community activities. . . ."

This case turns on the meaning of the phrase, "and other discarded material," contained in the statute's definitional provisions.

***

Under the final [EPA] rule, materials are considered "solid waste" if they are abandoned by being disposed of, burned, or incinerated; or stored, treated, or accumulated before or in lieu of those activities. In addition, certain recycling activities fall within EPA's definition. EPA determines whether a material is a RCRA solid waste when it is recycled by examining both the material or substance itself and the recycling activity involved. . . . Under the final rule, if a material constitutes "solid waste," it is subject to RCRA regulation unless it is directly reused as an ingredient or as an effective substitute for a commercial product, or is returned as a raw material substitute to its original manufacturing process. In the jargon of the trade, the latter category is known as the "closed-loop" exception. In either case, the material must not first be "reclaimed" (processed to recover a usable product or regenerated.) EPA exempts these activities "because they are like ordinary usage of commercial products."

***

Petitioners, American Mining Congress and American Petroleum Institute challenge the scope of EPA's final rule. Relying upon the statutory definition of "solid waste," petitioners contend that EPA's authority under RCRA is limited to controlling materials that are discarded or intended for discard. They argue that EPA's reuse and recycle rules, as applied to in-process secondary materials, regulate materials that have not been discarded, and therefore exceed EPA's jurisdiction. . . .

Because the issue is one of statutory interpretation, the principles enunciated in *Chevron U.S.A. Inc. v. NRDC,* 467 U.S. 837 (1984), and its progeny guide our inquiry.[4] In Chevron, a unanimous Supreme Court laid out a now familiar, general framework for analyzing agency interpretations of statutes. First, the reviewing court is to consider whether Congress "has directly spoken to the precise question at issue." This inquiry focuses first on the language and structure of the statute itself. If the answer is not yielded by the statute, then the court is to look to secondary indicia of intent, such as the measure's legislative history. . . .

Guided by these principles, we turn to the statutory provision at issue here. Congress, it will be recalled, granted EPA power to regulate "solid waste." Congress specifically defined "solid waste" as "discarded material." EPA then defined "discarded material" to include materials destined for reuse in an industry's ongoing production processes. The challenge to EPA's jurisdictional reach is founded, again, on the proposition that in-process secondary materials are outside the bounds of EPA's lawful authority. Nothing has been discarded, the argument goes, and thus RCRA jurisdiction remains untriggered.

The first step in statutory interpretation is, of course, an analysis of the language itself. As the Supreme Court has often observed, "the starting point in every case involving statutory construction is 'the language employed by Congress.'" In pursuit of Congress' intent, we "start with the assumption that the legislative purpose is expressed by the ordinary meaning of the words used." These sound principles governing the reading of statutes seem especially forceful in the context of the present case. Here, Congress defined "solid waste" as "discarded material." The ordinary, plain-English meaning of the word "discarded" is "disposed of," "thrown away" or "abandoned." Encompassing materials retained for immediate reuse within the scope of "discarded material" strains, to say the least, the everyday usage of that term. . . .

***

The question we face, then, is whether, in light of the National Legislature's expressly stated objectives and the underlying problems that motivated it to enact RCRA in the first instance, Congress was using the term "discarded" in its ordinary sense—"disposed of" or "abandoned"—or whether Congress was using it in a much more open-ended way, so as to encompass materials no longer useful in their original capacity though destined for immediate reuse in another phase of the industry's ongoing production process.

For the following reasons, we believe the former to be the case. RCRA was enacted, as the Congressional objectives and findings make clear, in an effort to help States deal with the ever-increasing problem of solid waste disposal by encouraging the search for and use of alternatives to existing methods of disposal (including recycling) and protecting health and the environment by regulating hazardous wastes. To fulfill these purposes, it seems clear that EPA need not regulate "spent" materials that are recycled and reused in an ongoing manufacturing or industrial process. These materials have not yet become part of the waste disposal problem; rather, they are destined for beneficial reuse or recycling in a continuous process by the generating industry itself. . . .

[O]ur analysis of the statute reveals clear Congressional intent to extend EPA's authority only to materials that are truly discarded, disposed of, thrown away, or abandoned. . . . Legislative history can be a legitimate guide to a statutory purpose obscured by ambiguity, but in the absence of a "clearly expressed legislative intention to the contrary," the language of the statute itself "must ordinarily be regarded as conclusive." Unless exceptional circumstances dictate otherwise, "when we find the terms of a statute unambiguous, judicial inquiry is complete."

***

We are constrained to conclude that, in light of the language and structure of RCRA, the problems animating Congress to enact it, and the relevant portions of the legislative history, Congress clearly and unambiguously expressed its intent that "solid waste" (and therefore EPA's regulatory authority) be limited to materials that are "discarded" by virtue of being disposed of, abandoned, or thrown away. While we do not lightly overturn an agency's reading of its own statute, we are persuaded that by regulating in-process secondary materials, EPA has acted in contravention of Congress' intent. Accordingly, the petition for review is Granted.

Questions and Comments for Discussion

1. Subsequent to the decision in this case, the EPA proposed amendments to the definition of solid waste to exclude certain in-process recycled secondary materials that are part of a continuous production or manufacturing process. What are some environmental policy concerns that might support EPA's original decision to treat some recycled waste products as waste for purposes of RCRA regulation?

2. One judge dissented in this opinion. In Judge Mikva's opinion,

> The court today strains to overturn the Environmental Protection Agency's interpretation of the Resource Conservation and Recovery Act to authorize the regulation of certain recycled industrial materials. Under today's decision, the EPA is prohibited from regulating in-process sec-

ondary materials that contribute to the ominous problem that Congress sought to eradicate by passing the RCRA. In my opinion, the EPA has adequately demonstrated that its interpretation is a reasonable construction of an ambiguous term in a statue committed to the agency's administration. We therefore are obliged to defer to the agency's interpretation under the principles of Chevron. . . .

3. To what extent do the conflicting opinions in this case (majority and dissenting opinions) illustrate the difficulty of applying the "plain meaning" rule under the Chevron test? Do you agree with Judge Mikva that the term "discarded material" is ambiguous, or do you agree with the majority that the intention of Congress is clear from the "plain meaning" of the words used in the statute?

Hazardous Waste under EPA Definition

Certain solid wastes are exempted from hazardous waste by EPA regulations. These include household waste and agricultural waste returned to the ground such as fertilizer, industrial wastewater discharges regulated under the CWA, irrigation return flows, and certain nuclear, mining, coal, and oil-drilling wastes.

Unless exempted from the definition of hazardous waste, a solid waste is deemed a hazardous waste under either of two tests: (1) It is listed as hazardous waste by the EPA or (2) it exhibits one of the following four hazardous waste characteristics:

1. *Ignitability* (poses a fire hazard during routine management)
2. *Corrosivity* (has the ability to corrode standard containers or dissolve toxic components of other wastes)
3. *Reactivity* (has the tendency to explode under normal conditions, to react violently with water, or to generate toxic gases)
4. *Toxicity* (exhibits the presence of one or more specified toxic materials)

If a waste is hazardous, those generating, transporting, storing, or disposing it are subject to RCRA requirements. Generators of waste are responsible for determining if it is hazardous, either because it is listed by the EPA or because it exhibits the characteristics set out above.

As required by the 1984 amendments to RCRA, the EPA has published a list of about 450 specific chemicals that are defined as toxic wastes. If a generator of waste demonstrates that its waste is fundamentally different from the waste listed, it may obtain an exemption from RCRA regulations. To do so, it must provide test data showing that the specific waste does not meet EPA criteria.

The EPA has adopted other rules broadly defining hazardous waste for purposes of RCRA regulation. Under the **mixture rule,** a mixture of a listed hazardous waste and solid waste is considered a hazardous waste unless it qualifies for an exemption. Under the EPA's **derived-from rule,** a waste that is generated from the treatment, storage, or disposal of a hazardous waste is also a hazardous waste, unless exempted. Finally, under the EPA's **contained-in rule,** soil, groundwater, surface water, and debris contaminated with hazardous waste are also regulated under Subtitle C.

The EPA also regulates recycling activities under RCRA. Regulated activities include (1) recycling in a manner constituting disposal, such as land application; (2) burning for energy recovery; (3) reclamation; and (4) speculative accumulation. In general, hazardous wastes destined for recycling are subject to RCRA regulations and storage facility requirements.

Any person who generates, transports, or owns or operates a **treatment, storage, and disposal** (TSD) **facility**, or who produces, markets, or burns hazardous waste-derived fuels, must file a notification form with the EPA, listing the reporting company and its location, and providing EPA identification numbers for the listed and characteristic hazardous wastes it manages.

Generator of Waste Requirements

Sections 3002 and 3003 of RCRA govern hazardous waste generators and transporters. EPA regulations issued under authority of those sections are published at 40 CFR 262 and 263. These establish the duties of generators and transporters of hazardous waste.

A **generator** is defined by EPA regulations as "any person, by site, whose act or process produces hazardous waste identified or listed in Part 261 of this chapter or whose act first causes hazardous waste to become subject to regulation." Under this definition, every plant site must evaluate and comply with generator requirements. A generator of hazardous waste must:

1. Obtain an EPA identification number within 90 days of beginning operation (available from the EPA regional office with jurisdiction over the facility)

2. Obtain a permit for the facility where waste is generated if the waste is held on site for more than 90 days before disposal

3. Use shipping containers specified by the Department of Transportation that meet labeling for shipment requirements

4. Prepare a *manifest* (shipping form) used for tracking the waste

5. Assure that the waste reaches the designated disposal facility

6. Periodically submit a summary of hazardous waste activities to the EPA

Small Quantity Generators

Before 1984, generators of 1,000 kilograms or more of hazardous waste per month were covered by RCRA requirements. Under the 1984 amendments, generators of between 100 and 1,000 kilograms of hazardous waste per month are now covered. These **small quantity generators** are governed by regulations which parallel existing generator standards but exempt smaller generators from the full manifest provisions. Small generators are permitted to store wastes on site for a longer period of time and are governed by reduced requirements for planning for emergencies and training employees. Small generator regulations govern an estimated 175,000 small businesses, including laundries, printers, and garages.

RCRA hazardous waste generator categories are as follows:

- *Large Quantity Generator*

  Generates more than 1,000 kg/month of hazardous waste, or generates more than 1 kg/month of extremely hazardous waste

  May store hazardous wastes on site for up to 90 days, or to a maximum quantity of 6,000 kg, without obtaining a RCRA Part B permit as a storage facility

- *Small Quantity Generator*

  Generates 100 to 1,000 kg/month of hazardous waste, or generates 1 kg/month or less of extremely hazardous waste

  May store hazardous wastes on site for up to 180 days (270 days if more than 200 miles from a TSDF facility) without obtaining a RCRA Part B permit as a storage facility

- *Conditionally Exempt Small Quantity Generator*

  Generates less than 100 kg/month of hazardous waste and no extremely hazardous waste

  May store hazardous wastes on site indefinitely, or until 100 kg is accumulated, without obtaining a RCRA Part B permit as a storage facility. When 100 kg has accumulated, the small quantity generator limitations are triggered.

The Hazardous Waste Manifest

The **Uniform Hazardous Waste Manifest** is a control and transport document that accompanies the hazardous waste at all times. The manifest must contain the generator's name, address, and EPA identification number; names and identification numbers of transporters; name and identification number of the facility designated to received the waste; description and identification number of the waste; quantity and number and type of containers; the generator's signature certifying that the waste meets EPA and Department of Transportation regulations; and a certification that the volume of waste has been minimized.

Copies of the manifest are prepared for all parties. The final copy is signed and returned to the generator by the TSD facility and must be kept by the generator for at least three years; however, because of its potential liability under CERCLA (discussed later in this chapter), generators commonly maintain RCRA manifests, and other records, much longer.

A generator who stores waste for more than ninety days is considered to operate a waste storage facility and must obtain a TSD permit. Small quantity generators may store wastes for 180 days (or for 270 days if over 200 miles from the disposal site) without obtaining a TSD permit. (See Appendix B for an example of a Uniform Hazardous Waste Manifest form.)

Transporter Requirements

Transporters of hazardous waste are governed by the EPA and **Department of Transportation** (DOT). A transporter is any person engaged in the off-site transportation of hazardous waste by air, rail, highway, or water. Transporters include both interstate and intrastate transporters. A generator who moves hazardous waste off site is a transporter for purposes of RCRA.

The EPA has promulgated standards for all transporters of hazardous wastes. These include labeling and packaging requirements, and other standards coordinated with DOT standards issued under the **Hazardous Materials Transportation Act** (49 U.S.C. 1801) discussed in the following section. These require transporters to:

1. Obtain an EPA identification number
2. Use the uniform manifest system (or shipping papers meeting DOT requirements for wastes traveling by rail or in bulk by water)
3. Deliver all wastes as specified on the manifest
4. Keep the manifest copy for three years
5. Comply with DOT requirements for reporting discharges and spills of wastes under the Hazardous Materials Transportation Act (HMTA)
6. Clean up any hazardous wastes discharged during transportation (in most cases, the discharge also must be reported to the National Response Center, which is charged with coordinating response to hazardous substances spills).

Transporters may hold a hazardous waste for up to ten days at a transfer facility without obtaining a RCRA storage permit. A transporter may become subject to the RCRA generator requirements if it mixes wastes by placing them into a single container or accumulates waste in a vehicle or vessel.

The Hazardous Materials Transportation Act

HMTA became law in 1975, and it gives the Department of Transportation (DOT) the authority to regulate movement of all substances within the United States which may pose a threat to health, safety, property, or the environment. This includes a broad range of substances, including RCRA hazardous wastes. Substances shipped in bulk by water are regulated separately by the U.S. Coast Guard. The HMTA regulates more than 30,000 hazardous materials, which are subject to rules requiring special packaging, labeling, handling, and routing. Shippers are primarily responsible for assuring compliance with HMTA. The shipper is required to classify the shipment according to DOT requirements, select an authorized package, mark and label the package as required by law, and certify compliance with DOT regulations.

All hazardous material must be classified according to the hazard it presents. Hazards are numbered, based on a classification scheme dividing hazardous materials into nine classes. A hazardous material is classified based on such factors as its flash point, boiling point, toxicity, pressure, and corrosivity.

Standards for Treatment, Storage, and Disposal (TSD) Facilities

EPA rules under RCRA governing the treatment, storage, or disposal of hazardous wastes are intended to ensure that wastes are handled safely. These EPA rules, published at 40 CFR 264, 265, and 276, include provisions governing emergencies, manifest handling, record keeping, waste treatment, storage, monitoring, closing a facility, and financial liability of the owner and operator.

The 1984 amendments to the act added several important provisions to TSD management regulations. Among other things, the amendments banned the disposal of various liquid wastes and hazardous wastes in landfills, imposed minimum technological requirements (double liners) for surface impoundments and landfills, and added controls on the marketing and burning of hazardous wastes as fuels. Congress also mandated that the EPA make a number of regulatory decisions and set a strict timetable for the EPA to implement a land disposal ban on untreated hazardous wastes and to establish treatment standards for the wastes.

Under EPA rule, a facility is a *treatment facility* if the operator utilizes any method, technique, or process designed to change the physical, chemical, or biological character or composition of hazardous waste. Under EPA rules, almost anything done to a hazardous waste qualifies as treatment.

A *storage facility* is one which holds hazardous waste for a temporary period of time. A *disposal* facility is a place at which hazardous waste is intentionally placed (on land or water), and at which the waste will remain after closure. Some TSD facilities are exempted by EPA regulation, including facilities disposing of hazardous waste by means of ocean disposal in conformance to a permit issued under the MPRSA; the disposal of hazardous waste by underground injection under permit issued under the Safe Drinking Water Act; POTW treating or storing wastes delivered to it; and TSD facilities regulated under a state program authorized by RCRA.

Under general RCRA requirements, owners and operators of TSD facilities must:

1. Analyze wastes entering the facility to ensure identities as specified on the manifest
2. Provide security at the site and undertake inspections monitoring safety, security, operating, and structural equipment
3. Train employees in handling emergencies and take special precautions preventing reactions between incompatible wastes
4. Maintain emergency equipment and inform local police, fire, and emergency response teams about the facility layout, possible hazards
5. Have a written plan for responding to emergencies

The owner or operator of the TSD facility is required to sign, date, and return a copy of the manifest to the transporter and the generator of the waste. He must also keep records of the wastes received at the site and report unmanifested wastes and releases of wastes, fires, explosions, or groundwater contamination. Other TSD requirements include groundwater monitoring requirements where hazardous waste is placed onto or into the land, waste storage and treatment requirements, and financial responsibility requirements upon closure of the facility.

Land Disposal Restrictions

The Hazardous and Solid Waste Amendments of 1984 (HSWA) establish a strong presumption against land disposal by prohibiting land disposal of hazardous wastes beyond specified dates in the law, unless the EPA determines such disposal to protect human health and the environment.

In RCRA Section 1002(b)(7) Congress stated "reliance on land disposal should be minimized or eliminated, and land disposal, particularly landfills and surface impoundments, should be the least favored method for managing hazardous wastes." *Land disposal* under EPA regulations includes any placement of hazardous waste in a landfill, surface impoundment, waste pile, injection well, land treatment facility, salt dome formation, or underground mine or cave. The EPA sets levels or methods of treatment to substantially diminish the toxicity of the waste. Wastes meeting those standards are not prohibited from land disposal.

Permit Requirements for TSD Facilities

Under RCRA, any TSD facility must obtain a permit from the EPA or the state if the state has taken over operation of the hazardous waste program. A facility which was in existence or under construction in 1980 had to seek an interim status permit. Such facilities needed to obtain a final permit by submitting a second application within six months after EPA request. The EPA must inform the public that a request for a permit application is pending, and must meet requirements for public notice, public comment, and public hearings before a permit is granted. Permits are effective for ten years, but may be reviewed, modified, or revoked by the EPA. Under the 1984 amendments, permits must be reviewed after five years and facilities inspected every two years.

Medical Waste

In 1988, Congress amended RCRA to include the Medical Waste Tracking Act, which required the EPA to develop a demonstration program for tracking medical waste, which includes blood and blood products, bandages, animal or human body parts, and contaminated equipment. Since the act was amended, forty-five states have issued regulations defining medical wastes and mandating disposal requirements.

State Hazardous Waste Programs

Congress authorized states to develop and carry out their own hazardous waste program in lieu of RCRA if the program is "equivalent" to and "consistent" with the federal program. States must also provide adequate enforcement of the requirements of Subsection C. Because Congress believed it was important to implement the 1984 amendments quickly, EPA regulations implementing the 1984 amendments take effect in authorized states the same day they are effective for the federal program. Because the EPA implements HSWA provisions until the state takes over authority, joint permitting of a TSD facility (that is, permitting by the EPA and state) is often required.

Enforcement Mechanisms and Citizen Suit Provisions

The EPA, the states, and the DOT, are all responsible for enforcing RCRA. The EPA may use compliance orders, administrative orders, and consent decrees to force compliance. Section 3007 authorizes the EPA to enter sites for compliance inspection, to collect samples of wastes, and to examine and copy records. Civil penalties of up to $25,000 per day and suspension or revocation of the hazardous waste permit are possible penalties for violation. In addition, it is a criminal offense to knowingly violate certain provisions of the law. Under Section 3008, an individual who knowingly violates RCRA in a way that places another person in imminent danger of death or serious bodily injury is subject to a penalty of $250,000 or 15 years' imprisonment or both. A defendant organization is liable for a $1 million fine in such cases.

The RCRA citizen suit provisions permit a person to bring civil action against a violator, or against the EPA administrator for failing to perform a nondiscretionary duty. The 1984 amendments expanded the citizen suit provision to authorize suits where past or present management or disposal of hazardous wastes has contributed to a situation presenting "imminent or substantial endangerment." In order to bring a citizen suit, the plaintiff must give notice to the violator, the EPA administrator, and the state in which the alleged violation occurs, 60 days prior to bringing the action.

The question of whether Section 7002, RCRA's citizen suit provision, gives the federal courts authority to award money judgments for costs incurred in cleaning up contaminated sites has been a frequently litigated issue. That section, 42 U.S.C. Section 6972, authorizes a private cause of action

> against any person . . . who has contributed or who is contributing to the past or present handling, storage, treatment, transportation, or disposal of any solid or hazardous waste which may present an imminent and substantial endangerment to health or the environment. . . .

The U.S. Supreme Court addressed this issue in *Meghrig v. KFC Western,* 116 S.Ct. 1251 (1996). KFC Western, Inc., after complying with a county order to clean up contamination on its property, brought action under the citizen suit provision of RCRA, attempting to recover its cleanup costs from the Meghrigs, prior owners of the property.

The district court had held that RCRA's citizen suit provision did not authorize such damages, and the court of appeals had reversed. The Supreme Court unanimously held that RCRA's provision does not permit recovery of past cleanup costs nor does it authorize a cause of action for the remediation of toxic waste that does not pose an "imminent and substantial endangerment" at the time the suit is filed. The court relied on its plain reading of the remedial scheme under RCRA, and the fact that provisions of CERCLA demonstrate that "Congress . . . demonstrated in CERCLA that it knew how to provide for the recovery of cleanup costs, and . . . the language used to define the remedies under RCRA does not provide that remedy."

Restraining Imminent or Substantial Endangerment to Health or the Environment

Under Section 7003 of RCRA, the EPA is authorized to bring a suit to restrain an "imminent or substantial endangerment to health or the environment." Utilizing this section, the United States brought an action against a chemical manufacturer, transporter of waste products, and officers and shareholders of a manufacturer, seeking to recover costs for cleanup of a hazardous waste site. One of the issues in the case was whether RCRA imposed strict liability upon past off-site generators and transporters of hazardous substances.

The district court had held that the defendants were not liable for response costs under Section 7003 of RCRA. The district court interpreted RCRA Section 7003(a) to require a finding of negligence in order to hold past off-site generators and transporters liable for response costs; consequently, it held that RCRA did not apply to past non-negligent off-site generators and transporters of hazardous substances. The government appealed that portion of the court's decision.

UNITED STATES v. NORTHEASTERN PHARMACEUTICAL

810 F.2d 726 (8th Cir. 1986)

McMILLIAN, Circuit Judge.

NEPACCO (Northeastern Pharmaceutical & Chemical Co.) was incorporated in 1966 under the laws of Delaware; its principal office was located in Stamford, Connecticut. . . . In 1974 its corporate assets were liquidated, and the proceeds were used to pay corporate debts and then distributed to the shareholders. Michaels formed NEPACCO, was a major shareholder, and was its president. Lee was NEPACCO's vice-president, the supervisor of its manufacturing plant located in Verona, Missouri, and also a shareholder. Mills was employed as shift supervisor at NEPACCO's Verona plant.

From April 1970 to January 1972 NEPACCO manufactured the disinfectant hexachlorophene at its Verona plant. NEPACCO leased the plant from Hoffman-Taff Inc; Syntex Agribusiness, Inc. (Syntex) is the successor to Hoffman-Taff. Michaels and Lee knew that NEPACCO's manufacturing process produced various hazardous and toxic byproducts, including 2,4,5-trichlorophenol

(TCP), 2,3,7,8-tetrachlorodibenzo-p-dioxin (TCDD or dioxin), and toluene. The waste byproducts were pumped into a holding tank which was periodically emptied by waste haulers. Occasionally, however, excess waste byproducts were sealed in 55-gallon drums and then stored at the plant.

In July 1971, Mills approached NEPACCO plant manager Bill Ray with a proposal to dispose of the waste-filled 55-gallon drums on a farm owned by James Denney located about seven miles south of Verona. Ray visited the Denney farm and discussed the proposal with Lee; Lee approved the use of Mills' services and the Denney farm as a disposal site. In mid-July 1971 Mills and Gerald Lechner dumped approximately 85 of the 55-gallon drums into a large trench on the Denney farm (Denney farm site) that had been excavated by Leon Vaughn. Vaughn then filled in the trench. Only NEPACCO drums were disposed of at the Denny farm site.

In October 1979, the Environmental Protection Agency (EPA) received an anonymous tip that hazardous wastes had been disposed of at the Denney farm. Subsequent EPA investigation confirmed that hazardous wastes had in fact been disposed of at the Denney farm and that the site was not geologically suitable for the disposal of hazardous wastes. Between January and April 1980 the EPA prepared a plan for the cleanup of the Denney farm site and constructed an access road and a security fence. . . .

In August 1980, the government filed its initial complaint against NEPACCO, the generator of the hazardous substances; Michaels and Lee, the corporate officers responsible for arranging for the disposal of the hazardous substances; Mills, the transporter of the hazardous substances; and Syntex, the owner and lessor of the Verona plant, seeking injunctive relief and reimbursement of response costs pursuant to RCRA sec. 7003 (Count I).

***

As an alternative basis for recovery of the response costs incurred before December 11, 1980, (the effective date of CERCLA), the government argues that it can also recover its response costs pursuant to RCRA sec. 7003(a). The district court did not reach the recovery issue because it held that under RCRA sec. 7003(a) (prior to amendments discussed below) proof of fault or negligence was required in order to impose liability upon past off-site generators and transporters. Because the government did not allege or prove negligence, the district court found no liability under RCRA sec. 7003(a) (prior to the 1984 amendments). The government argues that the standard of liability under RCRA sec. 7003(a) as initially enacted and as amended in 1984 is strict liability, not negligence, and that liability under RCRA can be imposed even though the acts of disposal occurred before RCRA became effective in 1976. We agree.

RCRA was initially enacted in 1976. In November 1984, after the district court's January 1984 decision in the present case, RCRA was again amended by the Hazardous and Solid Waste Amendments of 1984 (1984 amendments). We have considered the 1984 amendments and the accompanying legislative history and, for the reasons discussed below, we believe the 1984 amendments support the government's arguments about RCRA's standard and scope of liability and retroactivity.

The critical issue is the meaning of the phrase "contributing to." Before its amendment in 1984, RCRA sec. 7003(a) imposed liability upon any person "contributing to" "the handling, storage, treatment, transportation or disposal of any solid or hazardous waste" that "may present an imminent and substantial endangerment to health or the environment." The district court did not find either the statutory language or the statuary framework helpful in determining whether past non-negligent off-site generators and transporters were liable under RCRA sec. 7003(a) (prior to the 1984 amendments.) The district court then considered the legislative history of the 1984 amendments because "[t]he legislative history of the [RCRA] as originally enacted contains no specific discussion of the reach of section 7003 and no mention of the reasons for its insertion. The hastiness of the [RCRA's] passage in the final days of a congressional session has been well-documented. . . ."

[I]n November 1984, Congress passed and President Reagan signed the 1984 amendments, which were described as "clarifying" amendments and specifically addressed the standard and scope of liability of sec. 7003(a). As amended in 1984, RCRA sec. 7003(a) (new language underlined; deleted language in brackets) now provides in pertinent part:

> Notwithstanding any other provision of this chapter, upon receipt of evidence that the *past or present* handling, storage treatment, transportation or disposal of

any solid waste or hazardous waste may present an imminent and substantial endangerment to health or the environment, the Administrator may bring suit on behalf of the United States in the appropriate district court [to immediately restrain any person] *against any person (including any past or present generator, past or present transporter, or past or present owner or operator of a treatment, storage, or disposal facility) who has contributed or who is* contributing to such handling, storage, treatment, transportation or disposal [to stop] *to restrain such person from* such handling, storage, treatment, transportation, or disposal [or to take such other action as may be necessary] *to order such person to take such other action as may be necessary, or both.*

As amended, RCRA sec. 7003 specifically applies to *past* generators and transporters.

. . . From the legislative history of the 1984 amendments it is clear that Congress intended RCRA sec. 7003(a) as initially enacted and as amended, to impose liability without fault or negligence and to apply to the present conditions resulting from past activities. In other words, RCRA sec. 7003(a) as initially enacted and as amended, applies to past non-negligent off-site generators like NEPACCO and to non-negligent past transporters like Mills.

Appellants argue, however, that the 1984 amendments should not be applied to them because the 1984 amendments are not merely "clarifying" amendments but instead substantively changed the existing law. We disagree. First Congress itself expressly characterized the 1984 amendments as "clarifying" amendments. Second, as part of the legislative history of the 1984 amendments, Congress expressly stated what its intention had been when it initially passed the RCRA in 1976, even though the 1976 legislative history contained no specific discussion of the standard and scope of liability of sec. 7003(a). . . . [B]y passing the 1984 amendments, the 98th Congress made clear that the intention of the 94th Congress in enacting the RCRA in 1976 had been to impose liability upon past non-negligent off-site generators and transporters of hazardous waste.

Questions and Comments for Discussion

1. Strict retroactive liability means that a person can be held liable for the cost of cleaning up a contaminated site under Section 7003(a) of RCRA even though the disposal of the material was not negligent or illegal at the time. What are the policy implications of applying the law retroactively and imposing strict liability in cases like this one?

2. In the next section of this chapter you will see that the government also pursued response costs from defendants in this case under CERCLA. Questions on appeal in the case included whether CERCLA, like RCRA, could be applied retroactively.

Underground Storage Tanks

Underground storage tanks (USTs) are a major source of groundwater and soil contamination because the tanks corrode or fail for structural reasons. The EPA estimated that in 1988 there were over two million UST systems located at over 700,000 facilities nationwide, and roughly seventy-five percent of these were made of steel without any form of corrosion protection. Some estimate that it will cost $41 billion and take over thirty years to clean up the nation's leaking underground storage tanks.[5] As a result of concerns about these problems, Congress enacted Subtitle I in the 1984 amendments to RCRA to regulate underground storage tanks containing petroleum or other regulated substances.

The UST program affects an estimated 100,000 to 400,000 tanks containing regulated substances. Certain residential tanks, septic tanks, and tanks regulated under other provisions of the law are exempted from the program. Nonexempted underground storage tanks must meet certain technical performance standards. In addition, the UST program contains notice requirements to assist the EPA in identifying existing tanks. These requirements also include requirements that manufacturers and distributors inform owners about their RCRA obligations. Failure to notify the EPA about a tank (including those out of service since 1974) may result in up to $10,000 in fines.

The RCRA program also requires that releases from USTs be reported and cleaned up, and it sets financial responsibility requirements for persons who own and operate petroleum USTs. A new UST program was included in the Superfund amendments and Reauthorization Act of 1986, requiring states to make an inventory of underground storage tanks and requiring the EPA to establish financial responsibility regulations for owners of USTs.

THE COMPREHENSIVE ENVIRONMENTAL RESPONSE, COMPENSATION, AND LIABILITY ACT (CERCLA)

In 1978, public attention suddenly focused on the serious risks posed by abandoned hazardous waste sites following the discovery of massive chemical contamination at Love Canal near Niagara Falls, New York. The CERCLA Act of 1980, also known as "Superfund," was enacted in direct response to those concerns, because many felt that existing laws did not adequately address the need to clean up abandoned hazardous waste sites.

At the time CERCLA was passed, the EPA estimated that there were as many as 30,000 to 50,000 inactive, uncontrolled waste sites in the United States, of which 20–30 percent contained wastes from off-site generators. The EPA estimated cleanup of the most dangerous sites would cost between $13.1 and $22.1 billion.[6]

The National Priority List currently lists approximately 1,300 sites for federal cleanup action, but some experts suggest that the potential number of sites may actually tally in the tens of thousands,[7] and Superfund actually addresses only a tiny portion of contaminated sites.

CERCLA created a broad framework under which multiple parties, including past and present owners, operators, transporters, and generators, can be held jointly, severally, and strictly liable for the costs of cleaning up a contaminated site. Under CERCLA, individuals or companies may be held liable for the costs of cleanup, even though their contribution to the contamination at the site was slight and the disposal was legal at the time it occurred.[8]

Critics of Superfund argue it is expensive, complex, and sometimes unfair. There are many who say that Superfund simply has not worked very well as the number of sites requiring action continues to grow. As the date for reauthorization of Superfund approaches, many are calling for substantial changes in the process by which Superfund requires polluters to pay for cleanups. Most likely, Congress will make some adjustments when the act is reauthorized.

Basic Structure of the Act

CERCLA has four basic elements: (1) it establishes an information-gathering and analysis system, which enables federal and state governments to develop priorities for response actions at hazardous waste sites; (2) it establishes federal authority to respond to hazardous substance emergencies through removal and remedial actions; (3) it creates a Hazardous Substances Trust Fund (the Superfund) to pay for the costs of cleanup actions; and (4) it imposes liability on persons responsible for releases of hazardous substances.

In 1986, Congress extensively amended CERCLA by adopting SARA. SARA clarified some provisions of the original act, added new provisions, including Title III's Emergency Planning and Community Right to Know Act, and increased the Superfund from $1.6 billion to $8.5 billion for 1986 to 1991. In 1990, Congress reauthorized Superfund until September 1994 at a funding level of $5.1 billion. (See Appendix B for a graphic explanation of the Superfund process.)

The National Priorities List and the National Contingency Plan

CERCLA requires the EPA to develop criteria for determining priorities among hazardous waste sites. Using a rating system, the EPA ranks each site with respect to priority for cleanup. The **National Priorities List** (NPL), which is updated annually, is the EPA's list of abandoned or uncontrolled hazardous waste sites. About 1,300 sites are either on the list or have been proposed for listing by the EPA. The EPA's decision to place a site on the list is subject to notice and public comment.

The **National Contingency Plan** (NCP) is a primary document guiding CERCLA response actions. The NCP establishes procedures which the EPA and private parties must follow in conducting cleanup response actions. The NCP was first prepared as a part of the FWPCA and was expanded under CERCLA to emphasize procedures for responding to releases of hazardous substances.

Defining Hazardous Substances under CERCLA

Hazardous substances are broadly defined under CERCLA by incorporating definitions used in other environmental statutes. The term as used in CERCLA includes hazardous wastes under RCRA, hazardous substances and toxic pollutants under the CWA, hazardous air pollutants under the Clean Air Act, imminently hazardous substances and mixtures under the TSCA, and any additional substance the EPA designates as hazardous under CERCLA. Petroleum, including crude oil, is expressly excluded from the definition of hazardous waste under CERCLA, although petroleum contamination is addressed under RCRA.

The vast majority of CERCLA actions involve hazardous substances, although CERCLA permits EPA response to a release or threat of release of "any pollutant or contaminant." However, only sites contaminated with hazardous substances are subject to actions for recovery of cleanup costs from private parties.

Definition of Terms: "Release" and "Facility"

Liability under CERCLA attaches in the event of a *release* or substantial threat of release of a hazardous substance from a **facility** or vessel. The definition of release is very broad:

"any spilling, leaking, pumping, pouring, emitting, emptying, discharging, injecting, escaping, leaching, dumping, or disposing into the environment" of any quantity of hazardous waste constitutes a release under the act. The courts have also interpreted "substantial threat of a release" very broadly. For example, corroding and abandoned tanks have met the test of threatened releases under the act.[9]

Likewise the term *facility* is broadly defined. A facility is "any site or area where a hazardous substance has . . . come to be located," and includes buildings, structures, installations, equipment, pipes, and wells. Under this expansive definition, almost any site meets the test of facility.

CERCLA Response Actions

CERCLA authorizes the EPA to undertake two categories of response actions, a **removal action** or a **remedial action**. Removal actions are those which address emergency situations to promptly diminish the threat posed by a hazardous waste site. Remedial actions are long-term permanent cleanups. Some take years or even decades to complete, and are significantly more complex and costly actions than removal actions. Because the costs of permanent cleanup are so substantial, an important issue for potentially liable parties is the process by which the EPA selects the appropriate remedial action and remedies chosen. There are fewer administrative requirements imposed on an EPA removal action than remedial actions. For example, the courts have held that a site must be listed on the NPL before federally funded remedial action is taken.

In undertaking a cleanup, the EPA has two options. It may clean up the site itself and then seek to recover those costs from potentially responsible parties, or it can compel those parties to perform the cleanup. Before authorizing expenditure from the Superfund, the EPA usually tries to make the responsible party clean up the site, or to get the state or local government to take responsibility for the cleanup. About ninety percent of all cleanup actions are performed by the responsible parties.

Liability of Potentially Responsible Parties under CERCLA

Much of the litigation under CERCLA concerns Section 107, which defines those parties who may be responsible for the costs of cleanup. **Potentially responsible parties** (PRPs) under Section 107(a) of the act include:

a. Owners and operators of a vessel or facility

b. Any person who at the time of disposal of any hazardous substance owned or operated any facility at which such substances were disposed

c. Any person who by contract, agreement, or otherwise arranged for the transport of hazardous substances owned or possessed by such person to another's vessel or facility

d. Any person who accepts or has accepted any hazardous substance for transport once such hazardous substance causes the incurrence of response costs

Person is defined by the act as any "individual, firm, corporation, association, partnership, consortium, joint venture, commercial entity, United States Government, state, municipality, commission, political subdivision of a state, or interstate body."

The definition of potentially responsible party under CERCLA is very broad and inclusive, with the intent to expand the pool of parties who may be liable for cleanup costs. In addition, the courts have held that CERCLA incorporates the **strict liability** standard utilized in the CWA. Under principles of strict liability, a party's claims that it was not negligent or that its actions met standard industry practices at the time of disposal is not a defense to liability. In most cases involving a site with multiple PRPs, liability is **joint and several,** which means that one party may be liable for the entire costs of cleanup in cases where it is difficult to apportion liability (as in the case of commingling of hazardous substances at a site). However, an individual who pays for the entire cleanup may bring an action for *contribution* against other responsible persons under the act.

Most courts have held that CERCLA is also **retroactive,** which means that it includes PRPs dating back to the generation, transportation, and/or disposal of the hazardous materials. As a result, owners and operators who were responsible for the release of hazardous substances long before the act was passed may incur the same liability as present owners or operators of the site.

In the earlier RCRA section of this chapter, you read a portion of *United States v. NEPPACO,* a case where defendants appealed a finding of liability under RCRA and CERCLA for the costs of cleaning up a farm site contaminated with hazardous wastes, including dioxin and toluene. A portion of the opinion addressing CERCLA liability issues continues below.

UNITED STATES v. NORTHEASTERN PHARMACEUTICAL
810 F.2d 726 (8th Cir. 1986)

[*The facts of this case are set out on pages 345–347.*]

***

Appellants first argue the district court erred in applying CERCLA retroactively, that is, to impose liability for acts omitted before its effective date, December 11, 1980. CERCLA sec. 302(a) provides that "[u]nless otherwise provided, all provisions of this chapter shall be effective on December 11, 1980." Appellants argue that CERCLA should not apply to pre-enactment conduct that was neither negligent nor unlawful when committed. Appellants argue that all the conduct at issue occurred in the early 1970s, well before CERCLA became effective. Appellants also argue that there is no language supporting retroactive application in CERCLA's liability section, or in the legislative history. Appellants further argue that because CERCLA imposes a new kind of liability, retroactive application of CERCLA violates due process and the taking clause. We disagree.

The district court correctly found Congress intended CERCLA to apply retroactively. . . . Although CERCLA does not expressly provide for retroactivity, it is manifestly clear that Congress intended CERCLA to have retroactive effect. The language used in the key liability provision, CERCLA sec. 107, refers to actions and conditions in the past tense: "any person who at the time of disposal of any hazardous substances owned or operated. . . ." Further, the statutory scheme itself is overwhelmingly remedial and retroactive. . . . In order to be effective, CERCLA must reach past conduct.

CERCLA's backward-looking focus is confirmed by the legislative history. . . .

The district court also correctly found that retroactive application of CERCLA does not violate due process. Appellants argue CERCLA creates a new form of liability that is designed to deter and punish those who, according to current standards, improperly disposed of hazardous substances in the past. We disagree.

> It is by now well established that legislative Acts adjusting the burdens and benefits of economic life come to the Court with a presumption of constitutionality, and that the burden is on one complaining of a due process violation to establish that the legislature has acted in an arbitrary and irrational way. [L]egislation readjusting rights and burdens is not unlawful solely because it upsets otherwise settled expectations. This is true even though the effect of the legislation is to impose a new duty or liability based on past acts . . . (citations omitted).

***

Appellants also summarily argue retroactive application of CERCLA constitutes an unconstitutional taking of property. We disagree. First, because appellants do not have a property interest in the Denney farm site, we question appellants' standing to raise a takings issue. Second, we hesitate to characterize the government's cleanup as a taking at all; the government's cleanup of the Denney farm site has not deprived the property owner of any property interest. Instead, the government's cleanup of the site abated an "imminent and substantial endangerment" to the public health and the environment, thus eliminating a public nuisance and restoring value to the property by removing the hazardous substances.

***

Appellants argue the district court erred in finding them liable under CERLCA sec.

107(a)(1) as the "owners and operators" of a "facility" where hazardous substances are located. Appellants argue that, regardless of their relationship to the NEPACCO plant, they neither owned nor operated the Denny farm site, and that it is the Denney farm site, not the NEPACCO plant, that is a "facility" for purposes of "owner and operator" liability under CERCLA sec. 107(a)(1). We agree.

CERCLA defines the term "facility" in part as "any site or area where a hazardous substance has been deposited, stored, disposed of, or placed, or otherwise come to be located." The term "facility" should be construed very broadly to include "virtually any place at which hazardous wastes have been dumped, or otherwise disposed of." In the present case, however, the place where the hazardous substances were disposed of and where the government has concentrated its cleanup efforts is the Denney farm site, not the NEPACCO plant. . . .

CERCLA sec. 107(a)(3) imposes strict liability upon "any person" who arranged for the disposal or transportation for disposal of hazardous substances. As defined by statute, the term "person" includes both individuals and corporations and does not exclude corporate officers or employees. Congress could have limited the statutory definition of "person" but chose not to do so. Moreover, construction of CERCLA to impose liability upon only the corporation and not the individual corporate officers and employees who are responsible for making corporate decisions about the handling and disposal of hazardous substances would open an enormous, and clearly unintended, loophole in the statutory scheme.

First, Lee argues he cannot be held individually liable for having arranged for the transportation and disposal of hazardous substances under CERCLA sec. 107(a)(3) because he did not personally own or possess the hazardous substances. Lee argues NEPACCO owned or possessed the hazardous substances.

The government argues Lee "possessed" the hazardous substances within the meaning of CERCLA sec. 107(a)(3) because, as NEPACCO's plant supervisor, Lee had actual "control" over the NEPACCO plant's hazardous substances. We agree. It is the authority to control the handling and disposal of hazardous substances that is critical under the statutory scheme. The district court found that Lee, as plant supervisor, actually knew about, had immediate supervision over, and was directly responsible for arranging for the transportation and disposal of the NEPACCO plant's hazardous substances at the Denney farm site. We believe requiring proof of personal ownership or actual physical possession of hazardous substances as a precondition for liability under CERCLA sec. 107(a)(3) would be inconsistent with the broad remedial purposes of CERCLA.

[*The court concluded, among other things: (1) CERCLA applies retroactively, (2) RCRA imposes strict liability upon past off-site generators and transporters of hazardous substances, and (3) Lee and Michaels could be held individually liable.*]

Questions and Comments for Discussion

1.   Was the NEPACCO site a "facility" for purposes of CERCLA? Why or why not? Were defendants potentially liable as "owners or operators" of a facility for purposes of Section 107?

2.   Recall that Michaels was a major shareholder of NEPACCO and its president; Lee was NEPACCO's vice-president and supervisor of its manufacturing plant located in Verona, Missouri, and was also a shareholder. They conceded that NEPACCO was liable for arranging for the transportation and disposal of hazardous substances at the Denney farm site, but Lee argued that he could not be held individually liable for arranging for the transportation and disposal of hazardous substances because he did not "own or possess" the substances. The court concluded that CERCLA applied retroactively, and that Lee and Michaels could be held individually liable under CERCLA. Under what legal theory did the court hold Lee and Michaels personally liable? What are the policy implications of holding corporate officers individually liable in a case like this one?

3.   Lee also argued that he could not be held individually liable because he arranged for the transportation and disposal of the hazardous substances as a corporate officer or employee acting on behalf of NEPACCO. However, the court said Lee was individually liable because he personally arranged for the transportation and disposal of hazardous substances on behalf of NEPACCO and thus actually participated in NEPACCO's CERCLA violations. The court also held that Lee and Michaels were individually liable as "contributors" under RCRA. Unlike Lee, Michaels was not personally involved in the actual decision to transport and dispose of the hazardous substances. But the court said that "as NEPACCO's corporate president and as a major NEPACCO shareholder, Michaels was the individual in charge of and directly responsible for all of NEPACCO's operations, including those at the Verona plant, and he had the ultimate authority to control the disposal of NEPACCO's hazardous substances." The court concluded Lee could be held individually liable for arranging for the transportation and disposal of hazardous substances under CERCLA and both Lee and Michaels were individually liable for contributing to an imminent and substantial endangerment to health and the environment under RCRA.

4.   As this case suggests, liability has been imposed on individual corporate officers

and parent corporations under the broad coverage provisions of CERCLA and RCRA, even though under traditional notions of corporate law and its concept of limited liability, no individual liability would attach. Chapter 14 examines in greater depth corporate and individual civil and criminal liability for violation of environmental laws and regulations.

5.   While the vast majority of courts have upheld the retroactive effect of CERCLA, a district court in *U.S. v. Olin Corp.*, 927 F. Supp. 1502 (S.D. Ala. 1996) held that CERCLA could not be retroactively applied because (1) neither the express language of the statute nor its scant legislative history demonstrated a congressional intent to have CERCLA apply retroactively, and (2) Section 107(a) of CERCLA is not the sort of provision that must be understood to operate retroactively. . . . This decision prompted a flood of challenges until the decision was subsequently reversed in *U.S. v. Olin*, 107 F.3d 1506 (11th Cir. 1997).

6.   Relying on another recent Supreme Court decision in *U.S. v. Lopez*, 514 U.S. 549 (1995), which struck down the 1990 Gun-Free School Zones Act as an impermissible application of Congress' commerce power, the *Olin* court also concluded that CERCLA is unconstitutional because it exceeds Congress' power under the commerce clause. Other courts have declined to follow this court's opinion, and the decision was subsequently reversed.

Defenses to CERCLA Liability

There are very few defenses available in a CERCLA Section 107 cost recovery action. These include situations where a release was caused solely by:

1.   An act of God

2.   An act of war

3.   An act or omission of a third party (other than an employee, agent, or party with whom there is a contractual relationship) as long as the defendant exercised due care and took precautions against foreseeable acts of the third party

Most litigation focuses on the *third party defense* set out in number 3 above. If the defendant contributed to the release, the defense is unavailable because it was not "solely" caused by the third party. The *contract relationship* exception, in many cases, limits the defense because the third party has a direct or indirect contractual relationship with the defendant through a lease, employment contract, hauling contract, or real estate contract.

In the 1986 SARA amendments, Congress expanded the third party defense by creating the **innocent landowner defense.** Under this defense, a landowner who acquires contaminated property from a third party is not liable under CERCLA if the landowner acquired the property without knowledge of the contamination. In order to utilize the defense, the landowner must show that he undertook "all appropriate inquiry into the previous ownership and uses of the property consistent with good commercial or customary practice." This has given rise to an entire industry of environmental consulting firms, as purchasers conduct "due diligence" investigations necessary to establish this defense.

It is important to note that a person who transfers contaminated property to another without disclosing his knowledge of on-site waste disposal discovered during his ownership loses this defense. While this provision is clearly designed to protect subsequent purchasers, it may have a negative impact on the discovery and cleanup of hazardous waste sites. As a result, current owners may be wary of conducting environmental audits on their property because they are required to disclose any information discovered in the audit to a subsequent purchaser. Contract disclaimers and indemnification clauses which attempt to allocate CERCLA liability between individuals are discussed in Chapter 5.

Recoverable Response Costs

Response costs, which may be recovered under CERCLA, incorporate any costs associated with a response action, including sampling and monitoring costs, those associated with identifying and disposing of hazardous substances, and attorney's and consultant's fees. Damages also include "other necessary costs of response" incurred by any other person and "damages for injury to, destruction of, or loss of natural resources, including the reasonable costs of assessing such injury, destruction, or loss."

SARA expanded the list of recoverable costs to include all expenses associated with Superfund cleanup activities, including the costs of health assessment and health effects. However, there is still some controversy about whether private attorney's fees associated with a CERCLA case are recoverable. Damages to compensate individuals for personal injury or property damage are *not* recoverable under CERCLA, and individual plaintiffs still rely on common law remedies such as nuisance, trespass, negligence, and strict liability in recovering such damages.

Most CERCLA cases are settled without trial. Settlement gives PRPs greater control over the selection and implementation of remedial actions and minimizes the costs of litigation. To encourage settlement, the SARA amendments added settlement procedures which the EPA follows in negotiating settlement of a CERCLA response action. Settlements are ordinarily formalized in a consent decree (filed and signed by a federal court in a case involving judicial action), and consent orders (by administrative order). The U.S. Department of Justice must approve any settlement and consent order if the total response cost exceeds $500,000. The law also encourages early settlement with *de minimis* **parties,** who are parties who have disposed of relatively small quantities of hazardous substances at a site. In return for settlement payment, the EPA generally provides such parties a covenant not to sue, which relieves those parties from the obligation to pay for future remediation at the site.

CERCLA provides two different causes of action by which a party may recover some or all of the response costs incurred: a cost recovery action under Section 107(a) and a contribution action under Section 113(f)(1). Section 107(a) permits a party that has incurred necessary costs of response (consistent with NCP) to sue PRPs.

Section 113(f)(1), which was added by the SARA in 1986, permits "an action by and between jointly and severally liable parties for an appropriate division of the payment one of them has been compelled to make." The relative applicability of these two sections has been the focus of dispute in a number of cases. The courts have generally interpreted Section 103 to permit a court to order indemnification of a non-PRP plaintiff, while Section 113 authorizes the courts to allocate responsibility among PRPs.[10]

Community Right to Know

In addition to amending CERCLA, SARA added a new Title III, the **Emergency Planning and Community Right to Know Act** (EPCRA). This law was passed in response to the disaster in Bohpal, India, in December 1984, when the release of methyl isocyanate at a Union Carbide plant killed an estimated 3,000 people and injured thousands more. The act requires companies which make, process, or use chemicals to meet certain emergency preparedness requirements. These include a plan developed in coordination with community groups for response to chemical emergencies, disclosure of information on hazardous chemicals used or stored at the site, and notification of releases at the plant. The law also requires companies to submit copies of Material Safety Data Sheets (MSDS) for OSHA regulated chemicals to community groups, and to produce an annual inventory of toxic chemicals released into the environment.

Lender Liability under CERCLA

CERCLA contains a provision which exempts, from the definition of owner or operator, "a person, who, without participating in the management of a vessel or facility, holds indicia of ownership primarily to protect his security interest in the vessel or facility." This so-called **security interest exemption** is designed to protect lenders from liability if they merely retain a security interest in the property that is contaminated. In the past, the courts have narrowly construed this exemption. The courts have held that a lender that exercises control over the management of the borrower can lose its exemption and that lenders may lose the exemption if they take title on contaminated property through foreclosure and thus become an "owner" for purposes of the act. In 1997 Congress clarified the exemption in response to lenders' concerns.

The question of lender liability under CERCLA is an important one for lenders. Because the cleanup costs for contaminated property are often substantially greater than the market value of the property, commercial lenders are extremely wary of taking a security interest in property that may be contaminated. Lenders' concerns about potential liability as owners or operators under CERCLA greatly increased after the decision of the Eleventh Circuit Court of Appeals in the case that follows. The *Fleet Factors* decision became the focus of intense effort to change the law to clarify the "secured creditor" exemption under CERCLA.

In that case, Fleet had entered into a "factoring" agreement with Swainsboro Print Works (SPW), a cloth printing facility.[11] As collateral for Fleet's agreement to advance funds, Fleet obtained a security interest in SPW's facility, equipment, inventory, and fixtures. In August 1979, SPW filed for bankruptcy under Chapter 11, and the factoring agreement continued with court approval. In February 1981, SPW ceased operations and began to liquidate its inventory, and in December, 1981, SPW was adjudicated bankrupt.

In May 1981, Fleet foreclosed its security interest in some of SPW's inventory and equipment, and contracted with an industrial liquidator to auction off the collateral. Subsequently, on January 20, 1984, the EPA found toxic contamination at the site and incurred cleanup costs of nearly $400,000. The facility was subsequently conveyed to Emmanual County, Georgia, at a foreclosure sale to recover taxes.

The government sued the principal officers and stockholders of SPW and Fleet to recover its cost for cleaning up the site under CERCLA. Both the government and Fleet filed a motion for summary judgment on the question of Fleet's liability. The district court denied both motions and the parties appealed.

UNITED STATES v. FLEET FACTORS CORP.
901 F.2d 1550 (11th Cir. 1990)

KRAVITCH, Circuit Judge:

The Comprehensive Environmental Response Compensation and Liability Act was enacted by Congress in response to the environmental and public health hazards caused by the improper disposal of hazardous wastes. The essential policy underlying CERCLA is to place the ultimate responsibility for cleaning up hazardous waste on "those responsible for problems caused by the disposal of chemical poison." Accordingly, CERCLA authorizes the federal government to clean up hazardous waste dump sites and recover the cost of the effort from certain categories of responsible parties. . . . The district court, as a matter of law, rejected the government's claim that Fleet was a present owner of the facility. The court, however, found a sufficient issue of fact as to whether Fleet was an owner or operator of the SPW facility at the time the wastes were disposed to warrant the denial of Fleet's motion for summary judgment.

***

CERCLA also imposes liability on "any person who at the time of disposal of any hazardous substances owned or operated any . . . facility at which such hazardous substances were disposed of. . . ." CERCLA excludes from the definition of "owner or operator" any "person, who, without participating in the management of a . . . facility, holds indicia of ownership primarily to protect his security interest in the . . . facility." Fleet has the burden of establishing its entitlement to this exemption. There is no dispute that Fleet held an "indicia of ownership" in the facility through its deed of trust to SPW, and that this interest was held primarily to protect its security interest in the facility. The critical issue is whether Fleet participated in management sufficiently to incur liability under the statute. . . .

The court below . . . interpreted the statutory language to permit secured creditors to "provide financial assistance and general, and even isolated instances of specific, management advice to its debtors without risking CERCLA liability if the secured creditor does not participate in the day-to-day management of the business or facility either before or after the business ceases operation. . . ."

Although we agree with the district court's resolution of the summary judgment motion, we finds its construction of the statutory exemption too permissive towards secured creditors who are involved with toxic waste facilities. In order to achieve the "overwhelmingly remedial" goal of the CERCLA statutory scheme, ambiguous statutory terms should be construed to favor liability for the costs incurred by the government in responding to the hazards at such facilities. The district court's broad interpretation of the exemption would essentially require a secured creditor to be involved in the operations of a facility in order to incur liability. This construction ignores the plain language of the exemption and essentially renders it meaningless. Individuals and entities involved in the operations of a facility are already liable as operators under the express language of section 9607(a)92). Had Congress intended to absolve secured creditors from ownership liability, it would have done so. Instead, the statutory language chosen by Congress explicitly holds secured creditors liable if they participate in the management of a facility. . . .

Although similar, the phrase "participating in the management" and the term "operator" are not congruent. Under the standard we adopt today, a secured creditor may incur section 9607(a)(2) liability without being an operator by participating in the financial management of a facility to a degree indicating a capacity to influence the corporation's treatment of hazardous wastes. It is not necessary for the secured creditor actually to involve itself in the day-to-day operations of the facility in order to be liable—although such conduct will certainly lead to the loss of the protection of the statutory exemption. Nor is it necessary for the secured creditor to participate in management decisions relating to hazardous waste. Rather, a secured creditor will be liable if its involvement with the management of the facility is sufficiently broad to support the inference that it could affect hazardous waste disposal decisions if it so chose. . . .

Our interpretation of the exemption may be challenged as creating disincentives for lenders to extend financial assistance to businesses with potential hazardous waste problems and encouraging secured creditors to distance themselves from the management actions, particularly those related to hazardous wastes, of their debtors. As a result the improper treatment of hazardous wastes could be perpetuated rather than resolved. These concerns are unfounded.

Our ruling today should encourage potential creditors to investigate thoroughly the waste treatment systems and policies of potential debtors. If the treatment systems seem inadequate, the risk of CERCLA liability will be weighed into the terms of the loan agreement. Creditors, therefore, will incur no greater risk than they bargained for and debtors, aware that inadequate hazardous waste treatment will have a significant adverse impact on their loan terms, will have powerful incentives to improve their handling of hazardous wastes.

Similarly, creditors' awareness that they are potentially liable under CERCLA will encourage them to monitor the hazardous waste treatment systems and policies of their debtors and insist upon compliance with acceptable treatment standards as a prerequisite to continued and future financial support. Once a secured creditor's involvement with a facility becomes sufficiently broad that it can anticipate losing its exemption from CERCLA liability, it will have a strong incentive to address hazardous waste problems at the facility rather than studiously avoiding the investigation and amelioration of the hazard. . . .

***

We . . . conclude that the court properly denied Fleet's motion for summary judgment. . . . Because there remain disputed issues of material fact, the case is remanded for further proceedings consistent with this opinion.

Questions and Comments for Discussion

1. Much criticism was leveled at the courts' expansive interpretation of lender liability under CERLCA in this case. Lenders complained that the law encouraged plaintiffs to sue lenders as "deep pockets" and they argued they may be liable even though they had done everything they could to protect themselves.

Determining the proper scope of lender liability is inextricably entwined with broader economic and environmental policy decisions because exempting one segment of the business community from CERLCA liability means that someone else will have to pay those costs.

2. The court also addressed the question of lender liability and the scope of the secured creditor exemption in *In re Bergsoe Metal Corp.,* 910 F. 2d 668 (9th Cir. 1990). In the case, the Ninth Circuit Court

of Appeals held that a municipal corporation empowered to issue revenue bonds to promote industrial development was not liable for cleanup costs under CERCLA because it fell within the security interest exemption. Courts have held that taking title to the property through foreclosure does subject the lender to liability as an "owner." See *United States v. Maryland Bank & Trust Co.*, 632 F. Supp. 573 (D. Md. 1986).

3.   In April 1992, the EPA issued a rule that attempted to clarify the circumstances under which a lender may protect its security interest in property without incurring liability under CERCLA and RCRA, but the rule was successfully challenged as exceeding the EPA's authority. Congress included lender liability and fiduciary requirements under CERCLA in the Omnibus Consolidated Appropriations Act of 1997. The law specifies circumstances under which lenders will be liable for contamination of property they hold as collateral. The statute essentially codifies a portion of the EPA's lender liability rule.

COMMENTS AND SUMMARY

RCRA and CERCLA establish a partnership between the state and federal governments for addressing both past and present waste disposal activities. RCRA focuses on the tracking of hazardous materials and the management of active disposal sites; CERCLA was designed to address the problem of abandoned toxic waste sites. The regulatory programs established according to these acts are intricate and complex, and they are frequently criticized because they are too costly to business and do not incorporate economic incentives to encourage business to control hazardous waste risks.

CERCLA in particular has been criticized by industry as

a draconian system which hinders its economic growth and penalizes individual companies by requiring them to perform extensive and costly cleanups without regard to when the original disposal took place or the fact that a company may have exercised due care in handling hazardous materials.[12]

The slow pace of cleanup of abandoned waste sites has also frustrated Congress, the public, and industry alike. In the first nine years of Superfund, the EPA completed remedial activities at only 48 sites out of over 1,100 proposed or final NPL sites. Although SARA imposed deadlines on the EPA for cleanup of sites, the EPA expects actual site cleanup to grow to an average of 67 months under the new law.[13]

The costs of cleanup continue to climb. A 1994 Congressional Budget Office report suggested that the costs of cleaning up nonfederal hazardous waste sites in the United States could reach $120 billion for work that could take until 2075. The report's midrange estimate in present dollars was $75 billion for cleanups lasting through 2070, which translates to about $230 billion in actual spending over the period, accounting for inflation. Estimated costs for responsible parties based on the middle estimate was $43 billion.

Critics urge that the increasing costs of RCRA and CERCLA programs mandate a new approach, one which focuses on balancing the benefits against the costs of compliance, and they urge provisions designed to deter litigation. The Clinton administration has proposed a plan to provide less money for lawyers and more for cleanup. Initial provisions of the plan designed to slash litigation include:

- Bringing all parties to the bargaining table in order to determine through EPA-mediation the appropriate share of cleanup costs
- Establishing an annual $500 million assessment on the nation's commercial insurance companies to settle pre-1986 claims by corporate policyholders who decide to participate in the fund
- Reducing liability of small contributors to a waste site, and freeing purchasers of hazardous waste sites of liability for past contamination, although imposing some obligations related to the cleanup process[14]

Many are urging Congress to make these and other substantial changes in CERCLA when the act comes up for reauthorization. Industry, lenders, and insurers are particularly vocal in their opposition to CERCLA's liability scheme. They argue that the broad liability provisions of the act coupled with the enormous costs involved in hazardous waste site cleanup actually encourage parties to litigate rather than clean up the site. Because the cost of litigation is usually less than the costs of remedying the contamination, they argue that CERCLA'S liability scheme ultimately delays cleanup. Others, including many environmental organizations, will oppose major changes in CERCLA because they believe those changes will weaken the act. Arguments against making substantial changes in the law center on fears that "reforming" the law could remove the best financial incentives for companies to maintain environmentally sound disposal practices, and that eliminating industry responsibility for cleaning up abandoned contaminated sites will substantially deplete the resources available for such cleanup efforts. As a result of these conflicting concerns, the debate over reauthorization of CERCLA will likely be a lengthy and heated one.

GLOSSARY

CERCLA—Comprehensive Environmental Response, Compensation, and Liability Act of 1980.

CFR—Code of Federal Regulations

Contained-in rule—Under RCRA, soil, groundwater, surface water, and debris contaminated with hazardous waste are considered hazardous waste.

De minimis **parties**—Parties at a site which have disposed of relatively small quantities of hazardous substances.

Derived-from rule—Under RCRA, a waste generated from the treatment, storage, or disposal of a hazardous waste is also a hazardous waste unless exempted.

DOT—Department of Transportation.

EPCRA—Emergency Planning and Community Right to Know Act established in Title III of SARA.

Facility—Under CERCLA, any site at which hazardous waste has come to be located.

Generator—Under RCRA, a person whose act or process produces hazardous waste or whose act first causes hazardous waste to become subject to regulation.

HMTA—Hazardous Materials Transportation Act, which gives the Department of Transportation authority to regulate the movement of hazardous substances.

HSWA—Hazardous and Solid Waste Amendments (to RCRA) of 1984.

Innocent landowner defense—Under CERCLA, a landowner who acquired property after contamination is not liable if he had no knowledge of the contamination or no reason to know of the contamination.

Joint and several liability—All defendants are liable for the entire amount of damages imposed by the court.

Mixture rule—Under RCRA, a mixture of a listed hazardous waste and solid waste is considered hazardous waste unless exempted.

NCP—National Contingency Plan under CERCLA, which establishes procedures for cleanup response actions.

NPL—National Priorities List under CERCLA, in which the EPA ranks each hazardous waste site with respect to priority for cleanup.

PRP—Potentially responsible party under Section 107 of CERCLA.

RCRA—Resource Conservation and Recovery Act of 1976.

Remedial action—Long-term permanent cleanup responses under CERCLA.

Removal action—Short-term emergency response actions under CERCLA.

Response costs—Costs of cleanup which may be recovered under CERCLA.

Retroactive liability—liability imposed for acts done prior to passage of the law imposing such liability.

SARA—Superfund Amendments and Reauthorization Act of 1986.

Security interest exemption—Under CERCLA, exemption from liability for a person who, without participating in the management of a vessel or facility, holds indicia of ownership primarily to protect his security interest.

Small quantity generator—Under RCRA, generators of hazardous substances between 100 and 1,000 kilograms per month.

Strict liability—liability without proof of negligence.

TSD facility—A facility for the treatment, storage, or disposal of hazardous wastes.

Uniform Hazardous Waste Manifest—Control and transport document required by RCRA originating with the generator and accompanying the hazardous waste to the place of disposal.

UST—Underground storage tanks, regulated under Subtitle I of RCRA.

CASES FOR DISCUSSION

1.   Santa Fe Land Improvement Company sold 346 acres of land to the City of Richmond, California. Richmond hired Ferry to excavate and grade a portion of the land for a proposed housing development. While excavating the development site, Ferry spread some of the displaced soil over other parts of the property. The soil contained hazardous chemical compounds including paint thinner, lead, asbestos, and petroleum hydrocarbons. Richmond sued the present owner (Catellus) to recover part of the cost of removing the contaminated soil from the property. Catellus filed a third party complaint against Ferry for contribution under CERCLA, alleging that Ferry exacerbated the extent of the contamination by extracting the contaminated soil from the excavation site and spreading it over uncontaminated areas of the property. Can the excavator be liable as a

PRP under Section 107 of CERCLA? *Kaiser Aluminum v. Catellus Dev.*, 976 F.2d 1338 (9th Cir. 1992).

2.   For many years, Borden operated a phosphate fertilizer plant on a 114-acre tract of land in Texas City, Texas. As a by-product of the fertilizer manufacturing process, large quantities of phosphogypsum were produced. Phosphogypsum contains low levels of radioactivity. More highly radioactive sludges and scales from processing equipment were dumped into the pile, creating "hot" areas within the pile. During processing, radioactive materials became concentrated in manufacturing equipment, pipe, and filter cloths used in production, which were left near a junkyard on the property. Amoco purchased the property from Borden in 1977 "as is," accepting responsibility for removing the phosphogypsum. Amoco claimed it had no knowledge of its radioactive nature. Amoco brought an action for breach of contract and an action under CERLCA to recover its response costs. The trial court required Amoco to show that the property's radioactive emissions violated a quantitative threshold in order to meet the requirement of a "release" under CERCLA. Is there any quantitative requirement on the term "release" under CERCLA? *Amoco Oil Co. v. Borden, Inc.*, 889 F.2d 664 (5th Cir. 1989).

3.   A company appealed a judgment imposing joint and several liability in connection with chromium waste contamination of a local water supply at the site of a former chrome-plating shop. The EPA filed a cost recovery action against the three entities that performed chrome-plating activities at the site from 1971 to 1977. The appellant company introduced evidence that there was a reasonable basis for apportionment between the three entities because the chromium entered the groundwater as a result of similar operations by the three entitites who operated at mutually exclusive times. Assuming that a reasonable approximation of each defendant's individual contribution to the contamination can be made (based on the volume of chromium-contaminated water discharged into the environment by each party), should the court impose joint and several liability? *In re Bell Petroleum Services*, 3 F.3d 889 (5th Cir. 1993).

4.   A manufacturer argued that it should not be liable for response costs because the wastes it sent to New York City landfills contained only traces of hazardous metals. Do listed hazardous substances need to be present in any particular concentration at the disposal site to trigger liability under CERCLA? *New York City v. Exxon Corp.*, 744 F. Supp. 474 (DC SNY 1990).

5.   Does CERCLA authorize the present owner of a building to recover from a prior owner the cost of removing asbestos installed by the prior owner? The suit was brought under Section 107(a)(2) of CERCLA, which provides for recovery from "any person who at the time of disposal of any hazardous substance owned or operated any facility at which such hazardous substances were disposed of." *Stevens Creek Associates v. Barclays Bank of California*, 915 F2d 1355 (9th Cir. 1990).

6.   Can the United States be liable for cleanup costs at a site where the government controlled production of high-tenacity rayon for use during World War II? In the case, the War Production Board, later subsumed in the Department of Commerce, commissioned the plant to convert from textile rayon to high-tenacity rayon, leased the necessary equipment and installed it, ensured raw materials and a work force for production, and supervised employees at the plant. *FMC Corp. v. Department of Comerce*, 29 F.3d 833 (3d. Cir. 1994).

ENDNOTES

1. Mary Devine Worobec and Cheryl Hogue, *Toxic Substances Controls Guide* 2d ed., at 169 (BNA, 1992).

2. Roger W. Findley and Daniel A. Farber, *Environmental Law in a Nutshell* 3d ed., at 231 (West Publishing Company, 1992).

3. *Environmental Law Handbook,* at 60. (Government Institutes, Inc., 1993).

4. Authors note: The *Chevron* case is discussed in Chapter 8.

5. *Environmental Law Handbook* at 94 (Government Institutes, Inc., 1993).

6. Worobec and Hogue, 209.

7. *Environment Week,* March, 23, 1995. *Reilly Management Review on Schedule,* 19 (Environment Reporter, p. 2683).

8. One federeal court held that CERCLA cannot be retroactively applied and that it exceeds Congress' power under the commerce clause. This case was *U.S. v. Olin Corp.,* 927 F. Supp. 1502 (D.C. Ala. 1996). However, the Eleventh Circuit reversed in *U.S. v. Olin Corp.,* 107 F.3d 1506 (1997).

9. *New York v. Shore Realty Corp.,* 759 F.2d 1032 (2d Cir. 1985).

10. See *Catellus Development Corporation v. L.D. McFarland Co.,* 910 F. Supp. 1509 (D. Or. 1995).

11. A "factor's lien" is a method of inventory financing whereby a lender takes a lien on inventory in the borrower's possession.

12. *Environmental Law Handbook* at 267 (Government Institutes, Inc., 1993).

13. Roger C. Dower "Hazardous Wastes," in *Public Policies for Environmental Protection,* Robert R. Portney, ed. at 178 (Resources for the Future, 1990).

14

ENFORCING ENVIRONMENTAL LAWS: ISSUES IN CRIMINAL AND CORPORATE LIABILITY

INTRODUCTION

This chapter focuses on some of the significant legal and policy issues in criminal and corporate liability under federal and state environmental laws. Most of the major environmental laws today contain criminal penalties, as well as civil penalties, for violation of their provisions. For example, under the Clean Water Act (CWA), any person who knowingly discharges pollutants into U.S. waters from a point source without a permit has committed a federal crime. Transporting or disposing of hazardous waste without proper documentation under the Resource Conservation and Recovery Act (RCRA) is a criminal offense. Likewise, failure to notify the EPA of a discharge in violation of the Comprehensive Environmental Response, Compensation and Liability Act (CERCLA), and releasing pollutants in violation of standards of the Clean Air Act are violations of federal law.

The chapter examines the differences between civil and criminal law and discusses the increasing use of criminal laws to enforce compliance with environmental laws. First reviewed are general elements of a criminal offense, especially the requirement by particular environmental statutes of specific intent. Subsequent sections focus on special problems of corporate criminal and civil liability and the personal liability of corporate directors and officers for violations of environmental laws, as well as issues of shareholder and corporate successor liability. After exploring some constitutional defenses to criminal prosecution in environmental cases, we discuss sentencing issues and examine laws affecting environmental compliance, including securities law. The chapter concludes with an examination of the disasterous 1989 oil spill from the *Exxon Valdez* into the waters and shores of Prince William Sound, Alaska, and legal efforts to recover damages and punish the corporation and the captain of the tanker for damages. (See Appendix C for excerpts of penalties sections from various environmental laws.)

Compliance Issues

Although this chapter focuses on criminal and corporate liability for violations of environmental laws, it is important to note that there are many reasons why businesses and individuals voluntarily comply with environmental laws and regulations.

First, most people would agree that businesses and individuals have an ethical responsibility to avoid causing harm to the environment. Many would argue that the traditional view that a corporation's duties are fulfilled by market performance has given way to broader notions of social responsibility. Increasingly, there are those who maintain that corporations have responsibilities beyond the production of goods and services at a profit, and that they have a responsibility to address important social problems, especially those they have helped create. Under this theory, corporations have a broader constituency than stockholders, and they serve a wider range of human values than economic values alone.

Second, voluntary compliance is often good business. In addition to avoiding the possibility of fines and penalties and the potentially substantial costs of litigation, voluntary compliance programs frequently save companies money. In the Sun Company's 1995 "CERES Report and Health, Environment and Safety Review," the company documented a reduction of oil spills, a reduction of air permit exceedences, improvement in safety performance, and a reduction of fire losses as a result of continuing health/safety and environmental performance measures, presumably all amounting to substantial savings to the company.

Community environmental quality activities also benefit a company by increasing corporate goodwill and providing a forum for cooperative rather than confrontational ways to solve environmental problems. In addition, by encouraging research and participating in activities designed to share advances in environmental technology and management, and by committing to materials reduction, reuse, and recycling, companies can reduce production costs and increase profits. For all these reasons, voluntary compliance makes good business sense.

Voluntary Compliance as Regulatory Policy

As a part of its enforcement policies, the EPA has encouraged voluntary compliance with environmental laws. In 1996, the EPA reported that under its voluntary enforcement program, chemical manufacturers turned in nearly 11,000 scientific studies in the preceding five years. Concerned that manufacturers were withholding data required to be submitted under the TSCA, the EPA offered an amnesty program in which it reduced penalties for companies that turned in studies. Even so, the EPA has levied fines of $19 million on seventy-three chemical manufacturers for their belated disclosures. According to the report, many of the studies submitted during the amnesty period indicate that chemicals on the market may pose "substantial risks" to people or the environment.

CIVIL v. CRIMINAL LIABILITY

Most environmental statutes contain a *dual penalty structure,* which means that they provide for overlapping civil and criminal penalties for violations of the law. Although civil enforcement of environmental laws still predominates, criminal enforcement is increasing. Since penalties may be assessed under either system, why do prosecutors choose to prosecute many violations under the criminal law rather than civil? The answer lies in the differences between the two systems.

The **civil law** is generally designed to *compensate* victims and *deter* similar actions in the future. **Criminal laws,** on the other hand, are designed to deter future actions by *punishing* a wrongdoer. Civil law, criminal law, and administrative enforcement procedures are all designed to deter individuals from acting wrongfully. However, civil and administrative law sanctions generally are used in cases involving "non-moral" actions or omissions like negligence, while criminal law essentially addresses moral wrongdoing. In addition, a civil law is generally characterized as private law, while criminal law is considered public law. A criminal conviction carries with it the stigma of being labeled a "criminal."

Traditional legal theories generally provide that the criminal law serves the following four goals: *deterrence, incapacitation, rehabilitation, and retribution.* While all of these goals can be served through other systems, criminal remedies impose the severest consequences. Civil penalties are generally limited to payment of money damages and/or compliance with orders to cease similar actions in the future. Prosecution of an individual under criminal law carries the potential for payment of substantial fines; it also carries with it the potential for loss of the defendant's freedom through imprisonment in serious cases.

There are different factors involved in the government's decision to pursue a criminal rather than civil violation of a federal environmental statute. For example, the Department of Justice considers the *deterrent effect* on future illegal discharging or dumping, whether or not the defendant's actions were *deliberate,* whether the individual or company attempted to *conceal its activities,* whether the individual or company has *previous convictions* for similar activities, and whether the defendant *economically benefitted* from the illegal activity.[1] All of these factors frequently involve decisions ultimately concerned with the *moral culpability* of the offender.

ESTABLISHING CRIMINAL INTENT

Because crimes are wrongs against the public, rather than "private wrongs" against an individual, prosecutions against a defendant for violation of a criminal law are brought by an agent of the state. In state courts that person is usually called a *prosecutor,* and in the federal system, that person is a *United States attorney.* Crimes are actions prohibited by state and federal statutes, and are usually classified as felonies or misdemeanors, depending on the seriousness of the offense and the potential **sanction** (punishment) for violation.

Generally, in order to convict a person of a criminal offense, the state must prove that the defendant's actions violated an *existing statute;* second, the state must prove that the defendant violated each and every element of the statute *beyond a reasonable doubt;* and third, the state must prove that the defendant had the *legal capacity* to form the required criminal intent.

In most cases, the degree of criminal intent, or **mens rea,** required to convict a person of a crime is expressly stated in the statute, and the level of intent required for criminal violation depends on the words used in the statute. "Knowingly," "intentionally," "recklessly," or "negligently" are all degrees of criminal intent. The problem of establishing criminal intent may arise in cases involving prosecution of corporations and corporate officers for white collar crime, a term used to describe a wide variety of nonviolent offenses by businesses, including environmental crimes. Initially, the common law rejected the notion that a corporation could be criminally responsible for the actions of its employees because the corporation lacked the requisite criminal intent to commit the crime.

More recently, however, common law rules on corporate criminal liability have changed as corporations have grown in size and power. Today, American courts are willing to *impute* the criminal intent of corporate employees to the corporation under some circumstances.

Second, while an individual acting in his corporate capacity has always been subject to criminal liability for offenses he personally committed, recent decades have seen an expansion of corporate officer liability through *strict* or *vicarious liability.* A **strict liability offense** is one which dispenses of any requirement of proof of criminal intent. Under **vicarious liability,** a defendant may be criminally liable for the acts of third parties, for example, employees under his personal supervision or control. Thus, corporate directors and officers may be liable for violation of federal and state environmental laws under one or both of these theories. Some of the issues involved in strict liability and vicarious liability offenses are explored in following sections of this chapter.

Proving "Knowledge" under RCRA's Criminal Enforcement Provision

Use of the criminal law to attempt to control some environmental problems, such as climate changes and resource depletion, may not be effective or appropriate. On the other hand, most people agree that people and organizations who release toxic wastes into the environment in violation of federal pollution laws like RCRA, especially if that violation involves some degree of moral wrongdoing, should be subject to prosecution for violation of the criminal law.

As discussed earlier, prosecution for the violation must be based on the *express language* of the statute. One of the more important enforcement issues in environmental law has involved the *mens rea* (state of mind) element in the penalty provision of RCRA. In the following case, the court considered whether individual employees could be subject to prosecution for violation of provisions of the RCRA.

UNITED STATES v. JOHNSON & TOWERS, INC.
741 F.2d 662 (3rd Cir. 1984)

SLOVITER, *Circuit Judge*

Before us is the government's appeal from the dismissal of three counts of an indictment charging unlawful disposal of hazardous wastes under the Resource Conservation and Recovery Act. In a question of first impression regarding the statutory definition of "person," the district court concluded that the Act's criminal penalty provision imposing fines and imprisonment could not apply to the individual defendants. We will reverse.

The criminal prosecution in this case arose from the disposal of chemicals at a plant owned by Johnson & Towers in Mount Laurel, New Jersey. In its operations the company, which repairs and overhauls large motor vehicles, uses degreasers and other industrial chemicals that contain chemicals such as methylene chloride and trichlorethylene, classified as "hazardous wastes" under the Resource Conservation and Recovery Act (RCRA), and "pollutants" under the Clean Water Act. During the period relevant here, the waste chemicals from cleaning operations were drained into a holding tank and, when the tank was full, pumped into a trench. The trench flowed from the plant property into Parker's Creek, a tributary of the Delaware River. Under RCRA, generators of such wastes must obtain a permit for disposal from the Environmental Protection Agency (EPA) The EPA had neither issued nor received an application for a permit for Johnson & Towers' operations.

The indictment named as defendants Johnson & Towers and two of its employees, Jack Hopkins, a foreman, and Peter Angel, the service manager in the trucking department. According to the indictment, over a three-day period federal agents saw workers pump waste from the tank into the trench, and on the third day observed toxic chemicals flowing into the creek . . .

Johnson & Towers pled guilty to the RCRA counts. Hopkins and Angel pled not guilty, and then moved to dismiss [the indictment.] The court concluded that the RCRA criminal provision applies only to "owners and operators," i.e., those obligated under the statute to obtain a permit. Since neither Hopkins nor Angel was an "owner" or "operator," the district court granted the motion as to the RCRA charges. . . .

***

The single issue in this appeal is whether the individual defendants are subject to prosecution under RCRA's criminal provision, which applies to:

[a]*ny person* who—. . . .

(2) *knowingly* treats, stores, or disposes of any hazardous waste identified or listed under this subchapter either—

(A) without having obtained a permit under section 6925 of this title . . . or

(B) in knowing violation of any material condition or requirement of such permit. (42 U.S.C. sec. 6928(d).

The permit provision in 6925 . . . requires "each person owning or operating a facility for the treatment, storage, or disposal of hazardous waste identified or listed under this subchapter to have a permit" from the EPA.

The parties offer contrary interpretations of section 6928(d)(2)(A). Defendants consider it an administrative enforcement mechanism, applying only to those who come within section 6925 and fail to comply; the government reads it as penalizing anyone who handles hazardous waste without a permit or in violation of a permit. Neither party has cited another case, nor have we found one, considering the application of this criminal provision to an individual other than an owner or operator.

A.

As in any statutory analysis, we are obliged first to look to the language and then, if needed, attempt to divine Congress' specific intent with respect to the issue. The language of the particular section under consideration does not readily support either interpretation proffered by the opposing parties. . . .

However, if we view the statutory language in its totality, the congressional plan becomes more apparent. First, "person" is defined in the statute as "an individual, trust, firm, joint stock company, corporation (including a government corporation), partnership, association, State municipality, commission, political subdivision of a State, or any interstate body." 42 U.S.C. 6903(15) (1982). Had Congress meant in section 6928(d)(2)(A) to take aim more narrowly, it could have used more narrow language. Since it did not, we attribute to "any person" the definition given the term in section 6903(15).

Second, under the plain language of the statute the only explicit basis for exoneration is the existence of a permit covering the action. Nothing in the language of the statute suggests that we should infer another provision exonerating persons who knowingly treat, store or dispose of hazardous waste but are not owners or operators.

Finally, though the result may appear harsh, it is well established that criminal penalties attached to regulatory statutes intended to protect public health, in contrast to statutes based on common law crimes, are to be construed to effectuate the regulatory purpose.

III

Since we must remand this case to the district court because the individual defendants are indeed covered by section 6928(d)(2)(A), it is incumbent on us to reach the question of the requisite proof as to individual defendants under that section. The government argues that "knowingly" applies only to "treats, stores, or disposes" of any hazardous waste, and that it does *not* have to show that the defendant knew either that the waste was hazardous or that there was no permit. Thus, the government argues, it need prove only that (1) the defendant is a "person," (2) the defendant handled hazardous material, and (3) there was no permit for such disposal or treatment. We conclude that this interpretation is overly literal. We focus again on the statutory language.

If the word "knowingly" in section 6928(d)(2) referred exclusively to the acts of treating, storing or disposing, as the government contends, it would be an almost meaningless addition since it is not likely that one would treat, store or dispose of waste without knowledge of that action. At a minimum the word "knowingly" which introduces subsection (A), must also encompass knowledge that the waste material is hazardous. . . .

Whether "knowingly" also modifies subsection (A) presents a somewhat different question. . . . Since we have already concluded that this is a regulatory statute which can be classified as a "public welfare statute," there would be a reasonable basis for reading the statute without any *mens rea* requirement. . . . However, whatever policy justification might warrant applying such a construction as a matter of general principle, such a reading would be arbitrary and nonsensical when applied to this statute.

. . . Our conclusion that "knowingly" applies to all elements of the offense in section 6298(d)(2)(A) does not impose on the government as difficult a burden as it fears. . . . [U]nder certain regulatory statutes requiring "knowing" conduct the government need prove only knowledge of the actions taken and not of the statute forbidding them. . . . [T]he district court will be required to instruct the jury that in order to convict each defendant the jury must find that each knew that Johnson & Towers was required to have a permit, and knew that Johnson & Towers did not have a permit. Depending on the evidence, the district court may also instruct the jury that such knowledge may be inferred.

***

In summary, we conclude that the individual defendants are "persons" within section 6928(d)(2)(A), that all the elements of that offense must be shown to have been knowing, but that such knowledge, including that of the permit requirement, may be inferred by the jury as to those individuals who hold the requisite responsible positions with the corporate defendant.

Questions and Comments for Discussion

1.   What is the first rule of statutory interpretation utilized by the court in this case? How did the court interpret the word "person" in the statute under this rule?

2.   How did the court interpret the requirement of "knowingly"? Did this term only apply to "treats, stores, or disposes" of hazardous waste (Subsection 2), or did it also

apply to the requirement "without having obtained a permit" in Subsection 2(A) of the statute? What was the significance of the court's determination?

3. In subsequent cases, courts have taken different and, in some cases, a more liberal view of the requirement of "knowingly." For example, in *U.S. v. Dean*, 969 F.2d 187 (6th Cir. 1992), the sixth circuit concluded that knowledge of the permit requirement under RCRA was *not* a prerequisite to conviction for unlawful treatment, storage, or disposal of hazardous waste without a permit. In other cases, some courts have appeared to impose liability on corporate officers under the "Responsible Corporate Officer" (RCO) doctrine discussed in a following section of this chapter. Under this doctrine, the requisite willfulness or negligence of a corporate officer defendant may be imputed to him by virtue of his position of responsibility. There is, however, no consensus among jurisdictions as to whether the RCO doctrine exempts RCRA's "knowingly" requirement.

Most federal environmental statutes use the word "knowing" to define the standard of criminal intent required under the law. Some statutes, however, adopt lesser standards. The CWA adopts a negligence standard for misdemeanor violations of the act. That section was involved in prosecutions arising from the grounding of the *Exxon Valdez*, discussed at the end of this chapter, and in the prosecution of Ashland Oil as a result of its discharge of diesel fuel into the Monogahela River following the rupture of a storage tank.[2]

Even under a statute imposing the requirement of *knowingly*, the degree of proof required to prove a criminal violation appears to be somewhat less than that required under traditional criminal statutes. For example, in *U.S. v. Baytank Inc.*,[3] Baytank, a liquid chemical storage and transfer company in Houston, Texas, was convicted of illegally discharging pollutants into the Gulf of Mexico, of failing to report a hazardous chemical release, and of storing hazardous waste without a permit in violation of the Clean Water Act, Superfund, and RCRA. On appeal of the district court's grant of a new trial to defendants in the case, the court of appeals affirmed the grant of the new trial to individual corporate defendants because of possible jury confusion in the complex case. However, the court said that it would presume that chemical storage companies are familiar with relevant regulations, and it refused to place the burden on the government to prove that the company knew it was violating governmental regulations.

ISSUES IN CORPORATE LIABILITY

The Rule Limiting Corporate Liability

Modern corporations have helped facilitate enormous and rapid economic development in the last 150 years. Corporate law permits people to invest in and become owners of a corporation while limiting their liability or management responsibilities. This encourages investment and permits businesses greater capacity to raise necessary capital.

General corporate law recognizes several principle characteristics of a corporation. A corporation exists by permission of the state and is subject to state laws and regulations. For most purposes, it is considered a legal entity separate from its owners (shareholders) and its managers (officers and directors). It has a residence and domicile; it may acquire, hold, and convey property; and it may sue and be sued in its own name. In addition, harm to the corporation generally does not constitute harm to its shareholder, and the shareholder has no right or duty to manage the business of the corporation.

As noted previously, shareholders in the corporation have *limited liability,* which means that they are generally not liable for the debts of the corporation beyond their capital contribution.

Corporate Criminal Liability

Some environmental laws expressly impose civil liability on corporations. CERCLA imposes liability for site cleanup costs on corporations as "owners or operators, generators or transporters" based on the statutory language of the act, which specifically defines "person" to include an individual, firm, corporation, association, partnership, consortium, joint venture, or commercial entity.[4] Public policy may support imposing successor liability on purchasing corporations under the exceptions listed above.

A much different issue, however, concerns the extent to which *criminal law* should be used to punish corporations and deter actions which violate environmental protection laws. Corporations are generally included in the definition of "persons" for the purposes of criminal prosecution under current environmental regulations. Under the modern rule, a corporation can be liable for the criminal offenses committed by its employees if the employees are (1) acting within the scope of their employment and (2) acting for the benefit of the corporation. There are, however, legal issues and public policy question underlying the decision to seek criminal prosecution against a corporate entity.

First, which class of corporate employees should be used to impute intent to the corporation? Some have argued that only high corporate officers should be used; however, corporate policy often insulates high officers from responsibility for particular decisions. In cases involving crimes like "midnight dumping," the government may only be able to hold middle managers and subordinate employees responsible for violation of environmental laws. A second concern is the extent to which courts should permit a corporation's "due diligence" as a defense to prosecution. Those who favor the use of this defense argue that good faith corporate efforts to prevent violations should be a defense in enforcement actions. This approach, they argue, would encourage corporate compliance efforts. To date, however, most courts have rejected this defense.

If the decision is made to criminalize corporate behavior, the next question is how to *punish* a corporation. Presumably, the stigma of conviction affects corporate employees, some of whom may have done nothing wrong. Fines are often too small to act as an effective deterrent, and, like civil fines, may be passed on to consumers or absorbed by corporate shareholders. Further, some argue that punishment strategies assume that corporations are rational actors who will respond to the threats of deterrence. In reality, they say, many corporations are neither profit-maximizers nor rational actors, and the policies underlying the decisions of some managers may not be in the long-term interest of the corporation.

Despite these concerns, criminal enforcement of environmental laws continues to rise. In 1994, the EPA brought 2,249 federal enforcement actions with sanctions against companies and individuals who violated environmental laws. These actions included administrative penalty orders and civil and criminal judicial referrals. In 1994, the EPA also collected a record $165.2 million in fines, $36.8 million of which were criminal fines.[5]

When deciding whether to impose criminal sanctions on a corporation, courts tend to focus on the corporation's *control* over the violation. Even though the corporation could not control or abate the violation, criminal liability will arise if corporate policy knowingly diverges from environmental requirements. A corporation may be *vicariously liable* for its employees' violations if it directly or indirectly supervises the activity, for example, illegal dumping, if it could have prevented the violation with reasonable measures, or if its employees or agents were acting within the scope of their employment.

The question whether a corporation could be criminally liable for the wrongful acts of an **independent contractor,** who was hired by the company to dispose of hazardous waste, and over whom the company had no direct control, was at issue in the following case.

WASTE CONVERSION, INC. v. COMMONWEALTH OF PENNSYLVANIA
568 A.2d 738 (Pa. Commw. 1990)

OPINION BY: PALLADINO

Appellant was convicted of violating the Solid Waste Management Act following a non-jury trial. The pertinent facts are as follows. Appellant operates a hazardous and residual waste treatment, storage, and disposal facility in Montgomery County, Pennsylvania, under a Department of Environmental Resources (DER) license. Appellant hired Wills Trucking Company of Ohio (Wills) to transport processed waste to disposal facilities. Appellant's employees loaded nonhazardous waste into a truck owned and driven by Al Cullenen (Driver) who was an independent hauler hired by Wills. Driver was to transport the waste to a disposal site in Michigan.

Appellant's employees loaded Driver's truck to 83,500 pounds. Driver was traveling on Route 80 when he became aware that state police were operating a weigh station ahead. To avoid detection of the excessive weight, driver re-routed the truck to a back road. Unable to negotiate the hill, Driver backed down the road to a more level position. While attempting to redistribute the load by raising the bed of the trailer, a substantial amount of waste slid out of the truck and onto the side of the road. With a lighter load, Driver was able to negotiate the hill.

After an investigation by the Office of the Attorney General, the waste was traced to Appellant. Appellant, Driver and Wills were charged with violations of the Act. Only Appellant's case is before us.

[*Appellant raised several issues on appeal, including the constitutionality of the act, whether the trial court properly interpreted the Act, and whether the court erred in rejecting its "impossibility" defense.*]

***

Section 610(8)(i) of the act provides in pertinent part as follows: "It shall be unlawful for any person or municipality to:

. . . Consign, assign, sell, entrust, give or in any way transfer residual or hazardous waste which is at any time subsequently, by any such person or any other person;

(i) dumped or deposited or discharged in any manner into the surface of the earth or underground or into the waters of the Commonwealth unless a permit for the dumping or depositing or discharging of such residual or hazardous waste has first been obtained from the department.

The criminal penalties section of the Act under which Appellant was convicted and sentenced, states in pertinent part as follows:

(b) any person other than a municipal official exercising his official duties who violates any provision of this act, any rule or regulation of the department, any order of the department, or any term or condition of any permit, shall be guilty of a misdemeanor of the third degree and, upon conviction, shall be sentenced to pay a fine of not less than $1,000 but not more than $25,000 per day for each violation or to imprisonment for a period of more than one year, or both.

Appellant argues that the Act could impose absolute liability on a defendant for acts extraordinarily remote in time and place from a defendant's contact with the actual perpetrator and therefore violates due process on its face. However, this is not the case before us. . . . Appellant argues the ultimate waste dumper was an independent contractor whose actions were beyond Appellant's control. Without the ability to control the Driver's conduct, Appellant argues that the Act violates Appellant's right to substantive due process. . . . [6]

Appellant relies upon *Commonwealth v. Koczwara,* 397 Pa. 575 (1959) [where] the Supreme Court vacated the jail sentence of a tavern operator who was held vicariously liable for the liquor code violations of an employee. . . . The court noted that the actual violations were committed without the personal knowledge, participation or presence of the defendant. Appellant relies upon the following court language: "[o]ur own courts have stepped in time and again to protect a defendant from being held criminally responsible for acts about which he had no knowledge and over which he had little control." Appellant asserts that this language requires that a defendant must have at least some degree of control over the actual perpetrator to be held vicariously liable for his actions.

An examination of the Act reveals that Appellant can be deemed to have such control. . . .

The [Solid Waste Management] Act is a comprehensive scheme designed to protect the public from health and environmental hazards caused by inadequate solid waste practices. Appellant, as a corporation licensed to operate in this hazardous business, owes the highest duty of responsibility to insure that the citizens of this state are protected from the dangers necessarily a part of waste disposal. This was a principle reason for the legislature's imposition of strict vicarious liability. By undertaking the responsibility to dispose of waste, Appellant has assumed the duty to ensure that it is completed as required by the Act. Appellant cannot absolve itself of this responsibility by transferring it to independent contractors and claiming that it has no control over them. We hold that, because Appellant has assumed responsibility in the waste disposal process, Appellant maintains control of the independent contractors it hires for the purpose of its waste disposal duties. Appellant's failure to maintain control cannot be used as a defense to avoid liability.

Questions and Comments for Discussion

1. Whether a person is an independent contractor or an employee depends on the relationship between the person and the employer. There is no sharp line between the two designations, but the courts have devised a list of factors relevant in making that determination. The most important factor is the principal's (employer's) right to control the physical details of the work. Employees are generally subject to such control, whereas independent contractors generally contract with the employer to produce some result.

The distinction may be important in determining such things as the employer's liability for acts of the agent, application of various employment statutes, and tax laws. In this case, did the status of the driver as an independent contractor affect the liability of the employer under RCRA?

2. The court clearly rested its decision in this case on public policy concerns. What are those public policy concerns? To what extent is prosecution of the defendant company in this case likely to deter future similar incidents?

Personal Liability of Corporate Directors and Managers

Under traditional common law, even though a corporation may be strictly liable for the consequences of a management decision, a person who holds corporate office is not, for this reason alone, personally liable for management decisions. There are, however, exceptions to this rule.

Under the **personal participation theory,** an officer is liable for any wrongful acts she commits, regardless of whether she was on behalf of the corporation and within the scope of her duties. Corporate officers may be individually liable for response costs under CERCLA and abatement costs under RCRA, and may incur civil or criminal liability for violation of these and other federal and state environmental laws.

In addition, directors, officers, and managers may also be subject to criminal liability under the **derivative responsibility theory.** A responsible corporate official may be liable for corporate wrongdoing if he knew or should have known it was occurring, and failed to act to prevent or correct the situation. This makes managers responsible for monitoring the activities of subordinates.

The responsible relationship doctrine first developed in cases involving prosecutions under the FDCA of 1938. In the first significant decision under the FDCA,[7] the president and general manager of a Buffalo pharmaceutical company, and the company, were indicted for violations of the FDCA. The company employed twenty-six persons, all of whom worked on one floor and were directly supervised by the defendant. The government did not allege that the defendant possessed any knowledge of the facts underlying the violations; nevertheless the defendant was found criminally liable in his capacity as a corporate officer.

On appeal, the U.S. Supreme Court upheld defendant's conviction. It noted that the FDCA "dispenses with the conventional requirement for criminal conduct—awareness of some wrongdoing." The Court also found that the act was designed to protect the lives and health of the public, and the FDCA put the burden of acting at hazard upon a person standing in *responsible relation* to a danger. The RCO doctrine is applied to criminal public welfare statutes which impose the highest standard of care. It permits conviction of responsible corporate officials who have the power to prevent or correct violations of its provisions.

In *United States v. Park,* the U.S. Supreme Court further clarified the **responsible corporate officer doctrine** (RCO).[8] In *Park,* the chief executive officer of Acme Markets, was charged with violation of the FDCA by storing food in warehouses where it was exposed to rodent contamination. Acme was a national retail food chain with 36,000 employees, 874 retail outlets, and 16 warehouses. Following an inspection, the FDA notified Park of its violations at its Baltimore warehouse. Park then conferred with Acme's vice president for legal affairs, who told him that the Baltimore division vice president would be taking corrective action.

A subsequent FDA investigation in 1972 disclosed continued contamination at the Baltimore warehouse, and criminal charges were filed against the corporation and against Park. Park was convicted and fined $50 per count. On appeal, the court of appeals reversed his conviction; subsequently, however, the Supreme Court reversed the court of appeals decision and sustained Park's conviction. Justice Burger, writing for the Supreme Court, said:

> . . . [I]n providing sanctions which reach and touch the individuals who execute the corporate mission—and this is by no means necessarily confined to a single corporate agent or employee—the [Food and Drug] Act imposes not only a positive duty to seek out and remedy violations when they occur but also, and primarily, a duty to implement measures that will insure that violations will not occur. The duty imposed by Congress on responsible corporate

agents is, we emphasize, one that requires the highest standard of foresight and vigilance, but the Act, in its criminal aspect, does not require that which is objectively impossible. The theory upon which responsible corporate agents are held criminally accountable for 'causing' violations of the Act permits a claim that a defendant was 'powerless' to prevent or correct the violation to be raised defensively at a trial on the merits . . .

Turning to the jury charge in this case, it is arguable that isolated parts can be read as intimating that a finding of guilt could be predicated solely on Park's corporate position. Viewed as a whole, the charge did not permit the jury to find guilt solely on the basis of Park's position; rather, it fairly advised the jury that to find guilt it must find Park 'had a responsible relation to the situation,' and 'by virtue of his position . . . had authority and responsibility' to deal with the situation.

Under the RCO doctrine corporate officers may be subject to criminal prosecution for environmental crimes even if they committed no overt act and had no intention or knowledge of the wrongdoing. The government is only required to prove that the corporate officer was in a position to prevent or correct the violation and failed to do so.

Critics and supporters of the RCO doctrine continue to debate whether the application of the doctrine in criminal cases is the best and most fair way to achieve the public policy goals. A number of issues remain unresolved. Different standards may be used by courts in determining the degree of "responsibility and control" sufficient to establish the individual liability of corporate officers. Some have suggested that the "responsibility and control" test of the RCO doctrine actually amounts to a judicially imposed *negligence* standard. If so, a corporate officer is unlikely to be successfully prosecuted for an environmental crime unless he acted negligently in performing or failing to perform his duties.

Some also suggest that cases show distinctions in liability among different levels of employees within the corporation. Apparently, lower-level employees are much more likely to be the target of criminal prosecutions than upper-level management.

In addition, there is a difference of opinion whether the RCO doctrine may be used to substitute for *mens rea* in a criminal statute (as, for example, the requirement of "knowingly" under RCRA discussed in *Johnson & Towers Supra.*). This issue was directly addressed in a 1991 case where prosecutors argued that a corporate officer could be held criminally liable under the RCRA or the FIFRA simply by virtue of his direct responsibility for handling all environmental and safety matters.[9] The court concluded that the RCO doctrine should not apply to crimes where the federal government must prove specific criminal intent. The court said:

The 'responsible corporate officer' doctrine would allow a conviction without showing the requisite specific intent. None of the cases cited by the government supports the theory that a conviction may be had under a state of mind requirement other than that specified by Congress. In the instant case it is 'knowing,' not 'should have known' as the prosecution suggests.

Corporate Shareholder Liability and Successor Liability

Even though a corporation is a legal entity separate from its shareholders, in some cases a court may **pierce the corporate veil.** This means that, where necessary to promote justice, prevent inequity, or achieve some other important public purpose, a corporation's shareholders may lose their limited liability protection. An important issue in corporate environmental law is the question whether a shareholder of a corporation may be held personally liable for environmental cleanup costs incurred by the corporation under CERCLA or RCRA.[10]

CERCLA defines several classes of parties who may be liable for cleaning up facilities from which there is or may be a release of hazardous substances. These include current owners and operators, as well as owners and operators at the time of disposal, and arrangers and transporters of the waste. Generally, before a shareholder of a defendant corporation is liable for any damage-causing activities the courts must pierce the corporate veil. However, some courts have held that a shareholder of a company which owned a hazardous waste site could be directly liable as an "owner/operator."

In *State of New York v. Shore Realty Corp.,*[11] the court found that the corporation and its principle shareholder and owner, Leo Grande, could be liable for the response costs and common law nuisance costs of cleaning up the site. The court said that *persons* who may be liable under the statute include individuals as well as the corporation, and Leo Grande could be liable both as an "owner" and as an "operator" because he was in charge of the operation of the facility. Other courts, however, have rejected the reasoning in *Shore Realty* and have refused to impose liability on shareholders and officers without piercing the corporate veil because they do not believe the conclusion in *Shore* is authorized under the language or legislative history of CERCLA.[12]

In reality, the justification for imposing shareholder liability on an individual probably does not rest on the individual's status as shareholder but rather on the degree of his participation or responsibility for operating the hazardous site. And courts have consistently held that corporate managers may be held personally liable as *operators* under CERCLA if the facts indicate that the individual controlled corporate conduct and directed corporate activities which resulted in the contamination of the site.

Another legal issue is the extent to which a corporate *successor* may be liable for the actions of its predecessors under CERCLA and RCRA. The legal question in such cases is the extent to which a purchaser of all or a substantial proportion of a company's assets becomes liable for the environmental liabilities of the seller. Under common law, the purchaser of a company's stock and a surviving corporation in a **merger** was liable for the debts of the pre-transaction enterprise, but an **asset purchaser** was not responsible for the liabilities of the seller. However, courts have recognized several exceptions to this rule and have imposed CERCLA liability on asset purchasers in the following circumstances:

1. The purchaser corporation expressly or impliedly agreed to assume such obligations
2. The transaction amounted to a *de facto* consolidation or merger
3. The successor corporation is merely a continuation of the predecessor corporation
4. The transaction was fraudulently entered into in order to escape liability

The decision to impose CERCLA successor liability can cost a company millions of dollars. In one 1995 case, a U.S. District Court held a corporation liable for its predecessor's contamination under the theory that the company's 1964 acquisition of Whitmoyer Laboratories Inc. was a *de facto* merger (or a merger in fact) that caused the company to assume Whitmoyer's liabilities. The district court's decision meant that the purchasing company, Rohm and Haas, was responsible under CERCLA for more than ninety percent of the contamination that had occurred before it acquired the site. Cleanup costs at the site totaled more than $120 million dollars.[13]

Some Defenses to Environmental Enforcement Actions

In cases where an individual or corporation is charged with an environmental crime, the defendant may raise constitutional defenses to that prosecution. The subject of constitutional defenses against corporations and individuals is a complex one, and it is impossible to explore all the intricacies of these issues. Nevertheless, it is important to note that the Bill of Rights (the first ten Amendments to the U.S. Constitution) contains important provisions safeguarding the rights of criminal defendants.

The Fourth Amendment protects individuals from arbitrary and unreasonable governmental violations of their rights of privacy. Balancing those rights with the public's interest in enforcing criminal laws is often a difficult task. There are many cases where the courts have attempted to reconcile the government's legitimate interest in securing evidence of criminal wrongdoing with the need to protect citizens' legitimate expectations of privacy.

Under the Fourth Amendment, only *reasonable* privacy expectations are protected. Courts have extended protection of the Amendment to private dwellings and the areas immediately surrounding them, but have denied protection to areas where there is no reasonable expectation of privacy. Some of these issues and their impact on the enforcement of environmental laws, are illustrated in an important Fourth Amendment case, *Dow Chemical Co. v. United States.*

Dow Chemical Company operated a 2,000-acre chemical manufacturing facility at Midland, Michigan. The facility consisted of numerous covered buildings; manufacturing equipment and piping conduits between various buildings were plainly visible from the air. Dow maintained elaborate security around the perimeter of the complex, barring ground-level public views of these areas. It also investigated low-level flights by aircraft over the facility.

In early 1978, with Dow's consent, EPA officials inspected two power plants in the complex. Subsequently, Dow denied the EPA's request for a second inspection. The EPA, rather than seeking an administrative search warrant, hired a commercial aerial photographer. The photographer, using a standard floor-mounted aerial mapping camera, took aerial photographs of the facility from 12,000, 3,000, and 1,200 feet, all within navigable airspace.

Dow subsequently brought suit in the district court alleging that the EPA's action violated the Fourth Amendment. The district court granted Dow's motion for summary judgment, the sixth circuit reversed, and Dow appealed.

DOW CHEMICAL CO. v. UNITED STATES
476 U.S. 227 (1986)

BURGER, C.J.

Dow claims that the EPA's use of aerial photography was a "search" of an area that notwithstanding the large size of the plant, was within an "industrial curtilage" rather than an "open field," and that it had a reasonable expectation of privacy from such photography protected by the Fourth Amendment. In making this contention,

however, Dow concedes that a simple flyover with naked-eye observation, or the taking of a photograph from a nearby hillside overlooking such a facility, would give rise to no Fourth Amendment problem. . . .

Two lines of cases are relevant to the inquiry: the curtilage doctrine and the "open fields" doctrine. The curtilage area immediately surrounding a private house has long been given protection as a place where the occupants have a reasonable and legitimate expectation of privacy that society is prepared to accept.

As the curtilage doctrine evolved to protect much the same kind of privacy as that covering the interior of a structure, the contrasting "open fields" doctrine evolved as well. . . . [T]he Court has drawn a line as to what expectations are reasonable in the open areas beyond the curtilage of a dwelling: "open fields do not provide the setting for those intimate activities that the Fourth Amendment is intended to shelter from governmental interference or surveillance. . . ."

Dow plainly has a reasonable, legitimate, and objective expectation of privacy within the interior of its covered buildings. Moreover, it could hardly be expected that Dow would erect a huge cover over a 2,000 acre tract. Dow argues that its exposed manufacturing facilities are analogous to the curtilage surrounding a home because it has taken every possible step to bar access from ground level. . . .

Admittedly, Dow's enclosed plant complex does not fall precisely within the "open fields" doctrine. The area at issue here can perhaps be seen as falling somewhere between "open fields" and curtilage, but lacking some of the critical characteristics of both. Dow's inner manufacturing areas are elaborately secured to ensure they are not open or exposed to the public from the ground. Any actual physical entry by EPA into any enclosed area would raise significantly different questions, because "[t]he businessman, like the occupant of a residence, has a constitutional right to go about his business free from unreasonable official entries upon his private commercial property." The narrow issue raised by Dow's claim of search and seizure, however, concerns aerial observation of a 2,000 acre outdoor manufacturing facility *without* physical entry.

The Government has "greater latitude to conduct warrantless inspections of commercial property" because "the expectation of privacy that the owner of commercial property enjoys in such property differs significantly from the sanctity accorded an individual's home." Unlike a homeowner's interest in his dwelling, "[t]he interest of the owner of commercial property is not one in being free from any inspections." With regard to regulatory inspections, we have held that "[w]hat is observable by the public is observable without a warrant, by the Government inspector as well."

[Previous cases have] recognized that in the open field context, "the public and policy lawfully may survey lands from the air." Here, the EPA was not employing some unique sensory device that, for example, could penetrate the walls of buildings and record conversations in Dow's plants, offices, or laboratories, but rather a conventional, albeit precise, commercial camera commonly used in mapmaking. . . .

It may well be that surveillance of private property by using highly sophisticated surveillance equipment not generally available to the public, such as satellite technology, might be constitutionally proscribed absent a warrant. But the photographs here are not so revealing of intimate details as to raise constitutional concerns. The mere fact that human vision is enhanced somewhat, at least to the degree here, does not give rise to constitutional problems.

We conclude that the open areas of an industrial plant complex with numerous plant structures spread over an area of 2,000 acres are not analogous to the "curtilage" of a dwelling for purposes of aerial surveillance; such an industrial complex is more comparable to an open field and as such it is open to the view and observation of persons in aircraft lawfully in the public airspace immediately above or sufficiently near the area for the reach of cameras. . . .

Judgment for the EPA affirmed.

Questions and Comments for Discussion

1.   What is the "curtilage doctrine?" What is the "open fields" doctrine? Why were both doctrines at issue in this case?

2.   For what purpose might the EPA have wanted aerial photographs of the Dow Chemical Plant? Do you agree with the court that a person's reasonable expectation of privacy in a commercial complex is less than that in a residential complex? What are the policy implications of your answer?

Two other constitutional amendments which may be important in prosecution of environmental crimes are the Fifth Amendment and the due process clause of the Fourteenth Amendment, which specifically applies to the states. The Fifth Amendment and the due process clause guarantee basic procedural and substantive fairness in criminal cases. The Fifth Amendment also protects against compulsory testimonial self-incrimination: No "person . . . shall be compelled in any criminal case to be a witness against himself."

The right to silence protected by the Fifth Amendment is limited. Because it applies to testimonial admissions, the courts have permitted the police to compel an accused to furnish nontestimonial evidence. A particularly important Fifth Amendment issue for persons in business is the extent to which the Fifth Amendment protects business records and other documentary evidence.

In a series of decisions, the U.S. Supreme Court has drastically limited the scope of the protection of "private papers." A number of decisions have held that the private papers privilege is a personal privilege which cannot be asserted by a corporation or other collective entity. Under these decisions, an individual officer who has custody of an organization's records cannot assert a personal privilege to prevent their disclosure, even if the contents of such records incriminate the officer. Further, records required to be kept by the government (for example, RCRA manifests) are not entitled to any protection as "private papers."

Sentencing Problems and Other Enforcement Issues

During the 1970s, when modern environmental legislation was first enacted, the emphasis was on civil enforcement. In subsequent decades, however, the EPA, the Justice Department, and the FBI have increasingly viewed violations of environmental laws as criminal activity. In 1982, the Justice Department established an Environmental Crimes Unit, and the EPA has established a National Enforcement Investigations Center. The number of criminal prosecutions have increased steadily into the 1990s.[14]

As corporations and officers have increasingly become the target of criminal prosecution, some see this development particularly disturbing in light of the **federal sentencing guidelines,** which became effective in 1987. The Guidelines have substantially increased the probability that a convicted defendant will actually serve time in jail. The guidelines include specific provisions for sentencing environmental violators, and put environmental crimes on a par with other white collar crimes.

In developing the guidelines, the U.S. Sentencing Commission was aware that Congress had expressed views in favor of tougher penalties for white collar offenses. The guidelines force judges to take environmental crimes much more seriously than they have in the past.

The guidelines divide environmental offenses into four categories:

1.   Knowing endangerment of human life

2.   Offenses involving hazardous or toxic substances

3. Offenses involving other pollutants

4. Offenses against conservation and wildlife

The sentencing guidelines replace the traditional sentencing flexibility of judges. The guidelines thus remove virtually all discretion for sentencing for certain crimes, including environmental offenses. Prior to the guidelines, probation and suspension of sentences were common. Now judges no longer have the freedom to utilize such sentencing practices. The expansion of the RCO doctrine along with adoption of the federal sentencing guidelines means that the risk of criminal prosecution and actual jail time upon conviction has increased for corporate defendants convicted of environmental crimes.

Environmental Audits and the Corporate Defendant

Environmental audits should be an important part of corporate environmental policy. Through internal environmental audits, businesses can identify liabilities and address problems which can avert civil actions and criminal prosecutions. However, most environmental laws mandate disclosure of environmental liabilities; consequently, conducting an environmental audit may disclose liabilities which the company is required to report. As a result, the company may find itself liable for spills, releases, and other violations which it discovered voluntarily through the audit process.

Candor and full disclosure are essential if a company is to avoid liability under environmental laws and regulations; however, the possibility of incurring substantial fines and penalties upon discovering environmental liabilities during voluntary audits may discourage companies from trying to find and solve their environmental problems.

State legislatures, regulatory agencies, and the courts have acknowledged the need for effective environmental auditing and the consequences of disclosure. Some have advocated the development of a legal *privilege,* similar to the attorney's work-product privilege, which would protect the audit from discovery and from admission into evidence. In *Olen Properties Corp. v. Sheldahl Inc.,*[15] a court held that the attorney-client privilege protected environmental audit memoranda prepared by the company to assist the company's attorneys in complying with environmental laws. In addition, some courts have held that confidential minutes and reports in records of staff meetings held on a confidential basis should be entitled to a similar qualified privilege.

The EPA has a policy to protect businesses which disclose environmental violations voluntarily and address them quickly. Under the policy, such businesses would incur little if any punishment. Industry has also sought additional audit protection by lobbying for legislation which would protect the confidentiality of environmental audits and bar their admissibility into court. Prosecutors, environmentalists, and toxic tort plaintiffs have generally opposed an environmental audit privilege because they fear this would undermine the accountability of corporations for actions which harm health and the environment.

Prosecution under RICO for Environmental Crimes

Congress passed the **Racketeer Influenced and Corrupt Organizations Act** (RICO) as part of the Organized Crime Control Act of 1970. The broad language of the RICO statute has permitted the government to apply it in a wide variety of cases, many of which have little to do with organized crime. RICO is one of the most controversial statutes affecting business. Defenders argue that it is an effective tool for addressing illegal business activities; critics maintain it unduly favors prosecutors and plaintiffs in commercial litigation.

Under the criminal sections of RICO, it is a federal crime to (1) use income derived from a "pattern of racketeering activity" to acquire an interest in an enterprise, (2) acquire or maintain an interest in an enterprise through a pattern of racketeering activity, (3) conduct or participate in the affairs of an enterprise through a pattern of racketeering activity, or (4) conspire to do any of the preceding acts. *Racketeering* includes the commission of one of over thirty state or federal criminal offenses, called *predicate* criminal offenses. Almost any business fraud may constitute a racketeering activity.

RICO has been used to prosecute individuals and companies for environmental crimes. In 1990, for example, two men and their companies were convicted under RICO for operating an illegal seventy-acre landfill on Staten Island, N.Y.[16] Approximately fifty private carting companies had dumped garbage, asbestos, and medical and infectious waste at the site on a daily basis for more than four months in 1988. The men were sentenced to twelve years in prison and ordered to pay $250,000 fines. The judge described the case as one of the largest environmental crimes ever prosecuted in the United States, and called it a "highly complex scheme that was well thought out by the defendants."

Securities Violations

Corporate officers and directors should also be aware that the **Securities and Exchange Commission** (SEC) has increasingly scrutinized disclosures of potential environmental liabilities. In general, a public company must disclose information about its operations, including environmental matters, under the "line item" disclosure requirement of the Securities Act of 1933 and the Securities Exchange Act of 1934, and the general anti-fraud provisions of the 1934 act. Environmental disclosures must be made by various line items in a public company's disclosure documents. These include registration statements, quarterly reports, and annual reports filed under the securities acts.

Item 101 of Regulation S-K requires a public company to provide a general description of its business. In addition, it must disclose any material effects that compliance with federal, state, and local environmental laws may have on the capital expenditures, earnings, and the competitive position of the registrant.

Item 103 includes specific reporting requirements for environmental matters, and a public company must disclose any pending or contemplated administrative or judicial environmental proceeding material to the company's business or financial condition. Item 103 also requires an issuer to disclose any pending or contemplated proceeding arising under environmental laws if the government is a party to the proceeding and the proceeding involves potential sanctions of $100,000. "Proceeding" is construed broadly.

Item 303, the Management Discussion and Analysis Item, requires disclosure if a trend, demand, commitment, event, or uncertainty is both currently known to management and reasonably likely to have a material effect on the public company's financial condition or operation. General anti-fraud provisions of Rule 10b-5 also impose liability on public companies which make false statements or omit material facts in connection with the offer, purchase, or sale of securities. The rule also requires that any statement made by a public company be accurate and complete.

A 1990 agreement between the EPA and the SEC indicates that company statements will be scrutinized for disclosure of environmental liabilities. Under the agreement, the EPA will provide the SEC with information concerning public companies' compliance with environmental laws. This includes the names of parties receiving Superfund notice letters, a list of all cases filed under RCRA and CERCLA, a list of all recently concluded civil cases under federal environmental laws, a list of all criminal cases brought under federal environmental laws, a list of all facilities barred from government contracts under the CWA and the Clean Air Act, and a list of RCRA facilities subject to cleanup requirements.

A public company can minimize the risk of an SEC enforcement action by providing complete information of potential environmental liabilities. Disclosure also reduces the possibility of private lawsuits by shareholders claiming that the company failed to disclose known environmental problems.

Bankruptcy Law and the Environment

As laws creating environmental liabilities have grown, so has the cost of compliance with those laws. In some cases, a company faced with substantial cleanup costs may seek refuge under the federal bankruptcy code, but bankruptcy law cannot protect an individual or corporate entity from criminal penalties. This has created tension in the courts because the policies underlying enforcement of environmental laws and policies designed to give the bankrupt a "fresh start" under the bankruptcy code sometimes conflict.

The bankruptcy code has the primary purpose of relieving the honest debtor from the weight of oppressive indebtedness. Environmental laws, on the other hand, seek to hold violators responsible for injuries they cause the public as a result of their violations. Courts thus face the difficult policy question of balancing the concerns of environmental protection with the need to protect the bankrupt and his creditors.

Legal issues involved in this conflict include whether the state can force a bankruptcy debtor to correct violations of state anti-pollution laws, whether the automatic stay provision of bankruptcy law should operate against state or federal agencies seeking to enforce environmental laws under their police powers, and whether a federal bankruptcy court has the power to stay enforcement of a state's environmental laws.

Under the automatic stay provision of the bankruptcy code (which automatically halts other legal proceedings against the debtor), state enforcement of environmental laws must proceed unless (1) the state is acting solely to protect its pecuniary (money) interest in the debtor's estate, (2) the state is acting to enforce against the debtor what is in form or substance a money judgment, or (3) the state is acting to obtain property of the bankrupt's estate.

State enforcement actions taken to protect public health and safety or to prevent future public harm will pass the test set out above. Permitting debtors to avoid responsibility for money damages imposed under environmental statutes protects the interests of the debtor and other creditors, and ultimately enhances the debtor's opportunity to recover economic viability and eventually meet future environmental responsibilities.

ILLUSTRATING ISSUES: THE CASE OF THE EXXON VALDEZ

In the early hours of March 24, 1989, the oil tanker *Exxon Valdez* ran aground in the waters of Prince William Sound, Alaska. Over the next several days, the *Exxon Valdez* spilled approximately 240,000 barrels, or 11 million gallons, of crude oil, into the waters of one of the world's most productive and beautiful marine environments. Oil from the spill eventually spread over 800 miles, fouling shorelines, killing thousands of birds and marine mammals, contaminating fish and shellfish, and forcing the closure of many of the region's commercial fisheries. The *Exxon Valdez* was the worst oil spill in U.S. history, and one of the most significant environmental disasters of our time.

The *Exxon Valdez* spill dramatically demonstrated the potential risks of the nation's dependence on petroleum products and the hazards of oil transportation. The name itself has become a symbol for the power of man to wreak harm on the environment. Public outrage following the ecological disaster in the wake of the *Exxon Valdez* disaster also helped refashion the way the public views environmental regulations in general and the function of the civil and criminal law in deterring and preventing future environmental disasters. The disaster has even been credited with helping to influence value of environmental protection and quality of life over natural resource exploitation and the accumulation of material wealth.

Criminal prosecution of businesses and individuals for violation of laws resulting in ecological disasters like the *Exxon Valdez* spill increases public awareness of the costs of harming the environment, and encourages the public to view such harms seriously. Prosecution of individuals and businesses also helps assuage the public's anger and conveys the public's sense of moral outrage at the ecological effects of the disaster. The criminal prosecutions of the Exxon corporation and James Hazelwood, captain of the *Exxon Valdez,* also provided the government another mechanism for seeking penalties which could be applied toward the tremendous costs of cleaning up the effects of the spill.

The Prosecution of Captain Hazelwood

At the time the *Exxon Valdez* ran aground on Bligh Reef, Hazelwood was in his cabin, having turned the helm over to Third Mate Gregory Cousins a short time earlier.[17] Cousins immediately summoned Hazelwood to the bridge, and approximately twenty minutes after the grounding, Hazelwood reported the incident by radio to the Coast Guard Traffic Center in Valdez. The report sparked an immediate investigation by federal and state officials, yielding evidence that eventually led the state to indict Hazelwood on three criminal charges: reckless endangerment, operating a watercraft while intoxicated, and negligent discharge of oil. In a criminal trial in Anchorage, Alaska, Hazelwood was cleared of all but one misdemeanor charge, the reckless discharge of oil. He was sentenced to ninety days in jail and a $1000 fine, both suspended on condition that Hazelwood complete one year of probation, perform 1000 hours of community work, and pay $50,000 in restitution.

Prosecution of Hazelwood under state law created a serious problem for prosecutors because federal environmental law required him to disclose the spill to officials. The applicable federal statute provided:

> Any person in charge of a vessel or of an onshore facility or an offshore facility shall, as soon as he has knowledge of any discharge of oil or a hazardous substance from such vessel or facility in violation of paragraph (3) of this subsection, immediately notify the appropriate agency of the United States Government of such discharged. . . . Notification received pursuant to this paragraph or information obtained by the exploitation of such notification shall not be used against any such person in any criminal case, except a prosecution for perjury or for giving a false statement. 33 U.S.C. sec. 1321(b)(5).

Following a jury trial at which Hazelwood was convicted of negligent discharge of oil, Hazelwood appealed. The court of appeals reversed the conviction, holding that there was no independent source of evidence by which to convict the captain other than his report under the FWPCA. His report could not serve as a source for prosecution under the express language of the statute.

In 1993, the Supreme Court of Alaska affirmed the court of appeals decision in part, reversed in part, and remanded the case for further proceedings.[18] The central issue was the federal reporting requirement for oil and hazardous substance discharges, which included a statutory grant of immunity from criminal prosecution. For public policy reasons, the Alaskan Supreme Court held that evidence which would inevitably have been discovered should be admissible at Hazelwood's criminal trial.

The Corporate Defendants

Following the grounding of the *Exxon Valdez,* lawsuits were filed by thousands of individuals and businesses against the corporation, its subsidiary, Exxon Shipping, which owned the tanker, and the Alyeska Pipeline Service Co., which had first-strike responsibility for the cleanup. Plaintiffs claimed that the oil pollution had ruined commercial fishing and tourism, driven down property values, and damaged harvests. They argued that Exxon had acted recklessly by permitting Hazelwood, a man with a history of drinking problems, to pilot the tanker. Exxon was also the first to be charged with criminal felony violations of two maritime safety and anti-pollution rules.

In 1991, the federal district judge in charge of the case stunned many by refusing to accept a government plea agreement resolving civil claims and criminal charges against the company. The judge expressed difficulty with the concept that "we criminalize unintentional environmental accidents. In effect, criminalizing the killing of birds and sea otters, and so forth. Yet, we do not criminalize airline crashes, which result from negligence, and which kill people." However, Judge Holland said the $100 million fine, as negotiated by the parties, sent "the wrong message, suggesting that spill is a cost of doing business, which can be absorbed." Exxon was subsequently assessed a $150 million criminal fine.

The lawsuits were consolidated and three phases of the litigation were tried in 1994. Exxon admitted negligence but denied acting recklessly. In June 1994, an Alaskan jury found Exxon had acted recklessly, establishing the required prerequisite for *punitive damages* (damages awarded in a civil case to punish a defendant for wrongful behavior) in the case.

The Exxon Valdez Debate: What Did We Learn?

The Exxon oil spill continues to spark policy debate over corporate criminal liability. Civil law already mandates a corporate wrongdoer compensate victims for its wrongdoing. In cases of environmental catastrophes should large punitive fines and/or criminal sanctions be levied against corporate defendants in addition to civil penalties? Some argue that it is important to press harder for criminal penalties in cases where corporate managers are responsible for making decisions which profoundly impact the environment. Others consider the concept of criminal and excessive civil liability unfair, especially when liability is imposed on corporations and officers for the actions of remote low-level employees.

The *Exxon Valdez* case will be remembered as one of the worst ecological disasters of this century. Because it occurred as a result of human error, it is all the more tragic. Whether it is appropriate to use the criminal law to punish the corporation and individuals responsible for the spill is a policy decision that reflects society's attitude about the functions of the criminal law and the value it places on the environment. For now, it appears that the trend toward imposing criminal liability on corporations and employees for violation of environmental laws and regulations is likely to continue.

The CERES Principles

As a result of the *Exxon Valdez* oil spill, the Coalition for Environmentally Responsible Economies (CERES), a nonprofit membership organization of social investment professionals, environmental groups, religious organizations, pension trustees, and public interest groups, waged a campaign to compel public corporations to assume responsibility for and implement policies and procedures to protect the environment.

First released in 1989 as the **Valdez Principles,** the *CERES Principles* represent a ten-point corporate code of environmental conduct which asks industrial corporations to identify, disclose, remedy, and assume liability for the environmental consequences of their activities. Supporters argue that signing and adhering to the principles should, over the long term, help reduce a company's exposure to environmental liabilities both in the United States and abroad by forcing the companies to focus significant resources on environmental compliance matters. (See Appendix C for the complete text of the CERES Principles.)

GLOSSARY

Asset purchaser—A legal person who acquires the assets of another legal person for money.

Civil law—Law by which individuals are compensated for legal wrongs caused by others. Civil lawsuits are private as opposed to public actions. They include actions for damages under tort and contract law.

Criminal law—Law by which individuals are punished for violating state laws criminalizing certain behavior. Criminal lawsuits are public actions brought by the state against an individual or legal entity.

Derivative responsibility theory—Legal theory under which a corporate official may be liable for corporate wrongdoing if he knew or should have known it was occurring but failed to act to prevent or correct the situation.

Federal sentencing guidelines—1987 federal guidelines which include specific provisions for sentencing for certain crimes.

Independent contractor—One who contracts to do a piece of work according to his own methods and without being subject to the control of his employer except as to the result of the work.

Mens rea—Criminal intent under a criminal statute.

Merger—Union of two or more corporations by the transfer of property of all of one of them to the other.

Personal participation theory—Legal theory under which an officer of a corporation is liable for any wrongful acts she commits, regardless of whether they were on behalf of the corporation and within the scope of her duties.

Piercing the Corporate Veil—Legal doctrine by which courts, in some circumstances, reach beyond the limited liability of a corporation and hold shareholders responsible for its actions.

Responsible corporate officer doctrine (RCO)—Legal doctrine under which criminal intent may be imputed to a defendant by virtue of his position and responsibility.

RICO—The Racketeer Influenced and Corrupt Organizations Act of 1970.

Sanction—Punishment for violation of criminal law which may include such things as fines, public or private restitution, or incarceration.

SEC—Securities and Exchange Commission.

Strict liability offense—One which dispenses with the requirement of criminal intent.

Valdez Principles—A ten-point corporate code of environmental conduct sponsored by CERES, a project of the Social Investment Forum.

Vicarious liability—Theory under which a defendant may be criminally liable for the acts of a third party, for example, for the acts of an agent under his personal supervision or control.

CASES FOR DISCUSSION

1.   In *People v. O'Neil,* 550 N.E.2d 1090 (Ill. App. 1990), individual defendants and agents of Film Recovery Systems, Inc., were convicted in the death of Stefan Golab, a Film Recovery employee, from cyanide poisoning stemming from conditions in Film Recovery's plant in Elk Grove Village, Illinois. Corporate defendants Film Recovery and its sister corporation Metallic Marketing Systems were convicted of involuntary manslaughter in the same death. Can a corporation be held criminally responsible for offenses involving physical violence or specific intent under Illinois law?

2.   Mobil Oil Corporation was convicted of violating the Rivers and Harbors Act when simultaneous malfunctions in independent regulatory mechanisms caused the discharge of oil into a navigable waterway. The FWPCA granted immunity to persons in charge of notifying the appropriate agency of such discharge. Was Mobil an "owner-operator in charge" of the facility within the meaning of the law, and if so, is it entitled to immunity under the statute? *U.S. v. Mobil Oil Corp.,* 464 F.2d 1124 (5th Cir. 1972).

3.   A parent corporation appealed a decision holding it liable as both an owner and operator for the cleanup costs incurred by the EPA in response to a spill of trichlorethylene at a textile plant. The nominal owner of the site was a wholly owned subsidiary of the corporation prior to its 1977 dissolution. The government sought to recover its cleanup costs from the corporation under CERCLA based on director liability (the corporation as operator of the site) and indirect liability (the corporation as owner by piercing the corporate veil). The corporation argued that the parent company of a dissolved subsidiary cannot be liable on either ground. Is the corporation correct? *U.S. v. Kayser-Roth Corp.,* 910 F.2d 24 (1st Cir. 1990).

4.   Dean was convicted of three counts of storage and disposal of hazardous wastes without a permit in violation of 42 USC 6928(d)(2)(A). Dean was the production manager of a metal stamping, plating, and painting facility. The facility had not sought a RCRA permit

for treatment, storage, and disposal of hazardous waste. Dean had day-to-day supervision of the facility's production process and its employees. During plating operation, hazardous chemicals were drained through a pipe into an earthen lagoon outside the facility. Material Safety Data Sheets provided by the chemical manufacturer clearly stated that various chemicals in use at the plant were hazardous and were subject to state and federal pollution control laws. Dean contended that there was no evidence that he knew of RCRA's permit requirement. Should Dean's conviction be reversed because knowledge of the permit requirement is an element of the crime? *U.S. v. Dean*, 969 F.2d 187 (6th Cir. 1992).

5.   The government filed suit to recover some $1.3 million spent on the cleanup of a Superfund site in Texas. Among the defendants were a former owner of the site and a later corporate purchaser, from which the former owner sought indemnification under a corporate bylaw. Does the federal hazardous waste cleanup statute's provision for personal liability of corporate officers and directors nullify corporate bylaws that provide for indemnification of officers and directors for liability incurred "by reason of" such status? *U.S. v. Lowe*, 910 F.2d 24 (5th Cir. 1994).

ENDNOTES

1. *Eighth Survey of White Collar Crime: Environmental Crimes,* 30 Am. Crim. L. Rev. 565 (1993).

2. *U.S. v. Ashland Oil Co.,* 705 F. Supp. 270 (W.D. Pa. 1989).

3. 934 F.2d 599 (5th Cir. 1991).

4. Section 9601(21).

5. *New Records for Actions, Fines Set by EPA Despite Restructuring of Program,* 25 Envtl. Rep. 1501 (Dec. 2, 1994).

6. In arguing substantive due process in this case, appellants were essentially questioning whether the statute violated basic and fundamental notions of fairness.

7. *United States v. Dotterweich,* 320 U.S. 277 (1943).

8. 421 U.S. 658 (1975).

9. *United States v. White,* 766 F. Supp. 873 (E.D. Wash. 1991).

10. CERCLA and RCRA liability is discussed in Chapter 13 of this text.

11. 759 F.2d at 1032 (2d Cir. 1985).

12. *Joslyn Corporation v. T.L. James & Company, Inc.,* 696 F. Supp. 222 (W.D. La. 1988).

13. *SmithKline Beecham Corp. v. Rohm and Haas Co.,* 40 Env't. Rep. Cas. (BNA) 1538 (E.D. Pa. 1995), reversed and remanded on basis of contract indemnification provisions, 89 F.3d 154 (3rd Cir. 1996).

14. In 1990, for example, more than double the jail time was served in fiscal 1991 as in 1989. Criminal judgments also resulted in significantly longer sentences. *See* Lisa Ann Harig, *Ignorance Is Not Bliss: Responsible Corporate Officers Convicted of Environmental Crimes and the Federal Sentencing Guidelines,* 42 Duke L.J. 145, 146 (nt. 8) (1992).

15. *Olen Properties Corp. v. Sheldahl Inc.,* 24 Envtl. L. Rep. 20936 (C.D. Calif. 1994).

16. *U.S. v. Paccione,* 749 F. Supp. 476 (S.D.N.Y. 1990).

17. *Hazelwood v. State,* 866 P.2d 827 (Alaska 1993).

18. *Id.*

15

INTERNATIONAL LAW AND THE ENVIRONMENT

INTRODUCTION

Air, water, and land pollution know no national boundaries. As people become more concerned about global pollution issues, environmental concerns are increasingly impacting international law. Although international environmental law is a rapidly growing area of law, national governments are generally relunctant to surrender their sovereign powers through international **conventions** and treaties, and the economic implications of environmental regulation often limit their willingness to comprehensively address global environmental problems. Nevertheless, many nations have begun to address some of these important environmental issues, and this chapter examines some of the legal rules governing them. These rules are derived from a complicated web of domestic laws, bilateral treaties, and multilateral conventions, as well as general customs and principles of international law.

INTERNATIONAL ENVIRONMENTAL CONCERNS

This text has examined U.S. domestic laws addressing the problems of air, water, and land pollution. As scientists continue to explore and study the delicate, complicated ecosystems of the planet, it has become clear that pollution has international effects that reach beyond the boundaries of a particular state or country. Land pollution affects entire ecosystems, destroys the natural environment, and endangers the health of humans, animals, and plants. Air pollution may have long-range effects on the atmosphere, ozone layer, and the global environment. Acid rain, a kind of air pollution caused by increased sulphur from the burning of fossil fuels, pollutes the atmosphere and has been shown to cause damage to the forests of many nations. Concerns about photochemical smog (a mixture of smog and fog including nitrates, O_3 and NO_2), greenhouse gases, and depletion of the ozone layer have led many nations to enter into international treaties and conventions to address these worldwide concerns. The International Convention on the Law of the Sea recognizes the need for nations to address and to harmonize efforts to combat the problems of marine pollution.

Many nations have begun to address specific problems associated with urban pollution, including industrial pollution and the transportation and disposal of hazardous and toxic wastes across national boundaries, and to address international concerns about pesticide and insecticide pollution. The disastrous fire at the Chernobyl nuclear power plant focused the concerns of the international community on the problems associated with nuclear radiation. Most nations recognize the potentially devastating environmental effects of nuclear weapons tests and the spread of nuclear weapons. The Treaty on the Principles Governing the Activities of States in the Exploration and Use of Outer Space Including the Moon and Other Celestial Bodies established legal rules for the exploration and use of outer space. Among other things, it bars parties from placing objects carrying nuclear weapons of mass destruction into outer space, and provides that the moon and other celestial bodies are to be used exclusively for peaceful purposes.

SOURCES OF INTERNATIONAL ENVIRONMENTAL LAW

International environmental law, like all international law, consists of principles derived from several sources. These include customary practices, international conventions (or treaties), judicial decisions, resolutions of international organizations, and general principles or customs. **Customary international law** describes those guiding principles which nations generally recognize as part of international legal order. For example, sovereign nations generally recognize that countries have the right to use and conserve the marine resources of their coastal waters. Nations also generally recognize a responsibility not to harm the environment of another nation, and to warn another state if an event threatens another's environment.

An example of a legal decision resting on international custom is a 1941 arbitration decision in a dispute between the U.S. and Canada. In the *Trail Smelter Case,*[1] a Canadian mining and smelting company operated a smelter plant in British Columbia. Over a twelve-year period, emissions of sulfur dioxide fumes from the plant caused considerable damage to the state of Washington. The Canadian government agreed to pay damages under previous agreements and arbitration, but the U.S. asked the arbitration tribunal to issue an injunction barring further environmental damages to the state of Washington. In granting the injunction, the arbitration tribunal stated:

> To date, there has been no air pollution case dealt with by an international tribunal. The nearest analogy is that of water pollution, although there also no decision of an international tribunal has been found. There are, however, as regards both air pollution and water pollution, certain decisions by the Supreme Court of the United States that legitimately can be taken as a guide when no contrary rule prevails in international law. These decisions, taken as a whole, provide an adequate basis for the conclusion that, under principles of international law, no state has the right to use or permit the use of its territory in such a manner as to cause injury by fumes in or to the territory of another when the case is of serious consequence and the injury is established by clear and convincing evidence.

A second source of international environmental law includes *resolutions and declarations of international organizations.* The United Nations (UN) has addressed important global environmental issues. Its activities affect the environment in several important ways: first, it focuses the attention of the world community on significant environmental concerns; second, it coordinates the efforts of various states through treaties and international conventions; third, it creates specialized organizations, like the **United Nations Environment Program** (UNEP), which coordinates global environmental protection initiatives;

and, fourth, it introduces scientific and technological systems designed to address environmental problems.

The UN has also sponsored several important international conferences on the environment, such as the 1972 **Stockholm Conference on the Environment,** which ended with a Declaration on Principles of the International Law of the Environment. The Stockholm Conference has become a cornerstone of modern international environmental law. Since the declaration of the Stockholm Conference in 1972, over 140 international conventions and treaties on the environment have been concluded under the auspices of the UN and its specialized agencies. These treaties have addressed the preservation of wildlife, whale and seal catching, fisheries, protection of birds, conservation of living resources and plants, protection of rivers, seas, and oceans, the banning of nuclear weapons tests in the atmosphere, exploration of the seas, outer space and celestial bodies, and the banning of chemical weapons.

Other international organizations important in establishing international environmental policy include intergovernmental organizations which formulate and encourage public and private compliance with environmental policies. The **Organization for Economic Cooperation and Development** (OECD) is made up of the countries of Western Europe, Australia, Canada, Japan, New Zealand, and the U.S. The OECD has been responsible for establishing environmental policies which have led to environmental regulations adopted by international conventions.

The **International Law Commission,** created by the UN General Assembly, is charged with developing and codifying international law. The commission has proposed that willful acts of serious environmental pollution be regarded as crimes against the peace and security of mankind. The **World Health Organization** (WHO) and World Bank have also adopted policies addressing issues of international environmental concern. The World Bank adopted a policy which calls for the rejection of financing for environmentally destructive projects. However, the bank has been criticized for failing to follow this policy in the face of desirable economic development.

The **European Economic Community** (EEC) has, under the Maastrict Treaty, also established principal objectives of its policies and actions concerning the environment, and has called upon its members to cooperate in achieving these objectives. Other regional organizations like the **Organization of African Unity** (OAU) work to protect the global environment.

Nongovernmental organizations (NGOs) and worldwide "green" movements have been effective in pressuring governments to strengthen global environmental protections. These movements have generated global environmental concern which has led to the passage of domestic laws and international conventions. Other organizations, like the **International Council of Scientific Unions** (ICSU), consist of a broad-based federation of scientific organizations that continually update available environmental research and examine environmental issues. The World Conservation Union, or **International Union for the Conservation of Nature and Natural Resources** (IUCN), represents over sixty nations and many more universities and national nongovernmental organizations. The IUCN evaluates renewable natural resources and supports international conventions designed to conserve those resources. The **Worldwide Fund for Nature** (WWF) collects and distributes funds for global conservation activities, and pioneered the concept of "debt-for-nature" swaps, which involve the purchase of an underdeveloped nation's commercial debts in exchange for that country's agreement to promote conservation.

INTERNATIONAL TREATIES AND CONVENTIONS

The clearest sources of international environmental law are international conventions or treaties. Because of significant differences in the commitment by the various parties, these conventions contain only general principles rather than specific mandates, as they often limit the obligations and restrictions imposed on participating countries. Nevertheless, these conventions serve an important function by stating environmental goals and by requiring adopting nations to record and periodically report their environmental activities to international organizations. There are several landmark global initiatives, including international conventions as well as bilateral treaties, which form the basis of modern international environmental law. These include the 1972 Stockholm Conference, the 1987 Montreal Protocol, the 1989 Basel Convention, and the 1992 Earth Summit at Rio de Janeiro, Brazil.

The Stockholm Conference

The first "Earth Summit" occurred in 1972 at the UN Conference on the Human Environment in Stockholm. Under the auspices of the UN, delegations from over 100 nations as well as many organizations attended the conference. At the Stockholm Conference the global community came together to plan a framework for comprehensive consideration within the UN. Among other things, the Stockholm conference produced a Declaration on the Human Environment, affirming human responsibility to preserve the environment, a declaration of twenty-six principles concerning the environment, and recommendations for follow-up action. The Stockholm Declaration of Principles recognized the human right to a safe environment, the responsibility of nations to preserve natural ecosystems and wildlife, and the need to halt the release of substances and heat beyond levels consistent with human health and the earth's capacity to absorb them. The Stockholm conference also established a basic plan for worldwide environmental assessment and created "**Earthwatch,**" a program to facilitate international cooperation in research activities, monitoring, and exchange of information between nations.

Delegates at the Stockholm conference also confronted the serious problem that a nation's level of economic development substantially affects its willingness and ability to protect the environment. Delegates at the conference asserted that sound economic development is environmentally attainable with proper international cooperation and international financial assistance. They also affirmed that each nation has the sovereign right to plan and control its economic development and the exploitation of its natural resources; however, they also recognized a nation's obligation to prevent and abate extraterritorial environmental damage. The Stockholm conference called for financial and technical assistance for underdeveloped nations and urged national governments to develop international rules for liability and compensation for environmental damage that crosses national borders.

Following the Stockholm conference, global and regional conferences continued to address a wide range of international environmental issues. In 1982, the UN General Assembly declared the **World Charter for Nature,** which attempted to implement principles from the Stockholm conference. The World Charter recognized humans' responsibility to maintain the quality of nature and to conserve the world's natural resources, and it urged nations to incorporate conservation efforts into economic planning and domestic law making.

The growing awareness of the wide differences separating developed and developing nations, and the fact that many developing nations viewed environmental protection as a threat to their economic growth, led the World Commission on Environment and Development to issue its **Brundtland Report** in 1987. In this report, the commission stressed the importance of environmental protection for the developing world, and introduced the concept of **sustainable development.** This concept is defined as economic development which meets the demands of the present without compromising the ability of future generations to meet their own needs.

The Montreal Protocol

The ozone layer is a gaseous layer of molecules fifteen to thirty miles above the surface of the earth. The ozone layer absorbs and shields the earth from ultraviolet radiation. In the 1980s, scientists observed a significant hole developing in the ozone layer over the Antarctic each spring. While changes in the earth's ozone shield and climate occur naturally due to natural events such as volcanic eruptions, many believed that the emissions of man-made substances like chlorofluorocarbons (CFCs) substantially aggravated these natural changes.

CFCs and halons are chemicals that were widely used for air-conditioning, solvents, styrofoam, and spray aerosol propellants. Acting on this warning, fifty-seven nations signed the **Montreal Protocol on Substances that Deplete the Ozone Layer,** which became effective in 1989. Parties to this agreement agreed to freeze consumption of CFCs at 1986 levels and to cut production and consumption in half by 1999. Developing nations were given a ten-year exemption.

Following the effective date of the agreement, new scientific data indicated that CFCs were a greater threat than originally thought, and that a wider variety of chemicals than originally believed were destroying the ozone layer. In response to these new concerns, adopting countries reconvened and agreed to amendments which resulted in a more comprehensive and aggressive program to phase out CFCs. Participants also recognized the need to provide technical and financial support to developing nations and created a $240 million fund to assist developing nations in reaching the goals of the protocol.

The Montreal Protocol advanced the earlier 1985 Vienna Convention for the Protection of the Ozone Layer by establishing specific time schedules and control measures for limiting the use of ozone depleting chemicals. In the 1990 Clean Air Act, discussed in Chapter 10, the U.S. Congress mandated that the EPA take action in compliance with the provisions of the Montreal Protocol.

Many consider the Montreal Protocol to be a successful international initiative for two reasons: first, its specificity assured concrete results in reducing industrial sources of ozone depletion; and, second, its call for regular reassessment of the provisions of the agreement provides an opportunity for nations to quickly reconvene to address new scientific information and environmental concerns as they arise.

Basel Convention

The 1989 **Basel Convention on the Control of Transboundary Movements of Hazardous Wastes and Their Disposal** resulted from a conference convened by the United Nations Environment Programme (UNEP) to address problems caused by the international export of toxic and hazardous wastes. As developing nations struggle to improve their economic condition, many feared that these nations would become a dumping ground for the rest of the world. The Basel Convention was adopted by fifty-four countries, and it forbids the export of hazardous waste to any country whose government does not agree in advance to accept it. The agreement establishes a *notice and consent* structure for wastes covered by the agreement. Both exporting and importing nations must take necessary measures to assure environmentally safe methods of disposal of the shipped wastes.

Under the agreement, when a shipper intends to export hazardous wastes, it must first notify the export country, the import country, and any country through which the waste will be transported. Shipment cannot be made until written confirmation from those authorities is received. Further, all transboundary shipments of hazardous waste must be covered by insurance, and the convention requires an adopting nation to treat violations of its terms as criminal acts.

In 1994, at a conference on the Basel Convention in Geneva, Switzerland, all attending nations, including members of the Organization for Economic Cooperation and Development (OECD), unanimously approved a resolution calling for an immediate and total ban on hazardous waste exports to countries outside the OECD. The resolution has created controversy and its ultimate effect remains unclear.

The 1992 Earth Summit

In June 1992, delegates from over 150 countries, including the political leaders of 103 nations, more than 30,000 activists, world religious figures, and corporate CEOs convened in Rio De Janeiro for the **United Nations Conference on the Environment and Development** (UNCED). They gathered in three primary forums—governmental, nongovernmental, and a gathering of indigenous leaders. This 1992 Earth Summit gave participants the opportunity to exchange information and focused worldwide attention on environmental issues. The conference was based on a platform of five documents. Of these five, two were legally binding and were negotiated and prepared prior to UNCED: the Convention on Climate Change and the Convention on Biological Diversity. Other documents considered at the convention were Agenda 21, which comprised some 500 pages of discussion on solving environmental problems; the Rio Declaration, which sets out twenty-seven principles on how humankind can live in harmony with the earth; and the Statement of Forest Principles, which sets out a policy to maintain forests while utilizing them as an economic resource.

Two-and-a-half years of preparation preceded the twelve days of the Earth Summit. The Rio Declaration, Statement of Forest Principles, and Agenda 21 were agreed to in principle by consensus. Of the two signed treaties, several countries chose to sign one but not both documents.

The **Convention on Climate Change** was proposed in response to growing evidence that the earth is warming as a result of human activities, large-scale burning of fossil fuels, and massive cutting of forests which absorb carbon dioxide. Scientists have warned that the effects from global warming include rising sea levels and changes in rainfall and evaporation patterns which will lead to drought and desertification in some parts of the world, storms and flooding in others. Melting land ice could cause the sea to rise between three inches and a foot within the next forty years, flooding low-lying islands and coastal regions.

In response to alarm about the impact of climate change, delegates drafting the Convention on Climate Change detailed specific actions to address the problem. This ultimately led to a dispute among nations about specific targets and timetables for reducing emissions of carbon dioxide. Japan and the EEC favored a proposal mandating the stabilization of carbon emissions at 1990 levels by the year 2000, but the U.S. disputed the need for legislation and preferred voluntary adherence to this goal. Eventually, the document was signed without any set targets or timetables. The convention also addressed the need to control emissions of other greenhouse gases and for financial and technical aid to developing countries, especially the need to assist those countries in protecting their forests.

Prior to the Rio Conference, UNEP established the Intergovernmental Negotiating Committee for a Convention on Biological Diversity (INC). INC held five sessions to negotiate an agreement satisfactory to all countries. The ultimate document outlined the need to preserve biological diversity for present and future generations and sought to guarantee that royalties for medicines derived from plants in a developing country would go to that country in perpetuity, even if the medicines were synthesized. The **Convention on Biological Diversity** attracted the most media attention at the conference because the U.S. refused to sign it. U.S. President George Bush stated that the treaty did not adequately protect the intellectual property rights (patents) of industry. On June 4, 1993, President Clinton signed the Convention on Biological Diversity, but as of the end of 1996, the Senate had not yet ratified the agreement. The Clinton administration has declared that Senate ratification of the convention is a top foreign policy and environmental priority of the president's second term.

Just as in 1972 the UN Conference on the Human Environment adopted principles known as the Stockholm Declaration, in 1992 UNCED adopted a similar declaration called the Rio Declaration on Environment and Development. The 1992 declaration addressed environmental concerns which have emerged since 1972—most notably, the deterioration of the environment and the interrelationship between economic progress and environmental protection. The U.S. disagreed with the wording of some parts of the declaration, and issued a written statement listing its formal reservations.

The **Rio Declaration,** which is not legally binding, outlines the rights and responsibilities of countries toward the environment, and it attempts to balance principles important to both developed and developing nations. The twenty-seven principles of the Rio Declaration are set out in Appendix C. The **Statement of Forest Principles** ("The Non-Legally Binding Statement of Principles for a Global Consensus on the Management, Conservation and Sustainable Development of all Types of Forests"), reflects the first global consensus on forests. The statement includes a declaration that states have, in accordance with the charter of the UN and principles of international law, the sovereign and inalienable right to utilize, manage, and develop their forests in accordance with their developmental needs and level of socio-economic development. It declares that national forest policies should recognize and duly support the identity, culture, and rights of indigenous people and their communities. It recognizes the important role forests play in meeting energy requirements and declares that specific financial resources should be provided to developing countries with significant forested areas. It also declares that efforts should be taken to enhance forests around the world, and that all countries, notably developed countries, should take positive action toward reforestation and forest conservation.

Agenda 21, called The Manual for Planetary Survival by some, is a voluminous document identifying and addressing environmental problems which will trouble the planet into the twenty-first century, and it describes in detail courses of action necessary to address those problems. Agenda 21 is not a legally binding instrument, but is an important statement of policy and recommendations.

TRADE AND THE ENVIRONMENT

The impact of international trade on the global environment is a key issue in environmental policy debates. Liberalizing world trade is widely viewed as indispensable to the economic welfare of all nations, and free trade is central to efforts to promote "sustainable development." Environmental concerns have also been the source of tensions between nations. For example, the U.S. has quarreled with Norway over whaling, with Mexico over tuna fishing and the resulting dolphin deaths, with Japan over protection of endangered sea turtles, and with Brazil over rain forest preservation.

Some environmentalists argue that liberalizing trade between nations invites increased pollution and results in a loss of regulatory sovereignty. They see "free trade" as a synonym for anti-environmental policy making, driven by the desire for jobs and profits at the expense of the environment. They also fear that enforcement mechanisms under free trade agreements often permit obscure, unaccountable, and business-oriented international bureaucrats to control environmental policy.

Advocates of free trade, on the other hand, distrust the agenda of environmentalists, and they fear that environmental concerns will result in new forms of protectionism which will block foreign producers from entering markets and reduce the efficiency gained from trade. Trade advocates are also concerned that the use of penalties to enforce environmental agreements will break down the trading regime, and they object to efforts to adjust for differences in environmental standards.

Environmental Implications of International Trade Agreements

Increasingly, public attention has focused on the debate over the environmental implications of free trade agreements. Environmental concerns were central to the debate in 1993 over the **North American Free Trade Agreement** (NAFTA) and a focus of discussions during the "Uruguay Round" of global trade negotiations under the **General Agreement on Tariffs and Trade** (GATT). Clearly there are important environmental issues raised by bilateral and multi-lateral trade agreements like NAFTA and GATT. The following sections examine some of the environmental implications of these two important trade agreements.

Trade Agreements in General

Under the U.S. Constitution, the president has the power to enter into treaties with other nations, with the advice and consent of two-thirds of the Senate. The courts have broadly construed this treaty power and have held that the power extends to any issue involving negotiations with foreign governments, even if those issues substantially affect domestic issues.

The U.S. government has developed procedures for implementing international agreements. Some treaties give advance authority to the president to conclude supplemental agreements carrying out the terms of the original treaty without requiring new action by the legislative branch. These treaties are especially important for environmental accords where subsequent scientific data may require ongoing revisions to the original agreement.

In recent years, Congress has favored a *subsequent approval process*. In these cases, Congress enacts a treaty into law after the negotiations are complete. The treaty is not binding until it has been confirmed by both houses of Congress. Under the *fast-track* mechanism, the president must consult with Congress during the drafting of the proposal. Legislative committees then must report the bill to the floor within a short period of time and the debate is limited. Under this procedure, Congress must approve or reject the proposal (without amendments) within ninety days.

The executive branch is the dominant force in negotiating and drafting international agreements, and Congress has delegated authority to different executive agencies to coordinate trade regulation. The **U.S. Trade Representative** (USTR) is a cabinet-level post which carries the rank of ambassador. The trade representative coordinates and formulates international trade policy. The legal status of the USTR was a central issue in the *Public Citizen v. Office of the U.S. Trade Representative,* a case set out in the section of this chapter discussing NAFTA.

The president also influences environmental policy directly through issuance of executive orders. In 1994, President Clinton issued Executive Order No. 12898, which requires every executive agency to adopt an environmental justice strategy and requires research into environmental inequities which occur when poor and minority populations bear a disproportionate share of the burdens of pollution.

The General Agreement on Tariffs and Trade (GATT)

In 1944, during World War II, the U.S. and its allies determined that greater international cooperation and coordination would be required if future economic disasters and wars were to be prevented. As a result, they established the International Monetary Fund, the World Bank, and the International Trade Organization (ITO). Although the ITO never evolved into a viable trade organization, negotiators did establish the General Agreement on Tariffs and Trade, which was designed to assist in creating and maintaining international trade standards and tariff reductions.

GATT provides a regular mechanism for conducting multilateral trade negotiations. GATT sponsors rounds of negotiations, which last several years and are designed to remove global trade barriers. In 1993, over 100 countries were members of GATT; three-quarters of those members were from developing nations.

GATT is actually composed of approximately 200 different treaties which provide a legal framework for trade relations. To date, GATT members have conducted eight major trade rounds. The Uruguay Round began in 1986 and was completed in the 1990s. GATT has four major principles. First, trade tariffs are the only form of import protection permitted, and the system is designed to encourage reduction of import duties. Second, all members of GATT are given *most-favored nation* status. This means that, with some exceptions, any privilege or benefit granted to one GATT member must be extended to all other GATT members. Third, the principle of *national treatment* requires that imports from a member nation, once du 1ied and cleared from customs, may not be treated less favorably than domestic products. Finally, reduction of tariffs should occur on a *reciprocal* basis. Combined with most-favored nation status, this principle helps ensure a balanced and worldwide reduction in tariffs.

If a country fails to honor its GATT obligations, the member nation may utilize GATT's dispute settlement procedures. Under the procedures originally established by the agreement, nations first attempt to resolve the dispute through informal negotiations. If unsuccessful, GATT provides for a formal consultation process. If that fails, the GATT Council appoints a panel to assist the GATT membership in resolving the dispute. Within six months the GATT panel issues a report, which is then forwarded to the GATT Council for consideration. The council's decision on the adoption of the report must be given within fifteen months, and must be unanimous. The breaching nation is given a reasonable period of time to come into compliance with the council's recommendations. If it fails to do so, GATT members may permit the complaining country to suspend concessions it owes the non-complying nation. Such suspensions are, however, extremely rare.

A major issue affecting the global environment is GATT's prohibition against excluding products of member nations. In the past, GATT has tended to enforce trade access without regard for the environmentally harmful practices of some businesses, although GATT recognizes an exception if the product *directly* harms the health or environment. Consequently, the businesses of an environmentally progressive importing country may be at a competitive disadvantage in comparison with businesses of countries with less aggressive environmental regulations. This policy reflects trade advocates' fear that one nation's unilateral exclusion of foreign goods for environmental reasons could create an enormous loophole which might destroy the principles of free trade.

The Tuna-Dolphin Controversy   A 1991 GATT dispute over the importation of tuna between the U.S. and Mexico drew worldwide attention to the problems of trade and the environment. The controversy began when a U.S. District Court issued an injunction against the importation of yellowfin tuna from Mexico. Plaintiff environmental groups had sought the injunction against the domestic sale and importation of tuna caught in "purse seine" nets, a practice prohibited in the U.S. under MMPA. The government appealed the district court's decision, which held that the practice violated the MMPA, in the following case.

EARTH ISLAND INSTITUTE v. MOSBACHER
929 F.2d 1449 (9th Cir. 1991)

SCHROEDER, Circuit Judge

Congress enacted the MMPA in 1972 to address, among other problems, the tremendous number of dolphins killed by the purse seine method of fishing for yellowfin tuna in the eastern tropical Pacific Ocean. For unknown reasons, yellowfin tuna swim below schools of dolphins in that area. Thus, fishing vessels often set their purse seine nets on dolphins to catch the tuna below. The dolphins are frequently killed or maimed in this process. In the early 1970s, the United States fishing fleet was responsible for the slaughter of over 300,000 dolphins annually.

Although the Act brought about a material reduction in the number of dolphins killed by the United States fleet, dolphin slaughter by foreign nations remained a growing problem. By amendments to the Act in 1984 and 1988, Congress enacted specific standards intended to ensure that foreign tuna fishing fleets would reduce the number of dolphins killed and to protect certain endangered subspecies of dolphins. Such subspecies included the eastern spinner dolphin which is the subject to this law-

suit. The weapon Congress chose to bring about such reductions in killings was a mandatory embargo on the importation of yellowfin tuna to be imposed upon those countries whose fleets failed to meet the standards Congress established.

The statute mandates the Secretary of the Treasury to ban imports of yellowfin tuna products from a foreign nation until the Secretary of Commerce certifies that that nation's incidental kill rate of dolphins is comparable to that of the United States. The statute specifies that the total incidental kill rate of a foreign nation shall not be found comparable unless it is no more than 2.0 times the total incidental kill rate of the United States fleet. With respect to the eastern spinner dolphin, the statute additionally provides that the total number of eastern spinner dolphins killed by a foreign fleet cannot exceed fifteen percent of the total number of mammals killed by the fleet of that country.

[*The National Marine Fisheries Service (NMFS), which was responsible for implementing the provisions of the act, had pro-*

mulgated regulations implementing the requirements of the Marine Mammal Protection Act. Under its regulations, if a foreign nation had exceeded the limitations for a given year, and remained under embargo, the secretary could nevertheless "reconsider" the embargo and certify compliance based upon data only for the first six months following the year the limits were exceeded.]

***

The events giving rise to the preliminary injunction in this appeal are as follows. On June 25, 1990, Earth Island filed its first motion for a preliminary injunction in the federal district court for the northern district of California. Earth Island sought an "interim" embargo which would enjoin the importation of yellowfin tuna products pending NMFS' issuance of the comparability findings required by the MMPA. . . . Earth Island argued that, by the plain terms of the MMPA, an embargo was mandatory and the agency could not authorize imports until the requisite comparability findings were made; therefore, it argued, the agency was required to impose an embargo until after the relevant data had been reviewed. . . .

The government's primary argument is that the six-month "reconsideration" provision is within the discretion delegated by Congress to the agency for regulatory implementation of the Act. The government points to the deference the courts owe to agencies in matters of statutory interpretation. See, e.g., *Chevron,* 467 U.S. at 844, 104 S.Ct. at 2782 ("We have long recognized that considerable weight should be accorded to an executive department's con-

struction of a statutory scheme it is entrusted to administer.") The difficulty with this position is that agencies do not have discretion to issue regulations which conflict with statutory language and congressional purpose. This regulation clearly does. . . .

The government also suggests that regardless of the language used in the statute, the reconsideration provision should be upheld as a matter of policy because it offers an incentive to foreign countries to speed up their efforts to meet the statutory standards. The record in this case belies the existence of any incentive effect. The record demonstrates that the six-month reconsideration allows foreign nations and NMFS to withhold the release of negative findings until they have available a subsequent set of positive findings, as occurred with the 1989–90 data for Mexico. The result in this case was that Mexico, which had exceeded MMPA standards for an entire year, was subject to embargo for less than one day. Under this regulation, foreign nations could thus continually exceed MMPA limits for part of each year, yet never be subject to the ban. Because the reconsideration regulation creates such a potential for abuse, and has in fact already been used to circumvent the intent of Congress, we reject the government's argument that the reconsideration regulation offers a more effective incentive to foreign countries to reduce dolphin kill rates. . . .

Because the government's position is at odds with both the language and the purpose of MMPA, and the agency's intended role under it, we affirm the district court's order of October 4.

Questions and Comments for Discussion

1. What domestic environmental law was involved in this dispute? What agency was responsible for enforcing the law? How had the agency responsible for enforcing this law interpreted its application?

2. On what legal basis did the court strike down the agency regulation? What were the international policy implications of that regulation and the court's ruling?

The GATT Challenge   Following the decision in the above case, Mexico sought and obtained a GATT panel ruling that the tuna embargo violated GATT international trade rules. The panel concluded that the U.S. had violated GATT by instituting a ban under MMPA, and that U.S. embargoes on imports of tuna were inconsistent with U.S. GATT obligations, and was inconsistent with GATT's rules against prohibitions or restrictions on imports. While GATT restrictions theoretically do not prevent nations from excluding products that are environmentally offensive, or from adopting measures necessary to protect human, animal, or plant life, the GATT panel said that exception was not applicable here.

UNITED STATES RESTRICTIONS
ON IMPORTS OF TUNA
30 I.L.M. 1594 (1991)
Dispute Settlement Panel
General Agreement on Tariffs and Trade

CHAIRMAN SZEPESI AND MESSRS. RAMSAUER AND ROSELLI:

***

The Panel noted that under General Agreement, quantitative restrictions in imports are forbidden by Article XI:1 (of the General Agreement). . . . The Panel therefore found that the direct import prohibition on certain yellowfin tuna and certain yellowfin tuna products from Mexico and the provisions of the MMPA . . . were inconsistent with Article XI:1. . . .

The United States considered the prohibition of imports of certain yellowfin tuna and certain yellowfin tuna products from Mexico to be justified by Article XX(b) because they served solely the purpose of protecting dolphin life and health.[2]

The Panel recalled the finding of a previous panel that this paragraph of Article XX was intended to allow contracting parties to impose trade restrictive measures inconsistent with the General Agreement to pursue overriding public policy goals to the extent that such inconsistencies were unavoidable. The Panel considered that if the broad interpretation of Article XX(b) suggested by the United States were accepted, each contracting party could unilaterally determine the life or health protection policies from which other contracting parties could not deviate without jeopardizing their rights under the General Agreement. The General Agreement would then no longer constitute a multilateral framework for trade among all contracting parties but would provide legal security only in respect of trade between a limited number of contracting parties with identical internal regulations.

The Panel proceeded to examine whether the prohibition on imports of certain yellowfin tuna and certain yellowfin tuna products from Mexico and the MMPA provisions under which it was imposed could be justified under the exception in Article XX(g). . . .

The Panel considered that if the extra-jurisdictional interpretation of Article XX(g) suggested by the United States were accepted, each contracting party could unilaterally determine the conservation policies from which other contracting parties could not deviate without jeopardizing their rights under the General Agreement. The considerations that led the Panel to reject an extradictional application of Article XX(b) therefore apply also to Article XX(g). . . .

***

[A] contracting party is free to tax or regulate imported products and like domestic products as long as its taxes or regulations do not discriminate against imported products or afford protection to domestic producers, and a contracting party is also free to tax or regulate domestic production for environmental purposes. As a corollary to these rights, a contracting party may not restrict imports of a product merely because it originates in a country with environmental policies different from its own.

[*The panel found that the MMPA was inconsistent with the United States' obligations under GATT and requested the United States modify the MMPA to make it consistent with the General Agreement.*]

Questions and Comments for Discussion

The U.S. and Mexico subsequently resolved the dispute without requesting that the panel's decision be adopted by the full GATT Council. In October 1992, The U.S. Congress enacted the *International Dolphin Conservation Act*. Under this law, any nation currently under embargo could have the embargo lifted if it agreed to reduce dolphin mortality and abide by a five-year moratorium on the use of purse-seine nets.

Although the GATT Council never formally adopted the panel's recommendation, the now famous "tuna-dolphin" decision alarmed many by appearing to place trade obligations on a higher plane than environmental protection. The GATT ruling raised the specter of domestic environmental laws and regulations overridden by an obscure and environmentally insensitive international trade tribunal. The decision has been cited by environmental groups as evidence that GATT undermines domestic environmental protection standards, and many of the environmental concerns raised by the tuna-dolphin controversy spilled over into the more recent debate about NAFTA.

The Uruguay Round of GATT   On December 1, 1994, the Senate approved legislation implementing the Uruguay Round of GATT. The round included 117 participants and resulted in twenty-eight separate accords covering, among other things, agriculture, textiles, services, intellectual property, and foreign investment. The parties also agreed to form a **World Trade Organization** (WTO), a formal international body supporting GATT.

Environmentalists have complained that the most recent GATT bill, drafted jointly by the Clinton administration and Congress, contains no provisions addressing environmental concerns. Critics also fear that WTO, created to oversee the global trade pact, is too powerful, and that it will have the power to override domestic environmental laws. The administration, however, has insisted that the most recent round will not affect national sovereignty and substantive U.S. rights and obligations. Perhaps most controversial are new dispute-settlement procedures. Under the new organization, member countries provide the WTO with lists of trade experts. If a dispute arises, the WTO selects a panel from this list. Countries winning a case before the WTO may retaliate against the offending country.

In response to public concerns regarding the implications of new dispute settlement, the U.S. Congress included in its approval of the Uruguay Round of GATT comprehensive requirements to ensure monitoring of WTO dispute settlement proceedings involving U.S. laws, regulations, or policies. These requirements include mandates for the executive branch to keep Congress and the public advised of any WTO dispute resolution proceeding involving a U.S. law or regulation.

As the GATT and NAFTA controversies suggest, issues affecting consumers and the environment will continue to play an important role in the debate over future international trade agreements. In addition, trade and environmental issues are likely to re-emerge in future congressional debates over the president's authority to negotiate trade agreements.

Environmental Implications of NAFTA

In 1993, Congress approved the North American Free Trade Agreement (NAFTA). NAFTA created a free trade market among Canada, Mexico, and the U.S., thus combining the world's largest, eighth-largest, and thirteenth-largest economies into a North American market of 360 million people. NAFTA eliminated tariffs and other barriers to trade, and it also established a framework for supervising and implementing the provisions of the agreement.

Throughout its approval process, NAFTA generated a great deal of debate in the U.S. and Canada. The debate created some strange bedfellows as organized labor joined with environmentalists to oppose the agreement. The debate tended to focus on two important issues: the socioeconomic benefits of free trade versus job protection and the environment.

Environmentalists opposed to NAFTA expressed the fear that NAFTA would pose a threat to the environment and native cultures. They argued that further trade liberalization between the U.S. and Mexico would result in incremental environmental damage, citing as evidence the environmental conditions along the 2000-mile border between the U.S. and Mexico, an area contaminated by excessive air pollution, sewage in underground water, and toxic dumping. They also expressed fears that the agreement did not contain adequate provisions to remediate such damage, and they argued that NAFTA could be used to attack state environmental standards as illegal barriers to trade.

In response to these concerns, the Clinton administration sought a supplemental agreement for NAFTA to address environmental concerns. On September 14, 1993, the government released the *North American Free Trade Agreement Side Accord on the Environment* (the environmental side agreement). Among other things, the agreement sets up a dispute resolution process if a NAFTA signatory persistently fails to enforce its domestic environmental laws, and it sets out a plan for coordinating and financing environmental infrastructure. The agreement also requires all parties to inform each other of domestic decisions to ban or severely restrict a pesticide or other chemical.

The NAFTA side agreement also produced controversy. Mexico's failure to enforce its own environmental laws and the considerable disparity between wages and labor protection in Mexico and the U.S. and Canada raised public and congressional concern. However, because Mexico and Canada refused to surrender control over internal affairs and national sovereignty, the parties agreed in general to pursue environmental and trade policies compatible with NAFTA. NAFTA does not empower an international commission directly to enforce, enjoin, or penalize a nation for environmental offenses or unfair labor standards. It does direct NAFTA agencies to press investigation of complaints by other nations and to take remedial action by reporting and making recommendations to the government and NAFTA agencies.

Prior to congressional approval of NAFTA, several environmental groups pursued legal action to compel the U.S. **Office of the U.S. Trade Representative** (OTR) to produce an EIS for NAFTA before the agreement was submitted to Congress for ratification. Preparation of an EIS could have substantially delayed ratification of the agreement.

On June 30, 1994, a U.S. District Court ruled that the administration could not seek approval of NAFTA until it completed an environmental impact statement required by

NEPA (discussed in Chapter 9). Three weeks later, the Clinton administration filed an appeal in the case.

PUBLIC CITIZEN v. UNITED STATES TRADE REPRESENTATIVE
5 F.3d 549 (D.C. Cir. 1993)

MIKVA, C.J.

Appellees Public Citizen, Friends of the Earth, Inc., and the Sierra Club (collectively "Public Citizen") sued the Office of the United State Trade Representative, claiming that an environmental impact statement was required for the North American Free Trade Agreement ("NAFTA"). In its appeal of that ruling, the government contends that the trade representative's preparation of NAFTA without an impact statement is not "final agency action" under the Administrative Procedure Act ("APA") and therefore is not reviewable by this court. Because we conclude that NAFTA is not "final agency action" under the APA, we reverse the decision of the district court.

***

The National Environmental Policy Act ("NEPA") requires federal agencies to include an EIS "in every recommendation or report on proposals for legislation and other major Federal actions significantly affecting the quality of the human environment. . . ." In drafting NEPA, however, Congress did not create a private right of action. Accordingly, Public Citizen must rest its claim for judicial review on the Administrative Procedure Act.[3] Section 702 of the APA confers an action for injunctive relief on persons "adversely affected or aggrieved by agency action within the meaning of a relevant statute." Section 704, however, allows review only of "*final* agency action. . . ."

To determine whether an agency action is final, "[t]he core question is whether the agency has completed its decisionmaking process, *and* whether the result of that process is one that will directly affect the parties. . . ." This logic applies with equal force to NAFTA. Even though the OTR has completed negotiations on NAFTA, the agreement will have no effect on Public Citizen's members unless and until the president submits it to Congress. Like the reapportionment statute in Franklin,[4] the trade acts involve the president at the final stage of the process by providing for him to submit to Congress the final legal text of the agreement, a draft of the implementing legislation, and supporting information. The president is not obligated to submit any agreement to Congress, and until he does there is no final action. If and when the agreement is submitted to Congress, it will be the result of action by the president, action clearly not reviewable under the APA.

***

Public Citizen argues that applying [the rule under] *Franklin* in this case would effectively nullify NEPA's EIS requirement because often "some other step must be taken before" otherwise final agency actions will result in environmental harm. In support of this position, it catalogs a number of cases in which courts have reviewed NEPA challenges to agency actions that require the involvement of some other governmental or private entity before becoming final. Although we acknowledge the stringency of *Franklin's* "direct effect" requirement, we disagree that it represents the death knell of the legislative EIS. *Franklin* is limited to those cases in which the president has final constitutional or statutory responsibility for the final step necessary for the agency action directly to affect the parties. . . . [T]he requirement that the president, and not OTR, initiate trade negotiations and submit trade agreements and their implementing legislation to Congress indicates that Congress deemed the president's involvement essential to the integrity of international trade negotiations. When the president's role is not essential to the integrity of the process, however, APA review of otherwise final agency actions may well be available. . . .

The ultimate destiny of NAFTA has yet to be determined. Recently negotiated side agreements may well change the dimensions of the conflict that Public Citizen sought to

have resolved by the courts. More importantly, the political debate over NAFTA in Congress has yet to play out. Whatever the ultimate result, however, NAFTA's fate now rests in the hands of the political branches. The judiciary has no role to play.

In sum, under the reasoning and language of *Franklin v. Massachusetts,* the "final agency action" challenged in this case is the submission of NAFTA to Congress by the president. Because the trade acts vest in the president the discretion to renegotiate NAFTA before submitting it to Congress or to refuse to submit it at all, his action, and not that of the OTR, will directly affect Public Citizen's members. The president's actions are not "agency action" and thus cannot be reviewed under the APA. The district court's grant of summary judgment in favor of Public Citizen is, therefore, REVERSED.

Questions and Comments for Discussion

1.   What was the legal issue presented in this case? What law did the court apply in answering that legal question?

2.   To what extent do you think the timing of this case might have influenced the court's decision? Could the possibility of substantial delay of ratification of NAFTA (while the administration prepared an EIS) have been a factor in the court's interpretation and application of law in this case? To what extent was this case really about the appropriate separation of powers between the executive, legislative, and judicial branches of government?

3.   A concurring judge agreed that the injunction against the OTR must be set aside.

He did not quarrel with the majority's rationale; however, he said, "I am not prepared to say whether in NEPA cases, the act of proposing legislation constitutes final action under Section 704 of the APA. This is a troublesome question, bound to arise in future cases, and we should not stake out a position on it here." If an executive agency's proposal for legislation ultimately is a proposal by the executive branch, cannot one argue that *any* executive agency proposal for legislation will fail to meet the "final agency action" requirement of the APA?

Some have suggested that the appellate court's decision in *Public Citizen v. U.S. Trade Representative* will reshape the way environmental issues will be addressed in future international trade agreements. In denying judicial review to plaintiff environmental groups, the appellate court refused to force the administration to comply with NEPA in submitting international trade agreements to Congress for ratification. NEPA is one of the most powerful environmental public disclosure laws presently on the books. Thus some argue that the court's holding in this case substantially diminished the role of the public in the debate over the environmental implications of future trade agreements.

EXTRATERRITORIAL APPLICATION OF U.S. DOMESTIC LAWS

The question whether U.S. domestic environmental laws apply to the actions of the federal government or others outside the territorial U.S. is an important one for those concerned about the global environment. The U.S. Supreme Court has held that there must be clear evidence of congressional intent in order to apply a U.S. statute extraterritorially. Absent of clear intent, domestic environmental laws do not apply to the actions of American citizens or companies in other countries. In *Amlon Metals Inc. v. FMC Corp.*,[5] a U.S. District Court ruled that the RCRA did not apply extraterritorially to waste presenting a hazard in the United Kingdom. Amlon Metals had arranged for wastes generated by FMC Corporation in the U.S. to be shipped to the United Kingdom. After it discovered the waste contained hazardous substances, Amlon sought injunctive relief and damages from FMC under RCRA's citizen suit provisions. It alleged that the waste presented an "imminent and substantial danger" to workers in the United Kingdom. However, the district court ruled against Amlon in the case. It found no evidence of congressional intent to apply RCRA extraterritorially, and it noted that Congress had failed to prove a venue for citizen suits based on hazards from wastes in other countries.

In *Lujan v. Defenders of Wildlife*,[6] discussed in Chapter 8, the U.S. Supreme Court reversed a ruling by the court of appeals which had upheld regulations promulgated by the secretary of the interior under the Endangered Species Act (ESA). Those regulations limited the consultation requirements of the ESA to agency actions within the U.S. or on the high seas. In *Lujon*, the Supreme Court held that plaintiff environmental groups lacked standing to challenge the federal agency's decision. The Court found that plaintiffs had failed to demonstrate a specific injury or that the injury was redressable, and therefore the plaintiffs lacked standing to challenge the agency rule.

The Supreme Court has continued to reaffirm its rule of strict statutory construction in determining the applicability of U.S. laws outside the United States. However, in 1993, the U.S. Court of Appeals for the District of Columbia ruled that NEPA *does* apply to certain federal actions outside the U.S. This decision is important in that it suggests that environmental statutes which regulate the decision-making process of federal agencies may not raise the problem of extraterritoriality at all. Under the court's reasoning in the *Massey* case, an agency's decision making may be subject to the requirements of NEPA even if the actions at issue occur outside the U.S.

ENVIRONMENTAL DEFENSE FUND, INC. v. MASSEY
986 F.2d 528 (D.C. Cir. 1993)

MIKVA, Chief Judge.

The Environmental Defense Fund ("EDF") appeals the district court's order dismissing its action seeking declaratory and injunctive relief under the National Environmental Policy Act ("NEPA"). EDF alleges that the National Science Foundation ("NSF") violated NEPA by failing to prepare an environmental impact statement ("EIS") in accordance with [NEPA] Section 102(2)(C) before going forward with plans to incinerate food wastes in Antarctica. The district court dismissed EDF's action for lack of subject matter jurisdiction. The court explained that while Congress utilized broad language in NEPA, the statute nevertheless did not contain "a clear expression of legislative intent through a plain statement of extraterritorial statutory effect. . . ."

We reverse the district court's decision, and hold that the presumption against the extraterritorial application of statutes does not apply where the conduct regulated by the statute occurs primarily, if not exclusively, in the United States, and the alleged extraterritorial effect of the statute will be felt in Antarctica—a continent without a sovereign, and an area over which the United States has a great measure of legislative control. . . .

As both parties readily acknowledge, Antarctica is not only a unique continent, but somewhat of an international anomaly. Antarctica is the only content on earth which has never been, and is not now, subject to the sovereign rule of any nation. Since entry into force of the Antarctic Treaty in 1961, the United States and 39 other nations have agreed not to assert any territorial claims to the continent or to establish rights of sovereignty there. Hence, Antarctica is generally considered to be a "global commons" and frequently analogized to outer space.

Under the auspices of the United States Antarctica Program, NSF operates the McMurdo Station research facility in Antarctica. McMurdo Station is one of three year-round installations that the United States has established in Antarctica, and over which NSF exercises exclusive control. All of the installations serve as platforms or logistic centers for U.S. scientific research; McMurdo Station is the largest of the three, with more than 100 buildings and a summer population of approximately 1200.

Over the years, NSF has burned food wastes at McMurdo Station in an open land-

fill as a means of disposal. . . . [In 1991, NSF] decided to resume incineration in an "interim incinerator" until a state-of-the-art incinerator could be delivered to McMurdo Station. EDF contends that the planned incineration may produce highly toxic pollutants which could be hazardous to the environment, and that NSF failed to consider fully the consequences of its decision to resume incineration as required by the decision-making process established by NEPA.

***

As the district court correctly noted, the Supreme Court recently reaffirmed the general presumption against the extraterritorial application of statutes. Extraterritoriality is essentially and in common sense, a jurisdictional concept concerning the authority of a nation to adjudicate the rights of particular parties and to establish the norms of conduct applicable to events or persons outside its borders. More specifically, the extraterritoriality principle provides that "[r]ules of the United States statutory law, whether prescribed by federal or state authority, apply only to conduct occurring within, or having effect within, the territory of the United States. . . ." As stated by the Supreme Court, the primary purpose of this presumption against extraterritoriality is "to protect against the unintended clashes between our laws and those of other nations which could result in international discord."[7]

***

There are at least three general categories of cases for which the presumption against the extraterritorial application of statutes clearly does not apply. First, the presumption will not apply where there is an "affirmative intention" of the Congress clearly expressed to extend the scope of the statute to conduct occurring within other sovereign nations.

Second, the presumption is generally not applied where the failure to extend the scope of the statute to a foreign setting will result in adverse effects within the United States. . . . Finally, the presumption against extraterritoriality is not applicable when the conduct regulated by the government occurs within the United States. By definition, an extraterritorial application of a statute involves the regulation of conduct beyond U.S. borders. Even where the significant effects of the regulated conduct are felt outside U.S. borders, the statute itself does not present a problem of extraterritoriality, so long as the conduct which Congress seeks to regulate occurs largely within the United States.

***

NEPA is designed to control the decision-making process of U.S. federal agencies, not the substance of agency decisions. By enacting NEPA, Congress exercised its statutory authority to determine the factors an agency must consider when exercising its discretion, and created a process whereby American officials, while acting within the United States, can reach enlightened policy decisions by taking into account environmental effects. In our view, such regulation of U.S. federal agencies and their decisionmaking processes is a legitimate exercise of Congress' territoriality-based jurisdiction and does not raise extraterritoriality concerns . . . Section 102(2)(C) binds only American officials and controls the very essence of the government function: decision-making. Because the decisionmaking processes of federal agencies take place almost exclusively in this country and involve the workings of the United States government, they are uniquely domestic. . . .

***

Antarctica's unique status in the international arena further supports our conclusion that this case does not implicate the presumption against extraterritoriality. The Supreme Court explicitly stated that when applying the presumption against extraterritoriality, courts should look to see if there is any indication that Congress intended to extend the statute's coverage "beyond places over which the United States has sovereignty *or some measure of legislative control.*" Thus, where the U.S. has some real measure of legislative control over the region at issue, the presumption against extraterritoriality is much weaker. . . . And where there is no potential for conflict "between our laws and those of other nations," the purpose behind the presumption is eviscerated, and the presumption against extraterritoriality applies with significantly less force. . . .

CONCLUSION

Applying the presumption against extraterritoriality here would result in a federal agency being allowed to undertake actions significantly affecting the human environment in Antarctica, an area over which the United States has substantial interest and authority, without ever being held accountable for its failure to comply with the decisionmaking procedures instituted by Congress—even though such accountability, if it was enforced, would result in no conflict with foreign law or threat to foreign policy. NSF has provided no support for its proposition that conduct occurring within the United States is rendered exempt from otherwise applicable statutes merely because the effects of its compliance would be felt in the global commons. We therefore reverse the district court's decision, and remand for a determination of whether the environmental analyses performed by NSF, prior to its decision to resume incineration, failed to comply with Section 102(2)(C) of NEPA.

Reversed and remanded.

Questions and Comments for Discussion

1. What is the principle of "extraterritoriality" as defined by the court in this case? What is the purpose of the rule? Under what circumstances will a domestic environmental law be applied extraterritoriality? What are three exceptions to that rule?

2. On what basis did the court hold that NEPA did apply to the NSF's actions in Antarctica? Under the court's ruling would or should NEPA apply to federal agency decisions affecting projects in places other than Antarctica?

3. Extending NEPA's application to federal actions taking place outside the territorial limits of the U.S. was an important decision. Some have suggested that the decision may open the door to those who would extend NEPA's requirements to federal actions in foreign countries. What are the environmental, economic, and political ramifications of applying NEPA extraterritorialy?

Legal Actions by Foreign Citizens in U.S. Courts

U.S. courts in some cases have been willing to accept jurisdiction over environmental injury suits brought by foreign plaintiffs against American companies if they have a legal basis for doing so. In *Dow Chemical Company v. Alfaro,*[8] a Texas statute provided:

> An action for damages of a citizen of a foreign country may be enforced in the courts of this state, although the wrongful act takes place in a foreign country, if: (1) the laws of the foreign country give a right to maintain an action for damages; (2) the action is begun in this state within the time provided by the laws of this state for beginning the action; and (3) the foreign country of which the plaintiffs are citizens has equal treaty rights with the United States on behalf of its citizens.

In *Alfaro,* eighty-two Costa Rican employees of Standard Fruit Company sued Dow Chemical Company in a Texas district court. They claimed that while working on a banana plantation in Costa Rica, they were required to handle DBCP, a pesticide manufactured and supplied to Standard Fruit by Dow Chemical. They alleged that exposure to DBCP caused physical and mental damages, including sterility. Dow sought to dismiss the case under the doctrine of *forum non conveniens.*[9] The Texas court held that the statute applied because Costa Rica recognized plaintiffs' claims against Dow, the lawsuit was filed in a timely manner, and Costa Rica permits U.S. citizens to brings lawsuit before its courts.[10]

Bhopal, India   On the nights of December 2 and 3, 1984, winds blew deadly methyl isocyanate gas from a plant operated by Union Carbide India Limited (UCIL) into densely occupied parts of the city of Bhopal, India. The result was one of the most devastating industrial disasters in history, with deaths of over 2,000 persons and injuries to over 200,000. UCIL was incorporated under the laws of India, with fifty-and-nine-tenths percent of its stock owned by Union Carbide Corporation (UCC), an American company.

Four days after the accident, the first of some 145 consolidated personal injury actions arising out of the disaster were filed in federal district courts in the U.S. The plaintiffs sought relief in the U.S. against UCIL and UCC. Plaintiffs' decision to bring suit in the U.S. was attributed in part to the fact that the Indian courts did not have jurisdiction over UCC.

UCC moved to dismiss the plaintiffs' complaints on the ground of *forum non conveniens* and lack of standing (a legal doctrine discussed in Chapter 8 which determines whether a person is entitled to maintain a particular legal action). The district court agreed and dismissed the lawsuits on several conditions, including that UCC consent to the Indian court jurisdiction, that it agree to satisfy any judgment rendered by an Indian court against it, and that it be subject to discovery under the Federal Rules of Civil Procedure of the United States.

The Federal Court of Appeals subsequently affirmed the district court's decision with a few modifications of its conditions.[11] The court said:

> As the district court found, the record shows that the private interests of the respective parties weigh heavily in favor of dismissal on grounds of *forum non conveniens.* The many witnesses and source of proof are almost entirely located in India, where the accident occurred, and could not be compelled to appear for trial in the United States. The Bhopal plant at the time of the accident was operated by some 193 Indian nationals. . . . The great majority of documents bearing on the design, safety, start-up and operation of the plan, as well as the safety training of the plant's employees is located in India. . . .
>
> The plaintiffs seek to prove that the accident was caused by negligence on the part of UCC in originally contributing to the design of the plant and its provision for storage of excessive amounts of the gas at the plant. . . . [H]owever, UCC's contribution was limited and its involvement in plant operations terminated long before the accident.

Litigation in India continued for two years. On February 14, 1989, the Supreme Court of India entered an order of settlement of all litigations, claims, rights, and liabilities arising from the disaster at Bhopal. Under the terms of the settlement, UCC and UCIL agreed to pay $470 million to the Registrar of the Supreme Court of India to settle claims arising from the disaster.

Impact of U.S. Laws Abroad

Although U.S. courts have narrowly construed the applicability of environmental laws abroad, U.S. environmental laws still have substantial impact outside the United States. Many domestic laws affect businesses which import goods into the U.S. The EPA, for example, has adopted rules requiring that products manufactured outside the U.S. using a process with ozone-depleting substances be labeled as such if imported into the United States.

The U.S. courts have also ruled that they may exercise jurisdiction over foreign citizens and corporations responsible for violating U.S. environmental laws in the United States. In *U.S. v. Ivey,*[12] a Federal District Court in Michigan ruled that it had jurisdiction over a Canadian citizen and a Canadian corporation in a case to recover governmental costs incurred in cleaning up a Michigan Superfund site.

The U.S. has been a leader in enacting laws addressing the problems of environmental pollution, protection of wildlife and its habitat, ecosystems management, and natural resource preservation. These laws and the regulations enacted in conformance with them have provided other nations examples of ways to approach (and perhaps some ways not to approach) similar environmental problems within their borders. Some countries have adopted laws mandating the preparation of an EIS for significant government projects. Faced with the specter of thousands of toxic waste sites, and significant air, water, and land pollution in Europe, the EEC in 1992 proposed imposing civil liability under a scheme borrowed from CERCLA (discussed in Chapter 13).

The Global Environment and Problems of Enforcement

Environmental law has traditionally been a matter of domestic law, and cross-border environmental issues, with some notable exceptions, have not played a significant role in the development of international law. Neighboring nations have confronted regional pollution problems—for example, the transportation of hazardous wastes across national borders and the problem of acid rain between Canada and the U.S. To date there have been few major global initiatives, other than those addressing global warming and stratospheric ozone depletion, which have directly addressed international pollution problems.

International regulation may not always be a satisfactory means of addressing global environmental problems. First, customary law and general principles of law are slow to develop and therefore often unable to address immediate health and environmental hazards. Second, international agreements tend to set goals and policy but rarely impose precise obligations on participating nations, because the principle of national sovereignty also protects nations from being forced to comply with international agreements except by consent. The International Court of Justice is the only judicial forum which may conduct international litigation, but its jurisdiction is voluntary and depends upon a nation's consent for its power to adjudicate disputes.

In addition, major polluters throughout the world tend to be individual corporations and private individuals while international law tends to address the rights and obligations of nations. There are instances where nations have agreed to implement and enforce strict regulatory measures to address international environmental concerns, for example, amendments to the Montreal Protocol, but these instances have been rare.

EMERGING PROTECTION FOR THE ENVIRONMENT—ISO 14000

The International Organization for Standardization, or ISO, is a private organization formed to promote the adoption and use of uniform standards in international trade. Its standards for corporate environmental management are known as ISO 14000.

ISO 14000 standards are voluntary, but sponsors believe that they may eventually become mandatory for most firms engaged in international trade. This reflects the assumption that it is in the best interest of international trade to operate under a common and consistent set of environmental standards. ISO 14000 establishes a common vocabulary and shared management procedures which apply regardless of the jurisdiction in which international firms operate. The immediate goal of ISO 14000 is to establish common procedures for internal environmental controls, including audits, to assure compliance with applicable environmental laws and regulations. Some predict that the environmental management system specifications developed by the organization may become the model to determine compliance with applicable environmental laws.

Direct Regulation of Products

Within the last several years, a new regulatory approach for protecting the environment has emerged. This approach, which has significant international implications, calls for the direct regulation of products or manufacturing and disposal activities. Some nations have begun to adopt different kinds of product-related regulations designed to address environmental concerns. These include packaging and product "take-back" rules, content restrictions, "eco-labeling," and "eco-taxes." Such regulations potentially affect manufacturers throughout the world.

In June 1991, Germany enacted a packaging law which imposes strict packaging take-back requirements for manufacturers, importers and retailers doing business in Germany. Transport packaging, secondary packaging, sales packaging, and beverage containers are regulated under the German law.

Transport packaging includes any packing material used by a manufacturer or importer to protect or ensure the safety of the product. A manufacturer or importer and the retailer must take back such packaging, and must ensure that the materials are reused or recycled outside the public waste disposal system. Secondary packaging includes materials used to deter theft or for the purposes of product promotion such as blister packs and cartons. Sales packaging is used by consumers to transport and protect the product until use, and includes bags, wrappers, and cartons. In general, manufacturers, importers, and distributors must take back secondary and sales packaging from consumers (which is collected by retailers). As of January 1, 1993, non-returnable packaging requires a mandatory deposit which is re-paid when the packaging is returned.

It is still too early to assess the ultimate impact of the German packaging law, and there are many problems with its implementation. For example, it is sometimes difficult to differentiate between types of packing. And the "green dot" program, which helps manufacturers meet the requirements of the program, faces financial and legal challenges. The German program, however, has prompted other nations to undertake packaging take-back requirements. Canada, Belgium, the Netherlands, Sweden, and Austria have embarked on similar initiatives, and the European Union (EU) has created a take-back framework directive.

Some nations have developed regulations banning or restricting the use of certain chemicals in products, mandating the use of "environmentally friendly" materials. Directives of the EU have targeted mutagenic and carcinogenic compounds, chlorinated solvents, and creosote, and have restricted the use of cadmium in a variety of products. In 1995, restrictions extended to other chemical compounds, including urea formaldehyde resins and high-impact polystyrene, polypropylene, and paints. Several EU members have implemented these EU directives, including Denmark, Greece, Germany, the Netherlands, the United Kingdom, and Spain.

Several countries are also using eco-labeling to designate products as environmentally safe. Under most of these schemes, a product's impact on the environment is evaluated throughout its life cycle and through its disposal. Many countries are also examining the use of special taxes to penalize manufacturers using certain materials and to finance government-required recycling programs. As a result, manufacturers marketing products throughout the world will increasingly encounter specific environmentally based requirements. These in turn will influence product content and manufacturing and will in some cases inevitably conflict with principles of free trade, as the following case suggests.

RE DISPOSABLE BEER CANS: E.C. COMMISSION
v. DENMARK
Before the Court of Justice of the European Communities
Case 302/86, 20 September 1988

Opinion of the Advocate General (Sir Gordon Slynn)

This case raises a difficult and sensitive issue—the compatibility of measures taken to protect the environment with the fundamental rule of the EEC Treaty that quantitative restrictions and measures of equivalent effect in relation to imports into one member-State from another are unlawful.

It has long been the practice in Denmark to charge a deposit on the sale of bottles containing beer and soft beverages. The attraction of recovering the deposit was enough to encourage a high percentage of consumers to return the bottles voluntarily and so the countryside and open spaces were kept free of empty discarded bottles. It seems that the system worked well on a voluntary basis whilst the number of different bottles used was limited and, where soft drinks were marked by foreign manufacturers, they were frequently made under licence in Denmark or at least bottled in Denmark.

In the mid-1970s, however, Danish beer manufacturers began to use cans and different shaped bottles. It is said that there was thus competition not merely between the drinks but between the containers. And so to ensure that the deposit system continued to be effective, legislation was introduced. Act 297 of 8 June 1978 applied to, *inter alia,* containers used for drinks and was expressed to be an anti-pollution measure. It empowered the Minister to introduce rules limiting or prohibiting the use of certain materials and types of container . . . to promulgate rules introducing compulsory deposits for certain types of container and to fix the amount of such deposits. . . .

[*Following protests from producers of beverages and containers in other member-States, the Commission notified Denmark that its provisions were contrary to Article 30 of the EEC.[13] Denmark subsequently modified its regulation to permit beverages of the types in question to be sold in non-approved containers provided that the quantity sold did not exceed 3000 hecolitres a year per product, and imposing certain other restrictions. The Commission challenged that system, arguing that the Kingdom of Denmark had failed to fulfill its obligations under Article 30 of the EEC Treaty.*]

***

In my view, national measures taken for the protection of the environment are capable of constituting "mandatory requirements" recognized . . . as limiting the application in Article 30 of the Treaty in the absence of Community case. [This] does not, however, give member-States carte blanche—the level of protection required for one of the acceptable categories must not, as I see it, be excessive or unreasonable and the measures taken to achieve the requirement must be necessary and proportional. Moreover, the measures taken must be 'indistinctly applicable' in form and in substance to domestic producers and to producers from other member-States.

The measures taken by Denmark in relation to approved bottles are highly effective. The producer or importer supplies bottles and cases against a deposit to the wholesaler or retailer who in turn charges the retail purchaser the same deposit on the bottle. The retail purchaser can return the bottle to any retailer selling beer and soft drinks. He gets his deposit back. The retailer collects the various bottles and returns them down the chain to the producer or importer who finally refunds the deposit. Vehicles go out with cases of filled bottles and return with cases of empty bottles and the retailer, the wholesaler or the producer sorts out the different categories of bottles. In the result, it is said, 99 per cent of such bottles are returned and they may be used up to 30 times. Some bottles which are not returned by the purchaser are returned by enterprising children, the deposit repaid forming a valuable source of pocket money. The result is a cleaner countryside and a saving of raw materials. . . .

The Commission's case is that the measures adopted go too far. Moreover they discriminate against producers or importers from other member-States. Denmark replies that the steps taken are all essential to achieve a very high standard of environmental protection and that the system is an integrated one—approval, collection against deposit and reutilization—so that the removal of any of the conditions affects the efficiency of the system as a whole. . . .

Whilst fully recognizing the importance of environmental protection, and bearing in mind the Community's and member-States' increasing awareness of it, it seems to me that the Danish rules impose serious restrictions on the producers of beer and soft beverages in other member-States. In the first place, only approved bottles can be used, subject to the derogation in respect of 3,000 hectolitres per year per producer. Although it is said that so far no bottles have been refused approval, it is an essential argument of the Danish Government that the present system could not absorb more than 30 types of bottle. If increasingly producers from other member-States wish to sell beer in Denmark there is a risk that approval will not be given because withdrawal of an existing approval cannot be obtained. The result would be that producers outside Denmark would have to make or purchase bottles of a type already approved—at the sort of increased cost which [has been] recog-

nized to be a restriction on the free movement of goods. . . .

At first glance the requirement of a compulsory deposit system seems sensible and is effective. At the end of the day, however, it seems to me that, to the extent that non-approved bottles may be used, the system imposes certain restrictions on the importer from other member-States. Under the present system only approved bottles can be returned to any shop; non-approved bottles must be taken back to a retailer of the particular product. It may well be that as a result consumers will not buy imported beers if their deposit is more difficult to recover—though it is clearly possible that a purchaser of a foreign beer is likely to go back to the retailer for more, and to take his empty beer bottles with him. A compulsory deposit system may also be unworkable in respect of disposable containers. . . .

I am accordingly of the view that, even though on the surface indiscriminately applicable to Danish and non-Danish manufacturers, the rules bear in practice more heavily on the latter. . . .

I accepted, as Denmark contends, that it achieves the highest standard of environmental protection in respect of the collection of containers, though it obviously accepts the risk of certain kinds of bottle or container being left around the countryside (e.g., wine bottles which it is said are only left in small quantities).

I also accept that it may be difficult by other methods to achieve the same high standard. Yet it does not seem to me that Denmark must succeed in this application unless the commission can show that the same standard can be achieved by other specified means. There has to be a balancing of interests between the free movement of goods and environmental protection, even if in achieving the balance the high standard of the protection sought has to be reduced. The level of protection sought must be a reasonable level: I am satisfied that the various methods outlined in the Council directive and referred to at the hearing—e.g., selective collection by governmental authorities or private industry, a voluntary deposit system, penalties for litter, education of the public as to waste disposal—are capable of acheiving a reasonable standard which impinges less on the provisions of Article 30.

Accordingly, in my view, the commission is entitled to the declaration it seeks and to its costs of these proceedings.

Questions and Comments for Discussion

1.   How did the court in this case resolve the "difficult and sensitive issue—the compatibility of measures taken to protect the environment with the fundamental rule of the EEC Treaty that quantitative restrictions and measures of equivalent effect in relation to imports into one member-State from another are unlawful?"
2.   As this case suggests, European environmental regulation is similar to that of the U.S. in that it occurs at different levels. Member states may maintain stricter standards than those imposed by EEC institutions as long as they are not hidden barriers to trade. However, communitywide action is permitted only if it is better able to attain fundamental environmental policies than would national action. Thus, this approach defers to action by member states.

SUMMARY AND CONCLUSION

This chapter has examined international environmental law and highlighted some of the important international organizations which help establish international policy. It has focused on some of the significant global environmental initiatives designed to address specific international environmental concerns. These include the Stockholm Conference, the Montreal Protocol, the Basel Convention, and the 1992 UNCED (the Rio Conference).

The chapter has also addressed some of the important legal and policy issues raised by international trade agreements, and specifically discussed recent trade agreements such as NAFTA and GATT. It has also examined some important international legal issues affecting the environment, including the extraterritorial application of U.S. domestic laws, and the power of American courts to adjudicate environmental disputes involving foreign citizens and corporations. Finally, the development of direct product regulation designed to protect the environment and its impact on global environmental issues were reviewed and discussed.

Although recent international conferences like the Rio Conference focused world concern on the problems of the international environment, in reality there have been relatively few global initiatives directly addressing the problems of international environmental pollution. As we move into the twenty-first century, it is possible that increasing concern for the environment will lead to more global initiatives. However, it is important to keep in mind that, ultimately, international environmental issues are inextricably tied to issues of political sovereignty, economic development, trade, and international business. In the future, one can only hope that significant changes in the world's political environment and the increasing interdependence of nations through international trade and communications will also lead to an increased concern for the world's natural environment and a willingness to address those concerns.

GLOSSARY

Agenda 21—One of the "Five Pillars" of the Rio Conference (along with the Rio Declaration, Statement of Forest Principles, Convention on Climate Change, and Convention on Biological Diversity), the agenda is a lengthy document identifying and addressing global environmental problems and describing action necessary to address those problems.

Basel Convention—The Basel Convention on the Control of Transboundary Movements of Hazardous Wastes and Their Disposal. Agreement forbidding the export of hazardous waste to countries unless notice and consent is given.

Brundtland Report—Issued in 1987 by the World Commission on Environment and Development, this stressed the importance of environmental protection for the developing world and introduced the concept of sustainable development.

Convention—An international treaty or agreement.

Convention on Biological Diversity—A controversial proposal presented at the Rio Conference (which the U.S. refused to sign), this convention outlined the need to preserve biological diversity and addressed the financial interest of developing countries in plant and animal life.

Convention on Climate Change—Adopted at the Rio Conference, a convention generally recognizing the need to control emissions of carbon dioxide and other greenhouse gases.

Customary international law—General guiding principles recognized by nations as a source of international law.

"Earthwatch"—A program facilitating international cooperation in research activities, monitoring, and information exchange first established by the Stockholm Conference.

EEC—The European Economic Community established under the Maastrict Treaty.

GATT—The General Agreement on Tariffs and Trade.

ICSU—International Council of Scientific Unions, which undertakes and updates environmental research.

International Law Commission—Commission created by the United Nations General Assembly, charged with developing and codifying international law.

IUCN—The International Union for the Conservation of Nature and Natural Resources, or World Conservation Union, which evaluates renewable natural resources and supports international conventions designed to conserve such resources.

Montreal Protocol on Substances that Deplete the Ozone Layer—Effective in 1989, an international agreement wherein parties agreed to take certain specific actions to address the problem of changes in the atmospheric ozone layer.

NAFTA—The North American Free Trade Agreement.

NGOs—Nongovernmental organizations which are often very active and effective in lobbying for environmental policies to protect the environment.

OAU—Organization of African Unity.

OECD—Organization for Economic Cooperation and Development, responsible for adopting environmental policies which have led to international conventions.

OTR—Office of the United States Trade Representative.

Rio Declaration—Declaration of principles adopted at the 1972 Rio Conference for the ecologically sound management of the environment.

Statement of Forest Principles—A non-legally binding statement of principles for management, conservation, and sustainable development of forests adopted at the 1972 Rio Conference.

Stockholm Conference on the Environment—The first "Earth Summit," held in 1972, which adopted a Declaration on Principles of the International Law of the Environment.

Sustainable development—Economic development which meets the demands of the present without compromising the ability of future generations to meet their own needs.

UNCED—1992 United Nations Conference on the Environment and Development, also known as the *Rio Conference* and the *Earth Summit.*

UNEP—United Nations Environment Program, which coordinates global environmental initiatives.

USTR—U.S. Trade Representative, a cabinet-level post who coordinates and formulates international trade policy.

WHO—World Health Organization, created under the auspices of the United Nations.

World Charter for Nature—Adopted by the UN General Assembly in 1982, this charter recognizes humans' responsibility to maintain the quality of nature and to conserve the world's natural resources.

World Trade Organization—Organization created under the Uruguay Round of GATT to oversee the global trade agreement.

WWF—The Worldwide Fund for Nature, which collects and distributes funds for global conservation activities.

CASES FOR DISCUSSION

1.   A 1975 European Council Directive suggested a system of waste oil collection, including exclusive zones for collectors of waste oils, approval of collection firms, and indemnification of collectors. The directive was challenged in the European Court of Justice. Is the directive consistent with the European Community's commitment to free trade? *Waste Oils 240/83,* 1984 E.C.R. 531 (1984).

2.   Is a universal ban on waste importation promulgated by the Walloon region of Belgium a violation of the EEC treaty guaranteeing free trade among member nations? *Commission v. Belgium,* ECJ 9 July 1992.

3.   The U.S. Superfund Act of 1986 provided for excise taxes on imported petroleum and petroleum-produced products. Canada, Mexico, and the EEC challenged the taxes under GATT on the grounds that differential tax rates on imported and domestic petroleum violated the principle of national treatment for foreign goods. The U.S. argued the resulting differential was competitively insignificant and imposed for the purpose of cleaning up hazardous waste sites. Does the tax scheme violate GATT? *Superfund GATT,* BISD 34 SUPP. 136 (1987).

4.   Canadian statutes prohibited the export of unprocessed herring, roe, and pink and sockeye salmon, requiring that these fish first be landed in Canada for processing. The U.S. chal-

lenged the statute under GATT. Canada claimed an exemption under GATT exceptions permitting export prohibitions for ensuring quality or regulations relating to international marketing of a good, and permitting measures to protect a natural resource. Does the Canadian law violate GATT? *Herring and Salmon GATT,* BISD 35 Supp. 98 (1988).

5.   Under an amendment to the Magnuson Fishery Conservation and Management Act, the U.S. set minimum size requirements for domestic or imported lobsters sold in the United States. The regulations were meant to ensure U.S. lobster stocks would reach maturity and breed, thus sustaining the viability of the industry. The prohibition on imports of undersized lobsters, almost entirely from Canada, was designed to prevent American lobster dealers from fraudulently selling undersized U.S. lobsters as Canadian lobsters, to reduce the illegal American market for undersized lobsters. Canada, arguing that Canadian lobsters reach maturity at a smaller size due to colder waters, challenged the U.S. law as a GATT trade restriction. Is Canada correct? *Lobster Case,* Final Report of US-CANADA FTA Panel, 25 May 1990.

ENDNOTES

1.   3 R.Int'l Arb. Awards 1938 (1941).

2.   Article XX provides in part that: "Subject to the requirement that such measures are not applied in a manner which would constitute a means of arbitrary or unjustifiable discrimination between countries where the same conditions prevail, or a disguised restriction on international trade, nothing in this Agreement shall be construed to prevent the adoption or enforcement by any contracting party of measures . . . (b) necessary to protect human, animal or plant life, or health; . . . . (g) relating to the conservation of exhaustible natural resources if such measures are made effective in conjunction with restrictions on domestic production or consumption."

3.   The Administrative Procedure Act is discussed in Chapter 8.

4.   505 U.S. 788 (1992). [Author's note: This case involved a challenge to the method used by the Secretary of Commerce to calculate the 1990 census. The Supreme Court held that APA review was unavailable because the final action under the reapportionment statute was that of the president, and the president is not an agency.]

5.   775 F. Supp. 668 (S.D.N.Y. 1991).

6.   504 U.S. 555 (1992).

7.   The leading Supreme Court case on this issue is *Equal Employment Opportunity Commission v. Arabian American Oil Co.,* 499 U.S. 244 (1991). In that case, the Court held that Title VII of the 1964 Civil Rights Act did not apply extraterritorially to regulate the employment practices of United States firms employing American citizens abroad. The decision was subsequently superceded by statute as stated in *Stender v. Lucky Stores,* 780 F. Supp. 1302 (N.D. Cal. 1992).

8.   786 S.W.2d 674 (Tex. 1990).

9.   Under this doctrine a court may refuse to hear a case if, for the convenience of the parties and in the interest of justice, the action should be instituted in another forum.

10.   Subsequently, the holding in this case was superseded by statute. *'21' Int'l Holdings, Inc. v. Westinghouse Elec. Corp.,* 856 S.W.2d 479 (Tex. App. 1993).

11.   809 F.2d 195 (2d Cir. 1987).

12.   747 F. Supp. 1235 (E.D. Mich. 1990).

13.   Article 30 specifically establishes a prohibition against quantitative restrictions on imports among member states, including measures with an effect equivalent to trade restrictions.

COURT SYSTEMS

The United States Court System

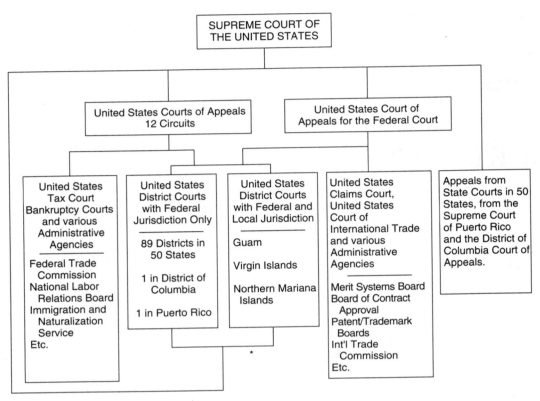

CALIFORNIA STATE COURT SYSTEM

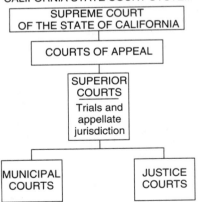

* Direct review by the Supreme Court of an order granting or denying an interlocutory or permanent injunction in a civil action to be heard and determined by a district court of three judges, and from an interlocutory or final judgment of a court of the United States holding an Act of Congress unconstitutional in any civil proceeding to which the United States or any of the agencies, or any officer or employee, is a party. (28 U.S.C.A. 44 1252, 1263)

The Federal Judicial Circuits

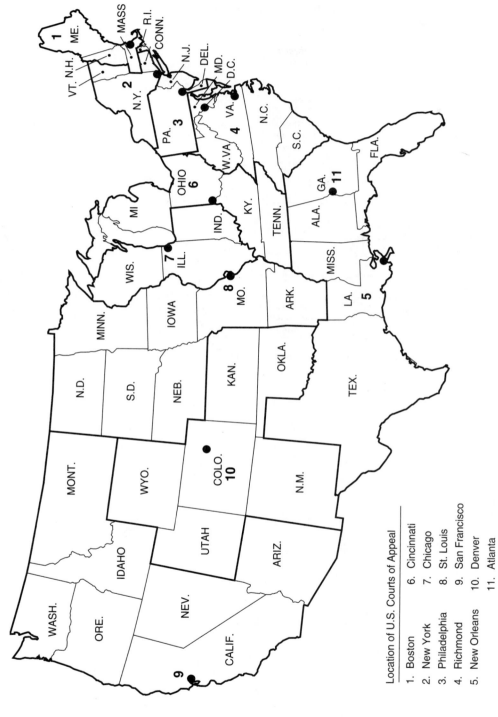

Location of U.S. Courts of Appeal

1. Boston
2. New York
3. Philadelphia
4. Richmond
5. New Orleans
6. Cincinnati
7. Chicago
8. St. Louis
9. San Francisco
10. Denver
11. Atlanta

District of Columbia: D.C. Circuit and Court of Appeals for Federal Circuit

Note: Hawaii and Alaska are in the 9th Circuit.

An Illustrative State Court System

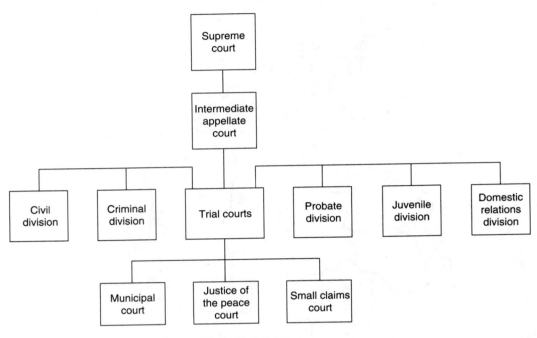

Courts of limited jurisdiction

SAMPLE HAZARDOUS WASTE FORM AND THE SUPERFUND PROCESS

Sample "Uniform Hazardous Waste Manifest" Form

SIGNATURE AND INFORMATION *MUST* BE LEGIBLE ON ALL COPIES

 INDIANA DEPARTMENT OF ENVIRONMENTAL MANAGEMENT
OFFICE OF SOLID AND HAZARDOUS WASTE MANAGEMENT
P.O. Box 7035
Indianapolis, IN 46207-7035

PLEASE PRINT OR TYPE   *(Form designed for use on elite (12-pitch) typewriter.)*   Form Approved. OMB No. 2050-0039. Expires 9-30-91

UNIFORM HAZARDOUS WASTE MANIFEST

1. Generator's US EPA ID No.	Manifest Document No.	2. Page 1 of	Information in the shaded areas is not required by Federal law, but items D, F, H and I are required by State law.
V A D 0 0 1 2 3 4 5 6 7	0 0 0 0 1		

3. Generator's Name and Mailing Address
GENERAL METAL PROCESSING CO.
501 MAIN ST.
SMALLTOWN, VA 23000

A. State Manifest Document Number
INA 0634599

B. State Generator's ID

4. Generator's Phone (804) 555 - 0509

5. Transporter 1 Company Name	6. Use EPA ID Number	C. State Transporter's ID
SAFETY HAULER	V A D 0 0 8 9 1 2 3 4 5	D. Transporter's Phone

7. Transporter 2 Company Name	8. Use EPA ID Number	E. State Transporter's ID
		F. Transporter's Phone

9. Designated Facility Name and Site Address
DISPOS-ALL, INC
1800 NORTH AVE
FRIENDLY TOWN, VA 2300

10. Use EPA ID Number
V A D 0 0 6 7 8 9 1 2 3

G. State Facility's ID

H. Facility's Phone

11. US DOT Description *(Including Proper Shipping Name, Hazard Class, and ID Number)*	12. Containers No.	Type	13. Total Quantity	14. Unit Wt/Vol.	I. Waste No.
a. HAZARDOUS WASTE, LIQUID OR SOLID, NOS ORM-E, NA9189	0 0 2	D M	0 0 1 1 0	GAL	
b. WASTE CYANIDE SOLUTION, NOS UN1935	0 0 1	D M	0 0 0 5 5	GAL	
c. WASTE FLAMMABLE LIQUID, NOS UN1993	0 0 1	D M	0 0 0 5 5	GAL	
d.					

J. Additional Descriptions for Materials Listed Above	K. Handling Codes for Wastes Listed Above

15. Special Handling Instructions and Additional Information

16. **GENERATOR'S CERTIFICATION:** I hereby declare that the contents of this consignment are fully and accurately described above by proper shipping name and are classified, packed, marked, and labeled, and are in all respects in proper condition for transport by highway according to applicable international and national government regulations.

If I am a large quantity generator, I certify that I have a program in place to reduce the volume and toxicity of waste generated to the degree I have determined to be economically practicable and that I have selected the practicable method of treatment, storage, or disposal currently available to me which minimizes the present and future threat to human health and the environment; OR, if I am a small quantity generator, I have made a good faith effort to minimize my waste generation and select the best waste management method that is available to me and that I can afford.

Printed/Typed Name	Signature	Month	Day	Year
JOSEPHINE K. DOE	*Josephine K. Doe*	0 8	3 0	8 6

17. Transporter 1 Acknowledgement of Receipt of Materials

Printed/Typed Name	Signature	Month	Day	Year

18. Transporter 2 Acknowledgement of Receipt of Materials

Printed/Typed Name	Signature	Month	Day	Year

19. Discrepancy Indication Space

20. Facility Owner or Operator: Certification of receipt of hazardous materials covered by this manifest except as noted Item 19.

Printed/Typed Name	Signature	Month	Day	Year

In case of a spill call the Indiana Office of Environmental Response at 317/241-4336 (day or night) and the National Response Center at 800/424-8802 or 202/426-2675.

GENERATOR

TRANSPORTER

FACILITY

INA 0634599

EPA Form 8700-22
Previous editions are obsolete.
State Form 11865 (R/4-89)

COPY 1. TSD MAIL TO TSD STATE

THE SUPERFUND PROCESS

| 1 Identification | 2 Assessment | 3 NPL Placement | 4 RI/FS | 5 Final Remedy |

The Comprehensive Environmental Response Compensation and Liability Act (CERCLA, also known as Superfund) was enacted by Congress in December 1980. The new law established a program to investigate and clean up actual and potential releases of hazardous substances at sites throughout the United States. In 1986, Congress reauthorized the law under the Superfund Amendments and Reauthorization Act (SARA), and increased the size of the fund from $1.6 billion to $8.5 billion. U.S. EPA administers the Superfund program in cooperation with individual states.

The Superfund process involves several steps after a potential site is initially identified (1). After a preliminary inspection of the site is conducted by the U.S. EPA or state agency, the site is evaluated for its potential impact on human health and the environment (2). If the site poses a serious enough threat to the community, it is placed on the National Priorities List (NPL), a roster of the nation's worst hazardous waste sites (3).

Sometime after the site is placed on the NPL, U.S. EPA plans and conducts a remedial investigation and feasibility study (RI/FS) (4). The RI is a long term study to identify the nature and extent of contamination at the site. The FS evaluates remedial alternatives for site conditions.

If potentially responsible parties (PRPs) can be identified and are willing to cooperate with U.S. EPA, one or more of the PRPs may conduct the RI/FS. All work conducted by the PRPs is closely monitored by state and federal agencies.

After the public has had an opportunity to comment on the alternatives presented in the FS, U.S. EPA chooses the most appropriate alternative as a final remedy for the site. The chosen remedy is then designed and implemented (5).

At each site where a long term investigation and clean up takes place, U.S. EPA prepares a community relations plan to provide information about community concerns and present a plan to enhance communication between U.S. EPA and the local community.

At any time during this process U.S. EPA may conduct an emergency response action if the site becomes an immediate threat to public health or the environment.

Site Related Documents Are Available at the Repository Or From the U.S. EPA
230 South Dearborn Street, Chicago, IL 60604

Pathways of Contamination

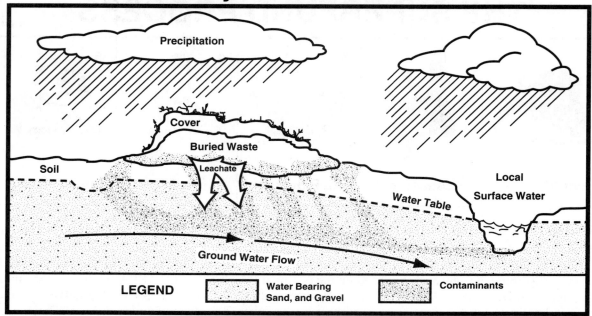

There are several potential pathways, or routes, by which an uncontrolled hazardous waste site may cause contamination problems in the surrounding community. The most common routes, shown in the illustration above, are described below.

AIR

Air may provide a route of contamination depending on factors such as wind speed and direction, humidity, and temperature. Tiny particles of hazardous substances may be dispersed as dust into the air and carried by the wind. Many volatile liquids form a gas or vapor when they evaporate in the air. Some airborne chemicals are harmful if they are inhaled or come in contact with the body.

The greatest risk is posed to individuals who are in locations of high concentrations of airborne contaminants. On-site workers are required to wear special equipment to minimize the risk of contact. The concentration of airborne contaminants decreases as they are dispersed over a wide area.

SURFACE WATER

There are several ways in which hazardous wastes may enter surface waters such as ponds, rivers or lakes. For example, when rain water runs down the sides of an elevated site (like the one in the illustration) toward the ground, contaminants present at the site may be dissolved or suspended in the runoff. The runoff drains away from the site toward an existing body of water, such as a nearby river. Once in the river, contaminants can be carried downstream toward nearby communities, which may use the river for recreation, food or a safe drinking water resource. If fish or other aquatic life consume contaminated water, the contaminants may be introduced into the food chain.

GROUND WATER

Many hazardous waste sites were in operation long before most people understood the interaction between substances present on the surface and ground water. Many hazardous waste sites are located directly above ground water sources. Therefore, contamination of ground-water supplies near a site is often a major concern.

Ground water is formed through a long process. Precipitation, such as rain, reaches the ground and then slowly moves through the soil, sand, gravel and/or rock into small cracks and crevices beneath the ground surface. These rock or sand and gravel formations are called aquifers. During a process which can take many years, the water is filtered as it moves through the aquifer, eventually providing a water source which is naturally pure. This water may then be withdrawn by wells for use as drinking water. An aquifer, and the ground water it contains, often covers a large geographic area.

Substances may be picked up (leached) by water or other liquid as it moves through and about the wastes at the site. This contaminated liquid, called leachate, may travel through the waste and be carried along as the waste moves through the soil into the aquifer. This process can go on for years. Water drawn from the aquifer through a well may also contain these substances. If an aquifer becomes contaminated, it is a very difficult, lengthy and expensive task to resolve the potential problems related to it. Waste facilities constructed according to current federal and state standards contain multiple safeguards to minimize the possibility of ground-water contamination.

APPENDIX
C

ENVIRONMENTAL PRINCIPLES AND LAWS

SELECTED PENALTIES SECTIONS FROM VARIOUS ENVIRONMENTAL LAWS

Federal Insecticide, Fungicide, and Rodenticide Act [FIFRA]

Section 136l Penalties (Federal Insecticide, Fungicide, and Rodenticide Act [FIFRA])

(a) *Civil penalties.*

(1) *In general.* Any registrant, commercial applicator, wholesaler, dealer, retailer, or other distributor who violates any provision of this subchapter may be assessed a civil penalty by the administrator of not more than $5,000 for each offense.

(2) *Private applicator.* Any private applicator or other person not included in paragraph (1) who violates any provision of this subchapter subsequent to receiving a written warning from the administrator or following a citation for a prior violation, may be assessed a civil penalty by the administrator of not more than $1,000 for each offense, except that any applicator not included under paragraph (1) of this subsection who holds or applies registered pesticides, or uses dilutions of registered pesticides, only to provide a service of controlling pests without delivering any applied pesticide to any person so served, and who violates any provision of this subchapter may be assessed a civil penalty by the administrator of not more than $500 for the first offense nor more than $1,000 for each subsequent offense.

(b) *Criminal penalties.*

(1) *In general.*

(A) Any registrant, applicant for a registration, or producer who knowingly violates any provision of this subchapter shall be fined not more than $50,000 or imprisoned not more than 1 year, or both.

(B)   Any commercial applicator of a restricted use pesticide, or any other person not described in subparagraph (a) who distributes or sells pesticides or devices, who knowingly violates any provision of this subchapter shall be fined not more than $25,000 or imprisoned for not more than 1 year, or both.

(3)   *Disclosure of information.* Any person, who, with intent to defraud, uses or reveals information relative to formulas of products acquired under the authority of section 136a of this title, shall be fined not more than $10,000, or imprisoned for not more than three years, or both.

(4)   *Acts of officers, agents, etc.* When construing and enforcing the provisions of this subchapter, the act, omission, or failure of any officer, agent, or other person acting for or employed by any person shall in every case be also deemed to be the act, omission, or failure of such person as well as that of the person employed.

Toxic Substances Control Act [TSCA]

Section 2615 Enforcement. (Toxic Substances Control Act [TSCA])

(a)   *Civil*
(1)   Any person who violates a provision of section 2614 of this title shall be liable to the United States for a civil penalty in an amount not to exceed $25,000 for each such violation. Each day such a violation continues shall, for purposes of this subsection, constitute a separate violation of section 2614 of this title.

(b)   *Criminal*
Any person who knowingly or willfully violates any provision of section 2614 of this title, shall, in addition to or in lieu of any civil penalty which may be imposed under subsection (a) of this section for such violation, be subject, upon conviction, to a fine of not more than $5,000 for each day of violation, or to imprisonment for not more than one year, or both.

Endangered Species Act

Section 1540 Penalties and Enforcement. (Endangered Species Act [ESA])

(a)   *Civil penalties*
(1)   Any person who knowingly violates, and any person engaged in business as an importer or exporter of fish, wildlife, or plants who violates any provision of this chapter, or any provision of any permit or certificate issued hereunder, or of any regulation issued in order to implement [enumerated] subsection[s] . . . of this title, may be assessed a civil penalty by the secretary of not more than $25,000 for each violation. . . .

No penalty may be assessed under this subsection unless such person is given notice and opportunity for a hearing with respect to such violation. Each violation shall be a separate offense. . . .

(3)   Notwithstanding any other provision of this chapter, no civil penalty shall be imposed if it can be shown by a preponderance of the evidence that the defendant committed an act based on a good faith belief that he was acting to protect himself or herself, a member of his or her family, or any other individual from bodily harm, from any endangered or threatened species.

(b)   *Criminal violations*

(1)   Any person who knowingly violates any provision of this chapter, of any permit or certificate issued hereunder, or of any regulation issued in order to implement [enumerated] subsection[s] of this title shall, upon conviction, be fined not more than $50,000 or imprisoned for not more than one year, or both. . . .

(3)   Notwithstanding any other provision of this chapter, it shall be a defense to prosecution under this subsection if the defendant committed the offense based on a good faith belief that he was acting to protect himself or herself, a member of his or her family, or any other individual, from bodily harm from any endangered or threatened species.

Federal Water Pollution Control Act [FWPCA]

Section 1319 Enforcement. (Federal Water Pollution Control Act [FWPCA])

(a)   *State enforcement; compliance orders*

(1)   Whenever, on the basis of any information available to him, the administrator finds that any person is in violation of any condition or limitation which implements [enumerated] section[s] of this title in a permit issued by a state under an approved permit program . . . he shall proceed under his authority in paragraph (3) of this subsection or he shall notify the person in alleged violation and such State of such finding. If beyond the thirtieth day after the administrator's notification the state has not commenced appropriate enforcement action, the administrator shall issue an order requiring such person to comply with such condition or limitation or shall bring a civil action in accordance with subsection (b) of this section.

(b)   The administrator is authorized to commence a civil action for appropriate relief, including a permanent or temporary injunction, for any violation for which he is authorized to issue a compliance order under subsection (a) of this section. . . .

(c)   *Criminal penalties*

(1)   *Negligent violations*

Any person who—

(A)   negligently violates [enumerated] section[s] of this title, or any permit condition or limitation implementing any of such sections in a permit issued under . . . this title by the administrator or by a state, or any requirement imposed in a pretreatment program approved under [enumerated] section[s] of this title or in a permit issued under . . . this title . . . or

(b)   negligently introduces into a sewer system or into a publicly owned treatment works any pollutant or hazardous substance which such person knew or reasonably should have known could cause personal injury or property damage or, other than in compliance with all applicable federal, state, or local requirements or permits, which causes such treatment works to violate any effluent limitation or condition in any permit issued to the treatment works under section 1342 of this title. . . .

Shall be punished by a fine of not less than $2,500 nor more than $25,000 per day of violation, or by imprisonment for not more than 1 year, or by both. If a conviction of a person is for a violation committed after a first conviction of such person under this paragraph, punishment shall be by a fine of not more than $50,000 per day of violation, or by imprisonment of not more than 2 years or by both.

(2)   *Knowing violations*

Any person who—

(A)   knowingly violates [enumerated] section[s] of this title, or any permit condition or limitation implementing any of such sections in a permit issued under section 1342 of this title . . . or any requirement imposed in a pretreatment program approved under . . . this title or in a permit issued under . . . this title . . . ; or

(B)   knowingly introduces into a sewer system or into a publicly owned treatment works any pollutant or hazardous substance which such person knew or reasonably should have known could cause personal injury or property damage or, other than in compliance with all applicable federal, state, or local requirements or permits, which causes such treatment works to violate any effluent limitation or condition in a permit issued to the treatment works under . . . this title . . . ;

shall be punished by a fine of not less than $5,000 nor more than $50,000 per day of violation, or by imprisonment for not more than 3 years, or by both. If a conviction of a person is for a violation committed after a first conviction of such person under this paragraph, punishment shall be by a fine of not more than $100,000 per day of violation, or by imprisonment of not more than 6 years, or by both.

(3)   *Knowing endangerment*

(A)   General rule

Any person who knowingly violates [enumerated] section[s] of this title, or any permit condition or limitation implementing any of such sections . . . or in a permit issued under . . . this title . . . , and who knows at that time that he thereby places another person in imminent danger of death or serious bodily injury, shall, upon conviction, be subject to a fine of not more than $250,000 or imprisonment of not more than 15 years, or both. A person which is an organization shall, upon conviction of violating this subparagraph, be subject to a fine of not more than $1,000,000. If a conviction of a person is for a violation committed after a first conviction of such person under this paragraph, the maximum punishment shall be doubled with respect to both fine and imprisonment.

(6)   *Responsible corporate officer as "person"*

For the purpose of this subsection, the term "person" means . . . any responsible corporate officer.

Solid Waste Disposal Act [SWDA]

Section 6928 Federal Enforcement. (Solid Waste Disposal Act [SWDA])

(a)   *Compliance orders*

(1)   Except as provided in paragraph (2), whenever on the basis of any information the administrator determines that any person has violated or is in violation of any requirement of this subchapter, the administrator may issue an order assessing a civil penalty for any past or current violation, requiring compliance immediately or within a specified time period, or both, or the administrator may commence a civil action in the United States district court in the district in which the violation occurred for appropriate relief, including a temporary or permanent injunction.

(2)   In the case of a violation of any requirement of this subchapter where such violation occurs in a state which is authorized to carry out a hazardous waste program under section 6926 of this title, the administrator shall give notice to the State in which

such violation has occurred prior to issuing an order or commencing a civil action under this section.

(3)   Any order issued pursuant to this subsection may include a suspension or revocation of any permit issued by the administrator or a state under this subchapter and shall state with reasonable specificity the nature of the violation. Any penalty assessed in the order shall not exceed $25,000 per day of noncompliance for each violation of a requirement of this subchapter. In assessing such a penalty, the administrator shall take into account the seriousness of the violation and any good faith efforts to comply with applicable requirements.

(d)   *Criminal penalties*

Any person who—

(1)   knowingly transports or causes to be transported any hazardous waste identified or listed under this subchapter to a facility which does not have a permit under this subchapter or pursuant to Title I of the Marine Protection, Research, and Sanctuaries Act,

(2)   knowingly treats, stores, or disposes of any hazardous waste identified or listed under this subchapter—

(A)   without a permit under this subchapter . . . ; or

(B)   in knowing violation of any material condition or requirement of such permit;

(C)   in knowing violation of any materials condition or requirement of any applicable interim status regulations or standards;

shall, upon conviction, be subject to a fine of not more than $50,000 for each day of violation, or imprisonment not to exceed two years (five years in the case of a violation of paragraph (1) or (2)), or both. If the conviction is for a violation committed after a first conviction of such person under this paragraph, the maximum punishment under the respective paragraph shall be doubled with respect to both fine and imprisonment.

(e)   *Knowing endangerment*

Any person who knowingly transports, treats, stores, disposes of, or exports any hazardous waste identified or listed under this subchapter or used oil not identified or listed as a hazardous waste under this subchapter in violation of paragraph (1)–(7) of subsection (d) of this section who knows at that time that he thereby places another person in imminent danger of death or serious bodily injury, shall, upon conviction, be subject to a fine of not more than $250,000 or imprisonment for not more than fifteen years, or both. A defendant that is an organization shall, upon conviction of violating this subsection, be subject to a fine of not more than $1,000,000.

THE CERES PRINCIPLES

By adopting these Principles, we publicly affirm our belief that corporations have a responsibility for the environment, and must conduct all aspects of their business as responsible stewards of the environment by operating in a manner that protects the Earth. We believe that corporations must not compromise the ability of future generations to sustain themselves. We will update our practices constantly in light of advances in technology and new understandings in health and environmental science. In collaboration with CERES, we will promote a dynamic process to ensure that the Principles are interpreted in a way that accommodates changing technology and environmental realities. We intend to make consistent, measurable progress in implementing these Principles and to apply them to all aspects of our operations throughout the world.

1. Protection of the Biosphere: We will reduce and make continual progress toward eliminating the release of any substance that may cause environmental damage to the air, water, or the earth or its inhabitants. We will safeguard all habitats affected by our operations and will protect open spaces and wilderness, while preserving biodiversity.

2. Sustainable Use of Natural Resources: We will make sustainable use of renewable natural resources, such as water, soils and forests. We will conserve nonrenewable natural resources through efficient use and careful planning.

3. Reduction and Disposal of Wastes: We will reduce and where possible eliminate waste through source reduction and recycling. All waste will be handled and disposed of through safe and responsible methods.

4. Energy Conservation: We will conserve energy and improve the energy efficiency of our internal operations and of the goods and services we sell. We will make every effort to use environmentally safe and sustainable energy sources.

5. Risk Reduction: We will strive to minimize the environmental, health and safety risks to our employees and the communities in which we operate through safe technologies, facilities and operating procedures and by being prepared for emergencies.

6. Safe Products and Services: We will reduce and where possible eliminate the use, manufacture or sale or products and services that cause environmental damage or health or safety hazards. We will inform our customers of the environmental impacts of our products or services and try to correct unsafe use.

7. Environmental Restoration: We will promptly and responsibly correct conditions we have caused that endanger health, safety or the environment. To the extent feasible, we will redress injuries we have caused to persons or damage we have caused to the environment and will restore the environment.

8. Informing the Public: We will inform, in a timely manner, everyone who may be affected by conditions caused by our company that might endanger health, safety or the environment. We will regularly seek advice and counsel through dialogue with persons in communities near our facilities. We will not take any action against employees for reporting dangerous incidents or conditions to management or to appropriate authorities.

9. Management Commitment: We will implement these Principles and sustain a process that ensures that the Board of Directors and Chief Executive Officer are fully informed about pertinent environmental issues and are fully responsible for environmental policy. In selecting our Board of Directors, we will consider demonstrated environmental commitment as a factor.

10. Audits and Reports: We will conduct an annual self-evaluation of our progress in implementing these Principles. We will support the timely creation of generally accepted environmental audit procedures. We will annually complete the CERES Report, which will be made available to the public.

Disclaimer: These Principles establish an environmental ethic with criteria by which investors and others can assess the environmental performance of companies. Companies that endorse these Principles pledge to go voluntarily beyond the requirements of the law. The terms "may" and "might" in Principles one and eight are not meant to encompass every imaginable consequence, no matter how remote. Rather, these Principles obligate endorsers to behave as prudent persons who are not governed by conflicting interests and who possess a strong commitment to environmental excellence and to human health and safety. These Principles are not intended to create new legal liabilities, expand existing rights or obligations, waive legal defenses or otherwise affect the legal position of any endorsing company, and are not intended to be used against an endorser in any legal proceeding for any purpose.

THE 27 PRINCIPLES OF THE RIO DECLARATION

Principle 1: Human beings are at the center of concerns for sustainable development. They are entitled to a healthy and productive life in harmony with nature.

Principle 2: States have, in accordance with the Charter of the United Nations and the principles of international law, the sovereign right to exploit their own resources pursuant to their own environmental and developmental policies, and the responsibility to ensure that activities within their jurisdiction or control do not cause damage to the environment of other States or of areas beyond the limits of national jurisdiction.

Principle 3: The right to development must be fulfilled so as to equitably meet developmental and environmental needs of present and future generations.

Principle 4: In order to achieve sustainable development, environmental protection shall constitute an integral part of the development process and cannot be considered in isolation from it.

Principle 5: All countries and all people shall cooperate in the essential task of eradicating poverty as an indispensable requirement for sustainable development, in order to decrease the disparities in standards of living and better meet the needs of the majority of the people of the world.

Principle 6: The special situation and needs of developing countries, particularly the least developed and those most environmentally vulnerable, shall be given special priority. International actions in the field of environment and development should also address the interests and needs of all countries.

Principle 7: States shall cooperate in a spirit of global partnership to conserve, protect and restore the health and integrity of the Earth's ecosystem. In view of the different contributions to global environmental degradation, States have common but differentiated responsibilities. The developed countries acknowledge the responsibility that they bear in the international pursuit of sustainable development in view of the pressures their societies place on the global environment and of the technologies and financial resources they command.

Principle 8: To achieve sustainable development and a higher quality of life for all people, States should reduce and eliminate unsustainable patterns of production and consumption and promote appropriate demographic policies.

Principle 9: States should cooperate to strengthen indigenous capacity-building for sustainable development by improving scientific understanding through exchanges of scientific and technological knowledge, and by enhancing the development, adaption, diffusion and transfer of technologies, including new and innovative technologies.

Principle 10: Environmental issues are best handled with the participation of all concerned citizens, at the relevant level. At the national level, each individual shall have appropriate access to information concerning the environment that is held by public authorities, including information on hazardous materials and activities in their communities, and the opportunity to participate in decision-making processes. States shall facilitate and encourage public awareness and participation by making information widely available. Effective access to judicial and administrative proceedings, including redress and remedy, shall be provided.

Principle 11: States shall enact effective environmental legislation. Environmental standards, management objectives and priorities should reflect the environmental and developmental context to which they apply. Standards applied by some countries may be inappropriate and of unwarranted economic and social cost to other countries, in particular developing countries.

Principle 12: States should cooperate to promote a supportive and open international economic system that would lead to economic growth and sustainable development in all countries, to better address the problems of environmental degradation. Trade policy measures for environmental purposes should not constitute a means of arbitrary or unjustifiable discrimination or a disguised restriction on international trade. Unilateral actions to deal with environmental challenges outside the jurisdiction of the importing country should be avoided. Environmental measures addressing transboundary pollution or global environmental problems should, as far as possible, be based on an international consensus.

Principle 13: States shall develop national law regarding liability and compensation for the victims of pollution and other environmental damage. States shall also cooperate in an expeditious and more determined manner to develop further international law regarding liability and compensation for adverse effects of environmental damage caused by activities within their jurisdiction or control to areas beyond their jurisdiction.

Principle 14: States should effectively cooperate to discourage or prevent the relocation and transfer to other States of any activities and substances that cause severe environmental degradation or are found to be harmful to human health.

Principle 15: In order to protect the environment, the precautionary approach shall be widely applied by States according to their capabilities. Where there are threats of serious or irreversible damage, lack of full scientific certainty shall not be used as a reason for postponing cost-effective measures to prevent environmental degradation.

Principle 16: National authorities should endeavor to promote the internalization of environmental costs and the use of economic instruments, taking into account the approach that the polluter should, in principle, bear the cost of pollution, with due regard to the public interest and without distorting international trade and investment.

Principle 17: Environmental impact assessment, as a national instrument, shall be undertaken for proposed activities that are likely to have a significant adverse impact on the environment and are subject to a decision of a competent national authority.

Principle 18: States shall immediately notify other States of any natural disasters or other emergencies that are likely to produce sudden harmful effects on the environment of those States. Every effort shall be made by the International community to help States so afflicted.

Principle 19: States shall provide prior and timely notification and relevant information to potentially affected States on activities that may have a significant adverse transboundary environmental effect and shall consult with those States at an early stage and in good faith.

Principle 20: Women have a vital role in environmental management and development. Their full participation is therefore essential to achieve sustainable development.

Principle 21: The creativity, ideals and courage of the youth of the world should be mobilized to forge a global partnership in order to achieve sustainable development and ensure a better future for all.

Principle 22: Indigenous people and their communities, and other local communities, have a vital role in environmental management and development because of their knowledge and traditional practices. States should recognize and duly support their identity, culture and interests and enable their effective participation in the achievement of sustainable development.

Principle 23: The environment and natural resources of people under oppression, domination and occupation shall be protected.

Principle 24: Warfare is inherently destructive of sustainable development. States shall therefore respect international law providing protection for the environment in times of armed conflict and cooperate in its further development, as necessary.

Principle 25: Peace, development and environmental protection are interdependent and indivisible.

Principle 26: States shall resolve all their environmental disputes peacefully and by appropriate means in accordance with the Charter of the United Nations

Principle 27: States and people shall cooperate in good faith and in a spirit of partnership in the fulfillment of the principles embodied in this Declaration and in the further development of international law in the field of sustainable development.

INDEX

Acid rain provisions, and Clean Air Act, 261
Acquisition, types of, 49
Acquisition of real property, 53–55
    by adverse possession, 53–55
    origin of title, 53
    by purchase, gift, or will, 53
Acts and agencies, glossary of, 24–26
Adjudication, vs. rule making, in ADA, 187
Administrative law, 32, 185–211
    Administrative Procedure Act, 187–95
    defined, 185
    delegation doctrine, 186
    Federal Advisory Committee Act, 195
    Federal Register Act, 195
    glossary of terms, 209–10
    judicial review of agency decision making,
        195–209
    National Environment Policy Act
        (NEPA), 195
    Negotiated Rulemaking Act of 1990, 195
    Paperwork Reduction Act, 195
    Regulatory Flexibility Act, 195
    scope of agency authority, 186
Administrative Procedure Act (APA),
        187–95
    application of delegation doctrine,
        191–94
    deference to agency opinion, 188–91
    general framework, 187
    and judicial review, 202
    rule making vs. adjudication, 187–88
    rule-making procedures under APA, 188,
        194–95
Administrative remedies, 28
Adversary system, 39–40
Adverse possession, theory of, 53–55, 58
Agencies and acts, glossary of, 24–26
Agenda 21, 395
Air pollution, controlling, 245–71
    and Clean Air Act of 1970, 246–68
    glossary of terms, 268–70
    indoor, 263–64

national ambient air quality standards
        (NAAQSs), 247–50
    overview, 246–47
    sources of, 247
    state implementation plans, 250–53
Air rights, sale of, 58
Alternative dispute resolution (ADR), 40
*American Mining Congress v. United States
        EPA,* 336–38
American Society for Testing and Materials
        (ASTM), 106–7
Appeals, 42–43
Army Corps of Engineers, 275
    and EPA memorandum of agreement,
        141, 292
"As is" clause, 110–13
Asbestos, 119, 325
Asbestos Hazard Emergency Response Act
        (AHERA), 325
    and TSCA, 325
Asset Conservation, Lender Liability and
        Deposit Insurance Protection Act of
        1996, 194
Asset purchaser, and successor liability, 377
*Association of National Advertisers v. Lun-
        gren,* 29–31
Assumption of risk, 92, 122
Atomic Energy Commission (AEC), 216

*Babbitt v. Sweet Home Chapter of Communi-
        ties for a Great Oregon,* 235–37
Bald and Golden Eagle Protection Act, 181
Basel Convention, 393–94
Best available control technology
        (BACT), 246
    and clean air standards, 266
Best available technology (BAT), 283–84, 286
    and Clean Water Act, 284
Best conventional pollutant control tech-
        nology (BCT), 283–84

Best practicable control technology (BPT), 283–84, 286
Bhopal, India, 356, 408–9
Biochemical oxygen demand (BOD), 15, 283–84
Biodiversity, 6–7
Biotechnology, and TSCA, 326
Boomer v. Atlantic Cement Company, 81–83
Bradley v. American Smelting and Refining, 77–79
Bubble theory, of air pollution, 247
Bureau of Land Management (BLM), 178
    and Department of the Interior, 178
    and FLMPA, 179

Calvert Cliffs' Coord. Com. v. United States A.E. Com'n, 216–18
Cause in fact, defined, 87
Caveat venditor approach, 123
CERES Principles, 386, 432–33
Chatham Steel Corp. et al. v. Brown et al., 36–38, 41–42
Chemical Mfrs. Ass'n. v. U.S. EPA, 317–20
Chemical Waste Management, Inc. v. Hunt, 164–66
Chernobyl nuclear power plant, 389
Chevron U.S.A. Inc. v. Natural Resources Defense Council, 188–91
Chlorofluorocarbons (CFCs), 261–62
Ciba-Geiby Corp. v. United States EPA, 309–11
Citizen suit provisions
    and Clean Water Act, 281
    and FIFRA exception, 281
    and NEPA exception, 281
    and RCRA, 344
Citizens to Preserve Overton Park v. Volpe, 196–97
Civil procedure, 39–43
    adversary system, 39–40
    appeals, 42–43
    commencing action, 40
    complaint, 40
    defendant's answer, 40–41
    motion for summary judgment, 41
    stages of litigation, 43
    summons, 40
Class action, defined, 92
Clean Air Act (CAA) of 1970, 246–68
    acid rain provisions, 261

glossary of terms, 300–301
hazardous air toxics, 258–60
indoor air pollution, 263
Indoor Air Quality Research Act, 264
mobile source fuels and fuel additives, 262–63
motor vehicle provisions, 263
national ambient air quality standards (NAAQSs), 247–50
new source performance standards, 254
and nitrogen oxide emissions, 261
Noise Pollution and Abatement Act, 264
nonattainment areas, 253–54
overview, 246–47
permit program, 255
policy implications of, 264–65
PSD program, 255–58
radon gas, 264
sources of, 247
standard setting under, 266–68
state implementation plans, 250–53
stratospheric ozone protection, 261–62
Clean Air Amendments of 1977 and 1990, 246. *See also* Clean Air Act
Clean Water Act (CWA), 273–304
    BAT, 284
    citizen suit provision, 281
    and conventional pollutants, 283–84
    effluent limitations for publicly owned treatment works, 288–89
    enforcement of, 295
    glossary of terms, 300–301
    hazardous substances spills, 294
    history of federal water pollution control, 273–74
    indirect dischargers, 288
    monitoring and reporting requirements, 282
    new source performance standards (NSPS), 285
    nonconventional pollutants, 285
    nonpoint source pollution, 293–94
    NPDES exclusions, 279–81
    ocean dumping, 294–95
    oil spills, 294
    permit program conditions, 282
    pollution discharge prohibition, 275–79
    pretreatment, 288
    Safe Drinking Water Act, 295–96
    technology-based limitations, 282–83

Clean Water Act (*cont.*)
   toxicants, 285
   variances, 285–87
   water quality standards, 284–85
   and wetlands protection, 289–93
Coalition for Environmentally Responsible
   Economies (CERES), 386
Coastal Zone Management Act (CZMA), 180
Code of Federal Regulations (CFR), 32
Command and control regulations, 15–16
Commerce Clause, of U.S. Constitution,
   157–69
   balancing test, 167–68
   dormant commerce clause, 163–66
   as source of federal regulatory power,
     158–62
   state as market participant, 168–69
   state regulation of waste, 163–66
Commerce power, and U.S. Constitution, 158
Common law remedies for environmental
   harms, 75–102
   cause in fact, 87–89
   defenses to negligence, 92–93
   glossary of terms, 99–100
   injury, 90–91
   multiple-party toxic torts cases, 91–92
   negligence, 84–87
   nuisance, 80–84
   proximate cause, 90
   strict liability, 93–96
   tort law, 76
   trespass, 76–80
Common law, defined, 32
Common law, English, 47
Community property, defined, 63
Community right to know, and CERCLA,
   355–56
Comprehensive Environmental Response,
   Compensation, and Liability Act
   (CERCLA), 333, 348–63
   and cleanup costs, 125, 191
   community right to know, 355–56
   defenses of liability, 354–55
   facility, defined, 349–50
   glossary of terms, 360
   hazardous substances defined under, 349
   and indemnification, 110
   and leasing of commercial industrial
     property, 117
   lender liability under, 356–59
   liability of parties, 350–51

   liability under, 104–7
   National Contingency Plan (NCP), 349
   National Priorities List (NPL), 349
   recoverable response costs, 355
   release, defined, 349–50
   response actions, 350
   structure of, 349
   Superfund, 333, 358
Concerned Area Residents for the Environ-
   ment v. Southview Farm, 276–79
Condemnation proceedings, and the Fifth
   Amendment, 145–46
Condominium, 63
Congressional intent, and the Silkwood case,
   172–73
Connecticut Unfair Trade Practices Act
   (CUTPA), 114
Constitutional issues, in land use regulation,
   144–45
Consumer Product Safety Act (CPSA), 326
Consumer Product Safety Commission
   (CPSC), 326
Contract law, 104–7
   and CERCLA liability, 104–7
   environmental audits, 106–7
   general principles of, 104–6
Contributory negligence, 122
Convention on Climate Change, 394
Conventional pollutants, and Clean Water Act,
   283–84
"Coping with Complexity" (Flournoy), 16–18
Corporate liability, 371–88
   bankruptcy law, 383
   corporate defendant and disclosure, 381
   criminal, 372–74
   defenses to enforcement, 378–80
   environmental audits, 381
   and *Exxon Valdez,* 383–86
   glossary of terms, 386–87
   personal liability of corporate directors and
     managers, 375–76
   and prosecution under RICO, 381–82
   rule limiting, 371–72
   securities violations, 382–83
   sentencing problems, 380–81
   shareholder, 376–77
   successor liability, 376–77
Corporate veil, and liability, 376
Corps of Engineers. *See* Army Corps of
   Engineers
Corrosion Proof Fittings v. EPA, 322–25

corrosivity, as hazardous waste characteristic, 339
Council on Environmental Quality (CEQ), 213, 215
Court, function of, 34
Courts of general jurisdiction, 34
Court structure, 33–43
  civil procedure, 39–43
  federal, 38–39
  state, 33–38
Court systems, 420–22
Covenants, 65–70
  restrictive, 69–70
  and right to light, 59
Critical habitat, time limits for listing, 233
Crude oil products, 262–63

Data disclosure, and TSCA, 321
DDT, 1, 309, 313
Declaratory relief, 27
Defenses of liability, and CERCLA, 354–55
Delaney Clause, 307
Delegation doctrine of APA, 186, 191–94
Department of Health, Education, and Welfare (HEW), 244
Department of the Interior, and BLM, 178
Department of Transportation (DOT), 341
Derby Refining Company v. City of Chelsea, 138–39
Derivative responsibility theory, of CERCLA, 375
Discarded material, defined, 335
Disclaimers of liability, 110–13
Discrimination, in land use regulation, 144–45
Disposal facility, defined, 342
Dormant commerce clause theory, 163
Dow Chemical Co. v. United States, 378–80
Dual penalty structure, of environmental statutes, 366
Due process requirements, 35

Eagles, 181
Earth Day (1970), 185
Earth Island Institute v. Mosbacher, 398–99
Earth Summit 1992, 394–95
Easements, 65–69
  defined, 65
  express, 68–69
  and right to light, 59
Economic Analysis of Law (Posner), 48–49

Economic Theory of Property Rights (Posner), 7
Effluent limitations for publicly owned treatment works, and Clean Water Act, 288–89
Emergency Planning and Community Right to Know Act (EPCRA), 355–56
Emergency registration exemption, from FIFRA, 308
Eminent domain, and the Fifth Amendment, 145
Enabling legislation, defined, 186
Endangered species, defined, 233
Endangered Species Act (ESA), 2, 229–44
  application to federal agencies, 234
  evaluation of, 237–41
  and federalism, 179
  glossary of terms, 241–42
  history, 229–32
  key provisions of, 233–34
  listing procedures, 233–34
  purposes, 229–32
  Section 4, 233–34
  Section 7, 234
  Section 9, 234–37
  Section 1540, 428
  "taking" prohibition, 234–37
Endangerment, and RCRA, 345–47
Enforcement of environmental law, 365–88
  civil vs. criminal liability, 366–67
  corporate liability, 371–86
  establishing criminal intent, 367–68
  general compliance, 366
  and RCRA, 344, 368–71
  voluntary compliance as regulatory policy, 366
Environmental audits, 106–7, 381
Environmental Defense Fund, Inc. v. Massey, 405–8
"Environmental Federalism" (Portney), 19–20
Environmental impact statement (EIS), 215–29
  contents of, 225–28
  and NEPA, 215–16, 228–29
  and record of decision, 225
  scope and timing, 221–25
  threshold requirements for, 218–21
Environmental implications of trade agreements, 396
Environmental law
  defined, 2–3
  enforcement of, 365–88

Environmental law (*cont.*)
  and future, 21–24
  government actions regulated by, 213–44
  history, 1–2
  values and goals, 3–8
Environmental Protection Agency (EPA), 1.
    See also National Environmental Pro-
    tection Act
  and hazardous waste treatment stan-
    dards, 333
  memorandum of agreement (MOA) with
    Corps of Engineers, 141
  and RCRA, 338–39
  tobacco trade groups and, 264
  and wetlands, 140
EPA v. National Crushed Stone Association,
    286–87
Environmental site assessment (ESA), 106
Estate, defined, 61
Estate for years, 63
"Ethical Strands of Environmental Law"
    (Freyfogle), 6–8
Ethics, and environment, 1
European Economic Community (EEC), 391
European Union (EU), 411
"Evolving Consensus" (Rosenberg), 21–23
Exactions, municipal, 140
Expanding landlord and tenant liability, 116–17
Extraterritorial application of domestic laws,
    405–14
  enforcement and global environment, 410
  impact of U.S. laws abroad, 409–10
  ISO 14000, 410–14
  legal actions by foreign citizens, 408–9
Exxon Valdez, 371, 383–86
  Captain Hazelwood prosecution, 384–85
  and CERES, 386
  corporate defendants, 385
  value of debate, 385–86

Facility, defined, 349–50
Federal Advisory Committee Act, 195
Federal Aviation Administration (FAA), 262
Federal court system, 38–39
  courts of appeal, 39
  district court, 38–39
  U.S. Supreme Court, 39
Federal Energy Regulatory Commission
    (FERC), 174
Federal Food, Drug, and Cosmetic Act
    (FFDCA), 303

Federal Hazardous Substances Act
    (FHSA), 326
Federal Insecticide, Fungicide, and Rodenti-
    cide Act (FIFRA), 1, 303–13
  and cancellation of registration, 311–12
  and citizen suit provisions, 281
  classification and certification, 308
  compared to TSCA, 327–29
  cost-benefit analysis under, 305
  and defective products, 119
  Delaney Clause, 307
  enforcement and penalties, 312
  FFDCA and pesticide, 306–7
  FQPA of 1996, 307
  glossary of terms, 329
  minor use registrations, 308–9
  1996 amendments to FIFRA, 307–8
  and other laws, 312–13
  overview, 305
  pesticide registration, 305–6
  pesticide tolerances in food, 306–7
  removal of pesticides from market, 309–11
  Section 3 of, 308
  special registrations, 308
  state authority to regulate pesticides, 312
  trade secrets and, 306
  use of data and, 306
Federal land management legislation, 178–79
Federal Land Policy and Management Act
    (FLPMA), 178
  and BLM, 179
  and sustained yield of public lands, 178
Federal public land laws, 175–82
  Coastal Zone Management Act, 180
  and ESA, 179
  Federal Wildlife Protection Acts, 180–81
  land management legislation, 178–79
  and NEPA, 179
  Surface Mining Control and Reclamation
    Act, 179–80
  wilderness protection laws, 181
Federal Register, 225, 233
Federal Register Act, 195
Federal sentencing guidelines, for corporate
    liability, 380
Federal Water Pollution Control Act
    (FWPCA), 274, 429–30. *See also*
    Clean Water Act
Federalism, 157–84
  Commerce Clause, 157–69
  defined, 157
  federal public land laws, 175–82

Federalism (*cont.*)
    glossary of terms, 182
    and interstate commerce, 157
    pre-emption of state laws affecting environment, 169–74
Fee simple absolute, defined, 61
Fertilizer, as hazardous waste, 338
FFDCA and pesticide, and FIFRA, 306–7
Fifth Amendment, and land use regulation, 144–46
Final Forest, The (Dietrich), 238–41
Finding of No Significant Impact (FONSI), 218
First Amendment, challenges to, 29
Flammable Fabrics Act (FFA), 326
Food and Drug Administration (FDA), 303
Food Quality Protection Act of 1996 (FQPA), 303, 307–8
    and FIFRA, 307
Free-market environmentalists, 15–16
Fundamentally different factors (FDF), 283–84
"Future Environmental Agenda for the U.S., The" (Babbitt), 6

Garb-Ko Inc. v. Lansing-Lewis Services, Inc., 111–13
General Agreement on Tariffs and Trade (GATT), 31, 397–98
    challenge, 400–402
    and most-favored nation status, 397
    Uruguay Round, 401
General Aviation Inc. v. The Cleveland Electric Illuminating Co., 56–58
General jurisdiction, courts of, 34
Generator of Waste Requirements, and RCRA, 339–40
Geo-Tech Reclamation Industries, Inc. v. Hamrick, 134–36
Ghen v. Rich, 49–50
Global issues, 2
Global warming, 2
Glossary of acts and agencies, 24–26
Gorton v. American Cyanamid Co., 120–22
Green marketing statute, 31

Hall v. Nascimento, 54–55, 63
Hardy v. Griffin, 114–16
Harm, defined, 235

Hazardous air toxics, and Clean Air Act, 258–60
Hazardous and Solid Waste Amendments (HSWA), 334
Hazardous Liquid Pipeline Safety Act of 1979 (HLPSA), 170–71
Hazardous Materials Transportation Act, and RCRA, 341–42
Hazardous substances defined under CERCLA, 349
Hazardous substances spills, and Clean Water Act, 294
Hazardous waste
    defined, 339
    RCRA definition of, 335–38
    regulating, 333–63
    sample form, 424
Hazardous waste manifest, and RCRA, 340–41
History of environmental law, 1–2
Hodel v. Virginia Surface Mining and Reclamation Association, 27, 158–61
Hoffman Homes, Inc. v. EPA, 279
Homestead Act of 1862, 49
Housing and Community Development Act of 1992, 114
Hybrid rule making, and APA, 195

Ignitability, as hazardous waste characteristic, 339
Implied warranties of habitability, 113
Implied warranty of merchantability, 107, 119
Importers and exporters, and TSCA, 326
In re Quechee Lakes Corp., 143–44
Indemnification agreements, 110, 118
Indiana Harbor Belt Railroad Co. v. American Cyanamid Co., 93–94
Indirect dischargers, and Clean Water Act, 288
Indoor air pollution, 263–64
Indoor Air Quality Research Act, 264
Inferior courts, defined, 33
Injunction
    and common law, 75
    vs. monetary legal remedy, 27
    and nuisance, 80
Innocent landowner defense, and CERCLA, 354
Insurer liability, 123–28
    contract interpretation, 124–25
    standard CGL policy language, 124–28

International Council of Scientific Unions (ICSU), 391

International Law Commission, 391

International law, 389–417
Basel Convention, 393–94
Earth Summit 1992, 394–95
glossary of terms, 415–16
and international trade, 395–414
Montreal Protocol, 393
sources of, 390–91
Stockholm Conference, 392–93
treaties and conventions, 392

International Organization for Standardization (ISO), 410–14
direct regulation of products, 411–14
ISO 14000, 410–14

International trade, 395–414

International Trade Organization (ITO), 397

International Union for the Conservation of Nature and Natural Resources (IUCN), 391

Interstate commerce, and federalism, 157

Irrigation return flows, as hazardous waste, 338

ISO 14000, 410–14

Jersey City Redevelopment Authority v. PPG Industries, 85–86, 94–96

Joint tenancy, 63

Judicial review of agency decision making, 195–209
and APA, 202
arbitrary and capricious test, 205
in excess cases, 205–8
failure to act, 208–9
and NAFTA, 201
scope of, 201–4
"standing" issue, 197–201
timing issues, 201

Jurisdiction
concurrent, 38
defined, 35
diversity, 38
federal question, 38
of state courts, 35

Kelley v. United States EPA, 192–94

Kinley Corp. v. Iowa Utilities Bd., 170–71

Kleppe v. Sierra Club, 222–25

Kleppe v. State of New Mexico, 175–77

Lake Erie, 1

Land development, state controls of, 140

Land disposal, defined, 343

Land use regulation, 133–56
challenges to, 153
constitutional issues in, 144–45
glossary of terms, 154
standards of review, 142–44
state controls of land development, 140
and "taking" issue, 145–53
wetlands regulations, 140–42
zoning, 133–40

Lead Industries Association, Inc. v. EPA, 248–50, 265

Lead-based paint, and TSCA, 325

Lease, defined, 48

Legal remedy, vs. injunction, 27

Legal system, 27–44
civil cases, 27–28
civil procedure, 39–43
court structure, 33
federal court system, 38–39
glossary of terms, 44
sources of law, 28–33
state court systems, 33–38

Legislation, as choice, 2

Lender liability, and CERCLA, 356–59

Liability, 103–31, 371–88. *See also* Warranties and disclaimers
avoiding, 117–19
under CERCLA, 104–7, 350–51, 356–59
contract law, 104–7
corporate, 371–88
and corporate veil, 376
disclaimers of, 110–13
glossary of terms, 129–30
insurer liability for environmental damages, 123–28
landlord and tenant, 116–17
product liability law, 119–23
strict, defined, 96
successor, 376–77
warranties and disclaimers, 107–19

Liability of parties, and CERCLA, 350–51

Lincoln Alameda Creek v. Cooper Industries, Inc., 105–6

Load disposal restrictions, and RCRA, 343
Long-arm statutes, 35
Love Canal, 1
Lowest achievable emmission rate
    (LAER), 254
Lucas v. South Carolina Coastal Council,
    150–53
Lujan v. Defenders of Wildlife et al.,
    199–201

Manifest, for shipping waste, 340
Manual for Planetary Survival, 395
Marine Mammal Protection Act (MMPA),
    2, 180
    and GATT, 401
Marine Protection, Research, and Sanctuaries
    Act (MPRSA), 294
Market-based incentives, vs. command and
    control regulations, 15–16
Maximum contamination level (MCL), 295
Maximum contaminant level goals
    (MCLG), 295
Medical waste, and RCRA, 343
Meehan v. State, 87–89
Memorandum of agreement, EPA and Corps
    of Engineers, 292
Mens rea, and criminal liability, 367
*Metropolitan Edison Co. et al. v. People
    Against Nuclear Energy,* 219–21
Mexico, and NAFTA, 402
Migratory Bird Treaty Act, 181
Mitigation banking, concept of, 292
Mobile source fuels and fuel additives, and
    Clean Air Act, 262–63
Monitoring and reporting requirements, and
    Clean Water Act, 282
Montreal Protocol on Substances that Deplete
    the Ozone Layer, 393
Most-favored nation status, and GATT, 397
Motor Vehicle Pollution Control Act, 245
Motor vehicle provisions, and Clean Air
    Act, 263
Multiple use of public lands, 178

NAFTA. *See* North American Free Trade
    Agreement
National ambient air quality standards
    (NAAQSs), 246–50
    and nitrogen oxides, 248

National Contingency Plan (NCP), 349
National Emissions Standards for Hazardous
    Air Pollutants (NESHAPs), 258
National Environmental Policy Act (NEPA),
    1, 195, 213–29
    action forcing provisions of, 215–18
    and CEQ, 215
    and citizen suit provisions, 281
    environmental impact statement, 215–29
    and federalism, 179
National Forest Management Act
    (NFMA), 179
National Forest Service, and NFMA, 179
National Marine Fisheries Services (NMFS),
    233, 398
National Park Service Act, 229
National Pollutant Discharge Elimination Sys-
    tem (NPDES), 274
    exclusions, and Clean Water Act, 279–81
    and stormwater discharge, 293
National Priorities List (NPL), 349
National Trails System Act Amendments of
    1983, 61
National Wildlife Refuge System (NWRS)
    Administration Act, 181
Natural environment, value of, 13–15
Natural Gas Pipeline Safety Act
    (NGPSA), 171
Natural Resources Defense Council
    (NRDC), 285
*Natural Resources Defense Council v. Envi-
    ronmental Protection Agency* (1991),
    256–58
*Natural Resources Defense Council, Inc. v.
    Morton,* 226–28
*Natural Resources Defense Council, Inc. v.
    U.S. Environmental Protecton Agency*
    (1987), 258–60
Navigable waters, defined, 279
Negligence, 92–93, 98
    defenses to, 92–93
    defined, 76
    and Velsicol, 98
Negotiated Rulemaking Act of 1990, 195
New Deal, 186
New source performance standards (NSPSs),
    265, 285
    and Clean Air Act, 254
    and Clean Water Act, 285
    for water, 285
Nitrogen oxides, as pollutants, 248, 261
Nixon, Richard M., 185

Noise pollution and abatement act, 264
    policy implications of, 264–65
    standard setting under, 266–68
Nollan v. California Coastal Commission,
    147–49
Nonattainment areas, and Clean Air Act,
    253–54
Nonconforming use, and zoning, 137
Nonconventional pollutants, and Clean Water
    Act, 285
Nongovernmental organizations (NGOs), 391
Nonpoint source pollution, 293
    and Clean Water Act, 293–94
    stormwater discharge, 293–94
North American Free Trade Agreement
    (NAFTA), 31, 402–4
    and judicial review, 201
    Side Accord on the Environment, 402
    and trade agreements in general, 396–97
Notice of Commencement (NOC) of Manu-
    facture or Import, 315
Nuisance, 80–84, 98
    public, 83–84
    public vs. private, 83
    and Velsicol, 98
Nuisance exception, and taking of prop-
    erty, 153

Occupational Safety and Health Act (OSHA)
    and agricultural workers, 313
    and indoor air pollution, 263
    and statutory jurisdiction, 205
Occurrence, defined, 134
Ocean dumping, and Clean Water Act,
    294–95
Office of Environmental Policy (OEP), 215
Office of Surface Mining (OSM), 180
Oil Pollution Act of 1990 (OPA), 2
Oil spills, and Clean Water Act, 294
Organization for Economic Cooperation and
    Development (OECD), 391
Organization of African Unity (OAU), 391
OSHA. *See* Occupational Safety and
    Health Act
Out-of-state waste, and state regulation,
    163–66
Outer Continental Shelf (OCS), 180
Outer Continental Shelf Lands Act
    (OCSLA), 180
Overton Park v. Volpe, 202–4
"Ownership and Ecology" (Freyfogle), 70–71

Ownership
    concepts, 61–62
    corporations, 64–65
    estates in land, 61–62
    future interests in land, 62
    for investment purposes, 64–65
    kinds of, 62–65
    landlord and tenant law, 63–64
    life estates, 62
    multiple ownership of property,
        62–63
    partnership, 64
Ownership states, 59
Ozone, and Clean Air Act, 261–62
Ozone layer, and Montreal Protocol, 393
Ozone nonattainment areas, 263

Packaging law, in Germany, 411
Paperwork Reduction Act, 195
Partition, defined, 64
Patz v. St. Paul Fire & Marine Ins. Co.,
    126–28
PCBs. *See* Polychlorinated biphenyls
People Against Nuclear Energy (PANE),
    219–21
Periodic tenancy, 63
Permit program, and Clean Air Act, 255
Permit program conditions, and Clean Water
    Act, 282
Person, defined, 350
Pesticide registration, and FIFRA, 305–6
Pesticide regulation, 303–31
Pesticide tolerances in food, and FIFRA,
    306–7
Pesticides, 309–12
    removal from market, 309–11
    state authority to regulate, 312
Planned unit development (PUD),
    defined, 139
Planning authority, establishing,
    136–37
Point source, defined, 275
Point source pollution, 293
Poison Prevention Packaging Act
    (PPPA), 326
Police power
    and real property, 150
    and regulation, 134
    and zoning, 134–36
Pollution discharge prohibition, and Clean
    Water Act, 275–79

Polychlorinated biphenyls (PCBs), 321
   regulating, 325
   spills, 51–52
   and TSCA, 325
Potentially responsible parties (PRPs), 41
Prah v. Maretti, 32, 60
Pre-emption of state laws by federal. *See*
   State laws
Premanufacture notice (PMN), 314–15
   approval of, 315
   requirements for new microorganisms, 326
   and TSCA, 314–15
Pretreatment, and Clean Water Act,
   274, 288
Prevention of significant deterioriation (PSD),
   255–58
   and Clean Air Act, 255–58
   PSD programs, 255–58
Prior appropriation doctrine, 61
Proctor & Gamble Co. v. Chicago, 167–68
Product liability, 119–23
   actions, 119
   causation, 122–23
   defenses in actions, 122
   summary of law, 123
Product misuse, 122
Property, 47–73
   acquisition of, 49–51
   acquisition of real property, 53–55
   defined, 48
   easements and covenants, 65–70
   glossary of terms, 71–72
   kinds of ownership, 62–65
   legal categories of, 51–53
   ownership concepts, 61–62
   property law, 47–73
   public vs. private property, 52–53
   public trust doctrine, 52–53
   real, defined, 48
   real vs. personal, 51–52
   sale or lease liability, 103–31
   scope of interests in real property,
   56–61
   tangible vs. intangible, 52
Property Clause, of U.S. Constitution, 175
PSD programs, 255–58
Public Citizen v. United States Trade Repre-
   sentative, 403–4
Public land laws, federal, 175–82
Public nuisance, defined, 83
Public policy, and unconscionable
   clause, 110

Publicly owned water treatment works
   (POTWs), 274, 279, 288
Punitive damages, 98–99
   defined, 96
   and Velsicol, 98

Quiet-title action, 62

Racketeer Influenced and Corrupt Organiza-
   tions Act (RICO), 381–82
Radon gas, 325
   and Clean Air Act, 264
   and TSCA, 325
Rails to Trails projects, 61
Re Disposable Beer Cans: E.C. Commission
   v. Denmark, 412–14
Reactivity, as hazardous waste characteris-
   tic, 339
Real vs. personal property, 51
Reasonably available control technology
   (RACT), 254
Record of decision (ROD), and EIS, 228
Recoverable response costs, and
   CERCLA, 355
Red-cockaded woodpecker, 235
"Reflexive Environmental Law" (Orts), 297
Refuse Act, 279
Regional special districts, and flood
   control, 142
Regulation
   command and control vs. market-based
   incentives, 15–16
   of existing chemicals, and TSCA,
   321–25
   land use, 133–56
   state vs. federal, 18–21
Regulatory Flexibility Act, 195
Release, defined, 349–50
Remedy of specific performance, 113
Residential and commercial leases, 113–16
Resource Conservation and Recovery Act
   (RCRA), 1, 333–48
   citizen suit provisions, 344
   and congressional intent, 173
   and endangerment, 345–47
   enforcement mechanisms, 344
   vs. EPA definition of hazardous waste,
   338–39
   Generator of Waste Requirements,
   339–40

RCRA (*cont.*)
    Hazardous Materials Transportation Act,
       341–42
    hazardous waste defined, 335–38
    hazardous waste manifest, 340–41
    load disposal restrictions, 343
    medical waste, 343
    overview, 334
    and SDWA, 295
    small quantity generators, 340
    state hazardous waste programs, 343–44
    structure of, 334–35
    transporter requirements, 341
    TSD facilities permit requirements, 343
    TSD facilities standards, 342–43
    and underground storage tanks, 347–48
Response actions, and CERCLA, 350
Responsible corporate officer doctrine
    (RCO), 375
Restrictive covenant, defined, 69
RICO. *See* Racketeer Influenced and Corrupt
    Organizations Act
Rio Declaration, 395, 434–36
Riparian doctrine, 61
Ripeness, doctrine of, 201
Risk, 16–18
    assessment, 16–18
    assumption of, 92, 122
    foreseeable, 90
Rivers and Harbors Appropriations Act of
    1899, 273–74
Roosevelt, Franklin D., 186
Rule making vs. adjudication, 187–88
Rule making under APA, 188, 194–95

Safe Drinking Water Act (SDWA), 273, 295–96
    1996 amendments, 296
Sale or lease liability, 103
Sanction, defined, 367
Scope of interests in real property, 56–61
    air rights, 56–58
    mineral rights, 58–59
    right to light, 59–61
    water rights, 61
Scoping, and EIS, 221
Section 3, of FIFRA, 308
Section 4, of ESA, 233–34
Section 7, of ESA, 234
Section 9, of ESA, 234–37
Securities and Exchange Commission
    (SEC), 382

Security interest exception, to CERCLA, 356
Sierra Club v. Colorado Refining Company,
    280–81
Sierra Club v. Morton, 8–12
Significant new use rule (SNUR), 315
Silent Spring (Carson), 3–5, 185
Silkwood v. Kerr-McGee Corp.,
    172–73
Solid Waste Disposal Act
    Section 6228, 430–31
Solid waste, regulating. *See* Resource Con-
    servation and Recovery Act
Sources of law, 28–33
    administrative law, 32
    common law, 32–33
    constitutional law, 28–31
    executive orders, 32
    state and federal statutes, 31–32
    treaties, 31
Special registrations, and FIFRA, 308
Spill prevention, control and countermeasure
    (SPCC) plans, 294
Spills, 294
*Standard Practices for Environmental Site
    Assessments,* 106
Standard State Zoning Enabling Act, 137
State court systems, 33–38
    inferior courts, 33
    jurisdiction of, 35
    state appellate courts, 34–38
    state trial courts, 33–34
State ex Rel Thornton v. Hay, 66–68
State hazardous waste programs, and RCRA,
    343–44
State implementation plans (SIPs), 251, 253
State laws, pre-emption by federal laws,
    169–74
    by congressional intent, 172–73
    express intention, 169–72
    incompatibility with congressional intent,
       173–74
    interference with federal policy
       objectives, 174
Statement of Forest Principles, 395
Statutes, defined, 31
Statutes of limitations, and product
    liability, 122
Sterling v. Velsicol Chemical Corporation,
    96–99
Stockholm Conference on the Environment,
    391–93
Storage facility, defined, 342

Stratospheric ozone protection, and Clean Air Act, 261–62
Strict liability, 93–96
    offense, 368
    theories of, 97–98
Subdivision, defined, 139
Subsurface rights. *See* Mineral rights
Superfund. *See* Comprehensive Environmental Response, Compensation, and Liability Act (CERCLA)
Superfund Amendments and Reauthorization Act of 1986 (SARA), 333
Superfund process, 425–26
Supremacy Clause, of U.S. Constitution, 28, 169–71
Surface Mining Control and Reclamation Act of 1977, 179–80
Sustained yield on public lands, 178
Sweet Home Chapter of Communities for a Great Oregon v. Babbitt, 235
Swin Resource System, Inc. v. Lycoming County, 168–69

"Taking"
    analysis, 150–53
    and endangered species, 234–35
    and ESA, 229
    Fifth Amendment requirements, 145–46
    in land use regulation, 145–53
    and nuisance exception, 153
    regulatory takings, 146–49, 237
    statutory definition of, 235
    takings analysis, 150–53
    and wetlands, 142
Technology-based limitations, and Clean Water Act, 282–83
Tenancy, 62–63
    in common, 62
    by the entireties, 63
    joint, 63
    periodic, 63
    at sufferance, 63
    at will, 63
Tennessee Valley Authority v. Hill, 230–32, 234, 237
Testing requirements, and TSCA, 316–20
Title, defined, 53
Tobacco trade groups, and EPA, 264
Torts
    defined, 75
    intentional, 96

negligence, 96
    toxic tort cases, 91
Total suspended solids (TSS), 283
Toxic substances, 303–31
    critical analysis, 328–29
    regulating, 303–31
    risk assessment, 327–28
    and TSCA, 303, 313–26
Toxic Substances Control Act (TSCA), 1, 302, 303, 313–26
    compared to FIFRA, 327–29
    screening new chemicals, 314–15
    Section 2615, 428
    and solid waste, 333
Toxic tort cases, 91
Toxicants, and Clean Water Act, 285
Toxicity, as hazardous waste characteristic, 339
Trade, international, 395–417
    environmental implications of trade agreements, 396
    and GATT, 397–98, 400–402
    and NAFTA, 402–4
    trade agreements in general, 396–97
    tuna-dolphin controversy, 398–99
Trade secrets
    and FIFRA, 306
    and TSCA, 321
"Tragedy of the Commons, The" (Hardin), 13
Transporter requirements, and RCRA, 341
Treaties, 31
Treatment facility, defined, 342
Treatment, storage, and disposal (TSD) facility, 335, 339
    and RCRA, 342–43
Treaty on the . . . Use of Outer Space, 390
Trespass, 76–80, 98
    and Velsicol, 98
Trial de novo, 33
Triple G Landfills, Inc. v. Board of Commissioners of Fountain County, Indiana, 136–37
Tuna-dolphin controversy, 398–401

Underground injection control (UIC) requirements, 296
Underground storage tanks (USTs), 347–48
Union Carbide Corporation (UCC), 408–9
Union Carbide India Limited (UCIL), 408–9
Union Electric Company v. Environmental Protection Agency, 250–53

United Nations Environment Program (UNEP), 390–91, 393
United States. *See also* U.S.
United States v. Fleet Factors Corp., 357–59
United States v. Johnson & Towers, Inc., 368–71
United States v. Lopez, 161–62
United States v. Northeastern Pharmaceutical, 345–47, 351–54
United States Restrictions on Imports of Tuna, 400–401
United States v. Riverside Bayview Homes, Inc., 279, 289–92
Unreasonable risk, and TSCA regulation of chemicals, 314
Uruguay Round of GATT, 401
U.S. *See also* United States
U.S. Constitution, 28
    Commerce Clause of, 157–69
    commerce power and, 158
    and condemnation proceedings, 145–46
    and eminent domain, 145
    and Fifth Amendment, 144–46
    and land use regulation, 144–45
    Property Clause of, 175
    and sources of law, 28–33
    Supremacy Clause of, 28, 169–71
U.S. Fish and Wildlife Services (FWS), 233
U.S. Forest Service (USFS), 179
U.S. Supreme Court, 39. *See also individual cases and* U.S. Constitution
U.S. Trade Representative (USTR), 396–97
Useful safe life, defined, 122

"Valuing Natural Environments" (Williams), 14
Vermont Yankee Nuclear Power Corp. v. Natural Res. D.C., 206–8
Versatile Metals, Inc. v. Union Corp., 108–9
Vicarious liability, 368

Warranties and disclaimers, 107–19. *See also* Liability
    "as is" clause, 110–13
    avoiding environmental liability, 117–19
    disclaimers of liability, 110–13
    expanding landlord and tenant liability, 116–17
    implied warranties of habitability, 113
    indemnification agreements, 110
    residential and commercial leases, 113–16
Waste, defined, 64
Waste Conversion, Inc. v. Commonwealth of Pennsylvania, 373–74
Water quality standards, and Clean Water Act, 284–85
Wetlands, 140–42, 289–93
    Alaska, 141
    defined under EPA, 140
    designation, 292
    flood plain regulation, 142
    mechanisms for protection, 293
    no net loss policy, 141
    protection under Clean Water Act, 289–93
    state protection, 142
Wild and Scenic Rivers Act (WSRA), 2, 181
Wilderness Act of 1964, 181
World Charter for Nature, 392
World Health Organization (WHO), 391
World Trade Organization (WTO), 401
Worldwide Fund for Nature (WWF), 391
Writ of certiorari, 39

Zoning, 133–40
    authority to zone, 134–36
    defined, 133
    and discrimination, 144–45
    exceptions from regulations, 137–39
    and nonconforming use, 137
    planning authority, 136–37
    and police power, 134–36
    regulation under code, 137
    subdivision regulations, 139–40